AFRO-AMERICAN WRITING
An Anthology of Prose and Poetry

AFRO-AMERICAN WRITING

An Anthology of Prose and Poetry

Edited by
Richard A. Long
and
Eugenia W. Collier

Second and Enlarged Edition

THE PENNSYLVANIA STATE UNIVERSITY PRESS
UNIVERSITY PARK AND LONDON

For
Arna Bontemps and Sterling Brown
poets and pioneers

Library of Congress Cataloging in Publication Data

Main entry under title:

Afro-American writing.

Includes index.
1. American literature—Afro-American authors.
2. American literature—20th century.
I. Long, Richard A., 1927–   . II. Collier, Eugenia W.
PS508.N3A37 1985   810'.8'0896073   83–43224
ISBN 0–271–00374–X
ISBN 0–271–00376–6 (pbk.)

Second printing, 1986

Contents

PART I: To the Civil War

PART II: The Civil War to World War I

PART IV: The Forties to 1970

xii

Preface

This anthology is designed for varied uses. For the general reader who wishes to gain a historical overview of Afro-American writing, it should be of considerable value, For a college course, it provides a total of fifty-five authors, a selection from whom will make possible several different approaches to the material: historical, generic, thematic. The selections also provide complementary reading for varied period courses in American literature.

The chief feature of this second and enlarged edition is the inclusion of Part V: The Seventies and Beyond, which introduces the work of seven prose writers and five poets who have come to prominence in recent years. Representative selections are presented from the fiction of Toni Morrison, Ishmael Reed, Toni Cade Bambara, and Alice Walker, and from the nonfiction of Albert Murray, Addison Gayle, and Maya Angelou. Under the heading "A Gathering of Poets" we have selected five exemplars from the widening circle whose work is enriching the poetic landscape of the seventies and eighties: Michael Harper, Larry Neal, Audre Lorde, Etheridge Knight, and June Jordan. The Select Chronology has been brought down through 1984.

In Parts I to IV we have increased the sampling of work by six writers whose reputations continue to grow—Frederick Douglass, Langston Hughes, Sterling Brown, James Baldwin, Hoyt W. Fuller, and Mari Evans—and have omitted a few writers now considered marginal. We also have made three reluctant omissions and several substitutions for reasons given below.

We are happy that a second and revised edition of this anthology has been made possible thanks to the good offices of Mr. Chris W. Kentera and the Pennsylvania State University Press. We are grateful to the New York University Press for its willingness to transfer its interests to us and to the new publisher. We are also grateful that all living authors and xiv

their publishers gave us permission to re-use selections from the first edition under generous conditions.

Many estates were unable to comply with our requests, but only Richard Wright and Countee Cullen are omitted in consequence. For other deceased authors we have been able to make substitutions fully representative of their work. We are especially grateful to Mr. George Bass, executor of the Langston Hughes estate; to Harold Ober Associates; to Mrs. Robert Hayden; and to the families of Hoyt Fuller and Margaret Danner.

In Part I we have supplemented the selections from Frederick Douglass by a portion from his last great oration, on the Republic of Haiti.

In Part III we have had reluctantly to omit the poetry selections from James Weldon Johnson, and we have substituted an autobiographical essay of Claude McKay's for the selection from *A Long Way From Home* and omitted one of his poems. We have substituted a short story of Zora Neale Hurston's for the autobiographical selection from *Dust Tracks on a Road*, finding the story more representative of her art. We have also substituted two shorter, less-known, "Simple" stories of Langston Hughes for a single longer one. We have been pleased to add a substantial critical essay by Sterling Brown to complete the picture of this important writer.

In Part IV we have supplemented the essay by James Baldwin with a short story and a poetic appreciation of a major American painter, and we have added a critical essay by Hoyt Fuller and two poems by Mari Evans.

To our respective institutions, Atlanta University and Howard University, we express appreciation for various kinds of help. The following libraries have been useful: Soper Library of Morgan State College, Library of Baltimore Community College, Trevor Arnett Library of Atlanta University, and the Enoch Pratt Free Library of Baltimore. Mrs. Lillian Miles Lewis, former curator of special collections at the Trevor Arnett Library, has extended many kindnesses. The staff of the Center of African and African-American Studies (CAAS) of Atlanta University has been of great assistance. Appreciation should be expressed to Misses Rutheen Samuels, Maggie Wanza, and Gwendolyn Marshall, CAAS assistants. Special appreciation is due Mrs. Harriette Washington Bell, former assistant to the director of CAAS, and to Miss Willie Jackson of the Afro-American Studies Program at Atlanta University. This work could scarcely have come to completion in the time available to us without the intelligent and willing collaboration of Miss Thelma Blair, to whom we are both most grateful.

For yeoman service in the manifold details of preparing the new edition, we are indebted to Pam Smith and Sara Dickerson.

Richard A. Long
Eugenia W. Collier

Acknowledgments

"The Watchers" and "Rhapsody," by William Stanley Braithwaite. Reprinted by permission of Coward, McCann & Geoghegan, The Putnam Publishing Group, from *Selected Poems* by William Stanley Braithwaite. Copyright 1948 by William Stanley Braithwaite.

"Bad Man Ballad." Collected, adapted and arranged by John A. Lomax and Alan Lomax. Copyright 1934 and renewed 1962 by Ludlow Music, Inc. Reprinted by permission of Ludlow Music, Inc.

"The Principles of the Universal Negro Improvement Association," "An Appeal to the Conscience of the Black Race to See Itself," and "Message from Atlanta Prison," by Marcus Garvey. Reprinted from *The Philosophy and Opinions of Marcus Garvey* by permission of A. Jacques Garvey.

"If We Must Die" and "Flame-Heart," by Claude McKay. Reprinted from *Selected Poems of Claude McKay*. Copyright 1953 by Twayne Publishers, Inc. Reprinted by permission of Twayne Publishers, a division of G. K. Hall & Co., Boston.

"Song of the Son," "Harvest Song," and "Avey" reprinted from *Cane*, by Jean Toomer, by permission of Liveright Publishing Corporation. Copyright 1923 by Boni & Liveright. Copyright renewed 1951 by Jean Toomer.

"Young Gal's Blues" from *Shakespeare in Harlem*, by Langston Hughes. Copyright 1927 by Alfred A. Knopf, Inc. and renewed 1955 by Langston Hughes. Reprinted by permission of Alfred A. Knopf, Inc.

"Song to a Negro Wash-woman," by Langston Hughes. Copyright 1941, and renewed, by Langston Hughes. Reprinted from *Golden Slippers*, edited by Arna Bontemps, by permission of Harold Ober Associates Incorporated.

"Dream Variation" from *Selected Poems*, by Langston Hughes. Copyright 1926 by Alfred A. Knopf, Inc. and renewed 1954 by Langston Hughes. Reprinted by permission of Alfred A. Knopf, Inc.

"The Doors of Life" from *Not Without Laughter*, by Langston Hughes. Copyright 1930 by Alfred A. Knopf, Inc. Reprinted by permission of the publisher.

"Simple Discusses Colleges and Color" and "Simple and the Rosenwald Fund" from *The Best of Simple*, by Langston Hughes. Copyright 1961 by Langston Hughes. Reprinted by permission of Hill and Wang, Inc., a division of Farrar, Straus & Giroux, Inc.

"Dance of the Abakweta," "Visit of the Professor of Aesthetics," and "Gold Is the Shade Esperanto," by Margaret Danner. "And Through the Caribbean Sea," by Margaret Danner from *Poem: Counterpoem.* Published by Broadside Press. Reprinted by permission of the author.

"Facing the Challenge of the New Age," by Martin Luther King, Jr. Originally published in *Phylon*, XVIII (1957). Reprinted by permission of *Phylon*.

"Dinner at Diop's," by Hoyt Fuller. Originally published in and copyrighted by *Southwest Review*. "Toward a Black Aesthetic," by Hoyt Fuller. Copyright 1971 by Hoyt Fuller. Reprinted by permission of the author's family.

"Black Jam for Dr. Negro," "Status Symbol," and "Vive Noir" from *I Am a Black Woman*, by Mari Evans. Published by William Morrow & Co., Inc., 1970. "The Writers" and "conceptuality" from *Nightstar*, by Mari Evans. Copyright 1981 by Mari Evans. Reprinted by permission of the author.

"Preface to a Twenty Volume Suicide Note" from *Preface to a Twenty Volume Suicide Note*, by Amiri Baraka. Copyright 1961 by LeRoi Jones. Reprinted by permission of the author.

"A Poem for Black Hearts" from *Black Magic Poetry 1961–1967*, by Amiri Baraka. Copyright 1969 by LeRoi Jones. Published by Bobbs-Merrill Company, Inc. Reprinted by permission of the author.

"State/Ment" from *Home*, by Amiri Baraka. Copyright 1961–1966 by LeRoi Jones. Published by William Morrow & Co. Reprinted by permission of the author.

"To Da-duh, In Memoriam," by Paule Marshall. Reprinted by permission of the author.

"But He Was Cool" and "Nigerian Unity" from *Don't Cry, Scream*, by Don L. Lee. Copyright 1969 by Haki Madhubuti. "Bloodsmiles" from *Black Pride*, by Haki Madhubuti. Copyright 1968 by Don L. Lee. "Mixed Sketches" from *We Walk the Way of the New World*, by Don L. Lee. Copyright 1970 by Haki Madhubuti. Published by Broadside Press. Reprinted by permission of the author.

"A Clutch of Social Science Fiction Fiction" from *The Omni-Americans*, by Albert Murray. Copyright 1970 by Albert Murray. Published by Outerbridge, 1970; Avon, 1971. Reprinted by permission of the author.

Introduction from *The Way of the New World*, by Addison Gayle, Jr. Copyright 1975 by Addison Gayle, Jr. Reprinted by permission of the author and Doubleday & Co., Inc.

Chapter 16 from *Gather Together in My Name*, by Maya Angelou. Copyright 1974 by Maya Angelou. Reprinted by permission of the author and Random House, Inc.

Pages 12–29 from *The Bluest Eye*, by Toni Morrison. Copyright 1970 by Toni Morrison. Published by Holt, Rinehart and Winston. Reprinted by permission of the author.

Sections 25–27 from *Mumbo Jumbo*, by Ishmael Reed. Copyright 1972 by Ishmael Reed. Reprinted by permission of the author and Doubleday & Co., Inc.

"Christmas Eve at Johnson's Drug N Goods" from *The Sea Birds Are Still Alive*, by Toni Cade Bambara. Copyright 1977 by Toni Cade Bambara. Published by Random House, 1977; Vintage Books edition, 1982. Reprinted by permission of the author and Random House, Inc.

"To Hell with Dying" from *In Love and Trouble*, by Alice Walker. Copyright 1973 by Alice Walker. Reprinted by permission of Harcourt Brace Jovanovich, Inc.

A Select Chronology of
Afro-American Prose and Poetry,
1760–1984

1760

Jupiter Hammon, "An Evening Thought"

1773

Phillis Wheatley, *Poems on Various Subjects, Religious and Moral*

1778

Jupiter Hammon, "An Address to Miss Phillis Wheatley"

1794

Richard Allen and Absalom Jones, *A Narrative of the Black People during the Late Awful Calamity in Philadelphia*

1829

David Walker, *Appeal*
George Moses Horton, *The Hope of Liberty* (re-issued as *Poems by a Slave* in 1837)

1841

Ann Plato, *Essays* (prose and Poetry)

1845

Narrative of the Life of Frederick Douglass
The Narrative of Lunsford Lane

1846

Narrative of William Hayden

1847

Narrative of William W. Brown, A Fugitive Slave

1848

William W. Brown, *Antislavery Harp*
Narratives of the Sufferings of Lewis and Milton Clarke
W. C. Pennington, *Fugitive Blacksmith*

1849

The Life of Josiah Henson
Narrative of Henry Box Brown
Narrative of the Life and Adventures of Henry Bibb

1850

Narrative of Sojourner Truth

1851

William Nell, *Services of Colored Americans in the Wars of 1776 and
1812*

1852

William W. Brown, *Three Years in Europe*
Martin R. Delany, *The Condition, Elevation, Emigration, and Destiny of the Colored People of the United States*

1853

William W. Brown, *Clotel, or the President's Daughter* (later versions in 1864 and 1867)
Solomon Northrop, *Twelve Years A Slave*

1854

Frances E. Harper, *Poems on Various Subjects*

1855

Frederick Douglass, *My Bondage and My Freedom*
William W. Brown, *Sketches of Places and People Abroad*
William C. Nell, *The Colored Patriots of the American Revolution*
Samuel R. Ward, *The Autobiography of a Fugitive Negro*

1856

Alexander Crummell, *The Duty of a Rising Christian State*

1857

Austin Stewart, *Twenty-Two Years a Slave and Forty Years a Freeman*
Frank J. Webb, *The Garies and Their Friends*

1859

Martin L. Delaney, *Blake, or the Huts of America*
The Rev. J. W. Loguen as a Slave and as a Freeman

1861

Martin R. Delaney, *The Official Report of the Niger Valley Exploring Party*

1863

William W. Brown, *The Black Man*

1866

Jacob Rhodes, *The Nation's Loss*

1867

William W. Brown, *The Negro in the American Rebellion*

1868

Elizabeth Keckley, *Behind the Scenes*

1869

Frances E. Harper, *Moses: A Story of the Nile*

1872

Frances E. Harper, *Sketches of Southern Life*
William Still, *The Underground Railroad*

1873

William W. Brown, *The Rising Son*
Islay Walden, *Miscellaneous Poems*

1874

Frances E. Harper, *Poems on Miscellaneous Subjects*

1877

Albery A. Whitman, *Not a Man, and Yet a Man*

1878

Henry O. Flipper, *The Colored Cadet at West Point*
James M. Trotter, *Music and Some Highly Musical People*

1879

Martin R. Delaney, *Principia of Ethnology*
J. Willis Menard, *Lays in Summer Lands*

1880

William W. Brown, *My Southern Home*

1881

Sam Lucas, *Careful Man Songster*

1882

Alexander Crummell, *The Greatness of Christ and Other Sermons*

1883

George W. Williams, *History of the Negro Race*

1884

Life and Times of Frederick Douglass
T. Thomas Fortune, *Black and White: Land, Labor, and Politics in the South*
Albery A. Whitman, *The Rape of Florida*

1885

T. Thomas Fortune, *The Negro in Politics*

1887

William J. Simmons, *Men of Mark*

1888

Daniel A. Payne, *Recollections of Seventy Years*
George W. Williams, *A History of the Negro Troops in the War of Rebellion*
Joseph T. Wilson, *The Black Phalanx*

1889

Alexander Crummell, *The Race Problem in America*

1891

Archibald H. Grimke, *Life of Charles Sumner*
Archibald H. Grimke, *William Lloyd Garrison*
Irvine G. Penn, *The Afro-American Press*

1893

Paul Laurence Dunbar, *Oak and Ivy*
Frances E. Harper, *Iola Leroy, or Shadows Uplifted*

1894

John Mercer Langston, *From the Virginia Plantation to the National Capital*

1895

James E. Campbell, *Echoes from the Cabin and Elsewhere*
Alexander Crummell, *Incidents of Hope for the Negro Race in America*
Paul Laurence Dunbar, *Majors and Minors*
Frances E. Harper, *Atlanta Offering: Poems*
Alice Moore (later Dunbar-Nelson), *Violets and other Tales*

1896

W. E. B. Du Bois, *The Suppression of the African Slave Trade*
Paul Laurence Dunbar, *Lyrics of Lowly Life*

1897

D. W. Davis, *Weh Down Souf'*

1898

Joseph S. Cotter, *Links of Friendship*
Paul Laurence Dunbar, *Folks from Dixie*
Paul Laurence Dunbar, *The Uncalled*

1899

Charles W. Chesnutt, *The Conjure Woman and Other Tales*
Charles W. Chesnutt, *The Wife of His Youth*
Charles W. Chesnutt, *Frederick Douglass*
W. E. B. Du Bois, *The Philadelphia Negro*
Paul Laurence Dunbar, *Lyrics of the Hearthside*
Sutton E. Griggs, *Imperium in Imperio*

1900

Charles W. Chesnutt, *The House Behind the Cedars*
Paul Laurence Dunbar, *The Love of Landry*
Paul Laurence Dunbar, *The Strength of Gideon*

1901

William S. Braithwaite, *The Canadian*
Charles W. Chesnutt, *The Marrow of Tradition*
Paul Laurence Dunbar, *The Fanatics*
Sutton E. Griggs, *Overshadowed*
Booker T. Washington, *Up From Slavery*
Albery A. Whitman, *An Idyl of the South*

1902

James D. Corothers, *The Black Cat Club*
Paul Laurence Dunbar, *The Sport of the Gods*
Sutton E. Griggs, *Unfettered*

1903

W. E. B. Du Bois, *The Souls of Black Folk*
Paul Laurence Dunbar, *Lyrics of Love and Laughter*
Paul Laurence Dunbar, *In Old Plantation Days*
Booker T. Washington and others, *The Negro Problem*

1904

William S. Braithwaite, *Lyrics of Life and Love*
Paul Laurence Dunbar, *The Heart of Happy Hollow*
Booker T. Washington, *Working With the Hands*

1905

James E. Campbell, *Echoes from the Cabin and Elsewhere*
Charles W. Chesnutt, *The Colonel's Dream*
Paul Laurence Dunbar, *Lyrics of Sunshine and Shadow*
T. Thomas Fortune, *Dreams of Life: Miscellaneous Poems*
Sutton E. Griggs, *The Hindered Hand*

1906

Joseph S. Cotter, *Caleb, the Degenerate*
Frances E. Harper, *Idylls of the Bible*

1907

Booker T. Washington, *The Life of Frederick Douglass*

1908

William S. Braithwaite, *The House of Falling Leaves*
Sutton E. Griggs, *Pointing the Way*
Kelly Miller, *Race Adjustment*

1909

Joseph S. Cotter, *A White Song and A Black One*
W. E. B. Du Bois, *John Brown*
Sutton E. Griggs, *Wisdom's Call*
William Pickens, *Abraham Lincoln*
Booker T. Washington, *The Story of the Negro*

1910

Benjamin Brawley, *The Negro in Literature and Art*
William Pickens, *The Heir of Slaves*

1911

W. E. B. Du Bois, *The Quest of the Silver Fleece*
Booker T. Washington, *My Larger Education*

1912

Joseph S. Cotter, *Negro Tales*
James W. Johnson, *The Autobiography of an Ex-Colored Man*
William Pickens, *Frederick Douglass*
Booker T. Washington, *The Man Farthest Down*

1913

Benjamin Brawley, *A Short History of the American Negro*
William H. Ferris, *The African Abroad*
Fenton Johnson, *A Little Dreaming*
William Pickens, *Fifty Years of Emancipation*

1914

John W. Cromwell, *The Negro in American History*
Kelly Miller, *Out of the House of Bondage*
Alice Dunbar Nelson, *Masterpieces of Negro Eloquence*

1915

W. E. B. Du Bois, *The Negro*
Fenton Johnson, *Visions of the Dusk*
Carter Woodson, *The Education of the Negro Prior to 1861*
John W. Work, *Folk Songs of the American Negro*

1916

Fenton Johnson, *Songs of the Soil*
William Pickens, *The New Negro*

1917

J. W. Johnson, *Fifty Years and Other Poems*
J. A. Rogers, *From Superman to Man*

1918

Benjamin Brawley, *Your Negro Neighbor*
Benjamin Brawley, *The Negro in Literature and Art* (revision)
Benjamin Brawley, *Africa and the War*
Joseph S. Cotter, Jr., *The Band of Gideon*
Maud Cuney-Hare, *The Message of the Trees*
Georgia D. Johnson, *The Heart of a Woman*
Kelly Miller, *An Appeal to Conscience*
Carter Woodson, *A Century of Negro Migration*

1919

William S. Braithwaite, *The Story of the Great War*
Benjamin Brawley, *Women of Achievement*
Kelly Miller, *History of the World War*
Clement Richardson, *National Cyclopedia of the Colored Race*

1920

W. E. B. Du Bois, *Darkwater*
James W. Johnson, *Self-Determining Haiti*
Robert R. Moton, *Finding a Way Out*

1921

Benjamin Brawley, *A Social History of the American Negro*
Leslie P. Hill, *The Wings of Oppression*
Claude McKay, *Spring in New Hampshire*
Kelly Miller, *Booker T. Washington Five Years After* (Pamphlet)
Carter Woodson, *The History of the Negro Church*

1922

Georgia D. Johnson, *Bronze*
James W. Johnson, *The Book of American Negro Poetry*
Claude McKay, *Harlem Shadows*
William Pickens, *The Vengeance of the Gods*
Charles Wesley, *The Collapse of the Confederacy*
Carter Woodson, *The Negro in Our History*

1923

Philosophy and Opinions of Marcus Garvey, ed. Amy Jacques Garvey
William Pickens, *Bursting Bonds*
Jean Toomer, *Cane*

1924

William S. Braithwaite, *Going Over Tindel*
W. E. B. Du Bois, *The Gift of Black Folk*
Jessie Fauset, *There Is Confusion*
Kelly Miller, *The Everlasting Stain*
Walter White, *Fire in the Flint*

1925

Countee Cullen, *Color*
James W. and J. Rosamond Johnson, *The Book of American Negro
    Spirituals*
Alain Locke, *The New Negro*
Carter Woodson, *Negro Orators and Their Orations*

1926

Blues: An Anthology, ed. W. C. Handy
Langston Hughes, *The Weary Blues*
William Pickens, *American Aesop*
Walter A. Roberts, *The Haunting Hand*
Eric Walrond, *Tropic Death*
Charles Wesley, *Negro Labor in the United States*
Walter White, *Flight*

1927

Countee Cullen, *Copper Sun*
Countee Cullen, *Ballad of the Brown Girl*
Countee, Cullen, *Caroling Dusk* (anthology)
Langston Hughes, *Fine Clothes to the Jew*
Charles W. Johnson, *Ebony and Topaz*
James W. Johnson, *God's Trombones*
Alain Locke, *Four Negro Poets*
Charles Wesley, *Negro Labor in the United States*

1928

W. E. B. Du Bois, *Dark Princess*
Jessie Fauset, *Plum Bun*
Rudolph Fisher, *The Walls of Jericho*
Leslie Hill, *Toussaint L'Ouverture*
Nella Larsen, *Quicksand*
Claude McKay, *Home to Harlem*
Carter Woodson, *African Myths with Proverbs*

1929

Countee Cullen, *The Black Christ*
Tyler Gordon, *Born to Be*
Nella Larsen, *Passing*
John F. Matheus, *Ouanga* (libretto)
Claude McKay, *Banjo*
Robert R. Moton, *What the Negro Thinks*
Wallace Thurman, *The Blacker the Berry*

Lorenzo Dow Turner, *Anti-Slavery Sentiment in American Literature*
Walter White, *Rope and Faggot*

POETS OF THE HARLEM RENAISSANCE

The following important poets were published only in magazines and anthologies during the twenties:

Gwendolyn Bennett
Arna Bontemps
Waring Cuney
Jessie Fauset
Frank Horne
Helene Johnson
Anne Spencer

1930

Langston Hughes, *Not Without Laughter*
Charles W. Johnson, *The Negro in American Civilization*
James W. Johnson, *Black Manhattan*
James W. Johnson, *St. Peter Relates An Incident*
Eslanda Goode Robeson, *Paul Robeson, Negro*
Carter G. Woodson, *The Rural Negro*

1931

Arna Bontemps, *God Sends Sunday*
Eva Dykes, Otelia Cromwell and Lorenzo Turner, *Readings From
      Negro Authors*
Jessie Fauset, *The Chinaberry Tree*
Langston Hughes, *Dear, Lovely Death*
James W. Johnson, *The Book of American Negro Poetry* (revision)
George Schuyler, *Black No More*
George Schuyler, *Slaves Today*

1932

Sterling Brown, *Southern Road*
Countee Cullen, *One Way to Heaven*

Rudolph Fisher, *The Conjure Man Dies*
Langston Hughes, *Scottsboro Limited*
Langston Hughes, *The Dream Keeper*
Langston Hughes and Arna Bontemps, *Popo and Fifine*
Claude McKay, *Gingertown*
Wallace Thurman, *Infants of the Spring*

1933

J. Mason Brewer, *Negrito: Negro Dialect Poems of the Southwest*
Jessie Fauset, *Comedy: American Style*
James W. Johnson, *Along This Way*
Alain Locke, *The Negro in America* (bibliography)
Claude McKay, *Banana Bottom*
Carter Woodson, *The Miseducation of the Negro*

1934

Horace M. Bond, *The Education of the Negro in the American Social Order*
D. O. W. Holmes, *The Evolution of the Negro College*
Langston Hughes, *The Ways of White Folks*
Zora Neale Hurston, *Jonah's Gourd Vine*
Charles Johnson, *Shadow of the Plantation*
James W. Johnson, *Negro Americans, What Now?*
Negro: An Anthology, ed. Nancy Cunard

1935

Benjamin Brawley, *Early Negro Writers*
Countee Cullen, *The Medea and Other Poems*
Frank Marshall Davis, *Black Man's Verse*
W. E. B. Du Bois, *Black Reconstruction*
George W. Henderson, *Ollie Miss*
Zora Neale Hurston, *Mules and Men*
Charles Wesley, *Richard Allen. Apostle of Freedom*

1936

Ralph J. Bunche, *A World View of Race*
Arna Bontemps, *Black Thunder*

Benjamin Brawley, *Paul Lawrence Dunbar*
Charles Johnson, *A Preface to Racial Understanding*
Alain Locke, *The Negro and His Music*
Carter G. Woodson, *The African Background Outlined*

1937

Arna Bontemps, *Sad-Faced Boy*
Benjamin Brawley, *The Negro Genius*
Sterling Brown, *The Negro in American Fiction*
Sterling Brown, *Negro Poetry and Drama*
Frank Marshall Davis, *I Am the American Negro*
Angelo Herndon, *Let Me Live*
Zora Neale Hurston, *Their Eyes Were Watching God*
George W. Lee, *River George*
Claude McKay, *A Long Way From Home*
Waters E. Turpin, *These Low Grounds*

1938

Benjamin Brawley, ed. *The Best Short Stories of P. L. Dunbar*
Frank Marshall Davis, *Through Sepia Eyes*
Langston Hughes, *A New Song*
Zora Neale Hurston, *Tell My Horse*
Georgia Douglass Johnson, *An Autumn Love Cycle*
Richard Wright, *Uncle Tom's Children*

1939

William Attaway, *Let Me Breathe Thunder*
Horace M. Bond, *Negro Education in Alabama*
Arna Bontemps, *Drums at Dusk*
W. E. B. Du Bois, *Black Folk: Then and Now*
E. Franklin Frazier, *The Negro Family in the United States*
Zora Neale Hurston, *Moses, Man of the Mountain*
Saunders Redding, *To Make A Poet Black*
Waters E. Turpin, *O Canaan!*
Carter Woodson, *African Heroes and Heroines*

1940

Countee Cullen, *The Lost Zoo*
W. E. B. Du Bois, *Dusk of Dawn*
Langston Hughes, *The Big Sea*
Alain Locke, *The Negro in Art*
Rayford W. Logan, *The Diplomatic Relations of the United States with Haiti*
McKay, Claude, *Harlem: Negro Metropolis*
Mary Church Terrell, *A Colored Woman in A White World*
Richard Wright, *Native Son*

1941

William Attaway, *Blood on the Forge*
Sterling Brown, Arthur P. Davis and Ulysses Lee, *The Negro Caravan*
W. C. Handy, *Father of the Blues: An Autobiography*
Richard Wright, *Twelve Million Black Voices*

1942

Eva Dykes, *The Negro in English Romantic Thought*
Lorenzo J. Greene, *The Negro in Colonial New England*
Langston Hughes, *Shakespeare in Harlem*
Zora Neale Hurston, *Dust Tracks on a Road*
George W. Lee, *Beale Street Sundown*
Saunders Redding, *No Day of Triumph*
Margaret Walker, *For My People*

1943

Langston Hughes, *Freedom's Plow*
Charles Johnson, *Patterns of Negro Segregation*
Carl R. Offord, *The White Face*
Roi Ottley, *New World A-Coming*
James A. Porter, *Modern Negro Art*
Chancellor Williams, *The Raven*

1944

Arthur H. Fauset, *Black Gods of the Metropolis*
Melvin B. Tolson, *Rendezvous with America*

1945

Gwendolyn Brooks, *A Street in Bronzeville*
St. Clair Drake and Horace Cayton, *Black Metropolis*
W. E. B. Du Bois, *Color and Democracy*
Chester Himes, *If He Hollers, Let Him Go*
Adam Clayton Powell, *Marching Blacks*
Richard Wright, *Black Boy*

1946

Brailsford K. Brazeal, *The Brotherhood of Sleeping Car Porters*
Owen Dodson, *Powerful Long Ladder*
Katherine Dunham, *Journey to Accompong*
Shirley Graham, *Paul Robeson, Citizen of the World*
George W. Henderson, *Jule*
Ann Petry, *The Street*
Era Bell Thompson, *American Daughter*
Robert C. Weaver, *Negro Labor*
Frank Yerby, *The Foxes of Harrow*

1947

W. E. B. Du Bois, *The World and Africa*
Chester Himes, *Lonely Crusade*
Langston Hughes, *Fields of Wonder*
Willard Motley, *Knock on Any Door*
Ann Petry, *Country Place*

1948

William S. Braithwaite, *Selected Poems*
Frank Marshall Davis, *47th Street Poems*
Hugh M. Gloster, *Negro Voices in American Fiction*
Zora Neale Hurston, *Seraph on the Suwanee*
Roi Ottley, *Black Odyssey*

Benjamin Quarles, *Frederick Douglass*
William Gardner Smith, *Last of the Conquerers*
Dorothy West, *The Living is Easy*

1949

Gwendolyn Brooks, *Annie Allen*
Shirley Graham, *Your Most Humble Servant* (Benjamin Banneker)
Robert Hayden and Myron O'Higgins, *The Lion and the Archer*
Langston Hughes, *One-Way Ticket*
Langston Hughes and Arna Bontemps, *The Poetry of the Negro, 1746-1949*

1950

William Demby, *Beetlecreek*
Langston Hughes, *Simple Speaks His Mind*
Saunders Redding, *Stranger and Alone*
Saunders Redding, *They Came in Chains*
William Gardner Smith, *Anger at Innocence*

1951

Arna Bontemps, *Chariot in the Sky*
Owen Dodson, *Boy at the Window*
Langston Hughes, *Montage of a Dream Deferred*
Saunders Redding, *On Being Negro In America*

1952

Helen M. Chesnutt, *Charles W. Chesnutt: Pioneer of the Color Line*
Ralph Ellison, *Invisible Man*
Langston Hughes, *Laughing to Keep From Crying*

1953

James Baldwin, *Go Tell It On The Mountain*
Gwendolyn Brooks, *Maud Martha*
Langston Hughes, *Simple Takes A Wife*
Claude McKay, *Selected Poems*
Ann Petry, *The Narrows*

Melvin B. Tolson, *Libretto for the Republic of Liberia*
Richard Wright, *The Outsider*

1954

Chester Himes, *The Third Generation*
John O. Killens, *Youngblood*
Carl R. Offord, *The Naked Fear*
William Gardner Smith, *South Street*
Richard Wright, *Black Power*

1955

James Baldwin, *Notes of A Native Son*
Robert E. Hayden, *Figure of Time*
Roi Ottley, *The Lonely Warrior* (Robert S. Abbott)

1956

James Baldwin, *Giovanni's Room*
Margaret Butcher, *The Negro in American Culture*
John H. Franklin, *From Slavery to Freedom*
Langston Hughes, *I Wonder As I Wander*
Pauli Murray, *Proud Shoes*
Richard Wright, *The Color Curtain*

1957

W. E. B. Du Bois, *The Ordeal of Mansart*
E. Franklin Frazier, *Black Bourgeosie*
E. Franklin Frazier, *The Negro in the United States*
Langston Hughes, *Simple Stakes A Claim*
Julian Mayfield, *The Hit*
Waters E. Turpin, *The Rootless*
Richard Wright, *Pagan Spain*
Richard Wright, *White Man, Listen!*

1958

Otelia Cromwell, *Lucretia Mott*
Benjamin Davis, *Communist Councilman From Harlem: An Auto-biography*
Langston Hughes, *Tambourines to Glory*
Martin Luther King, Jr., *Stride Toward Freedom*
Julian Mayfield, *The Long Night*
Saunders Redding, *The Lonesome Road*
Richard Wright, *The Long Dream*

1959

Frank L. Brown, *Turnbull Park*
Philip Butcher, *George W. Cable: The Northhampton Years*
W. E. B. Du Bois, *Mansart Builds A School*
Katherine Dunham, *A Touch of Innocence*
Paule Marshall, *Brown Girl, Brownstones*
Lawrence Reddick, *Crusader Without Violence* (Martin L. King, Jr.)
Gladys B. Sheppard, *Mary Church Terrell*

1960

Gwendolyn Brooks, *The Bean Eaters*
Owen Dodson, *The Confession Stone*
May Miller, *Into the Clearing*
John A. Williams, *The Angry Ones*

1961

James Baldwin, *Nobody Knows My Name*
Waring Cuney, *Puzzles*
Margaret Danner, *Impressions of African Art Forms*
W. E. B. Du Bois, *Worlds of Color*
Langston Hughes, *Ask Your Mama*
LeRoi Jones, *Preface to a 20 Volume Suicide Note*
Paule Marshall, *Soul Clap Hands and Sing*
Julian Mayfield, *The Grand Parade*
Benjamin Quarles, *The Negro in the American Revolution*
John A. Williams, *Night Song*
Richard Wright, *Eight Men*

1962

James Baldwin, *Another Country*
Robert Hayden, *A Ballad of Remembrance*
Langston Hughes, *Fight for Freedom: The Story of the N.A.A.C.P.*
William Melvin Kelly, *A Different Drummer*
Lewis E. Lomax, *The Negro Revolt*
May Miller, *Poems*
Benjamin Quarles, *Lincoln and the Negro*

1963

James Baldwin, *The Fire Next Time*
Arna Bontemps, *Personals*
Frank Horne, *Haverstraw*
Langston Hughes, *Something in Common and Other Stories*
John O. Killens, *And Then We Heard The Thunder*
Gordon Parks, *The Learning Tree*
Conrad Kent Rivers, *These Black Bodies and This Sunburnt Face*
William G. Smith, *The Stone Face*
Mary E. Vroman, *Esther*
Charles Wright, *The Messenger*
Richard Wright, *Lawd, Today*

1964

Lerone Bennett, *Confrontations in Black and White*
Ralph Ellison, *Shadow and Act*
Ernest J. Gaines, *Catherine Carmier*
Lorraine Hansberry, *The Movement*
Kristin Hunter, *God Bless the Child*
LeRoi Jones, *The Dead Lecturer*
William Melvin Kelly, *Dancers on the Shore*
Benjamin Quarles, *The Negro in the Making of America*

1965

James Baldwin, *Going to Meet the Man*
Lerone Bennett, *The Negro Mood*
Claude Brown, *Manchild in the Promised Land*
William Demby, *The Catacombs*

Ronald Fair, *Many Thousand Gone*
Autobiography of Malcolm X (with Alex Haley)
Langston Hughes, *Simple's Uncle Sam*
LeRoi Jones, *The System of Dante's Hell*
William Melvin Kelly, *A Drop of Patience*
John O. Killens, *Black Man's Burden*
Naomi Long Madgett, *Star by Star: Poems*
A. B. Spellman, *The Beautiful Days*
Howard Thurman, *The Luminous Darkness*
Melvin B. Tolson, *Harlem Gallery*
Henry Van Dyke, *Ladies of the Rachmaninoff Eyes*
Richard Wright, *Savage Holiday*

1966

Ronald L. Fair, *Hog Butcher*
Sam Greenlee, *The Spook Who Sat By The Door*
Rosa Guy, *Bird At My Window*
Robert Hayden, *Selected Poems*
Kristin Hunter, *The Landlord*
LeRoi Jones, *Home*
Loren Miller, *The Petitioners* (the Supreme Court and the Negro)
A. B. Spellman, *Four Lives in the Bebop Business*
Margaret Walker, *Jubilee*
Charles Wright, *The Wig*

1967

Stokely Carmichael and Charles V. Hamilton, *Black Power*
Harold Cruse, *The Crisis of the Negro Intellectual*
James A. Emmanuel, *Langston Hughes*
Langston Hughes, *The Panther and the Lash*
Frank Hercules, *I Want A Black Doll*
LeRoi Jones, *Tales*
William Melvin Kelly, *Dem*
John O. Killens, *'Sippi*
Charlene Hatcher Polite, *The Flagellants*
Ishmael Reed, *The Free Lance Pall Bearers*
John A. Williams, *The Man Who Cried I Am*

1968

James Baldwin, *Tell Me How Long the Train's Been Gone*
Gwendolyn Brooks, *In the Mecca*
Eldridge Cleaver, *Soul on Ice*
Harold Cruse, *Rebellion or Revolution*
W. E. B. Du Bois, *Autobiography*
James A. Emmanuel, *The Treehouse and Other Poems*
Mari Evans, *Where Is All the Music?*
Ernest Gaines, *Bloodline*
Nikki Giovanni, *Black Feeling, Black Talk*
Etheridge Knight, *Poems from Prison*
Jewel C. Latimore, *Black Essence*
Don L. Lee, *Black Pride*
Don L. Lee, *Think Black*
Audre Lorde, *First Cities*
Dudley Randall, *Cities Burning*
Dudley Randall and Margaret Danner, *Poem Counterpoem*
Mary E. Vroman, *Harlem Summer*

1969

Lerone Bennett, *Pioneers in Protest*
Gwendolyn Brooks, *Riot*
Lucille Clifton, *Good Times*
Mercer Cook and Stephen Henderson, *The Militant Black Writer*
W. Edward Farrison, *William Wells Brown*
Nikki Giovanni, *Black Judgment*
Ted Joans, *Black Pow-Wow; Jazz Poems*
Don L. Lee, *Don't Cry, Scream!*
James McPherson, *Hue and Cry*
Larry Neal, *Black Boogaloo*
Ishmael Reed, *Yellow Back Radio Broke Down*
Sonia Sanchez, *Homecoming*
John A. Williams, *Sons of Darkness, Sons of Light*
Sarah E. Wright, *This Child's Gonna Live*
Frank Yerby, *Speak Now*

1970

Maya Angelou, *I Know Why The Caged Bird Sings*
Robert H. Brisbane, *The Black Vanguard*
Cecil Brown, *The Life and Loves of Mr. Jiveass Nigger*
Mari Evans: *I Am A Black Woman*
Ronald L. Fair, *World of Nothing*
Ted Joans, *Afrodisia*
Don L. Lee, *We Walk the Way of the New World*
Paule Marshall, *The Chosen Place, The Timeless People*
Louise Meriwether, *Daddy Was A Number Runner*
Pauli Murray, *Dark Testament and Other Poems*
William G. Smith, *Return to Black America*

1971

Maya Angelou, *Just Give Me A Cool Drink of Water 'Fore I Die*
George Cain, *Blueschild Baby*
Ernest J. Gaines, *The Autobiography of Miss Jane Pittman*
Addison Gayle, *The Black Aesthetic*
Michael Harper, *History Is Your Own Heartbeat*
George E. Kent, *Blackness and the Adventure of Western Culture*
John O. Killens, *The Cotillion*
Don L. Lee (Haki R. Madhubuti), *Dynamite Voices*
Toni Morrison, *The Bluest Eye*
Dudley Randall, *The Black Poets*

1972

Houston Baker, *Long Black Song*
James Baldwin, *No Name in the Street*
Toni Cade Bambara, *Gorilla, My Love*
Arna Bontemps, *The Harlem Renaissance Remembered*
Gwendolyn Brooks, *Report from Part One*
Stephen Henderson, *Understanding the New Black Poetry*
Chester Himes, *The Quality of Hurt*
Ishmael Reed, *Mumbo Jumbo*
John A. Williams, *Captain Blackman*
Sherley Anne Williams, *Give Birth to Brightness*

1973

Alice Childress, *A Hero Ain't Nothin But a Sandwich*
Leon Forrest, *A Tree More Ancient than Eden*
Alice Walker, *Revolutionary Petunias and Other Poems*

1974

Maya Angelou, *Gather Together in My Name*
June Jordan, *Poems of Exile and Return*
John McClusky, *Look What They Done to My Song*
Albert Murray, *Train Whistle Guitar*
Larry Neal, *Hoodoo Hollerin' Bebop Ghosts*
Ishmael Reed, *The Last Days of Louisiana Red*
Ann Allen Shockley, *Loving Her*
Alice Walker, *In Love and Trouble*

1975

Maya Angelou, *Oh Pray My Wings Are Gonna Fit Me Well*
Robert Hayden, *Angle of Ascent*
Lance Jeffers, *When I Know the Power of My Black Hand*
Gayl Jones, *Corregidora*
Toni Morrison, *Sula*
John A. Williams, *Mothersill and the Foxes*

1976

Maya Angelou, *Singin' and Swingin' and Gettin' Merry Like Christmas*
Alex Haley, *Roots*
Chester Himes, *My Life of Absurdity*
Gayl Jones, *Eva's Man*
Eugene Redmond, *Drumvoices*
Alice Walker, *Meridian*

1977

Toni Cade Bambara, *The Sea-Birds Are Still Alive*
Owen Dodson, *Come Home Early, Child*
Leon Forrest, *The Bloodworth Orphans*
Michael Harper, *Images of Kin*

Lance Jeffers, *O Africa, Where I Baked My Bread*
Gayl Jones, *White Rat*
James Alan McPherson, *Elbow Room*
Toni Morrison, *Son of Solomon*
Larry Neal, *The Glorious Monster and the Bull of the Horn*
Richard Wright, *American Hunger*

1978

James Baldwin, *Just Above My Head*
Ernest J. Gaines, *In My Father's House*

1979

Lance Jeffers, *Grandsire*
Alice Walker, *Good Night, Willie Lee, I'll See You in the Morning*

1980

Toni Cade Bambara, *The Salt-Eaters*
Sterling A. Brown, *Collected Poems*
Ntozake Shange, *Nappy Edges*

1981

David Bradley, *The Chaneyville Incident*
Mari Evans, *Nightstar*
Gayl Jones, *Song for Anninho*
Toni Morrison, *Tar Baby*
Alice Walker, *You Can't Keep a Good Woman Down*

1982

Robert Hayden, *American Journal*
Gloria Naylor, *The Women of Brewster Place*
Ntozake Shange, *Sassafrass, Cypress, and Indigo*
Joyce Carol Thomas, *Marked by Fire*
Alice Walker, *The Color Purple*
John A. Williams, *Click Song*

1983

Maya Angelou, *Shaker Why Don't You Sing?*
Ernest J. Gaines, *A Gathering of Old Men*
Lance Jeffers, *Witherspoon*
Paule Marshall, *Praisesong for the Widow*
Claudia Tate, *Black Women Writers at Work*
Joyce Carol Thomas, *Bright Shadow*
Alice Walker, *In Search of Our Mothers' Gardens*

1984

Amiri Baraka, *The Autobiography of Leroi Jones/Amiri Baraka*
Amiri Baraka, *Daggers and Javelins*
Mari Evans, *Black Women Writers (1950–1980): A Critical Evaluation*
Audre Lorde, *Sister Outsider: Essays and Speeches*
Richard Perry, *Montgomery's Children*
Gloria Wade-Gayles, *No Crystal Stair: Visions of Race and Sex in Black Women's Fiction*
John Wideman, *Brothers and Keepers*
Jerome Dyson Wright, *Shadows of Hope*

Introduction

The cries of "Black Power!" that echoed down a dusty Southern
road in the early 1960s, drowning out the strains of "We Shall Overcome," announced the beginning of a new age of awareness for
Black Americans. The turmoil and trouble of the sixties, the tragedy
and the triumph, resulted in a renewed emphasis on blackness—its
meaning and its significance and the new direction in which America
must turn. Thus, Afro-Americans emerged rather suddenly from
their invisibility and became visible in many domains. This visibility is
not an unmixed blessing. The distortions of overemphasis are as brutal
as those of underemphasis. Today on every hand, strident voices,
black and white, are bringing us up to date on what the Afro-American was and is.

Definitions are increasingly important. The survival of a culture
—any culture—depends in large measure on the nature of its definitions of itself and of those aspects of life on which its survival depends: for example, what the past implies, what freedom means, who
the enemy is. The literature of a culture is a totality of its definitions,
a self-portrait of that culture. Knowledge of a literature, then, yields
valuable insight into the culture that produced it. In this crucial and
often mystifying age, Afro-American literature is involved in a general rage for scrutiny and redress. It is necessary for those who are
devoted to the study of this literature to conceptualize a view of the
Afro-American literary experience, if they are to relate effectively
the reality of the past with the perplexities of the present, in the task
of preparing for the uncertainty of the future.

First, then, what is to be included in the Afro-American literary
experience? All writings by Americans of African descent, whether
or not they write about that which is uniquely black? Writings by
nonblacks which treat the Afro-American experience with insight or

sympathy? Patronizing works by nonblacks? The philosophical issues posed by these questions have never been resolved to anybody's satisfaction. But some type of resolution is vital here in an anthology purporting to deal with the literature of black Americans.

It is our conviction that Afro-American literature is grounded in Afro-American life and that anyone who partakes of this life is molded by it. Even one who minimizes his blackness and writes from a Euro-American perspective is responding in his way to his experience as a black person. The works of William Stanley Braithwaite, for example, may be counted as part of the Afro-American literary experience, as well as the militantly black works of Malcolm X and Amiri Baraka (LeRoi Jones). A strange but legitimate bedfellow is the body of black folk tales collected and recorded by white Georgian Joel Chandler Harris.

There is a rationale for confining the study of the Afro-American literary experience to the works of Afro-American writers. At the moment of social crisis through which we are passing, such a study is of the highest existential relevance. There is no wall between the academy and the street. Our books are our weapons and the only ones which are likely to enable us to survive. Therefore, we must distinguish, as never before, between the profound and the superficial, between the felt and the observed, between soul and slick. We must scrutinize our heritage with sharper eyes than ever for those segments of truth which will be our passports into the future.

And here Euro-American works are not helpful. Writings by nonblacks are likely to be about the "American" experience; writings by blacks are almost certain to be from the Afro-American experience. And it is the depths of that experience which must now concern us. It is not surprising that most white writers dealing with Afro-American experience succeed in obtaining only a negative relevance, if indeed they are not irrelevant. It would indeed be strange if it were otherwise, for they neither have nor choose to have the perspective of the Afro-American. And what they report is shaped to the expectations of the white majority. Hence it is not a matter of wonder that most bestsellers about Afro-Americans have been written by whites. And those few bestsellers written by Afro-Americans have been largely misunderstood by whites. In other words, their success is a result of a collapse in communication.

The Afro-American literary experience, then, is contained in the writings that embody the Afro-American's spiritual journeying.

And that experience is today germane to any full consideration of the Afro-American in all of his dimensions.

What are the directions apparent in the literature of black Americans? We discern in the Afro-American literary experience two essential modes, two categories of vision: the simplistic and the oracular. Both may be associated with either hope or despair—the two poles around which Afro-American works cluster. Two classics of Afro-American literature illustrate the simplistic and oracular modes: *Up from Slavery* and *The Souls of Black Folk*. *Up from Slavery* presents the simplistic vision. It is not merely a question of the so-called Washington philosophy or of Washington's moral vision. There is a coalescence of form and content which serves to underscore the simplistic nature of the work. The underlying pattern is of the Horatio Alger myth based on the Calvinistic idea of wealth being a reward for work. *Up from Slavery* is filled with simplistic themes: uprightness, cleanliness, mother-love. It is optimistic. All will be well, though the where, when, and how are only obscurely hinted at.

In *The Souls of Black Folk* we find the oracular mode illustrated. Here all is complex; the canvas is crowded. The very language of Du Bois, modelled on nineteenth-century rhetoric, is intended to suggest the manifold dimensions of the Afro-American experience. The metaphor of the veil, and the two-ness of the black man's vision are the leitmotivs of a varied collection, one that includes historical and social essays and a short story. Most appropriately, the work embodies a conscious reply to the simplistic rhetoric and ideology of Booker T. Washington.

The further importance of these two works is that in addition to illustrating the two modes, the simplistic and the oracular, they each illustrate a major genre of Afro-American literature. These two genres, the life-story and the oration, were dominant before the Civil War. There were the slave narrative and the antislavery polemic, both of which reached their masterful pinnacle in the work of Frederick Douglass, sadly neglected as a literary master. The slave narrative attained a sort of climax in Douglass' *Narrative* and then received, as it were, the kiss of death, both historically and artistically, in *Up from Slavery*. Douglass, of course, practiced the oracular mode throughout his life. His editorial "Nemesis" fulfills all the demands the rhetoricians would place upon such a work, a work that is in fact an oration. Du Bois' work falls into the tradition of these orations, though they are the orations of the study rather than of the meeting hall. His eloquence is marshalled to move with passion and indignation the thinking man in his study rather than a crowd at a public meeting.

In addition to the two genres, the life-story and the oration, there also existed before the Civil War a rich folklore or popular literature for whose shape and content we are dependent upon tardy reporters with varying degrees of proficiency. Afro-American folklore, possessing as it does strong African roots, simply eludes attempts to cast it into Euro-American frames. It surfaced in the pre-Civil War epoch most prominently in an essentially poetic form—the biblical sermon. This was the true literature of the folk. It had its themes, its artifices, its almost universal public. And in spite of James Weldon Johnson's fears in 1927, it lives still, and has indeed acquired a secular lease on life.

Since the Civil War other genres have arisen. The essay assumed prominence during the dark years at the turn of the century when black thinkers wrestled with what was then known as the Negro Problem, and again during the twenties when black scholars assessed the place of the black artist in the scheme of things, and again in the fifties and sixties when every aspect of the black man's experience in America had to be scrutinized, and black thinkers wrestled with what had become known as the White Problem. Fiction also became increasingly important as an art form, as the image of the black man changed from Charles Chesnutt's conniving, obsequious Uncle Julius to the many faces of the Harlem Renaissance to Richard Wright's victimized Bigger Thomas to Ralph Ellison's faceless Invisible Man to the very strong, very black hero of the sixties. Poetry probed the innermost recesses of blackness, flowering most profusely in the Harlem Renaissance of the twenties and then again in the Black Renaissance of the sixties. In all genres the thrust has been increasingly toward the oracular rather than the simplistic mode as writers have discovered the materials of art in the varied nuances of Afro-American life.

Certain time cycles emerge. We distinguish the larger periods as

I. To the Civil War: the literature of the slave culture; art as an expression of suffering and an affirmation of manhood in the quest for freedom.

II. From the Civil War to the era of World War I: the literature of the newly freed citizens; the struggle for identity as reflected in literature.

5

III. From World War I to the era of World War II: the first flowering of Afro-American literature as high art, the Harlem Renaissance, its precursors and immediate descendants.

IV. From the mid-forties to the present: from protest to the Black Arts movement; new forms and expanded use of language as the quest for identity changes to self-discovery.*

All such divisions are, of course, artificial. Some writers extend over two or even three of the periods; some adhere only casually to the dominant thrust of the period. But time periods are convenient and economical, and they provide a workable taking-off point.

We must now turn our attention to a critical issue and an issue of criticism. This is the condemnation frequently made that Afro-American writers are lacking in universality, bound up as so many of them are by the theme of race and race-conflict, which is local, limited, parochial. Obviously, there are themes which are universal in some sense or other: love, death, and nature, for example. But any extensive treatment of such themes outside of lyric poetry has to be circumstantial, set in a given time and place. And no given time and place are universal. What is inherently universal about Dante's ten heavens and limbo, about Homer's libations to the gods and his funeral pyres of heroes, about Shakespeare's feudal kings? The answer is, very little. Or Melville's whaling ship or Mark Twain's river towns? The answer is, nothing.

The demand for universality in the writings of the Afro-American cloaks a disapproval which the critic cannot articulate: The writing of the Afro-American is the stain in the literature of this country which seriously challenges the myth of American perfection. Even the most liberal critic turns out to be a racist at this point. Fundamental wrong, fundamental error, fundamental injustice disturb the picture. And yet it is fundamental wrong, fundamental error, fundamental injustice that Afro-American literature must reflect to be true to itself, for it is a literature of oppression, it is a cry from the soul of an oppressed people. It is also a literature of protest, a cry for redress. And in its most recent manifestation it is preeminently a literature of liberation.

This, then, is the cycle of Afro-American literature; this is its dynamic course: from oppression through protest to liberation. This experience is a proper object of study and criticism both in itself and as a part of the larger pattern of the literature of the United States

*This cycle includes the writers who emerged to prominence in the seventies, some of whom came directly out of the Black Arts Movement, most of whom responded to it.

and the literature of the world. Only by seeing this experience as an entity, a totality, and then confronting it with other literary traditions will it be possible to draw from it what inheres therein, the vital and profound truths of the tragic dilemma of democracy and freedom denied in the plenitude of its unending assertion.

Part I

To the Civil War

Conventional accounts of the American experience present the American Revolution as the seed time of that peculiarly American blessing, liberty. Here we encounter the beginning of the almost continuous divergence of the black experience from the mainstream tradition, for the American Revolution modified the position of the blacks, who made up nearly one fourth of the population, mainly by transferring the ultimate authority for the maintenance of slavery from the British crown to the new republic. The change was imperceptible to the blacks. Though blacks were to be found, both slave and free, in most of the colonies at the time of the Revolution, it is Virginia which best encapsulates the history of the black man in the colonies. It was at Jamestown that the first blacks arrived in 1619 as indentured servants, the only form of servitude then known there. It was there in 1662 that slavery was declared hereditary, thus providing legal sanction for the sad history that ensued. Over a hundred years later, Thomas Jefferson of Virginia composed the Declaration of Independence, from which he was forced to delete a disapproval of slavery in order to have it adopted. However, by this time enlightened Virginians, at least, saw little future for slavery in the new United States, and Pennsylvania had gone one step further to organize an Abolition Society in 1775, a year before the emasculated Declaration.

In the colonies still further north, New York and Massachusetts, two literate domestic slaves had emerged, singing the blessedness of

Christian salvation. On Long Island, New York, Jupiter Hammon as early as 1760 wrote:

> Salvation comes by Christ alone,
>   The only Son of God
> Redemption now to every one
>   That loves his holy word.

It would be stretching the point to perceive in this any element distinctly Afro-American: Hammon was little more than a moral versifier. With Phillis Wheatley, Boston's prodigy, much more talent is in evidence, but her references to slavery are rare and illustrative, as in the poem "To the Right Honorable William, Earl of Dartmouth":

> Should you, my lord, while you pursue my song,
> Wonder from whence my love of Freedom sprung,
> Whence flow these wishes for the common good,
> By feeling hearts alone best understood,
> I, young in life, by seeming cruel fate
> Was snatch'd from Afric's fancy'd happy seat:
> What pangs excrutiating must molest,
> What sorrows labour in my parent's breast?
> Steel'd was the soul and by no misery mov'd
> That from a father seiz'd his babe belov'd
> Such, such my case. And can I then but pray
> Others may never feel tyrannic sway?

Both Hammon and Wheatley were to be used to bolster the claims of succeeding generations of abolitionists, black and white, that given the opportunity to pursue Christian pursuits and to develop pious personalities, blacks would be found not at all wanting in these respects.

Slavery began to expand rapidly and to reveal itself as the scourge it was to become in 1793, when a New England Yankee residing in Georgia invented the cotton gin, thus making a peculiar institution of dubious value an exceedingly profitable one. In the same year a Fugitive Slave Law was passed sanctioning the institution on a national level. Virginia again became a focus of Afro-American history with Gabriel's Revolt in 1800, chronicled in Arna Bontemps' novel *Black Thunder* (1936). From this point the lines were clearly drawn in the politics and pragmatics of slavery and freedom, and slavery, which was the condition of the overwhelming number of blacks, was the inexorable context for those who were free, North and South. Against this developing canvas the slave poet of North Carolina, George Moses Horton, uttered plaintively "The Slave's Complaint":

> Am I sadly cast aside,
> On misfortune's rugged tide?
> Will the world my pains deride
> Forever?
>
> Must I dwell in Slavery's night,
> And all pleasure take its flight,
> Far beyond my feeble sight,
> Forever?

The answer to Horton's query given by the slave power and its eloquent spokesmen, such as John C. Calhoun, was a profound echo; forever and ever. In their view black slavery was a blessing both for them and for the blacks, and only the scum of the earth could be opposed to such an idyllic system.

The real substance of Afro-American writing in the period between the development of the cotton kingdom and the passing of the Thirteenth Amendment is the protest against slavery. The most outright protest was David Walker's *Appeal* (1829), the rhetoric of which was so stinging that the pamphlet was outlawed in the South and a reward offered for the assassination of the author. Yet, it did not actually call for insurrection; it merely listed in emotional terms the nature of the blacks' oppression. Whether or not Walker's *Appeal* had any direct part in Nat Turner's famed revolt of 1831, Nat's own confession gives no clue, but the connection was surely made by his proslavery contemporaries, who feared the pen as much as the sword.

As interesting as David Walker's *Appeal* and closely associated with it in tone and spirit was *An Address to the Slaves of the United States of America*, written by Henry Highland Garnet and proposed for adoption to a national convention of free blacks in 1843. The essay, rejected by the convention as too provocative, was subsequently printed by Garnet and received wide circulation. Garnet's argument to his brothers in bondage, that it was sinful to submit voluntarily to slavery and that to do so incurred the penalty of eternal damnation, was an artful twisting of the proslavery argument urging submission with the prospect of eternal bliss.

One solution offered to the problem of blacks and to the problem of slavery (not always the same, since there were hundreds of thousands of free blacks) was that of colonization outside of the United States, preferably in Africa, though occasionally Haiti and other places were mentioned. The American Colonization Society had been founded in 1816. As early as 1822 it had sent settlers to what was to become, in 1847, Liberia. Actually, it was the free blacks who were the object of the colonization schemes. It was their troublesome presence which many whites, North and South, found most undesirable. The lure of colonization had limited appeal for Afro-Americans, and many whites who backed the scheme did so from the most ignoble motive—the elimination of the free blacks so that they could not influence those in slavery to aspire to liberty. Pro-colonization attracted little of the literary energies of Afro-Americans before the Civil War.

The most characteristic genre of Afro-American expression during the period before the Civil War was the slave narrative. Some of these were dictated to friendly antislavery whites. But many represented the individual effort of the author himself. Among those of considerable importance we should note the *Narrative of William Wells Brown* (1847) and Samuel R. Ward's, *The Autobiography of A Fugitive Slave* (1855). Ward's own experience in slavery was brief. His slave parents escaped with him from Maryland when he was a child of three. He was widely known as an antislavery lecturer. Exiled to Canada because of his antislavery activities, he found time there to compose his autobiography as a document in the struggle.

William Wells Brown, who achieved considerable fame in the pre-Civil War period as a writer, was another of the antislavery lecturers known both in the United States and in England. While in London for a five year period he published a novel, *Clotel; or the President's Daughter* (1853), which was subsequently revised and republished twice by him in the United States. He also wrote and published in 1858 a play, *The Escape: or a Leap for Freedom*. Both novel and play join his antislavery work and his *Narrative* in a common theme: protest against slavery.

The most brilliant figure to emerge in the struggle against slavery was Frederick Douglass, an escaped slave. His career as an antislavery lecturer began in 1841, and his oratorical skill and magnificent physical presence were themselves telling arguments against a system that denied liberty to such a man. In 1845 the *Narrative of the Life of Frederick Douglass* appeared and immediately became a popular work. With consummate literary skill Douglass told the story of his life as a slave and his escape from servitude. A revised version appeared in 1855 under the title *My Bondage and My Freedom*. Meanwhile Douglass lectured, edited a newspaper, and kept up a large correspondence with antislavery supporters in the United States and England.

The 1850s saw the lines being drawn more tightly between that part of the nation committed to eternal slavery for the black man and those who wished the institution (and usually also the blacks) out of the country. Black protest took many forms: conventions passing resolutions; support of the Underground Railroad, whose legendary figure is Harriet Tubman; and interminable lectures, usually before the converted. Among the remarkable platform speakers was the poet Frances E. W. Harper, whose career continued into the twentieth century and whose public declamations of her poems in the 1850s caused her audiences to buy her published poems by the thousands. One of her poems, "Eliza Harris," describes the character of that name from Harriet Beecher Stowe's antislavery novel *Uncle Tom's Cabin* (1852), itself the single most potent work in the annals of antislavery. Mrs. Harper's poem concludes:

But she's free!—yes, free from the land where the slave
From the hand of oppression must rest in the grave;
Where bondage and torture, where scourges and chains
Have plac'd on our banner indelible stains.

The bloodhounds have miss'd the scent of her way;
The hunter is rifled and foil'd of his prey;
Fierce jargon and cursing, with clanking of chains
Make sounds of strange discord on Liberty's plains.

With the rapture of love and fulness of bliss,
She placed on his brow a mother's fond kiss:—
O poverty, danger and death she can brave,
For the child of her love is no longer a slave!

The political events of the fifties ended the hopes for a nonviolent abolition of slavery. The Missouri Compromise was repealed in 1854 by the Kansas and Nebraska Act, thus encouraging the expansion of slavery. The Supreme Court rendered in 1857 the Dred Scott Decision, which sanctioned slavery in federal territory. John Brown's Raid of 1859, an armed attempt to free the slaves in West Virginia, ended disastrously with his execution. The acts of Secession, which followed the election of the pro-Union antislavery candidate Abraham Lincoln in 1860, brought about a situation in which the forcible abolition of slavery could be proposed as a matter of political and military expediency, and it was on this narrow ground that the stage was set for the Emancipation Proclamation and the Thirteenth Amendment.

PHILLIS WHEATLEY

(?1753-1784)

It is as a frail black child standing on a slave block in puritan Boston in 1761 that Phillis Wheatley enters the annals of American history. Purchased as a domestic servant by John Wheatley and christened by his family, she rapidly acculturated herself to her environment and was considered a prodigy. An ability to versify using the models available, chiefly adaptations of psalms and neo-classical poetry, brought her such acclaim that when she accompanied members of the Wheatley family to England in 1773 she was received by many distinguished people, and the Lord Mayor of London presented her with an edition of Paradise Lost. *It was in London in 1773 that* Poems, on Various Subjects, Religious and Moral *was published.*

Colonial America, a literary province of England, could hardly have been expected to produce many poets. Phillis Wheatley ranks with the best three or four who emerged between the colonization and the Revolution. Her achievement is, however, only relative, and she must be considered a minor English poet of her time whose interest for Afro-American literature is minimal. There was neither an Afro-American society for her to reflect nor an Afro-American audience to address. Nevertheless, the propaganda value of her achievement in the struggle of blacks in the United States has been extraordinary. The countless institutions and organizations named for her since early in the nineteenth century attest to the prestige of her attainment.

Of the poems presented here, "On Imagination" is simply a set piece in the manner of the English poetry of the time, utilizing the Miltonic diction that is normal for the genre. "To the University of Cambridge, in New England" (Harvard) is a greeting or compli-

mentary poem of occasion. "On Being Brought from Africa to America" offers, together with a passage on freedom in the poem which she addressed to Lord Dartmouth, one of the few allusions made by Phillis to her African home, of which she had probably blotted out all recollection. Her poems have been edited several times, notably by Heartman (1915), Ruth Wright (1930) and Julian D. Mason, Jr. (1966). Heartman's edition also includes her surviving letters.

On Imagination

Thy various works, imperial queen, we see.
How bright their forms! how decked with pomp by thee!
Thy wondr'ous acts in beauteous order stand,
And all attest how potent is thine hand.

From Helicon's refulgent heights attend,
Ye sacred choir, and my attempts befriend:
To tell her glories with a faithful tongue.
Ye blooming graces, triumph in my song.

Now here, now there, the roving Fancy flies,
Till some loved object strikes her wand'ring eyes,
Whose silken fetters all the senses bind,
And soft captivity involves the mind.

Imagination! who can sing thy force?
Or who describe the swiftness of thy course?
Soaring through air to find the bright abode,
Th' empyreal palace of the thundering God,
We on thy pinions can surpass the wind,
And leave the rolling universe behind:
From star to star the mental optics rove,
Measure the skies, and range the realms above.
There in one view we grasp the mighty whole,
Or with new worlds amaze th' unbounded soul.

Though Winter's frowns to Fancy's raptured eyes
The fields may flourish, and gay scenes arise;
The frozen deeps may break their iron bands,
And bid their waters murmur o'er the sands.
Fair Flora may resume her fragrant reign,
And with her flow'ry riches deck the plain;
Sylvanus may diffuse his honors round,
And all the forest may with leaves be crowned;
Show'rs may descend, and dews their gems disclose,
And nectar sparkle on the blooming rose.

Such is thy pow'r, nor are thine orders vain,
Oh, thou, the leader of the mental train;
In full perfection all thy works are wrought,
And thine the sceptre o'er the realms of thought.
Before thy throne the subject-passions bow,
Of subject-passions sov'reign ruler Thou;
At thy command joy rushes on the heart,
And through the glowing veins the spirits dart.

Fancy might now her siken pinions try
To rise from earth, and sweep th' expanse on high;
From Tithon's bed now might Aurora rise,
Her cheeks all glowing with celestial dies,
While a pure stream of light o'erflows the skies.

The monarch of the day I might behold,
And all the mountains tipped with radiant gold,
But I reluctant leave the pleasing views,
Which Fancy dresses to delight the Muse;
Winter austere forbids me to aspire,
And northern tempests damp the rising fire;
They chill the tides of Fancy's flowing sea,
Cease then, my song, cease th' unequal lay.

To the University of Cambridge, in New England

WHILE an intrinsic ardor prompts to write,
The muses promise to assist my pen;
'Twas not long since I left my native shore
The land of errors, and Egyptians gloom:
Father of mercy, 'twas thy gracious hand
Brought me in safety from those dark abodes.

Students, to you 'tis giv'n to scan the heights
Above, to traverse the ethereal space,
And mark the systems of revolving worlds.
Still more, ye sons of science, ye receive
The blissful news by messengers from heav'n,
How *Jesus*' blood for your redemption flows.
See him with hands outstretched upon the cross;
Immense compassion in his bosom glows;
He hears revilers, nor resents their scorn:
What matchless mercy in the Son of God!
When the whole human race by sin had fall'n,
He deign'd to die that they might rise again,
And share with him in the sublimest skies,
Life without death, and glory without end.

18

Improve your privileges while they stay,
Ye pupils, and each hour redeem, that bears
Or good or bad report of you to heav'n.
Let sin, that baneful evil to the soul,
By you be shunned, nor once remit your guard;
Suppress the deadly serpent in its egg.
Ye blooming plants of human race divine,
An *Ethiope* tells you 'tis your greatest foe;
Its transient sweetness turns to endless pain,
And in immense perdition sinks the soul.

On Being Brought from Africa to America

'Twas mercy brought me from my *Pagan* land,
Taught my benighted soul to understand
That there's a God, that there's a *Saviour* too:
Once I redemption neither sought nor knew.
Some view our race with scornful eye,
"Their color is a diabolic die."
Remember, Christians, Negroes, black as Cain,
May be refined, and join th' angelic train.

JUPITER HAMMON

(?1720-1800)

The slave-poet Jupiter Hammon is more a colonial curiosity than an authentic monument of Afro-American literature. His poetry is occasional, inspired by pious sentiment, and reflects acquiescence in an essentially benign divine order. Not enough is known of the circumstances of his life to relate any of his surviving broadsides to it. As a domestic servant with a literary bent living on rural Long Island, it may be supposed that his life was one of uneventful labor, reading and churchgoing.

Poems such as "An Evening Thought" (1761) and "A Winter Piece" (1782) reflect a bucolic piety in no way different from that of Euro-American writers of similar talents and temperament. Only in "An Address to Miss Phillis Wheatley" (1778) is there possibility of a quickened interest in Hammon's work. Expectation, however, is dashed in the wake of the poem's metred moralizing.

An Address to Miss Phillis Wheatley

1.

O, come, you pious youth! adore
 The wisdom of thy God,
In bringing thee from distant shore,
 To learn His holy word,

2.

Thou mightst been left behind,
 Amidst a dark abode;
God's tender mercy still combined,
 Thou hast the holy word.

3.

Fair Wisdom's ways are paths of peace,
 And they that walk therein,
Shall reap the joys that never cease,
 And Christ shall be their King.

4.

God's tender mercy brought thee here;
 Tossed o'er the raging main;
In Christian faith thou hast a share,
 Worth all the gold of Spain.

5.

While thousands tossed by the sea,
  And others settled down,
God's tender mercy set thee free
  From dangers that come down.

6.

That thou a pattern still might be,
  To youth of Boston town,
The blessed Jesus set thee free
  From every sinful wound.

7.

The blessed Jesus, who came down,
  Unveiled his sacred face,
To cleanse the soul of every wound,
  And give repenting grace.

8.

That we poor sinners may obtain
  The pardon of our sin,
Dear Blessed Jesus, now constrain,
  And bring us flocking in.

9.

Come, you, Phillis, now aspire,
  And seek the living God,
So step by step thou mayst go higher,
  Till perfect in the word.

10.

While thousands moved to distant shore,
  And others left behind,
The blessed Jesus still adore;
  Implant this in thy mind.

11.

Thou hast left the heathen shore;
  Through mercy of the Lord,
Among the heathen live no more;
  Come magnify thy God.

12.

I pray the living God may be,
  The shepherd of thy soul;
His tender mercies still are free,
  His mysteries to unfold.

13.

Thou, Phillis, when thou hunger hast,
  Or pantest for thy God,
Jesus Christ is thy relief,
  Thou hast the holy word.

14.

The bounteous mercies of the Lord
  Are hid beyond the sky,
And holy souls that have His word
  Shall taste them when they die.

15.

The bounteous mercies are from God,
  The merits of His Son;
The humble soul that loves His word
  He chooses for his own.

16.

Come, dear Phillis, be advised
  To drink Samaria's flood;
There nothing that shall suffice
  But Christ's redeeming blood.

17.

While thousands muse with earthly toys,
　And range about the street,
Dear Phillis, seek for heaven's joys,
　Where we do hope to meet.

18.

When God shall send his summons down,
　And number saints together,
Blessed angels chant (triumphant sound),
　Come live with me forever.

19.

The humble soul shall fly to God,
　And leave the things of time,
Start forth as 'twere at the first word,
　To taste things more divine.

20.

Behold! the soul shall waft away,
　Whene'er we come to die,
And leave its cottage made of clay,
　In twinkling of an eye.

21.

Now glory be to the Most High,
　United praises given,
By all on earth, incessantly,
　And all the host of heaven.

DAVID WALKER
(1785-1830)

Little is known of the man, but David Walker reveals himself in his Appeal *as one of the most passionate and radical of evangelists against the evil of slavery as an institution. The* Appeal *was printed in Boston in 1829. Its distribution and fame were sufficient to have it banned in several of the Southern states. Walker's own violent and mysterious death may have been a result of the tremors which his words evoked in the slave power.*

Walker was himself born in slavery in North Carolina, and like the many antislavery pamphleteers and lecturers who were to follow, he had personal experience of the institution he damned so resoundingly. The spirit of Walker's Appeal *animated his successors such as Douglass and Ward.*

From *David Walker's Appeal*

PREAMBLE.

My dearly beloved Brethren and Fellow Citizens:

Having travelled over a considerable portion of these United States, and having, in the course of my travels taken the most accurate observations of things as they exist—the result of my observations has warranted the full and unshakened conviction, that we, (colored people of these United States) are the most degraded, wretched, and abject set of beings that ever lived since the world began, and I pray God, that none like us ever may live again until time shall be no more. They tell us of the Israelites in Egypt, the Helots in Sparta, and of the Roman Slaves, which last, were made up from almost every nation under heaven, whose sufferings under those ancient and heathen nations were, in comparison with ours, under this enlightened and christian nation, no more than a cypher—or in other words, those heathen nations of antiquity, had but little more among them than the name and form of slavery, while wretchedness and endless miseries were reserved, apparently in a phial, to be poured out upon our fathers, ourselves and our children by *christian* Americans!

These positions, I shall endeavour, by the help of the Lord, to demonstrate in the course of this *appeal*, to the satisfaction of the most incredulous mind—and may God Almighty who is the father of our Lord Jesus Christ, open your hearts to understand and believe the truth.

The *causes*, my brethren, which produce our wretchedness and miseries, are so very numerous and aggravating, that I believe the pen only of a Josephus or a Plutarch, can well enumerate and explain them. Upon subjects, then, of such incomprehensible magnitude, so impenetrable, and so notorious, I shall be obliged to omit a large class of, and content myself with giving you an exposition of a few of those, which do indeed rage to such an alarming pitch, that they cannot but be a perpetual source of terror and dismay to every reflecting mind.

I am fully aware, in making this appeal to my much afflicted and suffering brethren, that I shall not only be assailed by those whose greatest earthly desires are, to keep us in abject ignorance and wretchedness, and who are of the firm conviction that heaven has designed us and our children to be slaves and *beasts of burden* to them and their children.—I say, I do not only expect to be held up to the public as an ignorant, impudent and restless disturber of the public peace, by such avaricious creatures, as well as a mover of insubordination—and perhaps put in prison or to death, for giving a superficial exposition of our miseries, and exposing tyrants. But I am persuaded, that many of my brethren, particularly those who are ignorantly in league with slave-holders or tyrants, who acquire their daily bread by the blood and sweat of their more ignorant brethren —and not a few of those too, who are too ignorant to see an inch beyond their noses, will rise up and call me cursed—Yea, the jealous ones among us will perhaps use more abject subtlety by affirming that this work is not worth perusing; that we are well situated and there is no use in trying to better our condition, for we cannot. I will ask one question here.—Can our condition be any worse?—Can it be more mean and abject? If there are any changes, will they not be for the better, though they may appear for the worst at first? Can they get us any lower? Where can they get us? They are afraid to treat us worse, for they know well, the day they do it they are gone. But against all accusations which may or can be preferred against me, I appeal to heaven for my motive in writing—who knows that my object is, if possible, to awaken in the breasts of my afflicted, degraded and slumbering brethren, a spirit of enquiry and investigation respecting our miseries and wretchedness in this *Republican Land of Liberty!!!!!*

The sources from which our miseries are derived and on which I shall comment, I shall not combine in one, but shall put them under distinct heads and expose them in their turn; in doing which, keeping truth on my side, and not departing from the strictest rules of morality, I shall endeavor to penetrate, search out, and lay them open for your inspection. If you cannot or will not profit by them, I shall have done *my* duty to you, my country and my God.

And as the inhuman system of *slavery*, is the *source* from which most of our miseries proceed, I shall begin with that *curse to nations;* which has spread terror and devastation through so many nations of antiquity, and which is raging to such a pitch at the present day in Spain and in Portugal. It had one tug in England, in France, and in the United States of America; yet the inhabitants thereof, do not learn wisdom, and erase it entirely from their dwellings and from all with whom they have to do. The fact is, the labor of slaves comes so cheap to the avaricious usurpers, and is (as they think) of such great utility to the country where it exists, that those who are actuated by sordid avarice only, overlook the evils, which will as sure as the Lord lives, follow after the good. In fact, they are so happy to keep in ignorance and degradation, and to receive the homage and the labor of the slaves, they forget that God rules in the armies of heaven and among the inhabitants of the earth, having his ears continually open to the cries, tears and groans of his oppressed people; and being a just and holy Being will at one day appear fully in behalf of the oppressed, and arrest the progress of the avaricious oppressors; for although the destruction of the oppressors God may not effect by the oppressed, yet the Lord our God will bring other destructions upon them—for not unfrequently will he cause them to rise up one against another, to be split and divided, and to oppress each other, and sometimes to open hostilities with sword in hand. Some may ask, what is the matter with this enlightened and happy people?—Some say it is the cause of political usurpers, tyrants, oppressors, &c. But has not the Lord an oppressed and suffering people among them? Does the Lord condescend to hear their cries and see their tears in consequence of oppression? Will he let the oppressors rest comfortably and happy always? Will he not cause the very children of the oppressors to rise up against them, and oftimes put them to death? "God works in many ways his wonders to perform."

I will not here speak of the destructions which the Lord brought upon Egypt, in consequence of the oppression and consequent groans of the oppressed—of the hundreds and thousands of Egyptians whom God hurled into the Red Sea for afflicting his people in their land—of the Lord's suffering people in Sparta or Lacedemon, the land of the truly famous Lycurgus—nor have I time to comment upon the cause which produced the fierceness with which Sylla usurped the title, and absolutely acted as dictator of the Roman people—the conspiracy of

Cataline—the conspiracy against, and murder of Caesar in the Senate house—the spirit with which Marc Antony made himself master of the commonwealth—his associating Octavius and Lipidus with himself in power,—their dividing the provinces of Rome among themselves—their attack and defeat on the plains of Phillipi the last defenders of their liberty, (Brutus and Cassius)—the tyranny of Tiberius, and from him to the final overthrow of Constantinople by the Turkish Sultan, Mahomed II., A. D. 1453. I say, I shall not take up time to speak of the *causes* which produced so much wretchedness and massacre among those heathen nations, for I am aware that you know too well, that God is just, as well as merciful!—I shall call your attention a few moments to that *christian* nation, the Spaniards, while I shall leave almost unnoticed that avaricious and cruel people, the Portuguese, among whom all true hearted christians and lovers of Jesus Christ, must evidently see the judgments of God displayed. To show the judgments of God upon the Spaniards I shall occupy but little time, leaving a plenty of room for the candid and unprejudiced to reflect.

All persons who are acquainted with history, and particularly the Bible, who are not blinded by the God of this world, and are not actuated solely by avarice—who are able to lay aside prejudice long enough to view candidly and impartially, things as they were, are, and probably will be, who are willing to admit that God made man to serve him *alone*, and that man should have no other Lord or Lords but himself—that God Almighty is the *sole proprietor* or *master* of the WHOLE human family, and will not on any consideration admit of a colleague, being unwilling to divide his glory with another.—And who can dispense with prejudice long enough to admit that we are men, notwithstanding our *improminent noses* and *woolly heads*, and believe that we feel for our fathers, mothers, wives and children as well as they do for theirs.—I say, all who are permitted to see and believe these things, can easily recognize the judgments of God among the Spaniards. Though others may lay the cause of the fierceness with which they cut each other's throats, to some other circumstances, yet they who believe that God is a God of justice, will believe that SLAVERY *is the principal cause.*

While the Spaniards are running about upon the field of battle cutting each other's throats, has not the Lord an afflicted and suffering people in the midst of them whose cries and groans in consequence of oppression are continually pouring into the ears of the God of justice? Would they not cease to cut each others throats if they could? But how can they? The very support which they draw from government to aid them in perpetrating such enormities, does it not arise in a great degree from the wretched victims of oppression among them? And yet they are calling for *Peace!—Peace ! !* Will any peace be given unto them? Their destruction may indeed be procrastinated awhile, but can it continue long while they are oppressing the Lord's people? Has He not the hearts of all men in His hand? Will he suffer one part of his creatures to go on oppressing another like brutes always, with impunity? And yet those avaricious wretches are calling for *Peace ! ! ! !* I declare it does appear to me, as though some nations think God is asleep, or that he made the Africans for nothing else but to dig their mines and work their farms, or they cannot believe history, sacred or profane. I ask every man who has a heart and is blessed with the privilege of believing—Is not God a God of justice to all his creatures? Do you say he is? Then if he gives peace and tranquility to tyrants, and permits them to keep our fathers, our mothers, ourselves and our children in eternal ignorance and wretchedness to support them and their families, would he be to us a God of *justice?* I ask O ye *christians ! ! !* who hold us and our children, in the most abject ignorance and degradation, that ever a people were afflicted with since the world began—I say, if God gives you peace and tranquility, and suffers you thus to go on afflicting us and our children, who have never given you the least provocation,— Would he be to us *a God of justice?* If you will allow that we are MEN, who feel for each other, does not the blood of our fathers and of us their children, cry aloud to the Lord of Sabaoth against you, for the cruelties and murders with which you have, and do continue to afflict us. But it is time for me to close my remarks on the suburbs, just to enter more fully into the interior of this system of cruelty and oppression.

HENRY HIGHLAND GARNET

(1815-1882)

Like Douglass, Garnet was born in slavery on the Eastern shore of Maryland. Like Ward, his parents took him as a child in their escape from slavery to New York, where he attended school with Ward and others who were to achieve fame in the cause of black liberation. Garnet's most famous work is An Address to the Slaves of the United States of America *(1843), a truly radical document.*

Garnet toured Europe, speaking against slavery, and was a missionary in Jamaica. After the abolition of slavery he achieved a certain degree of official approval and was named United States Representative to Liberia.

Alexander Crummell, who had been one of his schoolmates in New York, wrote The Eulogy of Henry Highland Garnet *(1882).*

An Address to the Slaves of the United States of America

PREFACE.

The following Address was first read at the National Convention held at Buffalo, N. Y., in 1843. Since that time it has been slightly modified, retaining, however, all of its original doctrine. The document elicited more discussion than any other paper that was ever brought before that, or any other deliberative body of colored persons, and their friends. Gentlemen who opposed the Address, based their objections on these grounds. 1. That the document was war-like, and encouraged insurrection; and 2. That if the Convention should adopt it, that those delegates who lived near the borders of the slave states, would not dare to return to their homes. The Address was rejected by a small majority; and now in compliance with the earnest request of many who heard it, and in conformity to the wishes of numerous friends who are anxious to see it, the author now gives it to the public, praying God that this little book may be borne on the four winds of heaven, until the principles it contains shall be understood and adopted by every slave in the Union.   H. H. G.

Troy, N. Y., April 15, 1848.

ADDRESS TO THE SLAVES OF THE U.S.

BRETHREN AND FELLOW CITIZENS:

Your brethren of the north, east, and west have been accustomed to meet together in National Conventions, to sympathize with each other, and to weep over your unhappy condition. In these meetings we have addressed all classes of the free, but we have never until this time, sent a word of consolation and advice to you. We have been contented in sitting still and mourning over your sorrows, earnestly hoping that before this day, your sacred liberties would have been restored. But, we have hoped in vain. Years have rolled on, and tens of thousands have been borne on streams of blood, and tears, to the shores of eternity. While you have been oppressed, we have also been partakers with you; nor can we be free while you are enslaved. We therefore write to you as being bound with you.

Many of you are bound to us, not only by the ties of a common humanity, but we are connected by the more tender relations of parents, wives, husbands, children, brothers, and sisters, and friends. As such we most affectionately address you.

Slavery has fixed a deep gulf between you and us, and while it shuts out from you the relief and consolation which your friends would willingly render, it afflicts and persecutes you with a fierceness which we might not expect to see in the fiends of hell. But still the Almighty Father of Mercies has left to us a glimmering ray of hope, which shines out like a lone star in a cloudy sky. Mankind are becoming wiser, and better—the oppressor's power is fading, and you, every day, are becoming better informed, and more numerous. Your grievances, brethren, are many. We shall not attempt, in this short address, to present to the world, all the dark catalogue of this nation's sins, which have been committed upon an innocent people. Nor is it indeed, necessary, for you feel them from day to day, and all the civilized world look upon them with amazement.

Two hundred and twenty-seven years ago, the first of our injured race were brought to the shores of America. They came not with glad spirits to select their homes, in the New World. They came not with their own consent, to find an unmolested enjoyment of the blessings of this fruitful soil. The first dealings which they had with men calling themselves Christians, exhibited to them the worst features of corrupt and sordid hearts; and convinced them that no cruelty is too great, no villainy, and no robbery too abhorrent for even enlightened men to perform, when influenced by avarice, and lust. Neither did they come flying upon the wings of Liberty, to a land of freedom. But, they came with broken hearts, from their beloved native land, and were doomed to unrequited toil, and deep degradation. Nor did the evil of their bondage end at their emancipation by death. Succeeding generations inherited their chains, and millions have come from eternity into time, and have returned again to the world of spirits, cursed, and ruined by American Slavery.

The propagators of the system, or their immediate ancestors very soon discovered its growing evil, and its tremendous wickedness, and secret promises were made to destroy it. The gross inconsistency of a people holding slaves, who had themselves "ferried o'er the wave," for freedom's sake, was too apparent to be entirely overlooked. The voice of Freedom cried, "emancipate your Slaves." Humanity supplicated with tears, for the deliverance of the children of Africa. Wisdom urged her solemn plea. The bleeding captive pled his innocence, and pointed to Christianity who stood weeping at the cross. Jehovah frowned upon the nefarious institution, and thunderbolts, red with vengeance, struggled to leap forth to blast the guilty wretches who maintained it. But all was vain. Slavery had stretched its dark wings of death over the land, the Church stood silently by— the priests prophesied falsely, and the people loved to have it so. Its throne is established, and now it reigns triumphantly.

Nearly three millions of your fellow citizens, are prohibited by law, and public opinion, (which in this country is stronger than law), from reading the Book of Life. Your intellect has been destroyed as much as possible, and every ray of light they have attempted to shut out from your minds. The oppressors themselves have become involved in the ruin. They have become weak, sensual, and rapacious. They have cursed you—they have cursed themselves—they have cursed the earth which they have trod. In the language of a Southern statesman, we can truly say, "even the wolf, driven back long since by the approach of man, now returns after the lapse of a hundred years, and howls amid the desolations of slavery."

The colonists threw the blame upon England. They said that the mother country entailed the evil upon them, and that they would rid themselves of it if they could. The world thought they were sincere, and the philanthropic pitied them. But time soon tested their sincerity. In a few years, the colonists grew strong and severed themselves from the British Government. Their Independence was declared, and they took their station among the sovereign powers of the earth. The declaration was a glorious document. Sages admired it, and the patriotic of every nation reverenced the Godlike sentiments which it contained. When the power of Government returned to their hands, did they emancipate the slaves? No; they rather added new links to our chains. Were they ignorant of the principles of

Liberty? Certainly they were not. The sentiments of their revolutionary orators fell in burning eloquence upon their hearts, and with one voice they cried, LIBERTY OR DEATH. O, what a sentence was that! It ran from soul to soul like electric fire, and nerved the arm of thousands to fight in the holy cause of Freedom. Among the diversity of opinions that are entertained in regard to physical resistance, there are but a few found to gainsay that stern declaration. We are among those who do not.

SLAVERY! How much misery is comprehended in that single word. What mind is there that does not shrink from its direful effects? Unless the image of God is obliterated from the soul, all men cherish the love of Liberty. The nice discerning political economist does not regard the sacred right, more than the untutored African who roams in the wilds of Congo. Nor has the one more right to the full enjoyment of his freedom than the other. In every man's mind the good seeds of liberty are planted, and he who brings his fellow down so low, as to make him contented with a condition of slavery, commits the highest crime against God and man. Brethren, your oppressors aim to do this. They endeavor to make you as much like brutes as possible. When they have blinded the eyes of your mind—when they have embittered the sweet waters of life—when they have shut out the light which shines from the word of God—then, and not till then has American slavery done its perfect work.

TO SUCH DEGRADATION IT IS SINFUL IN THE EXTREME FOR YOU TO MAKE VOLUNTARY SUBMISSION. The divine commandments, you are in duty bound to reverence, and obey. If you do not obey them you will surely meet with the displeasure of the Almighty. He requires you to love him supremely, and your neighbor as yourself—to keep the Sabbath day holy—to search the Scriptures—and bring up your children with respect for his laws, and to worship no other God but him. But slavery sets all these at naught, and hurls defiance in the face of Jehovah. The forlorn condition in which you are placed does not destroy your moral obligation to God. You are not certain of Heaven, because you suffer yourselves to remain in a state of slavery, where you cannot obey the commandments of the Sovereign of the universe. If the ignorance of slavery is a passport to heaven, then it is a blessing, and no curse, and you should rather desire its perpetuity than its abolition. God will not receive slavery, nor ignorance, nor any other state of mind, for love, and obedience to him. Your condition does not absolve you from your moral obligation. The diabolical injustice by which your liberties are cloven down, NEITHER GOD, NOR

ANGELS, NOR JUST MEN, COMMAND YOU TO SUFFER FOR A SINGLE MOMENT.
THEREFORE IT IS YOUR SOLEMN AND IMPERATIVE DUTY TO USE EVERY
MEANS, BOTH MORAL, INTELLECTUAL, AND PHYSICAL, THAT PROMISE SUC-
CESS. If a band of heathen men should attempt to enslave a race of
Christians, and to place their children under the influence of some
false religion, surely, heaven would frown upon the men who would
not resist such aggression, even to death. If, on the other hand, a
band of Christians should attempt to enslave a race of heathen men
and to entail slavery upon them, and to keep them in heathenism in
the midst of Christianity, the God of heaven would smile upon every
effort which the injured might make to disenthral themselves.

Brethren, it is as wrong for your lordly oppressors to keep you
in slavery, as it was for the man thief to steal our ancestors from the
coast of Africa. You should therefore now use the same manner of
resistance, as would have been just in our ancestors, when the bloody
foot prints of the first remorseless soul thief was placed upon the
shores of our fatherland. The humblest peasant is as free in the sight
of God, as the proudest monarch that ever swayed a sceptre. Liberty
is a spirit sent out from God, and like its great Author, is no respector
of persons.

Brethren, the time has come when you must act for yourselves.
It is an old and true saying, that "if hereditary bondmen would be
free, they must themselves strike the blow." You can plead your own
cause, and do the work of emancipation better than any others. The
nations of the old world are moving in the great cause of universal
freedom, and some of them at least, will ere long, do you justice. The
combined powers of Europe have placed their broad seal of disappro-
bation upon the African slave trade. But in the slave holding parts of
the United States, the trade is as brisk as ever. They buy and sell you
as though you were brute beasts. The North has done much—her
opinion of slavery in the abstract is known. But in regard to the
South, we adopt the opinion of the New York Evangelist—"We have
advanced so far, that the cause apparently waits for a more effectual
door to be thrown open than has been yet." We are about to point
you to that more effectual door. Look around you, and behold the
bosoms of your loving wives, heaving with untold agonies! Hear the
cries of your poor children! Remember the stripes your fathers bore.
Think of the torture and disgrace of your noble mothers. Think of
your wretched sisters, loving virtue and purity, as they are driven
into concubinage, and are exposed to the unbridled lusts of incarnate
devils. Think of the undying glory that hangs around the ancient

name of Africa:—and forget not that you are native-born American citizens, and as such, you are justly entitled to all the rights that are granted to the freest. Think how many tears you have poured out upon the soil which you have cultivated with unrequited toil, and enriched with your blood; and then go to your lordly enslavers, and tell them plainly, that YOU ARE DETERMINED TO BE FREE. Appeal to their sense of justice, and tell them that they have no more right to oppress you, than you have to enslave them. Entreat them to remove the grievous burdens which they have imposed upon you, and to remunerate you for your labor. Promise them renewed diligence in the cultivation of the soil, if they will render to you an equivalent for your services. Point them to the increase of happiness and prosperity in the British West Indies, since the act of Emancipation. Tell them in language which they cannot misunderstand, of the exceeding sinfulness of slavery, and of a future judgment, and of the righteous retributions of an indignant God. Inform them that all you desire, is FREEDOM, and that nothing else will suffice. Do this, and for ever after cease to toil for the heartless tyrants, who give you no other reward but stripes and abuse. If they then commence the work of death, they, and not you, will be responsible for the consequences. You had far better all die—*die immediately*, than live slaves, and entail your wretchedness upon your posterity. If you would be free in this generation, here is your only hope. However much you and all of us may desire it, there is not much hope of Redemption without the shedding of blood. If you must bleed, let it all come at once—rather, *die freemen, than live to be slaves.* It is impossible, like the children of Israel, to make a grand Exodus from the land of bondage. THE PHARAOHS ARE ON BOTH SIDES OF THE BLOOD-RED WATERS! You cannot remove en masse, to the dominions of the British Queen—nor can you pass through Florida, and overrun Texas, and at last find peace in Mexico. The propagators of American slavery are spending their blood and treasure, that they may plant the black flag in the heart of Mexico, and riot in the halls of the Montezumas. In the language of the Rev. Robert Hall, when addressing the volunteers of Bristol, who were rushing forth to repel the invasion of Napoleon, who threatened to lay waste the fair homes of England, "Religion is too much interested in your behalf, not to shed over you her most gracious influences."

You will not be compelled to spend much time in order to become inured to hardships. From the first moment that you breathed the air of heaven, you have been accustomed to nothing else but hardships. The heroes of the American Revolution were never put upon harder fare, than a peck of corn, and a few herrings per week. You have not become enervated by the luxuries of life. Your sternest energies have been beaten out upon the anvil of severe trial. Slavery has done this, to make you subservient to its own purposes; but it has done more than this, it has prepared you for any emergency. If you receive good treatment, it is what you could hardly expect; if you meet with pain, sorrow, and even death, these are the common lot of the slaves.

Fellow-men! patient sufferers! behold your dearest rights crushed to the earth! See your sons murdered, and your wives, mothers, and sisters, doomed to prostitution! In the name of the merciful God! and by all that life is worth, let it no longer be a debateable question, whether it is better to choose LIBERTY or DEATH!

In 1822, Denmark Veazie, of South Carolina, formed a plan for the liberation of his fellow men. In the whole history of human efforts to overthrow slavery, a more complicated and tremendous plan was never formed. He was betrayed by the treachery of his own people, and died a martyr to freedom. Many a brave hero fell, but History, faithful to her high trust, will transcribe his name on the same monument with Moses, Hampden, Tell, Bruce, and Wallace, Toussaint L'Ouverture, Lafayette and Washington. That tremendous movement shook the whole empire of slavery. The guilty soul thieves were overwhelmed with fear. It is a matter of fact, that at that time, and in consequence of the threatened revolution, the slave states talked strongly of emancipation. But they blew one blast of the trumpet of freedom, and then laid it aside. As these men became quiet, the slaveholders ceased to talk about emancipation: and now, behold your condition today! Angels sigh over it, and humanity has long since exhausted her tears in weeping on your account!

The patriotic Nathaniel Turner followed Denmark Veazie. He was goaded to desperation by wrong and injustice. By Despotism, his name has been recorded on the list of infamy, but future generations will number him among the noble and brave.

Next arose the immortal Joseph Cinque, the hero of the Amistad. He was a native African, and by the help of God he emancipated a whole ship-load of his fellow men on the high seas. And he now sings of liberty on the sunny hills of Africa, and beneath his native palm trees, where he hears the lion roar, and feels himself as free as that king of the forest. Next arose Madison Washington, that bright star of freedom, and took his station in the constellation of freedom.

He was a slave on board the brig Creole, of Richmond, bound to New Orleans, that great slave mart, with a hundred and four others. Nineteen struck for liberty or death. But one life was taken, and the whole were emancipated, and the vessel was carried into Nassau, New Providence. Noble men! Those who have fallen in freedom's conflict, their memories will be cherished by the true hearted, and the God-fearing, in all future generations; those who are living, their names are surrounded by a halo of glory.

We do not advise you to attempt a revolution with the sword, because it would be INEXPEDIENT. Your numbers are too small, and moreover the rising spirit of the age, and the spirit of the gospel, are opposed to war and bloodshed. But from this moment cease to labor for tyrants who will not remunerate you. Let every slave throughout the land do this, and the days of slavery are numbered. You cannot be more oppressed than you have been—you cannot suffer greater cruelties than you have already. RATHER DIE FREEMEN, THAN LIVE TO BE SLAVES. Remember that you are THREE MILLIONS.

It is in your power so to torment the God cursed slaveholders, that they will be glad to let you go free. If the scale was turned and black men were the masters, and white men the slaves, every destructive agent and element would be employed to lay the oppressor low. Danger and death would hang over their heads day and night. Yes, the tyrants would meet with plagues more terrible than those of Pharaoh. But you are a patient people. You act as though you were made for the special use of these devils. You act as though your daughters were born to pamper the lusts of your masters and overseers. And worse than all, you tamely submit, while your lords tear your wives from your embraces, and defile them before your eyes. In the name of God we ask, are you men? Where is the blood of your fathers? Has it all run out of your veins? Awake, awake; millions of voices are calling you! Your dead fathers speak to you from their graves. Heaven, as with a voice of thunder, calls on you to arise from the dust.

Let your motto be RESISTANCE! RESISTANCE! RESISTANCE!— No oppressed people have ever secured their liberty without resistance. What kind of resistance you had better make, you must decide by the circumstances that surround you, and according to the suggestion of expediency. Brethren, adieu. Trust in the living God. Labor for the peace of the human race, and remember that you are three millions.

GEORGE HORTON
(c.1800-c.1880)

*The third of the slave-poets known to American literature was
curiously enough a campus figure. The proximity (and accessibility)
of books on the campus of the University of North Caroline at Chapel
Hill served to make of George Horton a minor poet, adept at writing poems of dalliance commissioned by amorous undergraduates. He
had, however, more serious concerns, his freedom being the major
one. This gifted man received his freedom only with the abolition of
slavery, in spite of a bizarre effort to raise enough money to buy his
freedom by the sale of his verse.*

Poems by a Slave *(1837)*, Poetical Works *(1845)* and the Naked
Genius *(1865)* contain the works of Horton known to us. Of his
verse William H. Robinson, Jr., says, in Early Black American Poets:
"*There is not much thought in most of his work, his best pieces being
those that plead for his freedom with a sincerity that is believable,
despite the conventionally stilted syntax and the abstract language.*"

To Eliza

Eliza, tell thy lover why
Or what induced thee to deceive me?
  Fare thee well—away I fly—
I shun the lass who thus will grieve me.

Eliza, still thou art my song,
Although by force I may forsake thee;
  Fare thee well, for I was wrong
To woo thee while another take thee.

Eliza, pause and think awhile—
Sweet lass! I shall forget thee never:
  Fare thee well: although I smile,
I grieve to give thee up forever.

Eliza, I shall think of thee—
My heart I shall ever twine about thee;
  Fare thee well—but think of me,

Compell'd to live and die without thee,
  "Fare thee well!—and if forever,[1]
"Still forever fare thee well!"

The Art of a Poet

True nature first inspires the man,
But he must after learn to scan,
    And mark well every rule;
Gradual the climax then ascend,
And prove the contrast in the end,
    Between the wit and fool.

A fool tho' blind, may write a verse,
And seem from folly to emerge,
    And rime well every line;
One lucky, void of light, may guess
And safely to the point may press,
    But this does not refine.

Polish mirror, clear to shine,
And streams must run if they refine,
    And widen as they flow;
The diamond water lies concealed,
Till polished it is ne'er revealed,
    Its glory bright to show.

A bard must traverse o'er the world,
Where things concealed must rise unfurled,
    And tread the feet of yore;
Tho' he may sweetly harp and sing,
But strictly prune the mental wing,
    Before the mind can soar.

Slavery

When first my bosom glowed with hope,
    I gazed as from a mountain top
      On some delightful plain;
But oh! how transient was the scene—
It fled as though it had not been,
      And all my hopes were vain.

How oft this tantalyzing blaze
    Has led me through deception's maze;
      My friends became my foe—
Then like a plaintive dove I mourned;
To bitter all my sweets were turned,
      And tears began to flow.

Why was the dawning of my birth
Upon this vile, accursed earth,
      Which is but pain to me?
Oh! that my soul had winged its flight,
When I first saw the morning light,
      To worlds of liberty!

Come, melting Pity, from afar,
And break this vast, enormous bar
      Between a wretch and thee;
Purchase a few short days of time,
And bid a vassal rise sublime
      On wings of liberty.

Is it because my skin is black,
That thou should'st be so dull and slack,
   And scorn to set me free?
Then let me hasten to the grave,
The only refuge for the slave,
   Who mourns for liberty.

The wicked cease from troubling there;
No more I'd languish or despair—
   The weary there can rest!
Oppression's voice is heard no more,
Drudg'ry and pain and toil are o'er,
   Yes! there I shall be blest!

WILLIAM WELLS BROWN
(1815-1884)

Like Douglass and Ward a leading antislavery lecturer, William Wells Brown turned to the novel as an extension of his platform activity against slavery. He was born in Lexington, Kentucky, as a slave. From St. Louis, where he was working, he fled to Canada in 1834. While in England on a five-year stay he published the first of four versions of his novel, Clotel; or the President's Daughter *(1853) (later versions published in the United States were* Clotelle: A Tale of the Southern States *[1864] and* Clotelle; or the Colored Heroine *[1867]). Earlier, Brown had written the narrative of his own life in slavery in 1847.*

Brown also wrote and lectured on the history of the black man. He had lectured in Boston on the Revolution in Haiti as early as 1855. Published works included The Black Man *(1863) and* The Negro in the American Rebellion *(1867). In a more personal vein he wrote* The Rising Son *(1874) and* My Southern Home *(1880).*

A comprehensive study of Brown as a pioneer figure in black literature has been written by W. Edward Farrison (1969) and is indispensable for knowing Brown and his period.

From *Clotel, or the President's Daughter*

CHAPTER XIX

ESCAPE OF CLOTEL

> "THE fetters galled my weary soul—
>   A soul that seemed but thrown away:
> I spurned the tyrant's base control,
>   Resolved at least the man to play."

No country has produced so much heroism in so short a time, connected with escapes from peril and oppression, as has occurred in the United States among the fugitive slaves, many of whom show great shrewdness in their endeavours to escape from this land of bondage. A slave was one day seen passing on the high road from a border town in the interior of the state of Virginia to the Ohio river. The man had neither hat upon his head or coat upon his back. He was driving before him a very nice fat pig, and appeared to all who saw him to be a labourer employed on an adjoining farm. "No negro is permitted to go at large in the Slave States without a written pass from his or her master, except on business in the neighbourhood." "Where do you live, my boy?" asked a white man of the slave, as he passed a white house with green blinds. "Jist up de road, sir," was the answer. "That's a fine pig." "Yes, sir, marser like dis choat berry much." And the negro drove on as if he was in great haste. In this way he and the pig travelled more than fifty miles before they reached the Ohio river. Once at the river they crossed over; the pig was sold; and nine days after the runaway slave passed over the Niagara river, and, for the first time in his life, breathed the air of freedom. A few weeks later, and, on the same road, two slaves were seen passing; one was on horseback, the other was walking before him with his arms tightly bound, and a long rope leading from the man on foot to the one on horseback. "Oh, ho, that's a runaway rascal, I suppose," said a farmer, who met them on the road. "Yes, sir, he bin runaway, and I got him fast. Marser will tan his jacket for him nicely when he gets him." "You are a trustworthy fellow, I imagine," continued the farmer. "Oh yes, sir; marser puts a heap of confidence in this nigger." And the slaves travelled on. When the one on foot was fatigued they would change positions, the other being tied and driven on foot. This they called "ride and tie." After a journey of more than two hundred miles they reached the Ohio river, turned the horse loose, told him to go home, and proceeded on their way to Canada. However they were not to have it all their own way. There are men in the Free States, and especially in the states adjacent to the Slave States, who make their living by catching the runaway slave, and returning him for the reward that may be offered. As the two slaves above mentioned were travelling on towards the land of freedom, led by the North Star, they were set upon by four of these slave-catchers, and one of them unfortunately captured. The other escaped. The captured fugitive was put under the torture, and compelled to reveal the name of his owner and his place of residence. Filled with delight, the kidnappers started back with their victim. Overjoyed with the prospect of receiving a large reward, they gave themselves up on the third night to pleasure. They put up at an inn. The negro was chained to the bed-post, in the same room with his captors. At dead of night, when all was still, the slave arose from the floor upon which he had been lying, looked around, and saw that the white men were fast asleep. The brandy punch had done its work. With palpitating heart and trembling limbs he viewed his position. The door was fast, but the warm weather had compelled them to leave the window open. If he could but get his chains off, he might escape through the window to the piazza, and reach the ground by one of the posts that supported the piazza. The sleeper's clothes hung upon chairs by the bedside; the slave thought of the padlock key, examined the pockets and found it. The chains were soon off, and the negro stealthily making his way to the window: he stopped and said to himself, "These men are villains, they are enemies to all who like me are trying to be free. Then why not I teach them a lesson?" He then undressed himself, took the clothes of one of the men, dressed himself in them, and escaped through the window, and, a moment more, he was on the high road to Canada. Fifteen days later, and the writer of this gave him a passage across Lake Erie, and saw him safe in her Britannic Majesty's dominions.

We have seen Clotel sold to Mr. French in Vicksburgh, her hair cut short, and everything done to make her realise her position as a servant. Then we have seen her re-sold, because her owners feared she would die through grief. As yet her new purchaser treated her with respectful gentleness, and sought to win her favour by flattery and presents, knowing that whatever he gave her he could take back again. But she dreaded every moment lest the scene should change, and trembled at the sound of every footfall. At every interview with her new master Clotel stoutly maintained that she had left a husband in Virginia, and would never think of taking another. The gold watch and chain, and other glittering presents which he purchased for her, were all laid aside by the quadroon, as if they were of no value to her. In the same house with her was another servant, a man, who had from time to time hired himself from his master. William was his name. He could feel for Clotel, for he, like her, had been separated from near and dear relatives, and often tried to console the poor woman. One day the quadroon observed to him that her hair was growing out again. "Yes," replied William, "you look a good deal like a man with your short hair." "Oh," rejoined she, "I have often been told that I would make a better looking man than a woman. If I had the money," continued she, "I would bid farewell to this place." In a moment more she feared that she had said too much, and smilingly remarked, "I am always talking nonsense." William was a tall, full-bodied negro, whose very countenance beamed with intelligence. Being a mechanic, he had, by his own industry, made more than what he paid his owner; this he laid aside, with the hope that some day he might get enough to purchase his freedom. He had in his chest one hundred and fifty dollars. His was a heart that felt for others, and he had again and again wiped the tears from his eyes as he heard the story of Clotel as related by herself. "If she can get free with a little money, why not give her what I have?" thought he, and then he resolved to do it. An hour after, he came into the quadroon's room, and laid the money in her lap, and said, "There, Miss Clotel, you said if you had the means you would leave this place; there is money enough to take you to England, where you will be free. You are much fairer than many of the white women of the South, and can easily pass for a free white lady." At first Clotel feared that it was a plan by which the negro wished to try her fidelity to her owner; but she was soon convinced by his earnest manner, and the deep feeling with which he spoke, that he was honest. "I will take the money only on one condition," said she; "and that is, that I effect your escape as well as my own." "How can that be done?" he inquired. "I will assume the disguise of a gentleman and you that of a servant, and we will take passage on a steamboat and go to Cincinnati, and thence to Canada. Here William put in several objections to the plan. He feared detection, and he well knew that, when a slave is once caught when attempting to escape, if returned is sure to be worse treated than before. However, Clotel satisfied him that the plan could be carried out if he would only play his part.

The resolution was taken, the clothes for her disguise procured, and before night everything was in readiness for their departure. That night Mr. Cooper, their master, was to attend a party, and this was their opportunity. William went to the wharf to look out for a boat, and had scarcely reached the landing ere he heard the puffing of a steamer. He returned and reported the fact. Clotel had already packed her trunk, and had only to dress and all was ready. In less than an hour they were on board the boat. Under the assumed name of "Mr. Johnson," Clotel went to the clerk's office and took a private state room for herself, and paid her own and servant's fare. Besides being attired in a neat suit of black, she had a white silk handkerchief tied round her chin, as if she was an invalid. A pair of green glasses covered her eyes; and fearing that she would be talked to too much and thus render her liable to be detected, she assumed to be very ill. On the other hand, William was playing his part well in the servants' hall; he was talking loudly of his master's wealth. Nothing appeared as good on the boat as in his master's fine mansion. "I don't like dees steamboats no how," said William; "I hope when marser goes on a journey agin he will take de carriage and de hosses." Mr. Johnson (for such was the name by which Clotel now went) remained in his room, to avoid, as far as possible, conversation with others. After a passage of seven days they arrived at Louisville, and put up at Gough's Hotel. Here they had to await the departure of another boat for the North. They were now in their most critical position. They were still in a slave state, and John C. Calhoun, a distinguished slave-owner, was a guest at this hotel. They feared, also, that trouble would attend their attempt to leave this place for the North, as all persons taking negroes with them have to give bail that such negroes are not runaway slaves.

The law upon this point is very stringent: all steamboats and other public conveyances are liable to a fine for every slave that escapes by them, besides paying the full value for the slave. After a delay of four hours, Mr. Johnson and servant took passage on the steamer Rodolph, for Pittsburgh. It is usual, before the departure of the boats, for an officer to examine every part of the vessel to see that no slave secretes himself on board, "Where are you going?" asked the officer of William, as he was doing his duty on this occasion. "I am going with marser," was the quick reply. "Who is your master?" "Mr. Johnson, sir, a gentleman in the cabin." "You must take him to the office and satisfy that captain that all is right, or you can't go on this boat." William informed his master what the officer had said. The boat was on the eve of going, and no time could be lost, yet they knew not what to do. At last they went to the office, and Mr. Johnson, addressing the captain, said, "I am informed that my boy can't go with me unless I give security that he belongs to me." "Yes," replied the captain, "that is the law." "A very strange law indeed," rejoined Mr. Johnson, "that one can't take his property with him." After a conversation of some minutes, and a plea on the part of Johnson that he did not wish to be delayed owing to his illness, they were permitted to take their passage without farther trouble, and the boat was soon on its way up the river. The fugitives had now passed the Rubicon, and the next place at which they would land would be in a Free State. Clotel called William to her room, and said to him, "We are now free, you can go on your way to Canada, and I shall go to Virginia in search of my daughter." The announcement that she was going to risk her liberty in a Slave State was unwelcome news to William. With all the eloquence he could command, he tried to persuade Clotel that she could not escape detection, and was only throwing her freedom away. But she had counted the cost, and made up her mind for the worst. In return for the money he had furnished, she had secured for him his liberty, and their engagement was at an end.

After a quick passage the fugitives arrived at Cincinnati, and there separated. William proceeded on his way to Canada, and Clotel again resumed her own apparel, and prepared to start in search of her child. As might have been expected, the escape of those two valuable slaves created no little sensation in Vicksburgh. Advertisements and messages were sent in every direction in which the fugitives were thought to have gone. It was soon, however, known that they had left the town as master and servant; and many were the communications which appeared in the newspapers, in which the writers thought, or pretended, that they had seen the slaves in their disguise. One was to the effect that they had gone off in a chaise; one as master, and the other as servant. But the most probable was an account given by a correspondent of one of the Southern newspapers, who happened to be a passenger in the same steamer in which the slaves escaped, and which we here give:—

"One bright starlight night, in the month of December last, I found myself in the cabin of the steamer Rodolph, then lying in the port of Vicksburgh, and bound to Louisville. I had gone early on board, in order to select a good berth, and having got tired of reading the papers, amused myself with watching the appearance of the passengers as they dropped in, one after another, and I being a believer in physiognomy, formed my own opinion of their characters.

"The second bell rang, and as I yawningly returned my watch to my pocket, my attention was attracted by the appearance of a young man who entered the cabin supported by his servant, a strapping negro.

"The man was bundled up in a capacious overcoat; his face was bandaged with a white handkerchief, and its expression entirely hid by a pair of enormous spectacles.

"There was something so mysterious and unusual about the young man as he sat restless in the corner, that curiosity led me to observe him more closely.

"He appeared anxious to avoid notice, and before the steamer had fairly left the wharf, requested, in a low, womanly voice, to be shown his berth, as he was an invalid, and must retire early: his name he gave as Mr. Johnson. His servant was called, and he was put quietly to bed. I paced the deck until Tybee light grew dim in the distance, and then went to my berth.

"I awoke in the morning with the sun shining in my face; we were then just passing St. Helena. It was a mild beautiful morning, and most of the passengers were on deck, enjoying the freshness of the air, and stimulating their appetites for breakfast. Mr. Johnson soon made his appearance, arrayed as on the night before, and took his seat quietly upon the guard of the boat.

"From the better opportunity afforded by daylight, I found that he was a slight built, apparently handsome young man, with black hair and eyes, and of a darkness of complexion that betokened Spanish extraction. Any notice from others seemed painful to him; so to satisfy my curiosity, I questioned his servant, who was standing near, and gained the following information.

"His master was an invalid—he had suffered for a long time under a complication of diseases, that had baffled the skill of the best physicians in Mississippi he was now suffering principally with the 'rheumatism,' and he was scarcely able to walk or help himself in any way. He came from Vicksburgh, and was now on his way to Philadelphia, at which place resided his uncle, a celebrated physician, and through whose means he hoped to be restored to perfect health.

"This information communicated in a bold, off-hand manner, enlisted my sympathies for the sufferer, although it occurred to me that he walked rather too gingerly for a person afflicted with so many ailments."

After thanking Clotel for the great service she had done him in bringing him out of slavery, William bade her farewell. The prejudice that exists in the Free States against coloured persons, on account of their colour, is attributable solely to the influence of slavery, and is but another form of slavery itself. And even the slave who escapes from the Southern plantations, is surprised when he reaches the North, at the amount and withering influence of this prejudice. William applied at the railway station for a ticket for the train going to Sandusky, and was told that if he went by that train he would have to ride in the luggage-van. "Why?" asked the astonished negro. "We don't send a Jim Crow carriage but once a day, and that went this morning." The "Jim Crow" carriage is the one in which the blacks have to ride. Slavery is a school in which its victims learn much shrewdness, and William had been an apt scholar. Without asking any more questions, the negro took his seat in one of the first-class carriages. He was soon seen and ordered out. Afraid to remain in the town longer, he resolved to go by that train; and consequently seated himself on a goods' box in the luggage-van. The train started at its proper time, and all went on well. Just before arriving at the end of the journey, the conductor called on William for his ticket. "I have none," was the reply. "Well, then, you can pay your fare to me," said the officer. "How much is it?" asked the black man. "Two dollars." "What do you charge those in the passenger-carriage?" "Two dollars." "And do you charge me the same as you do those who ride in the best carriages?" asked the negro. "Yes," was the answer. "I shan't pay it," returned the man. "You black scamp, do you think you can ride on this road without paying your fare?" "No, I don't want to ride for nothing; I only want to pay what's right." "Well, launch out two dollars, and that's right." "No, I shan't; I will pay what I ought, and won't pay any more." "Come, come, nigger, your fare and be done with it," said the conductor, in a manner that is never used except by Americans to blacks. "I won't pay you two dollars, and that enough," said William. "Well, as you have come all the way in the luggage-van, pay me a dollar and a half and you may go." "I shan't do any such thing." "Don't you mean to pay for riding?" "Yes, but I won't pay a dollar and a half for riding up here in the freight-van. If you had let me come in the carriage where others ride, I would have paid you two dollars." "Where were you raised? You seem to think yourself as good as white folks." "I want nothing more than my rights." "Well, give me a dollar, and I will let you off." "No, sir, I shan't do it." "What do you mean to do then—don't you wish to pay anything?" "Yes, sir, I want to pay you the full price." "What do you mean by full price?" "What do you charge per hundred-weight for goods?" inquired the negro with a degree of gravity that would have astonished Diogenes himself. "A quarter of a dollar per hundred," answered the conductor. "I weigh just one hundred and fifty pounds," returned William, "and will pay you three eighths of a dollar." "Do you expect that you will pay only thirty-seven cents for your ride?" "This, sir, is your own price. I came in a luggage-van, and I'll pay for luggage." After a vain effort to get the negro to pay more, the conductor took the thirty-seven cents, and noted in his cash-book, "Received for one hundred and fifty pounds of luggage, thirty-seven cents." This, reader, is no fiction; it actually occurred in the railway above described.

Thomas Corwin, a member of the American Congress, is one of the blackest white men in the United States. He was once on his way to Congress, and took passage in one of the Ohio river steamers. As he came just at the dinner hour, he immediately went into the dining saloon, and took his seat at the table. A gentleman with his whole party of five ladies at once left the table. "Where is the captain," cried the man in an angry tone. The captain soon appeared, and it was sometime before he could satisfy the old gent, that Governor Corwin was not a nigger. The newspapers often have notices of mistakes made by innkeepers and others who undertake to accommodate the public, one of which we give below.

On the 6th inst., the Hon. Daniel Webster and family entered Edgartown, on a visit for health and recreation. Arriving at the hotel, without alighting from the coach, the landlord was sent for to see if suitable accommodation could be had. That dignitary apppearing, and surveying Mr. Webster, while the hon. senator addressed him, seemed woefully to mistake the dark features of the traveller as he sat back in the corner of the carriage, and to suppose him a *coloured man*, particularly as there were two coloured servants of Mr. W. outside. So he promptly declared that there was no room for him and his family, and he could not be accommodated there—at the same time suggesting that he might perhaps find accommodation at some of the huts "up back," to which he pointed. So deeply did the prejudice of looks possess him, that he appeared not to notice that the stranger introduced himself to him as Daniel Webster, or to be so ignorant as not to have heard of such a personage; and turning away, he expressed to the driver his astonishment that he should bring *black* people there for *him* to take in. It was not till he had been repeatedly assured and made to understand that the said Daniel Webster was a real live senator of the United States, that he perceived his awkward mistake and the distinguished honour which he and his house were so near missing.

In most of the Free States, the coloured people are disfranchised on account of their colour. The following scene, which we take from a newspaper in the state of Ohio, will give some idea of the extent to which this prejudice is carried.

"The whole of Thursday last was occupied by the Court of Common Pleas for this county in trying to find out whether one Thomas West was of the VOTING COLOUR, as some had very *constitutional doubts* as to whether his colour was orthodox, and whether his hair was of the official crisp! Was it not a dignified business? Four profound judges, four acute lawyers, twelve grave jurors, and I don't know how many venerable witnesses, making in all about thirty men, perhaps, all engaged in the profound, laborious, and illustrious business, of finding out whether a man who pays tax, works on the road, and is an industrious farmer, has been born according to the republican, Christian constitution of Ohio—so that he can vote! And they wisely, gravely, and 'JUDGMATICALLY' decided that he should not vote! What wisdom—what research it must have required to evolve this truth! It was left for the Court of Common Pleas for Columbian county, Ohio, in the United States of North America, to find out what Solomon never dreamed of—the courts of all civilised, heathen, or Jewish countries, never contemplated. Lest the wisdom of our courts should be circumvented by some such men as might be named, who are so near being born constitutionally that they might be taken for white by sight, I would suggest that our court be invested with SMELLING powers, and that if a man don't ex-hale the constitutional smell, he shall not vote! This would be an additional security to our liberties."

William found, after all, that liberty in the so-called Free States was more a name than a reality; that prejudice followed the coloured man into every place that he might enter. The temples erected for the worship of the living God are no exception. The finest Baptist church in the city of Boston has the following paragraph in the deed that conveys its seats to pewholders:

"And it is a further condition of these presents, that if the owner or owners of said pew shall determine hereafter to sell the same, it shall first be offered, in writing, to the standing committee of said society for the time being, at such price as might otherwise be obtained for it; and the said committee shall have the right, for ten days after such offer, to purchase said pew for said society, at that price, first deducting there-from all taxes and assessments on said pew then remaining unpaid. And if the said committee shall not so complete such purchase within said ten days, then the pew may be sold by the owner or owners thereof (after payment of all such ar-rears) to any one respectable *white person*, but upon the same conditions as are contained in this instrument; and immediate notice of such sale shall be given in writing, by the vendor, to the treasurer of said society."

Such are the conditions upon which the Rowe Street Baptist Church, Boston, disposes of its seats. The writer of this is able to put that whole congregation, minister and all, to flight, by merely putting his coloured face in that church. We once visited a church in New York that had a place set apart for the sons of Ham. It was a dark, dismal looking place in one corner of the gallery, grated in front like a hencoop, with a black border around it. It had two doors; over one was B. M.—black men; over the other B. W.—black women.

(1853)

FREDERICK DOUGLASS

(1817-1895)

Douglass, who was born a slave on a plantation in Maryland, is one of the giants of world history. The magnitude of his achievement is frequently overlooked by those who see him only as a great leader of the antislavery movement. A careful reading of his life and a study of his mind as reflected in the vast amount of writing he left will reveal a towering genius. He left three distinct autobiographies, each of which reveals the growth of a mind, and each of which is a triumph of literary art: Narrative of the Life of Frederick Douglass *(1845);* My Bondage and My Freedom *(1855);* Life and Times of Frederick Douglass *(1881-1892).*

As the editor of his own antislavery newspaper from 1847 to 1860, Douglass wrote regularly on a wide range of questions. Contributors to his paper included such other black reformers as Samuel Ward, William Wells Brown, and Martin Delany, as well as aspiring poets and essayists.

The position of Douglass in black esteem at the abolition of slavery was equalled only by that of Lincoln. He continued for three decades to be a central figure in the consciousness of black people. In a sense the leadership role, more symbolic than real, played by Douglass was assumed by Booker T. Washington, whose Atlanta speech was spoken, significantly, in the year of Douglass' death. Douglass, however, would have found the views of the Great Compromiser unacceptable.

Many eminent Afro-Americans have eulogized and written about

Douglass: Chesnutt wrote a biography of Douglass (1899), as did Booker T. Washington (1907) and William Pickens (1912). Students go today to the biography by the noted historian Benjamin Quarles (1948) and to the four-volume collection of Douglass' writings edited by Phillip Foner (1950-1955).

A large-scale edition of Douglass' writings, including letters, is underway at Yale University under the editorship of John Blassingame. The successive appearance of the many volumes of this edition will certainly reveal Douglass as one of the major voices of nineteenth-century America.

The Right to Criticize American Institutions

Speech before the American Anti-Slavery Society, May 11, 1847

I am very glad to be here. I am very glad to be present at this Anniversary, glad again to mingle my voice with those with whom I have stood identified, with those with whom I have laboured, for the last seven years, for the purpose of undoing the burdens of my brethren, and hastening the day of their emancipation.

I do not doubt but that a large portion of this audience will be disappointed, both by the *manner* and the *matter* of what I shall this day set forth. The extraordinary and unmerited eulogies, which have been showered upon me, here and elsewhere, have done much to create expectations which, I am well aware, I can never hope to gratify. I am here, a simple man, knowing what I have experienced in Slavery, knowing it to be a bad system, and desiring, by all Christian means, to seek its overthrow. I am not here to please you with an eloquent speech, with a refined and logical address, but to speak to you the sober truths of a heart overborne with gratitude to God that we have in this land, cursed as it is with Slavery, so noble a band to second my efforts and the efforts of others, in the noble work of undoing the yoke of bondage, with which the majority of the States of this Union are now unfortunately cursed.

Since the last time I had the pleasure of mingling my voice with the voices of my friends on this platform, many interesting and even trying events have occurred to me. I have experienced, within the last eighteen or twenty months, many incidents, all of which it would be interesting to communicate to you, but many of these I shall be compelled to pass over at this time, and confine my remarks to giving a general outline of the manner and spirit with which I have been hailed abroad, and welcomed at the different places which I have visited during my absence of twenty months.

You are aware, doubtless, that my object in going from this country, was to get beyond the reach of the clutch of the man who claimed to own me as his property. I had written a book, giving a history of that portion of my life spent in the gall and bitterness and degradation of Slavery, and in which, I also identified my oppressors as the perpetrators of some of the most atrocious crimes. This had deeply incensed them against me, and stirred up within them the purpose of revenge, and, my whereabouts being known, I believed it necessary for me, if I would preserve my liberty, to leave the shores of America, and take up my abode in some other land, at least until the clamor had subsided. I went to England, monarchical England, to get rid of Democratic Slavery; and I must confess that at the very threshold I was satisfied that I had gone to the right place. Say what you will of England—of the degradation—of the poverty—and there is much of it there,—say what you will of the oppression and suffering going on in England at this time, there is Liberty there, not only for the white man, but for the black man also. The instant that I stepped upon the shore, and looked into the faces of the crowd around me, I saw in every man a recognition of my manhood, and an absence, a perfect absence, of everything like that disgusting hate with which we are pursued in this country. [Cheers.] I looked around in vain to see in any man's face a token of the slightest aversion to me on account of my complexion. Even the cabmen demeaned themselves to me as they did to other men, and the very dogs and pigs of old England treated me as a man! I cannot, however, my friends, dwell upon this anti-prejudice, or rather the many illustrations of the absence of prejudice against colour in England, but will proceed, at once, to defend the right and duty of invoking English aid and English sympathy for the overthrow of American Slavery, for the education of coloured Americans, and to forward, in every way, the interests of humanity; inasmuch as the right of appealing to England for aid in overthrowing Slavery in this country has been called in question, in public meetings and by the press, in this city.

I cannot agree with my friend Mr. Garrison, in relation to my love and attachment to this land. I have no love for America, as such; I have no patriotism. I have no country. What country have I? The institutions of this country do not know me, do not recognize me as a man. I am not thought of, spoken of, in any direction, out of the anti-slavery ranks, as a man. I am not thought of, or spoken of, except as a piece of property belonging to some *Christian* slave-holder, and all the religious and political institutions of this country, alike pronounce me a slave and a chattel. Now, in such a country as this, I cannot have patriotism. The only thing that links me to this land is my family, and the painful consciousness that here there are three millions of my fellow-creatures, groaning beneath the iron rod of the worst despotism that could be devised, even in Pandemonium; that here are men and brethren, who are identified with me by their complexion, identified with me by their hatred of Slavery, identified with me by their love and aspirations for liberty, identified with me by the stripes upon their backs, their inhuman wrongs and cruel sufferings. This, and this only, attaches me to this land, and brings me here to plead with you, and with this country at large, for the dis-enthralment of my oppressed countrymen, and to overthrow this system of Slavery which is crushing them to the earth. How can I love a country that dooms three millions of my brethren, some of them my own kindred, my own brothers, my own sisters, who are now clanking the chains of Slavery upon the plains of the South, whose warm blood is now making fat the soil of Maryland and of Alabama, and over whose crushed spirits rolls the dark shadow of oppression, shutting out and extinguishing forever, the cheering rays of that bright sun of Liberty lighted in the souls of all God's children by the Omnipotent hand of Deity itself? How can I, I say, love a a country thus cursed, thus bedewed with the blood of my brethren? A country, the Church of which, and the Government of which, and the Constitution of which, is in favour of supporting and perpetuating this monstrous system of injustice and blood? I have not, I cannot have, any love for this country, as such, or for its Constitution. I desire to see its overthrow as speedily as possible, and its Constitution shivered in a thousand fragments, rather than this foul curse should continue to remain as now. [Hisses and Cheers.]

In all this, my friends, let me make myself understood. I do not hate America as against England, or against any other country, or land. I love humanity all over the globe. I am anxious to see right-eousness prevail in all directions. I am anxious to see Slavery over-thrown here; but, I never appealed to Englishmen in a manner calculated to awaken feelings of hatred or disgust, or to influence their prejudices towards America as a nation, or in a manner pro-vocative of national jealousy or ill-will; but I always appealed to their conscience—to the higher and nobler feelings of the people of that country, to enlist them in this cause. I always appealed to their manhood, that which preceded their being Englishmen, (to quote an expression of my friend Phillips,) I appealed to them as men, and I had a right to do so. They are men, and the slave is a man, and we have a right to call upon all men to assist in breaking his bonds, let them be born when, and live where they may.

But it is asked, "What good will this do?" or "What good has it done?" "Have you not irritated, have you not annoyed your American friends, and the American people rather, than done them good?" I admit that we have irritated them. They deserve to be irritated. I am anxious to irritate the American people on this question. As it is in physics, so in morals, there are cases which demand irritation, and counter irritation. The conscience of the American public needs this irritation. And I would *blister it all over, from centre to circumference*, until it gives signs of a purer and better life than it is now manifesting to the world.

But why expose the sins of one nation in the eyes of another? Why attempt to bring one people under the odium of another people? There is much force in this question. I admit that there are sins in almost every country which can be best removed by means confined exclusively to their immediate locality. But such evils and such sins pre-suppose the existence of a moral power in this immediate locality sufficient to accomplish the work of renovation. But where, pray, can we go to find moral power in this nation, sufficient to overthrow Slavery? To what institution, to what party shall we apply for aid? I say, we admit that there are evils which can be best removed by influences confined to their immediate locality. But in regard to American Slavery, it is not so. It is such a giant crime, so darkening to the soul, so blinding in its moral influence, so well calculated to blast and corrupt all the humane principles of our nature, so well adapted to infuse its own accursed spirit into all around it, that the people among whom it exists have not the moral power to abolish it. Shall we go to the Church for this influence? We have heard its character described. Shall we go to politicians or political parties? Have they the moral power necessary to accomplish this mighty task? They have not. What are they doing at this moment? Voting supplies for Slavery—voting supplies for the extension, the stability, the perpetuation of Slavery in this land. What is the Press doing? The same. The pulpit? Almost the same. I do not flatter myself that there is moral power in the land sufficient to overthrow Slavery, and I welcome the aid of England. And that aid will come. The growing intercourse between England and this country, by means of steam-navigation, the relaxation of the protective system in various countries in Europe, gives us an opportunity to bring in the aid, the moral and Christian aid of those living on the other side of the Atlantic. We welcome it, in the language of the resolution. We entreat our British friends to continue to send in their remonstrances across the deep, against Slavery in this land. And these remonstrances will have a powerful effect here. Sir, the Americans may tell of their ability, and I have no doubts they have it, to keep back the invader's hosts, to repulse the strongest force that its enemies may send against this country. It may boast, and it may *rightly* boast, of its capacity to build its ramparts so high that no foe can hope to scale them, to render them so impregnable as to defy the assault of the world. But, Sir, there is one thing it cannot resist, come from what quarter it may. It cannot resist TRUTH. You cannot build your forts so strong, nor your ramparts so high, nor arm yourself so powerfully, as to be able to withstand the overwhelming MORAL SENTIMENT against Slavery now flowing into this land. For example; prejudice against color is continually becoming weaker in this land and more and more consider this sentiment as unworthy a lodgment in the breast of an enlightened community. And the American abroad dare not now, even in a public conveyance, to lift his voice in defence of this disgusting prejudice.

I do not mean to say that there are no practices abroad which deserve to receive an influence favourable to their extermination, from America. I am most glad to know that Democratic freedom—not the bastard democracy, which, while loud in its protestations of regard for liberty and equality, builds up Slavery, and, in the name of Freedom, fights the battles of Despotism—is making great strides in Europe. We see abroad, in England especially, happy indications of the progress of American principles. A little while ago England was cursed by a Corn monopoly—by the giant monopoly, which snatched from the mouths of the famishing poor the bread which you sent them from this land. The community, the *people* of England, demanded its destruction, and they have triumphed. We have aided them, and they aid us, and the mission of the two nations, henceforth, is *to serve each other.*

Sir, it is said that, when abroad, I misrepresented my country on this question. I am not aware of any misrepresentation. I stated facts, and facts only. A gentleman of your own city, Rev. Dr. Cox, has taken particular pains to stigmatize me as having introduced the subject of Slavery illegitimately into the World's Temperance Convention. But what was the fact? I went to that Convention, not as a delegate. I went into it by the invitation of the Committee of the Convention. I suppose most of you know the circumstances, but I wish to say one word in relation to the spirit and the principle which animated me at the meeting. I went into it at the invitation of the Committee, and spoke not only at their urgent request, but by public announcement. I stood on the platform on the evening referred to, and heard some eight or ten Americans address the seven thousand people assembled in that vast Hall. I heard them speak of the temperance movement in this land. I heard them eulogize the temperance societies in the highest terms, calling on England to follow their' example; (and England may follow them with advantage to herself;) but I heard no reference made to the 3,000,000 of people in this country who are denied the privileges, not only of temperance, but of all other societies. I heard not a word of the American slaves, who, if seven of them were found together at a temperance meeting, or any other place, would be scourged and beaten by their cruel tyrants. Yes, nine-and-thirty lashes is the penalty required to be inflicted by the law if any of the slaves get together in a number exceeding seven, for any purpose however peaceable or laudable. And while these American gentlemen were extending their hands to me, and saying, "How do you do, Mr. Douglass? I am most happy to meet you here," &c. &c. I knew that, in America, they would not have touched me with a pair of tongs. I felt, therefore, that that was the place and the time to call to remembrance the 3,000,000 of slaves, whom I aspired to represent on that occasion. I did so, not maliciously, but with a desire, only, to subserve the best interests of my race. I besought the American delegates, who had at first responded to my speech with shouts of applause, when they should arrive at home to extend the borders of their temperance societies so as to include the 500,000 coloured people in the Northern States of the Union. I also called to mind the facts in relation to the mob that occurred in the city of Philadelphia, in the year 1842. I stated these facts to show to the British public how difficult it is for a coloured man in this country to do anything to elevate himself or his race from the state of degradation in which they are plunged; how difficult it is for him to be virtuous or temperate, or anything but a menial, an outcast. You all remember the circumstances of the mob to which I have alluded. A number of intelligent, philanthropic, manly coloured men, desirous of snatching their coloured brethren from the fangs of intemperance, formed themselves into a procession, and walked through the streets of Philadelphia with appropriate banners and badges and mottoes. I stated the fact that that procession was not allowed to proceed far, in the city of Philadelphia—the American city of Brotherly Love, the city of all others loudest in its boasts of freedom and liberty—before these noble-minded men were assaulted by the citizens, their banners torn in shreds and themselves trampled in the dust, and inhumanly beaten, and all their bright and fond hopes and anticipations, in behalf of their friends and their race, blasted by the wanton cruelty of their white fellow-citizens. And all this was done for no other reason than that they had presumed to walk through the street with temperance banners and badges, like human beings.

The statement of this fact caused the whole Convention to break forth in one general expression of intense disgust at such atrocious and inhuman conduct. This disturbed the composure of some of our American representatives, who, in serious alarm, caught hold of the skirts of my coat, and attempted to make me desist from my exposition of the situation of the coloured race in this country. There was one Doctor of Divinity there, the ugliest man that I ever saw in my life, who almost tore the skirts of my coat off, so vehement was he in his *friendly* attempts to induce me to yield the floor. But fortunately the audience came to my rescue, and demanded that I should go on, and I did go on, and, I trust, discharged my duty to my brethren in bonds and the cause of human liberty, in a manner not altogether unworthy the occasion.

I have been accused of *dragging* the question of Slavery into the Convention. I had a right to do so: It was the *World's* convention—not the Convention of any sect, or number of sects—not the Convention of any particular nation—not a man's or a woman's Convention, not a black man's nor a white man's Convention, but the *World's* Convention, the Convention of ALL, black as well as *white, bond* as well as *free*. And I stood there, as I thought, a representative of the 3,000,000 of men whom I had left in rags and wretchedness, to be devoured by the accused institution which stands by them, as with a drawn sword, ever ready to fall upon their devoted and defenceless heads. I felt, as I said to Dr. Cox, that it was demanded of me by conscience, to speak out boldly in behalf of those whom I had left behind. [Cheers.] And, Sir, (I think I may say this, without subjecting myself to the charge of egotism,) I deem it very fortunate for the friends of the slave, that Mr. Garrison and myself were there just at that time. Sir, the churches in this country have long repined at the position of the churches in England on the subject of Slavery. They have sought many opportunities to do away the prejudices of the English churches against American Slavery. Why, Sir, at this time there were not far from seventy ministers of the Gospel from Christian America, in England, pouring their leprous pro-slavery distilment into the ears of the people of that country, and by their prayers, their conversation, and their public speeches, seeking to darken the British mind on the subject of Slavery, and to create in the English public the same cruel and heartless apathy that prevails in this country in relation to the slave, his wrongs and his rights. I knew them by their continuous slandering of my race; and at this time, and under these circumstances, I deemed it a happy interposition of God, in behalf of my oppressed and misrepresented and slandered people, that one of their number should burst up through the dark incrustation of malice, and hate, and degradation, which had been thrown over them, and stand before the British public to open to them the secrets of the prison-house of bondage in America. [Cheers.] Sir, the slave sends no delegates to the Evangelical Alliance. [Cheers.] The slave sends no delegates to the World's Temperance Convention. Why? Because chains are upon his arms and fetters fast bind his limbs. He must be driven out to be sold at auction by some *Christian* slaveholder, and the money for which his soul is bartered must be appropriated to spread the Gospel among the heathen.

Sir, I feel that it is good to be here. There is always work to be done. Slavery is everywhere. Slavery goes everywhere. Slavery was in the Evangelical Alliance, looking saintly in the person of the Rev. Dr. Smythe; it was in the World's Temperance Convention in the person of the Rev. Mr. Kirk. Dr. Marsh went about saying, in so many words, that the unfortunate slaveholders in America were so peculiarly situated, so environed by uncontrollable circumstances, that they could not liberate their slaves; that if they were to emancipate them they would be, in many instances, cast into prison. Sir, it did me good to go around on the heels of this gentleman. I was glad to follow him around for the sake of my country, for the country is not, after all, so bad as the Rev. Dr. Marsh represented it to be.

My fellow-countrymen, what think ye he said of you, on the other side of the Atlantic? He said you were not only pro-slavery, but that you actually aided the slaveholder in holding his slaves securely in his grasp; that, in fact, you compelled him to be a slave-

holder. This I deny. You are not so bad as that. You do not compel
the slaveholder to be a slaveholder.

And Rev. Dr. Cox, too, talked a great deal over there; and among
other things he said, "that many slaveholders—dear Christian men!—
were sincerely anxious to get rid of their slaves"; and to show how
difficult it is for them to get rid of their human chattels, he put the
following case: A man living in a State, the laws of which compel
all persons emancipating their slaves to remove them beyond its limits,
wishes to·liberate his slaves, but he is too poor to transport them
beyond the confines of the State in which he resides; therefore he
cannot emancipate them—he is necessarily a slaveholder. But, Sir,
there was one fact, which I happened, fortunately, to have on hand
just at that time, which completely neutralized this very affecting
statement of the Doctor's. It so happens that Messrs. Gerrit Smith and
Arthur Tappan have advertised for the especial benefit of this
afflicted class of slaveholders that they have set apart the sum of
$10,000 to be appropriated in aiding them to remove their emancipated
slaves beyond the jurisdiction of the State, and that the money would
be forthcoming on application being made for it; but *no such application was ever made!* This shows that, however truthful the statements
of these gentlemen may be concerning the things of the world to
come, they are lamentably reckless in their statements concerning
things appertaining to this world. I do not mean to say that they
would designedly tell that which is false, but they did make the statements I have ascribed to them.

And Dr. Cox and others charge me with having stirred up war-
like feelings while abroad. This charge, also, I deny. The whole of
my arguments and the whole of my appeals, while I was abroad,
were in favour of anything else than war. I embraced every opportunity to propagate the principles of peace while I was in Great
Britain. I confess, honestly, that were I not a peace-man, were I a
believer in fighting at all, I should have gone through England, saying
to Englishmen, as Englishmen, there are 3,000,000 of men across the
Atlantic who are whipped, scourged, robbed of themselves, denied
every privilege, denied the right to read the Word of the God who
made them, trampled under foot, denied all the rights of human-
beings; go to their rescue; shoulder your muskets, buckle on your
knapsacks, and in the invincible cause of Human Rights and Universal
Liberty, go forth, and the laurels which you shall win will be as
fadeless and as imperishable as the eternal aspirations of the human
soul after that freedom which every being made after God's image

instinctively feels is his birth-right. This would have been my course had I been a war man. That such was not my course, I appeal to my whole career while abroad to determine.

> *Weapons of war we have cast from the battle;*
> TRUTH *is our armour, our watch-word is* LOVE;
> *Hushed be the sword, and the musketry's rattle,*
> *All our equipments are drawn from above.*
> *Praise then the God of Truth,*
> *Hoary age and ruddy youth,*
> *Long may our rally be*
> *Love, Light and Liberty,*
> *Ever our banner the banner of Peace*

From *My Bondage and My Freedom*

CHAPTER IV.

A GENERAL SURVEY OF THE SLAVE PLANTATION.

It is generally supposed that slavery, in the state of Maryland, exists in its mildest form, and that it is totally divested of those harsh and terrible peculiarities, which mark and characterize the slave system, in the southern and south-western states of the American union. The argument in favor of this opinion, is the contiguity of the free states, and the exposed condition of slavery in Maryland to the moral, religious and humane sentiment of the free states.

I am not about to refute this argument, so far as it relates to slavery in that State, generally; on the contrary, I am willing to admit that, to this general point, the argument is well grounded. Public opinion is, indeed, an unfailing restraint upon the cruelty and barbarity of masters, overseers, and slave-drivers, whenever and wherever it can reach them; but there are certain secluded and out-of-the way places, even in the state of Maryland, seldom visited by a single ray of healthy public sentiment—where slavery, wrapt in its own congenial, midnight darkness, *can*, and *does* develop all its malign and shocking characteristics; where it can be indecent without shame, cruel without shuddering, and murderous without apprehension or fear of exposure.

Just such a secluded, dark, and out-of-the-way place, is the "home plantation" of Col. Edward Lloyd, on the Eastern Shore, Maryland. It is far away from all the great thoroughfares, and is proximate to no town or village. There is neither school-house, nor town-house in its neighborhood. The school-house is unnecessary, for there are no children to go to school. The children and grand-children of Col. Lloyd were taught in the house, by a private tutor—a Mr. Page— a tall, gaunt sapling of a man, who did not speak a dozen words to a slave in a whole year. The overseers' children go off somewhere to school; and they, therefore, bring no foreign or dangerous influence from abroad, to embarrass the natural operation of the slave system of the place. Not even the mechanics—through whom there is an occasional out-burst of honest and telling indignation, at cruelty and wrong on other plantations—are white men, on this plantation. Its whole public is made up of, and divided into, three classes—SLAVE-HOLDERS, SLAVES and OVERSEERS. Its blacksmiths, wheelwrights, shoe-makers, weavers, and coopers, are slaves. Not even commerce, selfish and iron-hearted as it is, and ready, as it ever is, to side with the strong against the weak—the rich against the poor—is trusted or permitted within its secluded precints. Whether with a view of guarding against the escape of its secrets, I know not, but it is a fact, that every leaf and grain of the produce of this plantation, and those of the neighboring farms belonging to Col. Lloyd, are transported to Baltimore in Col. Lloyd's own vessels; every man and boy on board of which—except the captain—are owned by him. In return, everything brought to the plantation, comes through the same channel. Thus, even the glimmering and unsteady light of trade, which sometimes exerts a civilizing influence, is excluded from this "tabooed" spot.

Nearly all the plantations or farms in the vicinity of the "home plantation" of Col. Lloyd, belong to him; and those which do not, are owned by personal friends of his, as deeply interested in maintaining the slave system, in all its rigor, as Col. Lloyd himself. Some of his neighbors are said to be even more stringent than he. The Skinners, the Peakers, the Tilgmans, the Lockermans, and the Gipsons, are in the same boat; being slaveholding neighbors, they may have strengthened each other in their iron rule. They are on intimate terms, and their interests and tastes are identical.

Public opinion in such a quarter, the reader will see, is not likely to be very efficient in protecting the slave from cruelty. On the contrary, it must increase and intensify his wrongs. Public opinion seldom differs very widely from public practice. To be a restraint upon cruelty and vice, public opinion must emanate from a humane and virtuous community. To no such humane and virtuous community, is Col. Lloyd's plantation exposed. That plantation is a little nation of its own, having its own language, its own rules, regulations and customs. The laws and institutions of the state, apparently touch it nowhere. The troubles arising here, are not settled by the civil power of the state. The overseer is generally accuser, judge, jury, advocate and executioner. The criminal is always dumb. The overseer attends to all sides of a case.

There are no conflicting rights of property, for all the people are owned by one man; and they can themselves own no property. Religion and politics are alike excluded. One class of the population is too high to be reached by the preacher; and the other class is too low to be cared for by the preacher. The poor have the gospel preached to them, in this neighborhood only when they are able to pay for it. The slaves, having no money, get no gospel. The politician keeps away, because the people have no votes, and the preacher keeps away, because the people have no money. The rich planter can afford to learn politics in the parlor, and to dispense with religion altogether.

In its isolation, seclusion, and self-reliant independence, Col. Lloyd's plantation resembles what the baronial domains were, during the middle ages in Europe. Grim, cold, and unapproachable by all genial influences from communities without, *there it stands;* full three hundred years behind the age, in all that relates to humanity and morals.

This, however, is not the only view that the place presents. Civilization is shut out, but nature cannot be. Though separated from the rest of the world; though public opinion, as I have said, seldom gets a chance to penetrate its dark domain; though the whole place is stamped with its own peculiar, iron-like individuality; and though crimes, high-handed and atrocious, may there be committed, with almost as much impunity as upon the deck of a pirate ship,— it is, nevertheless, altogether, to outward seeming, a most strikingly interesting place, full of life, activity, and spirit; and presents a very favorable contrast to the indolent monotony and languor of Tucka-hoe. Keen as was my regret and great as was my sorrow at leaving the latter, I was not long in adapting myself to this, my new home. A man's troubles are always half disposed of, when he finds endurance his only remedy. I found myself here; there was no getting away; and what remained for me, but to make the best of it? Here were plenty of children to play with, and plenty of places of pleasant resort for boys of my age, and boys older. The little tendrils of affection, so rudely and treacherously broken from around the darling objects of my grandmother's hut, gradually began to extend, and to entwine about the new objects by which I now found myself sur-rounded.

There was a windmill (always a commanding object to a child's eye) on Long Point—a tract of land dividing Miles river from the Wye—a mile or more from my old master's house. There was a creek to swim in, at the bottom of an open flat space, of twenty acres or more, called "the Long Green"—a very beautiful playground for the children.

In the river, a short distance from the shore, lying quietly at anchor, with her small boat dancing at her stern, was a large sloop— the Sally Lloyd; called by that name in honor of a favorite daughter of the colonel. The sloop and the mill were wondrous things, full of thoughts and ideas. A child cannot well look at such objects with-out *thinking*.

Then here were a great many houses; human habitations, full of the mysteries of life at every stage of it. There was the little red house, up the road, occupied by Mr. Sevier, the overseer. A little nearer to my old master's stood a very long, rough, low building, literally alive with slaves, of all ages, conditions and sizes. This was called "the Long Quarter." Perched upon a hill, across the Long Green, was a very tall, dilapidated, old brick building—the architec-tural dimensions of which proclaimed its erection for a different purpose—now occupied by slaves, in a similar manner to the Long Quarter. Besides these, there were numerous other slave houses and huts, scattered around in the neighborhood, every nook and corner of which was completely occupied. Old master's house, a long, brick building, plain, but substantial, stood in the center of the plantation life, and constituted one independent establishment on the premises of Col. Lloyd.

Besides these dwellings, there were barns, stables, store-houses, and tobacco-houses; blacksmiths' shops, wheelwrights' shops, coopers' shops—all objects of interest; but, above all, there stood the grandest building my eyes had then ever beheld, called by everyone on the plantation, the "Great House." This was occupied by Col. Lloyd and his family. They occupied it; *I* enjoyed it. The great house was surrounded by numerous and variously shaped out-buildings. There were kitchens, wash-houses, dairies, summer-houses, green-houses, hen-houses, turkey-houses, pigeon-houses, and arbors, of many sizes and devices, all neatly painted, and altogether interspered with grand old trees, ornamental and primitive, which afforded delightful shade in summer, and imparted to the scene a high degree of stately beauty. The great house itself was a large, white, wooden building, with wings on three sides of it. In front, a large portico, extending the entire length of the building, and supported by a long range of columns, gave to the whole establishment an air of solemn grandeur. It was a treat to my young and gradually opening mind, to behold this elaborate exhibition of wealth, power, and vanity. The carriage entrance to the house was a large gate, more than a quarter of a mile distant from it; the intermediate space was a beautiful lawn, very neatly trimmed, and watched with the greatest care. It was dotted thickly over with delightful trees, shrubbery, and flowers. The road, or lane, from the gate to the great house, was richly paved with white pebbles from the beach, and, in its course, formed a complete circle around the beautiful lawn. Carriages going in and retiring from the great house, made the circuit of the lawn, and their passengers were permitted to behold a scene of almost Eden-like beauty. Outside this select inclosure, were parks, where—as about the residences of the English nobility—rabbits, deer, and other wild game, might be seen, peering and playing about, with none to molest them or make them afraid. The tops of the stately poplars were often covered with the red-winged black-birds, making all nature vocal with the joyous life and beauty of their wild, warbling notes. These all belonged to me, as well as to Col. Edward Lloyd, and for a time I greatly enjoyed them.

A short distance from the great house, were the stately mansions of the dead, a place of somber aspect. Vast tombs, embowered beneath the weeping willow and the fir tree, told of the antiquities of the Lloyd family, as well as of their wealth. Superstition was rife among the slaves about this family burying ground. Strange sights had been seen there by some of the older slaves. Shrouded ghosts, riding on great black horses, had been seen to enter; balls of fire had been seen to fly there at midnight, and horrid sounds had been repeatedly heard. Slaves know enough of the rudiments of theology to believe that those go to hell who die slaveholders; and they often fancy such persons wishing themselves back again, to wield the lash. Tales of sights and sounds, strange and terrible, connected with the huge black tombs, were a very great security to the grounds about them, for few of the slaves felt like approaching them even in the day time. It was a dark, gloomy and forbidding place, and it was difficult to feel that the spirits of the sleeping dust there deposited, reigned with the blest in the realms of eternal peace.

The business of twenty or thirty farms was transacted at this, called, by way of eminence, "great house farm." These farms all belonged to Col. Lloyd, as did, also, the slaves upon them. Each farm was under the management of an overseer. As I have said of the overseer of the home plantation, so I may say of the overseers on the smaller ones; they stand between the slave and all civil constitutions—their word is law, and is implicitly obeyed.

The colonel, at this time, was reputed to be, and he apparently was, very rich. His slaves, alone, were an immense fortune. These small and great, could not have been fewer than one thousand in number, and though scarcely a month passed without the sale of one or more lots to the Georgia traders, there was no apparent diminution in the number of his human stock: the home plantation merely groaned at a removal of the young increase, or human crop, then proceeded as lively as ever. Horse-shoeing, cart-mending, plow-repairing, coopering, grinding, and weaving, for all the neighboring farms, were performed here, and slaves were employed in all these branches. "Uncle Tony" was the blacksmith; "Uncle Harry" was the cartwright; "Uncle Abel" was the shoemaker, and all these had hands to assist them in their several departments.

These mechanics were called "uncles" by all the younger slaves, not because they really sustained that relationship to any, but according to plantation *etiquette*, as a mark of respect, due from the younger to the older slaves. Strange, and even ridiculous as it may seem, among a people so uncultivated, and with so many stern trials to look in the face, there is not to be found, among any people, a more rigid enforcement of the law of respect to elders, than they maintain. I set this down as partly constitutional with my race, and partly conventional. There is no better material in the world for making a gentleman, than is furnished in the African. He shows to others, and exacts for himself, all the tokens of respect which he is compelled to manifest toward his master. A young slave must approach the company of the older with hat in hand, and woe betide him, if he fails to acknowledge a favor, of any sort, with the accustomed *"tank'ee,"* &c. So uniformly are good manners enforced among slaves, that I can easily detect a "bogus" fugitive by his manners.

Among other slave notabilities of the plantation, was one called by everybody Uncle Isaac Copper. It is seldom that a slave gets a surname from anybody in Maryland; and so completely has the south shaped the manners of the north, in this respect, that even abolitionists make very little of the surname of a negro. The only improvement on the "Bills," "Jacks," "Jims," and "Neds" of the south, observable here is, that "William," "John," "James," "Edward," are substituted. It goes against the grain to treat and address a negro precisely as they would treat and address a white man. But, once in a while, in slavery as in the free states, by some extraordinary circumstance, the negro has a surname fastened to him, and holds it against all conventionalities. This was the case with Uncle Isaac Copper. When the "uncle" was dropped, he generally had the prefix "doctor," in its stead. He was our doctor of medicine, and doctor of divinity as well. Where he took his degree I am unable to say, for he was not very communicative to inferiors, and I was emphatically such, being but a boy seven or eight years old. He was too well established in his profession to permit questions as to his native skill, or his attainments. One qualification he undoubtedly had—he was a confirmed *cripple*; and he could neither work, nor would he bring anything if offered for sale in the market. The old man, though lame, was no sluggard. He was a man that made his crutches do him good service. He was always on the alert, looking up the sick, and all such as were supposed to need his counsel. His remedial prescriptions embraced four articles. For diseases of the body, *Epsom salts* and *castor oil*; for those of the soul, *the Lord's Prayer*, and *hickory switches!*

I was not long at Col. Lloyd's before I was placed under the care of Doctor Isaac Copper. I was sent to him with twenty or thirty other children, to learn the "Lord's Prayer." I found the old gentleman seated on a huge three-legged oaken stool, armed with several large hickory switches; and, from his position, he could reach—lame as he was—any boy in the room. After standing awhile to learn what was expected of us, the old gentleman, in any other than a devotional tone, commanded us to kneel down. This done, he commenced telling us to say everything he said. "Our Father"—this we repeated after him with promptness and uniformity; "Who art in heaven"—was less promptly and uniformly repeated; and the old gentleman paused in the prayer, to give us a short lecture upon the consequences of inattention, both immediate and future, and especially those more immediate. About these he was absolutely certain, for he held in his right hand the means of bringing all his predictions and warnings to pass. On he proceeded with the prayer; and we with our thick tongues and unskilled ears, followed him to the best of our ability. This, however, was not sufficient to please the old gentleman. Everybody, in the south, wants the privilege of whipping somebody else. Uncle Isaac shared the common passion of his country, and, therefore, seldom found any means of keeping his disciples in order short of flogging. "Say everything I say;" and bang would come the switch on some poor boy's undevotional head. *"What you looking at there"*—*"Stop that pushing"*—and down again would come the lash.

The whip is all in all. It is supposed to secure obedience to the slaveholder, and is held as a sovereign remedy among the slaves themselves, for every form of disobedience, temporal or spiritual. Slaves, as well as slaveholders, use it with an unsparing hand. Our devotions at Uncle Isaac's combined too much of the tragic and comic, to make them very salutary in a spiritual point of view; and it is due to truth to say, I was often a truant when the time for attending the praying and flogging of Doctor Isaac Copper came on.

The windmill under the care of Mr. Kinney, a kind hearted old Englishman, was to me a source of infinite interest and pleasure. The old man always seemed pleased when he saw a troop of darkey little urchins, with their tow-linen shirts fluttering in the breeze, approaching to view and admire the whirling wings of his wondrous machine. From the mill we could see other objects of deep interest. These were, the vessels from St. Michael's, on their way to Baltimore. It was a source of much amusement to view the flowing sails and complicated rigging, as the little crafts dashed by, and to speculate upon Baltimore, as to the kind and quality of the place. With so many sources of interest around me, the reader may be prepared to learn that I began to think very highly of Col. L.'s plantation. It was just a place to my boyish taste. There were fish to be caught in the creek, if one only had a hook and line; and crabs, clams and oysters were to be caught by wading, digging and raking for them. Here was a field for industry and enterprise, strongly inviting; and the reader may be assured that I entered upon it with spirit.

Even the much dreaded old master, whose merciless fiat had brought me from Tuckahoe, gradually, to my mind, parted with his terrors. Strange enough, his reverence seemed to take no particular notice of me, nor of my coming. Instead of leaping out and devouring me, he scarcely seemed conscious of my presence. The fact is, he was occupied with matters more weighty and important than either looking after or vexing me. He probably thought as little of my advent, as he would have thought of the addition of a single pig to his stock!

As the chief butler on Col. Lloyd's plantation, his duties were numerous and perplexing. In almost all important matters he answered in Col. Lloyd's stead. The overseers of all the farms were in some sort under him, and received the law from his mouth. The colonel himself seldom addressed an overseer, or allowed an overseer to address him. Old master carried the keys to all the store houses; measured out the allowance for each slave at the end of every month; superintended the storing of all goods brought to the plantation; dealt out the raw material to all the handicraftsmen; shipped the grain, tobocco, and all saleable produce of the plantation to market, and had the general oversight of the coopers' shop, wheelwrights' shop, blacksmiths' shop, and shoemakers' shop. Besides the care of these, he often had business for the plantation which required him to be absent two and three days.

Thus largely employed, he had little time, and perhaps as little disposition, to interfere with the children individually. What he was to Col. Lloyd, he made Aunt Katy to him. When he had anything to say or do about us, it was said or done in a wholesale manner; disposing of us in classes or sizes, leaving all minor details to Aunt Katy, a person of whom the reader has already received no very favorable impression. Aunt Katy was a woman who never allowed herself to act greatly within the margin of power granted to her, no matter how broad that authority might be. Ambitious, ill-tempered and cruel, she found in her present position an ample field for the exercise of her ill-omened qualities. She had a strong hold on old master—she was considered a first rate cook, and she really was very industrious. She was, therefore, greatly favored by old master, and as one mark of his favor, she was the only mother who was permitted to retain her children around her. Even to these children she was often fiendish in her brutality. She pursued her son Phil, one day, in my presence, with a huge butcher knife, and dealt a blow with its edge which left a shocking gash on his arm, near the wrist. For this, old master did sharply rebuke her, and threatened that if she ever should do the like again, he would take the skin off her back. Cruel, however, as Aunt Katy was to her own children, at times she was not destitute of maternal feling, as I often had occasion to know, in the bitter pinches of hunger I had to endure. Differing from the practice of Col. Lloyd, old master, instead of allowing so much for each slave, committed the allowance for all to the care of Aunt Katy, to be divided after cooking it, amongst us. The allowance, consisting of coarse corn-meal, was not very abundant—indeed, it was very slender; and in passing through Aunt Katy's hands, it was made more slender still, for some of us. William, Phil and Jerry were her children, and it is not to accuse her too severely, to allege that she was often guilty of starving myself and the other children, while she was literally cramming her own. Want of food was my chief trouble the first summer at my old master's. Oysters and clams would do very well, with an occasional supply of bread, but they soon failed in the absence of bread. I speak but the simple truth, when I say, I have often been so pinched with hunger, that I have fought with the dog—"Old Nep"—for the smallest crumbs that fell from the kitchen table, and have been glad when I won a single crumb in the combat. Many times have I followed, with eager step, the waiting-girl when she went out to shake the table cloth, to get the crumbs and small bones flung out for the cats. The water, in which meat had been boiled, was as eagerly sought for by me. It was a great thing to get the privilege of dipping a piece of bread in such water; and the skin taken from rusty bacon, was a positive luxury. Nevertheless, I sometimes got full meals and kind words from sympathizing old slaves, who knew my sufferings, and received the comforting assurance that I should be a man some day. "Never mind, honey—better day comin'," was even then a solace, a cheering consolation to me in my troubles. Nor were all the kind words I received from slaves. I had a friend in the parlor, as well, and one to whom I shall be glad to do justice, before I have finished this part of my story.

I was not long at old master's, before I learned that his surname was Anthony, and that he was generally called "Captain Anthony"— a title which he probably acquired by sailing a craft in the Chesapeake Bay. Col. Lloyd's slaves never called Capt. Anthony "old master," but always Capt. Anthony; and *me* they called "Captain Anthony Fed." There is not, probably, in the whole south, a plantation where the English language is more imperfectly spoken than on Col. Lloyd's. It is a mixture of Guinea and everything else you please. At the time of which I am now writing, there were slaves there who had been brought from the coast of Africa. They never used the "*s*" in indication of the possessive case. "Cap'n Ant'ney Tom," "Lloyd Bill," "Aunt Rose Harry," means "Captain Anthony's Tom," "Lloyd's Bill," &c. "*Oo you dem long to?*" means, "Whom do you belong to?" "*Oo dem got any peachy?*" means, "Have you got any peaches?" I could scarcely understand them when I first went among them, so broken was their speech; and I am persuaded that I could not have been dropped anywhere on the globe, where I could reap less, in the way of knowledge, from my immediate associates, than on this plantation. Even "Mas' Daniel," by his association with his father's slaves, had measurably adopted their dialect and their ideas, so far as they had ideas to be adopted. The equality of nature is strongly asserted in childhood, and childhood requires children for associates. *Color* makes no difference with a child. Are you a child with wants, tastes and pursuits common to children, not put on, but natural? then, were you black as ebony you would be welcome to the child of alabaster whiteness. The law of compensation holds here, as well as elsewhere. Mas' Daniel could not associate with ignorance without sharing its shade; and he could not give his black playmates his company, without giving them his intelligence, as well. Without knowing this, or caring about it, at the time, I, for some cause or other, spent much of my time with Mas' Daniel, in preference to spending it with most of the other boys.

Mas' Daniel was the youngest son of Col. Lloyd; his older brothers were Edward and Murray—both grown up, and fine looking men. Edward was especially esteemed by the children, and by me among the rest; not that he ever said anything to us or for us, which could be called especially kind; it was enough for us, that he never looked nor acted scornfully toward us. There were also three sisters, all married; one to Edward Winder; a second to Edward Nicholson; a third to Mr. Lownes.

The family of old master consisted of two sons, Andrew and Richard; his daughter, Lucretia, and her newly married husband, Capt. Auld. This was the house family. The kitchen family consisted of Aunt Katy, Aunt Esther, and ten or a dozen children, most of them older than myself. Capt. Anthony was not considered a rich slaveholder, but was pretty well off in the world. He owned about thirty "*head*" of slaves, and three farms in Tuckahoe. The most valuable part of his property was his slaves, of whom he could afford to sell one every year. This crop, therefore, brought him seven or eight hundred dollars a year, besides his yearly salary, and other revenue from his farms.

The idea of rank and station was rigidly maintained on Col. Lloyd's plantation. Our family never visited the great house, and the Lloyds never came to our home. Equal non-intercourse was observed between Capt. Anthony's family and that of Mr. Sevier, the overseer.

Such, kind reader, was the community, and such the place, in which my earliest and most lasting impressions of slavery, and of slave-life, were received; of which impressions you will learn more in the coming chapters of this book.

(1855)

Nemesis

At last our proud Republic is overtaken. Our National Sin has found us out. The National Head is bowed down, and our face is mantled with shame and confusion. No foreign arm is made bare for our chastisement. No distant monarch, offended at our freedom and prosperity, has plotted our destruction; no envious tyrant has prepared for our necks his oppressive yoke. Slavery has done it all. Our enemies are those of our own household. It is civil war, the worst of all wars, that has unveiled its savage and wrinkled front amongst us. During the last twenty years and more, we have as a nation been forging a bolt for our own national destruction, collecting and augmenting the fuel that now threatens to wrap the nation in its malignant and furious flames. We have sown the wind, only to reap the whirlwind. Against argument, against all manner of appeal and remonstrances coming up from the warm and merciful heart of humanity, we have gone on like the oppressors of Egypt, hardening our hearts

and increasing the burdens of the American slave, and strengthening
the arm of his guilty master, till now, in the pride of his giant power,
that master is emboldened to lift rebellious arms against the very
majesty of the law, and defy the power of the Government itself. In
vain have we plunged our souls into new and unfathomed depths of
sin, to conciliate the favor and secure the loyalty of the slaveholding
class. We have hated and persecuted the Negro; we have scourged
him out of the temple of justice by the Dred Scott decision; we have
shot and hanged his friends at Harper's Ferry; we have enacted laws
for his further degradation, and even to expel him from the borders of
some of our States; we have joined in the infernal chase to hunt him
down like a beast, and fling him into the hell of slavery; we have
repealed and trampled upon laws designed to prevent the spread of
slavery, and in a thousand ways given our strength, our moral and
political influence to increase the power and ascendency of slavery
over all departments of Government; and now, as our reward, this
slaveholding power comes with sword, gun and cannon to take the life
of the nation and overthrow the great American Government. Verily,
they have their reward. The power given to crush the Negro now
overwhelms the white man. The Republic has put one end of the
chain upon the ankle of the bondman, and the other end about its
own neck. They have been planting tyrants, and are now getting a
harvest of civil war and anarchy. The land is now to weep and howl,
amid ten thousand desolations brought upon it by the sins of two
centuries against millions on both sides of eternity. Could we write as
with lightning, and speak as with the voice of thunder, we should
write and cry to the nation, *Repent, Break Every Yoke, let the Oppressed Go Free for Herein alone is deliverance and safety!* It is not
too late. The moment is propitious, and we may even yet escape the
complete vengeance of the threatened wrath and fury, whose balls of
fire are already dropping to consume us. Now is the time to put an
end to the source of all our present national calamities. Now is the
time to change the cry of vengeance long sent up from the tasked and
toiling bondman, into a grateful prayer for the peace and safety of
the Government. Slaveholders have in their madness invited armed
abolition to march to the deliverance of the slave. They have furnished
the occasion, and bound up the fate of the Republic and that of the
slave in the same bundle, and the one and the other must survive or
perish together. Any attempt now to separate the freedom of the
slave from the victory of the Government over slaveholding rebels
and traitors; any attempt to secure peace to the whites while leaving

the blacks in chains; any attempt to heal the wounds of the Republic, while the deadly virus of slavery is left to poison the blood, will be labor lost. The American people and the Government at Washington may refuse to recognize it for a time; but the "inexorable logic of events" will force it upon them in the end; that the war now being waged in this land is a war for and against slavery; and that it can never be effectually put down till one or the other of these vital forces is completely destroyed. The irrepressible conflict, long confined to words and votes, is now to be carried by bayonets and bullets, and may God defend the right!

(1861)

Woman Suffrage Movement

The simplest truths often meet the sternest resistance, and are slowest in getting general acceptance. There are none so blind as those who will not see, is an old proverb. Usage and prejudice, like forts built of sand, often defy the power of shot and shell, and play havoc with their besiegers. No simpler proposition, no truth more self-evident or more native to the human soul, was ever presented to human reason or consciousness than was that which formed our late anti-slavery movement. It only affirmed that every man is, and of right ought to be, the owner of his own body; and that no man can rightfully claim another man as his property. And yet what a tempest and whirlwind of human wrath, what clouds of ethical and theological dust, this simple proposition created. Families, churches, societies, parties, and States were riven by it, and at last the sword was called in to decide the questions which it raised. What was true of this simple truth was also true as to the people's right to a voice in their own

Government, and the right of each man to form for himself his own religious opinions. All Europe ran blood before humanity and reason won this sacred right from priestcraft, bigotry, and superstition. What to-day seems simple, obvious, and undeniable, men looking through old customs, usages, and prejudices in other days denied altogether. Our friends of the woman's suffrage movement should bear this fact in mind, and share the patience of truth while they advocate the truth. It is painful to encounter stupidity as well as malice; but such is the fate of all who attempt to reform an abuse, to urge on humanity to nobler heights, and illumine the world with a new truth.

Now we know of no truth more easily made appreciable to human thought than the right of the woman to vote, or, in other words, to have a voice in the Government under which she lives and to which she owes allegiance. The very admission that woman owes allegiance, implies her right to vote. No man or woman who is not consulted can contract an obligation, or have an obligation created for him or her as the case may be. We can owe nothing by the mere act of another. Woman is not a censenting party to this Government. She has never been consulted. Ours is a Government of men, by men, each agreeing with all and all agreeing with each in respect to certain fundamental propositions, and women are wholly excluded. So far as respects its relation to woman, our Government is in its essence, a simple usurpation, a Government of force, and not of reason. We legislate for woman, and protect her, precisely as we legislate for and protect animals, asking the consent of neither.

It is nothing against this conclusion that our legislation has for the most part been eminently just and humane. A despotism is no less a despotism because the reigning despot may be a wise and good man. The principle is unaffected by the character of the man who for the moment may represent it. He may be kind or cruel, benevolent or selfish, in any case he rules according to his own sovereign will—and precisely such is the theoretical relation of our American Government toward woman. It simply takes her money without asking her consent and spends the same without in any wise consulting her wishes. It tells her that there is a code of laws which men have made, and which she must obey or she must suffer the consequences. She is absolutely in the hands of her political masters: and though these may be kind and tender hearted (the same was true of individual slave masters, as before stated), this in no wise mitigates the harshness of the principle—and it is against this principle we understand the woman's suffrage movement to be directed. It is intended to claim for woman a place by the side of man, not to rule over him, not to antagonize him, but to rule with him, as an equal subject to the solemn requirements of reason and law.

To ourselves the great truth underlying this woman's movement is just as simple, obvious, and indisputable as either of the great truths referred to at the beginning of this article. It is a part of the same system of truths. Its sources are individuality, rationality, and sense of accountability.

If woman is admitted to be a moral and intellectual being, possessing a sense of good and evil, and a power of choice between them, her case is already half gained. Our natural powers are the foundation of our natural rights; and it is a consciousness of powers which suggests the exercise of rights. Man can only exercise the powers he possesses, and he can only conceive of rights in presence of powers. The fact that woman has the power to say "I choose *this* rather than *that*" is all-sufficient proof that there is no natural reason against the exercise of that power. The power that makes her a moral and an accountable being gives her a natural right to choose the legislators who are to frame the laws under which she is to live, and the requirements of which she is bound to obey. By every fact and by every argument which man can wield in defence of his natural right to participate in government, the right of woman so to participate is equally defended and rendered unassailable.

Thus far all is clear and entirely consistent. Woman's natural abilities and possibilities, not less than man's, constitute the measure of her rights in all directions and relations, including her right to participate in shaping the policy and controlling the action of the Government under which she lives, and to which she is assumed to owe obedience. Unless it can be shown that woman is morally, physically, and intellectually incapable of performing the act of voting, there can be no natural prohibition of such action on her part. Usage, custom, and deeply rooted prejudices are against woman's freedom. They have been against man's freedom, national freedom, religious freedom, but these will all subside in the case of woman as well as elsewhere. The thought has already been conceived; the word has been spoken; the debate has begun; earnest men and women are choosing sides. Error may be safely tolerated while truth is left free to combat it, and nobody need fear the result. The truth can hurt nothing which ought not to be hurt, and it alone can make men and women free.

(1870)

Lecture on Haiti

World's Fair, Chicago, January 2, 1893

. . . From the beginning of our century until now, Haiti and its inhabitants, under one aspect or another, have, for various reasons, been very much in the thoughts of the American people. While slavery existed amongst us, her example was a sharp thorn in our side and a source of alarm and terror. She came into the sisterhood of nations through blood. She was described at the time of her advent, as a very hell of horrors. Her very name was pronounced with a shudder. She was a startling and frightful surprise and a threat to all slave-holders throughout the world, and the slave-holding world has had its questioning eye upon her career ever since.

By reason of recent events and the abolition of slavery, the enfranchisement of the Negro in our country, and the probable completion of the Nicaragua canal, Haiti has under another aspect, become, of late, interesting to American statesmen. More thought, more ink and paper have been devoted to her than to all the other West India Islands put together. This interest is both political and commercial, for Haiti is increasingly important in both respects. But aside from politics and aside from commerce, there is, perhaps, no equal number of people anywhere on the globe, in whose history, character and destiny there is more to awaken sentiment, thought and inquiry, than is found in the history of her people.

The country itself, apart from its people, has special attractions. First things have ever had a peculiar and romantic interest, simply because they are first things. In this, Haiti is fortunate. She has in many things been first. She has been made the theatre of great events. She was the first of all the cis-Atlantic world, upon which the firm foot of the progressive, aggressive and all-conquering white man was permanently set. Her grand, old tropical forests, fields and mountains, were among the first of the New World to have their silence broken by trans-Atlantic song and speech. She was the first to be invaded by the Christian religion and to witness its forms and ordinances. She was the first to see a Christian church and to behold the cross of Christ. She was also the first to witness the bitter agonies of the Negro bending under the blood-stained lash of Christian slave-holders. Happily too, for her, she was the first of the New World in

84

which the black man asserted his right to be free and was brave enough to fight for his freedom and fortunate enough to gain it.

In thinking of Haiti, a painful, perplexing and contradictory fact meets us at the outset. It is: that Negro slavery was brought to the New World by the same people from whom Haiti received her religion and her civilization. No people have ever shown greater religious zeal or have given more attention to the ordinances of the Christian church than have the Spaniards; yet no people were ever guilty of more injustice and blood-chilling cruelty to their fellowmen than these same religious Spaniards. Men more learned in the theory of religion than I am, may be able to explain and reconcile these two facts; but to me they seem to prove that men may be very pious, and yet very pitiless; very religious and yet practice the foulest crimes. These Spanish Christians found in Haiti a million of harmless men and women, and in less than sixty years they had murdered nearly all of them. With religion on their lips, the tiger in their hearts and the slave whip in their hands, they lashed these innocent natives to toil, death and extinction. When these pious souls had destroyed the natives, they opened the slave trade with Africa as a merciful device. Such, at least, is the testimony of history.

Interesting as Haiti is in being the cradle in which American religion and civilization were first rocked, its present inhabitants are still more interesting as having been actors in great moral and social events. These have been scarcely less portentous and startling than the terrible earthquakes which have some times moved their mountains and shaken down their towns and cities. The conditions in which the Republican Government of Haiti originated, were peculiar. The great fact concerning its people, is, that they were Negro slaves and by force conquered their masters and made themselves free and independent. As a people thus made free and having remained so for eighty-seven years, they are now asked to justify their assumption of statehood at the bar of the civilized world by conduct becoming a civilized nation.

The ethnologist observes them with curious eyes, and questions them on the ground of race. The statesman questions their ability to govern themselves; while the scholar and philanthropist are interested in their progress, their improvement and the question of their destiny.

But, interesting as they are to all these and to others, the people of Haiti, by reason of ancestral identity, are more interesting to the colored people of the United States than to all others, for the Negro, like the Jew, can never part with his identity and race. Color does for the one what religion does for the other and makes both distinct from the rest of mankind. No matter where prosperity or misfortune may chance to drive the Negro, he is identified with and shares the fortune of his race. We are told to go to Haiti; to go to Africa. Neither Haiti nor Africa can save us from a common doom. Whether we are here or there, we must rise or fall with the race. Hence, we can do about as much for Africa or Haiti by good conduct and success here as anywhere else in the world. The talk of bettering ourselves by getting rid of the white race, is a great mistake. It is about as idle for the black man to think of getting rid of the white man, as it is for the white man to think of getting rid of the black. They are just the two races which cannot be excluded from any part of the globe, nor can they exclude each other; so we might as well decide to live together here as to go elsewhere. Besides, for obvious reasons, until we can make ourselves respected in the United States, we shall not be respected in Haiti, Africa, or anywhere else.

Of my regard and friendship for Haiti, I have already spoken. I have, too, already spoken somewhat of her faults, as well, for they are many and grievous. I shall, however, show before I get through, that, with all her faults, you and I and all of us have reason to respect Haiti for her services to the cause of liberty and human equality throughout the world, and for the noble qualities she exhibited in all the trying conditions of her early history.

I have, since my return to the United States, been pressed on all sides to foretell what will be the future of Haiti—whether she will ever master and subdue the turbulent elements within her borders and become an orderly Republic. Whether she will maintain her liberty and independence, or, at last, part with both and become a subject of some one or another of the powerful nations of the world by which she seems to be coveted. The question still further is, whether she will fall away into anarchy, chaos and barbarism, or rise to the dignity and happiness of a highly civilized nation and be a credit to the colored race? I am free to say that I believe she will fulfill the latter condition and destiny. By one class of writers, however, such as Mr. Froude and his echoes, men and women who write what they know the prejudice of the hour will accept and pay for, this question has been vehemently answered already against Haiti and the possibilities of the Negro race generally.

They tell us that Haiti is already doomed—that she is on the downgrade to barbarism; and, worse still, they affirm that when the Negro is left to himself there or elsewhere, he inevitably gravitates to barbarism. Alas, for poor Haiti! and alas, for the poor Negro everywhere, if this shall prove true!

The argument as stated against Haiti, is, that since her freedom, she has become lazy; that she is given to gross idolatry, and that these evils are

on the increase. That voodooism, fetichism, serpent-worship and canni-
balism are prevalent there; that little children are fatted for slaughter and
offered as sacrifices to their voodoo deities; that large boys and girls run
naked through the streets of the towns and cities, and that things are generally going from bad to worse.

In reply to these dark and damning allegations, it will be sufficient
only to make a general statement. I admit at once, that there is much ignorance and much superstition in Haiti. The common people there believe
much in divinations, charms, witchcraft, putting spells on each other, and
in the supernatural and miracle working power of their voodoo priests
generally. Owing to this, there is a feeling of superstition and dread of
each other, the destructive tendency of which cannot be exaggerated. But
it is amazing how much of such darkness society has borne and can bear
and is bearing without falling to pieces and without being hopelessly abandoned to barbarism.

Let it be remembered that superstition and idolatry in one form or
another have not been in the past, nor are they in the present, confined to
any particular place or locality, and that, even in our enlightened age, we
need not travel far from our own country, from England, from Scotland,
from Ireland, France, Germany or Spain to find considerable traces of
gross superstition. We consult familiar spirits in America. Queen Victoria
gets water from the Jordan to christen her children, as if the water of that
river were any better than the water of any other river. Many go thousands of miles in this age of light to see an old seamless coat supposed to
have some divine virtue. Christians at Rome kiss the great toe of a black
image called St. Peter, and go up stairs on their knees, to gain divine favor. Here, we build houses and call them God's houses, and go into them
to meet God, as if the Almighty dwelt in temples made with men's hands.
I am not, myself, altogether free from superstition. I would rather sit at a
table with twelve persons than at one with thirteen; and would rather see
the new moon first over my right shoulder than over my left, though my
reason tells me that it makes no matter of difference over which shoulder I
see the new moon or the old. And what better is the material of one house
than that of another? Can man build a house more holy than the house
which God himself has built for the children of men? If men are denied a
future civilization because of superstition, there are others than the people
of Haiti who must be so denied. In one form or another, superstition will
be found everywhere and among all sorts of people, high or low. New
England once believed in witches, and yet she has become highly civilized.

Haiti is charged with the terrible crime of sacrificing little children to her voodoo gods, and you will want to know what I have to say about this shocking allegation. My answer is: That while I lived in Haiti I made diligent inquiry about this alleged practice so full of horror. I questioned many persons concerning it, but I never met a man who could say that he ever saw an instance of the kind; nor did I ever see a man who ever met any other man who said he had seen an act of human sacrifice. This I know is not conclusive, for strange things have sometimes been done in the name of God, and in the practice of religion. You know that our good father Abraham (not Abraham Lincoln) once thought that it would please Jehovah to have him kill his son Isaac and offer him a sacrifice on the altar. Men in all ages have thought to gain divine favor of their divinities or to escape their wrath by offering up to them something of great and special value. Sometimes it was the firstlings of the flock, and sometimes it was the fat of fed beasts, fed for the purpose of having it nice and acceptable to the divine being. As if a divine being could be greatly pleased with the taste or smell of such offerings. Men have become more sensible of late. They keep, smell and eat their fat beef and mutton themselves.

As to the little boys and girls running nude in the streets, I have to say, that while there are instances of the kind, and more of them than we, with the ideas of our latitude, would easily tolerate, they are nevertheless the exceptions to the general rule in Haiti. You will see in the streets of Port au Prince, one hundred decently dressed children to one that is nude; yet, our newspaper correspondents and six-day tourists in Haiti, would lead you to think that nudity is there the rule and decent clothing the exception. It should be remembered also, that in a warm climate like that of Haiti, the people consider more the comfort of their children in this respect than any fear of improper exposure of their little innocent bodies.

A word about snake worship. This practice is not new in the history of religion. It is as old as Egypt and is a part of our own religious system. Moses lifted up the serpent in the wilderness as a remedy for a great malady, and our Bible tells us of some wonderful things done by the serpent in the way of miraculous healing. Besides, he seems to have been on hand and performed marvelous feats in the Garden of Eden, and to have wielded a potent and mysterious influence in deciding the fate of mankind for time and eternity. Without the snake, the plan of salvation itself would not be complete. No wonder then that Haiti, having heard so much of the serpent in these respectable quarters and sublime relations, has *acquired* some respect for a divinity so potent and so ancient.

But the future of Haiti. What is it to be? Will it be civilization or barbarism? Will she remain an independent state, or be swallowed up by one or another of the great states? Whither is she tending? In considering these questions, we should allow no prejudice to influence us on the one hand or the other. If it be true that the Negro, left to himself, lapses into barbarism, as is alleged, the Negro above and beyond all others in the world should know it and should acknowledge it.

But it is said that the people of Haiti are lazy. Well, with the conditions of existence so easy and the performance of work so uninviting, the wonder is not that the men of Haiti are lazy, but that they work at all. But it is not true that the people of Haiti are as lazy as they are usually represented to be. There is much hard work done in Haiti, both mental and physical. This is true, not only of accessible altitudes where the air is cool and bracing, but it is so in the low lands, where the climate is hot, parching and enervating. No one can see the ships afloat in the splendid harbors of Haiti, and see the large imports and exports of the country, without seeing also that somebody there has been at work. A revenue of millions does not come to a country where no work is done.

Plainly enough, we should take no snap judgment on a question so momentous. It should not be determined by a dash of the pen and upon mere appearances of the moment. There are ebbs and flows in the tide of human affairs, and Haiti is no exception to this rule. There have been times in her history when she gave promise of great progress, and others, when she seemed to retrograde. We should view her in the broad light of her whole history, and observe well her conduct in the various vicissitudes through which she has passed. Upon such broad view I am sure Haiti will be vindicated.

It was once said by the great Daniel O'Connell, that the history of Ireland might be traced, like a wounded man through a crowd, by the blood. The same may be said of the history of Haiti as a free state. Her liberty was born in blood, cradled in misfortune, and has lived more or less in a storm of revolutionary turbulence. It is important to know how she behaved in these storms. As I view it, there is one great fundamental and soul-cheering fact concerning her. It is this: Despite all the trying vicissitudes of her history, despite all the machinations of her enemies at home, in spite of all temptations from abroad, despite all her many destructive revolutions, she has remained true to herself, true to her autonomy, and still remains a free and independent state. No power on this broad earth has yet induced or seduced her to seek a foreign protector, or has compelled her to bow her proud neck to a foreign government.

We talk of assuming protectorate over Haiti. We had better not attempt it. The success of such an enterprise is repelled by her whole history. She would rather abandon her ports and harbors, retire to her mountain fastnesses, or burn her towns and shed her warm, red, tropical blood over their ashes than to submit to the degradation of any foreign yoke, however friendly. In whatever may be the sources of her shame and misfortune, she has one source of great complacency; she lives proudly in the glory of her bravely won liberty and her blood-bought independence, and no hostile foreign foot has been allowed to tread her sacred soil in peace from the hour of her independence until now. Her future autonomy is at least secure. Whether civilized or savage, whatever the future may have in store for her, Haiti is the black man's country, now and forever.

In just vindication of Haiti, I can go one step further. I can speak of her, not only words of admiration, but words of gratitude as well. She has grandly served the cause of universal human liberty. We should not forget that the freedom you and I enjoy to-day; that the freedom that eight hundred thousand colored people enjoy in the British West Indies, the freedom that has come to the colored race the world over, is largely due to the brave stand taken by the black sons of Haiti ninety years ago. When they struck for freedom, they builded better than they knew. Their swords were not drawn and could not be drawn simply for themselves alone. They were linked and interlinked with their race, and striking for their freedom, they struck for the freedom of every black man in the world.

It is said of ancient nations, that each had its special mission in the world and that each taught the world some important lesson. The Jews taught the world a religion, a sublime conception of the Deity. The Greeks taught the world philosophy and beauty. The Romans taught the world jurisprudence. England is foremost among the modern nations in commerce and manufactures. Germany has taught the world to think, while the American Republic is giving the world an example of a Government by the people, of the people and for the people. Among these large bodies, the little community of Haiti, anchored in the Caribbean Sea, has her mission in the world, and a mission which the world had much need to learn. She has taught the world the danger of slavery and the value of liberty. In this respect she has been the greatest of all our modern teachers.

Speaking for the Negro, I can say, we owe much to Walker for his appeal, to John Brown for the blow struck at Harper's Ferry, and to Lundy and Garrison for their advocacy, and to the abolitionists in all the countries of the world. We owe much especially to Thomas Clarkson, to William Wilberforce, to Thomas Foxwell Buxton, and to the anti-slavery societies at home and abroad; but we owe incomparably more to Haiti than to them all. [Prolonged applause.] I regard her as the original pioneer emancipator of the nineteenth century. It was her one brave example that first of all startled the Christian world into a sense of the Negro's manhood. It was she who first awoke the Christian world to a sense of "the

danger of goading too far the energy that slumbers in a black man's arm."
Until Haiti struck for freedom, the conscience of the Christian world slept
profoundly over slavery. It was scarcely troubled even by a dream of this
crime against justice and liberty. The Negro was in its estimation a sheep-
like creature, having no rights which white men were bound to respect, a
docile animal, a kind of ass, capable of bearing burdens, and receiving
stripes from a white master without resentment, and without resistance.
The mission of Haiti was to dispel this degradation and dangerous delusion, and to give to the world a new and true revelation of the black man's
character. This mission she has performed and performed it well.

Until she spoke no Christian nation had abolished Negro slavery.
Until she spoke no Christian nation had given to the world an organized
effort to abolish slavery. Until she spoke the slave ship, followed by hun-
gry sharks, greedy to devour the dead and dying slaves flung overboard to
feed them, ploughed in peace the South Atlantic painting the sea with the
Negro's blood. Until she spoke, the slave trade was sanctioned by all the
Christian nations of the world, and our land of liberty and light included.
Men made fortunes by this internal traffic, and were esteemed as good
Christians, and the standing types and representations of the Saviour of
the World. Until Haiti spoke, the church was silent, and the pulpit was
dumb. Slave-traders lived and slave-traders died. Funeral sermons were
preached over them, and of them it was said that they died in the triumphs
of the Christian faith and went to heaven among the just.

To have any just conception or measurement of the intelligence, solidarity and manly courage of the people of Haiti when under the lead of
Toussaint L'Ouverture [Prolonged applause], and the dauntless Dessalines, you must remember what the conditions were by which they were
surrounded; that all the neighboring islands were slaveholding, and that to
no one of all these islands could she look for sympathy, support and cooperation. She trod the wine press alone. Her hand was against the Christian world, and the hand of the Christian world was against her. Hers was
a forlorn hope, and she knew that she must do or die.

In Greek or Roman history nobler daring cannot be found. It will
ever be a matter of wonder and astonishment to thoughtful men, that a
people in abject slavery, subject to the lash, and kept in ignorance of letters, as these slaves were, should have known enough, or have had left in
them enough manhood, to combine, to organize, and to select for themselves trusted leaders and with loyal hearts to follow them into the jaws of
death to obtain liberty.

In forecasting the future of this people, then, I insist that some importance shall be given to this and to another grand initial fact: *that the free-*

dom of Haiti was not given as a boon, but conquered as a right! Her people fought for it. They suffered for it, and thousands of them endured the most horrible tortures, and perished for it. It is well said that a people to whom freedom is given can never wear it as grandly as can they who have fought and suffered to gain it. Here, as elsewhere, what comes easily, is liable to go easily. But what man will fight to gain, that, man will fight to maintain. To this test Haiti was early subjected, and she stood this test like pure gold.

To re-enslave her brave self-emancipated sons of liberty, France sent in round numbers, to Haiti during the years 1802–1803, 50,000 of her veteran troops, commanded by her most experienced and skillful generals. History tells us what became of these brave and skillful warriors from France. It shows that they shared the fate of Pharaoh and his hosts. Negro manhood, Negro bravery, Negro military genius and skill, assisted by yellow fever and pestilence, made short work of them. The souls of them by thousands were speedily sent into eternity, and their bones were scattered on the mountains of Haiti, there to bleach, burn and vanish under the fierce tropical sun. Since 1804 Haiti has maintained national independence. I fling these facts at the feet of the detractors of the Negro and of Haiti. They may help them to solve the problem of her future. They not only indicate the Negro's courage, but demonstrate his intelligence as well.

No better test of the intelligence of a people can be had than is furnished in their laws, their institutions and their great men. To produce these in any considerable degree of perfection, a high order of ability is always required. Haiti has no cause to shrink from this test or from any other.

Human greatness is classified in three divisions: first, greatness of administration; second, greatness of organization; and the third, greatness of discovery, the latter being the highest order of human greatness. In all three of these divisions, Haiti appears to advantage. Her Toussaint L'Ouvertures, her Dessalines, her Christophes, her Petions, her Rigaud and others, their enemies being judges, were men of decided ability. They were great in all the three departments of human greatness. Let any man in our highly favored country, undertake to organize an army of raw recruits, and especially let any colored man undertake to organize men of his own color, and subject them to military discipline, and he will at once see the hard task that Haiti had on hand, in resisting France and slavery, and be led to admire the ability and character displayed by her sons in making and managing her armies and achieving her freedom.

But Haiti did more than raise armies and discipline troops. She organized a Government and maintained a Government during eighty-seven years. Though she has been ever and anon swept by whirlwinds of lawless turbulence, though she has been shaken by earthquakes of anarchy at home, and has encountered the chilling blasts of prejudice and hate from the outside world, though she has been assailed by fire and sword, from without and within, she has through all the machinations of her enemies, maintained a well defined civil government, and maintains it to-day.

She is represented at all the courts of Europe, by able men, and, in turn, she has representatives from all the nations of Europe in her capital.

She has her judiciary, her executive and legislative departments. She has her house of representatives and her senate. All the functions of government have been, and are now being, regularly performed within her domain. What does all this signify? I answer. Very much to her credit. If it be true that all the present and all the future rests upon all the past, there is a solid ground to hope for Haiti. There is a fair chance that she may yet be highly progressive, prosperous and happy.

Those who have studied the history of civilization, with the largest range of observation and the most profound philosophical generalization, tell us that men are governed by their antecedents; that what they did under one condition of affairs they will be likely to do under similar conditions, whenever such shall arise. Haiti has, in the past, raised many learned, able and patriotic men. She has made wise laws for her own government. Among her citizens she has had scholars and statesmen, learned editors, able lawyers and eminent physicians. She has now, men of education in the church and in her government, and she is now, as ever, in the trend of civilization. She may be slow and halting in the race, but her face is in the right direction.

The statement that she is on the down grade to barbarism is easily made, but hard to sustain.

It is not at all borne out by my observation and experience while in that country. It is my good fortune to possess the means of comparison, as to "what Haiti was and what Haiti is"; what she was twenty years ago, and what she is now. I visited that country twenty years ago and have spent much time there since, and I have no hesitation in saying that, with all that I have said of her revolutions and defective civilization, I can report a marked and gratifying improvement in the condition of her people, now, compared with what it was twenty years ago.

In Port au Prince, which may be taken as a fair expression of the general condition of the country, I saw more apparent domestic happiness, more wealth, more personal neatness, more attention to dress, more carriages rolling through the streets, more commercial activity, more schools, more well clothed and well cared for children, more churches, more teachers, more Sisters of Charity, more respect for marriage, more family comfort, more attention to sanitary conditions, more and better water supply, more and better Catholic clergy, more attention to religious observances, more elegant residences, and more of everything desirable than I saw there twenty years ago.

At that time Haiti was isolated. She was outside of telegraphic communication with the civilized world. She now has such connection. She has paid for a cable of her own and with her own money.

This has been accomplished under the much abused President Hyppolite. Then, there was no effort to light any of the streets. Now, the main streets are lighted. The streets are full of carriages at night but none are allowed to appear without lighted lamps, and every attention is given to the peace and good order of the citizens. There is much loud talk in Haiti, but blows are seldom exchanged between Haitians.

Even her revolutions are less sanguinary and ruthless now, than formerly. They have in many cases been attended with great disregard of private rights, with destruction of property and the commission of other crimes, but nothing of the kind was permitted to occur in the revolution by which President Hyppolite was raised to power. He was inaugurated in a manner as orderly as that of inducting into office any President of the United States.

Before we decide against the probability of progress in Haiti, we should look into the history of the progress of other nations. Some of the most enlightened and highly civilized states of the world of to-day, were, a few centuries ago, as deeply depraved in morals, manners and customs, as Haiti is alleged to be now. Prussia which is to-day the arbiter of peace and war in Europe and holds in her borders the profoundest thinkers of the nineteenth century, was, only three centuries ago like Haiti, the theatre of warring factions, and the scene of flagrant immoralities. France, England, Italy and Spain have all gone through the strife and turmoil of factional war, the like of which now makes Haiti a byword, and a hissing to a mocking earth. As they have passed through the period of violence, why may not Haiti do the same?

It should also be remembered that Haiti is still in her childhood. Give her time! Give her time!! While eighty years may be a good old age for a man, it can only be as a year in the life of a nation. With a people beginning a national life as Haiti did, with such crude material within, and such antagonistic forces operating upon her from without, the marvel is, not that she is far in the rear of civilization, but that she has survived in any sense as a civilized nation.

Though she is still an infant, she is out of the arms of her mother. Though she creeps, rather than walks, stumbles often and sometimes falls, her head is not broken, and she still lives and grows, and I predict, will yet be tall and strong. Her wealth is greater, her population is larger, her credit is higher, her currency is sounder, her progress is surer, her statesman are abler, her patriotism is nobler, and her government is steadier and firmer than twenty years ago. I predict that out of civil strife, revolution and war, there will come a desire for peace. Out of division will come a desire for union; out of weakness a desire for strength, out of ignorance a desire for knowledge, and out of stagnation will come a desire for progress. Already I find in her a longing for peace. Already she feels that she has had enough and more than enough of war. Already she perceives the need of education, and is providing means to obtain it on a large scale. Already she has added five hundred schools to her forces of education, within the two years of Hyppolite's administration. [Applause.] In the face of such facts; in the face of the fact that Haiti still lives, after being boycotted by all the Christian world; in the face of the fact of her known progress within the last twenty years—in the face of the fact that she has attached herself to the car of the world's civilization, I will not, I cannot believe that her star is to go out in darkness, but I will rather believe that whatever may happen of peace or war Haiti will remain in the firmament of nations, and, like the star of the north, will shine on and shine on forever. [Prolonged applause.]

Pamphlet, Chicago, 1893. Copy in Hispanic Division, Library of Congress.

SAMUEL WARD

(1817-1864)

Samuel Ward, whose parents, escaping from slavery, brought him as a child of three to New York state, became a leading figure of the antislavery circuit. Forced to leave New York because of his defiance of the fugitive slave laws, he went to Canada in 1851. From there he contributed to Frederick Douglass' North Star and wrote the Autobiography of A Fugitive Slave *(1855), which exhibits his literary powers.*

Ward was held in high esteem in the antislavery movement, because of both his courage and his eloquence. His relative isolation in Canada after 1851 from the direct currents of the struggle undoubtedly diminished the contribution he would have made.

From *Autobiography of a Fugitive Negro*

CHAPTER I

FAMILY HISTORY

I was born on the 17th October, 1817, in that part of the State of Maryland, U.S., commonly called the Eastern Shore. I regret that I can give no accurate account of the precise location of my birthplace. I may as well state now the reason of my ignorance of this matter. My parents were slaves. I was born a slave. They escaped, and took their then only child with them. I was not then old enough to know anything about my native place; and as I grew up, in the State of New Jersey, where my parents lived till I was nine years old, and in the State of New York subsequently, where we lived for many years, my parents were always in danger of being arrested and re-enslaved. To avoid this, they took every possible caution: among their measures of caution was the keeping of the children quite ignorant of their birthplace, and of their condition, whether free or slave, when born; because children might, by the dropping of a single word, lead to the betrayal of their parents. My brother, however, was born in New Jersey; and my parents, supposing (as is the general presumption) that to be born in a free State is to be born free, readily allowed us to tell where my brother was born; but *my* birthplace I was neither permitted to tell nor to know. Hence, while the secrecy and mystery thrown about the matter led me, most naturally, to suspect that I was born a slave, I never received direct evidence of it, from either of my parents, until I was four-and-twenty years of age; and then my mother informed my wife, in my absence. Generous reader, will you therefore kindly forgive my inability to say exactly where I was born; what gentle stream arose near the humble cottage where I first breathed—how that stream sparkled in the sunlight, as it meandered through green meadows and forests of stately oaks, till it gave its increased self as a contribution to the Chesapeake Bay—if I do not tell you the name of my native town and county, and some interesting details of their geographical, agricultural, geological, and revolutionary history—if I am silent as to just how many miles I was born from Baltimore the metropolis, or Annapolis the capital, of my native State? Fain would I satisfy you in all this; but I cannot, from sheer ignorance. I was born a slave—where? Wherever it was, it was where I dare not be seen or known, lest those who held my parents and ancestors in slavery should make a claim, hereditary or legal, in some form, to the ownership of my body and soul.

My father, from what I can gather, was descended from an African prince. I ask no particular attention to this, as it comes to me simply from tradition—such tradition as poor slaves may maintain. Like the sources of the Nile, my ancestry, I am free to admit, is rather difficult of tracing. My father was a pure-blooded Negro, perfectly black, with wooly hair; but, as is frequently true of the purest Negroes, of small, handsome features. He was about 5 feet 10 inches in height, of good figure, cheerful disposition, bland manners, slow in deciding, firm when once decided, generous and unselfish to a fault; and one of the most consistent, simple-hearted, straightforward Christians, I ever knew. What I have grouped together here concerning him you would see in your first acquaintance with him, and you would see the same throughout his entire life. Had he been educated, free, and admitted to the social privileges in early life for which nature fitted him, and for which even slavery could not, did not, altogether *unfit* him, my poor crushed, outraged people would never have had nor needed a better representation of themselves—a better specimen of the black gentleman. Yes: among the heaviest of my maledictions against slavery is that which it deserves for keeping my poor father— and many like him—in the midnight and dungeon of the grossest ignorance. Cowardly system as it is, it does not dare to allow the slave access to the commonest sources of light and learning.

After his escape, my father learned to read, so that he could enjoy the priceless privilege of searching the Scriptures. Supporting himself by his trade as a house painter, or whatever else offered (as he was a man of untiring industry), he lived in Cumberland County, New

Jersey, from 1820 until 1826; in New York city from that year until 1838; and in the city of Newark, New Jersey, from 1838 until May 1851, when he died, at the age of 68.

In April I was summoned to his bedside, where I found him the victim of paralysis. After spending some few days with him, and leaving him very much better, I went to Pennsylvania on business, and returned in about ten days, when he appeared still very comfortable; I then, for a few days, left him. My mother and I knew that another attack was to be feared—another, we knew too well, would prove fatal; but when it would occur was of course beyond our knowledge; but we hoped for the best. My father and I talked very freely of his death. He had always maintained that a Christian ought to have his preparation for his departure made, and completed in Christ, before death, so as when death should come he should have nothing to do BUT TO DIE. "That," said my father, "is enough to do at once: let repenting, believing, everything else, be sought at a proper time; let dying alone be done at the dying time." In my last conversation with him he not only maintained, but he *felt*, the same. Then, he seemed as if he might live a twelve-month; but eight-and-forty hours from that time, as I sat in the Rev. A. G. Beeman's pulpit, in New Haven, after the opening services, while singing the hymn which immediately preceded the sermon, a telegraphic despatch was handed me, announcing my father's death. I begged Mr. Beeman to preach; his own feelings were such, that he could not, and I was obliged to make the effort. No effort ever cost me so much. Have I trespassed upon your time too much by these details? Forgive the fondness of the filial, the bereaved, the fatherless.

My mother was a widow at the time of her marriage with my father, and was ten years his senior. I know little or nothing of her early life: I think she was not a mother by her first marriage. To my father she bore three children, all boys, of whom I am the second. Tradition is my only authority for my maternal ancestry: that authority saith, that on the paternal side my mother descended from Africa. Her mother, however, was a woman of light complexion; her grandmother, a mulattress; her great-grandmother, the daughter of an Irishman, named Martin, one of the largest slaveholders in Maryland— a man whose slaves were so numerous, that he did not know the number of them. My mother was of dark complexion, but straight silklike hair; she was a person of large frame, as tall as my father, of quick discernment, ready decision, great firmness, strong will, ardent temperament, and of deep, devoted, religious character. Though a woman, she was not of so pleasing a countenance as my father, and I am thought strongly to resemble her. Like my father, she was converted in early life, and was a member of the Methodist denomination (though a lover of all Christian denominations) until her death. This event, one of the most afflictive of my life, occurred on the first day of September, 1853, at New York. Since my father's demise I had not seen her for nearly a year; when, being about to sail for England, at the risk of being apprehended by the United States' authorities for a breach of their execrable republican Fugitive Slave Law, I sought my mother, found her, and told her I was about to sail at three p.m., that day (April 20th, 1853), for England. With a calmness and composure which she could always command when emergencies required it, she simply said, in a quiet tone, "To England, my son!" embraced me, commended me to God, and suffered me to depart without a murmur. It was our last meeting. May it be our last parting! For the kind sympathy shown me, upon my reception of the melancholy news of my mother's decease, by many English friends, I shall ever be grateful: the recollection of that event, and the kindness of which it was the occasion, will dwell together in my heart while reason and memory shall endure.

In the midst of that peculiarly bereaved feeling inseparable from realizing the thought that one is both fatherless and motherless, it was a sort of melancholy satisfaction to know that my dear parents were gone beyond the reach of slavery and the Fugitive Law. Endangered as their liberty always was, in the *free* Northern States of New York and New Jersey—doubly so after the law of 1851—I could but feel a great deal of anxiety concerning them. I knew that there was no living claimant of my parents' bodies and souls; I knew, too, that neither of them would tamely submit to re-enslavement: but I also knew that it was quite possible there should be creditors, or heirs at law; and that there is no State in the American Union wherein there were not free and independent democratic republicans, and *soi-disant* Christians, "ready, aye ready" to aid in overpowering and capturing a runaway, *for pay*. But when God was pleased to take my father in 1851, and my mother in 1853, I felt relief from my greatest earthly anxiety. Slavery had denied them education, property, caste, rights, liberty; but it could not deny them the application of Christ's blood, nor an admittance to the rest prepared for the righteous. They could not be buried in the same part of a common graveyard, with whites, in their native country; but they can rise at the sound of the first trump, in the day of resurrection. Yes, reader: we who are slaveborn derive a comfort and solace from the death of those dearest to us, if they have the sad misfortune to be BLACKS and AMERICANS, that you know not. God forbid that you or yours should ever have occasion to know it!

My eldest brother died before my birth: my youngest brother, Isaiah Harper Ward, was born April 5th, 1822, in Cumberland County, New Jersey; and died at New York, April 16th, 1838, in the triumphs of faith. He was a lad partaking largely of my father's qualities, resembling him exceedingly. Being the youngest of the family, we all sought to fit him for usefulness, and to shield him from the thousand snares and the ten thousand forms of cruelty and injustice which the unspeakably cruel prejudice of the whites visits upon the head and the heart of every black young man, in New York. To that end, we secured to him the advantages of the Free School, for coloured youth, in that city—advantages which, I am happy to say, were neither lost upon him nor unappreciated by him. Upon leaving school he commenced learning the trade of a printer, in the office of Mr. Henry R. Piercy, of New York—a gentleman who, braving the prejudices of his craft and of the community, took the lad upon the same terms as those upon which he took white lads: a fact all the more creditable to Mr. Piercy, as it was in the very teeth of the abominably debased public sentiment of that city (and of the whole country, in fact) on this subject. But ere Isaiah had finished his trade, he suddenly took a severe cold, which resulted in pneumonia, and—in death.

I expressed a doubt, in a preceding page, as to the legal validity of my brother's freedom. True, he was born in the nominally Free State of New Jersey; true, the inhabitants born in Free States are *generally* free. But according to slave law, "the child follows the condition of the mother, during life." My mother being born of a slave woman, and not being legally freed, those who had a legal claim to her had also a legal claim to her offspring, wherever born, of whatever paternity. Besides, at that time New Jersey had not entirely ceased to be a Slave State. Had my mother been legally freed before his birth, then my brother would have been born free, because born of a free woman. As it was, we were all liable at any time to be captured, enslaved, and re-enslaved—first, because we had been robbed of our liberty; then, because our ancestors had been robbed in like manner; and, thirdly and conclusively, in law, because we were black Americans.

I confess I never felt any personal fear of being retaken—

primarily because, as I said before, I knew of no legal claimants; but chiefly because I knew it would be extremely difficult to identify me. I was less than three years old when brought away: to identify me as a man would be no easy matter. Certainly, slaveholders and their more wicked Northern parasites are not very particularly scrupulous about such matters; but still, I never had much fear. My private opinion is, that he who would have enslaved me would have "caught a Tartar": for my peace principles never extended so far as to *either seek or accept peace at the expense of liberty*—if, indeed, a state of slavery can by any possibility be a state of peace.

I beg to conclude this chapter on my family history by adding, that my father had a cousin, in New Jersey, who had escaped from slavery. In the spring of 1826 he was cutting down a tree, which accidentally fell upon him, breaking both thighs. While suffering from this accident his master came and took him back into Maryland. He continued *lame* a very great while, without any *apparent* signs of amendment, until one fine morning he was gone! They never took him again.

Two of my father's nephews, who had escaped to New York, were taken back in the most summary manner, in 1828. I never saw a family thrown into such deep distress by the death of any two of its members, as were our family by the re-enslavement of these two young men. Seven-and-twenty years have past, but we have none of us heard a word concerning them, since their consignment to the living death, the temporal hell, of American slavery.

Some kind persons who may read these pages will accuse me of bitterness towards Americans generally, and slaveholders particularly: indeed, there are many *professional* abolitionists, on both sides of the Atlantic, who have no idea that a black man should feel towards and speak of his tormenters as a white man would concerning his. But suppose the blacks had treated *your* family in the manner the Americans have treated *mine*, for five generations: how would you write about these blacks, and their system of bondage? You would agree with me, that the 109th Psalm, from the 5th to the 21st verses inclusive, was written almost purposely for them.

(1855)

FRANCES HARPER

(1825-1911)

Born free in Baltimore, Maryland, Frances Ellen Watkins Harper was a lifelong reformer. Active in the antislavery movement until emancipation, she then devoted most of her attention to the temperance crusade. As a poet she was widely celebrated, taking her models from the reform poetry of both England and New England. Her poems are those of an eloquent platform reader and may be expected to have been far more impressive in her delivery than in cold print. Particularly would this be true of such poems as are presented here, which treat the theme of the moral degradation of slavery. Poems on Miscellaneous Subjects (1854) was frequently reprinted and reached a wide public.

Mrs. Harper also attempted fiction about both biblical and current themes. Examples of the first genre are Moses: A Story of the Nile *(1869) and* Idylls of the Bible *(1901). The second is illustrated by her novel* Iola Leroy, or Shadows Uplifted *(1892), which is probably modelled on Brown's* Clotel, *with its tragic mulatto theme, though Mrs. Harper manages to contrive a happy ending.*

The Slave Auction

The sale began—young girls were there,
    Defenceless in their wretchedness,
Whose stifled sobs of deep despair
    Revealed their anguish and distress.

And mothers stood with streaming eyes,
    And saw their dearest children sold;
Unheeded rose their bitter cries,
    While tyrants bartered them for gold.

And woman, with her love and truth—
    For these in sable forms may dwell—
Gazed on the husband of her youth,
    With anguish none may paint or tell.

And men, whose sole crime was their hue,
    The impress of their Maker's hand,
And frail and shrieking children, too,
    Were gathered in that mournful band.

Ye who have laid your love to rest,
    And wept above their lifeless clay,
Know not the anguish of that heart,
    Whose loved are rudely torn away.

Ye may not know how desolate
    Are husbands rudely forced to part,
And how a dull and heavy weight
    Will press the life-drops from the heart.

The Slave Mother

Heard you that shriek? It rose
    So wildly in the air,
It seemed as if a burdened heart
Was breaking in despair.

Saw you those hands so sadly clasped—
    The bowed and feeble head—
The shuddering of that fragile form—
    That look of grief and dread?

She is a mother, pale with fear,
    Her boy clings to her side,
And in her kirtle vainly tries
    His trembling form to hide.

He is not hers, although she bore
    For him a mother's pains;
He is not hers, although her blood
    Is coursing through his veins!

He is not hers, for cruel hands
    May rudely tear apart
The only wreath of household love
    That binds her breaking heart.

Bury Me in a Free Land

Make me a grave where'er you will,
In a lowly plain, or a lofty hill;
Make it among earth's humblest graves,
But not in a land where men are slaves.

I could not rest if around my grave
I heard the steps of a trembling slave;
His shadow above my silent tomb
Would make it a place of fearful gloom.

I could not rest if I heard the tread
Of a coffle gang to the shambles led,
And the mother's shriek of wild despair
Rise like a curse on the trembling air.

I could not sleep if I saw the lash
Drinking her blood at each fearful gash,
And I saw her babes torn from her breast,
Like trembling doves torn from their parent nest.

I'd shudder and start if I heard the bay
Of bloodhounds seizing their human prey,
And I heard the captive plead in vain
As they bound afresh his galling chain.

If I saw young girls from their mothers' arms
Bartered and sold for their youthful charms,
My eye would flash with a mournful flame,
My death-paled cheek grow red with shame.

I would sleep, dear friends, where bloated might
Can rob no man of his dearest right;
My rest shall be calm in any grave
Where none can call his brother a slave.

I ask no monument, proud and high,
To arrest the gaze of the passers-by;
All that my yearning spirit craves,
Is bury me not in a land of slaves.

SPIRITUALS

When the text of a spiritual is isolated and treated as a work of purely verbal art, considerable violence is done to its nature, far more so than when a ballad is so treated. In the spiritual, which is a lyric form, the musical elements merge completely with the verbal elements to create a whole that is on a plane different from that of lyric poetry in the usual sense of the term. Nevertheless the spiritual represents a kind of poetry of the people in several ways: It grows out of the experience of slavery shared by millions of black people in the American South; it was transmitted through several generations by the people, or more specifically by those among them with the gifts essential for such transmission. Exact and detailed information on the spiritual is no more available than for most other forms of popular art. Most speculations on the origin and development of the spirituals are merely that and are, in addition, often demonstrably inadmissible.

The spiritual is only one type of "slave song." Consequently, not every antebellum mention of the singing of the slaves necessarily refers to the spiritual. It may indeed be supposed that relatively few whites had occasion to hear the spirituals during their period of active creation, for they seem closely allied in mood and spirit to the prayer services conducted by the slaves for their personal consolation in remote and inaccessible places. The spirituals entered documentary history during the Civil War, when they were heard and commented upon by white commanders of black troops such as Thomas Wentworth Higginson and General Armstrong, later of Hampton Institute. But it was the Civil War which brought to an end the actual conditions which created and nurtured the spiritual. The tradition of singing spirituals in prayer services, of course, continued and may be considered to be yet alive, and an occasional new creation probably took place, but the Civil War marks the terminal point for the main corpus of the spiritual. The secularization of the spiritual by musically sophisticated groups such as the Fisk Jubilee Singers has no direct relation to the consideration of the spiritual as poetry of the people.

Musically the spiritual belongs to that vast matrix of song sprung from African roots and nurtured on American soil. Febrile attempts in the past to derive the spiritual from purely European sources have been made by persons fundamentally ignorant of African music and conveniently oblivious of the fact that the spiritual contains many elements inexplicable in European terms. The procedures of canto-metrics, developed through the researches of Alan Lomax and his associates, demonstrate unquestionably the Africanity of the spiritual. Textually, of course, we have to do with works in English; however, the imagery and syntax in these texts frequently defy the mentality and linguistic drift of the English language.

The group of texts presented here to represent the spiritual dem-onstrate recurrent themes: oppression, suffering, escape from adversity. The predominance of these themes has led some, including DuBois, to refer to them as sorrow songs, a designation that is misleading, since many spirituals deal with triumph and joy. When the spirituals allude to events, these are overwhelmingly taken from the Old Testament history of the Jews, a history illustrative of oppression and divine chastisement. The songs are less indebted to the New Testament, though it should not be surprising that the Crucifixion is often treated and is the subject of one of the noblest spirituals. Water is indeed the master symbol of the spiritual texts: It signifies cleansing, coolness, release from earthly care. The Christian rite of baptism is closely connected to this symbol, but West African lustration rites and river deities are probably also to be taken into account, as Herskovits has implied.

A massive and highly informative work on the spiritual is John Lovell's Black Song: The Forge and the Flame (1972). Of highest importance and value as a presentation of unexplored documentation of slave music is Dena J. Epstein, Sinful Tunes and Spirituals (1977). The essays by Alain Locke and Sterling Brown in this anthology are classic examples of Afro-American perspectives on the spiritual.

Sometimes I Feel Like a Motherless Child

Sometimes I feel like a motherless child,
Sometimes I feel like a motherless child,
Sometimes I feel like a motherless child,
A long ways from home;
A long ways from home.

True believer,
A long ways from home,
A long ways from home.

Sometimes I feel like I'm almos' gone,
Sometimes I feel like I'm almos' gone,
Sometimes I feel like I'm almos' gone;
Way up in de heab'nly lan'
Way up in de heab'nly lan'

True believer,
Way up in de heab'nly lan'
Way up in de heab'nly lan'

Sometimes I feel like a motherless child,
Sometimes I feel like a motherless child,
Sometimes I feel like a motherless child,
A long ways from home.

Go Down Moses

Go down, Moses
'Way down in Egypt land,
Tell ole—Pharaoh
To let my people go.

Go down, Moses
'Way down in Egypt land,
Tell ole—Pharaoh,
To let my people go.

When Israel was in Egypt land:
Let my people go,
Oppressed so hard they could not stand,
Let my people go.

Go down, Moses
'Way down in Egypt land,
Tell ole—Pharaoh,
To let my people go.

When spoke the Lord, bold Moses said:
Let my people go
If not I'll smite your first born dead,
Let my people go.

Go down, Moses
'Way down in Egypt land,
Tell ole—Pharaoh,
To let my people go.

Joshua Fit De Battle of Jericho

Joshua fit de battle ob
Jericho, Jericho, Jericho,
Joshua fit de battle ob Jericho,
An' de walls come tumblin' down.

You may talk about yo' king ob Gideon,
You may talk about yo' man ob Saul,
Dere's none like good ole Joshua
At de battle ob Jericho,

Up to de walls ob Jericho.
He marched with spear in han'
"Go blow dem ram horns"
Joshua a cried,
"Kase de battle am in my han."

Den de lam' ram sheep horns begin to blow,
Trumpets begin to soun'
Joshua commanded chillen to shout,
An' de walls come tumblin' down.

Dat mornin' Joshua fit de battle ob Jericho,
Jericho, Jericho,
Joshua fit de battle ob Jericho,
An' de walls come tumblin' down.

Steal Away to Jesus

Steal away,
Steal away,
Steal away to Jesus!

Steal away,
Steal away home,
I ain't got long to stay here.

Steal away,
Steal away,
Steal away to Jesus!

Steal away,
Steal away home,
I ain't got long to stay here.

My Lord, He calls me,
He calls me by the thunder,
The trumpet sounds within a my soul,
I ain't got long to stay here.

Roll, Jordan, Roll

Roll Jordan, roll,
Roll Jordan, roll,
I want to go to heav'n when I die,
To hear ol' Jordan roll.

O, brethren,
Roll Jordan roll,
Roll Jordan roll,
Wanter go to heav'n when I die,
To hear ol' Jordan roll.

Oh, brothers you oughter been dere,
Yes, my Lord
A sittin' up in de kingdom,
To hear ol' Jordan roll.

Sing it ovah,
Oh, roll.
O, Roll Jordan, roll,
Roll Jordan, roll,
I wanter go to heav'n when I die,
To hear ol' Jordan roll.

Crucifixion

They crucified my Lord,
An' He never said a mumbalin' word;
They crucified my Lord,
An' He never said a mumbalin' word,
Not a word, not a word, not a word.

They nailed him to the tree,
An' He never said a mumbalin' word;
They nailed him to the tree,
An' He never said a mumbalin' word.
Not a word, not a word, not a word.

They pierced him in the side,
An' He never said a mumbalin' word,
They pierced Him in the side,
An' He never said a mumbalin' word.
Not a word, not a word, not a word.

The blood came twinklin' down,
An' He never said a mumbalin' word;
The blood came twinklin' down,
An' He never said a mumbalin' word.
Not a word, not a word, not a word.

He bow'd His head an' died,
An' He never said a mumbalin' word,
He bow'd his head an' died,
An' He never said a mumbalin' word;
Not a word, not a word, not a word.

Part II

The Civil War
to World War I

The post-Civil War period in American culture has been aptly named the Gilded Age. Beneath a façade of gentility, Victorian morality, and burgeoning wealth was the dark reality of racism, robber barons, and violence. America's lofty ideals masked the pursuit of wealth and the indifference to humanity. The rich became richer as government gave monopolies full sway; the poor remained poor as social welfare was left to the conscience of the rich. Darwin had proposed the theory of the survival of the fittest; in nineteenth-century America, the fit were unquestionably the rich. Industry boomed, electricity came to the cities, the East and West coasts were linked by the Union Pacific Railroad and eventually the Panama Canal. Meanwhile, America limited immigration for Orientals, and the plight of the poor and the nonwhite continued to worsen as conditions on farm and in factory deteriorated.

American literature reflected the increasing vapidity of the culture. By the last decade of the nineteenth century all the great romantics were dead or silent. In their wake came writers of sentiment and cynicism: The Horatio Alger books, with their theme of rags-to-riches, portrayed the sagacious hero who, through cunning and good fortune, achieves success, that is, wealth. On a more artistic level, Mark Twain was writing cynical books about the evil in mankind; Henry James, Edith Wharton and later William Dean Howells were writing fiction picturing the narrow experience of the affluent. At the end of the century genteel realism merged into the naturalism of Jack London, Stephen Crane, Theodore Dreiser, and Upton Sinclair. In poetry there was the sequestered lyricism of the recluse, Emily Dickinson. A great deal of the literature of the era consisted of sentimental, moralistic preachments, signifying nothing—except perhaps the philosophical emptiness of a materialistic age.

For black Americans, these years were a time of toil and trouble, disillusion and despair. The bright hopes of freedom were soon dimmed by unspeakable conditions which the government not only permitted but often sanctioned. A succession of laws established strict segregation in nearly all areas of life, the Ku Klux Klan began its reign of terror, and the ballot was wrested from the eager hands of the new citizens. Lynchings and race riots occurred with monotonous frequency. The black American was left disfranchised, uneducated, and impoverished.

Meanwhile, black intellectuals struggled to work out a viable philosophy of survival in a hostile land and to implement this philosophy with practical measures. In retrospect, the period seems full of furious activity. Schools for blacks were founded, virtually all with the financial backing of white philanthropists. Fisk University, the Atlanta colleges, Howard University, and many others opened during these years. Black periodicals became the forum for the presentation of varying ideas about what direction to take: T. Thomas Fortune's *New York Age*, William Monroe Trotter's *Boston Guardian*, John H. Murphy's *Afro-American*, the *Washington Bee*, and others. Groups were formed to reach specific goals—Alexander Crummell's American Negro Academy, Booker T. Washington's National Business League, and, later, Carter G. Woodson's Association for the Study of Negro Life and History. Pressure groups were formed and became effective weapons in the struggle for civil rights—for example, T. Thomas Fortune's Afro-American Council and W. E. B. Du Bois' Niagara Movement, which prefigured the NAACP.

The quest for the way to full citizenship was led by the two outstanding figures of the period, Booker T. Washington and W. E. B. Du Bois, who advocated two different methods for reaching the same goal. Booker T. Washington himself was the personification of the Horatio Alger hero. He expressed great faith in middle-class values and based much of his philosophy on these values. An incredibly energetic man with a great deal of practical sagacity, he had clawed his way up from slavery to a pinnacle of power. Washington exercised tremendous control over black thought by manipulating people of influence: He controlled several newspapers and had decision-making power in government and private black-oriented activities. In his public pronouncements he advocated a policy of conciliation and gradualism as the means of obtaining civil rights. He felt that the black man must become educated for voting before he could reasonably demand the vote, must become economically self-sufficient, and must be "morally" acceptable in order to deserve full citizenship. Washington emphasized industrial education for black people at the expense of higher learning: A black youngster studying French while living in poverty was, to him, the height of the absurd.

Du Bois, whose genius always kept him ahead of his time, took a far more militant stand. In fiery editorials and scholarly essays he exposed the brutality of white America and demanded redress. He insisted that the ballot was the means of obtaining economic and educational advance, not vice versa. He stressed the importance of higher education to black youth, especially to the Talented Tenth, that intellectual elite of exceptional people whom he envisioned as the future leaders of the black movement. Whereas Washington saw salvation through material success (an idea perfectly consistent with the ethic of his time), Du Bois saw salvation through intelligent and educated men and women and through forthright demands for immediate civil rights.

The scholars, journalists, and religious leaders of the time argued on one side or the other, sometimes changed sides, or were equivocal. Editor T. Thomas Fortune changed from Du Bois' ideology to that of Washington; James Weldon Johnson changed from Washington to Du Bois; editor William Monroe Trotter remained firmly anti-Washington; Kelly Miller remained at a point midway between the two camps. For nearly twenty years the debate delineated the poles of black thought and formed the backbone of many progressive moves. For a while Washington's ideology dominated. In time, however, the Du Bois views prevailed. By the time of Washington's death in 1915, his influence had diminished considerably.

The literature of the period reflected the peculiarities of the culture. The times were more conducive to mental probing than to artistic creativity. There were few educated blacks to write or to read, few with sufficient respite from toil to become conscious artists, The educated individuals who did write were often plagued by the dilemmas which arose from having to work in an essentially white literary world. As a result, the body of imaginative literature of the age was not only thin, but pale.

By far the major form of literature was the essay. Historical, social, and personal essays, as well as speeches and editorials, record the thoughts of intellectual men seeking solutions to the so-called Negro Problem.

Scholars looked to the past with great interest. Immediately after the Civil War, William Wells Brown reported the black man's part in the conflict in *The Negro in the American Rebellion* (1867). Five years later, William Still published a valuable collection, *The Underground Rail Road: A Record of Facts, Authentic Narratives, Letters* (1872). Other useful historical essays on the war are contained in Joseph T. Wilson's *The Black Phalanx* (1888) and in George Washington Williams' *A History of the Negro Troops in the War of Rebellion* (1888). Additional histories which recorded the progress of the black American are *The Remarkable Achievement of the Afro-American* (1902), by J. W. Gibson and William F. Crogman, and *Fifty Years of Emancipation* (1913), by William Pickens. By far the most distinguished study was W. E. B. Du Bois' *The Suppression of the African Slave Trade to the United States* (1896). This work remains a landmark of scholarship in this area.

More numerous than historical studies were the essays that attempted to analyze the current situation and, often, to offer at least a partial solution. For the most part, though not entirely, these essays took stands in the conciliation versus militancy debate begun by the Washington-Du Bois controversy: The essay which started the controversy was Washington's speech at the Atlanta exposition in 1895, For the next twenty years Washington was reiterating the ideas of that address in other speeches, in articles, and in books like *Working with the Hands* (1904), *Putting the Most into Life* (1906), and *The Man Farthest Down* (1912).

W. E. B. Du Bois' response to Washington is contained in his collection of essays, *The Souls of Black Folk* (1903). This book is the most distinguished work published during the period. In lyrical prose and logical, lucid exposition, Du Bois examines the history, analyzes the present, and enunciates the goals of black people. The book had a profound effect on the intellectuals of his and of later generations; it is still being avidly read. Du Bois' aggressive demand for immediate remediation of wrongs continued in his editorials in the magazine of the NAACP, *The Crisis*, of which he was founder and editor.

Among other prominent thinkers who contributed to the discussion of the "problem" were T. Thomas Fortune, who published *Black and White: Land, Labor, and Politics in the South* (1884) and *The Negro in Politics* (1885), and Alexander Crummell, scholar and influential religious leader, who wrote *The Race Problem in America* (1889), *Incidents of Hope for the Negro Race in America* (1895) and *Civilization: The Primal Need of the Race* (1898).

All of these writers published individual essays and articles in periodicals. One of the most interesting was Kelly Miller's reply to Thomas Dixon's *The Leopard's Spots*. William Pickens wrote a number of sociological articles in leading magazines. The passionate anti-Washington editorials of William Monroe Trotter still make fascinating reading. Washington, Du Bois, and others contributed essays to a collection called *The Negro Problem* (1903). Washington and Du Bois collaborated on *The Negro in the South: His Economic Progress in Relation to His Moral and Religious Development* (1907).

Essays appeared that were not essentially political. The most important of these was Benjamin Brawley's *The Negro in Literature and Art in the United States* (1910). Brawley's careful scholarship gives the book lasting value. An earlier work significant to later generations was Irvine G. Penn's *The Afro-American Press and Its Editors* (1891).

Biography and autobiography, useful before the war as antislavery argument, now became a means of focusing on prominent blacks as a way to prove to black as well as to white readers that blacks really were not "like that." Many interesting works resulted. Elizabeth Keckley, who had worked for Mrs. Abraham Lincoln, published *Behind the Scenes; or, Thirty Years in the White House* (1868). This autobiography is still considered an excellent source of information about Lincoln and his family. Another interesting but less historically accurate work is William Wells Brown's *The Rising Son; or the Antecedents and Advancement of the Colored Race* (1874), which is generally considered autobiography, although it is written in the third person. Other autobiographical works were Henry Ossian Flipper's *The Colored Cadet at West Point* (1878), Bishop Daniel A. Payne's *Recollections of Seventy Years* (1899), John Mercer Langston's *From the Virginia Plantation to the National Capitol* (1894), and William Pickens' *The Heir of Slaves* (1910). By far the most popular autobiography of the time was Booker T. Washington's *Up from Slavery*, first serialized in *Outlook* magazine, and published in book form in 1901. William J. Simmons wrote a significant collective biography, *Men of Mark: Eminent, Progressive and Rising* (1887). Frederick Douglass was the subject of Booker T. Washington's *The Life of Frederick Douglass* (1907) and Williams Pickens' *Frederick Douglass and the Spirit of Freedom* (1912). Pickens published another biography, *Abraham Lincoln, Man and Statesman* (1909). Other white benefactors were the subjects of two biographies by Archibald H. Grimké, one of the intellectual leaders of the period: *William Lloyd Garrison* (1891) and *The Life of Charles Sumner* (1891). Perhaps the most scholarly study was Du Bois' *Life of John Brown* (1909),

There is little poetry or fiction of outstanding artistic value, although what exists provides interesting insights on the black psyche of the period.

The white public's degrading image of black people, superimposed on America's Victorian mediocrity, hovered over the imaginative literature. So dark was its shadow that the writer had few choices if he wanted to publish his work. Some writers combatted the stereotype by creating counterstereotypes. In their poetry and fiction one-dimensional characters muddle their way through hackneyed situations, speaking in stilted, rhetorical diction. Other writers reinforced the white public's stereotyped image, and in their works simple child-like Negroes dance, make love, and weep, talking all the while in plantation dialect. Some authors responded to the stereotype by ignoring the issue entirely and writing sentimental, moralistic works for the uplift of their readers, Of course, the limitations of all these works are obvious: there was very little rendering of the reality of black life, or any life at all, since the characters were generally pasteboard people caught up in unlikely situations.

Some poets, however, achieved a measure of success in their medium. Frances E. W. Harper, who had been a popular poet and lecturer before the war, published several volumes in the later years of the century—*Moses; A Story of the Nile* (1869), *Sketches of Southern Life* (1873), and several new editions of her collected poems. Albery A. Whitman, a minister who had been born a slave, published a long poem, "Not a Man Yet a Man" (1877), revised the next year as *Twasinta's Seminoles: or the Rape of Florida*. In 1901 he published *The Octoroon, An Idyl of the South*. Whitman was one of the scholarly poets later called "mockingbird" poets because their work resembled those of earlier poets in form and technique. Both Whitman and Mrs. Harper were passionate writers with a genuine devotion to poetry. In a different age, they might have excelled.

The star of the age in poetry was, of course, Paul Laurence

Dunbar. Equipped with a talent for writing lyrics, Dunbar followed in the wake of the white Southern local colorists who were so popular at the time. Although he wrote commemorative verses and romantic lyrics in standard English, his dialect poems were the ones that made him famous. Dunbar was an oddity to the white public. In any event, he became the first professional Negro poet, and published many volumes which went through many editions. Though his characters were more sympathetically portrayed than those of sentimentalized white apologists for the plantation system, the dialect poems yielded a sentimental image of black life.

James Edwin Campbell, who published *Echoes from the Cabin and Elsewhere* (1905), wrote in Gullah dialect. Other dialect poets were James David Carruthers and Daniel Webster Davis. Poems in dialect went over well as social recitations, but their range of possibilities was narrow. James Weldon Johnson later stated in the introduction to *God's Trombones* (1927) that dialect poetry was "limited to two stops: pathos and humor."

William Stanley Braithwaite chose a different way to react to the pressures of the white public. He largely ignored the question of race and urged other writers to free themselves from the shackles of racial themes. He himself wrote delicate lyrics on a number of subjects. Braithwaite became a recognized critic and anthologist of American literature. *Lyrics of Love and Life* (1905) and *The House of Falling Leaves* (1908) contain his own poems.

Always the exception to the current trend, W. E. B. Du Bois was writing a different kind of poetry from most others. In periodicals he was publishing individual poems on various aspects of black experience, especially those aspects involving the black man's reaction to oppression. Poems like "The Song of the Smoke" insisted on the strength and beauty of blackness in a manner which anticipated the emphasis on black awareness sixty years later.

In fiction, there was even less talent than in poetry. Frances E. W. Harper published *Iola Leroy* (1892), a novel with a trite plot and wooden characters—the tragic mulatto, the noble black lover. Sutton Griggs wrote novels of beautiful idealized Negroes. Paul Laurence Dunbar wrote short stories and several novels. Three of his novels, *The Uncalled* (1898), *The Love of Landry* (1900), and *The Fanatics* (1901), are about white characters. A fourth, *The Sport of the Gods* (1904), concerning a Negro family who migrate from the South to New York City, does begin to come to grips with social realities. But Dunbar's fiction in general is technically weak and ineffective.

By far the most talented writer of fiction was Charles W. Chesnutt. Chesnutt's "The Goophered Grapevine," which appeared in *The Atlantic Monthly* in 1887, was the first Afro-American story to appear in a major publication. Two volumes of stories appeared later —*The Conjure Woman* (1899) and *The Wife of His Youth* (1899) —and several novels, *The House Behind the Cedars* (1900), *The Marrow of Tradition* (1901), and *The Colonel's Dream* (1906). Chesnutt was a compelling story-teller and creator of characters.

ALEXANDER CRUMMELL
(1819-1898)

*A native of New York, Alexander Crummell became an Episco-
pal priest at the age of twenty-three. A few years later he traveled to
England, where he studied at Queen's College, Cambridge, and received his Bachelor of Arts degree in 1853. From England he traveled
to Liberia, where he remained for twenty years. Crummell was at
that time a militant nationalist in favor of black colonization in Liberia; he felt that the black man had no future in America. Although
he later modified this conviction, Crummell always advocated pride
in the African heritage.*

*In 1878 he relinquished the idea of colonization and returned to
the United States. Crummell's thought reflected social Darwinism in
its projected solution to the "Negro problem." He felt that economic
and social development and cultivation of high moral character would
be more effective than emphasis on the franchise and political agitation. He was convinced, too, of the black man's need for unity and
organization to achieve these ends. He was convinced that black
people primarily needed manual education, and denounced as evil
the overemphasis on higher education. Thus, Crummell anticipated
the ideas advocated by Booker T. Washington, whose thought later
dominated the age.*

*Paradoxically, he also anticipated the ideas of Washington's in-
tellectual adversary, W. E. B. Du Bois. Crummell's thinking broadened
so that he eventually rejected his earlier stand on industrial education
and economic success as the key to the racial problem and asserted*

that the hope of the black man lay in the hands of the college-educated black elite. Thus he enunciated the idea which Du Bois later developed into the theory of leadership of a Talented Tenth. In 1897, only a year before his death, Crummell founded the American Negro Academy, whose objectives included the fostering of intellectual tastes and the publication of scholarly works.

The Attitude of the American Mind
Toward the Negro Intellect

The American mind has refused to foster and to cultivate the Negro intellect. Join to this a kindred fact, of which there is the fullest evidence. Impelled, at times, by pity, a modicum of schooling and training has been given the Negro; but even this almost universally, with reluctance, with cold criticism, with microscopic scrutiny, with icy reservation, and at times, with ludicrous limitations.

Cheapness characterizes almost all the donations of the American people to the Negro:—Cheapness, in all the past, has been the regimen provided for the Negro in every line of his intellectual, as well as his lower life. And so, cheapness is to be the rule in the future, as well for his higher, as for his lower life:—cheap wages and cheap food, cheap and rotten huts; cheap and dilapidated schools; cheap and stinted weeks of schooling; cheap meeting houses for worship; cheap and ignorant ministers; cheap theological training; and now, cheap learning, culture and civilization!

Noble expectations are found in the grand literary circles in which Mr. Howells moves—manifest in his generous editing of our own Paul Dunbar's poems. But this generosity is not general, even in the world of American letters.

You can easily see this in the attempt, now-a-days, to sidetrack the Negro intellect, and to place it under limitations never laid upon any other class.

The elevation of the Negro has been a moot question for a generation past. But even to-day what do we find the general reliance of the American mind in determining this question? Almost universally the resort is to material agencies! The ordinary, and sometimes the *extraordinary* American is unable to see that the struggle of a degraded people for elevation is, in its very nature, a warfare, and that its main weapon is the cultivated and scientific mind.

Ask the great men of the land how this Negro problem is to be solved, and then listen to the answers that come from divers classes of our white fellow-citizens. The merchants and traders of our great cities tell us—"The Negro must be taught to work;" and they will pour out their moneys by thousands to train him to toil. The clergy in large numbers, cry out—"Industrialism is the only hope of the Negro"; for this is the bed-rock, in their opinion, of Negro evangelization! "Send him to Manual Labor Schools," cries out another set of philanthropists. "Hic haec, hoc, is going to prove the ruin of the Negro" says the Rev. Steele, an erudite Southern *Savant*. "You must begin at the bottom with the Negro," says another eminent authority—as though the Negro had been living in the clouds, and had never reached the bottom. Says the Honorable George T. Barnes, of Georgia—"The kind of education the Negro should receive should not be very refined nor classical, but adapted to his present condition:" as though there is to be no future for the Negro.

And so you see that even now, late in the 19th century, in this land of learning and science, the creed is—"Thus far and no farther," *i.e.* for the American black man.

One would suppose from the universal demand for the mere industrialism for this race of ours, that the Negro had been going daily to dinner parties, eating terrapin and indulging in champagne; and returning home at night, sleeping on beds of eiderdown; breakfasting in the morning in his bed, and then having his valet to clothe him daily in purple and fine linen—all these 250 years of his sojourn in this land. And then, just now, the American people, tired of all this Negro luxury, was calling him, for the first time, to blister his hands with the hoe, and to learn to supply his needs by sweatful toil in the cotton fields.

Listen a moment, to the wisdom of a great theologian, and withal as great philanthropist, the Rev. Dr. Wayland, of Philadelphia. Speaking, not long since, of the "Higher Education" of the colored people of the South, he said "that this subject concerned about 8,000,000 of our fellow-citizens, among whom are probably 1,500,000 voters. The education suited to these people is that which should be suited to white people under the same circumstances. These people are bearing the impress, which was left on them by two centuries of slavery and several centuries of barbarism. This education must begin at the bottom. It must first of all produce the power of self-support to assist them to better their condition. It should teach them good citizenship and should build them up morally. It should be, first, a good English education. They should be imbued with the knowledge of the Bible. They should have an industrial education. An industrial education leads to self-support and to the elevation of their condition. Industry is itself largely an education, intellectually and morally, and, above all, an education of character. Thus we should make these people self-dependent. This education will do away with pupils being taught Latin and Greek, while they do not know the rudiments of English."

Just notice the cautious, restrictive, limiting nature of this advice! Observe the lack of largeness, freedom and generosity in it. Dr. Wayland, I am sure, has never specialized just such a regimen for the poor Italians, Hungarians or Irish, who swarm, in lowly degradation, in immigrant ships to our shores. No! for them he wants, all Americans want, the widest, largest culture of the land; the instant opening, not simply of the common schools; and then an easy passage to the bar, the legislature, and even the judgeships of the nation. And they oft times get there.

But how different the policy with the Negro. *He* must have "an education which begins at the bottom." "He should have an industrial education," &c. His education must, first of all, produce the power of self-support &c.

Now, all this thought of Dr. Wayland is all true. But, my friends it is all false, too; and for the simple reason that it is only half truth. Dr. Wayland seems unable to rise above the plane of burden-bearing for the Negro. He seems unable to gauge the idea of the Negro becoming a thinker. He seems to forget that a race of thoughtless toilers are destined to be forever a race of senseless *boys;* for only beings who think are men.

How pitiable it is to see a great good man be-fuddled by a half truth. For to allege "Industrialism" to be the grand agency in the elevation of a race of already degraded labourers, is as much a mere platitude as to say, "they must eat and drink and sleep," for man cannot live without these habits. But they never civilize man; and *civilization* is the objective point in the movement for Negro elevation. Labor, just like eating and drinking, is one of the inevitabilities of life, one of its positive necessities. And the Negro has had it for centuries; but it has never given him manhood. It does not *now,* in wide areas of population, lift him up to moral and social elevation. Hence the need of a new factor in his life. The Negro needs light: . . . the light of civilization.

The Negro Race in this land must repudiate this absurd notion which is stealing on the American mind. The Race must declare that it is not to be put into a single groove; and for the simple reason (1) that *man* was made by his Maker to traverse the whole circle of existence, above as well as below; and that universality is the kernel of all true civilization, of all race elevation. And (2) that the Negro mind, imprisoned for nigh three hundred years, needs breadth and freedom, largeness, altitude, and elasticity; not stint nor rigidity, nor contractedness.

But the "Gradgrinds" are in evidence on all sides, telling us that the colleges and scholarships given us since emancipation, are all a mistake: and that the whole system must be reversed. The conviction is widespread that the Negro has no business in the higher walks of scholarship; that, for instance, Prof. Scarborough has no right to labor in philosophy; Professor Kelly Miller in mathematics; Professor DuBois, in history; Dr. Bowen, in theology; Professor Turner, in science; nor Mr. Tanner in art. There is no repugnance to the Negro buffoon, and the Negro scullion; but so soon as the Negro stands forth as an intellectual being, this toad of American prejudice, as at the touch of Ithuriel's spear, starts up a devil!

It is this attitude, this repellant, this forbidding attitude of the American mind, which forces the Negro in this land, to both recognize and to foster the talent and capacity of his own race, and to strive to put that capacity and talent to use for the race. I have detailed the dark and dreadful attempt to stamp that intellect out of existence. It is not only a past, it is also, modified indeed, a present fact; and out of it springs the need of just such an organization as the Negro Academy.

(1898)

T. THOMAS FORTUNE

(1856-1928)

Born a slave before the Civil War, T. Thomas Fortune eventually became the leading black journalist of his time. He was a vigorous fighter who voiced some of the most militant ideas of the Reconstruction period. Among his accomplishments are the establishment of the New York Age, *the nation's leading black newspaper at the end of the nineteenth century, and the founding of the Afro-American League, a civil rights group which came before Du Bois' Niagara Movement and the NAACP. At the end of his life he edited* The Negro World, *the publication of Marcus Garvey's Universal Negro Improvement Association.*

Fortune's career began early. From age ten he worked in various capacities that acquainted him with the convergent worlds of politics and journalism. From page in the Florida Senate to printer's devil to post-office worker, he gathered knowledge and skills. At twenty he began a two-year period as a student at Howard University. He taught for a year in Florida, then went to New York to work as a compositor for a New York newspaper.

In 1881 Fortune collaborated in founding and editing the New York Globe, *which for two years was a strong voice for the black man. The* Globe *suspended operations when Fortune and his partner disagreed on policy. A week later Fortune began the* New York Freeman, *which later changed its name to* New York Age. *The* Age *became a leading Afro-American organ during the 1880s and 1890s.*

Fortune's early essays were often militant. In 1883, for example, he advocated violent retribution for blacks who suffered indignities at the hands of whites: "One or two murders growing from this intolerable nuisance would break it up." By the 1890s, when many black leaders were becoming disillusioned with the possibilities of any real progress, Fortune became more conservative and supported the ideas of Booker T. Washington. The two were close friends, although the friendship was sometimes troubled.

In his later years Fortune returned to the less conservative attitudes which were probably closer to his natural bent. Earlier he had rejected the idea of Africa as motherland and had regarded it as merely an interesting foreign land. But, as mentioned above, during his final years he was editing The Negro World.

Many of Fortune's essays are available in editorials of the Age, *and in his collections* The Negro in Politics *(1885) and* Black and White: Land, Labor, and Politics in the South *(1884). For much of his career he was regarded as a brilliant firebrand. His more conservative stand may be found in his essay, "The Negro's Place in American Life at the Present Day," in* The Negro Problem *(1903). His more radical views may be found in* Black and White, *from which the following essay is taken.*

THE NEGRO AND THE NATION
From *Black and White*

The war of the Rebellion settled only one question: It forever settled the question of chattel slavery in this country. It forever choked the life out of the infamy of the Constitutional right of one man to rob another, by purchase of his person, or of his honest share of the produce of his own labor. But this was the only question permanently and irrevocably settled. Nor was this *the* all-absorbing question involved. The right of a State to secede from the so-called *Union* remains where it was when the treasonable shot upon Fort Sumter aroused the people to all the horrors of internecine war. And the measure of protection which the National government owes the individual members of States, a right imposed upon it by the adoption of the XIVth Amendment to the Constitution, remains still to be affirmed.

It was not sufficient that the Federal government should expend its blood and treasure to unfetter the limbs of four millions of people. There can be a slavery more odious, more galling, than mere chattel slavery. It has been declared to be an act of charity to enforce ignorance upon the slave, since to inform his intelligence would simply be to make his unnatural lot all the more unbearable. Instance the miserable existence of Æsop, the great black moralist. But this is just what the manumission of the black people of this country has accomplished. They are more absolutely under the control of the Southern whites; they are more systematically robbed of their labor; they are more poorly housed, clothed and fed, than under the slave régime; and they enjoy, practically, less of the protection of the laws of the State or of the Federal government. When they appeal to the Federal government they are told by the Supreme Court to go to the State authorities—as if they would have appealed to the one had the other given them that protection to which their sovereign citizenship entitles them!

Practically, there is no law in the United States which extends its protecting arm over the black man and his rights. He is, like the Irishman in Ireland, an alien in his native land. There is no central or auxiliary authority to which he can appeal for protection. Wherever he turns he finds the strong arm of constituted authority powerless to protect him. The farmer and the merchant rob him with absolute immunity, and irresponsible ruffians murder him without fear of punishment, undeterred by the law, or by public opinion —which connives at, if it does not inspire, the deeds of lawless violence. Legislatures of States have framed a code of laws which is more cruel and unjust than any enforced by a former slave State.

The right of franchise has been practically annulled in every one of the former slave States, in not one of which, to-day, can a man vote, think or act as he pleases. He must conform his views to the views of the men who have usurped every function of government— who, at the point of the dagger, and with shotgun, have made themselves masters in defiance of every law or precedent in our history as a government. They have usurped government with the weapons of the coward and assassin, and they maintain themselves in power by the most approved practices of the most odious of tyrants. These men have shed as much innocent blood as the bloody triumvirate of Rome. To-day, red-handed murderers and assassins sit in the high places of power, and bask in the smiles of innocence and beauty.

The newspapers of the country, voicing the sentiments of the people, literally hiss into silence any man who has the courage to protest against the prevailing tendency to lawlessness and bare-faced usurpation; while parties have ceased to deal with the question for other than purposes of political capital. Even this fruitful mine is well-nigh exhausted. A few more years, and the usurper and the man of violence will be left in undisputed possession of his blood-stained inheritance. No man will attempt to deter him from sowing broadcast the seeds of revolution and death. Brave men are powerless to combat this organized brigandage, complaint of which, in derision, has been termed "waving the bloody shirt."

Men organize themselves into society for mutual protection. Government justly derives its just powers from the consent of the governed. But what shall we say of that society which is incapable of extending the protection which is inherent in it? What shall we say of the government which has not power or inclination to insure the exercise of those solemn rights and immunities which it guarantees? To declare a man to be free, and equal with his fellow, and then to refrain from enacting laws powerful to insure him in such freedom and equality, is to trifle with the most sacred of all the functions of sovereignty. Have not the United States done this very thing? Have they not conferred freedom and the ballot, which are necessary the one to the other? And have they not signally failed to make omnipotent the one and practicable the other? The questions hardly require an answer. The measure of freedom the black man enjoys can be gauged by the power he has to vote. He has, practically, no voice in the government under which he lives. His property is taxed and his life is jeopardized, by states on the one hand and inefficient police regulations on the other, and no question is asked or expected of him. When he protests, when he cries out against this flagrant nullification of the very first principles of a republican form of government, the insolent question is asked: "What are you going to do about it?" And here lies the danger.

You may rob and maltreat a slave and ask him what he is going to do about it, and he can make no reply. He is bound hand and foot; he is effectually gagged. Despair is his only refuge. He knows it is useless to appeal from tyranny unto the designers and apologists of tyranny. Ignominious death alone can bring him relief. This was the case of thousands of men doomed by the institution of slavery. *But such is not the case with free men.* You cannot oppress and murder freemen as you would slaves: you cannot so insult them with the question, "What are you going to do about it?" When you ask free men that question you appeal to men who, though sunk to the verge of despair, yet are capable of uprising and ripping hip and thigh those who deemed them incapable of so rising above their condition. The history of mankind is fruitful of such uprisings of races and classes reduced to a condition of absolute despair. The American negro is no better and no worse than the Haytian revolutionists headed by Toussaint l'Overture, Christophe and the bloody Dessalines.

I do not indulge in the luxury of prophecy when I declare that the American people are fostering in their bosoms a spirit of rebellion which will yet shake the pillars of popular government as they have never before been shaken, unless a wiser policy is inaugurated and honestly enforced. All the indications point to the fulfilment of such declaration.

The Czar of Russia squirms upon his throne, not because he is necessarily a bad man, but because he is the head and center of a condition of things which squeezes the life out of the people. His subjects hurl infernal machines at the tyrant because he represents the system which oppresses them. But the evil is far deeper than the throne, and cannot be remedied by striking the occupant of it—*the throne itself must be rooted out and demolished.* So the Irish question has a more powerful motive to foment agitation and murder than the landlord and landlordism. The landlord simply stands out as the representative of the real grievance. To remove *him* would not remove the evil; agitation would not cease; murder would still stalk abroad at noon-day. *The real grievance is the false system which makes the landlord possible.* The appropriation of the fertile acres of the soil of Ireland, which created and maintains a privileged class, a class that while performing no labor, wrings from the toiler, in the shape of rents, so much of the produce of his labor that he cannot on the residue support himself and those dependent upon him aggravates the situation. It is this system which constitutes the real grievance and makes the landlord an odious loafer with abundant cash and the laborer a constant toiler always upon the verge of starvation. Evidently, therefore, to remove the landlord and leave the system of land monopoly would not remove the evil. Destroy the latter and the former would be compelled to go.

Herein lies the great social wrong which has turned the beautiful roses of freedom into thorns to prick the hands of the black men of the South; which made slavery a blessing, paradoxical as it may appear, and freedom a curse. It is this great wrong which has crowded the cities of the South with an ignorant pauper population, making desolate fields that once bloomed "as fair as a garden of the Lord," where now the towering oak and pine-tree flourish, instead of the corn and cotton which gladdened the heart and filled the purse. It was this gigantic iniquity which created that arrogant class who have exhausted the catalogue of violence to obtain power and the lexicon of sophistry for arguments to extenuate the exceeding heinousness of crime. How could it be otherwise? To tell a man he is free when he has neither money nor the opportunity to make it, is simply to mock him. To tell him he has no master when he cannot live except by permission of the man who, under favorable conditions, monopolizes all the land, is to deal in the most tantalizing contradiction of terms. But this is just what the United States did for the black man. And yet because he has not grown learned and wealthy in twenty years, because he does not own broad acres and a large bank account, people are not wanting who declare he has no capacity, that he is improvident by nature and mendacious from inclination.

(1884)

BOOKER T. WASHINGTON

(1856-1915)

Undoubtedly the most visible figure in black America at the turn of the century was Booker T. Washington. In an era when the work ethic superseded the Golden Rule, this ex-slave who became the spokesman for the newly freed millions seemed the sable archetype of American ideals. Enthroned at Tuskegee Institute, which he founded, Washington wielded the tremendous power vested in him by the white power structure which had chosen him leader of the blacks. Through wily manipulation of money and influence, Washington fully dominated the activity of black America, or at least the expression of thought by its spokesmen.

Washington was born in a log cabin on a plantation in Virginia. He was never certain of his birthdate. His father was said to be a white man on a neighboring plantation; this alleged white ancestry was sometimes given the credit for Washington's later achievements. His mother and her three children were slaves. After emancipation, when Booker was about seven, his mother and stepfather moved the family to West Virginia. Young Booker's boyhood years were harsh, marked by the back-breaking and often spirit-breaking toil of the ex-slaves. Even then, Washington seemed endowed with unusual drive and energy. From early childhood, he struggled for an education. In his entire life he never acquired the taste for leisure. At age sixteen he set out on foot for Hampton Institute, five hundred miles away, with one dollar and fifty cents in his pocket. He reached his goal, and with some financial aid from wealthy whites, he worked his way through to graduation. After teaching for a while and attending a seminary for a year, Washington returned to Hampton where he supervised the residence hall for young Indian men from the West who were being exposed to the Hampton way. In 1881 he founded Tuskegee Institute. In the years that followed, Washington built up the school, and he himself rose to a position of greater influence than any American black before him had known.

Washington's rise to eminence was greatly accelerated by his Atlanta Exposition Address in 1895. Having been chosen to speak for the black community, he said the things that were comforting to the whites. He praised white leaders for their help to the ignorant black masses. He characterized his race as "the most patient, faithful, law-abiding, and unresentful people the world has seen" and promised their everlasting support to the white South. He urged that blacks remain in the South and learn manual skills; he urged that they wait for citizenship to be awarded rather than demand it. He advocated social separation. In effect he laid responsibility on the black man for much of his own oppressed situation and absolved the white man of a great deal of guilt and responsibility. He disavowed the civil rights goals that were most repugnant to whites.

Following his speech, Washington was acclaimed as the leader of his people—especially by white America, who poured a small fortune into his hands for the construction of his school and for the support of other projects in which he was interested. Government sought his advice on many matters; black projects which did not meet his approval were usually denied aid from Federal and private sources. The mass media published anything he wrote or said, but often rejected the works of those opposed to him. Washington himself gained financial control of several newspapers.

He organized the National Negro Business League, was instrumental in furthering American assistance to Liberia, and participated in numerous projects concerning the educational, economic, and physical benefit of black people.

For a great many years Washington's conciliatory ideas dominated black thought. Many highly intelligent and respected men wrote in his support, and many black children were educated in terms of his ideas. His ideological grip, however, was finally broken by the opposition of W. E. B. Du Bois *and others.*

*Washington was not primarily a creative writer. His works were expository in nature, aimed mainly toward instruction on how to get ahead. Perhaps the subject of his address at the Hampton 1879 commencement was prophetic of his later works—"The Force That Wins." The titles of some of his works clearly reveal the drift of their content—*Sowing and Reaping *(1900),* Working with the Hands

(1904), Putting the Most Into Life *(1906)*, My Larger Education *(1911), and* The Man Farthest Down *(1912). He also wrote a great many speeches and articles. In 1907 he wrote a biography of Frederick Douglass, whose rise from slavery he admired. On many of these works he had the active assistance of his staff at Tuskegee.*

Washington's most popular work was his autobiography Up From Slavery *(1901), which falls into the Horatio Alger genre of an American success story. It presents a simplified and even falsified picture of black life in the United States, but served the purpose of solidifying his acceptance as a Negro leader by many sectors of American society. Understanding of the full complexity of Washington's thought and activity has been enhanced by the two-volume biography completed by Lewis R. Harlan, editor of the Booker T. Washington papers.*

From *Up from Slavery*

CHAPTER I

A SLAVE AMONG SLAVES

I was born a slave on a plantation in Franklin County, Virginia. I am not quite sure of the exact place or exact date of my birth, but at any rate I suspect I must have been born somewhere and at some time. As nearly as I have been able to learn, I was born near a cross-roads post-office called Hale's Ford, and the year was 1858 or 1859. I do not know the month or the day. The earliest impressions I can now recall are of the plantation and the slave quarters—the latter being the part of the plantation where the slaves had their cabins.

My life had its beginning in the midst of the most miserable, desolate, and discouraging surroundings. This was so, however, not because my owners were especially cruel, for they were not, as compared with many others. I was born in a typical log cabin, about fourteen by sixteen feet square. In this cabin I lived with my mother and a brother and sister till after the Civil War, when we were all declared free.

Of my ancestry I know almost nothing. In the slave quarters, and even later, I heard whispered conversations among the coloured people of the tortures which the slaves, including, no doubt, my ancestors on my mother's side, suffered in the middle passage of the slave ship while being conveyed from Africa to America. I have been unsuccessful in securing any information that would throw any accurate light upon the history of my family beyond my mother. She, I remember, had a half-brother and a half-sister. In the days of slavery not very much attention was given to family history and family records—that is, black family records. My mother, I suppose, attracted the attention of a purchaser who was afterward my owner and hers. Her addition to the slave family attracted about as much attention as the purchase of a new horse or cow. Of my father I know even less than of my mother. I do not even know his name. I have heard reports to the effect that he was a white man who lived on one of the near-by plantations. Whoever he was, I never heard of his taking the least interest in me or providing in any way for my rearing. But I do not find especial fault with him. He was simply another unfortunate victim of the institution which the Nation unhappily had engrafted upon it at that time.

The cabin was not only our living-place, but was also used as the kitchen for the plantation. My mother was the plantation cook. The cabin was without glass windows; it had only openings in the side which let in the light, and also the cold, chilly air of winter. There was a door to the cabin—that is, something that was called a door—but the uncertain hinges by which it was hung, and the large cracks in it, to say nothing of the fact that it was too small, made the room a very uncomfortable one. In addition to these openings there was, in the lower right-hand corner of the room, the "cat-hole,"—a contrivance which almost every mansion or cabin in Virginia possessed during the ante-bellum period. The "cat-hole" was a square opening, about seven by eight inches, provided for the purpose of letting the cat pass in and out of the house at will during the night. In the case of our particular cabin I could never understand the necessity for this convenience, since there were at least a half-dozen other places in the cabin that would have accommodated the cats. There was no wooden floor in our cabin, the naked earth being used as a floor. In the centre of the earthen floor there was a large, deep opening covered with boards, which was used as a place in which to store sweet potatoes during the winter. An impression of this potato-hole is very distinctly engraved upon my memory, because I recall that during the process of putting the potatoes in or taking them out I would often come into possession of one or two, which I roasted and thoroughly enjoyed. There was no cooking-stove on our plantation, and all the cooking for the whites and slaves my mother had to do over an open fireplace, mostly in pots and "skillets." While the poorly built cabin caused us to suffer with cold in the winter, the heat from the open fireplace in summer was equally trying.

The early years of my life, which were spent in the little cabin, were not very different from those of thousands of other slaves. My mother, of course, had little time in which to give attention to the training of her children during the day. She snatched a few moments for our care in the early morning before her work began, and at night after the day's work was done. One of my earliest recollections is that of my mother cooking a chicken late at night, and awakening her children for the purpose of feeding them. How or where she got it I do not know. I presume, however, it was procured from our owner's farm. Some people may call this theft. If such a thing were to happen now, I should condemn it as theft myself. But taking place at the time it did, and for the reason that it did, no one could ever make me believe that my mother was guilty of thieving. She was simply a victim of the system of slavery. I cannot remember having slept in a bed until after our family was declared free by the Emancipation Proclamation. Three children—John, my older brother, Amanda, my sister, and myself—had a pallet on the dirt floor, or, to be more correct, we slept in and on a bundle of filthy rags laid upon the dirt floor.

I was asked not long ago to tell something about the sports and pastimes that I engaged in during my youth. Until that question was asked it had never occurred to me that there was no period of my life that was devoted to play. From the time that I can remember anything, almost every day of my life has been occupied in some kind of labour; though I think I would now be a more useful man if I had had time for sports. During the period that I spent in slavery I was not large enough to be of much service, still I was occupied most of the time in cleaning the yards, carrying water to the men in the fields, or going to the mill, to which I used to take the corn, once a week, to be ground. The mill was about three miles from the plantation. This work I always dreaded. The heavy bag of corn would be thrown across the back of the horse, and the corn divided about evenly on each side; but in some way, almost without exception, on these trips, the corn would shift as to become unbalanced and would fall off the horse, and often I would fall with it. As I was not strong enough to reload the corn upon the horse, I would have to wait, sometimes for many hours, till a chance passer-by came along who would help me out of my trouble. The hours while waiting for some one were usually spent in crying. The time consumed in this way made me late in reaching the mill, and by the time I got my corn ground and reached home it would be far into the night. The road was a

lonely one, and often led through dense forests. I was always frightened. The woods were said to be full of soldiers who had deserted
from the army, and I had been told that the first thing a deserter
did to a Negro boy when he found him alone was to cut off his ears.
Besides, when I was late in getting home I knew I would always get
a severe scolding or a flogging.

I had no schooling whatever while I was a slave, though I remember on several occasions I went as far as the schoolhouse door
with one of my young mistresses to carry her books. The picture of
several dozen boys and girls in a schoolroom engaged in study made
a deep impression upon me, and I had the feeling that to get into a
schoolhouse and study in this way would be about the same as getting
into paradise.

So far as I can now recall, the first knowledge that I got of the
fact that we were slaves, and that freedom of the slaves was being
discussed, was early one morning before day, when I was awakened
by my mother kneeling over her children and fervently praying that
Lincoln and his armies might be successful, and that one day she and
her children might be free. In this connection I have never been able
to understand how the slaves throughout the South, completely ignorant as were the masses so far as books or newspapers were concerned, were able to keep themselves so accurately and completely
informed about the great National questions that were agitating the
country. From the time that Garrison, Lovejoy, and others began
to agitate for freedom, the slaves throughout the South kept in close
touch with the progress of the movement. Though I was a mere child
during the preparation for the Civil War and during the war itself,
I now recall the many late-at-night whispered discussions that I
heard my mother and the other slaves on the plantation indulge in.
These discussions showed that they understood the situation, and that
they kept themselves informed of events by what was termed the
"grape-vine" telegraph.

During the campaign when Lincoln was first a candidate for
the Presidency, the slaves on our far-off plantation, miles from any
railroad or large city or daily newspaper, knew what the issues involved were. When war was begun between the North and the
South, every slave on our plantation felt and knew that, though other
issues were discussed, the primal one was that of slavery. Even the
most ignorant members of my race on the remote plantations felt
in their hearts, with a certainty that admitted of no doubt, that the
freedom of the slaves would be the one great result of the war, if the

Northern armies conquered. Every success of the Federal armies and every defeat of the Confederate forces was watched with the keenest and most intense interest. Often the slaves got knowledge of the results of great battles before the white people received it. This news was usually gotten from the coloured man who was sent to the post-office for the mail. In our case the post-office was about three miles from the plantation and the mail came once or twice a week. The man who was sent to the office would linger about the place long enough to get the drift of the conversation from the group of white people who naturally congregated there, after receiving their mail, to discuss the latest news. The mail-carrier on his way back to our master's house would as naturally retail the news that he had secured among the slaves, and in this way they often heard of important events before the white people at the "big house," as the master's house was called.

I cannot remember a single instance during my childhood or early boyhood when our entire family sat down to the table together, and God's blessing was asked, and the family ate a meal in a civilized manner. On the plantation in Virginia, and even later, meals were gotten by the children very much as dumb animals get theirs. It was a piece of bread here and a scrap of meat there. It was a cup of milk at one time and some potatoes at another. Sometimes a portion of our family would eat out of the skillet or pot, while some one would eat from a tin plate held on the knees, and often using nothing but the hands with which to hold the food. When I had grown to sufficient size, I was required to go to the "big house" at meal-times to fan the flies from the table by means of a large set of paper fans operated by a pulley. Naturally much of the conversation of the white people turned upon the subject of freedom and the war, and I absorbed a good deal of it. I remember that at one time I saw two of my young mistresses and some lady visitors eating ginger-cakes, in the yard. At that time those cakes seemed to me to be absolutely the most tempting and desirable things that I had ever seen; and I then and there resolved that, if I ever got free, the height of my ambition would be reached if I could get to the point where I could secure and eat ginger-cakes in the way that I saw those ladies doing.

Of course as the war was prolonged the white people, in many cases, often found it difficult to secure food for themselves. I think the slaves felt the deprivation less than the white, because the usual diet for the slaves was corn bread and pork, and these could be raised on the plantation; but coffee, tea, sugar, and other articles which the whites had been accustomed to use could not be raised on the plantation, and the conditions brought about by the war frequently made it impossible to secure these things. The whites were often in great straits. Parched corn was used for coffee, and a kind of black molasses was used instead of sugar. Many times nothing was used to sweeten the so-called tea and coffee.

The first pair of shoes that I recall wearing were wooden ones. They had rough leather on the top, but the bottoms, which were about an inch thick, were of wood. When I walked they made a fearful noise, and besides this they were very inconvenient, since there was no yielding to the natural pressure of the foot. In wearing them one presented an exceedingly awkward appearance. The most trying ordeal that I was forced to endure as a slave boy, however, was the wearing of a flax shirt. In the portion of Virginia where I lived it was common to use flax as part of the clothing for the slaves. That part of the flax from which our clothing was made was largely the refuse, which of course was the cheapest and roughest part. I can scarcely imagine any torture, except, perhaps, the pulling of a tooth, that is equal to that caused by putting on a new flax shirt for the first time. It is almost equal to the feeling that one would experience if he had a dozen or more chestnut burrs, or a hundred small pinpoints, in contact with his flesh. Even to this day I can recall accurately the tortures that I underwent when putting on one of these garments. The fact that my flesh was soft and tender added to the pain. But I had no choice. I had to wear the flax shirt or none; and had it been left to me to choose, I should have chosen to wear no covering. In connection with the flax shirt, my brother John, who is several years older than I am, performed one of the most generous acts that I ever heard of one slave relative doing for another. On several occasions when I was being forced to wear a new flax shirt, he generously agreed to put it on in my stead and wear it for several days, till it was "broken in." Until I had grown to be quite a youth this single garment was all that I wore.

One may get the idea from what I have said, that there was bitter feeling toward the white people on the part of my race, because of the fact that most of the white population was away fighting in a war which would result in keeping the Negro in slavery if the South was successful. In the case of the slaves on our place this was not true, and it was not true of any large portion of the slave population in the South where the Negro was treated with anything like decency. During the Civil War one of my young masters was killed, and two were severely wounded. I recall the feeling of sorrow which existed among the slaves when they heard of the death of "Mars' Billy." It was no sham sorrow but real. Some of the slaves had nursed "Mars' Billy"; others had played with him when he was a child. "Mars' Billy" had begged for mercy in the case of others when the overseer or master was thrashing them. The sorrow in the slave quarter was only second to that in the "big house." When the two young masters were brought home wounded, the sympathy of the slaves was shown in many ways. They were just as anxious to assist in the nursing as the family relatives of the wounded. Some of the slaves would even beg for the privilege of sitting up at night to nurse their wounded masters. This tenderness and sympathy on the part of those held in bondage was a result of their kindly and generous nature. In order to defend and protect the women and children who were left on the plantations when the white males went to war, the slaves would have laid down their lives. The slave who was selected to sleep in the "big house" during the absence of the males was considered to have the place of honour. Any one attempting to harm "young Mistress" or "old Mistress" during the night would have had to cross the dead body of the slave to do so. I do not know how many have noticed it, but I think that it will be found to be true that there are few instances, either in slavery or freedom, in which a member of my race has been known to betray a specific trust.

As a rule, not only did the members of my race entertain no feelings of bitterness against the whites before and during the war, but there are many instances of Negroes tenderly caring for their former masters and mistresses who for some reason have become poor and dependent since the war. I know of instances where the former masters of slaves have for years been supplied with money by their former slaves to keep them from suffering. I have known of still other cases in which the former slaves have assisted in the education of the descendants of their former owners. I know of a case on a large plantation in the South in which a young white man, the son of the former owner of the estate, has become so reduced in purse and self-control by reason of drink that he is a pitiable creature; and yet, notwithstanding the poverty of the coloured people themselves on this plantation, they have for years supplied this young white man with the necessities of life. One sends him a little coffee or sugar, another a little meat, and so on. Nothing that the coloured people possess is too good for the son of "old Mars' Tom," who will perhaps never be permitted to suffer while any remain on the place who knew directly or indirectly of "old Mars' Tom."

I have said that there are few instances of a member of my race betraying a specific trust. One of the best illustrations of this which I know of is in the case of an ex-slave from Virginia whom I met not long ago in a little town in the state of Ohio. I found that this man had made a contract with his master, two or three years previous to the Emancipation Proclamation, to the effect that the slave was to be permitted to buy himself, by paying so much per year for his body; and while he was paying for himself, he was to be permitted to labour where and for whom he pleased. Finding that he could secure better wages in Ohio, he went there. When freedom came, he was still in debt to his master some three hundred dollars. Notwithstanding that the Emancipation Proclamation freed him from any obligation to his master, this black man walked the greater portion of the distance back to where his old master lived in Virginia, and placed the last dollar, with interest, in his hands. In talking to me about this, the man told me that he knew that he did not have to pay the debt, but that he had given his word to his master, and his word he had never broken. He felt that he could not enjoy his freedom till he had fulfilled his promise.

From some things that I have said one may get the idea that some of the slaves did not want freedom. This is not true. I have never seen one who did not want to be free, or one who would return to slavery.

I pity from the bottom of my heart any nation or body of people that is so unfortunate as to get entangled in the net of slavery. I have long since ceased to cherish any spirit of bitterness against the Southern white people on account of the enslavement of my race. No one section of our country was wholly responsible for its introduction, and, besides, it was recognized and protected for years by the General Government. Having once got its tentacles fastened on to the economic and social life of the Republic, it was no easy matter for the country to relieve itself of the institution. Then, when we rid ourselves of prejudice, or racial feeling, and look facts in the face, we must acknowledge that, notwithstanding the cruelty and moral wrong of slavery, the ten million Negroes inhabiting this country, who themselves or whose ancestors went through the school of American slavery, are in a stronger and more hopeful condition, materially, intellectually, morally, and religiously, than is true of an equal number of black people in any other portion of the globe. This is so to such an extent that Negroes in this country, who themselves or whose forefathers went through the school of slavery, are constantly returning to Africa as missionaries to enlighten those who remained in the fatherland. This I say, not to justify slavery—on the other hand, I condemn it as an institution, as we all know that in America it was established for selfish and financial reasons, and not from a missionary motive—but to call attention to a fact, and to show how Providence so often uses men and institutions to accomplish a purpose. When persons ask me in these days how, in the midst of what sometimes seem hopelessly discouraging conditions, I can have such faith in the future of my race in this country, I remind them of the wilderness through which and out of which, a good Providence has already led us.

Ever since I have been old enough to think for myself, I have entertained the idea that, notwithstanding the cruel wrongs inflicted upon us, the black man got nearly as much out of slavery as the white man did. The hurtful influences of the institution were not by any means confined to the Negro. This was fully illustrated by the life upon our own plantation. The whole machinery of slavery was so constructed as to cause labour, as a rule, to be looked upon as a badge of degradation, of inferiority. Hence labour was something that both races on the slave plantation sought to escape. The slave system on our place, in a large measure, took the spirit of self-reliance and self-help out of the white people. My old master had many boys and girls, but not one, so far as I know, ever mastered a single trade or special line of productive industry. The girls were not taught to cook, sew or to take care of the house. All of this was left to the slaves. The slaves, of course, had little personal interest in the life of the plantation, and their ignorance prevented them from learning how to do things in the most improved and thorough manner. As a result of the system, fences were out of repair, gates were hanging half off the hinges, doors creaked, window-panes were out, plastering had fallen but was not replaced, weeds grew in the yard. As a rule, there was food for whites and blacks, but inside the house, and on the dining-room table, there was wanting that delicacy and refinement of touch and finish which can make a home the most convenient, comfortable, and attractive place in the world. Withal there was a waste of food and other materials which was sad. When freedom came, the slaves were almost as well fitted to begin life anew as the master, except in the matter of book-learning and ownership of property. The slave owner and his sons had mastered no special industry. They unconsciously had imbibed the feeling that manual labour was not the proper thing for them. On the other hand, the slaves, in many cases, had mastered some handicraft, and none were ashamed, and few unwilling, to labour.

Finally the war closed, and the day of freedom came. It was a momentous and eventful day to all upon our plantation. We had been expecting it. Freedom was in the air, and had been for months. Deserting soldiers returning to their homes were to be seen every day. Others who had been discharged, or whose regiments had been paroled, were constantly passing near our place. The "grape-vine telegraph" was kept busy night and day. The news and mutterings of great events were swiftly carried from one plantation to another. In the fear of "Yankee" invasions, the silverware and other valuables were taken from the "big house," buried in the woods, and guarded by trusted slaves. Woe be to any one who would have attempted to disturb the buried treasure. The slaves would give the Yankee soldiers food, drink, clothing—anything but that which had been specifically intrusted to their care and honour. As the great day grew nearer, there was more singing in the slave quarters than usual. It was bolder, had more ring, and lasted later into the night. Most of the verses of the plantation songs had some reference to freedom. True, they had sung those same verses before, but they had been careful to explain that the "freedom" in these songs referred to the next world, and had no connection with life in this world. Now they gradually threw off the mask; and were not afraid to let it be known that the "freedom" in their songs meant freedom of the body in this world. The night before the eventful day, word was sent to the slave quarters to the effect that something unusual was going to take place at the "big house" the next morning. There was little, if any, sleep that night. All was excitement and expectancy. Early the next morning word was sent to all the slaves, old and young, to gather at the house. In company with my mother, brother, and sister, and a large number of other slaves, I went to the master's house. All of our master's family were either standing or seated on the veranda of the house, where they could see what was to take place and hear what was said. There was a feeling of deep interest, or perhaps sadness, on their faces, but not bitterness. As I now recall the impression they made upon me, they did not at the moment seem to be sad because of the loss of property, but rather because of parting with those whom they had reared and who were in many ways very close to them.

The most distinct thing that I now recall in connection with the scene was that some man who seemed to be a stranger (a United States officer, I presume) made a little speech and then read a rather long paper—the Emancipation Proclamation, I think. After the reading we were told that we were all free, and could go when and where we pleased. My mother, who was standing by my side, leaned over and kissed her children, while tears of joy ran down her cheeks. She explained to us what it all meant, that this was the day for which she had been so long praying, but fearing that she would never live to see.

For some minutes there was great rejoicing, and thanksgiving, and wild scenes of ecstasy. But there was no feeling of bitterness. In fact, there was pity among the slaves for our former owners. The wild rejoicing on the part of the emancipated coloured people lasted but for a brief period, for I noticed that by the time they returned to their cabins there was a change in their feelings. The great responsibility of being free, of having charge of themselves, of having to think and plan for themselves and their children, seemed to take possession of them. It was very much like suddenly turning a youth of ten or twelve years out into the world to provide for himself. In a few hours the great questions with which the Anglo-Saxon race had been grappling for centuries had been thrown upon these people to be solved. These were the questions of a home, a living, the rearing of children, education, citizenship, and the establishment and support of churches. Was it any wonder that within a few hours the wild rejoicing ceased and a feeling of deep gloom seemed to pervade the slave quarters? To some it seemed that, now that they were in actual possession of it, freedom was a more serious thing than they had expected to find it. Some of the slaves were seventy or eighty years old; their best days were gone. They had no strength with which to earn a living in a strange place and among strange people, even if they had been sure where to find a new place of abode. To this class the problem seemed especially hard. Besides, deep down in their hearts there was a strange and peculiar attachment to "old Marster" and "old Missus," and to their children, which they found it hard to think of breaking off. With these they had spent in some cases nearly a half-century, and it was no light thing to think of parting. Gradually, one by one, stealthily at first, the older slaves began to wander from the slave quarters back to the "big house" to have a whispered conversation with their former owners as to the future.

Speech at the Atlanta Exposition

Mr. President and Gentlemen of the Board of Directors and Citizens: One-third of the population of the South is of the Negro race. No enterprise seeking the material, civil, or moral welfare of this section can disregard this element of our population and reach the highest success. I but convey to you, Mr. President and Directors, the sentiment of the masses of my race when I say that in no way have the value and manhood of the American Negro been more fittingly and generously recognized than by the managers of this magnificent Exposition at every stage of its progress. It is a recognition that will do more to cement the friendship of the two races than any occurrence since the dawn of freedom.

Not only this, but the opportunity here afforded will awaken among us a new era of industrial progress. Ignorant and inexperienced, it is not strange that in the first years of our new life we began at the top instead of at the bottom; that a seat in Congress or the State Legislature was more sought than real estate or industrial skill; that the political convention or stump speaking had more attractions than starting a dairy farm or truck garden.

A ship lost at sea for many days suddenly sighted a friendly vessel. From the mast of the unfortunate vessel was seen a signal: "Water, water; we die of thirst!" The answer from the friendly vessel at once came back: "Cast down your bucket where you are." A second time the signal, "Water, water; send us water"; ran up from the distressed vessel, and was answered: "Cast down your bucket where you are." The captain of the distressed vessel, at last heeding the injunction, cast down his bucket, and it came up full of fresh, sparkling water from the mouth of the Amazon River. To those of my race who depend upon bettering their condition in a foreign land, or whom underestimate the importance of cultivating friendly relations with the Southern white man, who is his next door neighbor, I would say: "Cast down your bucket where you are"—cast it down in making friends in every manly way of the people of all races by whom we are surrounded.

Cast it down in agriculture, mechanics, in commerce, in domestic service, and in the professions. And in this connection it is well to bear in mind that whatever other sins the South may be called to bear, when it comes to business, pure and simple, it is in the South that the Negro is given a man's chance in the commercial world, and in nothing is this Exposition more eloquent than in emphasizing this chance. Our greatest danger is, that in the great leap from slavery to freedom we may overlook the fact that the masses of us are to live by the productions of our hands, and fail to keep in mind that we shall prosper in proportion as we learn to draw the line between the superficial and the substantial, the ornamental geegaws of life and the useful. No race can prosper till it learns that there is as much dignity in tilling a field as in writing a poem. It is at the bottom of life we must begin, and not at the top. Nor should we permit our grievances to overshadow our opportunities.

To those of the white race who look to the incoming of those of foreign birth and strange tongue and habits for the prosperity of the South, were I permitted I would repeat what I say to my own race, "Cast down your bucket where you are." Cast it down among the 8,000,000 Negroes whose habits you know, whose fidelity and love you have tested in days when to have proved treacherous mean the ruin of your firesides. Cast down your bucket among these people who have, without strikes and labor wars, tilled your fields, cleared your forests, builded your railroads and cities, and brought forth treasures from the bowels of the earth, and helped make possible this magnificent representation of the progress of the South. Casting down your bucket among my people, helping and encouraging them as you are doing on these grounds, and, with education of head, hand and heart, you will find that they will buy your surplus land, make blossom the waste places in your fields, and run your factories. While doing this, you can be sure in the future, as in the past, that you and your families will be surrounded by the most patient, faithful, law-abiding, and unresentful people that the world has seen. As we have proved our loyalty to you in the past, in nursing your children, watching by the sick bed of your mothers and fathers, and often following them with tear-dimmed eyes to their graves, so in the future, in our humble way, we shall stand by you with a devotion that no foreigner can approach, ready to lay down our lives, if need be, in defense of yours, interlacing our industrial, commercial, civil, and religious life with yours in a way that shall make the interests of both races one. In all things that are purely social we can be as separate as the fingers, yet one as the hand in all things essential to mutual progress.

There is no defense or security for any of us except in the highest intelligence and development of all. If anywhere there are efforts tending to curtail the fullest growth of the Negro, let these efforts be turned into stimulating, encouraging, and making him the most useful and intelligent citizen. Effort or means so invested will pay a thousand per cent interest. These efforts will be twice blessed—blessing him that gives and him that takes.

There is no escape through law of man or God from the inevitable:

"The laws of changeless justice bind
Oppressor with oppressed;
And close as sin and suffering joined
We march to fate abreast."

Nearly sixteen millions of hands will aid you in pulling the load upwards, or they will pull against you the load downwards. We shall constitute one-third and more of the ignorance and crime of the South, or one-third its intelligence and progress; we shall contribute one-third to the business and industrial prosperity of the South, or we shall prove a veritable body of death, stagnating, depressing, retarding every effort to advance the body politic.

Gentlemen of the Exposition, as we present to you our humble effort at an exhibition of our progress, you must not expect overmuch. Starting thirty years ago with ownership here and there in a few quilts and pumpkins and chickens (gathered from miscellaneous sources), remember the path that has led from these to the invention and production of agricultural implements, buggies, steam engines, newspapers, books, statuary, carving, paintings, the management of drugs stores and banks has not been trodden without contract with thorns and thistles. While we take pride in what we exhibit as a result of our independent efforts, we do not for a moment forget that our part in this exhibition would fall far short of your expectations but for the constant help that has come to our educational life, not only from the Southern States, but especially from Northern philanthropists, who have made their gifts a constant stream of blessing and encouragement.

The wisest among my race understand that the agitation of questions of social equality is the extremest folly, and that progress in the enjoyment of all the privileges that wil come to us must be the result of severe and constant struggle rather than of artificial forcing. No race that has anything to contribute to the markets of the world is long in any degree ostracized. It is important and right that all privileges of the law be ours, but it is vastly more important that we be prepared for the exercise of those privileges. The opportunity to earn a dollar in a factory just now is worth infinitely more than the opportunity to spend a dollar in an opera house.

In conclusion, may I repeat that nothing in thirty years has given us more hope and encouragement, and drawn us so near to you of the white race, as this opportunity offered by the Exposition; and here bending; as it were, over the altar that represents the results of the struggles of your race and mine, both starting practically empty-handed three decades ago, I pledge that, in your effort to work out the great and intricate problem which God has laid at the doors of the South, you shall have at all times the patient, sympathetic help of my race; only let this be constantly in mind that, while from representations in these buildings of the products of field, of forest, of mine, of factory, letters, and art, much good will come, yet far above and beyond material benefits will be the higher good, that let us pray God will come, in a blotting out of sectional differences and racial animosities and suspicions, in a determination to administer absolute justice, in a willing obedience among all classes to the mandates of law. This, coupled with our material prosperity, will bring into our beloved South a new heaven and a new earth.

WILLIAM E. B. DU BOIS

(1868-1963)

W. E. B. Du Bois was not only the most brilliant and prolific black scholar of the early twentieth century, but also the most influential. He lived to be well over ninety; his long career spanned seventy years of writing, speaking, and organizing for human peace, dignity, and justice. His commitment to black Americans broadened to encompass all people descended from Africa, which he called "the Spiritual Frontier of humankind," and eventually to encompass humankind itself in his efforts toward world peace. Because he remained well ahead of his time, his views were often controversial. Because he was an outspoken critic of society, he became increasingly alienated from his native land. He spent his last years as a citizen of Ghana, where he pursued his lifelong project, the Encyclopedia Africana. *Among his accomplishments were the founding of the Niagara Movement, one of the earliest attempts to organize a black pressure group; his part in establishing the NAACP; and four magazines which he founded and edited, including* Phylon, *the Atlanta University journal, and the extremely significant* The Crisis, *official publication of the NAACP.*

Du Bois was born in Great Barrington, Massachusetts, a small New England town with few black families. Years of study at Fisk and Harvard Universities and the University of Berlin brought him in contact with some of the most brilliant teachers of two continents. In 1895 he received his doctorate from Harvard. His dissertation, The Suppression of the African Slave Trade to the United States of America, 1638 to 1870, *became the first volume of the Harvard University Series in History.*

For fifteen years after the completion of his formal education, Du Bois was a college professor and researcher. After a year as Professor of Classics at Wilberforce University, he was appointed Assistant Instructor at the University of Pennsylvania, where he conducted sociological research on the condition of Negroes in Philadelphia. In 1899 the results of this study were published in a monograph, The Philadelphia Negro, a Sociological Study, *a work of lasting importance. From 1897 to 1910 Du Bois was Professor of History and Economics at Atlanta University. During these years he produced some of his major works. Fifteen volumes of* The Atlanta University Publications *(1897-1915), edited by Du Bois (the last four with Augustus Dill), remain among the best sources of information about blacks for that time.*

The Souls of Black Folk: Essays and Sketches *(1903) is a classic in the field of black writing. It triggered the long debate with Booker T. Washington and, in a sense, freed black intellectuals from the incubus of Washington's conciliatory stand. Du Bois' biography* John Brown *appeared in 1909.*

In 1910 Du Bois left Atlanta University to edit The Crisis. *For the next twenty-four years he conducted the magazine as a vital weapon of protest, a forum for black opinion, and an important outlet for black writing. Through* The Crisis *Du Bois became the philosopher-spokesman of black thought. In addition to the militant* Crisis, *Du Bois founded and edited* The Brownies' Book, *a magazine for black children, whose purpose was to teach them the beauty of their blackness. Meanwhile, Du Bois was addressing white audiences through articles published in leading white periodicals. During this period Du Bois wrote two novels,* The Quest of the Silver Fleece *(1911) and* Dark Princess *(1928). He collected essays and sketches and some poetry in* Darkwater *(1920), which was followed by* The Gift of Black Folk *(1924). The Pan-African Congresses also belong to these years.*

Du Bois left the NAACP and The Crisis *in 1934 after a quarrel over policy and returned to Atlanta University as Professor of Sociology. While at Atlanta University he published two books of history,* Black Reconstruction in America, 1860-1880 *(1935),* Black Folk: Then and Now *(1939), an autobiography,* Dusk of Dawn *(1940), and the prefatory volume of the* Encyclopedia of the Negro *(1945). Following his involuntary retirement from Atlanta University at the age of seventy-six, he rejoined the NAACP, where he remained until another break four years later.*

When he was eighty, Du Bois began another phase of his career. The last fifteen years of his life were spent working vigorously for world peace and African unity. In his last years he became a communist and a citizen of Ghana. Du Bois died in 1963 on the day before the March on Washington.

As a creative writer, Du Bois was probably at his best as essayist. His essays are extant in the Crisis *editorials and in several volumes.* The Souls of Black Folk, *the first volume of essays, was a landmark in black American literary history. In his introduction to the Fawcett edition, Saunders Redding describes the book as "fixing that moment in history when the American Negro began to reject the idea of the world's belonging to white people only, and think of himself, in concert, as a potential force in the organization of society." In flowing, poetic style, rich in metaphor and musical devices, the essays affirm the strength and dignity of black people, define their aspirations, and remind the nation of their contributions to its culture. The lyricism of the essays is superimposed on the firm mass of Du Bois' historical and sociological observations.* The Souls of Black Folk *was received with alarm by the white South, but the ideas became firmly implanted in black soil and have since grown to fruition.*

Du Bois wrote comparatively little poetry; however, what he did write is noteworthy. He preferred free verse to the confinement of conventional forms. "A Litany of Atlanta" (1906) is one of the earliest free verse poems by a black author. Du Bois' poetry is extremely passionate and replete with vivid images. Sometimes, as in "A Litany of Atlanta," the long intricate sentences make the poem nearly as much prose as poetry. Du Bois' poetry, like his prose, deals with black themes: the horror of a lynching in "A Litany of Atlanta," black beauty in "The Song of the Smoke," the strength of black women in "The Burden of Black Women," the irony of white American Christianity in "A Christmas Poem."

His novels are not altogether successful. The Quest of the Silver Fleece *is essentially a sociological study of the South after the Civil War.* Dark Princess *bespeaks Du Bois' commitment to Pan-Africanism. In both novels the characters are types rather than people, and the theme in each work is so important that it overshadows the other dimensions of the novel. Toward the end of his life Du Bois wrote a trilogy,* The Black Flame. *All three novels are heavy with historical data.*

In his brilliant articulation of a great cause and in his energetic exploration of many facets of that cause, Du Bois exerted a profound influence on several generations. While his work is a most valuable part of black literature, as important is his encouragement of black writers and his strong influence on the developing black psyche.

Under the editorship of Herbert Aptheker, Du Bois' private papers and previously unpublished writings are being issued by the University of Massachusetts Press. Under the same editor the previously published works are being issued by Kraus. There are important books on Du Bois by Frederick Broderick (1959), Elliot Rudwick (1959), and Arnold Rampersad (1976). Du Bois: Black Titan *(1970) by the editors of* Freedomways *and* W.E.B. Du Bois: A Profile *edited by Rayford Logan are important collections of essays about Du Bois. For a discussion of Du Bois bibliographers, of whom the chief are Parl Partington, Ernest Kaiser, and Aptheker, see "Du Bois: Of Matters Archival and Bibliographical,"* Phylon *XLII (March, 1981), 97–98.*

The Song of the Smoke

I am the smoke king,
I am black.
I am swinging in the sky.
I am ringing worlds on high:
I am the thought of the throbbing mills,
I am the soul of the soul toil kills,
I am the ripple of trading rills,

Up I'm curling from the sod,
I am whirling home to God.
I am the smoke king,
I am black.

I am the smoke king,
I am black.
I am wreathing broken hearts,
I am sheathing devils' darts;
Dark inspiration of iron times,
Wedding the toil of toiling climes
Shedding the blood of bloodless crimes,

Down I lower in the blue,
Up I tower toward the true,
I am the smoke king,
I am black.

I am the smoke king,
I am black.

I am darkening with song,
I am hearkening to wrong;
I will be as black as blackness can,
The blacker the mantle the mightier the man,
My purpl'ing midnights no day dawn may ban.

I am carving God in night,
I am painting hell in white.
I am the smoke king,
I am black.

I am the smoke king,
I am black.

I am cursing ruddy morn,
I am nursing hearts unborn;
Souls unto me are as mists in the night,
I whiten my blackmen, I beckon my white,
What's the hue of a hide to a man in his might!
Hail, then, grilly, grimy hands,

Sweet Christ, pity toiling lands!
Hail to the smoke king,
Hail to the black!

(1899)

A Litany of Atlanta

Done at Atlanta, in the Day of Death, 1906.

O Silent God, Thou whose voice afar in mist and mystery hath left our ears an-hungered in these fearful days—
Hear us, good Lord!

Listen to us, Thy children: our faces dark with doubt are made a mockery in Thy sanctuary. With uplifted hands we front Thy heaven, O God, crying:
We beseech Thee to hear us, good Lord!

We are not better than our fellows, Lord, we are but weak and human men. When our devils do deviltry, curse Thou the doer and the deed: curse them as we curse them, do to them all and more than ever they have done to innocence and weakness, to womanhood and home.
Have mercy upon us, miserable sinners!

And yet whose is the deeper guilt? Who made these devils? Who nursed them in crime and fed them on injustice? Who ravished and debauched their mothers and their grandmothers? Who bought and sold their crime, and waxed fat and rich on public iniquity?
Thou knowest, good God!

Is this Thy justice, O Father, that guile be easier than innocence, and the innocent crucified for the guilt of the untouched guilty?
Justice, O judge of men!

Wherefore de we pray? Is not the God of the fathers dead? Have not seers seen in Heaven's halls Thine hearsed and lifeless form stark amidst the black and rolling smoke of sin, where all along bow bitter forms of endless dead?
Awake, Thou that sleepest!

Thou art not dead, but flown afar, up hills of endless light through blazing corridors of suns, where worlds do swing of good and gentle men, of women strong and free—far from the cozenage, black hypocrisy, and chaste prostitution of this shameful speck of dust!
Turn again, O Lord, leave us not to perish in our sin!

From lust of body and lust of blood,
Great God, deliver us!

From lust of power and lust of gold,
Great God, deliver us!

From the leagued lying of despot and of brute,
Great God, deliver us!

A city lay in travail, God our Lord, and from her loins sprang twin Murder and Black Hate. Red was the midnight; clang, crack and cry of death and fury filled the air and trembled underneath the stars when church spires pointed silently to Thee. And all this was to sate the greed of greedy men who hide behind the veil of vengeance!
Bend us Thine ear, O Lord!

In the pale, still morning we looked upon the deed. We stopped our ears and held our leaping hands, but they—did they not wag their heads and leer and cry with bloody jaws: *Cease from Crime!* The word was mockery, for thus they train a hundred crimes while we do cure one.
Turn again our captivity, O Lord!

Behold this maimed and broken thing; dear God, it was an humble black man who toiled and sweat to save a bit from the pittance paid him. They told him: *Work and Rise.* He worked. Did this man sin? Nay, but some one told how some one said another did—one whom he had never seen nor known. Yet for that man's crime this man lieth maimed and murdered, his wife naked to shame, his children, to poverty and evil.

Hear us, O heavenly Father!

Doth not this justice of hell stink in Thy nostrils, O God? How long shall the mounting flood of innocent blood roar in Thine ears and pound in our hearts for vengeance? Pile the pale frenzy of blood-crazed brutes who do such deeds high on Thine altar, Jehovah Jireh, and burn it in hell forever and forever.

Forgive us, good Lord; we know not what we say!

Bewildered we are, and passion-tost, mad with the madness of a mobbed and mocked and murdered people; straining at the armposts of Thy Throne, we raise our shackled hands and charge Thee, God, by the bones of our stolen fathers, by the tears of our dead mothers, by the very blood of Thy crucified Christ: *What meaneth this?* Tell us the Plan; give us the Sign!

Keep not Thou silence, O God!

Sit no longer blind, Lord God, deaf to our prayer and dumb to our dumb suffering. Surely Thou too art not white, O Lord, a pale, bloodless, heartless thing?

Ah! Christ of all the Pities!

Forgive the thought! Forgive these wild, blasphemous words. Thou art still the God of our black fathers, and in Thy soul's soul sit some soft darkenings of the evening, some shadowings of the velvet night.

But whisper—speak—call, great God, for Thy silence is white terror to our hearts! The way, O God, show us the way and point us the path.

Whither? North is greed and South is blood; within, the coward, and without the liar. Whither? To Death?

Amen! Welcome dark sleep!

Whither? To life? But not this life, dear God, not this. Let the cup pass from us, tempt us not beyond our strength, for there is that clamoring and clawing within, to whose voice we would not listen, yet shudder lest we must,—and it is red, Ah! God! It is a red and awful shape.

Selah!

In yonder East trembles a star.
Vengeance is mine; I will repay, saith the Lord!

Thy will, O Lord, be done!
Kyrie Eleison!

Lord, we have done these pleading, wavering words.
We beseech Thee to hear us, good Lord!

We bow our heads and hearken soft to the sobbing of
women and little children.
We beseech Thee to hear us, good Lord!

Our voices sink in silence and in night.
Hear us, good Lord!

In night, O God of a godless land!
Amen!

In silence, O silent God.
Selah!

Of the Sorrow Songs
From *The Souls of Black Folk*

> I walk through the churchyard
>   To lay this body down;
> I know moon-rise, I know star-rise;
> I walk in the moonlight, I walk in the starlight;
> I'll lie in the grave and stretch out my arms,
> I'll go to judgment in the evening of the day,
> And my soul and thy soul shall meet that day,
>   When I lay this body down.
>
>   NEGRO SONG.

They that walked in darkness sang songs in the olden days—Sorrow Songs—for they were weary at heart. And so before each thought that I have written in this book I have set a phrase, a haunting echo of these weird old songs in which the soul of the black slave spoke to men. Ever since I was a child these songs have stirred me strangely. They came out of the South unknown to me, one by one, and yet at once I knew them as of me and of mine. Then in after years when I came to Nashville I saw the great temple builded of these songs towering over the pale city. To me Jubilee Hall seemed ever made of the songs themselves, and its bricks were red with the blood and dust of toil. Out of them rose for me morning, noon, and night, bursts of wonderful melody, full of the voices of my brothers and sisters, full of the voices of the past.

Little of beauty has America given the world save the rude grandeur God himself stamped on her bosom; the human spirit in this new world has expressed itself in vigor and ingenuity rather than in beauty. And so by fateful chance the Negro folk-song—the rhythmic cry of the slave—stands to-day not simply as the sole American music, but as the most beautiful expression of human experience born this side the seas. It has been neglected, it has been, and is, half despised, and above all it has been persistently mistaken and misunderstood; but notwithstanding, it still remains as the singular spiritual heritage of the nation and the greatest gift of the Negro people.

Away back in the thirties the melody of these slave songs stirred the nation, but the songs were soon half forgotten. Some, like "Near the lake where drooped the willow," passed into current airs and their source was forgotten; others were caricatured on the "minstrel" stage and their memory died away. Then in war-time came the singular Port Royal experiment after the capture of Hilton Head, and perhaps for the first time the North met the Southern slave face to face and heart to heart with no third witness. The Sea Islands of the Carolinas, where they met, were filled with a black folk of primitive type, touched and moulded less by the world about them than any others outside the Black Belt. Their appearance was uncouth, their language funny, but their hearts were human and their singing stirred men with a mighty power. Thomas Wentworth Higginson hastened to tell of these songs, and Miss McKim and others urged upon the world their rare beauty. But the world listened only half credulously until the Fisk Jubilee Singers sang the slave songs so deeply into the world's heart that it can never wholly forget them again.

There was once a blacksmith's son born at Cadiz, New York, who in the changes of time taught school in Ohio and helped defend Cincinnati from Kirby Smith. Then he fought at Chancellorsville and Gettysburg and finally served in the Freedman's Bureau at Nashville. Here he formed a Sunday-school class of black children in 1866, and sang with them and taught them to sing. And then they taught him to sing, and when once the glory of the Jubilee songs passed into the soul of George L. White, he knew his life-work was to let those Negroes sing to the world as they had sung to him. So in 1871 the pilgrimage of the Fisk Jubilee Singers began. North to Cincinnati they rode,—four half-clothed black boys and five girl-women,—led by a man with a cause and a purpose. They stopped at Wilberforce, the oldest of Negro schools, where a black bishop blessed them. Then they went, fighting cold and starvation, shut out of hotels, and cheerfully sneered at, ever northward; and ever the magic of their song kept thrilling hearts, until a burst of applause in the Congregational Council at Oberlin revealed them to the world. They came to New York and Henry Ward Beecher dared to welcome them, even though the metropolitan dailies sneered at his "Nigger Minstrels." So their songs conquered till they sang across the land and across the sea, before Queen and Kaiser, in Scotland and Ireland, Holland and Switzerland. Seven years they sang, and brought back a hundred and fifty thousand dollars to found Fisk University.

Since their day they have been imitated—sometimes well, by the singers of Hampton and Atlanta, sometimes ill, by straggling quartettes. Caricature has sought again to spoil the quaint beauty of the music, and has filled the air with many debased melodies which vulgar ears scarce know from the real. But the true Negro folk-song still lives in the hearts of those who have heard them truly sung and in the hearts of the Negro people.

What are these songs, and what do they mean? I know little of music and can say nothing in technical phrase, but I know something of men, and knowing them, I know that these songs are the articulate message of the slave to the world. They tell us in these eager days that life was joyous to the black slave, careless and happy. I can easily believe this of some, of many. But not all the past South, though it rose from the dead, can gainsay the heart-touching witness of these songs. They are the music of an unhappy people, of the children of disappointment; they tell of death and suffering and unvoiced longing toward a truer world, of misty wanderings and hidden ways.

The songs are indeed the siftings of centuries; the music is far more ancient than the words, and in it we can trace here and there signs of development. My grandfather's grandmother was seized by an evil Dutch trader two centuries ago; and coming to the valleys of the Hudson and Housatonic, black, little, and lithe, she shivered and shrank in the harsh north winds, looked longingly at the hills, and often crooned a heathen melody to the child between her knees. thus:

> Do bana coba gene me, gene me!
> Do bana coba, gene me, gene me!
> Ben d'nuli, nuli, nuli, nuli, bend'le.

The child sang it to his children and they to their children's children, and so two hundred years it has travelled down to us and we sing it to our children, knowing as little as our fathers what its words may mean, but knowing well the meaning of its music.

This was primitive African music; it may be seen in larger form in the strange chant which heralds "The Coming of John":

"You may bury me in the East,
You may bury me in the West,
But I'll hear the trumpet sound in that morning,"

—the voice of exile.

Ten master songs, more or less, one may pluck from this forest of melody—songs of undoubted Negro origin and wide popular currency, and songs peculiarly characteristic of the slave. One of these I have just mentioned. Another whose strains begin this book is "Nobody knows the trouble I've seen." When, struck with a sudden poverty, the United States refused to fulfill its promises of land to the freedmen, a brigadier-general went down to the Sea Islands to carry the news. An old woman on the outskirts of the throng began singing this song; all the mass joined with her, swaying. And the soldier wept.

The third song is the cradle-song of death which all men know, —"Swing low, sweet chariot,"—whose bars begin the life story of "Alexander Crummell." Then there is the song of many waters, "Roll, Jordan, roll," a mighty chorus with minor cadences. There were many songs of the fugitive like that which opens "The Wings of Atalanta," and the more familiar "Been a-listening." The seventh is the song of the End and the Beginning—"My Lord, what a mourning! when the stars begin to fall"; a strain of this is placed before "The Dawn of Freedom." The song of groping—"My way's cloudy" —begins "The Meaning of Progress"; the ninth is the song of this chapter—"Wrestlin' Jacob, the day is a-breaking,"—a pæan of hopeful strife. The last master song is the song of songs—"Steal away,"— sprung from "The Faith of the Fathers."

There are many others of the Negro folk-songs as striking and characteristic as these, as, for instance, the three strains in the third, eighth, and ninth chapters; and others I am sure could easily make a selection on more scientific principles. There are, too, songs that seem to be a step removed from the more primitive types: there is the maze-like medley, "Bright sparkles," one phrase of which heads "The Black Belt"; the Easter carol, "Dust, dust and ashes"; the dirge, "My mother's took her flight and gone home"; and that burst of melody hovering over "The Passing of the First-Born"—"I hope my mother will be there in that beautiful world on high."

These represent a third step in the development of the slave song, of which "You may bury me in the East" is the first, and songs like "March on" (chapter six) and "Steal away" are the second. The first is African music, the second Afro-American, while the third is a blending of Negro music with the music heard in the foster land. The result is still distinctively Negro and the method of blending original, but the elements are both Negro and Caucasian. One might go further and find a fourth step in this development, where the songs of white America have been distinctively influenced by the slave songs or have incorporated whole phrases of Negro melody, as "Swanee River" and "Old Black Joe." Side by side, too, with the growth has gone the debasements and imitations—the Negro "minstrel" songs, many of the "gospel" hymns, and some of the contemporary "coon" songs,—a mass of music in which the novice may easily lose himself and never find the real Negro melodies.

In these songs, I have said, the slave spoke to the world. Such a message is naturally veiled and half articulate. Words and music have lost each other and new and cant phrases of a dimly understood theology have displaced the old sentiment. Once in a while we catch a strange word of an unknown tongue, as the "Mighty Myo," which figures as a river of death; more often slight words or mere doggerel are joined to music of singular sweetness. Purely secular songs are few in number, partly because many of them were turned into hymns by a change of words, partly because the frolics were seldom heard by the stranger, and the music less often caught. Of nearly all the songs, however, the music is distinctly sorrowful. The ten master songs I have mentioned tell in word and music of trouble and exile, of strife and hiding; they grope toward some unseen power and sigh for rest in the End.

The words that are left to us are not without interest, and, cleared of evident dross, they conceal much of real poetry and meaning beneath conventional theology and unmeaning rhapsody. Like all primitive folk, the slave stood near to Nature's heart. Life was a "rough and rolling sea" like the brown Atlantic of the Sea Islands; the "Wilderness" was the home of God, and the "lonesome valley" led to the way of life. "Winter'll soon be over," was the picture of life and death to a tropical imagination. The sudden wild thunder-storms of the South awed and impressed the Negroes,—at times the rumbling seemed to them "mournful," at times imperious:

> "My Lord calls me,
> He calls me by the thunder,
> The trumpet sounds it in my soul."

The monotonous toil and exposure is painted in many words. One sees the ploughmen in the hot, moist furrow, singing:

> "Dere's no rain to wet you,
> Dere's no sun to burn you,
> Oh, push along, believer,
> I want to go home."

The bowed and bent old man cries, with thrice repeated wail:

> "O Lord, keep me from sinking down,"

and he rebukes the devil of doubt who can whisper:

> "Jesus is dead and God's gone away."

Yet the soul-hunger is there, the restlessness of the savage, the wail of the wanderer, and the plaint is put in one little phrase:

> "My soul wants something that's new, that's new."

Over the inner thoughts of the slaves and their relations one with another the shadow of fear ever hung, so that we get but glimpses here and there, and also with them, eloquent omissions and silences. Mother and child are sung, but seldom father; fugitive and weary wanderer call for pity and affection, but there is little of wooing and wedding; the rocks and the mountains are well known, but home is unknown. Strange blending of love and helplessness signs through the refrain:

"Yonder's my ole mudder,
Been waggin' at det hill so long;
'Bout time she cross over,
Git home bime-by."

Elsewhere comes the cry of the "motherless" and the "Farewell, farewell, my only child."

Love-songs are scarce and fall into two categories—the frivolous and light, and the sad. Of deep successful love there is omnious silence, and in one of the oldest of these songs there is a depth of history and meaning:

"Poor Rosy, poor gal;
Poor Rosy, poor gal;
Rosy break my poor heart,
Hear'n shall-a-be my home."

A black woman said of the song, "It can't be sung without a full heart and a troubled sperrit." The same voice sings here that sings in the German folk-song:

"Jetz Geh i' an's brunele, trink' aber net."

Of death the Negro showed little fear, but talked of it familiarly and even fondly as simply a crossing of the waters, perhaps—who knows?—back to his ancient forests again. Later days transfigured his fatalism, and amid the dust and dirt the toiler sang:

"Dust, dust and ashes, fly over my grave,
But the Lord shall bear my spirit home."

The things evidently borrowed from the surrounding world
undergo characteristic change when they enter the mouth of the
slave. Especially is this true of Bible phrases. "Weep, O captive daughter of Zion," is quaintly turned into "Zion, weep-a-low," and the
wheels of Ezekiel are turned every way in the mystic dreaming of
the slave, till he says:

"There's a little wheel a-turnin' in-a-my heart."

As in olden time, the words of these hymns were improvised by
some leading minstrel of the religious band. The circumstances of the
gathering, however, the rhythm of the songs, and the limitations of
allowable thought, confined the poetry for the most part to single or
double lines, and they seldom were expanded to quatrains or longer
tales, although there are some few examples of sustained efforts,
chiefly paraphrases of the Bible. Three short series of verses have
always attracted me,—the one that heads this chapter, of one line of
which Thomas Wentworth Higginson has fittingly said, "Never, it
seems to me, since man first lived and suffered was his infinite longing
for peace uttered more plaintively." The second and third are descrip-
tions of the Last Judgment,—the one a late improvisation, with some
traces of outside influence:

"Oh, the stars in the elements are falling,
And the moon drips away into blood,
And the ransomed of the Lord are returning unto God,
Blessed be the name of the Lord."

And the other earlier and homelier picture from the low coast lands:

"Michael, haul the boat ashore,
Then you'll hear the horn they blow,
Then you'll hear the trumpet sound,
Trumpet sound the world around,
Trumpet sound for rich and poor,
Trumpet sound the Jubilee,
Trumpet sound for you and me."

Through all the sorrow of the Sorrow Songs there breathes a hope—a faith in the ultimate justice of things. The minor cadences of despair change often to triumph and calm confidence. Sometimes it is faith in life, sometimes a faith in death, sometimes assurance of boundless justice in some fair world beyond. But whichever it is, the meaning is always clear: that sometimes, somewhere, men will judge men by their souls and not by their skins. Is such a hope justified? Do the Sorrow Songs sing true?

The silently growing assumption of this age is that the probation of races is past, and that the backward races of to-day are of proven inefficiency and not worth the saving. Such an assumption is the arrogance of peoples irreverent toward Time and ignorant of the deeds of men. A thousand years ago such an assumption, easily possible, would have made it difficult for the Teuton to prove his right to life. Two thousand years ago such dogmatism, readily welcome, would have scouted the idea of blond races ever leading civilization. So woefully unorganized is sociological knowledge that the meaning of progress, the meaning of "swift" and "slow" in human doing, and the limits of human perfectability, are veiled, unanswered sphinxes on the shores of science. Why should Æschylus have sung two thousand years before Shakespeare was born? Why has civilization flourished in Europe, and flickered, flamed, and died in Africa? So long as the world stands meekly dumb before such questions, shall this nation proclaim its ignorance and unhallowed prejudices by denying freedom of opportunity to those who brought the Sorrow Songs to the Seats of the Mighty?

Your country? How came it yours? Before the Pilgrims landed we were here. Here we have brought our three gifts and mingled them with yours: a gift of story and song—soft, stirring melody in an ill-harmonized and unmelodious land; the gift of sweat and brawn to beat back the wilderness, conquer the soil, and lay the foundations

of this vast economic empire two hundred years earlier than your
weak hand could have done it; the third, a gift of the Spirit. Around
us the history of the land has centred for thrice a hundred years;
out of the nation's heart we have called all that was best to throttle
and subdue all that was worst; fire and blood, prayer and sacrifice,
have billowed over this people, and they have found peace only in
the altars of the God of Right. Nor has our gift of the Spirit been
merely passive. Actively we have woven ourselves with the very
warp and woof of this nation,—we fought their battles, shared their
sorrow, mingled our blood with theirs, and generation after generation have pleaded with a headstrong, careless people to despise not
Justice, Mercy, and Truth, lest the nation be smitten with a curse.
Our song, our toil, our cheer, and warning have been given to this
nation in blood-brotherhood. Are not these gifts worth the giving?
Is not this work and striving? Would America have been America
without her Negro people?

Even so is the hope that sang in the songs of my fathers well
sung. If somewhere in this whirl and chaos of things there dwells
Eternal Good, pitiful yet masterful, then anon in His good time
America shall rend the Veil and the prisoned shall go free. Free, free
as the sunshine trickling down the morning into these high windows
of mine, free as yonder fresh young voices welling up to me from
the caverns of brick and mortar below—swelling with song, instinct
with life, tremulous treble and darkening bass. My children, my little
children, are singing to the sunshine, and thus they sing:

> Let us cheer the weary traveller,
> Cheer the weary traveller,
> Let us cheer the weary traveller
> Along the heavenly way.

And the traveller girds himself, and sets his face toward the
Morning, and goes his way.

(1903)

Crime and Lynching

A favorite argument with shallow thinkers is: Stop crime and lynching will cease. Such a statement is both historically and logically false. Historically, lynching leads to lynching, burning to burning; and lynching for great crimes to lynching for trivial offenses. Moreover, lynching as practised to-day in the United States is not the result of crime—it is a cause of crime, on account of the flagrant, awful injustice it inflicts in so many cases on innocent men . . .

What now must be the feeling of the Negroes . . . ? Are they appalled at their own wickedness? Do they see that the wages of sin is death? Not they. They despise the white man's justice, hate him, and whenever they hear of Negro "crime" in the future they will say: "It's a white man's lie."

Not only this, but these people know how criminals are made and they pity rather than condemn them. Take, for instance, the cries throughout the South against "vagrants." It means the call for the State enslavement of any man who does not work for a white man at the white man's price. The most outrageous laws and arrests are made under the excuse of vagrancy. In Atlanta, on October 15, thirty-seven laborers were arrested at night in their lodging house as "vagrants." In Texas five laborers were arrested as vagrants and proved their hard, steady jobs. "But," remarks the Galveston Tribune chirpily:

"The State chose to prosecute under a different portion of the law, alleging loitering about houses of ill-fame. The court explained, as he has done before, that a person can be a vagrant yet be steadily employed, the law being general in its effect and covering many points upon which a conviction can be had on a charge of vagrancy."

Suppose now a mischievous boy or a loiterer or a laborer out of work is thrown into jail as a vagrant, what happens to him?

From a thousand examples, let us choose but one from a Texas report on a local "chain gang":

"The day's program was invariably this: Up at 4:30 o'clock in the morning, trot two to five miles to the cane fields, work there in squads until noon, when fifteen to twenty minutes would be allowed for the eating of a cold dinner; driven hard during the afternoon and brought back by starlight at night in the same dog trot they went out in the morning. The weak must keep up with the strong in his work or be punished. Convicts slept in their underclothes or naked, as it happened to rain or shine during the day. If it rained they hung up their clothes to dry and slept without. One convict testified that he had frequently taken his clothes from the nail frozen stiff. One man was on a farm a year, and during that time the bedclothes were not washed and were sunned but twice."

Thus desperate criminals are manufactured and turned out day by day.

Can we stop this by lynching? No. The first step toward stopping crime is to stop lynching. The next step is to treat black men like human beings.

(1912)

The Souls of White Folk
From *Darkwater*

. . . I know many souls that toss and whirl and pass, but none there are that intrigue me more than the Souls of White Folk,

Of them I am singularly clairvoyant. I see in and through them. I view them from unusual points of vantage. Not as a foreigner do I come, for I am native, not foreign, bone of their thought and flesh of their language. Mine is not the knowledge of the traveler or the colonial composite of dear memories, words and wonder. Nor yet is my knowledge that which servants have of masters, or mass of class, or capitalist of artisan. Rather I see these souls undressed and from the back and side. I see the working of their entrails. I know their thoughts and they know that I know. This knowledge makes them now embarrassed, now furious! They deny my right to live and be and call me misbirth! My word is to them mere bitterness and my soul, pessimism. And yet as they preach and strut and shout and threaten, crouching as they clutch at rags of facts and fancies to hide their nakedness, they go twisting, flying by my tired eyes and I see them ever stripped—ugly, human.

The discovery of personal whiteness among the world's peoples is a very modern thing—a nineteenth and twentieth century matter, indeed. The ancient world would have laughed at such a distinction. The Middle Age regarded skin color with mild curiosity; and even up into the eighteenth century we were hammering our national mani-kins into one, great, Universal Man, with fine frenzy which ignored color and race even more than birth. Today we have changed all that, and the world in a sudden, emotional conversion has discovered that it is white and by that token, wonderful!

This assumption that of all the hues of God whiteness alone is inherently and obviously better than brownness or tan leads to curious acts; even the sweeter souls of the dominant world as they discourse with me on weather, weal, and woe are continually playing above their actual words an obligato of tune and tone, saying:

"My poor, un-white thing! Weep not nor rage. I know, too well, that the curse of God lies heavy on you. Why? That is not for me to say, but be brave! Do your work in your lowly sphere, praying the good Lord that into heaven above, where all is love, you may, one day, be born—white!"

I do not laugh. I am quite straight-faced as I ask soberly:

"But what on earth is whiteness that one should so desire it?" Then always, somehow, some way, silently but clearly, I am given to understand that whiteness is the ownership of the earth forever and ever, Amen!

Now what is the effect on a man or a nation when it comes passionately to believe such an extraordinary dictum as this? That nations are coming to believe it is manifest daily. Wave on wave, each with increasing virulence, is dashing this new religion of whiteness on the shores of our time. Its first effects are funny: the strut of the Southerner, the arrogance of the Englishman amuck, the whoop of the hoodlum who vicariously leads your mob. Next it appears dampening generous enthusiasm in what we once counted glorious; to free the slave is discovered to be tolerable only in so far as it freed his master! Do we sense somnolent writhings in black Africa or angry groans in India or triumphant banzais in Japan? "To your tents, O Israel!" These nations are not white!

After the more comic manifestations and the chilling of generous enthusiasm come subtler, darker deeds. Everything considered, the title to the universe claimed by White Folk is faulty. It ought, at least, to look plausible. How easy, then, by emphasis and omission to make children believe that every great soul the world ever saw was a white man's soul; that every great thought the world ever knew was a white man's thought; that every great deed the world ever did was a white man's deed; that every great dream the world ever sang was a white man's dream. In fine, that if from the world were dropped everything that could not fairly be attributed to White Folk, the world would, if anything, be even greater, truer, better than now. And if all this be a lie, is it not a lie in a great cause?

Here it is that the comedy verges to tragedy. The first minor note is struck, all unconsciously, by those worthy souls in whom consciousness of high descent brings burning desire to spread the gift abroad—the obligation of nobility to the ignoble. Such sense of duty assumes two things: a real possession of the heritage and its frank appreciation by the humble-born. So long, then, as humble black folk, voluble with thanks, receive barrels of old clothes from lordly and generous whites, there is much mental peace and moral satisfaction. But when the black man begins to dispute the white man's title to certain alleged bequests of the Fathers in wage and position, authority and training; and when his attitude toward charity is sullen anger rather than humble jollity; when he insists on his human right to swagger and swear and waste—then the spell is suddenly broken and the philanthropist is ready to believe that Negroes are impudent, that the South is right, and that Japan wants to fight America.

After this the descent to Hell is easy. On the pale, white faces which the great billows whirl upward to my tower I see again and again, often and still more often, a writing of human hatred, a deep and passionate hatred, vast by the very vagueness of its expressions. Down through the green waters, on the bottom of the world, where men move to and fro, I have seen a man—an educated gentleman—grow livid with anger because a little, silent, black woman was sitting by herself in a Pullman car. He was a white man. I have seen a great, grown man curse a little child, who had wandered into the wrong waiting-room, searching for its mother: "Here, you damned black—." He was white. In Central Park I have seen the upper lip of a quiet, peaceful man curl back in a tigerish snarl of rage because black folk rode by in a motor car. He was a white man. We have seen, you and I, city after city drunk and furious with ungovernable lust of blood; mad with murder, destroying, killing, and cursing; torturing human victims because somebody accused of crime happened to be of the same color as the mob's innocent victims and because that color was not white! We have seen—Merciful God! in these wild days and in the name of Civilization, Justice, and Motherhood—what have we not seen, right here in America, of orgy, cruelty, barbarism, and murder done to men and women of Negro descent.

Up through the foam of green and weltering waters wells this great mass of hatred, in wilder, fiercer violence, until I look down and know that today to the millions of my people no misfortune could happen—of death and pestilence, failure and defeat—that would not make the hearts of millions of their fellows beat with fierce, vindictive joy! Do you doubt it? Ask your own soul what it would say if the next census were to report that half of black America was dead and the other half dying.

Unfortunate? Unfortunate. But where is the misfortune? Mine? Am I, in my blackness, the sole sufferer? I suffer. And yet, somehow, above the suffering, above the shackled anger that beats the bars, above the hurt that crazes there surges in me a vast pity—pity for a people imprisoned and enthralled, hampered and made miserable for such a cause, for such a phantasy!

Conceive this nation, of all human peoples, engaged in a crusade to make the "World Safe for Democracy"! Can you imagine the United States protesting against Turkish atrocities in Armenia, while the Turks are silent about mobs in Chicago and St. Louis; what is Louvain compared with Memphis, Waco, Washington, Dyersburg, and Estill Springs? In short, what is the black man but America's Belgium, and how could America condemn in Germany that which she commits, just as brutally, within her own borders?

A true and worthy ideal frees and uplifts a people; a false ideal imprisons and lowers. Say to men, earnestly and repeatedly: "Honesty is best, knowledge is power; do unto others as you would be done by." Say this and act it and the nation must move toward it, if not to it. But say to a people: "The one virtue is to be white," and the people rush to the inevitable conclusion, "Kill the 'nigger'!"

Is not this the record of present America? Is not this its headlong progress? Are we not coming more and more, day by day, to making the statement "I am white," the one fundamental tenet of our practical morality? Only when this basic, iron rule is involved is our defense of right nation-wide and prompt. Murder may swagger, theft may rule and prostitution may flourish and the nation gives but spasmodic, intermittent and lukewarm attention. But let the murderer be black or the thief brown or the violator of womanhood have a drop of Negro blood, and the righteousness of the indignation sweeps the world. Nor would this fact make the indignation less justifiable did not we all know that it was blackness that was condemned and not crime.

In the awful cataclysm of World War, where from beating, slandering, and murdering us the white world turned temporarily aside to kill each other, we of the Darker Peoples looked on in mild amaze . . .

Consider our chiefest industry—fighting. Laboriously the Middle Ages built its rules of fairness—equal armament, equal notice, equal conditions. What do we see today? Machine-guns against assegais; conquest sugared with religion; mutilation and rape masquerading as culture—all this, with vast applause at the superiority of white over black soldiers!

War is horrible! This the dark world knows to its awful cost. But has it just become horrible, in these last days, when under essentially equal conditions, equal armament, and equal waste of wealth white men are fighting white men, with surgeons and nurses hovering near? . . .

Behold little Belgium and her pitiable plight, but has the world forgotten Congo? What Belgium now suffers is not half, not even a tenth, of what she has done to black Congo since Stanley's great dream of 1880. . . .

Harris declares that King Leopold's régime meant the death of twelve million natives, "but what we who were behind the scenes felt most keenly was the fact that the real catastrophe in the Congo was desolation and murder in the larger sense. The invasion of family life, the ruthless destruction of every social barrier, the shattering of every tribal law, the introduction of criminal practices which struck the chiefs of the people dumb with horror—in a word, a veritable avalanche of filth and immorality overwhelmed the Congo tribes. . . ."

Here is a civilization that has boasted much. Neither Roman nor Arab, Greek nor Egyptian, Persian nor Mongol ever took himself and his own perfectness with such disconcerting seriousness as the modern white man. We whose shame, humiliation, and deep insult his aggrandizement so often involved were never deceived. We looked at him clearly, with world-old eyes, and saw simply a human thing, weak and pitiable and cruel, even as we are and were.

These super-men and world-mastering demi-gods listened, however, to no low tongues of ours, even when we pointed silently to their feet of clay. Perhaps we, as folk of simpler soul and more primitive type, have been most struck in the welter of recent years by the utter failure of white religion. We have curled our lips in something like content as we have witnessed glib apology and weary explanation. Nothing of the sort deceived us. A nation's religion is its life, and as such white Chistianity is a miserable failure.

Nor would we be unfair in this criticism: We know that we, too, have failed, as you have, and have rejected many a Buddha, even as you have denied Christ; but we acknowledge our human frailty, while you, claiming super-humanity, scoff endlessly at our shortcomings. . . .

Yet the fields of Belgium laughed, the cities were gay, art and science flourished; the groans that helped to nourish this civilization fell on deaf ears because the world round about was doing the same sort of thing elsewhere on its own account.

As we saw the dead dimly through rifts of battlesmoke and heard faintly the cursings and accusations of blood brothers, we darker men said: This is not Europe gone mad; this is not aberration nor insanity; this *is* Europe; this seeming Terrible is the real soul of white culture—back of all culture—stripped and visible today. . . .

Europe has never produced and never will in our day bring forth a single human soul who cannot be matched and over-matched in every line of human endeavor by Asia and Africa. . . .

Why, then, is Europe great? Because of the foundations which the mighty past have furnished her to build upon: the iron trade of ancient, black Africa, the religion and empire-building of yellow Asia, the art and science of the "dago" Mediterranean shore, east, south, and west, as well as north. And where she has builded securely upon this great past and learned from it she has gone forward to greater and more splendid human triumph; but where she has ignored this past and forgotten and sneered at it, she has shown the cloven hoof of poor, crucified humanity—she has played, like other empires gone, the world fool!

If, then, European triumphs in culture have been greater, so, too, may her failures have been greater. How great a failure and a failure in what does the World War betoken? . . . What is that breath of life, thought to be so indispensable to a great European nation? Manifestly it is expansion overseas; it is colonial aggrandizement which explains, and alone adequately explains, the World War. How many of us today fully realize the current theory of colonial expansion, of the relation of Europe which is white, to the world which is black and brown and yellow? Bluntly put, that theory is this: It is the duty of white Europe to divide up the darker world and administer it for Europe's good.

This Europe has largely done. The European world is using black and brown men for all the uses which men know. Slowly but surely white culture is evolving the theory that "darkies" are born beasts of burden for white folk. It were silly to think otherwise, cries the cultured world, with stronger and shriller accord. The supporting arguments grow and twist themselves in the mouths of merchant, scientist, soldier, traveler, writer, and missionary; Darker peoples are dark in mind as well as in body; of dark, uncertain, and imperfect descent; of frailer, cheaper, stuff; they are cowards in the face of mausers and maxims; they have no feelings, aspirations, and loves; they are fools, illogical idiots—"half-devil and half-child."

Such as they are civilization must, naturally, raise them, but soberly and in limited ways. They are not simply dark white men. They are not "men" in the sense that Europeans are men. To the very limited extent of their shallow capacities lift them to be useful to whites, to raise cotton, gather rubber, fetch ivory, dig diamonds— and let them be paid what men think they are worth—white men who know them to be well-nigh worthless.

Such degrading of men by men is as old as mankind and the invention of no one race or people. Ever have men striven to conceive of their victims as different from the victors, endlessly different, in soul and blood, strength and cunning, race and lineage. It has been left, however, to Europe and to modern days to discover the eternal world-wide mark of meanness—color! . . .

This theory of human culture and its aims has worked itself through warp and woof of our daily thought with a thoroughness that few realize. Everything great, good, efficient, fair, and honorable is "white"; everything mean, bad, blundering, cheating, and dishonorable is "yellow"; a bad taste is "brown"; and the devil is "black." The changes of this theme are continually rung in picture and story, in newspaper heading and moving-picture, in sermon anl school book, until, of course, the King can do no wrong—a White Man is always right and a Black Man has no rights which a white man is bound to respect.

There must come the necessary despisings and hatreds of these savage half-men, this unclean *canaille* of the world—these dogs of men. All through the world this gospel is preaching. It has its literature, it has its priests, it has its secret propaganda and above all— it pays!

There's the rub—it pays. Rubber, ivory, and palm-oil; tea, coffee, and cocoa; bananas, oranges, and other fruit; cotton, gold, and copper—they, and a hundred other things which dark and sweating bodies hand up to the white world from their pits of slime, pay and pay well, but of all that the world gets the black world gets only the pittance that the white world throws it disdainfully.

Small wonder, then, that in the practical world of things-that-be there is jealousy and strife for the possession of the labor of dark millions, for the right to bleed and exploit the colonies of the world where this golden stream may be had, not always for the asking, but surely for the whipping and shooting. It was this competition for the labor of yellow, brown, and black folks that was the cause of the World War. Other causes have been glibly given and other contributing causes there doubtless were, but they were subsidiary and subordinate to this vast quest of the dark world's wealth and toil.

Colonies, we call them, these places where "niggers" are cheap and the earth is rich; they are those outlands where like a swarm of hungry locusts white masters may settle to be served as kings, wield the lash of slave-drivers, rape girls and wives, grow as rich as Croesus and send homeward a golden stream. . . .

The cause of war is preparation for war; and of all that Europe has done in a century there is nothing that has equaled in energy, thought, and time her preparation for wholesale murder. The only adequate cause of this preparation was conquest and conquest, not in Europe, but primarily among the darker peoples of Asia and Africa; conquest, not for assimilation and uplift, but for commerce and degradation. For this, and this mainly, did Europe gird herself at frightful cost for war. . . .

Thus the world market most wildly and desperately sought today is the market where labor is cheapest and most helpless and profit is most abundant. This labor is kept cheap and helpless because the white world despises "darkies." If one has the temerity to suggest that these workingmen may walk the way of white workingmen and climb by votes and self-assertion and education to the rank of men, he is howled out of court. They cannot do it and if they could, they shall not, for they are the enemies of the white race and the whites shall rule forever and forever and everywhere. Thus the hatred and despising of human beings from whom Europe wishes to extort her luxuries has led to such jealousy and bickering between European nations that they have fallen afoul of each other and have fought like crazed beasts. Such is the fruit of human hatred.

But what of the darker world that watches? Most men belong to this world. With Negro and Negroid, East Indian, Chinese, and Japanese they form two-thirds of the population of the world. A belief in humanity is a belief in colored men. If the uplift of mankind must be done by men, then the destinies of this world will rest ultimately in the hands of darker nations.

What, then, is this dark world thinking? It is thinking that as wild and awful as this shameful war was, *it is nothing to compare with that fight for freedom which black and brown and yellow men must and will make unless their oppression and humiliation and insult at the hands of the White World cease. The Dark World is going to submit to its present treatment just as long as it must and not one moment longer.*

Let me say this again and emphasize it and leave no room for mistaken meaning: The World War was primarily the jealous and avaricious struggle for the largest share in exploiting darker races. As such it is and must be but the prelude to the armed and indignant protest of these despised and raped peoples. . . .

If Europe hugs this delusion, then this is not the end of world war—it is but the beginning. . . .

For two or more centuries America has marched proudly in the van of human hatred—making bonfires of human flesh and laughing at them hideously, and making the insulting of millions more than a matter of dislike—rather a great religion, a world war-cry: Up white, down black; to your tents, O white folk, and world war with black and parti-colored mongrel beasts!

Instead of standing as a great example of the success of democracy and the possibility of human brotherhood America has taken her place as an awful example of its pitfalls and failures, so far as black and brown and yellow peoples are concerned. . . .

I will not believe that all that was must be, that all the shameful drama of the past must be done again today before the sunlight sweeps the silver seas.

If I cry amid this roar of elemental forces, must my cry be in vain, because it is but a cry—a small and human cry amid Promethean gloom?

Back beyond the world and swept by these wild, white faces of the awful dead, why will this Soul of White Folk—this modern Prometheus—hang bound by his own binding, tethered by a fable of the past? I hear his mighty cry reverberating through the world, "I am white!" Well and good, O Prometheus, divine thief! Is not the world wide enough for two colors, for many little shinings of the sun? Why, then, devour your own vitals if I answer even as proudly, "I am black!"

The Comet
From *Darkwater*

He stood a moment on the steps of the bank, watching the human river that swirled down Broadway. Few noticed him. Few ever noticed him save in a way that stung. He was outside the world—"nothing!" as he said bitterly. Bits of the words of the walkers came to him.

"The comet?"

"The comet—"

Everybody was talking of it. Even the president, as he entered, smiled patronizingly at him, and asked:

"Well, Jim, are you scared?"

"No," said the messenger shortly.

"I thought we'd journeyed through the comet's tail once," broke in the junior clerk affably.

"Oh, that was Halley's," said the president; "this is a new comet, quite a stranger, they say—wonderful, wonderful! I saw it last night. Oh, by the way, Jim," turning again to the messenger, "I want you to go down into the lower vaults today."

The messenger followed the president silently. Of course, they wanted *him* to go down to the lower vaults. It was dangerous for more valuable men. He smiled grimly and listened.

"Everything of value has been moved out since the water began to seep in," said the president; "but we miss two volumes of old records. Suppose you nose around down there,—it isn't very pleasant, I suppose."

"Not very," said the messenger, as he walked out.

"Well, Jim, the tail of the new comet hits us at noon this time," said the vault clerk, as he passed over the keys; but the messenger passed silently down the stairs. Down he went beneath Broadway, where the lim light filtered through the feet of hurrying men; down to the dark basement beneath; down into the blackness and silence beneath that lowest cavern. Here with his dark lantern he groped in the bowels of the earth, under the world.

He drew a long breath as he threw back the last great iron door and stepped into the fetid slime within. Here at last was peace, and he groped moodily forward. A great rat leaped past him and cobwebs crept across his face. He felt carefully around the room, shelf by shelf, on the muddied floor, and in crevice and corner. Nothing. Then he went back to the far end, where somehow the wall felt different. He sounded and pushed and pried. Nothing. He started away. Then something brought him back. He was sounding and working again when suddenly the whole black wall swung as on mighty hinges, and blackness yawned beyond. He peered in; it was evidently a secret vault—some hiding place of the old bank unknown in newer times. He entered hesitatingly. It was a long narrow room with shelves, and at the far end, an old iron chest. On a high shelf lay the two missing volumes of records, and others. He put them carefully aside and stepped to the chest. It was old, strong, and rusty. He looked at the vast and old-fashioned lock and flashed his light on the hinges. They were deeply incrusted with rust. Looking about, he found a bit of iron and began to pry. The rust had eaten a hundred years, and it had gone deep. Slowly, wearily, the old lid lifted, and with a last, low groan lay bare its treasure—and he saw the dull sheen of gold!

"Boom!"

A low, grinding, reverberating crash struck upon his ear. He started up and looked about. All was black and still. He groped for his light and swung it about him. Then he knew! The great stone door had swung to. He forgot the gold and looked death squarely in the face. Then with a sigh he went methodically to work. The cold sweat stood on his forehead; but he searched, pounded, pushed, and worked until after what seemed endless hours his hand struck a cold bit of metal and the great door swung again harshly on its hinges, and then, striking against something soft and heavy, stopped. He had just room to squeeze through. There lay the body of the vault clerk, cold and stiff. He stared at it, and then felt sick and nauseated. The air seemed unaccountably foul, with a strong, peculiar odor. He stepped forward, clutched at the air, and fell fainting across the corpse.

He awoke with a sense of horror, leaped from the body, and groped up the stairs, calling to the guard. The watchman sat as if asleep, with the gate swinging free. With one glance at him the messenger hurried up to the sub-vault. In vain he called to the guards. His voice echoed and re-echoed weirdly. Up into the great basement he rushed. Here another guard lay prostrate on his face, cold and still. A fear arose in the messenger's heart. He dashed up to the cellar floor, up into the bank. The stillness of death lay everywhere and everywhere bowed, bent, and stretched the silent forms of men. The messenger paused and glanced about. He was not a man easily moved; but the sight was appalling! "Robbery and murder," he whispered slowly to himself as he saw the twisted, oozing mouth of the president where he lay half-buried on his desk. Then a new thought seized him: If they found him here alone—with all this money and all these dead men—what would his life be worth? He glanced about, tiptoed cautiously to a side door, and again looked behind. Quietly he turned the latch and stepped out into Wall Street.

How silent the street was! Not a soul was stirring, and yet it was high-noon—Wall Street? Broadway? He glanced almost wildly up and down, then across the street, and as he looked, a sickening horror froze in his limbs. With a choking cry of utter fright he lunged, leaned giddily against the cold building, and stared helplessly at the sight.

In the great stone doorway a hundred men and women and children lay crushed and twisted and jammed, forced into that great, gaping doorway like refuse in a can—as if in one wild, frantic rush to safety, they had crushed and ground themselves to death. Slowly the messenger crept along the walls, wetting his parched mouth and trying to comprehend, stilling the tremor in his limbs and the rising terror in his heart. He met a business man, silk-hatted and frock-coated, who had crept, too, along that smooth wall and stood now stone dead with wonder written on his lips. The messenger turned his eyes hastily away and sought the curb. A woman leaned wearily against the signpost, her head bowed motionless on her lace and silken bosom. Before her stood a street car, silent, and within—but the messenger but glanced and hurried on. A grimy newsboy sat in the gutter with the "last edition" in his uplifted hand: "Danger!" screamed its black headlines. "Warnings wired around the world. The Comet's tail sweeps past us at noon. Deadly gases expected. Close doors and windows. Seek the cellar." The messenger read and staggered on. Far out from a window above, a girl lay with gasping face and sleevelets on her arms. On a store step sat a little, sweet-faced girl looking upward toward the skies, and in the carriage by her lay—but the messenger looked no longer. The cords gave way—the terror burst in his veins, and with one great, gasping cry he sprang desperately forward and ran,—ran as only the frightened run, shrieking and fighting the air until with one last wail of pain he sank on the grass of Madison Square and lay prone and still.

When he arose, he gave no glance at the still and silent forms on the benches, but, going to a fountain, bathed his face; then hiding himself in a corner away from the drama of death, he quietly gripped himself and thought the thing through: The comet had swept the earth and this was the end. Was everybody dead? He must search and see.

He knew that he must steady himself and keep calm, or he would go insane. First he must go to a restaurant. He walked up Fifth Avenue to a famous hostelry and entered its gorgeous, ghost-haunted halls. He beat back the nausea, and, seizing a tray from dead hands, hurried into the street and ate ravenously, hiding to keep out the sights.

"Yesterday, they would not have served me," he whispered, as he forced the food down.

Then he started up the street,—looking, peering, telephoning, ringing alarms; silent, silent all. Was nobody—nobody—he dared not think the thought and hurried on.

Suddenly he stopped still. He had forgotten. My God! How could he have forgotten? He must rush to the subway—then he almost laughed. No—a car; if he could find a Ford. He saw one. Gently he lifted off its burden, and took his place on the seat. He tested the throttle. There was gas. He glided off, shivering, and drove up the street. Everywhere stood, leaned, lounged, and lay the dead, in grim and awful silence. On he ran past an automobile, wrecked and overturned; past another, filled with a gay party whose smiles yet lingered on their death-struck lips; on past crowds and groups of cars, pausing by dead policemen; at 42nd Street he had to detour to Park Avenue to avoid the dead congestion. He came back on Fifth Avenue at 57th and flew past the Plaza and by the park with its hushed babies and silent throng, until as he was rushing past 72nd Street he heard a sharp cry, and saw a living form leaning wildly out an upper window. He gasped. The human voice sounded in his ears like the voice of God.

"Hello—hello—help, in God's name!" wailed the woman. "There's a dead girl in here and a man and—and see yonder dead men lying in the street and dead horses—for the love of God go and bring the officers—" And the words trailed off into hysterical tears.

He wheeled the car in a sudden circle, running over the still body of a child and leaping on the curb. Then he rushed up the steps and tried the door and rang violently. There was a long pause, but at last the heavy door swung back. They stared a moment in silence. She had not noticed before that he was a Negro. He had not thought of her as white. She was a woman of perhaps twenty-five—rarely beautiful and richly gowned, with darkly-golden hair, and jewels. Yesterday, he thought with bitterness, she would scarcely have looked at him twice. He would have been dirt beneath her silken feet. She stared at him. Of all the sorts of men she had pictured as coming to her rescue she had not dreamed of one like him. Not that he was not human, but he dwelt in a world so far from hers, so infinitely far, that he seldom even entered her thought. Yet as she looked at him curiously he seemed quite commonplace and usual. He was a tall, dark workingman of the better class, with a sensitive face trained to stolidity and a poor man's clothes and hands. His face was soft and slow and his manner at once cold and nervous, like fires long banked, but not out.

So a moment each paused and gauged the other; then the thought of the dead world without rushed in and they started toward each other.

"What has happened?" she cried. "Tell me! Nothing stirs. All is silence! I see the dead strewn before my window as winnowed by the breath of God,—and see—" She dragged him through great, silken hangings to where, beneath the sheen of mahogany and silver, a little French maid lay stretched in quiet, everlasting sleep, and near her a butler lay prone in his livery.

The tears streamed down the woman's cheeks and she clung to his arm until the perfume of her breath swept his face and he felt the tremors racing through her body.

"I had been shut up in my dark room developing pictures of the comet which I took last night; when I came out—I saw the dead!

"What has happened?" she cried again.

He answered slowly:

"Something—comet or devil—swept across the earth this morning and—many are dead!"

"Many? Very many?"

"I have searched and I have seen no other living soul but you."

She gasped and they stared at each other.

"My—father!" she whispered.

"Where is he?"

"He started for the office."

"Where is it?"

"In the Metropolitan Tower."

"Leave a note for him here and come."

Then he stopped.

"No," he said firmly—"first, we must go—to Harlem."

"Harlem!" she cried. Then she understood. She tapped her foot at first impatiently. She looked back and shuddered. Then she came resolutely down the steps.

"There's a swifter car in the garage in the court," she said.

"I don't know how to drive it," he said.

"I do," she answered.

In ten minutes they were flying to Harlem on the wind. The Stutz rose and raced like an airplane. They took the turn at 110th Street on two wheels and slipped with a shriek into 135th.

He was gone but a moment. Then he returned, and his face was gray. She did not look, but said:

"You have lost—somebody?"

"I have lost—everybody," he said, simply—"unless—"

He ran back and was gone several minutes—hours they seemed to her.

"Everybody," he said, and he walked slowly back with something film-like in his hand which he stuffed into his pocket.

"I'm afraid I was selfish," he said. But already the car was moving toward the park among the dark and lined dead of Harlem— the brown, still faces, the knotted hands, the homely garments, and the silence—the wild and haunting silence. Out of the park, and down Fifth Avenue they whirled. In and out among the dead they slipped and quivered, needing no sound of bell or horn, until the great, square Metropolitan Tower hove in sight. Gently he laid the dead elevator boy aside; the car shot upward. The door of the office stood open. On the threshold lay the stenographer, and, staring at her, sat the dead clerk. The inner office was empty, but a note lay on the desk, folded and addressed but unsent:

Dear Daughter:

I've gone for a hundred mile spin in Fred's new Mercedes. Shall not be back before dinner. I'll bring Fred with me.

J. B. H.

"Come," she cried nervously. "We must search the city."

Up and down, over and across, back again—on went that ghostly search. Everywhere was silence and death—death and silence! They hunted from Madison Square to Spuyten Duyvel; they rushed across the Williamsburg Bridge; they swept over Brooklyn; from the Battery and Morningside Heights they scanned the river. Silence, silence everywhere, and no human sign. Haggard and bedraggled they puffed a third time slowly down Broadway, under the broiling sun, and at last stopped. He sniffed the air. An odor—a smell—and with the shifting breeze a sickening stench filled their nostrils and brought its awful warning. The girl settled back helplessly in her seat.

"What can we do?" she cried.

It was his turn now to take the lead, and he did it quickly.

"The long distance telephone—the telegraph and the cable— night rockets and then—flight!"

She looked at him now with strength and confidence. He did not look like men, as she had always pictured men; but he acted like one and she was content. In fifteen minutes they were at the central telephone exchange. As they came to the door he stepped quickly before her and pressed her gently back as he closed it. She heard him moving to and fro, and knew his burdens—the poor, little burdens he bore. When she entered, he was alone in the room. The grim switchboard flashed its metallic face in cryptic, sphinx-like immobility. She seated herself on a stool and donned the bright earpiece. She looked at the mouthpiece. She had never looked at one so closely before. It was wide and black, pimpled with usage; inert; dead; almost sarcastic in its unfeeling curves. It looked—she beat back the thought —but it looked,—it persisted in looking like—she turned her head and found herself alone. One moment she was terrified; then she thanked him silently for his delicacy and turned resolutely, with a quick intaking of breath.

"Hello!" she called in low tones. She was calling to the world. The world *must* answer. Would the world *answer?* Was the world—

Silence!

She had spoken too low.

"Hello!" she cried, full-voiced.

She listened. Silence! Her heart beat quickly. She cried in clear, distinct, loud tones: "Hello—hello—hello!"

What was that whirring? Surely—no—was it the click of a receiver?

She bent close, she moved the pegs in the holes, and called and called, until her voice rose almost to a shriek, and her heart hammered. It was as if she had heard the last flicker of creation, and the evil was silence. Her voice dropped to a sob. She sat stupidly staring into the black and sarcastic mouthpiece, and the thought came again. Hope lay dead within her. Yes, the cable and the rockets remained; but the world—she could not frame the thought or say the word. It was too mighty—too terrible! She turned toward the door with a new fear in her heart. For the first time she seemed to realize that she was alone in the world with a stranger, with something more than a stranger,—with a man alien in blood and culture—unknown, perhaps unknowable. It was awful! She must escape—she must fly; he must not see her again. Who knew what awful thoughts—

She gathered her silken skirts deftly about her young, smooth limbs—listened, and glided into a side-hall. A moment she shrank back: the hall lay filled with dead women; then she leaped to the door and tore at it, with bleeding fingers, until it swung wide. She looked out. He was standing at the top of the alley,—silhouetted, tall and black, motionless. Was he looking at her or away? She did not know—she did not care. She simply leaped and ran—ran until she found herself alone amid the dead and the tall ramparts of towering buildings.

She stopped. She was alone. Alone! Alone on the streets—alone in the city—perhaps alone in the world! There crept in upon her the sense of deception—of creeping hands behind her back—of silent, moving things she could not see,—of voices hushed in fearsome conspiracy. She looked behind and sideways, started at strange sounds and heard still stranger, until every nerve within her stood sharp and quivering, stretched to scream at the barest touch. She whirled and flew back, whimpering like a child, until she found that narrow alley again and the dark silent figure silhouetted at the top. She stopped and rested; then she walked silently toward him, looked at him timidly; but he said nothing as he handed her into the car. Her voice caught as she whispered:

"Not—that."

And he answered slowly: "No—not that!"

They climbed into the car. She bent forward on the wheel and sobbed, with great, dry, quivering sobs, as they flew toward the cable office on the east side, leaving the world of wealth and prosperity for the world of poverty and work. In the world behind them were death and silence, grave and grim, almost cynical, but always decent; here it was hideous. It clothed itself in every ghastly form of terror, struggle, hate, and suffering. It lay wreathed in crime and squalor, greed and lust. Only in its dread and awful silence was it like to death everywhere.

Yet as the two, flying and alone, looked upon the horror of the world, slowly, gradually, the sense of all-enveloping death deserted them. They seemed to move in a world silent and asleep,—not dead. They moved in quiet reverence, lest somehow they wake these sleeping forms who had, at last, found peace. They moved in some solemn, world-wide *Friedhof*, above which some mighty arm had waved its magic wand. All nature slept until—until, and quick with the same startling thought, they looked into each other's eyes—he, ashen, and she, crimson, with unspoken thought. To both, the vision of a mighty beauty—of vast, unspoken things, swelled in their souls; but they put it away.

Great, dark coils of wire came up from the earth and down from the sun and entered this low lair of witchery. The gathered lightnings of the world centered here, binding with beams of light the ends of the earth. The doors gaped on the gloom within. He paused on the threshold.

"Do you know the code?" she asked.

"I know the call for help—we used it formerly at the bank."

She hardly heard. She heard the lapping of the waters far below,—the dark and restless waters—the cold and luring waters, as they called. He stepped within. Slowly she walked to the wall, where the water called below, and stood and waited. Long she waited, and he did not come. Then with a start she saw him, too, standing beside the black waters. Slowly he removed his coat and stood there silently. She walked quickly to him and laid her hand on his arm. He did not start or look. The waters lapped on in luring, deadly rhythm. He pointed down to the waters, and said quietly:

"The world lies beneath the waters now—may I go?"

She looked into his stricken, tired face, and a great pity surged within her heart. She answered in a voice clear and calm, "No."

Upward they turned toward life again, and he seized the wheel. The world was darkening to twilight, and a great, gray pall was falling mercifully and gently on the sleeping dead. The ghastly glare of reality seemed replaced with the dream of some vast romance. The girl lay silently back, as the motor whizzed along, and looked half-consciously for the elf-queen to wave life into this dead world again. She forgot to wonder at the quickness with which he had learned to drive her car. It seemed natural. And then as they whirled and swung into Madison Square and at the door of the Metropolitan Tower she gave a low cry, and her eyes were great! Perhaps she had seen the elf-queen?

The man led her to the elevator of the tower and deftly they ascended. In her father's office they gathered rugs and chairs, and he wrote a note and laid it on the desk; then they ascended to the roof and he made her comfortable. For a while she rested and sank to dreamy somnolence, watching the worlds above and wondering. Below lay the dark shadows of the city and afar was the shining of the sea. She glanced at him timidly as he set food before her and took a shawl and wound her in it, touching her reverently, yet tenderly. She looked up at him with thankfulness in her eyes, eating what he served. He watched the city. She watched him. He seemed very human,—very near now.

"Have you had to work hard?" she asked softly.

"Always," he said.

"I have always been idle," she said. "I was rich."

"I was poor," he almost echoed.

"The rich and the poor are met together," she began, and he finished:

"The Lord is the Maker of them all."

"Yes," she said slowly; "and how foolish our human distinctions seem—now," looking down to the great dead city stretched below, swimming in unlightened shadows.

"Yes—I was not—human, yesterday," he said.

She looked at him. "And your people were not my people," she said; "but today—" She paused. He was a man,—no more; but he was in some larger sense a gentleman,—sensitive, kindly, chivalrous, everything save his hands and—his face. Yet yesterday—

"Death, the leveler!" he muttered.

"And the revealer," she whispered gently, rising to her feet with great eyes. He turned away, and after fumbling a moment sent a rocket into the darkening air. It arose, shrieked, and flew up, a slim path of light, and, scattering its stars abroad, dropped on the city below. She scarcely noticed it. A vision of the world had risen before her. Slowly the mighty prophecy of her destiny overwhelmed her. Above the dead past hovered the Angel of Annunciation. She was no mere woman. She was neither high nor low, white nor black, rich nor poor. She was primal woman; mighty mother of all men to come and Bride of Life. She looked upon the man beside her and forgot all else but his manhood, his strong, vigorous manhood—his sorrow and sacrifice. She saw him glorified. He was no longer a thing apart, a creature below, a strange outcast of another clime and blood, but her Brother Humanity incarnate, Son of God and great All-Father of the race to be.

He did not glimpse the glory in her eyes, but stood looking outward toward the sea and sending rocket after rocket into the unanswering darkness. Dark-purple clouds lay banked and billowed in the west. Behind them and all around, the heavens glowed in dim, weird radiance that suffused the darkening world and made almost a minor music. Suddenly, as though gathered back in some vast hand, the great cloud-curtain fell away. Low on the horizon lay a long, white star—mystic, wonderful! And from it fled upward to the pole, like some wan bridal veil, a pale, wide sheet of flame that lighted all the world and dimmed the stars.

In fascinated silence the man gazed at the heavens and dropped his rockets to the floor. Memories of memories stirred to life in the dead recesses of his mind. The shackles seemed to rattle and fall from his soul. Up from the crass and crushing and cringing of his caste leaped the lone majesty of kings long dead. He arose within the shadows, tall, straight, and stern, with power in his eyes and ghostly scepters hovering to his grasp. It was as though some mighty Pharaoh lived again, or curled Assyrian lord. He turned and looked upon the lady, and found her gazing straight at him.

Silently, immovably, they saw each other face to face—eye to eye. Their souls lay naked to the night. It was not lust; it was not love—it was some vaster, mightier thing that needed neither touch of body nor thrill of soul. It was a thought divine, splendid.

Slowly, noiselessly, they moved toward each other—the heavens above, the seas around, the city grim and dead below. He loomed from out the velvet shadows vast and dark. Pearl-white and slender, she shone beneath the stars. She stretched her jeweled hands abroad. He lighted up his mighty arms, and they cried each to the other, almost with one voice, "The world is dead."

"Long live the—"

"Honk! Honk!" Hoarse and sharp the cry of a motor drifted clearly up from the silence below. They started backward with a cry and gazed upon each other with eyes that faltered and fell, with blood that boiled.

"Honk! Honk! Honk! Honk!" came the mad cry again, and almost from their feet a rocket blazed into the air and scattered its stars upon them. She covered her eyes with her hands, and her shoulders heaved. He dropped and bowed, groped blindly on his knees about the floor. A blue flame spluttered lazily after an age, and she heard the scream of an answering rocket as it flew.

Then they stood still as death, looking to opposite ends of the earth.

"Clang—crash—clang!"

The roar and ring of swift elevators shooting upward from below made the great tower tremble. A murmur and babel of voices swept in upon the night. All over the once dead city the lights blinked, flickered, and flamed; and then with a sudden clanging of doors the entrance to the platform was filled with men, and one with white and flying hair rushed to the girl and lifted her to his breast. "My daughter!" he sobbed.

Behind him hurried a younger, comelier man, carefully clad in motor costume, who bent above the girl with passionate solicitude and gazed into her staring eyes until they narrowed and dropped and her face flushed deeper and deeper crimson.

"Julia," he whispered; "my darling, I thought you were gone forever."

She looked up at him with strange, searching eyes.

"Fred," she murmured, almost vaguely, "is the world—gone?"

"Only New York," he answered; "it is terrible—awful! You know,—but you, how did you escape—how have you endured this horror? Are you well? Unharmed?"

"Unharmed!" she said.

"And this man here?" he asked, encircling her drooping form with one arm and turning toward the Negro. Suddenly he stiffened anl his hand flew to his hip. "Why!" he snarled. "It's—a—nigger—Julia! Has he—has he dared—"

She lifted her head and looked at her late companion curiously and then dropped her eyes with a sigh.

"He has dared—all, to rescue me," she said quietly, "and I—thank him—much." But she did not look at him again. As the couple turned away, the father drew a roll of bills from his pockets.

"Here, my good fellow," he said, thrusting the money into the man's hands, "take that,—what's your name?"

"Jim Davis," came the answer, hollow-voiced.

"Well, Jim, I thank you. I've always liked your people. If you ever want a job, call on me." And they were gone.

The crowd poured up and out of the elevators, talking and whispering.

"Who was it?"

"Are they alive?"

"How many?"

"Two!"

"Who was saved?"

"A white girl and a nigger—there she goes."

"A nigger? Where is he? Let's lynch the damned—"

"Shut up—he's all right—he saved her."

"Saved hell! He had no business—"

"Here he comes."

Into the glare of the electric lights the colored man moved slowly, with the eyes of those that walk and sleep.

"Well, what do you think of that?" cried a bystander; "of all New York, just a white girl and a nigger!"

The colored man heard nothing. He stood silently beneath the glare of the light, gazing at the money in his hand and shrinking as he gazed; slowly he put his other hand into his pocket and brought out a baby's filmy cap, and gazed again. A woman mounted to the platform and looked about, shading her eyes. She was brown, small, and toil-worn, and in one arm lay the corpse of a dark baby. The crowd parted and her eyes fell on the colored man; with a cry she tottered toward him.

"Jim!"

He whirled and, with a sob of joy, caught her in his arms.

WILLIAM MONROE TROTTER

(1872-1934)

One of the most colorful individuals of the early days of the twentieth century was William Monroe Trotter, fiery editor of the Boston Guardian. *His uncompromising stand on the civil and human rights of black people was prophetic of our times.*

Trotter was a Bostonian, who was graduated from Harvard in 1895. He became a real estate broker, but in 1901 he realized his ambition to become a newspaperman by establishing, with George Washington Forbes, the Boston Guardian. *By no coincidence the newspaper plant was located in the same building in which William Lloyd Garrison had published* The Liberator *and in which Harriet Beecher Stowe's* Uncle Tom's Cabin *had been printed.*

In a time when Negro newspapers were generally conservative and heavily influenced by the Booker T. Washington policy of accommodation, the Guardian *was outspoken in its demands for full equality and became the most insistent voice against Washington. Trotter pushed the battle beyond the walls of his newspaper office. In 1903 Trotter and Forbes attended the meeting of the Afro-American Council, where Washington spoke. They tried to get the attention of the chairman, T. Thomas Fortune, but were never recognized. Later that year when Washington spoke at Columbus Avenue African Zion Church in Boston, Trotter and several friends disrupted his speech to protest Washington's alleged control over communication media. Trotter and his friends were arrested.*

Partly as a result of this incident, W. E. B. Du Bois, Trotter, and others organized the Niagara Movement, a pressure group to work for black people's civil rights. When that group later merged with the newly formed NAACP, Trotter refused to join because he did not approve of white leadership in the organization.

Trotter responded to many challenges. In 1910 he demonstrated against the anti-Negro play The Clansman, *based on Thomas Dixon's novel, and had a tumultuous interview with Woodrow Wilson over discrimination in government employment. In 1919, denied a passport, Trotter obtained a job as second cook on a transatlantic ship and appeared in Paris as a delegate from the National Equal Rights League to the Peace Conference.*

Trotter eventually lost many followers, who considered him too passionate and impulsive. Nevertheless, he never retreated in his fight for the black man's human rights.

A study of Trotter by Stephen R. Fox is The Guardian of Boston: William Monroe Trotter *(1970).*

Why Be Silent?

Under the caption, "Principal Washington Defines His Position,"
the Tuskegee Student, the official organ of Tuskegee, prints the
institute letter in which Mr. Washington said: "We cannot elevate
and make useful a race of people unless there is held out to them the
hope of reward for right living. Every revised constitution throughout
the southern states has put a premium upon intelligence, ownership
of property, thrift and character." This little sheet begins by saying
that the letter "appeared in all of the important papers of the country
on Nov. 28. It has been unstintingly praised from one section of the
country to the other for its clarity and forcefulness of statement, and
for its ringing note of sincerity." Although such words are to be
expected from the employes of the school they are for the most part
only too true. It is true that, although the letter was sent to the Age
Herald of Birmingham, Alabama, it appeared simultaneously "in all
the important papers of the country." Then its effect must be admitted to have been greater than if any other Negro had written it,
for admittedly no other Negro's letter could have obtained such
wide publicity. If it had in it aught that was injurious to the Negro's
welfare or to his manhood rights, therefore, such worked far more
damage than if any other Negro or any other man, save the president
himself, had written the words.

What man is there among us, whether friend or foe of the author
of the letter, who was not astounded at the reference to the disfranchising constitutions quoted above? "Every revised constitution
throughout the southern states has put a premium upon intelligence,
ownership of property, thrift and character," and all the more so
because Mr. Washington had not been accused by even the southerners of opposing these disfranchising constitutions. . . . If the state-

ment is false, if it is misleading, if it is injurious to the Negro, all the more blamable and guilty is the author because the statement was gratuitous on his part.

Is it the truth? Do these constitutions encourage Negroes to be thrifty, to be better and more intelligent? For this sort of argument is the most effective in favor of them. . . . Where is the Negro who says the law was or is ever intended to be fairly applied? . . . If so, then every reputable Negro orator and writer, from Hon. A. H. Grimke on, have been mistaken. If so, every Negro clergyman of standing, who has spoken on the subject . . . has been misinformed. We happen to know of an undertaker who has an enormous establishment in Virginia, who now can't vote. Is that encouraging thrift? Two letter carriers, who have passed the civil service examinations, are now sueing because disfranchised. Is that encouraging intelligence? . . . Even a Republican candidate for governor in Virginia recently said Negro domination was to be feared if 10 Negroes could vote because they could have the balance of power. Mr. Washington's statement is shamefully false and deliberately so.

But even were it true, what man is a worse enemy to a race than a leader who looks with equanimity on the disfranchisement of his race in a country where other races have universal suffrage by constitutions that make one rule for his race and another for the dominant race, by constitutions made by conventions to which his race is not allowed to send its representatives, by constitutions that his race although endowed with the franchise by law are not allowed to vote upon, and are, therefore, doubly illegal, by constitutions in violation to the national constitution, because, forsooth, he thinks such disfranchising laws will benefit the moral character of his people. Let our spiritual advisers condemn this idea of reducing a people to serfdom to make them good.

But what was the effect of Mr. Washington's letter on the northern white people? . . .

No thinking Negro can fail to see that, with the influence Mr. Washington wields in the North and the confidence reposed in him by the white people on account of his school, a fatal blow has been given to the Negro's political rights and liberty by his statement. The benevolence idea makes it all the more deadly in its effect. It comes very opportunely for the Negro, too, just when Roosevelt declares the Negro shall hold office, . . . when Congress is being asked to enforce the Negro's constitutional rights, when these laws are being carried to the Supreme Court. And here Mr. Washington, having gained sufficient influence through his doctrines, his school and his elevation by the President, makes all these efforts sure of failure by killing public sentiment against the disfranchising constitutions.

And Mr. Washington's word is the more effective for, discreditable as it may seem, not five Negro papers even mention a statement that belies all their editorials and that would have set aflame the entire Negro press of the country, if a less wealthy and less powerful Negro had made it. Nor will Negro orators nor Negro preachers dare now to pick up the gauntlet thrown down by the great "educator." Instead of being universally repudiated by the Negro race his statement will be practically universally endorsed by its silence because Washington said it, though it sounds the death-knell of our liberty. The lips of our leading politicians are sealed, because, before he said it, Mr. Washington, through the President, put them under obligation to himself. Nor is there that heroic quality now in our race that would lead men to throw off the shackles of fear, of obligation, of policy and denounce a traitor though he be a friend, or even a brother. It occurs to none that silence is tantamount to being virtually an accomplice in the treasonable act of this Benedict Arnold of the Negro race.

O, for a black Patrick Henry to save his people from this stigma of cowardice; to rouse them from their lethargy to a sense of danger; to score the tyrant and to inspire his people with the spirit of those immortal words: "Give Me Liberty or Give Me Death."

(1902)

CHARLES W. CHESNUTT

(1858-1932)

Charles Waddell Chesnutt was the first Afro-American to gain stature as a writer of fiction. Although his stories and novels may now be outdated in terms of their image of black realities, Chesnutt is respected as a literary groundbreaker. His works reflect considerable talent and attain artistic power that is surprising when one considers the severe stresses imposed upon black artists at the turn of the century.

Chesnutt was born in Cleveland, Ohio, two years before the Civil War. A year after the war ended, the Chesnutt family moved to North Carolina, the birthplace of his parents. It was here, during the days of his youth, that he absorbed the folk culture that would later become the basis of his first successful stories. At the age of sixteen, Chesnutt was teaching in North Carolina; at twenty-three he was a school principal. Two years later he left the South, worked as a newspaperman and stenographer in New York, then finally settled down in his birthplace, Cleveland, where he became a member of the bar. Between stenography and the practice of law, he supported himself while he began his career as a writer of fiction.

"The Goophered Grapevine," Chesnutt's first published story, appeared in the Atlantic Monthly *in 1887. It was based upon the folk culture which had become so familiar to Chesnutt in North Carolina. Other stories in this vein followed; these were collected in 1899 in* The Conjure Woman and Other Tales.

For a decade, while these stories were appearing in the Atlantic Monthly, *Chesnutt's public did not suspect that he was not white. Indeed, there was nothing in these stories to testify to the author's color. Like white local colorists Joel Chandler Harris and Thomas*

Nelson Page, Chesnutt created an elderly black Uncle who tells plantation tales in dialect. The voice of the author, however, speaks in the clipped Northern accents of the wealthy white landowner to whom Uncle Julius and his stories are interpreted through white perceptions to a white audience.

Still, The Conjure Woman *stories bear certain signs of blackness. Uncle Julius is not the garrulous old darky weaving romantic tales of the good old days of slavery. Rather, he is a wily old man, wise in the necessities of survival, who by appearing ingenuous and childlike actually manipulates his white folks into doing things advantageous to himself. Also, the tales are rooted in genuine black folk material. An occasional dash of irony in* The Conjure Woman *pieces reveals the black face beneath the white mask. Saunders Redding, in his critical volume* To Make a Poet Black, *says of these early stories, "Nearly all the stories of this first collection are tragic with the fatal consequences of human actions and prejudices. It is not the weak pseudo-tragedy of propaganda, it is not pathos and tears in which Chesnutt deals—it is fundamental stuff of life translated into the folk terms of a people who knew true tragedy."*

Chesnutt's second collection of stories, also published in 1899, was The Wife of His Youth and Other Stories of the Color Line. These stories dealt with the theme particularly poignant to Chesnutt: the problems of the Afro-American of mixed blood, who belonged neither to the black world nor to the white. With compassion and irony, Chesnutt probes the absurdity of the mulatto's situation. Working sometimes with satire, as in "A Matter of Principle," sometimes with bitter irony, as in "The Sheriff's Children," Chesnutt examines the isolation of the blue-veined people with an interest not often shown by black authors.

Some of Chesnutt's stories do not deal with black people at all. Of these, "Baxter's Procrustes," published in the Atlantic Monthly, June, 1904, is probably the best. Here Chesnutt writes in a Jamesian fashion of brilliant, cultured people, about as far from goophered grapevines as one can get.

Chesnutt wrote three novels, but they were never as successful as his stories. The objectivity of the stories was lost; the novels seldom rose above propaganda. The first novel, The House Behind the Cedars (1900), is probably the best. Chesnutt's craftsmanship is excellent, and there is fervor in his delivery. The other two novels, The Marrow of Tradition (1901) and The Colonel's Dream (1905), contain more anger than order.

Chesnutt also wrote a biography of Frederick Douglass, and several essays and speeches. After 1905 Chesnutt fell silent. In 1928 he was awarded the Spingarn Medal "for pioneer work as a literary artist depicting the life and struggle of Americans of Negro descent."

In spite of his early reluctance to reveal his race, a reluctance which was imposed on him by white racism, Chesnutt was essentially an honest writer, writing from his own knowledge and experience. Speaking especially of Chesnutt's early works, Saunders Redding says in To Make a Poet Black, "He worked with dangerous, habit-ridden material with passive calm and fearlessness. Considering more than the emotional factors that lay behind the American race problem, he exposed the Negro to critical analysis . . . He is the most solid representative of prose fiction that the Negro could boast before the 1920's."

An important addition to our knowledge of Chesnutt is provided by Sylvia L. Render, The Short Fiction of Charles W. Chesnutt (rev. ed. 1981).

The Goophered Grapevine

Some years ago my wife was in poor health, and our family doctor, in whose skill and honesty I had implicit confidence, advised a change of climate. I shared, from an unprofessional standpoint, his opinion that the raw winds, the chill rains, and the violent changes of temperature that characterized the winters in the region of the Great Lakes tended to aggravate my wife's difficulty, and would undoubtedly shorten her life if she remained exposed to them. The doctor's advise was that we seek, not a temporary place of sojourn, but a permanent residence, in a warmer and more equable climate. I was engaged at the time in trade in cotton and naval stores. This business activity was not immediately apparent to my unaccustomed eyes. Indeed, when I first saw the town, there brooded over it a calm that seemed almost sabbatic in its restfulness, though I learned later on that underneath its somnolent exterior the deeper currents of life—love and hatred, joy and despair, ambition and avarice, faith and friendship—flowed not less steadily than in livelier latitudes.

We found the weather delightful at that season, the end of summer, and were hospitably entertained. Our host was a man of means and evidently regarded our visit as a pleasure, and we were therefore correspondingly at our ease, and in a position to act with the coolness of judgment desirable in making so radical a change in our lives. My cousin placed a horse and buggy at our disposal, and himself acted as our guide until I became somewhat familiar with the country.

I found that grape-culture, while it had never been carried on to any great extent, was not entirely unknown in the neighborhood. Several planters thereabouts had attempted it on a commercial scale, in former years, with greater or less success; but like most Southern industries, it had felt the blight of war and had fallen into desuetude.

I went several times to look at a place that I though might suit me. It was a plantation of considerable extent, that had formerly belonged to a wealthy man by the name of McAdoo. The estate had been for years involved in litigation between disputing heirs, during which period shiftless cultivation had well-nigh exhausted the soil. There had been a vineyard of some extent on the place, but it had not been attended to since the war, and had lapsed into utter neglect. The vines—here partly supported by decayed and broken-down trellises, there twining themselves among the branches of the slender saplings which had sprung up among them—grew in wild and unpruned luxuriance, and the few scattered grapes they bore were the undisputed prey of the first comer. The site was admirably adapted to grape-raising; the soil, with a little attention, could not have been better; and with the native grape, the luscious scuppernong, as my main reliance in the beginning, I felt sure that I could introduce and cultivate successfully a number of other varieties.

One day I went over with my wife to show her the place. We drove out of the town over a long wooden bridge that spanned a spreading mill-pond, passed the long whitewashed fence surrounding the county fair-ground, and struck into a road so sandy that the horse's feet sank to the fetlocks. Our route lay partly up hill and partly down, for we were in the sand-hill county; we drove past cultivated farms, and then by abandoned fields grown up in scrub-oak and short-leaved pine, and once or twice through the solemn aisles of the virgin forest, where the tall pines, well-nigh meeting over the narrow road, shut out the sun, and wrapped us in cloistral solitude. Once, at a cross-roads, I was in doubt as to the turn to take, and we sat there waiting ten minutes—we had already caught some of the native infection of restfulness—for some human being to come along, who could direct us on our way. At length a little negro girl appeared, walking straight as an arrow, with a piggin full of water on her head. After a little patient investigation, necessary to overcome the child's shyness, we learned what we wished to know, and at the end of about five miles from the town reached our destination.

We drove between a pair of decayed gateposts—the gate itself had long since disappeared—and up a straight sandy lane, between two lines of rotting rail fence, partly concealed by jimson-weeds and briers, to the open space where a dwelling-house had once stood, evidently a spacious mansion, if we might judge from the ruined chimneys that were still standing, and the brick pillars on which the sills rested. The house itself, we had been informed, had fallen a victim to the fortunes of war.

We alighted from the buggy, walked about the yard for a while, and then wandered off into the adjoining vineyard. Upon Annie's complaining of weariness I led the way back to the yard, where a pine log lying under the spreading elm afforded a shady though somewhat hard seat. One end of the log was already occupied by a venerable-looking colored man. He held on his knees a hat full of grapes, over which he was smacking his lips with great gusto; and a pile of grapeskins near him indicated that the performance was no new thing. We approached him at an angle from the rear, and were close to him before he perceived us. He respectfully rose as we drew near, and was moving away, when I begged him to keep his seat.

"Don't let us disturb you," I said. "There is plenty of room for us all."

He resumed his seat with some embarrassment. While he had been standing, I had observed that he was a tall man, and though slightly bowed by the weight of years, apparently quite vigorous. He was not entirely black, and this fact, together with the quality of his hair, which was about six inches long and very bushy, except on the top of his head, where he was quite bald, suggested a slight strain of other than Negro blood. There was a shrewdness in his eyes, too, which was not altogether African, and which, as we afterwards learned from experience, was indicative of a corresponding shrewdness in his character. He went on eating his grapes, but did not seem to enjoy himself quite so well as he had apparently done before he became aware of our presence.

"Do you live around here?" I asked, anxious to put him at his ease.

"Yas, suh. I lives des ober yander, behine de nex' san'hill, on de Lumberton plank-road."

"Do you know anything about the time when this vineyard was cultivated?"

"Lawd bless you, suh, I knows all about it. Dey ain' na'er a man in dis settlement w'at won' tell you ole Julius McAdoo 'uz bawn en raise' on dis yer same plantation. Is you de Norv'n gemman w'at's gwine ter buy de ole vimya'd?"

"I am looking at it," I replied; "but I don't know that I shall care to buy unless I can be reasonably sure of making something out of it."

"Well, suh, you is a stranger ter me, en I is a stranger to you, en we is bofe strangers ter one anudder, but 'f I 'uz in yo' place, I wouldn't buy dis vimya'd."

"Why not?" I asked.

"Well, I dunno whe'r you b'lieves in conj'in' er not—some er de w'ite folks don't, er says dey don't—but de truf er de matter is dat dis yer ole vimya'd is goophered."

"Is what?" I asked, not grasping the meaning of this unfamiliar word.

"Is goophered—cunju'd, bewitch'."

He imparted this information with such solemn earnestness and with such an air of confidential mystery that I felt somewhat interested, while Annie was evidently much impressed, and drew closer to me.

"How do you know it is bewitched?" I asked.

"I wouldn' spec' fer you ter b'lieve me 'less you know all 'bout de fac's. But ef you en young miss dere doan' min' lis'nin' ter a ole nigger run on a minute er two w'ile you er restin', I kin 'spain to you how it all happen'."

We assured him that we would be glad to hear how it all happened, and he began to tell us. At first the current of his memory—or imagination—seemed somewhat sluggish; but as his embarrassment wore off, his language flowed more freely, and the story acquired perspective and coherence. As he became more and more absorbed in the narrative, his eyes assumed a dreamy expression, and he seemed to lose sight of his auditors, and to be living over again in monologue his life on the old plantation.

"Ole Mars Dugal' McAdoo," he began, "bought dis place long many years befo' de wah, en I 'member well we'en he sot out all dis yer part er de plantation in scuppernon's. De vimes growed monst'us fas', en Mars Dugal' made a thousan' gallon er scuppernon' wine eve'y year.

"Now, ef dey's an'thing a nigger lub, nex' ter 'possum, en chick'n, en watermillyums, it's scuppernon's. Dey ain' nuffin dat kin stan' up side'n de scuppernon' fer sweetness; sugar ain't a suckumstance ter scuppernon'. W'en de season is nigh 'bout ober, en de grapes begin ter swivel up des a little wid de wrinkles er ole age—we'n de skin git sof' en brown—den de scuppernon' make you smack yo' lip en roll yo' eye en wush fer mo'; so I reckon it ain' very 'stonishin' dat niggers lub scuppernon'.

"Dey wuz a sight er niggers in de naberhood er de vimya'd. Dere wuz ole Mars Henry Brayboy's niggers, en ole Mars Jeems McLean's niggers, en Mars Dugal's own niggers; den dey wuz a settlement er free niggers en po' buckrahs down by de Wim'l'ton Road, en Mars Dugal' had de only vimya'd in de naberhood. I reckon it ain' so much so nowadays, but befo' de wah, in slab'ry times, a nigger didn' mine going' fi' er ten mile in a night w'en dey wuz sump'n good ter eat at de yuther een'.

"So atter a w'ile Mars Dugal' begin ter miss his scuppernon's. Co'se he 'cuse' de niggers er it, but dey all 'nied it ter de las'. Mars

Dugal' sot spring guns en steel traps, en he en de obseah sot up nights once't or twice't, tel one night Mars Dugal'—he 'uz a monst'us keerless man—got his leg shot full er cow-peas. But somehow er nudder dey couldn' nebber ketch none er de niggers. I dunner how it happen, but it happen des like I tell you, en de grapes kep' on a-goin' des de same.

"But bimeby ole Mars Dugal' fix' up a plan ter stop it. Dey wuz a cunjuh 'oman livin' down 'mongs' de free niggers on de Wim'l'ton Road, en all de darkies fum Rockfish ter Beaver Crick wuz feared er her. She could wuk de mos' powerfulles' kin' er goopher—could make people hab fits, er rheumatiz', er mak 'em des dwinel away en die; en dey say she went out ridin' de niggers at night, fer she wuz a witch 'sides bein' a cunjuh 'oman. Mars Dugal' hearn 'bout Aun' Peggy's doin's, en begun ter 'flect whe'r er no he couldn' git her ter he'p him keep de niggers off'n de grapevimes. One day in de spring er de year, ole miss pack' up a basket er chick'n en poun'cake, en a bottle er scuppernon' wine, en Mars Dugal' tuk it in his buggy en driv over ter Aun' Peggy's cabin. He tuk de basket in, en had a long talk wid Aun' Peggy.

"De nex' day Aun' Peggy come up ter de vimya'd. De niggers seed her slippin' 'round, en dey soon foun' out what she 'uz doin' dere. Mars Dugal' had hi'ed her ter goopher de grapevimes. She sa'ntered 'roun' 'mongs' de vimes, en tuk a leaf fum dis one, en a grape-hull fum dat one, en den a little twig fum here, en a little pinch er dirt fum dere—en put it all in a big black bottle, wid a snake's toof en a speckle hen's gall en some ha'rs fum a black cat's tail, en den fill' de bottle wid scuppernon' wine. W'en she got de goopher all ready en fix', she tuk 'n went out in de woods en buried it under de root uv a red oak tree, en den come back en tole one er de niggers she done goopher de grapevimes, en ae'r a nigger w'at eat dem grapes 'ud be sho ter die inside'n twel' mont's.

"Atter dat de niggers let de scuppernon's 'lone, en Mars Dugal' didn' hab no' casion ter fine no mo' fault; en de season wuz mos' gone, w'en a strange gemman stop at de plantation one night ter see Mars Dugal' on some business; en his coachman, seein' de scuppernon's growin' so nice en sweet, slip 'roun' behine de smoke-house en et all de scuppernon's he could hole. Nobody didn' notice it at de time, but dat night, on de way home, de gemman's hoss runned away en kill' de coachman. W'en we hearn de noos, Aun' Lucy, de cook, she up'n say she seed de strange nigger eat'n' er de scuppernon's behine de smoke-house; en den we knowed de goopher had be'en er wukkin'. Den one er de nigger chilluns runned away from de quarters one day, en got in de scuppernon's, en died de nex' week. White folks say he die' er de fevuh, but de niggers knowed it wuz de goopher. So you k'n be sho de darkies didn' hab much ter do wid dem scuppernon' vimes.

"W'en de scuppernon' season 'uz ober fer dat year, Mars Dugal' foun' he had made fifteen hund'ed gallon er wine; en one er de niggers hearn him laffin' wid de obserseah fit ter kill, en sayin' dem fifteen hund'ed gallon er wine wuz monst'us good intrus' on de ten dollars he laid out on de vimya'd. So I 'low ez he paid Aun' Peggy ten dollars fer to goopher de grapevimes.

"De goopher didn' wuk no mo' tel de nex summer, w'en 'long to'ds de middle er de season one er de fiel' han's died; en ez dat lef' Mars Dugal' sho't er han's, he went off ter town fer ter buy anudder. He fotch de noo nigger home wid 'im. He wuz er ole nigger, er de color er a gingy-cake, en ball ez a hossapple on de top er his head. He wuz a peart ole nigger, do', en could do a big day's wuk.

"Now it happen dat one er de niggers on de nex' plantation, one er ole Mars Henry Brayboy's niggers, had runned away de day befo', en tuk ter de swamp, en ole Mars Dugal' en some er de yuther nabor w'ite folks had gone out wid dere guns en dere dogs fer ter he'p 'em hunt fer de nigger; en de han's on our own plantation wuz all so flusterated dat we fuhgot ter tell de noo han' 'bout de goopher on de scuppernon' vimes. Co'se he smell de grapes en see de vimes, an atter dahk de fus' thing he done wuz ter slip off ter de grapevimes 'dout sayin' nuffin ter nobody. Nex' mawnin' he tole some er de niggers 'bout de fine bait er scuppernon' he et de night befo'.

"W'en dey tole 'im 'bout de goopher on de grapevines, he 'uz dat tarrified dat he turn pale, en look des like he gwine ter die right in his tracks. De oberseah come up en axed w'at 'uz de matter; en w'en dey tole 'im Henry been eaten' er de scuppernon's, en got de goopher on 'im, he gin Henry a big drink er w'iskey, en 'low dat de nex' rainy day he take 'im ober ter Aun' Peggy's, en see ef she wouldn' take de goopher off'n him, seein' ez he didn't know nuffin' erbout it tel he done et de grapes.

"Sho nuff, it rain de nex' day, en de oberseah went ober ter Aun' Peggy's wid Henry. En Aun' Peggy say dat bein' ez Henry didn' know 'bout de goopher, en et de grapes in ign'ance er de conseq'ences, she reckon she mought be able ter take de goopher off'n him. So she fotch out er bottle wid some cunjuh medicine in it, en po'd some out in a go'd fer Henry ter drink. He manage ter git it down; he say it tas'e like w'iskey wid sump'n bitter in it. She 'lowed dat 'ud keep de goopher off'n him tel de spring; but w'en de sap begin ter rise in de grapevimes he ha' ter come en see her ag'in, en she tell him w'at he's ter do.

"Nex' spring, w'en de sap commence' ter rise in de scuppernon' vime, Henry tuk a ham one night. Whar'd he git de ham? I doan know; dey wa'n't no hams on de plantation 'cep'n' w'at 'uz in de smokehouse, but I never see Henry 'bout de smokehouse. But ez I wuz a-sayin', he tuk de ham ober ter Aun' Peggy's; en Aun' Peggy tole 'im dat w'en Mars Dugal' begin ter prune de grapevimes, he must go en take 'n scrape off de sap what it ooze out'n de cut een's er de vimes, en 'n'int his ball head wid it; en ef he do dat once't a year de goopher wouldn't wuk agin 'im long ez he done it. En bein' ez he fotch her de ham, she fix' it so he kin eat all de scuppernon' he want.

"So Henry 'n'int his head wid de sap out'n de big grapevime des ha'f way 'twix de quarters en de big house, en de goopher nebber wuk agin him dat summer. But the beatenes' thing you eber see happen ter Henry. Up ter dat time he wuz ez ball ez a sweeten' 'tater, but des ez soon ez de young leaves begun ter come out on de grapevimes, de ha'r begun ter grow out on Henry's head, en by de middle er de summer he had de bigges' head er ha'r on de plantation. Befo' dat, Henry had tol'able good ha'r 'roun' de aidges, but soon ez de young grapes begun ter come, Henry's ha'r begun to quirl all up in little balls, des like dis yer reg'lar grapy ha'r, en by de time de grapes got ripe his head look des like a bunch er grapes. Combin' it didn' do no good; he wuk at it ha'f de night wid er Jim Crow, en think he git it straighten' out, but in de mawnin' de grapes 'ud be dere des de same. So he gin it up, en tried ter keep de grapes down by havin' his ha'r cut sho't.

"But dat wa'n't de quares' thing 'bout de goopher. When Henry come ter de plantation, he wuz gittin' a little ole and stiff in de j'ints. But dat summer he got des ez spry en libely ez any young nigger on de plantation; fac', he got so biggity dat Mars Jackson, de oberseah, ha' ter th'eaten ter whip 'im ef he didn' stop cuttin' up his didos en behave hisse'f. But de mos' cur'ouses' thing happen' in de fall, when de sap begin ter go down in de grapevimes. Fus, when de grapes 'uz gethered, de knots begun ter straighten out'n Henry's ha'r; en w'en de leaves begin ter fall, Henry's ha'r commence' ter drap out; en when de vimes 'uz bar', Henry's head wuz baller'n it wuz in de spring, en he begin ter git ole en stiff in de j'ints ag'in, en paid no mo' 'tention ter de gals dyoin' er de whole winter. En nex' spring, w'en he rub de sap on ag'in, he got young ag'in, en so soopl en libely dat none er de young niggers on de plantation couldn' jump, ner dance, ner hoe ez much cotton ez Henry. But in de fall er de year his grapes 'mence' ter straighten out, en his j'ints ter git stiff, en his ha'r drap off, en de rheumatiz begin ter wrastle wid 'im.

"Now, ef you'd 'a' knowed ole Mars Dugal' McAdoo, you'd 'a' knowed dat it ha' ter be a mighty rainy day when he couldn' fine sump'n fer his niggers ter do, en it ha' ter be a mighty little hole he couldn' crawl thoo, en ha'ter be a monst'us cloudy night when a dollar git by him in de dahkness; en w'en he see how Henry git young in de spring en ole in de fall, he 'lowed ter hisse'f ez how he could make mo' money out'n Henry dan by wukkin' him in de cotton-fiel'. 'Long de nex' spring, atter de sap 'mence' ter rise, en Henry 'n'int 'is head en sta'ted fer ter git young en soopl, Mars Dugal' up'n tuk Henry ter town, en sole 'im for fifteen hunder' dollars. Co'se de man w'at bought Henry didn' know nuffin 'bout de goopher, en Mars Dugal' didn't see no 'casion fer ter tell 'im. Long to'ds de fall, w'en de sap went down, Henry begin ter git ole ag'in same ez yuzhal, en his noo marster begin ter git skeered les'n he gwine ter lose his fifteen-hunder'-dollar nigger. He sent fer a mighty fine doctor, but de med'cine didn' 'pear ter do no good; de goopher had a good holt. Henry tole de doctor 'bout de goopher, but de doctor des laff at 'im.

"One day in de winter Mars Dugal' went ter town, en wuz santerin' 'long de Main Street, w'en who should he meet but Henry's noo master. Dey said 'Hoddy,' en Mars Dugal' ax 'im ter hab a seegyar; en atter dey run on awhile 'bout de craps en de weather, Mars Dugal' ax 'im, sorter keerless, like ez ef he des thought of it—

" 'How you like de nigger I sole you las' spring?'

"Henry's marster shuck his head en knock de ashes off'n his seegyar.

" 'Spec' I made a bad bahgin when I bought dat nigger. Henry done good wuk all de summer, but sence de fall set in he 'pears ter be sorter pinin' away. Dey ain' nuffin pertickler de matter wid 'im—leastways de doctor say so—'cep'n' a tech er de rheumatiz; but his ha'r is all fell out, en ef he don't pick up his strenk mighty soon, I spec' I'm gwine ter lose 'im.'

"Dey smoked on awhile, en bimeby ole mars say, 'Well, a bahgin's a bahgin, but you en me is good fren's, en I doan wan' ter see you lose all de money you paid fer dat nigger; en ef w'at you say is so, en I ain't 'sputin' it, he ain't wuf much now. I spec's you wukked him too ha'd dis summer, er e'se de swamps down here don't agree wid de san'-hill nigger. So you des lemme know, en ef he gits any wusser, I'll be willin' ter gib yer five hund'ed dollars for 'im, en take my chances on his livin'.'

"Sho' nuff, when Henry begun ter draw up wid de rheumatiz en it look like he gwine ter die fer sho, his noo marster sen' fer Mars Dugal', en Mars Dugal' gin him what he promus, en brung Henry home ag'in. He tuk good keer uv 'im dyoin' er de winter—give 'im w'iskey ter rub his rheumatiz, en terbaker ter smoke, en all he want ter eat—'caze a nigger w'at he could make a thousan' dollars a year off'n didn' grow on eve'y huckleberry bush.

"Nex' spring, w'en de sap rise en Henry's ha'r commence' ter sprout, Mars Dugal' sole 'im ag'in, down in Robeson County dis time; en he kep' dat sellin' business up fer five year er mo'. Henry nebber say nuffin 'bout de goopher ter his noo marsters, 'caze he know he gwine ter be tuk good keer uv de nex' winter, w'en Mars Dugal' buy him back. En Mars Dugal' made 'nuff money off'n Henry ter buy anudder plantation ober on Beaver Crick.

"But 'long 'bout de een 'er dat five year dey come a stranger ter stop at de plantation. De fus' day he 'uz dere he went out wid Mars Dugal' en spent all de mawnin' lookin' ober de vimya'd, en atter dinner dey spent all de evenin' playin' kya'ds. De niggers soon 'skivver' dat he wuz a Yankee, en dat he come down ter Norf C'lina fer ter l'arn de w'ite folks how to raise grapes en make wine. He promus Mars Dugal' he c'd make de grapevimes b'ar twice't ez many grapes, en dat de noo winepress he wuz a-sellin' would make mo' d'n twice't ez many gallons er wine. En ole Mars Dugal' des drunk it all in, des 'peared ter be bewitch' wit dat Yankee. W'en de darkies see dat Yankee runnin' 'roun' de vimya'd en diggin' under de grape-vimes, dey shuk dere heads, en 'lowed dat dey feared Mars Dugal' losin' his min'. Mars Dugal' had all de dirt dug away fum under de roots er all de scuppernon' vimes, an' let 'em stan' dat away fer a week er mo'. Den dat Yankee made de niggers fix up a mixtry er lime en ashes en manyo, en po' it 'roun' de roots er de grapevimes. Den he 'vise Mars Dugal' fer ter trim de vimes close't, en Mars Dugal' tuck 'n done eve'ything de Yankee tole him ter do. Dyoin' all er dis time, mine yer, dis yer Yankee wuz libbin' off'n de fat er de lan', at de big house, en playin' kya'ds wid Mars Dugal' eve'y night; en dey say Mars Dugal' los' mo'n a thousan' dollars dyoin' er de week dat Yankee wuz a-ruinin' de grapevimes.

"W'en de sap ris nex' spring, ole Henry 'n'inted his head ez yuzhal, en his ha'r 'mence' ter grow des de same ez it done eve'y year.

De scuppernon' vimes growed monst's fas', en de leaves wuz greener en thicker dan dey eber be'n dyoin' my rememb'ance; en Henry's ha'r growed out thicker dan eber, en he 'peared ter git younger 'n younger, en soopler; en seein' ez he wuz sho't er han's dat spring, havin' tuk in consid'able noo groun', Mars Dugal' 'git de crap in en de cotton chop'. So he kep' Henry on de plantation.

"But 'long 'bout time fer de grapes ter come on de scuppernon' vimes, dey 'peared ter come a change ober 'em; de leaves witherd en swivel' up, en de young grapes turn' yaller, n bimeby eve'ybody on de plantation could see dat de whole vimya'd wuz dyin'. Mars Dugal' tuk'n water de vimes en done all he could, but 't wa'n no use; dat Yankee had done bus' de watermillyum. One time de vimes picked up a bit, en Mars Dugal' 'lowed dey wuz gwine ter come out ag'in; but dat Yankee done dug too close under de roots, en prune de branches too close ter de vime, en all dat lime en ashes done burn de life out'm de vimes, en dey des kep' a-with'in' en a-swivelin'.

"All dis time de goopher wuz a-wukkin'. When de vimes sta'ted ter wither, Henry 'mence' ter complain er his rheumatiz; en when de leaves begin ter dry up, his ha'r 'mence' ter drap out. When de vimes fresh' up a bit, Henry'd git peart ag'in, en when de vimes wither' ag'in, Henry'd git ole ag'in, en des kep' gittin' mo' fitten fer nuffin; he des pined away, en pined away, en fin'ly tuk ter his cabin; en when de big vime whar he got de sap ter 'n'int his head withered en turned yaller en died, Henry died too—des went out sorter like a cannel. Dey didn't 'pear ter be nuffin de matter wid 'im, 'cep'n de rheumatiz, but his strenk des dwinel' away 'tel he didn' hab ernuff lef' ter draw his bref. De goopher had got de under holt, en th'owed Henry dat time fer good en all.

"Mars Dugal' tuk on might'ly 'bout losin' his vimes en his nigger in de same year; en he swo' dat ef he could git holt er dat Yankee he'd wear 'im ter a frazzle, en den chaw up de frazzle; en he'd done it, too, for Mars Dugal' 'uz a monst'us brash man w'en he once git started. He sot de vimy'd out ober ag'in, but it wuz th'ee er fo' year befo' de vimes got ter b'arin' any scuppernon's.

"W'en de wah broke out, Mars Dugal' raise' a comp'ny, en went off ter fight de Yankees. He say he wuz mighty glad wah come, en he des want ter kill a Yankee fer eve'y dollar he los' 'long er dat grape-raisin' Yankee. En I 'spec' he would 'a' done it, too, ef de Yankees hadn' 's'picioned sump'en en killed him fus'. Atter de s'render, ole Miss move' ter town, de niggers all scattered 'way fum de planta-tion, en de vimya'd ain' be'n cultervated sence."

"Is that story true?" asked Annie doubtfully, but seriously, as the old man concluded his narrative.

"It's des ez true ez I'm a-settin' here, miss. Dey's a easy way ter prove it: I kin lead de way right ter Henry's grave ober yonder in de plantation buryin'-groun'. En I tell yer w'at, marster, I wouldn' 'vise you to buy dis yer ole vimya'd, 'caze de goopher's on it yit, en dey ain' no tellin' w'en it's gwine ter crap out."

"But I thought you said all the old vines died."

"Dey did 'pear ter die, but a few un 'em come out ag'in, en is mixed in 'mongs' de yuthers. I ain' skeered ter eat de grapes 'caze I knows de old vimes fum de noo ones, but wid strangers dey ain 'no tellin' w'at mought happen. I wouldn' 'vise yer ter buy dis vimya'd."

I bought the vineyard, nevertheless, and it has been for a long time in a thriving condition, and is often referred to by the local press as a striking illustration of the opportunities open to Northern capital in the development of Southern industries. The luscious scuppernong holds first rank among our grapes, though we cultivate a great many other varieties; and our income from grapes packed and shipped to the Northern markets is quite considerable. I have not noticed any developments of the goopher in the vineyard, although I have a mild suspicion that our colored assistants do not suffer from want of grapes during the season.

I found, when I bought the vineyard, that Uncle Julius had occupied a cabin on the place for many years, and derived a respectable revenue from the product of the neglected grapevines. This, doubtless, accounted for his advice to me not to buy the vineyard, though whether it inspired the goopher story I am unable to state. I believe, however, that the wages I paid him for his services as coachman, for I gave him employment in that capacity, were more than an equivalent for anything he lost by the sale of the vineyard.

PAUL LAURENCE DUNBAR

(1872-1906)

Paul Laurence Dunbar, the son of ex-slaves, rose from an elevator boy composing verses to an internationally known poet. Like other black writers in the turbulent days following the Civil War, Dunbar was artistically inhibited by the distorted image of black people which was comfortable for the white book-buying public. Nevertheless, Dunbar was a lyricist of considerable ability, who proved to the literary public (who discounted the magnificent folk culture then extant) that a black man could be an artist.

Dunbar was born in Dayton, Ohio, in 1872. From youth he was a black prodigy in a white world. The only black student in his high school class, he was tremendously popular because of what Benjamin Brawley calls "his modest and yet magnetic personality." Notwithstanding this modesty and magnetism, after high school Dunbar had to work at one of the few jobs open to black youngsters—that of elevator boy.

Dunbar's first volume of poems was Oak and Ivy, *privately published in 1893. It was followed two years later by a second collection,* Majors and Minors. *Dunbar had to sell these books himself. He began to give readings of his poems and soon built up a following. The poems came to the attention of William Dean Howells, who reviewed them in* Harper's Weekly.

In 1896 Dunbar published the volume which made him famous, Lyrics of Lowly Life. *Howells wrote his widely known introduction to this work, praising the dialect poems:*

[The precious difference in temperament] between the

races is best preserved and most charmingly suggested by Dun-
bar in those pieces of his where he studies the moods and traits
of his race in its own accents of our English . . . They are
really not dialect so much as personal attempts and failures for
the written and spoken language . . . pieces which . . . de-
scribed the range between appetite and emotion, with certain
lifts far beyond it and above it . . . He reveals in these a finely
ironical perception of the Negro's limitations, with a tenderness
for them which I think so very rare as to be almost quite new.
I should say, perhaps, that it was this humorous quality Mr.
Dunbar has added to our literature, and it would be this which
would most distinguish him, now and hereafter."

Read in the light of today's perceptions, the introduction reveals
the white critic's clouded vision of black realities. Although Howells
undoubtedly felt that he was praising Dunbar to the highest, he was
actually putting the kiss of death on any possibility of Dunbar's acceptance as a serious artist.

However, fame and some fortune followed the publication of
Lyrics of Lowly Life. *Dunbar gave readings in England in 1897, and
in the same year began a short period as an aide in the Library of
Congress. In 1899 he went South for the first time to give readings.
Meanwhile, he wrote many articles and stories, and four novels, in
addition to more poems. Numerous collections of his works appeared.*

In spite of his popular success, Dunbar was restless and dissatis-
fied. He was haunted by a feeling of failure because the dialect poems,
not the standard poems, were considered the more important. He was
haunted, too, by the spectre of early death, and, in fact, succumbed
to tuberculosis in 1906 at the age of thirty-three.

Assessments of Dunbar's work vary from Vernon Loggins' pronouncement that the publication of Lyrics of Lowly Life *is "the
"greatest single event in the history of American Literature" to the
feeling among some current black writers that Dunbar was an Uncle
Tom. Several certainties emerge, however: that Dunbar was a highly
talented lyricist; that his writing took on the configuration imposed
upon it by the necessity to survive in a white literary world; and
that he himself valued his standard English poems more highly than
the popular dialect pieces.*

One must come to grips with these dialect pieces. Dunbar wrote
them to gain an audience, knowing the fad exploited by *Thomas Nel-*

son Page, Joel Chandler Harris, and other white apologists for slavery. Dialect was not natural to Dunbar, who never even traveled South until after most of the dialect pieces had been written. From the folk speech he heard in his native Ohio, Dunbar constructed a patch-work dialect which is much like a Northern white's idea of "darky" talk. The form of the dialect poems is conventional literary form, and does not in any way resemble that of folk poetry. By substituting "funny spelling" for standard English, Dunbar produced graceful, quaint poems. The subject matter of the dialect poems is the simple pleasures and sorrows of a childlike people who could be comical or pathetic—seldom anything else. The poems were sympathetic to black people; but a comparison of any Dunbar dialect poem with a spiritual or with folk blues will reveal that the Dunbar poem is about, but not from, black life.

Dunbar speaks more truly in his standard English poems. In conventional forms Dunbar lauds notable people, finds nature a sympathetic companion, enjoys attractive women, and otherwise sings of things which through the ages have inspired poets. However, several obviously personal poems deal effectively with themes that vitally concerned Dunbar: his sense of impending death; his reactions to the damage inflicted upon the black man by American racism; his feelings of failure; his bitter disappointment that his dialect poems were so highly favoured while the standard English poems in which he expressed his powerful emotions were less popular.

Dunbar's stories were generally weak, although a few attained some degree of interest. Three of the novels concern white characters—The Uncalled (1898), The Love of Landry (1900), and The Fanatics (1901), The white public's image of the black man would not permit serious portrayal of black characters. The first novel is particularly revealing in that the leading character is Dunbar's own alter ego, facing a conflict Dunbar himself faced—but in the novel he is white. A fourth novel, The Sport of the Gods (1902), concerns black characters, but is technically weak.

Obviously Dunbar's scope was severely limited by the pressures of the times. Yet his contribution to black literature is considerable. He proved that a black writer could be a popular success—could, indeed, support himself with his pen. He broke the ground for poets to come. In the current upsurge of poetry which reflects black life, black rhythms, black language, we can perhaps detect the spectre of Dunbar.

There is a useful bibliography of Dunbar by E.W. Metcalf, Jr. (1975).

An Antebellum Sermon

We is gathahed hyeah, my brothahs,
    In dis howlin' wildaness,
Fu' to speak some words of comfo't
    To each othah in distress.
An' we chooses fu' ouah subjic'
    Dis—we'll 'splain it by an' by;
"An' de Lawd said, 'Moses, Moses,'
    An' de man said, 'Hyeah am I.' "

Now ole Pher'oh, down in Egypt,
    Was de wuss man evah bo'n,
An' he had de Hebrew chillun
    Down dah wukin' in his co'n;
'T well de Lawd got tiahed o' his foolin',
    An' sez he: "I'll let him know—
Look hyeah, Moses, go tell Pher'oh
    Fu' to let dem chillun go."

"An' ef he refuse to do it,
    I will make him rue de houah,
Fu' I'll empty down on Egypt
    All de vials of my powah."
Yes, he did—an' Pher'oh's ahmy
    Was n't wuth a ha'f a dime;
Fu' de Lawd will he'p his chillun,
    You kin trust him evah time.

An' yo' enemies may 'sail you
    In de back an' in de front;
But de Lawd is all aroun' you,
    Fu' to ba' de battle's brunt.
Dey kin fo'ge yo' chains an' shackles
    F'om de mountains to de sea;
But de Lawd will sen' some Moses
    Fu' to set his chillun free.

An' de lan' shall hyeah his thundah,
    Lak a blas' f'om Gab'el's ho'n,
Fu' de Lawd of hosts is mighty
    When he girds his ahmor on.
But fu' feah some one mistakes me,
    I will pause right hyeah to say,
Dat I'm still a-preachin' ancient,
    I ain't talkin' 'bout to-day.

But I tell you, fellah christuns,
    Things 'll happen mighty strange;
Now, de Lawd done dis fu' Isrul,
    An' his ways don't nevah change,
An' de love he showed to Isrul
    Was n't all on Isrul spent;
Now don't run an' tell yo' mastahs
    Dat I's preachin' discontent.

'Cause I is n't; I'se a-judgin'
    Bible people by deir ac's;
I'se a-givin' you de Scriptuah,
    I'se a-handin' you de fac's.
Cose ole Pher'oh b'lieved in slav'ry
    But de Lawd he let him see,
Dat de people he put bref in,—
    Evah mothah's son was free.

An' dahs othahs thinks lak Pher'oh,
    But dey calls de Scriptuah liar,
Fu' de Bible says "a servant
    Is a-worthy of his hire."
An' you cain't git roun' nor thoo dat,
    An' you cain't git ovah it,
Fu' whatevah place you git in,
    Dis hyeah Bible too 'll fit.

So you see de Lawd's intention,
    Evah sence de worl' began,
Was dat His almighty freedom
    Should belong to evah man,
But I think it would be bettah,
    Ef I'd pause agin to say,
Dat I'm talkin' 'bout ouah freedom
    In a Bibleistic way.

But de Moses is a-comin',
    An' he's comin', suah and fas'
We kin hyeah his feet a-trompin',
    We kin hyeah his trumpit blas'.
But I want to wa'n you people,
    Don't you git too briggity;
An' don't you git to braggin'
    'Bout dese things, you wait an' see.

But when Moses wif his powah
    Comes an' sets us chillun free,
We will praise de gracious Mastah
    Dat has gin us liberty;
An' we'll shout ouah halleluyahs,
    On dat mighty reck'nin' day,
When we'se reco'nised ez citiz'—
    Huh uh! Chillun, let us pray!

We Wear the Mask

We wear the mask that grins and lies,
It hides our cheeks and shades our eyes,—
This debt we pay to human guile;
With torn and bleeding hearts we smile,
And mouth with myriad subtleties.

Why should the world be over-wise,
In counting all our tears and sighs?
Nay, let them only see us, while
    We wear the mask.

We smile, but, O great Christ, our cries
To thee from tortured souls arise.
We sing, but oh the clay is vile
Beneath our feet, and long the mile;
But let the world dream otherwise,
    We wear the mask.

The Poet

He sang of life, serenely sweet.
    With, now and then, a deeper note.
    From some high peak, nigh yet remote,
He voiced the world's absorbing beat.

He sang of love when earth was young,
    And Love, itself, was in his lays.
    But ah, the world, it turned to praise
A jingle in a broken tongue.

Ere Sleep Comes Down to Soothe the Weary Eyes

Ere sleep comes down to soothe the weary eyes,
Which all the day with ceaseless care have sought
The magic gold which from the seeker flies;
Ere dreams put on the gown and cap of thought,
And make the waking world a world of lies,—
Of lies most palpable, uncouth, forlorn,
That say life's full of aches and tears and sighs,—
Oh, how with more than dreams the soul is torn,
Ere sleep comes down to soothe the weary eyes.

Ere sleep comes down to soothe the weary eyes,
How all the griefs and heartaches we have known
Come up like pois'nous vapors that arise
From some base witch's caldron, when the crone,
To work some potent spell, her magic plies.
The past which held its share of bitter pain,
Whose ghost we prayed that Time might exorcise,
Comes up, is lived and suffered o'er again,
Ere sleep comes down to soothe the weary eyes.

Ere sleep comes down to soothe the weary eyes,
What phantoms fill the dimly lighted room;
What ghostly shades in awe-creating guise
Are bodied forth within the teeming gloom.
What echoes faint of sad and soul-sick cries,
And pangs of vague inexplicable pain
That pay the spirit's ceaseless enterprise,
Come thronging through the chambers of the brain,
Ere sleep comes down to soothe the weary eyes.

Ere sleep comes down to soothe the weary eyes,
Where ranges forth the spirit far and free?
Through what strange realms and unfamiliar skies
Tends her far course to lands of mystery?
To lands unspeakable—beyond surmise,
Where shapes unknowable to being spring,
Till, faint of wing, the Fancy fails and dies
Much wearied with the spirit's journeying,
Ere sleep comes down to soothe the weary eyes.

Ere sleep comes down to soothe the weary eyes,
How questioneth the soul that other soul,—
The inner sense which neither cheats nor lies,
But self exposes unto self, a scroll
Full writ with all life's acts unwise or wise,
In characters indelible and known;
So, trembling with the shock of sad surprise,
The soul doth view its awful self alone,
Ere sleep comes down to soothe the weary eyes.

Ere sleep comes down to soothe the weary eyes,
The last dear sleep whose soft embrace is balm,
And whom sad sorrow teaches us to prize
For kissing all our passions into calm,
Ah, then, no more we heed the sad world's cries,
Or seek to probe th' eternal mystery,
Or fret our souls at long-withheld replies,
At glooms through which our visions cannot see,
Ere sleep comes down to soothe the weary eyes.

The Lynching of Jube Benson

Gordon Fairfax's library held but three men, but the air was dense with clouds of smoke. The talk had drifted from one topic to another much as the smoke wreaths had puffed, floated, and thinned away. Then Handon Gay, who was an ambitious young reporter, spoke of a lynching story in a recent magazine, and the matter of punishment without trial put new life into the conversation.

"I should like to see a real lynching," said Gay rather callously.

"Well, I should hardly express it that way," said Fairfax, "but if a real, live lynching were to come my way, I should not avoid it."

"I should," spoke the other from the depths of his chair, where he had been puffing in moody silence. Judged by his hair, which was freely sprinkled with gray, the speaker might have been a man of forty-five or fifty, but his face, though lined and serious, was youthful, the face of a man hardly past thirty.

"What! you, Dr. Melville? Why, I thought that you physicians wouldn't weaken at anything."

"I have seen one such affair," said the doctor gravely; "in fact, I took a prominent part in it."

"Tell us about it," said the reporter, feeling for his pencil and notebook, which he was, nevertheless, careful to hide from the speaker.

The men drew their chairs eagerly up to the doctor's, but for a minute he did not seem to see them, but sat gazing abstractedly into the fire; then he took a long draw upon his cigar and began:

"I can see it all very vividly now. It was in the summertime and about seven years ago. I was practicing at the time down in the little town of Bradford. It was a small and primitive place, just the location for an impecunious medical man, recently out of college.

"In lieu of a regular office, I attended to business in the first of two rooms which I rented from Hiram Daly, one of the more prosperous of the townsmen. Here I boarded and here also came my patients—white and black—whites from every section, and blacks from 'nigger town,' as the west portion of the place was called.

"The people about me were most of them coarse and rough, but they were simple and generous, and as time passed on I had about abandoned my intention of seeking distinction in wider fields and determined to settle into the place of a modest country doctor. This was rather a strange conclusion for a young man to arrive at, and I will not deny that the presence in the house of my host's beautiful young daughter, Annie, had something to do with my decision. She was a girl of seventeen or eighteen, and very far superior to her surroundings. She had a native grace and a pleasing way about her that made everybody that came under her spell her abject slave. White and black who knew her loved her, and none, I thought, more deeply and respectfully than Jube Benson, the black man of all work about the place.

"He was a fellow whom everybody trusted—an apparently steady-going, grinning sort, as we used to call him. Well, he was completely under Miss Annie's thumb, and as soon as he saw that I began to care for Annie, and anybody could see that, he transferred some of his allegiance to me and became my faithful servitor also. Never did a man have a more devoted adherent in his wooing than did I, and many a one of Annie's tasks which he volunteered to do gave her an extra hour with me. You can imagine that I liked the boy, and you need not wonder any more that, as both wooing and my practice waxed apace, I was content to give up my great ambitions and stay just where I was.

"It wasn't a very pleasant thing, then, to have an epidemic of typhoid break out in the town that kept me going so that I hardly had time for the courting that a fellow wants to carry on with his sweetheart while he is still young enough to call her his girl. I fumed, but duty was duty, and I kept to my work night and day. It was now that Jube proved how invaluable he was as coadjutor. He not only took messages to Annie, but brought sometimes little ones from her to me, and he would tell me little secret things that he had overheard her say that made me throb with joy and swear at him for repeating his mistress's conversation. But, best of all, Jube was a perfect Cerberus, and no one on earth could have been more effective in keeping away or deluding the other young fellows who visited the

Dalys. He would tell me of it afterwards, chuckling softly to himself, 'An,' Doctah, I say to Mistah Hemp Stevens, " 'Scuse us, Mistah Stevens, but Miss Annie, she des gone out," an' den he go outer de gate lookin' moughty lonesome. When Sam Elkins come, I say, "Sh, Mistah Elkins, Miss Annie, she done tuk down," an' he say, "What, Jube, you don' reckon hit de—" Den he stop an' look skeert, an' I say, "I feared hit is, Mistah Elkins," an' sheks my haid ez solemn. He goes outer de gate lookin' lak his bes' frien' done daid, an' all de time Miss Annie behine de cu'tain ovah de po'ch des a-laffin' fit to kill.'

"Jube was a most admirable liar, but what could I do? He knew that I was a young fool of a hypocrite, and when I would rebuke him for these deceptions, he would give way and roll on the floor in an excess of delighted laughter until from very contagion I had to join him—and, well, there was no need of my preaching when there had been no beginning to his repentance and when there must ensue a continuance of his wrong-doing.

"This thing went on for over three months, and then, pouf! I was down like a shot. My patients were nearly all up, but the reaction from overwork made me an easy victim of the lurking germs. Then Jube loomed up as a nurse. He put everyone else aside, and with the doctor, a friend of mine from a neighboring town, took entire charge of me. Even Annie herself was put aside, and I was cared for as tenderly as a baby. Tom, that was my physician and friend, told me all about it afterward with tears in his eyes. Only he was a big, blunt man, and his expressions did not convey all that he meant. He told me how Jube had nursed me as if I were a sick kitten and he my mother. Of how fiercely he guarded his right to be the sole one to 'do' for me, as he called it, and how, when the crisis came, he hovered, weeping but hopeful, at my bedside until it was safely passed, when they drove him, weak and exhausted, from the room. As for me, I knew little about it at the time, and cared less. I was too busy in my fight with death. To my chimerical vision there was only a black but gentle demon that came and went, alternating with a white fairy, who would insist on coming in on her head, growing larger and larger and then dissolving. But the pathos and devotion in the story lost nothing in my blunt friend's telling.

"It was during the period of a long convalescence, however, that I came to know my humble ally as he really was, devoted to the point of abjectness. There were times when, for very shame at his goodness to me, I would beg him to go away, to do something else. He would go, but before I had time to realize that I was not being ministered to, he would be back at my side, grinning and puttering just the same. He manufactured duties for the joy of performing them. He pretended to see desires in me that I never had, because he liked to pander to them, and when I became entirely exasperated and ripped out a good round oath, he chuckled with the remark, 'Dah, now, you sholy is gittin' well. Nevah did hyeah a man anywhaih nigh Jo'dan's sho' cuss lak dat.'

"Why, I grew to love him, love him, oh, yes, I loved him as well—oh, what am I saying? All human love and gratitude are damned poor things; excuse me, gentlemen, this isn't a pleasant story. The truth is usually a nasty thing to stand.

"It was not six months after that that my friendship to Jube, which he had been at such great pains to win, was put to too severe a test.

"It was in the summertime again, and, as business was slack, I had ridden over to see my friend, Dr. Tom. I had spent a good part of the day there, and it was past four o'clock when I rode leisurely into Bradford. I was in a particularly joyous mood and no premonition of the impending catastrophe oppressed me. No sense of sorrow, present or to come, forced itself upon me, even when I saw men hurrying through the almost deserted streets. When I got within sight of my home and saw a crowd surrounding it, I was only interested sufficiently to spur my horse into a jog trot, which brought me up to the throng, when something in the sullen, settled horror in the men's faces gave me a sudden, sick thrill. They whispered a word to me, and without a thought save for Annie, the girl who had been so surely growing into my heart, I leaped from the saddle and tore my way through the people to the house.

"It was Annie, poor girl, bruised and bleeding, her face and dress torn from struggling. They were gathered round her with white faces, and oh! with what terrible patience they were trying to gain from her fluttering lips the name of her murderer. They made way for me and I knelt at her side. She was beyond my skill, and my will merged with theirs. One thought was in our minds.

" 'Who?' I asked.

"Her eyes half opened. 'That black—' She fell back into my arms dead.

"We turned and looked at each other. The mother had broken down and was weeping, but the face of the father was like iron.

" 'It is enough,' he said; 'Jube has disappeared.' He went to the door and said to the expectant crowd, 'She is dead.'

"I heard the angry roar without swelling up like the noise of a flood, and then I heard the sudden movement of many feet as the men separated into searching parties, and laying the dead girl back upon her couch, I took my rifle and went out to join them.

"As if by intuition the knowledge had passed among the men that Jube Benson had disappeared, and he, by comment consent, was to be the object of our search. Fully a dozen of the citizens had seen him hastening toward the woods and noted his skulking air, but as he had grinned in his old good-natured way, they had, at the time, thought nothing of it. Now, however, the diabolical reason of his slyness was apparent. He had been shrewd enough to disarm suspicion, and by now was far away. Even Mrs. Daly, who was visiting with a neighbor, had seen him stepping out by a back way, and had said with a laugh, 'I reckon that black rascal's a-running off somewhere.' Oh, if she had only known!

" 'To the woods! To the woods!' that was the cry; and away we went, each with the determination not to shoot, but to bring the culprit alive into town, and then to deal with him as his crime deserved.

"I cannot describe the feelings I experienced as I went out that night to beat the woods for this human tiger. My heart smoldered within me like a coal, and I went forward under the impulse of a will that was half my own, half some more malignant power's. My throat throbbed drily, but water or whisky would not have quenched my thirst. The thought has come to me since, that now I could interpret the panther's desire for blood and sympathize with it, but then I thought nothing. I simply went forward and watched, watched with burning eyes for a familiar form that I had looked for as often before with such different emotions.

"Luck or ill-luck, which you will, was with our party, and just as dawn was graying the sky, we came upon our quarry crouched in the corner of a fence. It was only half light, and we might have passed, but my eyes caught sight of him, and I raised the cry. We leveled our guns and he rose and came toward us.

" 'I t'ought you wa'n't gwine see me,' he said sullenly; 'I didn't mean no harm.'

" 'Harm!'

"Some of the men took the word up with oaths, others were ominously silent.

"We gathered around him like hungry beasts, and I began to see terror dawning in his eyes. He turned to me, 'I's moughty glad you's hyeah, Doc,' he said; 'you ain't gwine let 'em whup me.'

" 'Whip you, you hound,' I said, 'I'm going to see you hanged,' and in the excess of my passion I struck him full on the mouth. He made a motion as if to resent the blow against such great odds, but controlled himself.

" 'W'y, Doctah,' he exclaimed in the saddest voice I have ever heard, 'w'y, Doctah! I ain't stole nuffin' o' yo'n, an' I was comin' back. I only run off to see my gal, Lucy, ovah to de Centah.

" 'You lie!' I said, and my hands were busy helping others bind him upon a horse. Why did I do it? I don't know. A false education, I reckon, one false from the beginning. I saw his black face glooming there in the half light, and I could only think of him as a monster. It's tradition. At first I was told that the black man would catch me, and when I got over that, they taught me that the devil was black, and when I recovered from the sickness of that belief, here were Jube and his fellows with faces of menacing blackness. There was only one conclusion: This black man stood for all the powers of evil, the result of whose machinations had been gathering in my mind from childhood up. But this has nothing to do with what happened.

"After firing a few shots to announce our capture, we rode back into town with Jube. The ingathering parties from all directions met us as we made our way up to the house. All was very quiet and orderly. There was no doubt that it was, as the papers would have said, a gathering of the best citizens. It was a gathering of stern, determined men, bent on a terrible vengeance.

"We took Jube into the house, into the room where the corpse lay. At the sight of it he gave a scream like an animal's, and his face went the color of storm-blown water. This was enough to condemn him. We divined rather than heard his cry of 'Miss Ann, Miss Ann; oh, my God! Doc, you don't t'ink I done it?'

"Hungry hands were ready. We hurried him out into the yard. A rope was ready. A tree was at hand. Well, that part was the least of it, save that Hiram Daly stepped aside to let me be the first to pull upon the rope. It was lax at first. Then it tightened, and I felt the quivering soft weight resist my muscles. Other hands joined and Jube swung off his feet.

"No one was masked. We knew each other. Not even the culprit's face was covered, and the last I remember of him as he went into the air was a look of sad reproach that will remain with me until I meet him face to face again.

"We were tying the end of the rope to a tree, where the dead man might hang as a warning to his fellows, when a terrible cry chilled us to the marrow.

" 'Cut 'im down, cut 'im down; he ain't guilty. We got de one. Cut him down, fu' Gawd's sake. Here's de man; we foun' him hidin' in de barn!'

"Jube's brother, Ben, and another Negro came rushing toward us, half dragging, half carrying a miserable-looking wretch between them. Someone cut the rope and Jube dropped lifeless to the ground.

" 'Oh, my Gawd, he's daid, he's daid!' wailed the brother, but with blazing eyes he brought his captive into the center of the group, and we saw in the full light the scratched face of Tom Skinner, the worst white ruffian in town; but the face we saw was not as we were accustomed to see it, merely smeared with dirt. It was blackened to imitate a Negro's.

"God forgive me; I could not wait to try to resuscitate Jube. I knew he was already past help; so I rushed into the house and to the dead girl's side. In the excitement they had not yet washed or laid her out. Carefully, carefully, I searched underneath her broken fingernails. There was skin there. I took it out, the little curled pieces, and went with it into my office.

"There, determinedly, I examined it under a powerful glass, and read my own doom. It was the skin of a white man, and in it were embedded strands of short brown hair or beard.

"How I went out to tell the waiting crowd I do not know, for something kept crying in my ears, 'Blood guilty! Blood guilty!'

"The men went away stricken into silence and awe. The new prisoner attempted neither denial nor plea. When they were gone, I would have helped Ben carry his brother in, but he waved me away fiercely. 'You he'ped murder my brothah, you dat was his frien'; go 'way, go 'way! I'll tek him home myse'f.' I could only respect his wish, and he and his comrade took up the dead man and between them bore him up the street on which the sun was now shining full.

"I saw the few men who had not skulked indoors uncover as they passed, and I—I—stood there between the two murdered ones, while all the while something in my ears kept crying 'Blood guilty! Blood guilty!' "

The doctor's head dropped into his hands and he sat for some time in silence, which was broken by neither of the men; then he rose, saying, "Gentlemen, that was my last lynching."

KELLY MILLER

(1863-1939)

During the first years of the new century, when the debate between Booker T. Washington and W. E. B. Du Bois delineated the poles of black thinking on many issues, Kelly Miller represented the view of a great many intellectuals who favored adopting a middle ground. A leading educator and essayist of his time, he was influential in molding opinions of black leaders for the first quarter of the century.

Kelly Miller was born in Winnsboro, South Carolina, during the Civil War. His boyhood years saw the abridgement of black people's civil rights and the tides of racial hatred and violence that took place South and North during Reconstruction and the years that followed. Miller was educated at Howard University and Johns Hopkins, then became a teacher of mathematics and eventually a dean at Howard University. He was active in many of the attempts to resolve the "Negro problem," and was a well-known lecturer and writer of articles, essays, and pamphlets.

Miller agreed with Booker T. Washington that industrial education was desirable for black people, but he insisted that in order for the race to rise economically and politically it was also necessary for a large number of young people to receive higher education. Miller felt that the solution to the race problem lay in racial unity and in political and economic independence. As he grew older he tended more to the side of the protesters than to that of the accommodaters.

As an essayist Miller wrote in a clear, straightforward style. His emotion is restrained but clearly evident, especially in the later essays. He makes effective use of time-honored rhetorical devices such as analogy, contrast, and exemplification. His works are deliberate and scholarly but not pedantic. His tone is moderate, for he is attempting to harmonize divergent views in search of the racial solidarity he espoused. In general, Miller's views are outdated in terms of today's conditions and attitudes. His works are worthy of study because of their statement of the problem and their demonstration of the thinking of many Negro leaders.

Miller's essays are collected in several volumes. The first, Race Adjustment *(1908), expresses his early, more conservative views. The essays in* Out of the House of Bondage *(1914) present his views on education, politics, crime, and other aspects of Afro-America fifty years after emancipation.* An Appeal to Conscience *(1918) reflects Miller's increased militancy after World War I. The element of protest is presented with moderation, but also with firmness and logic. Other works by Miller are the* History of the World War and the Important Part Taken by the Negroes *(1919) and* The Everlasting Stain *(1924).*

An Open Letter to Thomas Dixon, Jr.

September, 1905.

Mr. Thomas Dixon, Jr.

Dear Sir:—

I am writing you this letter to express the attitude and feeling of
ten millions of your fellow citizens toward the evil propagandism of
race animosity to which you have lent your great literary powers.
Through the widespread influence of your writings you have become
the chief priest of those who worship at the shrine of race hatred and
wrath. This one spirit runs through all your books and published
utterances, like the recurrent theme of an opera. As the general trend
of your doctrine is clearly epitomized and put forth in your contribution to the *Saturday Evening Post* of August 19, I beg to consider
chiefly the issues therein raised. You are a white man born in the midst
of the civil war, I am a Negro born during the same stirring epoch.
You were born with a silver spoon in your mouth, I was born with an
iron hoe in my hand. Your race has inflicted accumulated injury and
wrong upon mine, mine has borne yours only service and good will.
You express your views with the most scathing frankness; I am sure,
you will welcome an equally candid expression from me.

Permit me to acknowledge the personal consideration which you
have shown me. You will doubtless recall that when I addressed The
Congregational Ministers, of New York City, some year or more ago,
you asked permission to be present and listened attentively to what I
had to say, although as might have been expected, you beat a precipi-
tous retreat when luncheon was announced. In your article in the
Post you make several references to me and to other colored men
with entire personal courtesy. So far as I know you have never
varied from this rule in your personal dealings with members of my

race. You are merciless, however, in excoriating the race as a whole, thus keenly wounding the sensibilities of every individual of that blood. I assure you that this courtesy of personal treatment will be reciprocated in this letter, however sharply I may be compelled to take issue with the views you set forth and to deplore your attitude. I shall endeavor to indulge in no bitter word against your race nor against the South, whose exponent and special pleader you assume to be.

I fear that you have mistaken personal manners, the inevitable varnish of any gentleman of your antecedents and rearing, for friendship to a race which you hold in despite. You tell us that you are kind and considerate to your personal servants. It is somewhat strange that you should deem such assurance necessary, any more than it is necessary for you to assure us that you are kind to and fond of your horse or your dog. But when you write yourself down as "one of their best friends," you need not be surprised if we retort the refrain of the ritual: "From all such proffers of friendship, good Lord deliver us."

Your fundamental thesis is that "no amount of education of any kind, industrial, classical or religious, can make a Negro a white man or bridge the chasm of the centuries which separates him from the white man in the evolution of human history." This doctrine is as old as human oppression. Calhoun made it the arch stone in the defense of Negro slavery—and lost.

This is but a recrudescence of the doctrine which was exploited and exploded during the antislavery struggle. Do you recall the school of proslavery scientists who demonstrated beyond doubt that the Negro's skull was too thick to comprehend the substance of Aryan knowledge? Have you not read in the discredited scientific books of that period, with what triumphant acclaim it was shown that the Negro's shape and size of skull, facial angle, and cephalic configuration rendered him forever impervious to the white man's civilization? But all enlightened minds are now as ashamed of that doctrine as they are of the onetime dogma that the Negro had no soul. We become aware of mind through its manifestations. Within forty years of only partial opportunity, while playing as it were in the back yard of civilization, the American Negro has cut down his illiteracy by over fifty per cent; has produced a professional class, some fifty thousand strong, including ministers, teachers, doctors, lawyers, editors, authors, architects, engineers and all higher lines of listed pursuits in which white men are engaged; some three thousand Negroes have taken collegiate degrees, over three hundred being from the best institutions in the North and West established for the most favored white youth; there is scarcely a first-class institution in America, excepting some three or four in the South, that is without colored students who pursue their studies generally with success, and sometimes with distinction; Negro inventors have taken out four hundred patents as a contribution to the mechanical genius of America; there are scores of Negroes who, for conceded ability and achievements, take respectable rank in the company of distinguished Americans.

It devolves upon you, Mr. Dixon, to point out some standard, either of intelligence, character, or conduct to which the Negro can not conform. Will you please tell a waiting world just what is the psychological difference between the races? No reputable authority, either of the old or the new school of psychology, has yet pointed out any sharp psychic discriminant. There is not a single intellectual, moral, or spiritual excellence attained by the white race to which the Negro does not yield an appreciative response. If you could show that the Negro was incapable of mastering the intricacies of Aryan speech, that he could not comprehend the intellectual basis of European culture, or apply the apparatus of practical knowledge, that he could not be made amenable to the white man's ethical code or appreciate his spiritual motive, then your case would be proved. But in default of such demonstration, we must relegate your eloquent pronouncement to the realm of generalization and prophecy, an easy and agreeable exercise of the mind in which the romancer is ever prone to indulge.

The inherent, essential, and unchangeable inferiority of the Negro to the white man lies at the basis of your social philosophy. You disdain to examine the validity of your fondly cherished hope. You follow closely in the wake of Tom Watson, in the June number of his homonymous magazine. You both hurl your thesis of innate racial inferiority at the head of Booker T. Washington. You use the same illustrations, the same arguments, set forth in the same order of recital, and for the most part in identical language. This seems to be an instance of great minds, or at least of minds of the same grade, running in the same channel.

These are your words: "What contribution to human progress have the millions of Africa who inhabit this planet made during the past four thousand years? Absolutely nothing." These are the words of Thomas Watson spoken some two months previous: "What does civilization owe to the Negro race? Nothing! Nothing!! Nothing!!!" You answer the query with the most emphatic negative noun and the strongest qualifying adjective in the language. Mr. Watson, of a more ecstatic temperament, replies with the same noun and six exclamation points. One rarely meets, outside of yellow journalism, with such lavishness of language, wasted upon a hoary dogma. A discredited dictum that has been bandied about the world from the time of Canaan to Calhoun, is revamped and set forth with as much ardor and fervency of feeling as if discovered for the first time and proclaimed for the illumination of a waiting world.

But neither boastful asseveration on your part nor indignant denial on mine will affect the facts of the case. That Negroes in the average are not equal in developed capacity to the white race, is a proposition which it would be as simple to affirm as it is silly to deny. The Negro represents a backward race which has not yet taken a commanding part in the progressive movement of the world. In the great cosmic scheme of things, some races reach the limelight of civilization ahead of others. But that temporary forwardness does not argue inherent superiority is as evident as any fact of history. An unfriendly environment may hinder and impede the one, while fortunate circumstances may quicken and spur the other. Relative superiority is only a transient phase of human development. You tell us that "The Jew had achieved a civilization—had his poets, prophets, priests, and kings, when our Germanic ancestors were still in the woods cracking cocoanuts and hickory-nuts with the monkeys." Fancy some learned Jew at that day citing your query about the contribution of the Germanic races to the culture of the human spirit, during the thousands of years of their existence! Does the progress of history not prove that races may lie dormant and fallow for ages and then break suddenly into prestige and power? Fifty years ago you doubtless would have ranked Japan among the benighted nations and hurled at their heathen heads some derogatory query as to their contribution to civilization. But since the happenings at Mukden and Port Arthur, and Portsmouth, I suppose that you are ready to change your mind. Or maybe since the Jap has proved himself "a first-class fighting man," able to cope on equal terms with the best breeds in Europe, you will claim him as belonging to the white race, notwithstanding his pig eye and yellow pigment.

The Negro enters into the inheritance of all the ages on equal terms with the rest, and who can say that he will not contribute his quota of genius to enrich the blood of the world?

The line of argument of every writer who undertakes to belittle the Negro is a well-beaten path. Liberia and Haiti are bound to come in for their share of ridicule and contemptuous handling. Mr. Watson calls these experiments freshly to mind, lest we forget. We are told all about the incapacity of the black race for self-government, the relapse into barbarism and much more of which we have heard before; and yet when we take all the circumstances into account, Haiti presents to the world one of the most remarkable achievements in the annals of human history. The panegyric of Wendell Phillips on Toussaint L'Ouverture is more than an outburst of rhetorical fancy; it is a just measure of his achievements in terms of his humble environment and the limited instrumentalities at his command. Where else in the course of history has a slave, with the aid of slaves, expelled a powerfully intrenched master class, and set up a government patterned after civilized models and which without external assistance or reinforcement from a parent civilization, has endured for a hundred years in face of a frowning world? When we consider the difficulties that confront a weak government, without military or naval means to cope with its more powerful rivals, and where commercial adventurers are ever and anon stirring up internal strife, thus provoking the intervention of stronger governments, the marvel is that the republic of Haiti still endures, the only self-governing state of the Antilles. To expect as effective and proficient government to prevail in Haiti as at Washington would be expecting more of the black men in Haiti than we find in the white men of South America. And yet, I suspect that the million Negroes in Haiti are as well governed as the corresponding number of blacks in Georgia, where only yesterday eight men were taken from the custody of the law and lynched without judge or jury. It is often charged that these people have not maintained the pace set by the old master class, that the plantations are in ruin and that the whole island wears the aspect of dilapidation. Wherever a lower people overrun the civilization of a higher, there is an inevitable lapse toward the level of the lower. When barbarians and semi-civilized hordes of northern Europe overran the southern peninsulas, the civilization of the world was wrapped in a thousand years of darkness. Relapse inevitably precedes the rebound. Is there anything in the history of Haiti contrary to the law of human development?

You ask: "Can you change the color of the Negro's skin, the kink of his hair, the bulge of his lip, or the beat of his heart, with a spelling book or a machine?" This rhetorical outburst does great credit to your literary skill, and is calculated to delight the simple; but analysis fails to reveal in it any pregnant meaning. Since civilization is not an attribute of the color of skin, or curl of hair, or curve of lip, there is no necessity for changing such physical peculiarities, and if there was, the spelling book and the machine would be very unlikely instruments for its accomplishment. But why, may I ask, would you desire to change the Negro's heart throb, which already beats at a normal human pace? You need not be so frantic about the superiority of your race. Whatever superiority it may possess, inherent or acquired, will take care of itself without such rabid support. Has it ever occurred to you that the people of New England blood, who have done and are doing most to make the white race great and glorious in this land, are the most reticent about extravagant claims to everlasting superiority? You protest too much. Your loud pretensions, backed up by such exclamatory outbursts of passion, make upon the reflecting mind the impression that you entertain a sneaking suspicion of their validity.

Your position as to the work and worth of Booker T. Washington is pitiably anomalous. You recite the story of his upward struggle with uncontrolled admiration: "The story of this little ragged, barefooted pickaninny, who lifted his eyes from a cabin in the hills of Virginia, saw a vision and followed it, until at last he presides over the richest and most powerful institution in the South, and sits down with crowned heads and presidents, has no parallel even in the Tales of the Arabian Nights." You say that his story appeals to the universal heart of humanity. And yet in a recent letter to the *Columbia States,* you regard it as an unspeakable outrage that Mr. Robert C. Ogden should walk arm in arm with this wonderful man who "appeals to the heart of universal humanity," and introduce him to the lady clerks in a dry goods store. Your passionate devotion to a narrow dogma has seriously impaired your sense of humor. The subject of your next great novel has been announced as "The Fall of Tuskegee." In one breath you commend the work of this great institution, while in another you condemn it because it does not fit into your preconceived scheme in the solution of the race problem. The Tuskegee ideal: "to make Negroes producers, lovers of labor, independent, honest, and good" is one which you say that only a fool or a knave can find fault with, because, in your own words, "it rests squarely upon the eternal verities." Over against this you add with all the condemnatory emphasis of italics and exclamation point: "*Tuskegee is not a servant training school!*" And further: "Mr. Washington is not training Negroes to take their places in the industries of the South in which white men direct and control them. He is not training students to be servants and come at the beck and call of any man. He is training them to be masters of men, to be independent, to own and operate their own industries, plant their own field, buy and sell their own goods." All of which you condemn by imperative inference ten times stronger than your faint and forced verbal approval. It is a heedless man who wilfully flaunts his little philosophy in the face of "the eternal verities." When the wise man finds that his prejudices are running against fixed principles in God's cosmic plan, he speedily readjusts them in harmony therewith. Has it never occurred to you to reexamine the foundation of the faith, as well as the feeling, that is in you, since you admit that it runs afoul of the "eternal verities?"

Mr. Washington's motto, in his own words, is that "the Negro has been worked; but now he must learn to work." The man who works for himself is of more service to any community than the man whose labor is exploited by others. You bring forward the traditional bias of the slave regime to modern conditions, viz.: that the Negro did not exist in his own right and for his own sake, but for the benefit of the white man. This principle is as false in nature as it is in morals. The naturalists tell us that throughout all the range of animal creation, there is found no creature which exists for the sake of any other, but each is striving after its own best welfare. Do you fear that the Negro's welfare is incompatible with that of the white man? I commend to you a careful perusal of the words of Mr. E. Gardner Murphy who, like yourself, is a devoted Southerner, and is equally zealous to promote the highest interest of that section: "Have property, peace and happiness ever been successfully or permanently based upon indolence, inefficiency, and hopelessness? Since time began, has any human thing that God has made taken damage to itself or brought damage to the world through knowledge, truth, hope, and honest toil?" Read these words of your fellow Southerner, Mr. Dixon, meditate upon them; they will do you good as the truth doeth the upright heart.

You quote me as being in favor of the amalgamation of the races. A more careful reading of the article referred to would have convinced you that I was arguing against it as a probable solution of the race problem. I merely stated the intellectual conviction that two races cannot live indefinitely side by side, under the same general regime without ultimately fusing. This was merely the expression of a belief, and not the utterance of a preference nor the formulation of a policy. I know of no colored man who advocates amalgamation as a feasible policy of solution. You are mistaken. The Negro does not "hope and dream of amalgamation." This would be self-stultification with a vengeance. If such a policy were allowed to dominate the imagination of the race, its women would give themselves over to the unrestrained passion of white men, in quest of tawny offspring, which would give rise to a state of indescribable moral debauchery. At the same time you would hardly expect the Negro, in derogation of his common human qualities, to proclaim that he is so diverse from God's other human creatures as to make the blending of the races contrary to the law of nature. The Negro refuses to become excited or share in your frenzy on this subject. The amalgamation of the races is an ultimate possibility, though not an immediate probability. But what have you and I to do with ultimate questions, anyway? Our concern is with duty, not destiny.

But do you know, Mr. Dixon, that you are probably the foremost promoter of amalgamation between the two races? Wherever you narrow the scope of the Negro by preaching the doctrine of hate, you drive thousands of persons of lighter hue over to the white race carrying more or less Negro blood in their train. The blending of the races is less likely to take place if the self-respect and manly opportunity of the Negro are respected and encouraged, than if he is to be forever crushed beneath the level of his faculties for dread of the fancied result. Hundreds of the composite progeny are daily crossing the color line and carrying as much of the despised blood as an albicant skin can conceal without betrayal. I believe that it was Congressman Tillman, brother of the more famous Senator of that name, who stated on the floor of the constitutional convention of South Carolina, that he knew of four hundred white families in that State who had a taint of Negro blood in their veins. I personally know, or know of, fifty cases of transition in the city of Washington. It is a momentous thing for one to change his caste. The man or woman who affects to deny, ignore, or scorn the class with whom he previously associated is usually deemed deficient in the nobler qualities of human nature. It is not conceivable that persons of this class would undergo the self-degradation and humiliation of soul necessary to cross the great "social divide" unless it be to escape for themselves

and their descendants an odious and despised status. Your oft expressed and passionately avowed belief that the progressive development of the Negro would hasten amalgamation is not borne out by
the facts of observation. The refined and cultivated class among
colored people are as much disinclined to such unions as the whites
themselves. I am sorry that you saw fit to characterize Frederick
Douglass as "a bombastic vituperator." You thereby gave poignant
offense to ten millions of his race who regard him as the best embodi-
ment of their possibilities. Besides millions of your race rate him
among the foremost and best beloved of Americans. How would you
feel if some one should stigmatize Jefferson Davis or Robert E. Lee
in such language, these beau ideals of your Southern heart? But I
will not undertake to defend Frederick Douglass against your calum-
niations. I am frank to confess that I do not feel that he needs it.
The point I have in mind to make about Mr. Douglass is that he has
a hold upon the affection of his race, not on account of his second
marriage, but in spite of it. He seriously affected his standing with
his people by that marriage.

It seems to me, Mr. Dixon, that this frantic abhorrence of amalgamation is a little late in its appearance. Whence comes this stream of
white blood, which flows with more or less spissitude, in the veins
of some six out of ten million Negroes? The Afro-American is hardly
a Negro at all, except constructively; but a new creature. Who
brought about this present approachment between the races? Do you
not appreciate the inconsistency in the attitude and the action on the
part of many of the loudmouthed advocates of race purity? It is said
that old Father Chronos devoured his offspring in order to forestall
future complications. Bue we do not learn that he put a bridle upon
his passion as the surest means of security. The most effective service
you can render to check the evil of amalgamation is to do missionary
work among the males of your own race. This strenuous advocacy
of race purity in face of proved proneness for miscegenation affords
a striking reminder of the lines of Hudibras:—

The self-same thing they will abhor,
One way, and long another for.

Again, you say that "we have spent about $800,000,000 on Negro education since the war." This statement is so very wide of the mark, that I was disposed to regard it as a misprint, if you had not reinforced it with an application implying a like amount. In the report of the Bureau of Education for 1901, the estimated expenditure for Negro education in all the former slave States since the Civil War was put down at $121,184,568. The amount contributed by Northern philanthropy during that interval is variously estimated from fifty to seventy-five millions. Your estimate is four times too large. It would be interesting and informing to the world if you would reveal the source of your information. These misstatements of fact are not of so much importance in themselves, as that they serve to warn the reader against the accuracy and value of your general judgments. It would seem that your derive your figures of arithmetic from the same source from which you fashion your figures of speech. You will not blame the reader for not paying much heed to your sweeping generalizations, when you are at such little pains as to the accuracy of easily ascertainable data.

Your proposed solution of the race problem by colonizing the Negroes in Liberia reaches the climax of absurdity. It is difficult to see how such a proposition could emanate from a man of your reputation. Did you consult Cram's Atlas about Liberia? Please do so. You will find that it has an area of 48,000 square miles and a population of 1,500,000, natives and immigrants. The area and population are about the same as those of North Carolina, which, I believe, is your native State. When you tell us that this restricted area, without commerce, without manufacture, without any system of organized industry, can support every Negro in America, in addition to its present population, I beg mildly to suggest that you recall your plan for revision before submitting it to the judgment of a critical world. Your absolute indifference to and heedlessness of the facts, circumstances, and conditions involved in the scheme of colonization well befit the absurdity of the general proposition.

The solution of the race problem in America is indeed a grave and serious matter. It is one that calls for statesmanlike breadth of view, philanthropic tolerance of spirit, and exact social knowledge. The whole spirit of your propaganda is to add to its intensity and aggravation. You stir the slumbering fires of race wrath into an uncontrollable flame. I have read somewhere that Max Nordau, on reading *The Leopard's Spots*, wrote to you suggesting the awful responsibility you had assumed in stirring up enmity between race and race. Your teachings subvert the foundations of law and established order. You are the high priest of lawlessness, the prophet of anarchy. Rudyard Kipling places this sentiment in the mouth of the reckless stealer of seals in the Northern Sea: "There's never a law of God nor man runs north of fifty-three." This description exactly fits the brand of literature with which you are flooding the public. You openly urge your fellow citizens to override all law, human and divine. Are you aware of the force and effect of these words? "Could fatuity reach a sublimer height than the idea that the white man will stand idly by and see the performance? What will he do when put to the test? He will do exactly what his white neighbor in the North does when the Negro threatens his bread—kill him!" These words breathe out hatred and slaughter and suggest the murder of innocent men whose only crime is quest for the God-given right to work. You poison the mind and pollute the imagination through the subtle influence of letters. Are you aware of the force and effect of evil suggestion when the passions of men are in a state of unstable equilibrium? A heterogeneous population, where the elements are, on any account, easily distinguishable, is an easy prey for the promotor of wrath. The fuse is already prepared for the spark. The soul of the mob is stirred by suggestion of hatred and slaughter, as a famished beast at the smell of blood. The rabble responds so much more readily to an appeal to passion than to reason. To wantonly stir up the fires of race antipathy is as execrable a deed as flaunting a red rag in the face of a bull at a summer's picnic, or raising a false cry of "fire" in a crowded house. Human society could not exist one hour except on the basis of law, which holds the baser passions of men in restraint.

In our complex situation it is only the rigid observance of law re-enforced by higher moral restraint that can keep these passions in bound. You speak about giving the Negro a "square deal." Even among gamblers, a "square deal" means to play according to the rules of the game. The rules which all civilized States have set for themselves are found in the Ten Commandments, the Golden Rule, the Sermon on the Mount, and the organic law of the land. You acknowledge no such restraints when the Negro is involved, but waive them all aside with frenzied defiance. You preside at every crossroad lynching of a helpless victim; wherever the midnight murderer rides with rope and torch, in quest of the blood of his black brother, you ride by his side; wherever the cries of the crucified victim go up to God from the crackling flame, behold you are there; when women and children, drunk with ghoulish glee, dance around the funeral pyre and mock the death groans of their fellow man and fight for ghastly souvenirs, you have your part in the inspiration of it all. When guilefully guided workmen in mine and shop and factory, goaded by a real or imaginary sense of wrong, begin the plunder and pillage of property and murder of rival men, your suggestion is justifier of the dastardly doings. Lawlessness is gnawing at the very vitals of our institutions. It is the surpreme duty of every enlightened mind to allay rather than spur on this spirit. You are hastening the time when there is to be a positive and emphatic show of hands—not of white hands against black hands, God forbid; not of Northern hands against Southern hands, heaven forfend; but a determined show of those who believe in law and God and constituted order, against those who would undermine and destroy the organic basis of society, involving all in a common ruin. No wonder Max Nordau exclaimed: "God, man, are you aware of your responsibility!"

But do not think, Mr. Dixon, that when you evoke the evil spirit, you can exorcise him at will. The Negro in the end will be the least of his victims. Those who become inoculated with the virus of race hatred are more unfortunate than the victims of it. Voltaire tells us that it is more difficult and more meritorious to wean men of their prejudices than it is to civilize the barbarian. Race hatred is the most malignant poison that can afflict the mind. It freezes up the fount of inspiration and chills the higher faculties of the soul. You are a greater enemy to your own race than you are to mine.

I have written you thus fully in order that you may clearly understand how the case lies in the Negro's mind. If any show of feeling or bitterness of spirit crops out in the treatment or between the lines, it is wholly without vindictive intent; but is the inevitable outcome of dealing with issues that verge upon the deepest human passion.

Yours truly,
KELLY MILLER.

WILLIAM STANLEY BRAITHWAITE
(1878-1962)

*William Stanley Braithwaite was an astute critic and talent*ed *lyric poet whose editorial work gave impetus to the New Poetry movement in American literature. Born of West Indian ancestry in Boston, he had little formal education but taught himself through wide reading and careful observation. In addition to being a poet, Braithwaite became an editor with the* Boston Transcript *and* New Poetry Review. *He edited anthologies of Restoration, Georgian, and Victorian verse. From 1913 to 1929 he edited annual anthologies of magazine verse printing the early works of many modern masters. He contributed critical essays to such publications as* Forum, Scribner's, Century Magazine, *and* The Atlantic Monthly.

His own poems are contained in Lyrics of Life and Love *(1904),* The House of Falling Leaves *(1908) and* Selected Poems *(1948). His poems, written in a traditional nineteenth-century lyric style, are slight structures seeking philosophical truth as well as beauty. They are carefully executed, subtle, and often cryptic. They have nothing to do with the life of the black man of that time. Braithwaite felt that racial themes were too limiting for the artist to deal with and that they tended more toward propaganda than toward art.*

Twenty-three years after his first novel, The Canadian *(1901), Braithwaite wrote a second,* Going Over Tindel *(1924). Other prose works are* The House Under Arcturus: An Autobiography *(1940) and* The Bewitched Parsonage, *a biography of the Brontes.*

During the thirties and forties Braithwaite taught English litera-ture at Atlanta University, where he was a colleague of Du Bois.

Philip Butcher has edited The William Stanley Braithwaite Reader *(1972).*

The Watchers

Two women on the lone wet strand,
    (The wind's out with a will to roam)
The waves wage war on rocks and sand,
    (And a ship is long due home.)

The sea sprays in the women's eyes—
    (Hearts can writhe like the sea's wild foam)
Lower descend the tempestuous skies,
    (For the wind's out with a will to roam.)

"O daughter, thine eyes be better than mine,"
    (The waves ascend high as yonder dome)
"North or south is there never a sign?"
    (And a ship is long due home.)

They watcher there all the long night through—
    (The wind's out with a will to roam)
Wind and rain and sorrow for two,—
    (And heaven on the long reach home.)

Rhapsody

I am glad daylong for the gift of song,
For time and change and sorrow;
For the sunset wings and the world-end things
Which hang on the edge of tomorrow.
I am glad for my heart whose gates apart
Are the entrance-place of wonders,
Where dreams come in from the rush and din
Like sheep from the rains and thunders.

The Negro in American Literature

True to his origin on this continent, the Negro was projected into literature by an over-mastering and exploiting hand. In the generations that he has been so voluminously written and talked about he has been accorded as little artistic justice as social justice. Antebellum literature imposed the distortions of moralistic controversy and made the Negro a wax-figure of the market place: post-bellum literature retaliated with the condescending reactions of sentiment and caricature, and made the Negro a *genre* stereotype. Sustained, serious or deep study of Negro life and character has thus been entirely below the horizons of our national art. Only gradually through the dull purgatory of the Age of Discussion, has Negro life eventually issued forth to an Age of Expression.

Perhaps I ought to qualify this last statement that the Negro was *in* American literature generations before he was part of it as a creator. From his very beginning in this country the Negro has been, without the formal recognition of literature and art, creative. During more than two centuries of an enslaved peasantry, the race has been giving evidence, in song and story lore, of an artistic temperament and psychology precious for itself as well as for its potential use and promise in the sophisticated forms of cultural expression. Expressing itself with poignancy and a symbolic imagery unsurpassed, indeed, often unmatched, by any folk-group, the race in servitude was at the same time the finest national expression of emotion and imagination and the most precious mass of raw material for literature America was producing. Quoting these stanzas of James Weldon Johnson's *O Black and Unknown Bards*, I want you to catch the real point of its assertion of the Negro's way into domain of art:

> O black and unknown bards of long ago,
>   How came your lips to touch the sacred fire?
> How, in your darkness, did you come to know
>   The power and the beauty of the minstrel's lyre?
> Who first from midst his bonds lifted his eyes?
>   Who first from out the still watch, lone and long,
> Feeling the ancient faith of prophets rise
>   Within his dark-kept soul, burst into song?

How misdirected was the American imagination, how blinded by the dust of controversy and the pall of social hatred and oppression, not to have found it irresistibly urgent to make literary use of the imagination and emotion it possessed in such abundance.

Controversy and moral appeal gave us *Uncle Tom's Cabin,*— the first conspicuous example of the Negro as a subject for literary treatment. Published in 1852, it dominated in mood and attitude the American literature of a whole generation; until the body of Reconstruction literature with its quite different attitude came into vogue. Here was sentimentalized sympathy for a down-trodden race, but one in which was projected a character, in Uncle Tom himself, which has been unequalled in its hold upon the popular imagination to this day. But the moral gain and historical effect of Uncle Tom have an artistic loss and setback. The treatment of Negro life and character, overlaid with these forceful stereotypes, could not develop into artistically satisfactory portraiture.

Just as in the anti-slavery period, it had been impaled upon the dilemmas of controversy, Negro life with the Reconstruction, became involved in the paradoxes of social prejudice. Between the Civil War and the end of the century the subject of the Negro in literature is one that will some day inspire the literary historian with a magnificent theme. It will be magnificent not because there is any sharp emergence of character or incidents, but because of the immense paradox of racial life which came up thunderingly against the principles and doctrines of democracy, and put them to the severest test that they had known. But in literature, it was a period when Negro life was a shuttlecock between the two extremes of humor and pathos. The Negro was free, and was not free. The writers who dealt with him for the most part refused to see more than skin-deep, —the grin, the grimaces and the picturesque externalities. Occasionally there was some penetration into the heart and flesh of Negro characters, but to see more than the humble happy peasant would have been to flout the fixed ideas and conventions of an entire generation. For more than artistic reasons, indeed against them, these writers refused to see the tragedy of the Negro and capitalized his comedy. The social conscience had as much need for this comic mask as the Negro. However, if any of the writers of the period had possessed gifts of genius of the first caliber, they would have penetrated this deceptive exterior of Negro life, sounded the depths of tragedy in it, and produced a masterpiece.

American literature still feels the hold of this tradition and its indulgent sentimentalities. Irwin Russell was the first to discover the happy, care-free, humorous Negro. He became a fad. It must be sharply called to attention that the tradition of the ante-bellum Negro is a post-bellum product, stranger in truth than in fiction. Contemporary realism in American fiction has not only recorded his passing, but has thrown serious doubts upon his ever having been a very genuine and representative view of Negro life and character. At best this school of Reconstruction fiction represents the romanticized high-lights of a régime that as a whole was a dark, tragic canvas. At most, it presents a Negro true to type for less than two generations. Thomas Nelson Page, kindly perhaps, but with a distant view and a purely local imagination did little more than paint the conditions and attitudes of the period contemporary with his own manhood, the restitution of the over-lordship of the defeated slave owners in the Eighties. George W. Cable did little more than idealize the aristocratic tradition of the Old South with the Negro as a literary foil. The effects, though not the motives of their work, have been sinister. The "Uncle" and the "Mammy" traditions, unobjectionable as they are in the setting of their day and generation, and in the atmosphere of sentimental humor, can never stand as the great fiction of their theme and subject: the great period novel of the South has yet to be written. Moreover, these type pictures have degenerated into reactionary social fetishes, and from that descended into libelous artistic caricature of the Negro; which has hampered art quite as much as it has embarrassed the Negro.

Of all of the American writers of this period, Joel Chandler Harris has made the most permanent contribution in dealing with the Negro. There is in his work both a deepening of interest and technique. Here at least we have something approaching true portraiture. But much as we admire this lovable personality, we are forced to say that in the Uncle Remus stories the race was its own artist, lacking only in its illiteracy the power to record its speech. In the perspective of time and fair judgment the credit will be divided, and Joel Chandler Harris regarded as a sort of providentially provided amanuensis for preserving the folk tales and legends of a race. The three writers I have mentioned do not by any means exhaust the list of writers who put the Negro into literature during the last half of the nineteenth century. Mr. Howells added a shadowy note to his social record of American life with *An Imperative Duty* and prophesied the Fiction of the Color Line. But his moral scruples—the persistent artistic vice in all his novels—prevented him from consummating a just union between his heroine with a touch of Negro blood and his hero. It is useless to consider any others, because there were none who succeeded in creating either a great story or a great character out of Negro life. Two writers of importance I am reserving for discussion in the group of Negro writers I shall consider presently. One ought perhaps to say in justice to the writers I have mentioned that their non-success was more largely due to the limitations of their social view than of their technical resources. As white Americans of their day, it was incompatible with their conception of the inequalities between the races to glorify the Negro into the serious and leading position of hero or heroine in fiction. Only one man that I recall, had the moral and artistic courage to do this, and he was Stephen Crane in a short story called *The Monster*. But Stephen Crane was a genius, and therefore could not besmirch the integrity of an artist.

With Thomas Dixon, of *The Leopard's Spots*, we reach a distinct stage in the treatment of the Negro in fiction. The portraiture here descends from caricature to libel. A little later with the vogue of the "darkey-story," and its devotees from Kemble and McAllister to Octavus Roy Cohen, sentimental comedy in the portrayal of the Negro similarly degenerated to blatant but diverting farce. Before the rise of a new attitude, there represented the bottom reaction, both in artistic and social attitude. Reconstruction fiction was passing out in a flood of propagandist melodrama and ridicule. One hesitates to lift this material up to the plane of literature even for the purposes of comparison. But the gradual climb of the new literature of the Negro must be traced and measured from these two nadir points. Following *The Leopard's Spots*, it was only occasionally during the next twenty years that the Negro was sincerely treated in fiction by white authors. There were two or three tentative efforts to dramatize him. Sheldon's *The Nigger*, was the one notable early effort. And in fiction Paul Kester's *His Own Country* is, from a purely literary point of view, its outstanding performance. This type of novel failed, however, to awaken any general interest. This failure was due to the illogical treatment of the human situations presented. However indifferent and negative it may seem, there is the latent desire in most readers to have honesty of purpose and a full vision in the artist: and especially in fiction, a situation handled with gloves can never be effectively handled.

The first hint that the American artist was looking at this subject with full vision was in Torrence's *Granny Maumee*. It was drama, conceived and executed for performance on the stage, and therefore had restricted appeal. But even here the artist was concerned with the primitive instincts of the Race, and, though faithful and honest in his portrayal, the note was still low in the scale of racial life. It was only a short time, however, before a distinctly new development took place in the treatment of Negro life by white authors. This new class of work honestly strove to endow the Negro life with purely æsthetic vision and values, but with one or two exceptions, still stuck to the peasant level of race experience, and gave, unwittingly, greater currency to the popular notion of the Negro as an inferior, superstitious, half-ignorant and servile class of folk. Where they did in a few isolated instances recognize an ambitious impulse, it was generally defeated in the course of the story.

Perhaps this is inevitable with an alien approach, however well-intentioned. The folk lore attitude discovers only the lowly and the naïve: the sociological attitude finds the problem first and the human beings after, if at all. But American art in a reawakened seriousness, and using the technique of the new realism, is gradually penetrating Negro life to the core. George Madden Martin, with her pretentious foreword to a group of short stories, *The Children in the Mist*—and this is an extraordinary volume in many ways—quite seriously tried, as a Southern woman, to elevate the Negro to a higher plane of fictional treatment and interest. In succession, followed Mary White Ovington's *The Shadow*, in which Miss Ovington daringly created the kinship of brother and sister between a black boy and white girl, had it brought to disaster by prejudice, out of which the white girl rose to a sacrifice no white girl in a novel had hitherto accepted and endursed; then Shands' *White and Black,* as honest a piece of fiction with the Negro as a subject as was ever produced by a Southern pen —and in this story, also, the hero, Robinson, making an equally glorious sacrifice for truth and justice as Miss Ovington's heroine; Clement Wood's *Nigger,* with defects of treatment, but admirable in purpose, wasted though, I think, in the effort to prove its thesis on wholly illogical material; and lastly, T. S. Stribling's *Birthright,* more significant than any of these other books, in fact, the most significant novel on the Negro written by a white American, and this in spite of its totally false conception of the character of Peter Siner.

Mr. Stribling's book broke ground for a white author in giving us a Negro hero and heroine. There is an obvious attempt to see objectively. But the formula of the Nineties,—atavistic race-heredity, still survives and protrudes through the flesh and blood of the characters. Using Peter as a symbol of the man tragically linked by blood to one world and by training and thought to another, Stribling portrays a tragic struggle against the pull of lowly origins and sordid environment. We do not deny this element of tragedy in Negro life,—and Mr. Stribling, it must also be remembered, presents, too, a severe indictment in his painting of the Southern conditions which brought about the disintegration of his hero's dreams and ideals. But the preoccupation, almost obsession of otherwise strong and artistic work like O'Neill's *Emperor Jones, All God's Chillun Got Wings,* and Culbertson's *Goat Alley* with this same theme and doubtful formula of hereditary cultural reversion suggests that, in spite of all good intentions, the true presental of the real tragedy of Negro life is a task still left for Negro writers to perform. This is especially true for those phases of culturally representative race life that as yet have scarcely at all found treatment by white American authors. In corroborating this, let me quote a passage from a recent number of the *Independent*, on the Negro novelist which reads:

> "During the past few years stories about Negroes have been extremely popular. A magazine without a Negro story is hardly living up to its opportunities. But almost every one of these stories is written in a tone of condescension. The artists have caught the contagion from the writers, and the illustrations are ninety-nine times out of a hundred purely slapstick stuff. Stories and pictures make a Roman holiday for the millions who are convinced that the most important fact about the Negro is that his skin is black. Many of these writers live in the South or are from the South. Presumably they are well acquainted with the Negro, but it is a remarkable fact that they almost never tell us anything vital about him, about the real human being in the black man's skin. Their most frequent method is to laugh at the colored man and woman, to catalogue their idiosyncrasies, their departure from the norm, that is, from the ways of the whites. There seems to be no suspicion in the minds of the writers that there may be a fascinating thought life in the minds of the Negroes, whether of the cultivated or of the most ignorant type. Always the Negro is interpreted in the terms of the white man. White-man psychology is applied and it is no wonder that the result often shows the Negro in a ludicrous light."

I shall have to run back over the years to where I began to survey the achievement of Negro authorship. The Negro as a creator in American literature is of comparatively recent importance. All that was accomplished between Phyllis Wheatley and Paul Laurence Dunbar, considered by critical standards, is negligible, and of historical interest only. Historically it is a great tribute to the race to have produced in Phyllis Wheatley not only the slave poetess in eighteenth century colonial America, but to know she was as good, if not a better, poetess than Ann Bradstreet whom literary historians give the honor of being the first person of her sex to win face as a poet in America.

Negro authorship may, for clearer statement, be classified into three main activities: Poetry, Fiction, and the Essay, with an occasional excursion into other branches. In the drama, until very recently, practically nothing worth while has been achieved, with the exception of Angelina Grimke's *Rachel*, notable for its sombre craftsmanship. Biography has given us a notable life story, told by himself, Booker T. Washington. Frederick Douglass's story of his life is eloquent as a human document, but not in the graces of narration and psychologic portraiture, which has definitely put this form of literature in the domain of the fine arts. Indeed, we may well believe that the efforts of controversy, of the huge amount of discursive and polemical articles dealing chiefly with the race problem, that have been necessary in breaking and clearing the impeded pathway of racial progress, have absorbed and in a way dissipated the literary energy of many able Negro writers.

Let us survey briefly the advance of the Negro in poetry. Behind Dunbar, there is nothing that can stand the critical test. We shall always have a sentimental and historical interest in those forlorn and pathetic figures who cried in the wilderness of their ignorance and oppression. With Dunbar we have our first authentic lyric utterance, an utterance more authentic, I should say, for its faithful rendition of Negro life and character than for any rare or subtle artistry of expression. When Mr. Howells, in his famous introduction to the *Lyrics of Lowly Life*, remarked that Dunbar was the first black man to express the life of his people lyrically, he summed up Dunbar's achievement and transported him to a place beside the peasant poet of Scotland, not for his art, but precisely because he made a people articulate in verse.

The two chief qualities in Dunbar's work are, however, pathos and humor, and in these he expresses that dilemma of soul that characterized the race between the Civil War and the end of the nineteenth century. The poetry of Dunbar is true to the life of the Negro and expresses characteristically what he felt and knew to be the temper and condition of his people. But its moods reflect chiefly those of the era of Reconstruction and just a little beyond,—the limited experience of a transitional period, the rather helpless and subservient era of testing freedom and reaching out through the difficulties of life to the emotional compensations of laughter and tears. It is the poetry of the happy peasant and the plaintive minstrel. Occasionally, as in the sonnet to *Robert Gould Shaw* and the *Ode to Ethiopia* there broke through Dunbar, as through the crevices of his spirit, a burning and brooding aspiration, an awakening and virile consciousness of race. But for the most part, his dreams were anchored to the minor whimsies; his deepest poetic inspiration was sentiment. He expressed a folk temperament, but not a race soul. Dunbar was the end of a régime, and not the beginning of a tradition, as so many careless critics, both white and colored, seem to think.

After Dunbar many versifiers appeared,—all largely dominated by his successful dialect work. I cannot parade them here for tag or comment, except to say that few have equalled Dunbar in this vein of expression, and none have deepened it as an expression of Negro life. Dunbar himself had clear notions of its limitations;—to a friend in a letter from London, March 15, 1897, he says: "I see now very clearly that Mr. Howells has done me irrevocable harm in the dictum he laid down regarding my dialect verse." Not until James W. Johnson published his *Fiftieth Anniversary Ode* on the emancipation in 1913, did a poet of the race disengage himself from the background of mediocrity into which the imitation of Dunbar snared Negro poetry. Mr. Johnson's work is based upon a broader contemplation of life, life that is not wholly confined within any racial experience, but through the racial he made articulate that universality of the emotions felt by all mankind. His verse possesses a vigor which definitely breaks away from the brooding minor undercurrents of feeling which have previously characterized the verse of Negro poets. Mr. Johnson brought, indeed, the first intellectual substance to the content of our poetry, and a craftsmanship which, less spontaneous than that of Dunbar's, was more balanced and precise.

Here a new literary generation begins; poetry that is racial in substance, but with the universal note, with the conscious background of the full heritage of English poetry. With each new figure somehow the gamut broadens and the technical control improves. The brilliant succession and maturing powers of Fenton Johnson, Leslie Pinckney Hill, Everett Hawkins, Lucien Watkins, Charles Bertram Johnson, Joseph Cotter, Georgia Douglas Johnson, Roscoe Jameson and Anne Spencer bring us at last to Claude McKay and the poets of the younger generation and a poetry of the masterful accent and high distinction. Too significantly for mere coincidence, it was the stirring year of 1917 that heard the first real masterful accent in Negro poetry.

In the September *Crisis* of that year, Roscoe Jameson's *Negro Soldiers* appeared:

> These truly are the Brave,
> These men who cast aside
> Old memories to walk the blood-stained pave
> Of Sacrifice, joining the solemn tide
> That moves away, to suffer and to die
> For Freedom—when their own is yet denied!
> O Pride! A Prejudice! When they pass by
> Hail them, the Brave, for you now crucified.

The very next month, under the pen name of Eli Edwards, Claude McKay printed in *The Seven Arts*, "The Harlem Dancer."

With Georgia Johnson, Anne Spencer and Angelina Grimke, the Negro woman poet significantly appears. Mrs. Johnson especially has voiced in true poetic spirit the lyric cry of Negro womanhood. In spite of lapses into the sentimental and the platitudinous, she has an authentic gift. Anne Spencer, more sophisticated, more cryptic but also more universal, reveals quite another aspect of poetic genius. Indeed, it is interesting to notice how to-day Negro poets waver between the racial and the universal notes.

Claude McKay, the poet who leads his generation, is a genius meshed in this dilemma. His work is caught between the currents of the poetry of protest and the poetry of expression; he is in turn the violent and strident propagandist, using his poetic gifts to clothe arrogant and defiant thoughts, and then the pure lyric dreamer, contemplating life and nature with a wistful sympathetic passion. When the mood of *Spring in New Hampshire* or the sonnet *The Harlem Dancer* possesses him, he is full of that spirit and power of beauty that flowers above any and all men's harming. How different in spite of the admirable spirit of courage and defiance, are his poems of which the sonnet *If We Must Die* is a typical example. Negro poetic expression hovers for the moment, pardonably perhaps, over the race problem, but its highest allegiance is to Poetry—it must soar.

Let me refer briefly to a type of literature in which there have been many pens, but a single mind. Dr. Du Bois is the most variously gifted writer which the race has produced. Poet, novelist, sociologist, historian and essayist, he has produced books in all these fields with the exception, I believe, of a formal book of poems, and has given to each the distinction of his clear and exact thinking, and of his sensitive imagination and passionate vision. *The Souls of Black Folk* was the book of an era; it was a painful book, a book of tortured dreams woven into the fabric of the sociologist's document. This book has more profoundly influenced the spiritual temper of the race than any other written in its generation. It is only through the intense, passionate idealism of such substance as makes *The Souls of Black Folk* such a quivering rhapsody of wrongs endured and hopes to be fulfilled that the poets of the race with compelling artistry can lift the Negro into the only full and complete nationalism he knows—that of the American democracy. No other book has more clearly revealed to the nation at large the true idealism and high aspiration of the American Negro.

In this book, as well as in many of Dr. Du Bois's essays, it is often my personal feeling that I am witnessing the birth of a poet, phoenix-like, out of a scholar. Between *The Souls of Black Folk* and *Darkwater*, published four years ago, Dr. Du Bois has written a number of books, none more notable, in my opinion, than his novel *The Quest of the Silver Fleece*, in which he made Cotton the great protagonist of fate in the lives of the Southern people, both white and black. I only know of one other such attempt and accomplishment in American fiction—that of Frank Norris—and I am somehow of the opinion that when the great epic novel of the South is written this book will prove to have been its forerunner. Indeed, the Negro novel is one of the great potentialities of American literature. Must it be written by a Negro? To recur to the article from which I have already quoted:

> "The white writer seems to stand baffled before the enigma and so he expends all his energies on dialect and in general on the Negro's minstrel characteristics. . . . We shall have to look to the Negro himself to go all the way. It is quite likely that no white man can do it. It is reasonable to suppose that his white psychology will always be in his way. I am not thinking at all about a Negro novelist who shall arouse the world to the horror of the deliberate killings by white mobs, to the wrongs that condemn a free people to political serfdom. I am not thinking at all of the propaganda novel, although there is

enough horror and enough drama in the bald statistics of each one of the annual Moton letters to keep the whole army of writers busy. But the Negro novelist, if he ever comes, must reveal to us much more than what a Negro thinks about when he is being tied to a stake and the torch is being applied to his living flesh; much more than what he feels when he is being crowded off the sidewalk by a drunken rowdy who may be his intellectual inferior by a thousand leagues. Such a writer, to succeed in a big sense, would have to forget that there are white readers; he would have to lose self-consciousness and forget that his work would be placed before a white jury. He would have to be careless as to what the white critic might think of it; he would need the self-assurance to be his own critic. He would have to forget for the time being, at least, that any white man ever attempted to dissect the soul of a Negro."

What I here quote is both an inquiry and a challenge! Well informed as the writer is, he does not seem to detect the forces which are surely gathering to produce what he longs for.

The development of fiction among Negro authors has been, I might almost say, one of the repressed activities of our literary life. A fair start was made the last decade of the nineteenth century when Chestnutt and Dunbar were turning out both short stories and novels. In Dunbar's case, had he lived, I think his literary growth would have been in the evolution of the Race novel as indicated in *The Uncalled* and the *Sport of the Gods*. The former was, I think, the most ambitious literary effort of Dunbar; the latter was his most significant; significant because, thrown against the background of New York City, it displayed the life of the race as a unit, swayed by currents of existence, of which it was and was not a part. The story was touched with that shadow of destiny which gave to it a purpose more important than the mere racial machinery of its plot. But Dunbar in his fiction dealt only successfully with the same world that gave him the inspiration for his dialect poems; though his ambition was to "write a novel that will deal with the educated class of my own people." Later he writes of *The Fanatics:* "You do not know how my hopes were planted in that book, but it has utterly disappointed me." His contemporary, Charles W. Chestnutt, was concerned more primarily with the fiction of the Color Line and the contacts and conflicts of its two worlds. He was in a way more successful. In the five volumes to his credit, he has revealed himself as a fiction writer of a very high order. But after all Mr. Chestnutt is a story-teller of genius transformed by racial earnestness into the novelist of talent. His natural gift would have found freer vent in a flow of short stories like Bret Harte's, to judge from the facility and power of his two volumes of short stories, *The Wife of His Youth and Other Stories* and *The Conjure Woman*. But Mr. Chestnutt's serious effort was in the field of the novel, where he made a brave and partially successful effort to correct the distortions of Reconstruction fiction and offset the school of Page and Cable. Two of these novels, *The Marrow of Tradition* and *The House Behind the Cedars*, must be reckoned among the representative period novels of their time. But the situation was not ripe for the great Negro novelist. The American public preferred spurious values to the genuine; the coinage of the Confederacy was at literary par. Where Dunbar, the sentimentalist, was welcome, Chestnutt, the realist, was barred. In 1905 Mr. Chestnutt wrote *The Colonel's Dream*, and thereafter silence fell upon him.

From this date until the past year, with the exception of *The Quest of the Silver Fleece*, which was published in 1911, there has been no fiction of importance by Negro authors. But then suddenly there comes a series of books, which seems to promise at least a new phase of race fiction, and possibly the era of the major novelists. Mr. Walter White's novel *The Fire in the Flint* is a swift moving straightforward story of the contemporary conflicts of black manhood in the South. Coming from the experienced observation of the author, himself an investigator of many lynchings and riots, it is a social document story of first-hand significance and importance; too vital to be labelled and dismissed as propaganda, yet for the same reason too unvarnished and realistic a story to be great art. Nearer to the requirements of art comes Miss Jessie Fauset's novel *There is Confusion*. Its distinction is to have created an entirely new milieu in the treatment of the race in fiction. She has taken a class within the race of established social standing, tradition and culture, and given in the rather complex family story of *The Marshalls* a social document of unique and refreshing value. In such a story, race fiction, detaching itself from the limitations of propaganda on the one hand and genre fiction on the other, emerges from the color line and is incorporated into the body of general and universal art.

Finally in Jean Toomer, the author of *Cane*, we come upon the very first artist of the race, who with all an artist's passion and sympathy for life, its hurts, its sympathies, its desires, its joys, its defeats and strange yearnings, can write about the Negro without the surrender or compromise of the artist's vision. So objective is it, that we feel that it is a mere accident that birth or association has thrown him into contact with the life he has written about. He would write just as well, just as poignantly, just as transmutingly, about the peasants of Russia, or the peasants of Ireland, had experience brought him in touch with their existence. *Cane* is a book of gold and bronze, of dusk and flame, of ecstasy and pain, and Jean Toomer is a bright morning star of a new day of the race of literature.

(1924)

FENTON JOHNSON
(1888-1958)

    Fenton Johnson is included in the annals of black American poetry not only because of his poems themselves, but also because his works anticipated the Harlem Renaissance.

    Born and reared in Chicago, Johnson began writing at the age of nine. Later he attended the University of Chicago. He taught school for a year, but then decided that the academic life was not for him and subsequently became a magazine editor and publisher.

    In 1912 Johnson collected his poems in a volume, A Little Dreaming. *The poems are conventional; some are in dialect. The most impressive poem is a 300-line blank verse work, "The Vision of Lazarus." The rest are undistinguished.*

    Shortly after, Johnson's works underwent a change. Casting aside the conventional mold, he turned to a free form of poetry in which the irregular and unrhymed lines and the rhythms were determined by the theme. In this use of free form, solid imagery, and actual speech rather than romantic bombast, Johnson was related to the New Poetry Movement. His poetry deals with real-life situations, which it conveys in simple, concrete language. In halting rhythms and jagged lines he portrays the chaotic world of the black man, caught in the illogic of racism. He hits existential depths more characteristic of later generations than of his own.

    The poems in the later manner are collected in Visions of the Dusk *(1915) and* Songs of the Soil *(1916).*

The Scarlet Woman

Once I was good like the Virgin Mary and the Minister's wife.
My father worked for Mr. Pullman and white people's tips; but he
    died two days after his insurance expired.
I had nothing, so I had to go to work.
All the stock I had was a white girl's education and a face that
    enchanted the men of both races.
Starvation danced with me.
So when Big Lizzie, who kept a house for white men, came to me
    with tales of fortune that I could reap from the sale of my
    virtue I bowed my head to Vice.
Now I can drink more gin than any man for miles around.
Gin is better than all the water in Lethe.

Aunt Jane Allen

State Street is lonely today. Aunt Jane Allen has driven her chariot to Heaven.

I remember how she hobbled along, a little woman, parched of skin, brown as the leather of a satchel and with eyes that had scanned eighty years of life.

Have those who bore her dust to the last resting place buried with her the basket of aprons she went up and down State Street trying to sell?

Have those who bore her dust to the last resting place buried with her the gentle word *Son* that she gave to each of the seed of Ethiopia?

The Old Repair Man

God is the Old Repair Man.
When we are junk in Nature's storehouse he takes us apart.
What is good he lays aside; he might use it some day.
What has decayed he buries in six feet of sod to nurture the weeds.
Those we leave behind moisten the sod with their tears;
But their eyes are blind as to where he has placed the good.
Some day the Old Repair Man
Will take the good from its secret place
And with his gentle, strong hands will mold
A more enduring work—a work that will defy Nature—
And we will laugh at the old days, the troubled days,
When we were but a crude piece of craftsmanship,
When we were but an experiment in Nature's laboratory. . . .
It is good we have the Old Repair Man.

FOLKLORE
TALE, SONG AND SERMON

The demise of chattel slavery opened another chapter in the black saga of toil and trouble in America. The masses poured forth their experiences in songs which are a valuable source for historians seeking to fathom the truth of blackness. The years following the Civil War saw the development of three types of songs, rooted in slavery but gathering deeper significance in the early chaotic years of "freedom": worksongs, blues and ballads.

Like the spirituals and slave seculars, these songs are a synthesis of African and Euro-American culture, amid the oppression which pervades the life of the black American. The result is a strong body of folk songs, economical in language, warmly emotional, often bitter and ironic, and laced with satiric humor.

The worksongs are direct descendents of the songs which the West African farmers sang as they worked their fields. For the African and for his cultural heirs, songs were a necessary tool, a complement to labor. In Afro-American worksongs, as in West African, the rhythm of the work often sets the rhythm for the song: the swing of the hammer, the hoist of the shovel.

Another African trait in the worksongs is the leader-and-response pattern—the same pattern seen in many spirituals and in the "Amen, Brother!" and "Tell it, Lord!" responses of black congregations. On work gangs the song leader had a vital function in keeping the work going. He would establish a pattern, which would be picked up by the crew and then repeated throughout the song; meanwhile, the work would be getting done. For example, the leader would sing a solo line, each time followed by a set response from the group:

Leader: *Hyah come de cap'm*
Group: *Stan' right steddy*
Leader: *Walkin' lak Samson*
Group: *Stan' right steddy*
Leader: *-A big Goliath*
Group: *Stan' right steddy*
Leader: *He totin' his talker*
Group: *Stan' right steddy*

Or, the leader would sing a line, and the group would repeat it throughout the song. Or, the leader and group would sing in unison. There are many patterns, all well known to the workers.

The subject matter of the worksongs reflects, of course, the harsh life of the worker. Many workers led virtually nomadic lives; they wandered from town to town seeking employment or—since a black man would often be arrested for the most trifling offenses—evading the police. Worksongs reflected their loneliness, their alienation, their longing for home. Other themes were love, religion, weariness, exploits of other workers, and the effects of unceasing poverty and toil. Prison songs comprise a large segment of the worksongs. Men on chain gangs or prison farms could express in songs their hopelessness, their sense of injustice, their worry over loved ones—especially women—on the outside. Often they sang of other prisoners who had escaped. Worksongs, including prison songs, usually have an aspect of social protest.

The blues are closely related to worksongs in themes, but differ somewhat in treatment and form. Whereas the worksongs involve the feelings of the group, the blues express intensely individual personal feelings. Also, the worksongs are somewhat more varied in mood; the blues almost always express personal misery.

This, in fact, is what the blues are all about: capturing misery in song and therefore making it bearable. Subjects for the blues are simply those things that would make one blue: love problems, prison, natural disasters, hard times, homesickness and loneliness.

Blues lyric form is the next step in development after the one-line or two-line repetition of the hollers and the responsive patterns of the worksongs. With variations, the blues stanza basically consists of three lines: The first states the problem or situation; the second repeats the first, often with variation; the third is the punch line which completes the first two. Thus:

> *I'm leavin' in the morning, Mama, and I don't know*
> *where to go.*
> *I'm leavin' in the morning, Mama, and I don't know*
> *where to go.*
> *Cause the woman I been livin' with for twenty years,*
> *Mama, says she don't want me no more.*

The blues have been popularized and commercialized and synthesized, but the sensitive listener can separate the slick commercial blues package from the genuine passion sung by such greats as Blind Lemon Jefferson, Ma Rainey, Bessie Smith, Josh White, and Huddie Ledbetter (Leadbelly). Worksongs and ballads exist in other cultures; only black people have the blues.

Ballads, like worksongs and the blues, show African traces. The African love of music and penchant for storytelling combine in the wealth of ballads created by black Americans. Many ballads bear the imprint of Euro-American culture. Black variations on white folk ballads exist in "Casey Jones," "Frankie and Johnny," "Barb'ry Allen," and others. Here and there, lines appear in black ballads that have been sung in the story-songs of white America and Europe. But by and large, the ballads of black people are distinctly their own creation. The vast majority of the ballads are black-originated, and all reflect the realities of folk life. They sing the exploits of heroes like John Henry, steel-driving man, or villains like Stagolee, who killed a man over a Stetson hat. Prison, love, and hard times are themes of ballads as is the case in other types of folk expressions. Unlike worksongs and blues, the ballad tells a story chronologically and fairly completely. Also, the ballad lacks the intense personal feeling of the blues, since the song is about somebody else, not the singer.

While not precisely a musical type, the black folk sermon is very close to the song types. Moreover, its recitative mode of presentation and its frequent incorporation of song distinguishes it sharply from the declamatory Euro-American sermon. The black folk sermon has its standard themes and typical rhetorical devices. A study of the folk sermon must draw upon the theory of oral composition developed in recent years to account for epic poetry. The black folk preacher was every inch an artist appealing to a critical but generous audience. His progenitor is the African story teller, sure of his technique and of the responses of his audience.

Folklore is important in a study of black literature for several *reasons. In the 1920s black writers began to find in folklore themes, language, and rhythms which they incorporated into carefully wrought works. More important, these works are often infused with the spirit of black experience missing in the dialect poems of the Dunbar school. Sterling Brown wrote particularly effective poems in the style of worksongs and ballads; his Slim Greer has the "feel" of a ballad hero. Langston Hughes adapted the form and content of blues for many poems. James Weldon Johnson turned to the folk sermon for the artistic re-creations of* God's Trombones.

Folklore is vital in measuring the accuracy of a writer's image of black experience. This lore refutes the image of the black man shaped and defeated by an oppressive system, for it is expressive of hardships, and certainly of suffering and injustice—but not of defeat.

T'appin

TOLD BY CUGO LEWIS, PLATEAU, ALABAMA.

BROUGHT TO AMERICA FROM WEST COAST AFRICA, 1859.

It was famine time an' T'appin had six chillun. Eagle hide behin' cloud an' he went crossed de ocean an' go gittin' de palm oil; got de seed to feed his chillun wid it. T'appin see it, say "hol' on, it har' time. Where you git all dat to feed your t'ree chillun? I got six chillun, can't you show me wha' you git all dat food?" Eagle say, "No, I had to fly 'cross de ocean to git dat." T'appin say, "Well, gimme some o' you wings an' I'll go wid you." Eagle say, "A' right. When shall we go?" T'appin say, "'Morrow mornin' by de firs' cock crow." So 'morrow came but T'appin didn' wait till mornin'. T'ree 'clock in de mornin' T'appin come in fron' Eagle's house say, "Cuckee—cuckoo—coo." Eagle say, "Oh, you go home. Lay down. 'Tain't day yit." But he kep' on, "Cuckoo, cuckoo, coo," an' bless de Lor', Eagle got out, say, "What' you do now?" T'appin say, "You put t'ree wings on this side an' t'ree on udda side." Eagle pull out six feathers an' put t'ree on one side an' t'ree on de udda. Say, "Fly, le's see." So T'appin commence to fly. One o' de wings fall out. But T'appin said, "Da's all right, I got de udda wings. Le's go." So dey flew an' flew; but when dey got over de ocean all de eagle wings fell out. T'appin about to fall in de water. Eagle went out an' ketch him. Put him under his wings. T'appin say, "I don' like dis." Eagle say, "Why so?" T'appin say, "Gee it stink here." Eagle let him drop in ocean. So he went down, down, down to de underworl'. De king o' de underworl' meet him. He say, "Why you come here? Wha' you doin' here?" T'appin say, "King, we in te'bul condition on de earth. We can't git nothin' to eat. I got six chillun an' I can't git nothin' to eat for dem. Eagle he on'y got t'ree an' he go 'cross de ocean an' git all de food he need. Please gimme sumpin' so I kin feed my chillun." King say, "A' right, a' right," so he go an' give T'appin a dipper. He say to T'appin, "Take dis dipper. When you want food for your chillun say:

> Bakon coleh
> Bakon cawbey
> Bakon cawhubo lebe lebe.

So T'appin carry it home an' go to de chillun. He say to dem, "Come here." When dey all come he say:

> Bakon coleh
> Bakon cawbey
> Bakon cawhubo lebe lebe.

Gravy, meat, biscuit, ever'ting in de dipper. Chillun got plenty now. So one time he say to de chillun, "Come here. Dis will make my fortune. I'll sell dis to de King." So he showed de dipper to de King. He say:

> Bakon coleh
> Bakon cawbey
> Bakon cawhubo lebe lebe.

Dey got somet'ing. He feed ev'ryone. So de King went off, he call ev'ryboda. Pretty soon ev'ryboda eatin'. So dey ate an' ate, ev'ryt'ing. meats, fruits, and all like dat. So he took his dipper an' went back home. He say, "Come, chillun." He try to feed his chillun; nothin' came. (You got a pencil dere, ain't you?) When it's out it's out. So T'appin say, "Aw right, I'm going back to de King an' git him to fixa dis up." So he went down to de underworl' an' say to de King, "King, wha' de matter? I can't feeda my chillun no mora." So de King say to him, "You take dis cow hide an' when you want somepin' you say:

> Sheet n oun
> n-jacko
> nou o quaako.

So T'appin went offi an' he came to cross roads. Den he said de magic:

> Sheet n oun
> n-jacko
> nou o quaako.

De cowhide commence to beat um. It beat, beat. Cowhide said, "Drop, drop." So T'appin drop an' de cowhide stop beatin'. So he went home. He called his chillun in. He gim um de cowhide an' tell dem what to say, den he went out. De chillun say:

> Sheet n oun
> n-jacko
> nou o quaako.

De cowhide beat de chillun. It say, "Drop, drop." Two chillun dead an' de others sick. So T'appin say, "I will go to de King." He calls de King, he call all de people. All de people came. So before he have de cowhide beat, he has a mortar made an' gets in der an' gets all covered up. Den de King say:

> Sheet n oun
> n-jacko
> nou o quaako.

So de cowhide beat, beat. It beat everyboda, beat de King too. Dat cowhide beat, beat, beat right t'roo de mortar wha' was T'appin an'

beat marks on his back, an' da's why you never fin' T'appin in a
clean place, on'y under leaves or a log.

(Collected by Arthur Huff Fauset, 1925)

John Henry

When John Henry was a little fellow,
    You could hold him in the palm of your hand,
He said to his pa, "When I grow up
    I'm gonna be a steel-driving man.
        Gonna be a steel-driving man."

When John Henry was a little baby,
    Setting on his mammy's knee,
He said "The Big Bend Tunnel on the C. & O. Road
    Is gonna be the death of me,
        Gonna be the death of me."

One day his captain told him,
    How he had bet a man
That John Henry would beat his steam-drill down,
    Cause John Henry was the best in the land,
        John Henry was the best in the land.

John Henry kissed his hammer,
    White man turned on steam,
Shaker held John Henry's trusty steel,
    Was the biggest race the world had ever seen,
        Lord, biggest race the world ever seen.

John Henry on the right side
    The steam drill on the left,
"Before I'll let your steam drill beat me down,
    I'll hammer my fool self to death,
        Hammer my fool self to death."

John Henry walked in the tunnel,
    His captain by his side,
The mountain so tall, John Henry so small,
    He laid down his hammer and he cried,
        Laid down his hammer and he cried.

Captain heard a mighty rumbling,
    Said "The mountain must be caving in,
John Henry said to the captain,
    "It's my hammer swinging in de wind,
        My hammer swinging in de wind."

John Henry said to his shaker,
    "Shaker, you'd better pray;
For if ever I miss this piece of steel,
    Tomorrow'll be your burial day,
        Tomorrow'll be your burial day."

John Henry said to his shaker,
    "Lordy, shake it while I sing,
I'm pulling my hammer from my shoulders down,
    Great Gawdamighty, how she ring,
        Great Gawdamighty, how she ring!"

John Henry said to his captain,
    "Before I ever leave town,
Gimme one mo' drink of dat tom-cat gin,
    And I'll hammer dat steam driver down,
        I'll hammer dat steam driver down."

John Henry said to his captain,
    "Before I ever leave town,
Gimme a twelve-pound hammer wid a whale-bone handle,
    And I'll hammer dat steam driver down,
        I'll hammer dat steam drill on down."

John Henry said to his captain,
    "A man ain't nothin' but a man,
But before I'l let dat steam drill beat me down,
    I'll die wid my hammer in my hand,
        Die wid my hammer in my hand."

The man that invented the steam drill
    He thought he was mighty fine,
John Henry drove down fourteen feet,
    While the steam drill only made nine,
        Steam drill only made nine.

"Oh, lookaway over yonder, captain,
    You can't see like me,"
He gave a long and loud and lonesome cry,
    "Lawd, a hammer be the death of me,
        A hammer be the death of me!"

John Henry had a little woman,
    Her name was Polly Ann,
John Henry took sick, she took his hammer,
    She hammered like a natural man,
        Lawd, she hammered like a natural man.

John Henry hammering on the mountain
    As the whistle blew for half-past two,
The last words his captain heard him say,
    "I've done hammered my insides in two,
        Lawd, I've hammered my insides in two."

The hammer that John Henry swung
    It weighed over twelve pound,
He broke a rib in his left hand side
    And his intrels fell on the ground,
        And his intrels fell on the ground.

John Henry, O, John Henry,
    His blood is running red,
Fell right down with his hammer to the ground,
    Said, "I beat him to the bottom but I'm dead,
    Lawd, beat him to the bottom but I'm dead."

When John Henry was laying there dying,
    The people all by his side,
The very last words they heard him say,
    "Give me a cool drink of water 'fore I die,
    Cool drink of water 'fore I die."

John Henry had a little woman,
    The dress she wore was red,
She went down the track, and she never looked back,
    Going where her man fell dead,
        Going where her man fell dead.

John Henry had a little woman,
    The dress she wore was blue,
De very last words she said to him,
    "John Henry, I'll be true to you,
        John Henry, I'll be true to you."

"Who's gonna shoes yo' little feet,
    Who's gonna glove yo' hand,
Who's gonna kiss yo' pretty, pretty cheek,
    Now you done lost yo' man?
        Now you done lost yo' man?"

"My mammy's gonna shoes my little feet,
    Pappy gonna glove my hand,
My sister's gonna kiss my pretty, pretty cheek,
    Now I done lost my man,
        Now I done lost my man."

They carried him down by the river,
    And buried him in the sand,
And everybody that passed that way,
    Said, "There lies that steel-driving man,
        There lies a steel-driving man."

They took John Henry to the river,
    And buried him in the sand,
And every locomotive come a-roaring by,
    Says "There lies that steel-drivin' man,
        Lawd, there lies a *steel*-drivin' man."

Some say he came from Georgia,
    And some from Alabam,
But its wrote on the rock at the Big Bend Tunnel,
    That he was an East Virginia man,
        Lord, Lord, an East Virginia man.

Bad Man Ballad

Late las' night I was a-makin' my rounds,
Met my woman an' I blowed her down,
Went on home an' I went to bed,
Put my hand cannon right under my head.

Early nex' mornin' 'bout de risin' o' de sun,
I gets up-a for to make-a my run.
I made a good run but I made it too slow,
Got overtaken in Mexico.

Standin' on de corno', readin' of a bill,
Up step a man name o' Bad Texas Bill;
"Look here, bully, ain' yo' name Lee Brown?
B'lieve you are de rascal shot yo' woman down."

"Yes, oh, yes," says. "This is him.
If you got a warrant, jes' read it to me."
He says; "You look like a fellow that knows what's bes'.
Come 'long wid me—you're under arres'."

When I was arrested, I was dressed in black;
Dey put me on a train, an' dey brought me back.
Dey boun' me down in de county jail;
Couldn' get a human for to go my bail.

Early nex' mornin' 'bout half pas' nine,
I spied ol' jedge drappin' down de line.
I heered ol' jailer when he cleared his th'oat,
"Nigger, git ready for de deestreec' cote."

Deestreec' cote is now begin,
Twelve big jurymen, twelve hones' men.
Five mo' minutes up step a man,
He was holdin' my verdic' in his right han.'

Verdic' read murder in de firs' degree.
I said, "O Lawd, have mercy on me."
I seed ol' jedge when he picked up his pen,
Say, "I don' think you'll ever kill a woman ag'in.

"This here killin' of women natchly got to stop,
I don't know whether to hang you er not.
Ninety-nine years on de hard, hard groun',
'Member de night you blowed de woman down."

Here I is, bowed down in shame,
I got a number instead of a name.
Here for de res' of my nachul life,
An' all I ever done is kill my wife. . . .

The Remnant
A Sermon

Brothers and sisters, being a duty-bound servant of God, I stand before you to-night. I am a little hoarse from a cold. But if you will bear with me a little while we will try to bring you a message of "Thus sayeth the Lord." If God is willing we will preach. The hell-hounds are so swift on our trail that we have to go sometime whether we feel like it or not. So we are here to-night to hear what the spirit has to say.

It always make my heart glad when I run back in my mind and see what a powerful God this is we serve. And every child . . . Pray with me a little while children—that has been borned of the spirit, I mean born until he can feel it, ought to feel proud that he is serving a captain who has never lost a battle, a God that can speak and man live, but utter his voice and man lay down and die. A God that controls play across the heaven. Oh, ain't He a powerful God? He stepped out on the scope of time one morning and declared 'I am God and there's none like me. I'm God and there is none before me. In my own appointed time I will visit the iniquities of the earth. I will cut down on the right and on the left. But a remnant I will save.' Ain't you glad, then, children that he always spares a remnant? Brothers (pray with me a little while), we must gird up our loins. We who are born of the spirit should cling close to the Master, for he has promised to be a shelter in the time of storm; a rock in a weary land. Listen at Him when He says 'behold I lay in Zion, a stone, a tried stone.' . . . What need have we to worry about earthly things. They are temporal and will fade away. But we, the born of God have laid hold on everlasting life. Every child that has had his soul delivered from death and hell (Pray with me brothers) stayed at hell's dark door until he got his orders is a traveler. His home is not in this world. He is but a sojourner in a weary land. Brothers! this being true we ought to love one another; we ought to be careful how we entertain strangers. If your neighbor mistreat you, do good for evil, for a-way by and by our God that sees all we do and hears all we say will come and woe be unto him that has offended one of these His "Little Ones." I know the way gets awful dark sometimes; and it looks like everything is against us, but listen what Job said, 'All the days of my appointed time I will wait on the Lord till my change comes!' Sometimes we wake up in the dark hours of midnight, briny tears flowing down our cheeks (Ah, pray with me a little longer, Brothers). We cry and don't know what we are crying about. Brother, If you have been truly snatched from the greedy jaws of Hell, your feet taken out of the miry clay and placed on the rock, the sure foundation, you will shed tears sometime. You just feel like you want to run away somewhere. But listen at the Master when he says: 'Be still and know that I am God. I have heard your groans but I will not put on you a burden you cannot bear.' We ought to rejoice and be glad for while some day they think, we know we have been born of God because we have felt His power, tasted His love, waited at Hell's dark door for orders, got a through ticket straight through from hell to heaven; we have seen the travel of our soul; He dressed us up, told us we were His children, sent us back into this low land of sorrows to tarry until one sweet day when He shall send the angels of death to bear our soul from this old earthly tabernacle and bear it back home to glory, I say back home because we been there once and every since that day we have been making our way back." "Brothers! A-ha! Glory to God! The Captain is on board now, Brothers. Sit still and hear the word of God, a-ha; away back, away back brothers, a-ha! Before the wind ever blowed, a-ha! Before the flying clouds, a-ha! Or before ever the earth was made, a-ha! Our God had us in mind. Ha! oh, brothers, oh brothers! Ha! ain't you glad then, a-ha! that our God, Ha! looked down through time one morning, a-ha! saw me and you, a-ha! ordained from the very beginning that we should be his children, a-ha! the work of His Almighty hand, a-ha! Old John the Revelator, a-ha! a-looking over yonder, a-ha! in bright glory, a-ha! Oh, what do you see, John! Ha! I see a number, a-ha! Who are these, a-ha! I heard the angel Gabriel when he answered, a-ha! 'These are they that come up through hard trials and great tribulations, a-ha! who washed their robes, a-ha! and made them white in the blood of the lamb, a-ha! They are now shouting around the throne of God,' a-ha! Well, oh brothers! Oh, brothers! Ain't you glad that you have already been in the dressing room, had your everlasting garments fitted on and sandals on your feet. We born of God, a-ha! are shod for traveling, a-ha! Oh, Glory to God! It won't be long before some of us here, a-ha! will bid farewell, a-ha! take the wings of the morning, a-ha! where there'll be no more sin and sorrow, a-ha! no more weeping and mourning, a-ha! We can just walk around, brother, a-ha! Go over and shake hands with old Moses, a-ha! See Father Abraham, a-ha! Talk with Peter, Matthew, Luke and John, a-ha! And, Oh yes, Glory to God! we will want to see our Saviour, the Lamb that was slain, Ha! They tell me that His face outshines the sun, a-ha! but we can look on him, a-ha! because we will be like Him; and then oh brother, Oh brother, we will just fly from Cherubim to Cherubim, There with the angels we will eat off the welcome table, a-ha! Soon! Soon! we will all be gathered together over yonder. Brothers, ain't you glad you done died the sinner death and don't have to die no more? When we rise to fly that morning, we can fly with healing in our wings. . . . Now, if you don't hear my voice no more, a-ha! remember, I am a Hebrew child, a-ha! Just meet me over yonder, a-ha! on the other side of the River of Jordan, away back in the third heaven.

Backwater Blues

When it rain five days an' de skies turned dark as night
When it rain five days an' de skies turned dark as night
Then trouble taken place in the lowland that night

I woke up this mornin', can't even get outa mah do'
I woke up this mornin', can't even get outa mah do'
That's enough trouble to make a po' girl wonder where she wanta go

They rowed a little boat about five miles 'cross the pond
Then they rowed a little boat about five miles 'cross the pond
I packed all mah clothes, th'owed 'em in, an' they rowed me along

When it thunder an' a-lightnin', an' the wind begin to blow
When it thunder an' a-lightnin', an' the wind begin to blow
An' thousan' people ain' got no place to go

Then I went an' stood up on some high ol' lonesome hill
I went an' stood up on some high ol' lonesome hill
An' looked down on the house where I used to live

Backwater blues done cause me to pack mah things an' go
Backwater blues done cause me to pack mah things an' go
Cause mah house fell down an' I cain' live there no mo'

O-o-o-oom, I cain' move no mo'
O-o-o-oom, I cain' move no mo'
There ain' no place fo' a po' ol' girl to go

(Bessie Smith)

Part III

World War I
to World War II

Most social historians view the period in the United States between the end of World War I and the onset of the Depression as
one of considerable individual crisis, for which the career of the
novelist F. Scott Fitzgerald has become a major symbol. Each of the
various names by which the period is now known reveals some aspect
of life during that time as perceived by those who lived it: the Jazz
Age, the Roaring Twenties, the Prohibition Era, Normalcy. If the
chief tonality of the period, however, is gaiety, albeit a frenetic and
half-hearted gaiety, the period between the beginning of the Depression and the end of World War II (1932 to 1945) is by contrast regarded as one of frustration, anguish, and suffering. The entire epoch
under review may be said to have been launched by the ending of a
war fought to make the world safe for democracy (to use that war's
most cherished slogan), and is itself ended by a war for the so-called
four freedoms—freedom from want, freedom of worship, freedom
of speech, and freedom from fear.

As is usually true, however, the conventional view, common
to textbooks and orators, bears little relation to the view of black
Americans, since they are not usually consulted in its construction.
The intellectuals of the black American community rallied reluctantly
to the support of the First World War in the hope that the slogans

about democracy might have some real meaning. The masses, ever more trustful and optimistic, sought in every way to be counted in. Thousands of blacks entered the services—the draft in any case being democratically extended to them. There was wholesale emigration from the South to centers of war production in the East and the Midwest. In the pages of Du Bois' *Crisis* and of such big-city weeklies as Robert Abbott's *Chicago Defender*, black folk were exhorted to make the most of their opportunities for work and to prepare for fuller participation in the democracy to come. The mass-oriented weeklies and Du Bois' necessarily intellectualist editorials in the *Crisis* were joined by the contrary views of A. Phillip Randolph and Chandler Owen in the *Messenger*, which was founded in 1917 as a socialist review. The *Messenger* preached the standard socialist view that the war was merely a symptomatic event of capitalism and should be resisted by the working classes everywhere. The *Messenger*, despite its passion and brilliance, had little following in the black community.

Quite otherwise was the impact of Marcus Garvey, who also preached disbelief in the promises of democracy. As wartime events seemed to bear out his analyses, he was to conquer a huge following among the black masses with his talk of African redemption and black nationhood, to be implemented by black economic independence. Two incidents which seemed to justify Garvey's stand were the so-called Houston Affair, in which black troops were victims of military injustice, and the infamous St. Louis Massacre, both of which occurred in 1917. The latter event brought no support to the view that the sympathies of the working classes, black and white, were essentially one.

The apologetic tradition, which is recurrent throughout the history of Afro-American expression, was represented in 1918 by Benjamin Brawley's *Your Negro Neighbor* and by Kelly Miller's *An Appeal to Conscience*. The prolific Brawley also published in this year *Africa and the War*, as well as a new edition of *The Negro in Literature and Art*, which had originally appeared in 1910.

The famous post-war Race Riots of 1919, in Illinois, Arkansas, Texas, Nebraska, and elsewhere, gave further impetus to Garvey's views represented in his weekly paper *The Negro World*, the organ of the UNIA—the United Negro Improvement Association. *The Negro World*, a well edited newspaper, contained many editorials, speeches, and even poems by Garvey himself, and justified its international claims by publishing pages in Spanish and French. Kelly

Miller, true to the apologetic tradition, published in 1919 a lavishly illustrated *History of the Great War* in which the role of blacks is fully presented.

The Peace Conference of 1919 gave new impetus to the Pan-African idea. Du Bois, long interested in Africa and in Pan-Africanism, organized a conference in Paris, known subsequently as the First Pan-African Congress, with the hope of influencing the treaty-makers to apply the principle of self-determination to Africa as well as to Europe. Though his movement had its Pan-African aspects, Garvey did not participate in this conference, which did not prevent him from being associated with it in the minds—and even the secret reports—of some European governments who regarded both Garvey and Du Bois with suspicion. Subsequent Pan-African Congresses were held in 1921, 1923, 1927, and 1945. Du Bois was the prime mover in all the Congresses except the last, held in Manchester, England, of which he was Honorary Chairman.

Another aspect of Pan-Africanism was concern with black people in the western hemisphere. Garvey was himself from Jamaica; many of his followers were West Indians from Jamaica and other islands. The UNIA had branches throughout the West Indies and Central America, particularly in Panama. The NAACP was especially interested in Haiti, the Black Republic, which had been occupied by the United States since 1915. The NAACP secretary, James Weldon Johnson, was part of a fact-finding commission to that country and published his findings in a series of articles, collected in the book *Self-Determining Haiti* (1920). Johnson himself claims, with justice, to have begun the American literary and artistic interest in Haiti. In Afro-American expression, one may cite as examples of this interest Leslie Pinckney Hill's poetic drama *Toussaint L'Ouverture* (1928), the opera *Ouanga* dealing with Dessalines, with a libretto by John F. Matheus and music by Clarence Cameron White, the juvenile *Popo and Fifine* (1932) by Hughes and Bontemps, and Alain Locke's *La role du nègre dans la culture des Amériques* (1943), delivered as lectures in Haiti and published there.

World War I and its aftermath brought large concentrations of blacks into many big American cities. It is no accident that for a number of reasons Harlem in New York's Manhattan should have been the largest of these and should have become the symbol for the others. There is an euphoric evocation of Harlem, its life and its origins by James Weldon Johnson in *Black Manhattan* (1930), written when the Harlem Renaissance of the twenties was already on the wane. The designation Harlem Renaissance or Negro Renaissance is used to cover that period of Afro-American expression which parallels the Jazz Age. It has some obvious rapport with the Jazz Age but is properly not of it, though it was blacks who ironically enough provided the sources of jazz.

The Harlem Renaissance was the era of the "New Negro." In 1916 William Pickens had written a book with that title, possibly echoing Du Bois' *The Negro* (1915). Garvey frequently used the phrase in his speeches, and it received an historic consecration as the title of Alain Locke's anthology of 1925, which included Locke's title essay interpreting the spirit of the new Negro. Alain Locke's interpretation was a highly nuanced one, taking into account not only the social dimensions of Afro-American life but the implications for group experience provided by African origins and the Afro-American folk background. It is significant that in the volume *The New Negro* there appear essays by Locke on the spirituals, African art, and on the younger black writers.

The Harlem Renaissance was nourished by the pages of *The Crisis*, whose literary editor during most of the twenties was Jessie Fauset, novelist and poet, and by *Opportunity*, founded in 1923 and edited by Charles S. Johnson. Each journal conducted literary contests which provided impetus and reward for young black writers looking for stimulation and guidance.

Two writers whose work helped initiate the Harlem Renaissance but who stand ironically a little apart from it are Claude McKay and Jean Toomer. McKay was born in Jamaica and had already published two volumes of dialect verse there before he came to the United States. His carefully crafted sonnets on the themes of lynching and racial injustice originally appeared in avant-garde and leftist publications before the twenties. During the twenties he lived mainly outside the United States though publishing several books through American houses. Toomer published *Cane* in 1923 and then, for reasons not fully explicable, fell into a silence which was never to be broken by similar work. Both writers, then, were curiously present and absent throughout the period, but their presence was in no sense that of Arna Bontemps, Countee Cullen, or Langston Hughes, nor yet that of Zora Neale Hurston, Rudolph Fisher, or Wallace Thurman, all of whom were well known on the Harlem scene at some point in the twenties.

Among older writers of the Renaissance was Jessie Fauset, whose bourgeois novels of color and caste within Negro life look back to

Chesnutt and whose work falls into a niche with those of the younger Nella Larsen. The work of William Stanley Braithwaite, W. E. B. Du Bois, Benjamin Brawley, and especially James Weldon Johnson provided continuity with the past. Braithwaite retained his preeminent position as an American anthologist, whose racial identity was unsuspected by the larger public, and included black poets in his anthologies. James Weldon Johnson edited the *Book of American Negro Poetry* in 1922 and revised it in 1931. He published *God's Trombones* and reissued *The Autobiography of an Ex-Colored Man* in 1927.

The Stock Market Crash of 1929 presaged the Depression which was to dominate the next decade until the eve of World War II. The Depression effectively ended the Harlem Renaissance. Negro artists were a luxury America could ill afford in its hour of adversity. Gay Harlem was deprived of its visitors from downtown as a general decline of interest in the Afro-American affected all his arts. The crucial point is that the Harlem Renaissance, despite the folk and ancestral emphases of Alain Locke, had in fact been largely for white consumption. The group of black readers eager for the next work of Hughes or Cullen was not large enough to provide economic independence for the authors. When Arna Bontemps' novel *Black Thunder* was published in 1936, it did not earn anything beyond the advance in royalties. For less popular writers, the expected readership was not large enough to justify economically the publication of their works.

One result of this situation was a minor flourishing of works directed to the juvenile market. Cullen, Bontemps, and Shirley Graham were conspicuous among writers who pursued various goals by means of appealing to this special and slightly more certain audience.

The thirties had its extravagances: the Father Divine Movement was one of many. It had its real suffering: starving sharecroppers and breadlines. It had its Scottsboro Case, which was to black America what the Sacco-Vanzetti Case had been to liberal America in the twenties. Countee Cullen wrote one of his few topical poems on Scottsboro. There was the Angelo Herndon Case alluded to in Langston Hughes' drama *Angelo Herndon Jones* (1936) and described in the protagonist's own words in Herndon's *I Want to Live* (1937).

Afro-American poetry in the thirties was far more concerned with "problems" than it had been in the twenties. New poets such as Frank Marshall Davis and Margaret Walker Alexander sang embittered songs of deprivation and social ills.

The WPA writers project, particularly in New York and Chicago, was a welcome means of support for talented black writers during the latter thirties. Among those associated with the project were Richard Wright, Margaret Walker Alexander, and Ralph Ellison.

A major motif of Afro-American writing in the thirties was the notion of the unity of the working class and a consequent de-emphasis of racial distinctiveness. Hughes was won over to this point of view and expressed it in many poems. Younger writers such as Richard Wright began their careers influenced by the Communist formulation of the idea. Communist dialectic provided material for Wright's masterpiece, *Native Son*, but he had already abandoned the movement.

Nineteen-forty, the year of *Native Son*, was the year in which the 70-year-old Du Bois published a powerful autobiographical essay *Dusk of Dawn* and established *Phylon*, the Atlanta University review of race and culture; in which Hughes published the first part of his autobiography, *The Big Sea*, which took his life to 1930, the end of the Harlem Renaissance and the onset of the Depression; in which Claude McKay published his *Harlem: Negro Metropolis*. It was also the year in which it became clear that the United States would enter the war then raging in Europe. No one suspected that U.S. entry would be provoked by a Japanese attack on Pearl Harbor. Just as the Depression had brought a conclusion to the Harlem Renaissance, World War II brought a conclusion to the characteristic Afro-American expression of the thirties. Minor concessions were made to demands formulated by black leaders: a weak Fair Employment Practices Commission was established by executive order; a segregated air training squadron was created. These, however, mainly provided cold storage for the grievances of black Americans. The air of emergency and uncertainty however—and perhaps the paper shortage—cast a pall on black writers that lasted until 1945.

JAMES WELDON JOHNSON
(1871-1938)

A man of many talents and skills, James Weldon Johnson was by turn a teacher, principal, lawyer, song lyricist, consular official, civil rights worker, novelist, anthologist-critic, and the poet who immortalized the Afro-American folk sermon both for its indigenous audience and the world. He was born in Jacksonville, Florida, where he spent his childhood and early manhood. He studied at Atlanta University and was one of the early graduates of that school. At the close of his life he was teaching literature and creative writing at Fisk University, where the poet Samuel Allen (Paul Vesey) was one of his pupils.

It was in the collaboration with his younger brother J. Rosamond Johnson, the composer, that he wrote the stirring words of the anthem "Lift Every Voice and Sing," so beloved of generations of black folk. The two collaborated regularly on songs for the early musical-comedy stage, including "Under the Bamboo Tree," cited by T. S. Eliot in The Wasteland. *They later edited two volumes of* Negro Spirituals *(1925; 1926). Johnson published anonymously in 1912 the haunting novel of the color-line,* The Autobiography of an Ex-Colored Man, *where appeared for the first time in print glimpses of the sporting and early jazz life of New York City, as well as authentic scenes of the rural black South. He collected his poems in 1917 in* Fifty Years and Other Poems, *"Fifty Years" being a commemorative poem on the Emancipation Proclamation.*

The early poetry of Johnson belongs to the late nineteenth century tradition of sentimental poetry in so far as its techniques and verse forms are concerned, seldom rising above the mediocrity characteristic of American poetry in the period 1890-1910, during which it was written for the most part. In purpose, however, Johnson's early verse was a species of propaganda, designed sometimes overtly, sometimes obliquely, to advance to a reading public the merits and the grievances of blacks.

The second decade of the twentieth century was a period of innovation and change in American poetry. The establishment of Poetry *Magazine, the Imagist manifesto, the appearance of Frost, Masters, Sandburg, Lindsay and Pound all bespeak the new spirit. The annual anthologies of Magazine verse edited by William Stanley Braithwaite beginning in 1913 which were one of the chief forums of the new spirit despite Braithwaite's own conservatism were surely well-perused by his friend James Weldon Johnson. Accordingly, it is not surprising to find a sudden modification in Johnson's poetic practice develop during this decade, for his poem "The Creation" precedes by almost a decade its publication with companion pieces in* God's Trombones *in 1927.*

Johnson is actively associated with the Harlem Renaissance, which he helped initiate with his strategic anthology, The Book of American Negro Poetry, *published in 1922 and revised, with the addition of the poets of the Renaissance, in 1931. Johnson himself published* God's Trombones; Seven Negro Sermons in Verse *(1927) with an important introductory essay on the Afro-American folk sermon. In the same year,* The Autobiography *was re-issued with Johnson indicated as the author. In 1930 Johnson celebrated his love of New York with the informal history* Black Manhattan, *a graceful marriage of research and personal reminiscence. In the same year he issued privately the ironical poem, "St. Peter Relates an Incident of the Resurrection Day," republished with other poems in 1935.*

His own life and his social philosophy are best summarized in the autobiography Along This Way *(1933), and the work based on his many years as NAACP secretary,* Negro Americans, What Now? *(1934).*

The Winter, 1971, issue of Phylon, *devoted to James Weldon Johnson, contains several informative articles.*

Harlem: The Culture Capital

In the history of New York, the significance of the name Harlem has changed from Dutch to Irish to Jewish to Negro. Of these changes, the last has come most swiftly. Throughout colored America, from Massachusetts to Mississippi, and across the continent to Los Angeles and Seattle, its name, which as late as fifteen years ago had scarcely been heard, now stands for the Negro metropolis. Harlem is indeed the great Mecca for the sight-seer, the pleasure-seeker, the curious, the adventurous, the enterprising, the ambitious and the talented of the whole Negro world; for the lure of it has reached down to every island of the Carib Sea and has penetrated even into Africa.

In the make-up of New York, Harlem is not merely a Negro colony or community, it is a city within a city, the greatest Negro city in the world. It is not a slum or a fringe, it is located in the heart of Manhattan and occupies one of the most beautiful and healthful sections of the city. It is not a "quarter" of dilapidated tenements, but is made up of new-law apartments and handsome dwellings, with well-paved and well-lighted streets. It has its own churches, social and civic centers, shops, theaters and other places of amusement. And it contains more Negroes to the square mile than any other spot on earth. A stranger who rides up magnificent Seventh Avenue on a bus or in an automobile must be struck with surprise at the transformation which takes place after he crosses One Hundred and Twenty-fifth Street. Beginning there, the population suddenly darkens and he rides through twenty-five solid blocks where the passers-by, the shoppers, those sitting in restaurants, coming out of theaters, standing in doorways and looking out of windows are practically all Negroes; and then he emerges where the population as suddenly becomes white again. There is nothing just like it in any other city in the country, for there is no preparation for it; no change in the character of the houses and streets; no change, indeed, in the appearance of the people, except their color.

Negro Harlem is practically a development of the past decade, but the story behind it goes back a long way. There have always been colored people in New York. In the middle of the last century they lived in the vicinity of Lispenard, Broome and Spring Streets. When Washington Square and lower Fifth Avenue was the center of aristocratic life, the colored people, whose chief occupation was domestic service in the homes of the rich, lived in a fringe and were scattered in nests to the south, east and west of the square. As late as the '80's the major part of the colored population lived in Sullivan, Thompson, Bleecker, Grove, Minetta Lane and adjacent streets. It is curious to note that some of these nests still persist. In a number of the blocks of Greenwich Village and Little Italy may be found small groups of Negroes who have never lived in any other section of the city. By about 1890 the center of colored population had shifted to the upper Twenties and lower Thirties west of Sixth Avenue. Ten years later another considerable shift northward had been made to West Fifty-third Street.

The West Fifty-third Street settlement deserves some special mention because it ushered in a new phase of life among colored New Yorkers. Three rather well-appointed hotels were opened in the street and they quickly became the centers of a sort of fashionable life that hitherto had not existed. On Sunday evenings these hotels served dinner to music and attracted crowds of well-dressed diners. One of these hotels, The Marshall, became famous as the headquarters of Negro talent. There gathered the actors, the musicians, the composers, the writers, the singers, dancers and vaudevillians. There one went to get a close-up of Williams and Walker, Cole and Johnson, Ernest Hogan, Will Marion Cook, Jim Europe, Aida Overton, and of others equally and less known. Paul Laurence Dunbar was frequently there whenever he was in New York. Numbers of those who loved to shine by the light reflected from celebrities were always to be found. The first modern jazz band ever heard in New York, or, perhaps anywhere, was organized at The Marshall. It was a playing-singing-dancing orchestra, making the first dominant use of banjos, saxophones, clarinets and trap drums in combination, and was called The Memphis Students. Jim Europe was a member of that band, and out of it grew the famous Clef Club, of which he was the noted leader, and which for a long time monopolized the business of "entertaining" private parties and furnishing music for the new dance craze. Also in the Clef Club was "Buddy" Gilmore who originated trap drumming as it is now practised, and set hundreds of white men to juggling their sticks and doing acrobatic stunts while they manipulated a dozen other noise-making devices aside from their drums. A good many well-known white performers frequented The Marshall and for seven or eight years the place was one of the sights of New York.

The move to Fifty-third Street was the result of the opportunity to get into newer and better houses. About 1900 the move to Harlem began, and for the same reason. Harlem had been overbuilt with large, new-law apartment houses, but rapid transportation to that section was very inadequate—the Lenox Avenue Subway had not yet been built—and landlords were finding difficulty in keeping houses on the east side of the section filled. Residents along and near Seventh Avenue were fairly well served by the Eighth Avenue Elevated. A colored man, in the real estate business at this time, Philip A. Payton, approached several of these landlords with the proposition that he would fill their empty or partially empty houses with steady colored tenants. The suggestion was accepted, and one or two houses on One Hundred and Thirty-fourth Street east of Lenox Avenue were taken over. Gradually other houses were filled. The whites paid little attention to the movement until it began to spread west of Lenox Avenue; they then took steps to check it. They proposed through a financial organization, the Hudson Realty Company, to buy in all properties occupied by colored people and evict the tenants. The Negroes countered by similar methods. Payton formed the Afro-American Realty Company, a Negro corporation organized for the purpose of buying and leasing houses for occupancy by colored people. Under this counter stroke the opposition subsided for several years.

But the continually increasing pressure of colored people to the west over the Lenox Avenue dead line caused the opposition to break out again, but in a new and more menacing form. Several white men undertook to organize all the white people of the community for the purpose of inducing financial institutions not to lend money or renew mortgages on properties occupied by colored people. In this effort they had considerable success, and created a situation which has not yet been completely overcome, a situation which is one of the hardest and most unjustifiable the Negro property owner in Harlem has to contend with. The Afro-American Realty Company was now defunct, but two or three colored men of means stepped into the breach. Philip A. Payton and J. C. Thomas bought two five-story apartments, dispossessed the white tenants and put in colored. J. B. Nail bought a row of five apartments and did the same thing. St. Philip's Church bought a row of thirteen apartment houses on One Hundred and Thirty-fifth Street, running from Seventh Avenue almost to Lenox.

The situation now resolved itself into an actual contest. Negroes not only continued to occupy available apartment houses, but began to purchase private dwellings between Lenox and Seventh Avenues. Then the whole movement, in the eyes of the whites, took on the aspect of an "invasion"; they became panic-stricken and began fleeing as from a plague. The presence of one colored family in a block, no matter how well bred and orderly, was sufficient to precipitate a flight. House after house and block after block was actually deserted. It was a great demonstration of human beings running amuck. None of them stopped to reason why they were doing it or what would happen if they didn't. The banks and lending companies holding mortgages on these deserted houses were compelled to take them over. For some time they held these houses vacant, preferring to do that and carry the charges than to rent or sell them to colored people. But values dropped and continued to drop until at the outbreak of the war in Europe property in the northern part of Harlem had reached the nadir.

In the meantime the Negro colony was becoming more stable; the churches were being moved from the lower part of the city; social and civic centers were being formed; and gradually a community was being evolved. Following the outbreak of the war in Europe Negro Harlem received a new and tremendous impetus. Because of the war thousands of aliens in the United States rushed back to their native lands to join the colors and immigration practically ceased. The result was a critical shortage in labor. This shortage was rapidly increased as the United States went more and more largely into the business of furnishing munitions and supplies to the warring countries. To help meet this shortage of common labor Negroes were brought up from the South. The government itself took the first steps, following the practice in vogue in Germany of shifting labor according to the supply and demand in various parts of the country. The example of the government was promptly taken up by the big industrial concerns, which sent hundreds, perhaps thousands, of labor agents into the South who recruited Negroes by wholesale. I was in Jacksonville, Fla., for a while at that time, and I sat one day and watched the stream of migrants passing to take the train. For hours they passed steadily, carrying flimsy suit cases, new and shiny, rusty old ones, bursting at the seams, boxes and bundles and impedimenta of all sorts, including banjos, guitars, birds in cages and what not. Similar scenes were being enacted in cities and towns all over that region. The first wave of the great exodus of Negroes from the South was on. Great numbers of these migrants headed for New York or eventually got there, and naturally the majority went up into Harlem. But the Negro population of Harlem was not swollen by migrants from the South alone; the opportunity for Negro labor exerted its pull upon the Negroes of the West Indies, and those islanders in the course of time poured into Harlem to the number of twenty-five thousand or more.

These new-comers did not have to look for work; work looked for them, and at wages of which they had never even dreamed. And here is where the unlooked for, the unprecedented, the miraculous happened. According to all preconceived notions, these Negroes suddenly earning large sums of money for the first time in their lives should have had their heads turned; they should have squandered it in the most silly and absurd manners imaginable. Later, after the United States had entered the war and even Negroes in the South were making money fast, many stories in accord with the tradition came out of that section. There was the one about the colored man who went into a general store and on hearing a phonograph for the first time promptly ordered six of them, one for each child in the house. I shall not stop to discuss whether Negroes in the South did that sort of thing or not, but I do know that those who got to New York didn't. The Negroes of Harlem, for the greater part, worked and saved their money. Nobody knew how much they had saved until congestion made expansion necessary for tenants and owner-ship profitable for landlords, and they began to buy property. Persons who would never be suspected of having money bought property. The Rev. W. W. Brown, pastor of the Metropolitan Baptist Church, repeatedly made "Buy Property" the text of his sermons. A large part of his congregation carried out the injunction. The church itself set an example by purchasing a magnificent brownstone church building on Seventh Avenue from a white congregation. Buying property became a fever. At the height of this activity, that is, 1920-21, it was not an uncommon thing for a colored washerwoman or cook to go into a real estate office and lay down from one thousand to five thousand dollars on a house. "Pig Foot Mary" is a character in Harlem. Everybody who knows the corner of Lenox Avenue and One Hundred and Thirty-fifth Street knows "Mary" and her stand, and has been tempted by the smell of her pigsfeet, fried chicken and hot corn, even if he has not been a customer. "Mary," whose real name is Mrs. Mary Dean, bought the five-story apartment house at the corner of Seventh Avenue and One Hundred and Thirty-seventh Street at a price of $42,000. Later she sold it to the Y. W. C. A. for dormitory purposes. The Y. W. C. A. sold it recently to Adolph Howell, a leading colored undertaker, the price given being $72,000. Often companies of a half dozen men combined to buy a house—these combinations were and still are generally made up of West Indians—and would produce five or ten thousand dollars to put through the deal.

When the buying activity began to make itself felt, the lending companies that had been holding vacant the handsome dwellings on and abutting Seventh Avenue decided to put them on the market. The values on these houses had dropped to the lowest mark possible and they were put up at astonishingly low prices. Houses that had been bought at from $15,000 to $20,000 were sold at one-third those figures. They were quickly gobbled up. The Equitable Life Assurance Company held 106 model private houses that were designed by Stanford White. They are built with courts running straight through the block and closed off by wrought-iron gates. Every one of these houses was sold within eleven months at an aggregate price of about two million dollars. To-day they are probably worth about 100 per cent more. And not only have private dwellings and similar apartments been bought but big elevator apartments have been taken over. Corporations have been organized for this purpose. Two of these, The Antillian Realty Company, composed of West Indian Negroes, and the Sphinx Securities Company, composed of American and West Indian Negroes, represent holdings amounting to approximately $750,000. Individual Negroes and companies in the South have invested in Harlem real estate. About two years ago a Negro institution of Savannah, Ga., bought a parcel for $115,000 which it sold a month or so ago at a profit of $110,000.

I am informed by John E. Nail, a successful colored real estate dealer of Harlem and a reliable authority, that the total value of property in Harlem owned and controlled by colored people would at a conservative estimate amount to more than sixty million dollars. These figures are amazing, especially when we take into account the short time in which they have been piled up. Twenty years ago Negroes were begging for the privilege of renting a flat in Harlem. Fifteen years ago barely a half dozen colored men owned real property in all Manhattan. And down to ten years ago the amount that had been acquired in Harlem was comparatively negligible. To-day Negro Harlem is practically owned by Negroes.

The question naturally arises, "Are the Negroes going to be able to hold Harlem?" If they have been steadily driven northward for the past hundred years and out of less desirable sections, can they hold this choice bit of Manhattan Island? It is hardly probable that Negroes will hold Harlem indefinitely, but when they are forced out it will not be for the same reasons that forced them out of former quarters in New York City. The situation is entirely different and without precedent. When colored people do leave Harlem, their homes, their churches, their investments and their businesses, it will be because the land has become so valuable they can no longer afford to live on it. But the date of another move northward is very far in the future. What will Harlem be and become in the meantime? Is there danger that the Negro may lose his economic status in New York and be unable to hold his property? Will Harlem become merely a famous ghetto, or will it be a center of intellectual, cultural and economic forces exerting an influence throughout the world, especially upon Negro peoples? Will it become a point of friction between the races in New York?

I think there is less danger to Negroes of New York of losing out economically and industrially than to the Negroes of any large city in the North. In most of the big industrial centers Negroes are engaged in gang labor. They are employed by thousands in the stockyards in Chicago, by thousands in the automobile plants in Detroit; and in those cities they are likely to be the first to be let go, and in thousands, with every business depression. In New York there is hardly such a thing as gang labor among Negroes, except among the longshoremen, and it is in the longshoremen's unions, above all others, that Negroes stand on an equal footing. Employment among Negroes in New York is highly diversified; in the main they are employed more as individuals than as non-integral parts of a gang. Furthermore, Harlem is gradually becoming more and more a self-supporting community. Negroes there are steadily branching out into new businesses and enterprises in which Negroes are employed. So the danger of great numbers of Negroes being thrown out of work at once, with a resulting economic crisis among them, is less in New York than in most of the large cities of the North to which Southern migrants have come.

These facts have an effect which goes beyond the economic and industrial situation. They have a direct bearing on the future character of Harlem and on the question as to whether Harlem will be a point of friction between the races in New York. It is true that Harlem is a Negro community, well defined and stable; anchored to its fixed homes, churches, institutions, business and amusement places; having its own working, business and professional classes. It is experiencing a constant growth of group consciousness and community feeling. Harlem is, therefore, in many respects, typically Negro. It has many unique characteristics. It has movement, color, gayety, singing, dancing, boisterous laughter and loud talk. One of its outstanding features is brass band parades. Hardly a Sunday passes but that there are several of these parades of which many are gorgeous with regalia and insignia. Almost any excuse will do—the death of an humble member of the Elks, the laying of a cornerstone, the "turning out" of the order of this or that. In many of these characteristics it is similar to the Italian colony. But withal, Harlem grows more metropolitan and more a part of New York all the while. Why is it then that its tendency is not to become a mere "quarter"?

I shall give three reasons that seem to me to be important in their order. First, the language of Harlem is not alien; it is not Italian or Yiddish; it is English. Harlem talks American, reads American, thinks American. Second, Harlem is not physically a "quarter." It is not a section cut off. It is merely a zone through which four main arteries of the city run. Third, the fact that there is little or no gang labor gives Harlem Negroes the opportunity for individual expansion and individual contacts with the life and spirit of New York. A thousand Negroes from Mississippi put to work as a gang in a Pittsburgh steel mill will for a long time remain a thousand Negroes from Mississippi. Under the conditions that prevail in New York they would all within six months become New Yorkers. The rapidity with which Negroes become good New Yorkers is one of the marvels to observers.

These three reasons form a single reason why there is small probability that Harlem will ever be a point of race friction between the races in New York. One of the principal factors in the race riot in Chicago in 1919 was the fact that at that time there were 12,000 Negroes employed in gangs in the stockyards. There was considerable race feeling in Harlem at the time of the hegira of white residents due to the "invasion," but that feeling, of course, is no more. Indeed, a number of the old white residents who didn't go or could not get away before the housing shortage struck New York are now living peacefully side by side with colored residents. In fact, in some cases white and colored tenants occupy apartments in the same house. Many white merchants still do business in thickest Harlem. On the whole, I know of no place in the country where the feeling between the races is so cordial and at the same time so matter-of-fact and taken for granted. One of the surest safeguards against an outbreak in New York such as took place in so many Northern cities in the summer of 1919 is the large proportion of Negro police on duty in Harlem.

To my mind, Harlem is more than a Negro community; it is a large scale laboratory experiment in the race problem. The statement has often been made that if Negroes were transported to the North in large numbers the race problem with all of its acuteness and with new aspects would be transferred with them. Well, 175,000 Negroes live closely together in Harlem, in the heart of New York —75,000 more than live in any Southern city—and do so without any race friction. Nor is there any unusual record of crime. I once heard a captain of the 38th Police Precinct (the Harlem precinct) say that on the whole it was the most law-abiding precinct in the city. New York guarantees its Negro citizens the fundamental rights of American citizenship and protects them in the exercise of those rights. In return the Negro loves New York and is proud of it, and contributes in his way to its greatness. He still meets with discriminations, but possessing the basic rights, he knows that these discriminations will be abolished.

I believe that the Negro's advantages and opportunities are greater in Harlem than in any other place in the country, and that Harlem will become the intellectual, the cultural and the financial center for Negroes of the United States, and will exert a vital influence upon all Negro peoples.

(1925)

ALAIN LOCKE

(1886-1954)

Alain Locke was born and attended school in Philadelphia. After graduating from Central High School, he finished the two-year course in the Normal School. He then went to Harvard, where he was later named a Rhodes scholar.

Mentor of the Harlem Renaissance, and adviser and encourager of black writers and artists from the early twenties to the fifties, Alain Locke is a major figure of Afro-American letters and thought. His education at Harvard, Oxford, and Berlin made of him an esthete whose familiarity with the world of art and literature was encyclopedic. He was equally a social scientist and an analyst of culture in the fullest sense. He was a teacher of philosophy at Howard University from 1912 until a year before his death. During these years he read and wrote constantly on questions of race, culture and esthetics. He was the preeminent black critic of literature, plastic art, and music. His versatility is indicated in The New Negro *(1925), an outgrowth of the Harlem number of the magazine* Survey Graphic *(March, 1925), in which he wrote of music, art, and literature, and provided a bibliography and an interpretive essay on the spirit of* The New Negro.

Together with Du Bois, Carter Woodson, and William Leo Hansberry, with whom he shared a Harvard background, Alain Locke was one of those who demanded of black Americans an identification with Africa at a time when such demands were wasted breath. He was one of the few black intellectuals to perceive in certain aspects of the Garvey Movement the basis for a cultural strategy for black Americans generally. Locke's contribution to the origins of Negritude have been recognized by Senghor and Damas. Richard A. Long has used the term *"ancestralism"* to describe *Locke's cultural theory respecting the African background.*

Locke's association with Opportunity, *the journal of the Urban League, was an enduring one. It began in 1923 and lasted until the demise of the journal in the forties. For* Opportunity *and later for* Phylon *he did an important annual survey of the literature of race, and he also contributed to many other journals and to the yearbook of the* Encyclopedia Britannica.

A founder of the Associates in Negro Folk Education, Locke issued under that trademark in 1936 two brief but important studies, Negro Art: Past and Present *and* The Negro and His Music. *In 1940 his illustrated work* The Negro in Art, *which presented blacks as subjects and creators, and which provided a sampling of African art, was published. Two years later he edited an important anthology with Bernhard S. Stern,* When Peoples Meet: A Study in Race and Culture Contact. *In 1943 Locke delivered in Haiti a series of lectures published in that country as* La Rôle du Nègre dans la Culture des Amériques. *At the end of his life Locke was working on what was to be his magnum opus,* The Negro in American Culture, *but he was able to complete very little of it. Margaret Just Butcher's work of that title is based in part on Locke's notes.*

Locke has been the subject of a series of National Endowment seminars conducted at Atlanta University by Richard A. Long. Studies inspired by these seminars include Alain Locke: Reflections On A Modern Renaissance Man, *ed. by Russell J. Linneman and "Alain Locke: A Comprehensive Bibliography of his Published Writings" compiled by John Edgar Tidwell and John Wright (*Callaloo IV, 1-3*). An important selection of Locke's writings is available in* The Critical Temper of Alain Locke *by Jeffrey C. Stewart.*

Apropos of Africa

Except from the point of view of religious missionarism, it has been until recently almost impossible to cultivate generally in the mind of the American Negro an abiding and serious interest in Africa. Politically, economically, scientifically, culturally, the great concerns of this great continent have engaged the Caucasian and primarily the European mind. The sooner we recognize as a fact this painful paradox, that those who have naturally the greatest interests in Africa have of all other peoples been least interested, the sooner will it be corrected. With notable exceptions, our interest in Africa has heretofore been sporadic, sentimental and unpractical. And,—as for every fact, there is of course a reason: the dark shadow of slavery has thrown Africa, in spite of our conscious wishes, into a sort of chilly and terrifying eclipse, against which only religious ardor could kindle an attractive and congenial glow of interest. The time has come, however, with the generation that knows slavery only as history, to cast off this spell, and see Africa at least with the interest of the rest of the world, if not indeed with a keener, more favored, regard. There are parallels, we must remember, for this: Except for the prosperous Tories, England was a bogey to the American colonists; from the thirties to the nineties, the average Irishman was half-ashamed of Erin in spite of lapses into occasional fervent sentimentalism; and even with the sturdy Jewish sense of patrimony, Zionism has had its difficulties in rekindling the concrete regard for the abandoned fatherland. Only prosperity looks backward. Adversity is afraid to look over its own shoulder. But eventually all peoples exhibit the homing instinct and turn back physically or mentally, hopefully and helpfully, to the land of their origin. And we American Negroes in this respect cannot, will not, be an exception.

The very same facts that have frustrated the healthy, vigorous interest in Africa and things African, have focused whatever interest there was upon the West Coast,—erroneously regarded because of the accidents of the slave-trade as our especial patrimony, if we ever had any. But the colored millions of America represent every one of the many racial stocks of Africa, are descended from the peoples of almost every quarter of the continent, and are culturally the heirs of the entire continent. The history of the wide dispersion of the slave-trade and trading-posts will establish this in the mind of any open-minded person, and an anthropological investigation of American Negro types would conclusively prove this. If the Negro is interested in Africa, he should be interested in the whole of Africa; if he is to link himself up again with his past and his kin, he must link himself up with all of the African peoples. As the physical composite of eighty-five per cent at least of the African stocks, the American Negro is in a real sense the true Pan-African, and certainly even apart from this, on the grounds of opportunity and strategic position, should be the leader in constructive Pan-African thought and endeavor. Enlightened imperialism,—but who can visualize enlightened imperialism,—would have seen in the American Negro just those resources of leadership and devoted interest which it would have needed, and could have utilized if its real aims had been the development, and not merely the exploitation of this great continent and its varied peoples. But it is rather against than with the wish of the interested governments, that the American Negro must reach out toward his rightful share in the solution of African problems and the development of Africa's resources.

II.

With a more practical and enlightened vision, the question of the redemption of Africa has become with us the question of the regeneration of Africa. We now see that the missionary condescension of the past generations in their attitude toward Africa was a pious but sad mistake. In taking it, we have fallen into the snare of enemies and have given grievous offence to our brothers. We must realize that in some respects we need what Africa has to give us as much as, or even more than, Africa needs what we in turn have to give her; and that unless we approach Africa in the spirit of the finest reciprocity, our efforts will be ineffectual or harmful. We need to be the first of all

Westerners to rid ourselves of the insulting prejudice, the insufferable bias of the attitude of "civilizing Africa,"—for she is not only our mother but in the light of most recent science is beginning to appear as the mother of civilization in general. On the other hand, the average African of the enlightened classes has his characteristic bias,—his pride of blood and bias of clan,—so that the meeting of mind between the African and the Afro-American is dependent upon a broadening of vision and a dropping of prejudices from both sides. The African must dismiss his provincialism, his political-mindedness, his pride of clan; the Afro-American, his missionary condescension, his religious parochialism, and his pride of place. The meeting of the two will mean the inauguration of a new era for both. Above all, it must be recognized that for the present the best channels of cooperative effort lie along economic and educational lines, and that religion and politics, with their inevitable contentiousness and suspicions, are far less promising ways of approach and common effort. America offers the African his greatest educational opportunity; Africa offers the Afro-American his greatest economic opportunity. So we may truly say that the salvation of the one is in the other's hands. I am aware that this is not to many a self-evident proposition, but sober thought will prove to the far-sighted what the logic of the course of events must ultimately justify for the multitude.

But here on this point we have, strangely enough, the feeling of the masses, more ready and ripe for action than the minds of the leaders and the educated few. The Garvey movement has demonstrated that conclusively. Perhaps in the perspective of time, that will appear to have been its chief service and mission,—to have stirred the race mind to the depths with the idea of large-scale cooperation between the variously separated branches of the Negro peoples. This is without doubt the great constructive idea in the race life during the last decade, and must become the center of constructive endeavor for this and the next generation. Unfortunately obscured by the controversy between its radical exponents in the Garvey movement and its liberal exponents, Dr. Du Bois and the sponsors of the Pan-African Congress, and still more unfortunately but temporarily discredited by the financial mal-administration of Mr. Garvey's over-ambitious ventures, the idea has seemed to suffer a fatal set-back. But each branch of the movement has done yeoman service, in spite of great obstacles and unfortunate mistakes,—for publicity for the idea is for the present the main thing; its successful working out is a matter of painstaking experiment and endeavor. Each has temporarily failed in what it considered to be its main objective, and what, if realized, would have been a great service both to the cause of the race and humanity at large. The esetablishment of a great tropical African State, under international mandate, was one of the most constructive and promising proposals in all the grand agenda of the Peace Conference. If Mr. Wilson had sponsored it, fewer of his fourteen points would have been shattered by selfish European diplomacy, and not only America, but the American Negro would have had an official share and a responsible opportunity in the guardianship and development of this great continent. Many forces combined to crush the idea; but when the secret history of the Conference becomes public, General Smuts will probably appear as the most blameworthy opponent of the scheme. Time will, however, eventually justify this idea and acclaim its brilliant sponsor, and out of the desperate exigencies of the near future we may yet see it brought forward in altered form in the councils of the League of Nations, although the greatest practical opportunity, the disposal of the German colonies in Africa, has been irrevocably missed. Similarly, but for internal rather than external causes, the main objective of the Garvey movement has foundered. Wholly self-initiated and self-supported trade intercourse with Africa would have been in itself a wonderful demonstration of practical economic ability on the part of American Negroes as well as of a modern and constructive interest in their African brethren. It is more of a pity, more of a reproach, that this was not realized. But in both cases the idea has survived its initial defeat. Journalistically the Garvey movement has made a permanent contribution to the Afro-American press, and has built bridges of communication for the future. The first great span in the archway, communication, exchange of thought and information between American Negroes and their brothers in the West Indies, can be optimistically regarded as already established. With greater difficulty, three Pan-African Congresses have been trying to construct the broader spans of communication and publicity between us and Africa. The greatest difficulty is in bringing African interests together; that task once achieved, it will be comparatively easy to link up with the American groups. This is especially the problem of the Third Pan-African Congress, which has just concluded its sessions. In the present situation when national feeling, especially that of the French and Belgian contingents, threatens to disrupt the feeble unity of action already achieved, it is very necessary that the American Negro, the most disinterested party, should assume very direct leadership and responsibility for the movement, insisting upon keeping dominant the Pan-African character of the scheme. This is Dr. DuBois' purpose in holding the conference at what is considered by many formerly enthusiastic members as a singularly inappropriate time. Quixotic as it may seem to run counter to the wishes of many African delegates, such a course is undoubtedly right; but, pending its justification, the Pan-African idea is just now at the most critical point of its career. The European press and public opinion have always shown keenest interest, appreciating the important potentialities of this movement; it is the apathy and disinterestedness of the American, and especially the Afro-American press, which is the strange and disappointing feature of the situation. If the movement should lag, it will be an indictment of the intelligence, perspicacity, and race-mindedness of the American Negro.

III.

The great reason for this unfortunate apathy of interests is the lack of widespread and matter of fact information about Africa. Our interests are fed on sentiment, and not with knowledge. Our first duty is to cultivate every opportunity for the diffusion among us of the knowledge of Africa both of today and of the past. Travel, exchange of students, the spread of journalistic and academic information are for the moment of paramount importance. In a decade in which the study of African art and archeology has come to the very forefront of scholarship, it is both a reproach and a handicap to have no recognized experts of our own in these fields. Instead of being reluctant, our Negro colleges should be eager to develop special scholarship in these directions; in the cultural field, here is their special and peculiar chance to enter the academic arena and justify themselves. The pioneer work of the *Journal of Negro History*, under Dr. Carter G. Woodson, and of Howard University in the courses of the history of African civilizations, under Mr. Leo Hansberry, deserve not mere passing interest and praise but the financial support of the people and the active participation of the talented tenth. And both must eventually culminate, the sooner, the better, for the present is a very psychological moment in African studies, in well-planned and well-supported research investigation in Africa. Later I shall write more specifically about the problems and opportunities of research in this field as they have come under observation in the *reconnaisance* trip I have been able to undertake; for the moment it will suffice to quote, by permission, the following representative opinion from a letter of Mr. Arthur Weigall, former Chief Inspector of Antiquities for Upper Egypt, to that most eminent of archeologists, Sir William Flinders-Petrie: "The study of the history and traditions of the African races by their own students is, I think, most interesting, and I am sure you will find the idea of an African mind applying itself to ancient African manners and customs a very promising one." Out of over a score of most eminent authorities interviewed on this subject, all save two have substantially concurred in this opinion, and these two were investigators who strictly relegate ethnological matters to the findings of anthropometry and, naturally enough, consider physical anthropology too scientifically neutral for there to be any advantage or peculiar point to our participation. On the other hand, even they were willing to admit that in the question of folk-lore and comparative study of customs, psychological *rapport* and *entree* to the groups studied were of paramount importance, and that with respect to the study of African peoples, the employment of trained colored investigators would inaugurate a new era in this important, but admittedly unsatisfactory, field of research.

IV.

As an instance of the effectiveness of an identity of interest of this sort, one might cite the case of the Museum for Coptic Antiquities in Cairo. In ten years, six of them almost useless to the project because of the war, and with only limited private funds, but with the great intangible capital of group loyalty and cooperation. Murcos Samaika Pasha has assembled in competition with the great endowed museums of Europe and America a collection of Coptic antiquities which almost rivals the best in any line of special collection and in variety outmatches all. Artistically housed in the buildings adjacent to El Moallaka Church, Old Cairo, and maintained as part of that beautiful and historic structure, it is really one of the treasures of Cairo, and though quite off the beaten track, its register of prominent public and academic visitors attests the power of attraction of anything unique and distinctive. For this people, the martyrs and guardians of Christianity in Africa, and their interesting history and institutions, we should cultivate a very special and intimate interest. Certainly it was most pleasant to be assured by their most representative men that they regard us with a brotherly and lively interest and would welcome more cordial and intimate relations. Ethnologists may argue and dispute all they like, but a felt brotherhood and kinship is pragmatically a fact—and these ancient and rather exemplary people feel a kinship of blood and religion between us. After all, there is no greater difference of ethnic strain between us if as much as between the North and the South German or the Frenchman of Provence and the Frenchman of Flanders. Certainly with our access to the technique of western scientific scholarship, some of us ought to come to the study of the history of the people and their historically important branch of Christianity; for here, with very few exceptions, there is a definite case of the bias and disparagement of alien investigators. Just as the sympathetic call of Samaika Pasha coaxed out of many a hidden corner treasures unknown or inaccessible to the western antiquarian, so in the research history of the Coptic and the Abyssinian church, racial sympathy would open many a closed door and make accessible much that is hidden. We have not merely the word and opinion of this leader of the Egyptian Copts but by a fortunate coincidence of travel, the word and invitation of the august Abuna of the Church of Abyssinia, who has recently made a pilgrimage to Jerusalem where, incidentally, the patriarchate of this historic branch of Christianity maintains a votive church.

V.

While our active interests in Africa must of necessity and of reason remain educational and eventually economic, there is every reason why we should be keenly interested in the political fortunes of all African peoples. The apathy of our general public opinion in the matter of the proposed American loan and economic protection to Liberia was a shameful dereliction, which should not be allowed to repeat itself on any matter of African politics. Assessing at the lowest value, the motives of this project, and supposing even that it could have militated somewhat against Liberian sovereignty—a too pessimistic and undeserved assumption, especially in view of the moral force of the League of Nations, we may warrantably ask, what better guarantee of fair and considerate treatment could the Liberians have had than the force of the American Negro electorate, if properly awake and intelligently directed? Minorities have as their best protection today the court of world opinion; if they do not live on an international scale and in the eyes of the world, they are doomed even in the twentieth century to medieval conditions and hardships. Witness the effectiveness of that fine voice in the League of Nations, the former Haytian representative, Monsieur Bellegarde, who ought to have the esteem and gratitude of the entire world of colored people. European statesmen and publicists felt and acknowledged the force of this man; his recall was a calamity to our larger international interest. The success and strength of the Jew, still very precariously situated in some parts of the world, has been his international scale of organization, promoted first of all by his religion, and latterly through many other channels of cooperative race effort, of which Zionism is only one phase. Mr. Ford's phrase is true,—the international Jew; but it is an unwarrantable calumny because his inferences are wrong. In the first place, the Jew has been made international by persecution and forced dispersion,—and so, potentially, have we. In the second place, as a minority threatened here and there, its only intelligent safeguard has been international appeal and international organization. To relieve pressure in one place very often pressure has to be strategically applied in another, and the Jewish people have perforce become masters in this intelligent and modern strategy of group action. And if the international mind is to be for all people the eventual achievement, the Jew has simply the temporary advantage of having acquired it a little in advance of the rest of the world.

There is much value to us in this great example. We have for the present, in spite of Mr. Garvey's hectic efforts, no Zionistic hope or intention. But for protection and mutual development, we must develop the race mind and race interest on an international scale. For that reason, we should be most vitally interested in the idea of the League of Nations and all kindred movements. For that reason, it should be a matter of the profoundest satisfaction that an African State, with almost unassailable sovereignty, has recently achieved recognition and admittance; and on the basis of an enlightened initiative of its own. It was my privilege to meet and congratulate the able envoy,—His Excellency Belata Herony, in Egypt, on his way from Geneva to Addis Ababa; a man of modern view and twentieth century skill and what is more important, international vision. At a time when warrantably he might have been naturally and pardonably nationalistic and characteristic in sentiment, one found his dominant mood that of internationalism and the progressive interests of the darker races the world over. Politically he represents

Abyssinia; morally, however, I am sure, our interests and those of
Negroes everywhere on progressive world legislation and in event
of an appeal on any necessary question to the court of world opinion.
We already know from the cordial and interested behavior of this
man on his American visit, what a vivid sense of racial interest he
has. Counselled in another direction, the entire mission regarded the
colored people of America as brothers, and the feeling of kinship
was warmly reciprocated. To congratulations offered in the name
of our group, his reply, with greetings and assurances of warm
interest, was a forecast of progressive reform and development for
Abyssinia which proclaimed it, in my judgment, the most promising
and strategic center of African development in the near future, a
forecast that in itself was tantamount to a cordial invitation for closer
relations and cooperative help. I repeat, of the many, here is special
reason for more active and enlightened interest in Africa.

(1924)

The Negro Spirituals

The Spirituals are really the most characteristic product of the
race genius as yet in America. But the very elements which make
them uniquely expressive of the Negro make them at the same time
deeply representative of the soil that produced them. Thus, as
unique spiritual products of American life, they become nationally
as well as racially characteristic. It may not be readily conceded now
that the song of the Negro is America's folk-song; but if the Spirituals are what we think them to be, a classic folk expression, then
this is their ultimate destiny. Already they give evidence of this
classic quality. Through their immediate and compelling universality

of appeal, through their untarnishable beauty, they seem assured of the immortality of those great folk expressions that survive not so much through being typical of a group or representative of a period as by virtue of being fundamentally and everlastingly human. This universality of the Spirituals looms more and more as they stand the test of time. They have outlived the particular generation and the peculiar conditions which produced them; they have survived in turn the contempt of the slave owners, the conventionalizations of formal religion, the repressions of Puritanism, the corruptions of sentimental balladry, and the neglect and disdain of second-generation respectability. They have escaped the lapsing conditions and the fragile vehicle of folk art, and come firmly into the context of formal music. Only classics survive such things.

In its disingenuous simplicity, folk art is always despised and rejected at first; but generations after, it flowers again and transcends the level of its origin. The slave songs are no exception; only recently have they come to be recognized as artistically precious things. It still requires vision and courage to proclaim their ultimate value and possibilities. But while the first stage of artistic development is yet uncompleted, it appears that behind the deceptive simplicity of Negro song lie the richest undeveloped musical resources anywhere available. Thematically rich, in idiom of rhythm and harmony richer still, in potentialities of new musical forms and new technical traditions so deep as to be accessible only to genius, they have the respect of the connoisseur even while still under the sentimental and condescending patronage of the amateur. Proper understanding and full appreciation of the Spirituals, in spite of their present vogue, is still rare. And the Negro himself has shared many of the common and widespread limitations of view with regard to them. The emotional intuition which has made him cling to this folk music has lacked for the most part that convinced enlightenment that eventually will treasure the Spirituals for their true musical and technical values. And although popular opinion and the general conception have changed very materially, a true estimate of this body of music cannot be reached until many prevailing preconceptions are completely abandoned. For what general opinion regards as simple and transparent about them is in technical ways, though instinctive, very intricate and complex, and what is taken as whimsical and child-like is in truth, though naïve, very profound.

It was the great service of Dr. DuBois in his unforgettable chapter on the Sorrow Songs in *The Souls of the Black Folk* to give them a serious and proper social interpretation, just as later Mr. Krehbiel in his *Afro-American Folk Songs* gave them their most serious and adequate musical analysis and interpretation. The humble origin of these sorrow songs is too indelibly stamped upon them to be ignored or overlooked. But underneath broken words, childish imagery, peasant simplicity, lies, as Dr. Du Bois pointed out, an epic intensity and a tragic profundity of emotional experience, for which the only historical analogy is the spiritual experience of the Jews and the only analogue, the Psalms. Indeed they transcend emotionally even the very experience of sorrow out of which they were born; their mood is that of religious exaltation, a degree of ecstasy indeed that makes them in spite of the crude vehicle a classic expression of the religious emotion. They lack the grand style, but never the sublime effect. Their words are colloquial, but their mood is epic. They are primitive, but their emotional artistry is perfect. Indeed, spiritually evaluated, they are among the most genuine and outstanding expressions of Christian mood and feeling, fit musically and emotionally, if not verbally, of standing with the few Latin hymns, the handful of Gregorian tunes, and the rarest of German chorals as a not negligible element in the modicum of strictly religious music that the Christian centuries have produced.

Perhaps there is no such thing as intrinsically religious music; certainly the traceable interplay of the secular and the religious in music would scarcely warrant an arbitrary opinion in the matter. And just as certainly as secular elements can be found in all religious music are there discoverable sensuous and almost pagan elements blended into the Spirituals. But something so intensely religious and so essentially Christian dominates the blend that they are indelibly and notably of this quality. The Spirituals are spiritual. Conscious artistry and popular conception alike should never rob them of this heritage, it is untrue to their tradition and to the folk genius to give them another tone. That they are susceptible of both crude and refined secularization is no excuse. Even though their own makers worked them up from the "shout" and the rhythmic elements of the sensuous dance, in their finished form and basic emotional effect all of these elements were completely sublimated in the sincere intensities of religious seriousness. To call them Spirituals and treat them otherwise is a travesty.

It was the Negro himself who first took them out of their original religious setting, but he only anticipated the inevitable by a generation—for the folk religion that produced them is rapidly vanishing.

Noble as the purpose of this transplanting was, damage was done to the tradition. But we should not be ungrateful, for surely it was by this that they were saved to posterity at all. Nevertheless it was to an alien atmosphere that the missionary campaigning of the Negro schools and colleges took these songs. And the concert stage has but taken them an inevitable step further from their original setting. We should always remember that they are essentially congregational, not theatrical, just as they are essentially a choral not a solo form. In time, however, on another level, they will get back to this tradition,—for their next development will undoubtedly be, like that of the modern Russian folk music, their use in the larger choral forms of the symphonic choir, through which they will reachieve their folk atmosphere and epic spirituality.

It is a romantic story told in the *Story of the Jubilee Singers*, and retold in Professor Work's *Folk Song of the American Negro;* the tale of that group of singers who started out from Fisk University in 1871, under the resolute leadership of George L. White, to make this music the appeal of the struggling college for philanthropic support. With all the cash in the Fisk treasury, except a dollar held back by Principal Adam K. Spence, the troupe set out to Oberlin, where, after an unsuccessful concert of current music, they instantly made an impression by a program of Negro Spirituals. Henry Ward Beecher's invitation to Brooklyn led to fame for the singers, fortune for the college, but more important than these things, recognition for the Spirituals. Other schools, Hampton, Atlanta, Calhoun, Tuskegee joined the movement, and spread the knowledge of these songs far and wide in their concert campaigns. Later they recorded and published important collections of them. They thus were saved over that critical period of disfavor in which any folk product is likely to be snuffed out by the false pride of the second generation. Professor Work rightly estimates it as a service worth more racially and nationally than the considerable sums of money brought to these struggling schools. Indeed, as he says, it saved a folk art and preserved as no other medium could the folk temperament, and by maintaining them introduced the Negro to himself. Still the predominant values of this period in estimating the Spirituals were the sentimental, degenerating often into patronizing curiosity on the one side, and hectic exhibitionism on the other. Both races condescended to meet the mind of the Negro slave, and even while his moods were taking their hearts by storm, discounted the artistry of genius therein.

It was only as the musical appreciation of the Spirituals grew
that this interest changed and deepened. Musically I think the Spirituals are as far in advance of their moods as their moods are in
advance of their language. It is as poetry that they are least effective.
Even as folk poetry, they cannot be highly rated. But they do have
their quaint symbolisms, and flashes, sometimes sustained passages of
fine imagery, as in the much quoted

> I know moonlight, I know starlight
> > I lay dis body down
> I walk in de graveyard, I walk troo de graveyard
> > To lay dis body down.
>
> I lay in de grave an' stretch out my arms,
> > I lay dis body down.
> I go to de judgment in de evenin' of de day
> > When I lay dis body down,
> An' my soul an' yo' soul will meet de day
> > I lay dis body down.

or

> Bright sparkles in de churchyard
> > Give light unto de tomb;
> Bright summer, spring's over—
> > Sweet flowers in their bloom.
>
> My mother once, my mother twice, my mother,
> > she'll rejoice,
> In the Heaven once, in the Heaven twice,
> > she'll rejoice.
> May the Lord, He will be glad of me
> In the Heaven, He'll rejoice.

or again

> My Lord is so high, you can't get over Him,
> My Lord is so low, you can't get under Him,
> > You must come in and through de Lamb.

In the latter passages, there is a naïveté, and also a faith and fervor, that are mediæval. Indeed one has to go to the Middle Ages to find anything quite like this combination of childlike simplicity of thought with strangely consummate artistry of mood. A quaintly literal, lisping, fervent Christianity, we feel it to be the evangelical and Protestant counterpart of the naïve Catholicism of the tenth to the thirteenth centuries. And just as there we had quaint versions of Bernard of Clairvaux and Saint Francis in the Virgin songs and Saints Legends, so here we have Bunyan and John Wesley percolated through a peasant mind and imagination, and concentrated into something intellectually less, but emotionally more vital and satisfying. If the analogy seems forced, remember that we see the homely colloquialism of the one through the glamorous distance of romance, and of the other, through the disillusioning nearness of social stigma and disdain. How regrettable though, that the very qualities that add charm to the one should arouse mirthful ridicule for the other.

Over-keen sensitiveness to this reaction, which will completely pass within a half generation or so, has unfortunately caused many singers and musicians to blur the dialect and pungent colloquialisms of the Spirituals so as not to impede with irrelevant reactions their proper artistic and emotional effect. Some have gone so far as to advocate the abandonment of the dialect versions to insure their dignity and reverence. But for all their inadequacies, the words are the vital clues to the moods of these songs. If anything is to be changed, it should be the popular attitude. One thing further may be said, without verging upon apologetics, about their verbal form. In this broken dialect and grammar there is almost invariably an unerring sense of euphony. Mr. Work goes so far as to suggest—rightly, I think—that in many instances the dropped, elided, and added syllables, especially the latter, are a matter of instinctive euphonic sense following the requirements of the musical rhythm, as, for example, "The Blood came a twinklin' down" from "The Crucifixion" or "Lying there fo' to be heal" from "Blind Man at the Pool." Mr. Work calls attention to the extra beat syllable, as in "De trumpet soun's it in-a' my soul," which is obviously a singing device, a subtle phrase-molding element from a musical point of view, even if on verbal surface value, it suggests illiteracy.

Emotionally, these folks songs are far from simple. They are not only spread over the whole gamut of human moods, with the traditional religious overtone adroitly insinuated in each instance, but there is further a sudden change of mood in the single song, baffling to formal classification. Interesting and intriguing as was Dr. Du Bois's analysis of their emotional themes, modern interpretation must break with that mode of analysis, and relate these songs to the folk activities that they motivated, classifying them by their respective song-types. From this point of view we have essentially four classes, the almost ritualistic prayer songs or pure Spirituals, the freer and more unrestrained evangelical "shouts" or camp-meeting songs, the folk ballads so overlaid with the tradition of the Spirituals proper that their distinctive type quality has almost been unnoticed until lately, and the work and labor songs of strictly secular character. In choral and musical idiom closely related, these song types are gradually coming to be regarded as more and more separate, with the term Spiritual reserved almost exclusively for the songs of intensest religious significance and function. Indeed, in the pure Spirituals one can trace the broken fragments of an evangelical folk liturgy, with confession, exhortation, "mourning," conversion and "love-feast" rejoicing as the general stages of a Protestant folk-mass. The instinctive feeling for these differences is almost wholly lost, and it will require the most careful study of the communal life as it still lingers in isolated spots to set the groupings even approximately straight. Perhaps after all the final appeal will have to be made to the sensitive race interpreter, but at present many a half secularized ballad is mistaken for a "spiritual," and many a camp-meeting shout for a folk hymn. It is not a question of religious content or allusion,—for the great majority of the Negro songs have this—but a more delicate question of caliber of feeling and type of folk use. From this important point of view, Negro folk song has yet to be studied.

The distinctiveness of the Spirituals after all, and their finest meaning resides in their musical elements. It is pathetic to notice how late scientific recording has come to the task of preserving this unique folk art. Of course the earlier four-part hymn harmony versions were travesties of the real folk renditions. All competent students agree in the utter distinctiveness of the melodic, harmonic and rhythmic elements in this music. However, there is a regrettable tendency, though a very natural one in view of an inevitable bias of technical interest, to over-stress as basically characteristic one or other of these elements in their notation and analysis. Weldon Johnson thinks the characteristic beauty of the folk song is harmonic, in distinction to the more purely rhythmic stress in the secular music of the Negro, which is the basis of "ragtime" and "jazz"; while Krehbiel, more academically balances these elements, regarding the one as the African component in them, and the other as the modifying influence of the religious hymn. "In the United States," he says, "the rhythmic element, though still dominant, has yielded measurably to the melodic, the dance having given way to religious worship, sensual bodily movement to emotional utterance." But as a matter of fact, if we separate or even over-stress either element in the Spirituals, the distinctive and finer effects are lost. Strain out and emphasize the melodic element *a la* Foster, and you get only the sentimental ballad; emphasize the harmonic idiom, and you get a cloying sentimental glee; over-emphasize the rhythmic idiom and instantly you secularize the product into syncopated dance elements. It is the fusion, and that only, that is finely characteristic; and so far as possible, both in musical settings and in the singing of the Negro Spirituals, this subtle balance of musical elements should be sought after and maintained. The actual mechanics of the native singing, with its syllabic quavers, the off-tones and tone glides, the improvised interpolations and, above all, the subtle rhythmic phrase balance, has much to do with the preservation of the vital qualities of these songs.

Let us take an example. There is no more careful and appreciative student of the Spirituals than David Guion; as far as is possible from a technical and outside approach, he has bent his skill to catch the idiom of these songs. But contrast his version of "God's Goin' to Set Dis Worl' on Fire" with that of Roland Hayes. The subtler rhythmic pattern, the closer phrase linkage, the dramatic recitative movement, and the rhapsodic voice glides and quavers of the great Negro tenor's version are instantly apparent. It is more than a question of musicianship, it is a question of feeling instinctively qualities put there by instinct. In the process of the art development of this material the Negro musician has not only a peculiar advantage but a particular function and duty. Maintaining spiritual kinship with the best traditions of this great folk art, he must make himself the recognized vehicle of both its transmission and its further development.

At present the Spirituals are at a very difficult point in their musical career; for the moment they are caught in the transitional stage between a folk-form and an art-form. Their increasing concert use and popularity, as Carl Van Vechten has clearly pointed out in a recent article, has brought about a dangerous tendency toward sophisticated over-elaboration. At the same time that he calls attention to the yeoman service of Mr. Henry T. Burleigh in the introduction of the Spirituals to the attention and acceptance of the concert stage,

Mr. Van Vechten thinks many of his settings tincture the folk spirit with added concert furbelows and alien florid adornments. This is true. Even Negro composers have been perhaps too much influenced by formal European idioms and mannerisms in setting these songs. But in calling for the folk atmosphere, and insisting upon the folk quality, we must be careful not to confine this wonderfully potential music to the narrow confines of "simple versions" and musically primitive molds. While it is proper to set up as a standard the purity of the tradition and the maintenance of idiom, it is not proper to insist upon an arbitrary style or form. When for similar reasons, Mr. Van Vechten insists in the name of the folk spirit upon his preference for the "evangelical renderings" of Paul Robeson's robust and dramatic style as over against the subdued, ecstatic and spiritually refined versions of Roland Hayes, he overlooks the fact that the folk itself has these same two styles of singing, and in most cases discriminates according to the mood, occasion and song type, between them. So long as the peculiar quality of Negro song is maintained, and the musical idiom kept unadulterated, there is and can be no set limitation. Negro folk song is not midway its artistic career as yet, and while the preservation of the original folk forms is for the moment the most pressing necessity, an inevitable art development awaits them, as in the past it has awaited all other great folk music.

The complaint to be made is not against the art development of the Spirituals, but against the somewhat hybrid treatment characteristic of the older school of musicians. One of the worst features of this period has been the predominance of solo treatment and the loss of the vital sustained background of accompanying voices. In spite of the effectiveness of the solo versions, especially when competently sung by Negro singers, it must be realized more and more that the proper idiom of Negro folk song calls for choral treatment. The young Negro musicians, Nathaniel Dett, Carl Diton, Ballanta Taylor, Edward Boatner, Hall Johnson, Lawrence Brown and others, while they are doing effective solo settings, are turning back gradually to the choral form. Musically speaking, only the superficial resources in this direction have been touched as yet; just as soon as the traditional conventions of four-part harmony and the oratorio style and form are broken through, we may expect a choral development of Negro folk song that may equal or even outstrip the phenomenal choral music of Russia. With its harmonic versatility and interchangeable voice parts, Negro music is only conventionally in the four-part style, and with its skipped measures and interpolations it is at the very least potentially polyphonic. It can therefore undergo without breaking its own boundaries, intricate and original development in directions already the line of advance in modernistic music.

Indeed one wonders why something vitally new has not already been contributed by Negro folk song to modern choral and orchestral musical development. And if it be objected that it is too far a cry from the simple folk spiritual to the larger forms and idioms of modern music, let us recall the folk song origins of the very tradition which is now classic in European music. Up to the present, the resources of Negro music have been tentatively exploited in only one direction at a time,—melodically here, rhythmically there, harmonically in a third direction. A genius that would organize its distinctive elements in a formal way would be the musical giant of his age. Such a development has been hampered by a threefold tradition, each aspect of which stands in the way of the original use of the best in the Negro material. The dominance of the melodic tradition has played havoc with its more original harmonic features, and the oratorio tradition has falsely stereotyped and overlaid its more orchestral choral style, with its intricate threading in and out of the voices. Just as definitely in another direction has the traditional choiring of the orchestra stood against the opening up and development of the Negro and the African idioms in the orchestral forms. Gradually these barriers are being broken through. Edgar Varese's *Integrales*, a "study for percussion instruments," presented last season by the International Composers' Guild, suggests a new orchestral technique patterned after the characteristic idiom of the African "drum orchestra." The modernistic, *From the Land of Dreams*, by Grant Still, a young Negro composer who is his student and protége, and Louis Grünberg's setting for baritone and chamber orchestra of Weldon Johnson's *The Creation: a Negro Sermon*, are experimental tappings in still other directions into the rich veins of this new musical ore. In a recent article (*The Living Age*, October, 1924), Darius Milhaud sums up these characteristic traits as "the possibilities of a thoroughgoing novelty of instrumental technique." Thus Negro music very probably has a great contribution yet to make to the substance and style of contemporary music, both choral and instrumental. If so, its thematic and melodic contributions from Dvorák to Goldmark's recent *Negro Rhapsody* and the borrowings of rhythmical suggestions by Milhaud and Stravinsky are only preluding experiments that have proclaimed the value of the Negro musical idioms, but have not fully developed them. When a body of folk music is really taken up into musical tradition, it is apt to do more than contribute a few new themes. For when the rhythmic and harmonic basis of music is affected, it is more than a question of superstructure, the very foundations of the art are in process of being influenced.

In view of this very imminent possibility, it is in the interest of musical development itself that we insist upon a broader conception and a more serious appreciation of Negro folk song, and of the Spiritual which is the very kernel of this distinctive folk art. We cannot accept the attitude that would merely preserve this music, but must cultivate that which would also develop it. Equally with treasuring and appreciating it as music of the past, we must nurture and welcome its contribution to the music of to-morrow. Mr. Work has aptly put it in saying: "While it is now assured that we shall always preserve these songs in their original forms, they can never be the last word in the development of our music. . . . They are the starting point, not our goal; the source, not the issue, of our musical tradition."

(1925)

MARCUS GARVEY
(1887-1940)

Marcus Garvey, who was born in Jamaica, shares with Booker T. Washington, whom he admired and whose educational enterprise he had hoped to emulate in Jamaica, the distinction of being one of the few black leaders to have had a genuine mass following in the United States. The differences between the two are obvious. Washington's primacy was conferred by the establishment, and became an amiable legend; Garvey's was achieved against considerable odds and was maintained for only a brief period. The UNIA (Universal Negro Improvement Association), the organizational arm of the Garvey movement, was chartered in New York in 1917. Its nationwide growth was arrested by Garvey's indictment in 1923 in connection with alleged business irregularities. Its prospects for survival dimmed when Garvey was imprisoned in 1925 and deported in 1927 upon the commutation of his five-year sentence. But for several years Garvey's was a name and a personality of the first importance, for he provided untold millions of lowly black Americans with a sense of pride in themselves and in Africa.

Garvey's program, never articulated in detail, had two major objectives: black self-sufficiency through the establishment of capitalistic structures owned by blacks, and African redemption, to be consummated in a United States of Africa. Both goals were quasi-utopian and modelled too closely on European models which had never proved especially beneficial to black people. Garvey, though a well-read, self-educated man, had little real knowledge of business or of Africa, and his success was largely due to his prophetic demeanor and the need it fulfilled.

Garvey's African scheme was taken seriously enough, however,

by colonial nations to cause them to ban The Negro World, *the organ
of the UNIA, to which Garvey contributed essays, speeches, and
poems.*

Garvey's personal absence from the United States, the incompe-
tence and treachery of his lieutenants, and the coming of the Depression had virtually destroyed the UNIA by 1930. Its enterprises were
bankrupt, its following, disconsolate and defeated. Garvey attempted
to develop a political base in Jamaica in the early thirties. Discouraged,
he went to London in 1935 where he attempted to maintain his international position through writing and correspondence.

Garvey's speeches and writings were edited by his wife, Amy
Jacques Garvey, and published in two volumes (1923; 1925). Mrs.
Garvey's personal history of the movement, Garvey and Garveyism
(1963), naturally contains considerable material of interest. Black
Moses (1955), a study of Garvey by Edmund Cronon, is also of in-
terest. Norman Hodges is doing a joint biography of Garvey and
Mrs. Garvey.

Garvey's career has been illuminated by the volumes of The Marcus Garvey and Universal Negro Improvement Association Papers, *being edited by
Robert A. Hill (1983–   ).*

The Principles of the Universal Negro
Improvement Association

SPEECH DELIVERED AT LIBERTY HALL,
NOVEMBER 25, 1922.

Over five years ago the Universal Negro Improvement Association placed itself before the world as the movement through which the new and rising Negro would give expression of his feelings. This Association adopts an attitude not of hostility to other races and peoples of the world, but an attitude of self-respect, of manhood rights on behalf of 400,000,000 Negroes of the world.

We represent peace, harmony, love, human sympathy, human rights and human justice, and that is why we fight so much. Wheresoever human rights are denied to any group, wheresoever justice is denied to any group, there the U. N. I. A. finds a cause. And at this time among all the peoples of the world, the group that suffers most from injustice, the group that is denied most of those rights that belong to all humanity, is the black group of 400,000,000. Because of that injustice, because of that denial of our rights, we go forth under the leadership of the One who is always on the side of right to fight the common cause of humanity; to fight as we fought in the Revolutionary War, as we fought in the Civil War, as we fought in the Spanish-American War, and as we fought in the war between 1914-18 on the battle plains of France and of Flanders. As we fought on the heights of Mesopotamia; even so under the leadership of the U. N. I. A., we are marshaling the 400,000,000 Negroes of the world to fight for the emancipation of the race and of the redemption of the country of our fathers.

We represent a new line of thought among Negroes. Whether

you call it advanced thought or reactionary thought, I do not care. If it is reactionary for people to seek independence in government, then we are reactionary. If it is advanced thought for people to seek liberty and freedom, then we represent the advanced school of thought among the Negroes of this country. We of the U. N. I. A. believe that what is good for the other folks is good for us. If government is something that is worth while; if government is something that is appreciable and helpful and protective to others, then we also want to experiment in government. We do not mean a government that will make us citizens without rights or subjects without consideration. We mean a kind of government that will place our race in control even, as other races are in control of their own governments.

That does not suggest anything that is unreasonable. It was not unreasonable for George Washington, the great hero and father of the country, to have fought for the freedom of America, giving to us this great republic and this great democracy; it was not unreasonable for the Liberals of France to have fought against the Monarchy to give to the world French Democracy and French Republicanism; it was no unrighteous cause that led Tolstoi to sound the call of liberty in Russia, which has ended in giving to the world the social democracy of Russia, an experiment that will probably prove to be a boon and a blessing to mankind. If it was not an unrighteous cause that led Washington to fight for the independence of this country, and led the Liberals of France to establish the Republic, it is therefore not an unrighteous cause for the U. N. I. A. to lead 400,000,000 Negroes all over the world to fight for the liberation of our country.

Therefore the U. N. I. A. is not advocating the cause of church building, because we have a sufficiently large number of churches among us to minister to the spiritual needs of the people, and we are not going to compete with those who are engaged in so splendid a work; we are not engaged in building any new social institutions, and Y. M. C. A. or Y. W. C. A. because there are enough social workers engaged in those praise-worthy efforts. We are not engaged in politics because we have enough local politicians, Democrats, Socialists, Soviets, etc., and the political situation is well taken care of. We are not engaged in domestic politics, in church building or in social uplift work, but we are engaged in nation building.

In advocating the principles of this Association we find we have been very much misunderstood and very much misrepresented by men from within our own race, as well as others from without. Any reform movement that seeks to bring about changes for the benefit of humanity is bound to be misrepresented by those who have always taken it upon themselves to administer to, and lead the unfortunate, and to direct those who may be placed under temporary disadvantages. It has been so in all other movements whether social or political; hence those of us in the Universal Negro Improvement Association who lead, do not feel in any way embarrassed about this misrepresentation, about this misunderstanding as far as the Aims and Objects of the Universal Negro Improvement Association go. But those who probably would have taken kindly notice of this great movement, have been led to believe that this movement seeks, not to develop the good within the race, but to give expression to that which is most destructive and most harmful to society and to government.

I desire to remove the misunderstanding that has been created in the minds of millions of peoples throughout the world in their relationship to the organization. The Universal Negro Improvement Association stands for the Bigger Brotherhood; the Universal Negro Improvement Association stands for human rights, not only for Negroes, but for all races. The Universal Negro Improvement Association believes in the rights of not only the black race, but the white race, the yellow race and the brown race. The Universal Negro Improvement Association believes that the white man has as much right to be considered, the yellow man has as much right to be considered, the brown man has as much right to be considered as well as the black man of Africa. In view of the fact that the black man of Africa has contributed as much to the world as the white man of Europe and the brown man and yellow man of Asia, we of the Universal Negro Improvement Association demand that the white, yellow and brown races give to the black man his place in the civilization of the world. We ask for nothing more than the rights of 400,000,000 Negroes. We are not seeking, as I said before, to destroy or disrupt the society or the government of other races, but we are determined that 400,000,000 of us shall unite ourselves to free our motherland from the grasp of the invader. We of the Universal Negro Improvement Association are determined to unite 400,000,000 Negroes for their own industrial, political, social and religious emancipation.

We of the Universal Negro Improvement Association are determined to unite the 400,000,000 Negroes of the world to give expression to their own feeling; we are determined to unite the 400,000,000

Negroes of the world for the purpose of building a civilization of their own. And in that effort we desire to bring together the 15,000,000 of the United States, the 180,000,000 in Asia, the West Indies and Central and South America, and the 200,000,000 in Africa. We are looking toward political freedom on the continent of Africa, the land of our fathers.

The Universal Negro Improvement Association is not seeking to build up another government within the bounds or borders of the United States of America. The Universal Negro Improvement Association is not seeking to disrupt any organized system of government, but the Association is determined to bring Negroes together for the building up of a nation of their own. And why? Because we have been forced to it. We have been forced to it throughout the world; not only in America, not only in Europe, not only in the British Empire, but wheresoever the black man happens to find himself, he has been forced to do for himself.

To talk about Government is a little more than some of our people can appreciate just at this time. The average man does not think that way, just because he finds himself a citizen or a subject of some country. He seems to say, "Why should there be need for any other government?" We are French, English or American. But we of the U. N. I. A. have studied seriously this question of nationality among Negroes—this American nationality, this British nationality, this French, Italian or Spanish nationality, and have discovered that it counts for nought when that nationality comes in conflict with the racial idealism of the group that rules. When our interests clash with those of the ruling faction, then we find that we have absolutely no rights. In times of peace, when everything is all right, Negroes have a hard time, wherever we go, wheresoever we find ourselves, getting those rights that belong to us, in common with others whom we claim as fellow citizens; getting that consideration that should be ours by right of the constitution, by right of the law; but in the time of trouble they make us all partners in the cause, as happened in the last war, when we were partners, whether British, French or American Negroes. And we were told that we must forget everything in an effort to save the nation.

We have saved many nations in this manner, and we have lost our lives doing that before. Hundreds of thousands—nay, millions of black men, lie buried under the ground due to that old-time camouflage of saving the nation. We saved the British empire; we saved the French empire; we saved this glorious country more than once; and all that we have received for our sacrifices, all that we have received for what we have done, even in giving up our lives, is just what you are receiving now, just what I am receiving now.

You and I fare no better in America, in the British empire, or in any other part of the white world; we fare no better than any black man wheresover he shows his head. And why? Because we have been satisfied to allow ourselves to be led, educated, to be directed by the other fellow, who has always sought to lead in the world in that direction that would satisfy him and strengthen his position. We have allowed ourselves for the last 500 years to be a race of followers, following every race that has led in the direction that would make them more secure.

The U. N. I. A. is reversing the old-time order of things. We refuse to be followers any more. We are leading ourselves. That means, if any saving is to be done, later on, whether it is saving this one nation or that one government, we are going to seek a method of saving Africa first. Why? And why Africa? Because Africa has become the grand prize of the nations. Africa has become the big game of the nation hunters. To-day Africa looms as the greatest commercial, industrial and political prize in the world.

The difference between the Universal Negro Improvement Association and the other movements of this country, and probably the world, is that the Universal Negro Improvement Association seeks independence of government, while the other organizations seek to make the Negro a secondary part of existing governments. We differ from the organizations in America because they seek to subordinate the Negro as a secondary consideration in a great civilization, knowing that in America the Negro will never reach his highest ambition, knowing that the Negro in America will never get his constitutional rights. All those organizations which are fostering the improvement of Negroes in the British Empire know that the Negro in the British Empire will never reach the height of his constitutional rights. What do I mean by constitutional rights in America? If the black man is to reach the height of his ambition in this country—if the black man is to get all of his constitutional rights in America—then the black man should have the same chance in the nation as any other man to become president of the nation, or a street cleaner in New York. If the black man in the British Empire is to have all his constitutional rights it means that the Negro in the British Empire should have at least the same right to become premier of Great Britain as he has to become street cleaner in the city of London. Are they prepared to give us such political equality? You and I can live in the United States of America for 100 more years, and our generations may live for 200 years or for 5000 more years, and so long as there is a black and white population, when the majority is on the side of the white race, you and I will never get political justice or get political equality in this country. Then why should a black man with rising ambition, after preparing himself in every possible way to give expression to that highest ambition, allow himself to be kept down by racial prejudice within a country? If I am as educated as the next man, if I am as prepared as the next man, if I have passed through the best schools and colleges and universities as the other fellow, why should I not have a fair chance to compete with the other fellow for the biggest position in the nation? I have feelings, I have blood, I have senses like the other fellow; I have ambition, I have hope. Why should he, because of some racial prejudice, keep me down and why should I concede to him the right to rise above me, and to establish himself as my permanent master? That is where the U. N. I. A. differs from other organizations. I refuse to stultify my ambition, and every true Negro refuses to stultify his ambition to suit any one, and therefore the U. N. I. A. decides if America is not big enough for two presidents, if England is not big enough for two kings, then we are not going to quarrel over the matter; we will leave one president in America, we will leave one king in England, we will leave one president in France and we will have one president in Africa. Hence, the Universal Negro Improvement Association does not seek to interfere with the social and political systems of France, but by the arrangement of things to-day the U. N. I. A. refuses to recognize any political or social system in Africa except that which we are about to establish for ourselves.

We are not preaching a propaganda of hate against anybody. We love the white man; we love all humanity, because we feel that we cannot live without the other. The white man is as necessary to the existence of the Negro as the Negro is necessary to his existence, There is a common relationship that we cannot escape. Africa has certain things that Europe wants, and Europe has certain things that Africa wants, and if a fair and square deal must bring white and black with each other, it is impossible for us to escape it. Africa has oil, diamonds, copper, gold and rubber and all the minerals that Europe wants, and there must be some kind of relationship between Africa and Europe for a fair exchange, so we cannot afford to hate anybody.

The question often asked is what does it require to redeem a race and free a country? If it takes man power, if it takes scientific intelligence, if it takes education of any kind, or if it takes blood, then the 400,000,000 Negroes of the world have it.

It took the combined man power of the Allies to put down the mad determination of the Kaiser to impose German will upon the world and upon humanity. Among those who suppressed his mad ambition were two million Negroes who have not yet forgotten how to drive men across the firing line. Surely those of us who faced German shot and shell at the Marne, at Verdun, have not forgotten the order of our Commander-in-Chief. The cry that caused us to leave America in such mad haste, when white fellow citizens of America refused to fight and said, "We do not believe in war and therefore, even though we are American citizens, and even though the nation is in danger, we will not go to war." When many of them cried out and said, "We are German-Americans and we can not fight," when so many white men refused to answer to the call and dodged behind all kinds of excuses, 400,000 black men were ready without a question. It was because we were told it was a war of democracy; it was a war for the liberation of the weaker peoples of the world. We heard the cry of Woodrow Wilson, not because we liked him so, but because the things he said were of such a nature that they appealed to us as men. Wheresoever the cause of humanity stands in need of assistance, there you will find the Negro ever ready to serve.

He has done it from the time of Christ up to now. When the whole world turned its back upon the Christ, the man who was said to be the Son of God, when the world cried out "Crucify Him," when the world spurned Him and spat upon Him, it was a black man, Simon, the Cyrenian, who took up the cross. Why? Because the cause of humanity appealed to him. When the black man saw the suffering Jew, struggling under the heavy cross, he was willing to go to His assistance, and he bore that cross up to the heights of Calvary. In the spirit of Simon, the Cyrenian, 1900 years ago, we answered the call of Woodrow Wilson, the call of a large humanity, and it was for that that we willingly rushed into the war from America, from the West Indies, over 100,000; it was for that that we rushed into the war from Africa, 2,000,000 of us. We met in France, Flanders and in Mesopotamia. We fought unfalteringly. When the white men faltered and fell back on their battle lines, at the Marne and at Verdun, when they ran away from the charge of the German hordes, the black hell fighters stood before the cannonade, stood before the charge, and again they shouted, "There will be a hot time in the old town to-night."

We made it so hot a few months after our appearance in France and on the various battle fronts, we succeeded in driving the German hordes across the Rhine, and driving the Kaiser out of Germany, and out of Potsdam into Holland. We have not forgotten the prowess of war. If we have been liberal minded enough to give our life's blood in France, in Mesopotamia and elsewhere, fighting for the white man, whom we have always assisted, surely we have not forgotten to fight for ourselves, and when the time comes that the world will again give Africa an opportunity for freedom, surely 400,000,000 black men will march out on the battle plains of Africa, under the colors of the red, the black and the green.

We shall march out, yes, as black American citizens, as black British subjects, as black French citizens, as black Italians or as black Spaniards, but we shall march out with a greater loyalty, the loyalty of race. We shall march out in answer to the cry of our fathers, who cry out to us for the redemption of our own country, our motherland, Africa.

We shall march out, not forgetting the blessings of America. We shall march out, not forgetting the blessings of civilization. We shall march out with a history of peace before and behind us, and surely that history shall be our breastplate, for how can man fight better than knowing that the cause for which he fights is righteous? How can man fight more gloriously than by knowing that behind him is a history of slavery, a history of bloody carnage and massacre inflicted upon a race because of its inability to protect itself and fight? Shall we not fight for the glorious opportunity of protecting and forever more establishing ourselves as a mighty race and nation, never more to be disrespected by men. Glorious shall be the battle when the time comes to fight for our people and our race.

We should say to the millions who are in Africa to hold the fort, for we are coming 400,000,000 strong.

An Appeal to the Conscience of the Black Race
to See Itself

It is said to be a hard and difficult task to organize and keep together large numbers of the Negro race for the common good. Many have tried to congregate us, but have failed, the reason being that our characteristics are such as to keep us more apart than together.

The evil of internal division is wrecking our existence as a people, and if we do not seriously and quickly move in the direction of a readjustment it simply means that our doom becomes imminently conclusive.

For years the Universal Negro Improvement Association has been working for the unification of our race, not on domestic-national lines only, but universally. The success which we have met in the course of our effort is rather encouraging, considering the time consumed and the environment surrounding the object of our concern.

It seems that the whole world of sentiment is against the Negro, and the difficulty of our generation is to extricate ourselves from the prejudice that hides itself beneath, as well as above, the action of an international environment.

Prejudice is conditional on many reasons, and it is apparent that the Negro supplies, consciously or unconsciously, all the reasons by which the world seems to ignore and avoid him. No one cares for a leper, for lepers are infectious persons, and all are afraid of the disease, so, because the Negro keeps himself poor, helpless and undemonstrative, it is natural also that no one wants to be of him or with him.

Progress is the attraction that moves humanity, and to whatever people or race this "modern virtue" attaches itself, there will you find the splendor of pride and self-esteem that never fail to win the respect and admiration of all.

It is the progress of the Anglo-Saxons that singles them out for the respect of all the world. When their race had no progress or achievement to its credit, then, like all other inferior peoples, they paid the price in slavery, bondage, as well as through prejudice. We cannot forget the time when even the ancient Briton was regarded as being too dull to make a good Roman slave, yet today the influence of that race rules the world.

It is the industrial and commercial progress of America that causes Europe and the rest of the world to think appreciatively of the Anglo-American race. It is not because one hundred and ten million people live in the United States that the world is attracted to the republic with so much reverence and respect—a reverence and respect not shown to India with its three hundred millions, or to China with its four hundred millions. Progress of and among any people will advance them in the respect and appreciation of the rest of their fellows. It is such a progress that the Negro must attach to himself if he is to rise above the prejudice of the world.

The reliance of our race upon the progress and achievements of others for a consideration in sympathy, justice and rights is like a dependence upon a broken stick, resting upon which will eventually consign you to the ground.

The Universal Negro Improvement Association teaches our race self-help and self-reliance, not only in one essential, but in all those things that contribute to human happiness and well-being. The disposition of the many to depend upon the other races for a kindly and sympathetic consideration of their needs, without making the effort to do for themselves, has been the race's standing disgrace by which we have been judged and through which we have created the strongest prejudice against ourselves.

There is no force like success, and that is why the individual makes all efforts to surround himself throughout life with the evidence of it. As of the individual, so should it be of the race and nation. The glittering success of Rockefeller makes him a power in the American nation; the success of Henry Ford suggests him as an object of universal respect, but no one knows and cares about the bum or hobo who is Rockefeller's or Ford's neighbor. So, also, is the world attracted by the glittering success of races and nations, and pays absolutely no attention to the bum or hobo race that lingers by the wayside.

The Negro must be up and doing if he will break down the prejudice of the rest of the world. Prayer alone is not going to improve our condition, nor the policy of watchful waiting. We must strike out for ourselves in the course of material achievement, and by our own effort and energy present to the world those forces by which the progress of man is judged.

The Negro needs a nation and a country of his own, where he can best show evidence of his own ability in the art of human progress. Scattered as an unmixed and unrecognized part of alien nations and civilizations is but to demonstrate his imbecility, and point him out as an unworthy derelict, fit neither for the society of Greek, Jew nor Gentile.

It is unfortunate that we should so drift apart, as a race, as not to see that we are but perpetuating our own sorrow and disgrace in failing to appreciate the first great requisite of all peoples—organization.

Organization is a great power in directing the affairs of a race or nation toward a given goal. To properly develop the desires that are uppermost, we must first concentrate through some system or method, and there is none better than organization. Hence, the Universal Negro Improvement Association appeals to each and every Negro to throw in his lot with those of us who, through organization, are working for the universal emancipation of our race and the redemption of our common country, Africa.

No Negro, let him be American, European, West Indian or African, shall be truly respected until the race as a whole has emancipated itself, through self-achievement and progress, from universal prejudice. The Negro will have to build his own government, industry, art, science, literature and culture, before the world will stop to consider him. Until then, we are but wards of a superior race and civilization, and the outcasts of a standard social system.

The race needs workers at this time, not plagiarists, copyists and mere imitators; but men and women who are able to create, to originate and improve, and thus make an independent racial contribution to the world and civilization.

The unfortunate thing about us is that we take the monkey apings of our "so-called leading men" for progress. There is no progress in aping white people and telling us that they represent the best in the race, for in that respect any dressed monkey would represent the best of its species, irrespective of the creative matter of the monkey instinct. The best in a race is not reflected through or by the action of its apes, but by its ability to create of and by itself. It is such a creation that the Universal Negro Improvement Association seeks.

Let us not try to be the best or worst of others, but let us make the effort to be the best of ourselves. Our own racial critics criticise us as dreamers and "fanatics," and call us "benighted" and "ignorant," because they lack racial backbone. They are unable to see themselves creators of their own needs. The slave instinct has not yet departed from them. They still believe that they can only live or exist through the good graces of their "masters." The good slaves have not yet thrown off their shackles; thus, to them, the Universal Negro Improvement Association is an "impossibility."

It is the slave spirit of dependence that causes our "so-called leading men" (apes) to seek the shelter, leadership, protection and patronage of the "master" in their organization and so-called advancement work. It is the spirit of feeling secured as good servants of the master, rather than as independents, why our modern Uncle Toms take pride in laboring under alien leadership and becoming surprised at the audacity of the Universal Negro Improvement Association in proclaiming for racial liberty and independence.

But the world of white and other men, deep down in their hearts, have much more respect for those of us who work for our racial salvation under the banner of the Universal Negro Improvement Association, than they could ever have in all eternity for a group of helpless apes and beggars who make a monopoly of undermining their own race and belittling themselves in the eyes of self-respecting people, by being "good boys" rather than able men.

Surely there can be no good will between apes, seasoned beggars and independent minded Negroes who will at least make an effort to do for themselves. Surely, the "dependents" and "wards" (and may I not say racial imbeciles?) will rave against and plan the destruction of movements like the Universal Negro Improvement Association that expose them to the liberal white minds of the world as not being representative of the best in the Negro, but, to the contrary, the worst. The best of a race does not live on the patronage and philanthropy of others, but makes an effort to do for itself. The best of the great white race doesn't fawn before and beg black, brown or yellow men; they go out, create for self and thus demonstrate the fitness of the race to survive; and so the white race of America and the world will be informed that the best in the Negro race is not the class of beggars who send out to other races piteous appeals annually for donations to maintain their coterie, but the groups within us that are honestly striving to do for themselves with the voluntary help and appreciation of that class of other races that is reasonable, just and liberal enough to give to each and every one a fair chance in the promotion of those ideals that tend to greater human progress and human love.

The work of the Universal Negro Improvement Association is clear and clean-cut. It is that of inspiring an unfortunate race with pride in self and with the determination of going ahead in the creation of those ideals that will lift them to the unprejudiced company of races and nations. There is no desire for hate or malice, but every wish to see all mankind linked into a common fraternity of progress and achievement that will wipe away the odor of prejudice, and elevate the human race to the height of real godly love and satisfaction.

Message from Atlanta Prison

August 1, 1925.

Fellow members of the Universal Negro Improvement Association and co-workers in the cause of African Redemption:

It is with feeling of deep love and thoughts of a great future for the Negro race that I address you.

My months of forcible removal from among you, being imprisoned as a punishment for advocating the cause of our real emancipation, have not left me hopeless or despondent; but to the contrary, I see a great ray of light and the bursting of a mighty international political cloud which will bring you complete freedom.

We have gradually won our way back into the confidence of the

God of Africa, and He shall speak with the voice of thunder, that shall shake the pillars of a corrupt and unjust world, and once more restore Ethiopia to her ancient glory.

Our enemies have seemingly triumphed for a while, but the final battle when staged will bring us complete success and satisfaction.

The wicked and obstructive elements of our own race who have tried to defeat us shall meet their Waterloo, and when they fall we feel sure they shall not rise again. For many years since our general emancipation, certain elements composed chiefly of a few octoroons and quadroons who hate the blood of our race (although part of us) with greater venom, scorn and contempt than the most prejudiced of other races, have tried to undermine and sell us out to the mighty powers of oppression, and within recent years, they have succeeded in getting the ear of the leading statesmen of the world, and have influenced them to treat the bulk of us Negroes as dogs, reserving for themselves, their kind and class, all the privileges and considerations that, as a race, would have been otherwise granted us and merited.

The National Association for the Advancement of Colored People, although pretending to be interested in and working for the race, is really and truly the active representative of this class. I trust you will not believe that my opposition to the National Association for the Advancement of Colored People is based upon any other motive than that of preventing them from destroying the Negro race that they so much despise and hate.

I am always glad and ever willing to co-operate with all Negro organizations that mean good by the race, but I am perfectly convinced and satisfied that the present executive personnel of the National Association for the Advancement of Colored People is not serious nor honest in intent toward the black race.

When they shall have removed their white and colored officers who believe in the racial extermination of the Negro type, and honestly promote a program for race uplift, then we can co-operate with them for the general good, until then we regard them as among the greatest enemies of our race. They teach race amalgamation and inter-marriage as the means of destroying the moral purity of the Negro race and our absorption within the white race which is nothing less than race suicide.

You must not forget that we have enemies also within our own organization—men whose motives are selfish and who are only seeking the "loaves and fishes" and not honest in heart in serving the people. Yet we have to make the "wheat and tare" grow together till the day of harvest. It is impossible to know all our enemies at one and the same time. Some are our enemies because they do not want to see the Negro rise; some because the organization supplies the opportunity for exploitation; others because they are unable to resist the temptation of the evil one would have them betray us in our most righteous effort of racial love and freedom.

I feel that my imprisonment has helped to open the eyes of the world to your true position, and has made friends to your cause. Men and women of other races who were mis-informed and deceived by our enemies, are now seeing the light. The graves that the enemies of race pride and purity dug for us may yet entomb them.

Hold fast to the ideal of a dignified Negro race. Let us work together as one people, whether we are octoroons, quadroons, mulattoes or blacks for the making of a nation of our own, for in that alone lies our racial salvation.

The few who do not want to be with us will find out their mistake sooner or later, but as for us, let us all unite as one people. It is no fault of ours that we are what we are—if we are black, brown, yellow or near white, the accident is not ours, but the time has now come for us to get together and make of ourselves a strong healthy race.

The National Association for the Advancement of Colored People wants us all to become white by amalgamation, but they are not honest enough to come out with the truth. To be a Negro is no disgrace, but an honor, and we of the Universal Negro Improvement Association do not want to become white. We do not seek for the whiteman's company more than he would seek after ours. We are proud and honorable. We love our race and respect and adore our mothers. We are as proud as our fathers were in the days of old, and even though we have passed through slavery in the western world, we shall not hang down our heads for Ethiopia shall again return to her Glory.

The Universal Negro Improvement Association is a union of all groups within the race. We love each other with pride of race and great devotion and nothing in the world shall come between us.

The truth has to be told so that we may know from whence our troubles cometh. Yet we must never, even under the severest pressure, hate or dislike ourselves. Even though we oppose the present leaders of the National Association for the Advancement of Colored

People, we must remember that we are all members of one race, rent asunder by circumstances. Let us help them by advice and conversion. Men like DuBois need our sympathy. We should teach them to love themselves, at least, have respect for the blood of their mothers—our mothers, who have suffered so much to make us what we are. We should take the truth to the innocent members of the National Association and save them from the mis-leadership of the white and colored persons who seek to destroy our race by miscegenation and use them as a pawn towards that end, and to foster their own class interest. Let us reach out and convert these unfortunate people and thus save them from a grave error. They should not be left to the tender mercies of their vile leaders, for they are good people and of our race, they mean good, but are mis-directed.

I have to return many thanks to you, the members of the Universal Negro Improvement Association, for the loyal support you have given me during my trials and troubles, suffered for you. I can realize that you have at all times done your best for me, even as I have done the best for you, as God has directed me to see. If it were not for you I would have been left helpless and comfortless. I shall never forget you. If it were not for you the members and some of the officers of local divisions, I would have been left penniless and helpless to fight my enemies and the great powers against me, and to even in the slightest way give protection to my wife whom I neglected and cheated for the cause that I so much love.

It is surprising how those we serve and help most can be ungrateful and unkind in our absence, and generally seek to take advantage of the one who cannot help himself. My name I leave with you the people. For you I have built up an organization of international standing. Every sacrifice has been made. My youth, money and ability were freely given for the cause. The cause you now see. It was not made in a day, but it took years of steady work and sacrifice. Others will now try to take advantage of my predicament to rob and exploit you in my name and blame the absent and helpless, but ever remember that from nothing, I raised up an organization through which you may see the light; let others, if they may, show the ability to carry on that which they have found, and not seek to exploit, to ruin and then blame the absent one as is so easy to do. It was during my absence in the West Indies when I was helpless to act, that the traitors within and enemies without did the deeds of dishonor that placed me for the Black Star Line where I am. Let not the same characters succeed to enrich themselves at the cost of the name of one who cannot protect himself or protect you. You must protect yourselves—the time has come. My full tale of warning is not to be told here, but suffice it to say that on you I rely for the ultimate success of our great effort, and but for you I would have been hopelessly defeated in the great struggle to "keep the fire burning." Probably I should not have expected better for even our Blessed Master feared worse when his chief disciples failed him. I am not complaining, but I warn you against treachery, deceit, self-seeking, dishonesty and racial disloyalty. Personally, as I have so often stated, I counted the cost years ago, but the responsibility is not all mine, but equally that of the one whom I love with great devotion and fondness. You, I feel sure, have done your duty by her and will continue to shield and protect her, while, because of my imprisonment for you, I find it impossible to do my duty.

The God of our Fathers will raise up friends for the cause of Africa, and we who have struggled in the wilderness for all this time shall surely see the promised land.

Hold fast to the Faith. Desert not the ranks, but as brave soldiers march on to victory. I am happy, and shall remain so, as long as you keep the flag flying.

I hope to be with you again with greater energy and force to put the program over. I have yet to let my real voice and soul be heard in Europe, Asia and continental America in plea for the Negro's rights and for a free and redeemed Africa. Yet, I have not spoken. I await the summons of my God for the greater work that must be done. In the meanwhile pray for success and pray for me.

CLAUDE McKAY

(1890-1948)

Though born in Jamaica, Claude McKay is acclaimed by Afro-America as one of its own. McKay published two volumes of dialect verse in Jamaica before leaving to attend school in the United States: Constab Ballads *and* Songs from Jamaica *(both 1912). Ironically, his first "American" volume,* Spring in New Hampshire *(1920), was published in England. Between leaving Jamaica and taking up temporary residence in London, McKay had seen the United States, North and South, had lived in Harlem, sampled the bohemian life of Greenwich Village, and had written many poems, including some stirring ones on racial injustice. The most famous of these, "If We Must Die," a poem inspired by lynching, became outstandingly popular.*

In 1922 he published Harlem Shadows *and made a trip to the Soviet Union, not so much as an admirer of the Russian Revolution as in a spirit of open curiosity, though his contacts with communists in New York and London were influential in exciting that interest. McKay developed an attachment for the Russian people, but his enthusiasm for communism, Russian and otherwise, was always slight. After the early twenties, he turned his attention to prose fiction and wrote three novels:* Home to Harlem *(1928),* Banjo *(1929), and* Banana Bottom *(1933). His short stories, written over a period of more than a decade, were collected in* Gingertown *(1932). Some of the stories are drawn from his memories of Jamaica and others reflect the Harlem milieu.*

In Banjo, *set in Marseilles, McKay presents what may be called a folk or nonintellectual Pan-Africanist vision of the world derived from observing blacks from Africa, the West Indies, and elsewhere in mutual encounter in the French port city. Theirs he perceived as the life of spontaneity, free from the ratiocination and hypocrisy of Europe. A similar theme in a Jamaican setting is pursued in* Banana Bottom.

In 1937 McKay published an autobiography, A Long Way From Home, *in which his alienation from his black literary contemporaries is made manifest. He wrote an account of New York's famed ghetto in* Harlem: Negro Metropolis *(1940). Poems were collected in* Selected Poems *(1953).*

If We Must Die

If we must die, let it not be like hogs
Hunted and penned in an inglorious spot,
While round us bark the mad and hungry dogs,
Making their mock at our accurséd lot.
If we must die, O let us nobly die,
So that our precious blood may not be shed
In vain; then even the monsters we defy
Shall be constrained to honor us though dead!
O kinsmen! we must meet the common foe!
Though far outnumbered let us show us brave,
And for their thousand blows deal one deathblow!
What though before us lies the open grave?
Like men we'll face the murderous, cowardly pack,
Pressed to the wall, dying, but fighting back!

Flame-Heart

So much have I forgotten in ten years,
    So much in ten brief years! I have forgot
What time the purple apples come to juice,
    And what month brings the shy forget-me-not.
I have forgot the special, startling season
    Of the pimento's flowering and fruiting;
What time of year the ground doves brown the fields
        And fill the noonday with their curious fluting.
I have forgotten much, but still remember
The poinsettia's red, blood-red in warm December.

I still recall the honey-fever grass,
    But cannot recollect the high days when
We rooted them out of the ping-wing path
    To stop the mad bees in the rabbit pen.
I often try to think in what sweet month
    The languid painted ladies used to dapple
The yellow by-road mazing from the main,
    Sweet with the golden threads of the rose-apple.
I have forgotten—strange—but quite remember
The poinsettia's red, blood-red in warm December.

What weeks, what months, what time of the mild year
    We cheated school to have our fling at tops?
What days our wine-thrilled bodies pulsed with joy
    Feasting upon blackberries in the copse?
Oh some I know! I have embalmed the days,
    Even the sacred moments when we played,
All innocent of passion, uncorrupt,
    At noon and evening in the flame-heart's-shade.
We were so happy, happy, I remember,
Beneath the poinsettia's red in warm December.

Boyhood in Jamaica

My village was beautiful, sunny, sparsely populated. It was set upon a hill. Except when it was foggy or raining, it was always bathed by the sun. The hills came like chains from the other villages—James Hill, Tare-mont, Croft's Hill, Frankfield, and Ballad's River. They came to form a centre in my village of Sunny Ville.

The village was set, something like a triangle, between two streams. The parochial or dirt road, along which it grew on both sides, jutted off abruptly from the main macadamized road. We were about twenty-one families living between those two streams—one so large we called it a river, the other just a tributary which further down emptied itself into a larger river. Our lives were linked with streams. In fact, the Indian word *Xaymaca* means "land of springs."

The road was red, very red. I remember during the rainy season how that red clay would cake up on the legs and feet of the old folks going to work their patches of land, and the kids going to school. On Sunday, dur-ing that kind of weather, the peasant men went to Church with their shoes slung over their shoulders, and the peasant woman carrying theirs either on their arms and on their heads. When they got to the brook near the Church, they would wash their feet, put on their shoes, and step gingerly on the grass leading to the Church doors. What used to tickle us children was the quietness of the Church and the squeaking of the shoes of our el-ders, as they walked down the aisle to the front benches.

Sometimes the rainy season came in with a fierce hurricane which would sweep everything before it, uprooting the strongest trees and de-stroying the best crops of bananas, sugar cane, corn and yams. Sometimes it knocked down the peasants' huts. Everything was flattened like reeds by a wind. Fortunately the hurricanes did not come regularly—sometimes for five or six years we did not have one, and again suddenly we might have two within a period of two years.

Many of the peasants believed that hurricanes, like floods, diseases, and other evils, were caused by Obi or Obeah, a West African god. Obeahmen who could appease the god, or who could pit their strength against his by exorcism, were accordingly popular. We loved the hurri-cane though the aftermath was sheer misery. With all the best crops destroyed and the fruit trees uprooted, the villages were faced with starvation. Somehow I recall that we always used to pull through. Those peasants who had money saved up (and most of them did) used to buy barrels and bags of flour from the town. We would mix it with corn meal and make all kinds of food—johnny cakes, dumplings and mush.

Most of the time there was hardly any way of telling the seasons. To us in Jamaica, as elsewhere in the tropics, there were only two seasons—the rainy season and the dry season. We had no idea of spring, summer, autumn and winter like the peoples of northern lands. Springtime, however, we did know by the new and lush burgeoning of grasses and the blossoming of trees, although we had blooms all the year round. The mango tree was especially significant of spring, because it was one of the few trees that used to shed its leaves. Then, in springtime, the new leaves sprouted—very tender, a kind of sulphur brown, as if they had been singed by fire. Soon afterwards the white blossoms came out and we knew that we would be eating juicy mangoes by August. Cedric Dover and myself had a grand time in 1937 talking about mangoes and other things. He boasted about his mango fool and was thrilled when he found that I knew it too, although he insisted that we could not have made it better than it was in Calcutta.

I also recall the high ground above the church where we had our cricket field. Every boy in Jamaica plays cricket. It is one of the gifts that the English have bestowed on their colonies and dependencies. It is a much more difficult and subtle game than baseball, which we also play in Jamaica.

Ever since I was a boy, our crack Jamaican cricket teams, consisting of white men, brown men and black men, have gone abroad to compete with Englishmen, Scotsmen, Welshmen, Canadians, Australians, New Zealanders and East Indians. I have never heard of them competing with South Africans. Some of the black and brown cricketers came from our lowest social groups, but they knew how to wield a bat dexterously. I have never heard of Englishmen and other whites losing prestige because they played cricket with black and brown men. I have never heard of coloured populations anywhere getting "out of hand" because white men played cricket with their sons. I do know that the game of cricket helped to draw tighter "the bonds of Empire" and helped coloured and whites to understand each other better.

I have heard supposedly cultivated white Americans bandy about the phrase "that's not cricket," but I am sure they repeat the phrase as they learned it from Englishmen, without a fundamental understanding—just as those who have travelled in France with ears atuned to the language might say "Je m'en fiche" without knowning the difference between that and "Je m'en fou." One has to live with a language to know its symbolism.

One of the happiest periods of those times were moonlit nights on which we made what was called a moonshine baby. In every peasant's home there was a yard, a plot of ground around the house, the surface of which was hardened. It is in this yard that coffee, cocoa and pimento are dried and made ready for the markets. Now, in our village, my father possessed a huge barbecue yard which was built out of stones and cement. Thus built it could last for many years. Many of the children of the village came to father's barbecue to play in the late evening. We would do the ring plays, and hide and seek, which kids in every country play.

But on moonlit nights we would make moonshine babies. First, we went out into the garden and picked up bits of broken crockery, which we broke up into pieces about the size of a shilling. When we thought we had enough, one of us would be chosen to lie down on his back with his arms and feet stretched out. Then the others would take those broken bits of plates, of which only the white parts were used, and outline the form of the one who was lying down. This procedure took us quite a long time, because sometimes the subject would be fidgety, always stirring, moving an arm or a foot. Finally, when we were finished, a number of us would pick up the subject, being careful not to disturb the pieces of crockery; and then we would have there on the barbecue the outline of a boy, which we called the moonshine baby.

To us children, it was very weird, something like a great enlarged china doll which we ourselves had made. We would hold hands, form a circle, dance around it and sing. Sometimes our parents would come out to see what we were doing, and tell us whether our efforts were good or bad. I am not quite sure, but I think father told us that the making of these moonshine babies was an old African custom and that different villages used to compete in the making of them.

But amongst us there was no competition. We made the moonshine babies for the sheer fun of the thing. In the daytime we played cricket and softball, went swimming and running. In the evening we made moonshine babies, or we went to some neighbour's house, where there was fiddling, and there we sang and danced. We lived cooperatively, we lived together.

The direction of our schooling was, of course, English. And it was so successful that we really believed we were little black Britons. In this connection, one of the interesting things I remember was a long list of words which were called "Americanisms." The American pronunciations were different from the English. For instance, "which," "what," "where," and "when" were pronounced respectively "wich," "wat," "were," and "wen." My brother said the Americans aspirated such words, but that ours was the way of the cultivated English.

I have known many Americans who thought that such pronunciations were Cockney. There were other expressions which we were told not to use, such as "that fast," "that high," and "that good." My brother insisted that we should always say "as fast as that," "as high as that," and "as good as that." I remember also that the last letter of the alphabet we pronounced "zed," whilst the Americans say "zee."

There were many words we accented on the first syllable which they said were accented on the middle syllable in America: "in'flu-ence and in-flu'ence" for example. Words like labour and favour we spelled English-wise with the "u" in. Mr. Jekyll once said the Americans used the Spanish form, whilst the English preferred the French. I have forgotten many of these words but I do remember "schedule." This word was known to every Jamaican school child, because every elementary school had a schedule for the week's work tacked up over the teacher's desk. In Jamaica, as in England, we all pronounced it "shedule."

In my brother's school I became fascinated by one of the older girls. Agnes was very pretty. She was a light mulatto with very black hair, buxom body, and a face that radiated sunshine. We did not see each other often outside school hours, but during the recess periods we would get together in a ring and play "Drop the handkerchief." We would pass notes in the classroom and Agnes started to write me long letters. I did not know what to write in reply. My friend, the stable-boy, used to write my letters for me.

One day my brother discovered some letters from Agnes that I had hidden in the "what-not." Among them was a reply that the stable-boy had written for me. My brother took the letters to his wife; they both read them and thought that Agnes and I were wrong in writing such letters. They thought that the letters were very passionate, not the kind that children should be writing to each other. My brother whipped me for the first time. He said he was astonished that a small boy like me could have such adult thoughts. Agnes was very angry when she heard about the beating and the finding of the letters by my brother. The beating did not change us—beatings never change anybody.

The other school children now knew about us, but we hugged our love very closely. It was my first love. But before I could even be aware of it Agnes had blossomed into a young woman and I was still just a boy in knee-pants. Then she left the village and I never heard from her again. Years later I learned that she had died miserably in one of the brothels in Kingston. I wrote a poem to her in the Jamaican dialect. Strangely, it was never published in any of my books and I can recall no words to reproduce here; but friends who read it said it was one of my most touching poems.

The second year after my brother had taken over Palmyra there was a great flood. The waters gushed out of the vast sink holes, spreading over the land, covering the sugar cane and peas and yam hills. The flood lasted for days. The main road, which led to the neighbouring parish of St. Ann's was under water for a quarter of a mile. From the neighbouring villages the young people came to Boghole in boats during the moonlight evenings and on Sunday. They made a picnic atmosphere and paid the boatman to take them all over the flooded areas, while they ate sandwiches and fruit, chattered and sang. I remember one of these songs:

> The boat is filled with sail and oar
> Then row, row, row . . .
> Over the beautiful waves we go
> Then row, row, row,
> So merrily, merrily, oh . . .

We sang a great deal in Jamaica. There were the songs we learned at school, and there were the songs we made up for almost every occasion. A peasant mother, for example, would give her pretty daughter good advice in this way: "Tell them gals, oh tell them gals, We don't want no bonga (ugly) man here." Especially important were the songs we sang during clearing and planting. These were known as "Jamma Songs," or field songs, and were of the leader-response type. They were a little like the calypsos of today, while some distinctly resembled the flamencos of Spain and Morocco. And above all they were community songs for community work. They were not made in the mind of an individual intent on his individualism. They grew from a way of life.

Then we had a literary debating society, where we discussed such things as Chinese and East Indian immigration into Jamaica, and why these people were forced to leave their homes to work for so much less than the Jamaican native, whose wages were just a pittance anyhow. We debated also about the British Empire and its rôle in the world. We compared it with the Spanish Empire, because every schoolchild had some knowledge of the Spanish Armada. We also knew that Jamaica was Spanish before it was taken by the English. We felt it would fall as the Spanish Empire had done.

We still have many of the romantic names, like St. Jago de la Vega, Rio Cobre, Rio Minho, Montego Bay, Santa Cruz and Savanna la Mar. We had also the titillating names of our Jewish population, who had come to us from Spain and Portugal at the begining of the sixteenth century. Such names as de Cardova, de Lindo, Delgado, Delevante, Del Ano, de Paseo, Demendez, D'Aguilar, Enriquez, Morales, and Andrade. Just like the English and the Scots and some of our Negroes, they had shops in the city and towns, and they were also landed proprietors and shrewd politicians. In everything that was done in the Islands they took a part, and there was little thought of discrimination against them; or against Chinese, East Indians, mulattoes and Negroes, who had risen to the position where they could take part in the management of the Island's affairs. In spite of its poverty, Jamaica was like a beautiful garden in its human relationships.

There were no societies for better "race relations." Illegitimate children had as good a chance in the world as those born in wedlock. We all grew up together like wild flowers. Up there in the hills where I was born, it was no stranger for one to be born a poet than if he were born in the city. Although a boy could be less educated, because he was born in the country rather than in the city, he would never be considered stupid or unintelligent.

In many cases, there are families of peasants, and of the upper classes too, who have lived together all of their lives without benefit of marriage. They raise their children as well as they can, and send them to school and college. They remain very happy, unless a revivalist comes along to give them religion and marry them. After living together for twenty-five or thirty years happily, the reaction sets in in many such cases and they end in separation. It is always dangerous to outrage the patterns of a culture.

I know of a case of one of our village women who was a very pretty but illiterate quadroon. She went to a town twenty-five miles away and there lived with a Sephardic Jewish merchant named de Lindo. They had two girls who were educated in England. When they returned they were unhappy with their illiterate mother. They felt closer to the father, who had had a good education. Since their father had a lot of money, the girls went in for much socializing. They visited Kingston and attended the Governor's balls and garden parties, as well as the Archbishop's lawn parties and other social functions. Generally they had a good time, though everybody knew they were born out of wedlock.

After a few years the father became very ill. He had been fond of his woman, and as a last gesture he desired to marry her. She also wanted to be married to him, because she was religious and wanted to re-enter Church circles. When the two girls heard of their father's desire they became furious and opposed him. They said that if he married their mother they would never admit that she was their legal mother. The mother wept very much, but that made no difference to the girls. They thought merely of their higher social status, which would now be sullied by having an illiterate mother on their hands. So old de Lindo died without being able to marry his woman; but the girls were happy. The mother was well provided for. She went back to the village and the girls went to the city.

On January 7, 1907, the great earthquake hit Kingston.

. . . With only my underwear on, I was lying on my bed reading a Wild West thriller. Then suddenly I felt as if some great giant had crushed in the walls of the house. I was on the first floor and, as I ran out into the yard, I saw bricks from a nearby building falling down. People were running along the streets and screaming. I vividly remember that there was a cocoanut tree in the yard and a man had climbed it. He reached almost into the bower, where he shouted: "I'm going up to heaven, Lord! I'm going up to heaven!"

Then there came three more shocks and soon there were dead bodies everywhere. The city was ablaze. All traffic was stopped. I went out that afternoon to go to the centre of the city, where my cousin lived. The bricks had piled up in the streets. There were dead bodies all around. The groans of those who were trapped, and the stench of burning bodies, turned me back.

Soon the marauders began to loot right and left. . . . Then a cry went up that the American Marines were on the heels of the looters and that some of them had been shot. . . . Then we learned that the Governor of the Island had protested to the Rear Admiral of the United States warship for sending his Marines ashore armed and without the permission of the Government.

But our Governor's protest created an international incident. The Rear Admiral said he had been insulted. Washington referred the incident to London, which asked the Governor to apologize. The Governor said he wouldn't, for he felt he was right and all the people backed him up. The coloured people were very happy indeed to say that Jamaica was not the United States, where coloured people are kicked around. So the Governor resigned; but he lived in Jamaica for the rest of his days and was treated like a hero by the natives. In the British Empire, for all its wickedness, there have always been men of exceptionally high principles.

Finally, my people found a Trades Master in lovely little Brown's

Town in the parish of St. Ann. My master was a light mulatto, somewhat crabbed, yet kindly in a way. He was a jack-of-all-trades, a wheelwright, a carriage builder and an excellent cabinet maker. Those were the days, as I knew them in Jamaica, when people indulged in their fancy homemade furniture. We certainly had some wonderful native workmen. That was the period before the invasion of the modern Grand Rapids American furniture. . . .

Although St. Ann's soil was stony, it was wonderful for pimento and coffee. Sometimes we would leave the highway and go into the fields and sit under the pimento trees, just talking and reading poetry while the jontwits feasted and twitted on the ripe blue pimento fruit. This is not the red Spanish pimento with which most Americans are familiar. Our pimento tree belongs to the myrtle family. The bark is something between that of the poplar and the eucalyptus. The ripe berries are blue, exactly like blueberries. When we dry them for the market, they turn black.

My mother didn't care very much about what people did and why and how they did it. She only wanted to help them if they were in trouble. She wanted to help those who were outcast, poor and miserable. She loved us so much because she loved all people—it was a rich, warm love.

As I remember, my mother had few relatives around. She was quite brown, with two wonderful strands of hair reaching down to her shoulders when plaited. The legend goes that her people came from Madagascar. I remember some of her folks from the little townlet of Frankfield who sometimes came to visit her; and they were of the same type as my mother, but I never enquired about them. People of all kinds were just people to me. I had a romantic feeling about the different kinds of human groups and nations, until I came to America and saw race hatred in its most virulent form.

Father's origins were more definite. He was descended from West Africans, I believe of the Ashanti nation. Sometimes when he became angry with us boys for any foolish practice he would say to us: "Your grandfather was a slave and knew how cruel the white man could be. You boys don't know anything about life." My father was a wonderful teller of African stories and, besides, he would tell us about African customs. I vividly remember his telling us that when Ashanti mothers gave birth to albino babies they were regarded as types who were mixed up with magic. They were ill-omens who were exposed until they died.

Mr. Walter Jekyll and I liked each other immediately. He was about fifty-odd years old, myself eighteen. He read my poetry one day. Then he laughed a lot, and I became angry because I thought he was laughing at me. All these poems I had given him to read had been done in straight English; but there was one short one about an ass that was laden with native vegetables, for the market, who had suddenly sat down in the middle of the road and wouldn't get up. Its owner was talking to it in the Jamaican dialect, telling it to get up. That was the poem that Mr. Jekyll was laughing about. He then told me that he did not like my poems in straight English . . . they were repetitious. "But this," said he, holding up the donkey poem, "this is the real thing. The Jamaica dialect has never been put into literary form except in my Annansy stories. Now is your chance as a native boy to put the Jamaica dialect into literary language. I am sure that your poems will sell."

I was not very enthusiastic about this statement, because to us who were getting an education in the English schools, the Jamaican dialect was considered a vulgar tongue. It was the language of the peasants. All cultivated people spoke English, straight English. However, later on I began thinking seriously of what Mr. Jekyll had proposed, and as I knew so many pieces in the dialect, which were based on our local songs of the draymen, the sugar mills, and the farm lands, I decided to do some poems in dialect.

Most of the poems that were published in Jamaica at that time were repetitious and not very good. Our poets thought it was an excellent thing if they could imitate the English poets. We had poetry societies for the nice people. There were "Browning Clubs," where the poetry of Robert Browning was studied but not understood. I had read my poems before many of these societies and the members used to say: "Well, he's very nice and pretty, you know, but he's not a real poet as Browning and Byron and Tennyson are poets." I used to think I would show them something. Someday I would write poetry in straight English and amaze them and confound them. They thought I was not serious, simply because I wrote poems in the dialect, which they did not consider becoming or profound.

The people of Jamaica were a curious lot—as if God had planted a garden of mixed humanity there. The greatest drawback in the Island was its extreme poverty. Otherwise, the different groups of people lived very happily together. The Negroes, that is, the blacks and dark browns, were about ninety per cent of the population. Next to them, we had the landed mulattoes, that is, the light browns. They were the middle class of the Island, possessing most of its wealth. Then we had the British officials and our missionaries, who were mostly English, Scots and Irish.

We also had the Jews who owned large stores in Kingston, but there was not much feeling against them. I never heard the word "Christ-killer" until I came to America. Later, I learned from an English friend that our Jews were Sephardic Jews, who came to the island from Spain and Portugal during the Inquisition, and had had time to integrate. He also told me that they were a different type of Jew from the Ashkenazi Jews, who came from Russia, Germany, Poland and the Balkans. To the people of the Island the Jews were romantic, and we all spoke of them as the "Chosen People of God." They were handsome, with their black hair and extremely white skin—something like what we usually imagine the Spanish people look like. They participated in the life of the Island much as the whites did.

Then we also had Chinese and Indians, Hindus and Mohammedans, who married our native women and had beautiful children. Indeed, as I have said, the people of Jamaica were like an exotic garden planted by God. And today I see them as something more. I see them as a rising people, and sometimes I think that the Negroes amongst them will give leadership to the Negroes of the world in the great struggle that lies ahead.

I remember an American who was fined for abusing a peasant woman. The judge could not get a civil word out of him, and we were all pretty sure that he was neither sorry for what he had done, nor ashamed of the way he had conducted himself. He was just a proud, prejudiced American, with so little to be proud of.

And that is the main danger of Americanization. The carriers are prejudiced and materialistic. Most Americans, it seems to me, from the extreme left to the far right, believe that what the rest of the world needs is more sanitation and material luxury: enamel bathtubs, gleaming wash basins, and two bottles of milk for every person. They don't realize that millions in other countries don't like and won't drink milk as American adults do. Or that there are millions of Moslems and Hindus who insist that water for washing must be poured onto the body, as has been done from the most ancient times.

Sometimes I wonder if this dominating materialism is not the major problem of the modern world. Communism and Christianity can become reconciled, as Islam and Christianity were eventually reconciled. But how can we reconcile the conquering forces of American industrial materialism—the American Way of Life—with those vast forces that still cling to the traditional human values which America holds in such contempt?

The tea meetings were dandy affairs which were always in a yard, in a barbecue. A large booth was built chiefly of plaited palm leaves and at night the merry-making would start. We got all the "wine" we needed to drink and the elder men got their rum. Our favourite wine was orange and cola and we had a lot of ginger beer. The tea meetings started with dancing, chiefly quadrilles in my days. They went on late into the night. We had good fiddlers, and specialized in selling an unusual kind of bread, shaped like a crown or a gate, which the young men bought for their girls. Sometimes a young man who did not have a steady girl would buy one for his mother.

The big thing about the loaves of bread was their competitive scale. They were not auctioned off until about midnight. Then a man who was a good seller would stand up on the table and cry out: "Ladies and Gentlemen. We are ready to sell the gate and the crown of our village." Now for some reason no man in a given village wanted his gate or crown to be sold to a man of another village. So the competition was keen. Many of the men in the village, who did not have enough money as individuals, would get together in a gang and get enough money to prevent single individuals from a neighbouring village from outbidding them. It was all very exciting, especially as the women prodded their men on with such phrases as "Go to it, Marse George! Take that crown away from here for to crown you a chicken. Taremont needs a little pulling down, for it is too high and mighty." And the women would wag their heads and laugh while the auctioneer would say: "Now, boys, what are you going to do about it—are you going to let the crown of Taremont go to Croftshill?"

Then, finally, the boys of a village would band themselves together and make the purchase for THE girl of their village. Then the auctioneer would be as pleased as punch, for sometimes a loaf worth ten cents would go for more than ten dollars. After the selling of the crown-bread, the same procedure was adopted for the gate, which represented the opening into the village. Then men did not feel safe if an outsider purchased the village gate, so they got together and also bought the gate. After this prize money had been made, there was a lot of singing and dancing, and the tea meetings would generally break up around dawn.

Going to America was the greatest event in the history of our hills, for America was the supposedly golden land of education and opportunity. . . . We thought of England, France, Germany and the rest of Europe—some of our children were being educated there—but we all thought of America in a different sense. It was the new land to which all people who had youth, and a youthful mind, turned. Surely there would be opportunity in this land, even for a Negro.

Our general opinion of American Negroes was that they were clowns more or less. All those that we saw in Kingston on the street were the happy-go-lucky clowning types who sang "coon" songs for the white men and seemed to like doing so. I soon learned in America that we had an entirely wrong impression of the American Negro. But our Negroes were proud though poor. They would not sing clowning songs for white men and allow themselves to be kicked around by them.

At last I went off to Port Antonio, where my ticket was waiting for me. Soon I was on the boat and settled in my cabin. The weather was wonderful. The sea was as blue as the sky, but I hardly enjoyed it. I was ill all the way until I landed at Charleston, South Carolina. Where in all America could one land and find more beauty and moral ugliness at the same time?

I was in another world, a new world which grew into many worlds that engulfed me, though something of me was always separate, something that belonged to the beautiful green hills of my boyhood. I have sought to recapture their charm and influence, which in a wider sense is the shaping influence that makes the difference between the white and coloured worlds. I have tried to do this simply and honestly, without bitterness or excessive comment, as my final literary duty. For the creeping pressure of disease tells me that this is my last book, and I will never again see my green hills and the people I loved so much.

It is the farewell testimony of a man who was bitter because he loved, who was both right and wrong because he hated the things that destroyed love, who tried to give back to others a little of what he had got from them and the continuous adventure of being a black man in a white society. Happily, as I move on, I see that adventure changing for those who will come after me. For this is the century of the coloured world.

JEAN TOOMER
(1894-1967)

Cane *(1923), which has erroneously been called a novel, a book of poems and stories, and even a drama, defies classification. In fact, it is a curiously unified assemblage of stories, sketches, poems, and "Kabnis," a novella with formalized dialogue. Jean Toomer, like* Cane, *his single contribution to Afro-American writing, also defies classification. He was born in Washington, D.C., where his complexion and social origins assigned him to the mulatto elite.* Cane *springs largely from a contact of a few months with rural Georgia, though the locus of its second part is the urban extra-South, chiefly his native city.*

Toomer is hailed by Alain Locke and by William Stanley Braithwaite in The New Negro. *(See the final paragraph of Braithwaite's essay in this volume.) Yet he is absent from Johnson's anthology of 1931. Between these dates Toomer had precipitated that break with black America which is a part of his post-*Cane *story, and Johnson was either enjoined or dissuaded from mentioning him as an Afro-American poet.*

In the prose sections of Cane, *Toomer invests his black characters with total and indisputable dignity. In the poetry, written in a variety of forms, where we have echoes both of Tennyson and the Imagist poets, Toomer uses the stuff of black life and his own reaction to it. In turn subjective and objective, he writes in a fashion not precisely realized before. The book contains themes and clichés which are staples of the literature of the South: The black-white triangle, lynching, the emptiness of front-porch life, the lonesome wailing of the freight train are all present.*

The impact of Cane *on writers of the Harlem Renaissance, as well as on writers of subsequent generations, has been great.* Cane *has been the subject of a large amount of criticism and commentary, much of it of dubious worth. Darwin Turner, the leading Toomer scholar, has edited Toomer's* The Wayward and The Seeking.

Song of the Son

Pour O pour that parting soul in song,
O pour it in the sawdust glow of night,
Into the velvet pine-smoke air to-night,
And let the valley carry it along.
And let the valley carry it along.

O land and soil, red soil and sweet-gum tree,
So scant of grass, so profligate of pines,
Now just before an epoch's sun declines
Thy son, in time, I have returned to thee,
Thy son, I have in time returned to thee.

In time, for though the sun is setting on
A song-lit race of slaves, it has not set;
Though late, O soil, it is not too late yet
To catch thy plaintive soul, leaving, soon gone,
Leaving, to catch thy plaintive soul soon gone.

O Negro slaves, dark purple ripened plums,
Squeezed and bursting in the pine-wood air,
Passing, before they stripped the old tree bare
One plum was saved for me, one seed becomes

An everlasting song, a singing tree,
Caroling softly souls of slavery,
What they were, and what they are to me,
Caroling softly souls of slavery.

Harvest Song

I am a reaper whose muscles set at sundown. All my oats are cradled.
But I am too chilled, and too fatigued to bind them. And I hunger.

I crack a grain between my teeth. I do not taste it.
I have been in the fields all day. My throat is dry. I hunger.

My eyes are caked with dust of oatfields at harvest-time.
I am a blind man who stares across the hills, seeking stack'd fields of
    other harvesters.

It would be good to see them . . . crook'd, split, and iron-ring'd
    handles of the scythes. It would be good to see them, dust-caked
    and blind. I hunger.

(Dusk is a strange fear'd sheath their blades are dull'd in.)
My throat is dry. And should I call, a cracked grain like the oats . . .
    eoho—

I fear to call. What should they hear me, and offer me their grain,
    oats, or wheat, or corn? I have been in the fields all day. I fear
    I could not taste it. I fear knowledge of my hunger.

My ears are caked with dust of oatfields at harvest-time.
I am a deaf man who strains to hear the calls of other harvesters
    whose throats are also dry.

It would be good to hear their songs . . . reapers of the sweet-stalk'd
    cane, cutters of the corn . . . even though their throats cracked
    and the strangeness of their voices deafened me.

I hunger. My throat is dry. Now that the sun has set and I am chilled, I fear to call. (Eoho, my brothers!)

I am a reaper. (Eoho!) All my oats are cradled. But I am too fatigued to bind them. And I hunger. I crack a grain. It has no taste to it. My throat is dry . . .

O my brothers, I beat my palms, still soft, against the stubble of my harvesting. (You beat your soft palms, too.) My pain is sweet. Sweeter than the oats or wheat or corn. It will not bring me knowledge of my hunger.

Avey

For a long while she was nothing more to me than one of those skirted beings whom boys at a certain age disdain to play with. Just how I came to love her, timidly, and with secret blushes, I do not know. But that I did was brought home to me one night, the first night that Ned wore his long pants. Us fellers were seated on the curb before an apartment house where she had gone in. The young trees had not outgrown their boxes then. V Street was lined with them. When our legs grew cramped and stiff from the cold of the stone, we'd stand around a box and whittle it. I like to think now that there was a hidden purpose in the way we hacked them with our knives. I like to feel that something deep in me responded to the trees, the young trees that whinnied like colts impatient to be let free . . . On the particular night I have in mind, we were waiting for the top-floor light to go out. We wanted to see Avey leave the flat. This night she stayed longer than usual and gave us a chance to complete the plans of how we were going to stone and beat that feller on the top floor out of town. Ned especially had it in for him. He was about to throw a brick up at the window when at last the room went dark. Some minutes passed. Then Avey, as unconcerned as if she had been paying an old-maid aunt a visit, came out. I don't remember what she had on, and all that sort of thing. But I do know that I turned hot as bare pavements in the summertime at Ned's boast: "Hell, bet I could get her too if you little niggers weren't always spying and crabbing everything." I didnt say a word to him. It wasnt my way then. I just stood there like the others, and something like a fuse burned up inside of me. She never noticed us, but swung along lazy and easy as anything. We sauntered to the corner and watched her till her door banged to. Ned repeated what he'd said. I didnt seem to care. Sitting around old Mush-Head's bread box, the discussion began. "Hang if I can see how she gets away with it," Doc started. Ned knew, of course. There was nothing he didn't know when it came to women. He dilated on the emotional needs of girls. Said they werent much different from men in that respect. And concluded with the solemn avowal: "It does em good." None of us liked Ned much. We all talked dirt; but it was the way he said it. And then too, a couple of the fellers had sisters and had caught Ned playing with them. But there was no disputing the superiority of his smutty wisdom. Bubs Sanborn, whose mother was friendly with Avey's, had overhead the old ladies talking. "Avey's mother's ont her," he said. We thought that only natural and began to guess at what would happen. Some one said she'd marry that feller on the top floor. Ned called that a lie because Avey was going to marry nobody but him. We had our doubts about that, but we did agree that she'd soon leave school and marry some one. The gang broke up, and I went home, picturing myself as married.

Nothing I did seemed able to change Avey's indifference to me. I played basket-ball, and when I'd make a long clean shot she'd clap with the others, louder than they, I thought. I'd meet her on the street, and there'd be no difference in the way she said hello. She never took the trouble to call me by my name. On the days for drill, I'd let my voice down a tone and call for a complicated maneuver when I saw her coming. She'd smile appreciation, but it was an impersonal smile, never for me. It was on a summer excursion down to Riverview that she first seemed to take me into account. The day had been spent riding merry-go-rounds, scenic-railways, and shoot-the-chutes. We had been in swimming and we had danced. I was a crack swimmer then. She didnt know how. I held her up and showed her how to kick her legs and draw her arms. Of course she didnt learn in one day, but she thanked me for bothering with her. I was also somewhat of a dancer. And I had already noticed that love can start on a dance floor. We danced. But though I held her tightly in my arms, she was way away. That college feller who lived on the top floor was somewhere making money for the next year. I imagined that she was thinking, wishing for him. Ned was along. He treated her until his money gave out. She went with another feller. Ned got sore. One by one the boys' money gave out. She left them. And they got sore. Every one of them but me got sore. This is the reason, I guess, why I had her to myself on the top deck of the *Jane Mosely* that night as we puffed up the Potomac, coming home. The moon was brilliant. The air was sweet like clover. And every now and then, a salt tang, a stale drift of sea-weed. It was not my mind's fault if it went romancing. I should have taken her in my arms the minute we were. stowed in that old lifeboat. I dallied, dreaming. She took me in hers. And I could feel by the touch of it that it wasnt a man-to-woman love. It made me restless. I felt chagrined. I didnt know what it was, but I did know that I couldnt handle it. She ran her fingers through my hair and kissed my forehead. I itched to break through her tenderness to passion. I wanted her to take me in her arms as I knew she had that college feller. I wanted her to love me passionately as she did him. I gave her one burning kiss. Then she laid me in her lap as if I were a child. Helpless. I got sore when she started to hum a lullaby. She wouldnt let me go. I talked. I knew damned well that I could beat her at that. Her eyes were soft and misty, the curves of her lips were wistful, and her smile seemed indulgent of the irrelevance of my remarks. I gave up at last and let her love me, silently, in her own way. The moon was brilliant. The air was sweet like clover, and every now and then, a salt tang, a stale drift of sea-weed. . .

The next time I came close to her was the following summer at Harpers Ferry. We were sitting on a flat projecting rock they give the name of Lover's Leap. Some one is supposed to have jumped off it. The river is about six hundred feet beneath. A railroad track runs up the valley and curves out of sight where part of the mountain rock had to be blasted away to make room for it. The engines of this valley have a whistle, the echoes of which sound like iterated gasps and sobs. I always think of them as crude music from the soul of Avey. We sat there holding hands. Our palms were soft and warm against each other. Our fingers were not tight. She would not let them be. She would not let me twist them. I wanted to talk. To explain what I meant to her. Avey was as silent as those great trees whose tops we looked down upon. She has always been like that. At least, to me. I had the notion that if I really wanted to, I could do with her just what I pleased. Like one can strip a tree. I did kiss her. I even let my hands cup her breasts. When I was through, she'd seek my hand and hold it till my pulse cooled down. Evening after evening we sat there. I tried to get her to talk about that college feller. She never would. There was no set time to go home. None of my family had come down. And as for hers, she didnt give a hang about them. The general gossips could hardly say more than they had. The boarding-house porch was always deserted when we returned. No one saw us enter, so the time was set conveniently for scandal. This worried me a little, for I thought it might keep Avey from getting an appointment in the schools. She didnt care. She had finished normal school. They could give her a job if they wanted to. As time went on, her indifference to things began to pique me; I was ambitious. I left the Ferry earlier than she did. I was going off to college. The more I thought of it, the more I resented, yes, hell, thats what it was, her downright laziness. Sloppy indolence. There was no excuse for a healthy girl taking life so easy. Hell! she was no better than a cow. I was certain that she was a cow when I felt an udder in a Wisconsin stock-judging class. Among those energetic Swedes, or whatever they are, I decided to forget her. For two years I thought I did. When I'd come home for the summer she'd be away. And before she returned, I'd be gone. We never wrote; she was too damned lazy for that. But what a bluff I put up about forgetting her. The girls up that way, at least the ones I knew, havent got the stuff: they dont know how to love. Giving themselves completely was tame beside just the holding of Avey's hand. One day I received a note from her. The writing, I decided, was slovenly. She wrote on a torn bit of note-book paper. The envelope had a faint perfume that I remembered. A single line told me she had lost her school and was going away. I comforted myself with the reflection that shame held no pain for one so indolent as she. Nevertheless, I left Wisconsin that year for good. Washington had seemingly forgotten her. I hunted Ned. Between curses, I caught his opinion of her. She was no better than a whore. I saw her mother on the street. The same old pinch-beck, jerky-gaited creature that I'd always known.

Perhaps five years passed. The business of hunting a job or something or other had bruised my vanity so that I could recognize it. I felt old. Avey and my real relation to her, I thought I came to know. I wanted to see her. I had been told that she was in New York. As I had no money, I hiked and bummed my way there. I got work in a ship-yard and walked the streets at night, hoping to meet her. Failing in this, I saved enough to pay my fare back home. One evening in early June, just at the time when dusk is most lovely on the eastern horizon, I saw Avey, indolent as ever, leaning on the arm of a man, strolling under the recently lit arc-lights of U Street. She had almost passed before she recognized me. She showed no surprise. The puff over her eyes had grown heavier. The eyes themselves were still sleepy-large, and beautiful. I had almost concluded—indifferent. "You look older," was what she said. I wanted to convince her that I was, so I asked her to walk with me. The man whom she was with, and whom she never took the trouble to introduce, at a nod from her, hailed a taxi, and drove away. That gave me a notion of what she had been used to. Her dress was of some fine, costly stuff. I suggested the park, and then added that the grass might stain her skirt. Let it get stained, she said, for where it came from there are others.

I have a spot in Soldier's Home to which I always go when I want the simple beauty of another's soul. Robins spring about the lawn all day. They leave their footprints in the grass. I imagine that the grass at night smells sweet and fresh because of them. The ground is high. Washington lies below. Its light spreads like a blush against the darkened sky. Against the soft dusk sky of Washington. And when the wind is from the South, soil of my homeland falls like a fertile shower upon the lean streets of the city. Upon my hill in Soldier's Home. I know the policeman who watches the place of nights. When I go there alone, I talk to him. I tell him I come there to find the truth that people bury in their hearts. I tell him that I do not come there with a girl to do the thing he's paid to watch out for. I look deep in his eyes when I say these things, and he believes me. He comes over to see who it is on the grass. I say hello to him. He greets me in the same way and goes off searching for other black splotches upon the lawn. Avey and I went there. A band in one of the buildings a fair distance off was playing a march. I wished they would stop. Their playing was like a tin spoon in one's mouth. I wanted the Howard Glee Club to sing "Deep River," from the road. To sing "Deep River, Deep River," from the road. . . Other than the first comments, Avey had been silent. I started to hum a folk-tune. She slipped her hand in mine. Pillowed her head as best she could upon my arm. Kissed the hand that she was holding and listened, or so I thought, to what I had to say. I traced my development from the early days up to the present time, the phase in which I could understand her. I described her own nature and temperament. Told how they needed a larger life for their expression. How incapable Washington was of understanding that need. How it could not meet it. I pointed out that in lieu of proper channels, her emotions had overflowed into paths that dissipated them. I talked, beautifully I thought, about an art that would be born, an art that would open the way for women the likes of her. I asked her to hope, and build up an inner life against the coming of that day. I recited some of my own things to her. I sang, with a strange quiver in my voice, a promise-song. And then I began to wonder why her hand had not once returned a single pressure. My old-time feeling about her laziness came back. I spoke sharply. My policeman friend passed by. I said hello to him. As he went away, I began to visualize certain possibilities. An immediate and urgent passion swept over me. Then I looked at Avey. Her heavy eyes were closed. Her breathing was as faint and regular as a child's in slumber. My passion died. I was afraid to move lest I disturb her. Hours and hours, I guess it was, she lay there. My body grew numb. I shivered. I coughed. I wanted to get up and whittle at the boxes of young trees. I withdrew my hand. I raised her head to waken her. She did not stir. I got up and walked around. I found my policeman friend and talked to him. We both came up, and bent over her. He said it would be all right for her to stay there just so long as she got away before the workmen came at dawn. A blanket was borrowed from a neighbor house. I sat beside her through the night. I saw the dawn steal over Washington. The Capitol dome looked like a gray ghost ship drifting in from sea. Avey's face was pale, and her eyes were heavy. She did not have the gray crimson-splashed beauty of the dawn. I hated to wake her. Orphan-woman. . .

LANGSTON HUGHES
(1902-1967)

Langston Hughes was born in Joplin, Missouri, and spent his early years in Kansas and Cleveland. His writing career spanned four decades, during which he was never inactive. As writer, adviser, and confidante, he was constantly in the forefront of Afro-American literary activity from the first appearance of his poems in the Crisis *in the early twenties until his death. He died less than a year after he had attended the First World Festival of Negro Arts in Dakar, at which he received homage from black writers and artists from all over the world who had found inspiration in his life and work.*

Alain Locke perceived in Langston Hughes a young black artist who would take the materials of folk life and transmute them into high art, and Locke was accordingly lavish in his early praise of Hughes. The centrality of the folk orientation was always the dominant feature of Hughes' work, from his early adaptation of the blues as a form for lyric poetry to his creation of that quintesssential folk-commentator, Jesse B. Semple, protagonist of the saga of Simple.

The astonishing feature of Langston Hughes' art is his unerring re-creation of the imagery, idiom, and syntax of black speech. This was not the result of chance, for Hughes' own spontaneous speech was quite different from that of the folk. His achievement was that of a connoisseur in love with the speech of black folk and with the folk themselves.

Many of the poems which Hughes published in various volumes are collected in Selected Poems of Langston Hughes *(1959). Subsequent volumes are* Ask Your Mama *(1961) and* The Panther and the Lash *(1967). He wrote only two novels,* Not Without Laughter *(1930), in which he portrays the black life of a small Kansas town with marvelous richness and projects alternate black life styles with insight and compassion, and* Tambourines to Glory *(1959), a tale of the commercialization of religion in Harlem. There are two autobiographies,* The Big Sea *(1940) and* I Wonder as I Wander *(1956). Some of his plays are collected in* Five Plays *(1963). Short-story collections are* The Ways of White Folks *(1934),* Laughing to Keep from Crying *(1952), and* Something in Common *(1963). Early Simple sketches are collected in* The Best of Simple *(1961); a later volume is* Simple's Uncle Sam *(1965). Hughes also wrote an historical work,* Fight for Freedom: The Story of the NAACP *(1962).*

Hughes has been the subject of a large amount of critical writing. An earlier study is that by James Emanuel (1967). Therman B. O'Daniel edited Langston Hughes, Black Genius: A Critical Evaluation *(1971), which includes a bibliography. Faith Berry's biography,* Langston Hughes: Before and Beyond Harlem *(1983) fills in Hughes' earlier career in considerable detail.*

Young Gal's Blues

I'm gonna walk to de graveyard
'Hind ma friend, Miss Cora Lee.
Gonna walk to de graveyard
'Hind ma dear friend Cora Lee.
Cause when I'm dead some
Body'll have to walk behind me.

I'm going to de po' house
To see ma old Aunt Clew.
Goin' to de po' house
To see ma old Aunt Clew.
When I'm old an' ugly
I'll want to see somebody, too.

De po' house is lonely
An' de grave is cold.
O, de po' house is lonely,
De graveyard grave is cold.
But I'd rather be dead than
To be ugly an' old.

When love is gone what
Can a young gal do?
When love is gone, O,
What can a young gal do?
Keep on a-lovin' me, daddy,
Cause I don't want to be blue.

Song to a Negro Wash-woman

Oh, wash-woman,
Arms elbow-deep in white suds,
Soul washed clean,
Clothes washed clean,
I have many songs to sing you
Could I but find the words.

Was it four o'clock or six o'clock on a winter afternoon,
I saw you wringing out the last shirt in Miss White
Lady's kitchen? Was it four o'clock or six o'clock? I
don't remember.

But I know, at seven one spring morning you were on
Vermont Street with a bundle in your arms going to
wash clothes.

And I know I've seen you in the New York subway in
the late afternoon coming home from washing clothes.

Yes, I know you, wash-woman.

I know how you send your children to school, and high-
school, and even college.
I know how you work to help your man when times are
hard.
I know how you build your house up from the washtub
and call it home.
And how you raise your churches from white suds for the
service of the Holy God.

I've seen you singing, wash-woman. Out in the backyard garden under the apple trees, singing, hanging white clothes on long lines in the sunshine.

And I've seen you in church on Sunday morning singing, praising your Jesus because some day you're going to sit on the right hand side of the Son of God and forget you ever were a wash-woman.

And the aching back and the bundles of clothes will be unremembered then.

Yes, I've seen you singing.

So for you,
O singing wash-woman,
For you, singing little brown woman,
Singing strong black woman,
Singing tall yellow woman,
Arms deep in white suds,
Soul washed clean,
Clothes washed clean,
For you I have
Many songs to sing
Could I but find the words.

Dream Variation

To fling my arms wide
In some place of the sun,
To whirl and to dance
Till the white day is done.
Then rest at cool evening
Beneath a tall tree
While night comes on gently,
    Dark like me—
That is my dream!

To fling my arms wide
In the face of the sun,
Dance! Whirl! Whirl!
Till the quick day is done.
Rest at pale evening . . .
A tall, slim tree . . .
Night coming tenderly
    Black like me.

The Doors of Life
From *Not Without Laughter*

During Sandy's second year at high school Tempy was busy sewing for the local Red Cross and organizing Liberty Bond clubs among the colored population of Stanton. She earnestly believed that the world would really become safe for democracy, even in America, when the war ended, and that colored folks would no longer be snubbed in private and discriminated against in public.

"Colored boys are over there fighting," she said. "Our men are buying hundreds of dollars' worth of bonds, colored women are aiding the Red Cross, our clubs are sending boxes to the camps and to the front. White folks will see that the Negro can be trusted in war as well as peace. Times will be better after this for all of us."

One day a letter came from Annjee, who had moved to Chicago. She said that Sandy's father had not long remained in camp, but had been sent to France almost immediately after he enlisted, and she didn't know what she was going to do, she was so worried and alone! There had been but one letter from Jimboy since he left. And now she needed Sandy with her, but she wasn't able to send for him yet. She said she hoped and prayed that nothing would happen to his father at the front, but every day there were colored soldiers' names on the casualty list.

"Good thing he's gone," grunted Tempy when she read the letter as they were seated at the supper-table. Then, suddenly changing the subject, she asked Sandy: "Did you see Dr. Frank Crane's beautiful article this morning?"

"No, I didn't," said the boy.

"You certainly don't read as much as you did last winter," complained his aunt. "And you're staying out entirely too late to suit me. I'm quite sure you're not at the movies all that time, either. I want these late hours stopped, young man. Every night in the week out somewhere until ten and eleven o'clock!"

"Well, boys do have to get around a little, Tempy," Mr. Siles objected. "It's not like when you and I were coming up."

"I'm raising this boy, Mr. Siles," Tempy snapped. "When do you study, James? That's what I want to know."

"When I come in," said Sandy, which was true. His light was on until after twelve almost every night. And when he did not study late, his old habit of lying awake clung to him and he could not go to sleep early.

"You think too much," Buster once said. "Stop being so smart; then you'll sleep better."

"Yep," added Jimmy Lane. "Better be healthy and dumb than smart and sick like some o' these college darkies I see with goggles on their eyes and breath smellin' bad."

"O, I'm not sick," objected Sandy, "but I just get to thinking about things at night—the war, and white folks, and God, and girls, and—O, I don't know—everything in general."

"Sure, keep on thinking," jeered Buster, "and turn right ashy after while and be all stoop-shouldered like Father Hill." (The Episcopalian rector was said to be the smartest colored man in town.) "But I'm not gonna worry about being smart myself. A few more years, boy, and I'll be in some big town passing for white, making money, and getting along swell. And I won't need to be smart, either—I'll be ofay! So if you see me some time in St. Louis or Chi with a little blond on my arm—don't recognize me, hear! I want my kids to be so yellow-headed they won't have to think about a color line."

And Sandy knew that Buster meant what he said, for his light-skinned friend was one of those people who always go directly towards the things they want, as though the road is straight before them and they can see clearly all the way. But to Sandy himself nothing ever seemed quite that clear. Why was his country going stupidly to war? . . . Why were white people and colored people so far apart? Why was it wrong to desire the bodies of women? . . . With his mind a maelstrom of thoughts as he lay in bed night after night unable to go to sleep quickly, Sandy wondered many things and asked himself many questions.

Sometimes he would think about Pansetta Young, his class-mate with the soft brown skin, and the pointed and delicate breasts of her doll-like body. He had never been alone with Pansetta, never even kissed her, yet she was "his girl" and he liked her a great deal. Maybe he loved her! . . . But what did it mean to love a girl? Were you supposed to marry her then and live with her for ever? . . . His father had married his mother—good-natured, guitar-playing Jimboy—but they weren't always together, and Sandy knew that Jimboy was enjoying the war now, just as he had always enjoyed everything else.

"Gee, he must of married early to be my father and still look so young!" he thought. "Suppose I marry Pansetta now!" But what did he really know about marriage other than the dirty fragments he had picked up from Jimmy and Buster and the fellows at the pool hall?

On his fifteenth birthday Tempy had given him a book written for young men on the subject of love and living, called *The Doors of Life*, addressed to all Christian youths in their teens—but it had been written by a white New England minister of the Presbyterian faith who stood aghast before the flesh; so its advice consisted almost entirely in how to pray in the orthodox manner, and in how *not* to love.

"Avoid evil companions lest they be your undoing (see Psalms cxix, 115-20); and beware of lewd women, for their footsteps lead down to hell (see Proverbs vii, 25-7)," said the book, and that was the extent of its instructions on sex, except that it urged everyone to marry early and settle down to a healthy, moral, Christian life. . . . But how could you marry early when you had no money and no home to which to take a wife, Sandy wondered. And who were evil companions. Neither Aunt Hager nor Annjee had ever said anything to Sandy about love in its bodily sense; Jimboy had gone away too soon to talk with him; and Tempy and her husband were too proper to discuss such subjects; so the boy's sex knowledge consisted only in the distorted ideas that youngsters whisper; the dirty stories heard in the hotel lobby where he had worked; and the fact that they sold in drugstores articles that weren't mentioned in the company of nice people.

But who were nice people anyway? Sandy hated the word "nice." His Aunt Tempy was always using it. All of her friends were nice, she said, respectable and refined. They went around with their noses in the air and they didn't speak to porters and washwomen—though they weren't nearly so much fun as the folks they tried to scorn. Sandy liked Cudge Windsor or Jap Logan better than he did Dr. Mitchell, who had been to college—and never forgotten it.

Sandy wondered if Booker T. Washington had been like Tempy's friends? Or if Dr. Du Bois was a snob just because he was a college man? He wondered if those two men had a good time being great. Booker T. was dead, but he had left a living school in the South. Maybe he could teach in the South, too, Sandy thought, if he ever learned enough. Did colored folks need to know the things he was studying in books now? Did French and Latin and Shakespeare make people wise and happy? Jap Logan never went beyond the seventh grade and he was happy. And Jimboy never attended school much either. Maybe school didn't matter. Yet to get a good job you had to be smart—and white, too. That was the trouble, you had to be white!

"But I want to learn!" thought Sandy as he lay awake in the dark after he had gone to bed at night. "I want to go to college. I want to go to Europe and study. 'Work and make ready and maybe your chance will come,' it said under the picture of Lincoln on the calendar given away by the First National Bank, where Earl, his white friend, already had a job promised him when he came out of school. . . . It was not nearly so difficult for white boys. They could work at anything—in stores, on newspapers, in offices. They could become president of the United States if they were clever enough. But a colored boy. . . . No wonder Buster was going to pass for white when he left Stanton.

"I don't blame him," thought Sandy. "Sometimes I hate white people, too, like Aunt Harrie used to say she did. Still, some of them are pretty decent—my English-teacher, and Mr. Prentiss where I work. Yet even Mr. Prentiss wouldn't give me a job clerking in his shop. All I can do there is run errands and scrub the floor when everybody else is gone. There's no advancement for colored fellows. If they start as porters, they stay porters for ever and they can't come up. Being colored is like being born in the basement of life, with the door to the light locked and barred—and the white folks live upstairs. They don't want us up there with them, even when we're respectable like Dr. Mitchell, or smart like Dr. Du Bois. . . . And guys like Jap Logan—well, Jap don't care anyway! Maybe it's best not to care, and stay poor and meek waiting for heaven like Aunt Hager did. . . . But I don't want heaven! I want to live first!" Sandy thought. "I want to live!"

He understood then why many old Negroes said: "Take all this world and give me Jesus!" It was because they couldn't get this world anyway—it belonged to the white folks. They alone had the power to give or withhold at their back doors. Always back doors— even for Tempy and Dr. Mitchell if they chose to go into Wright's Hotel or the New Albert Restaurant. And no door at all for Negroes if they wanted to attend the Rialto Theatre, or join the Stanton Y. M. C. A., or work behind the grilling at the National Bank.

The Doors of Life. . . . God damn that simple-minded book that Tempy had given him! What did an old white minister know about the doors of life for him and Pansetta and Jimmy Lane, for Willie-Mae and Buster and Jap Logan and all the black and brown and yellow youngsters standing on the threshold of the great beginning in a Western town called Stanton? What did an old white minister know about the doors of life anywhere? And, least of all, the doors to a Negro's life? . . . Black youth. . . . Dark hands knocking, knocking! Pansetta's little brown hands knocking on the doors of life! Baby-doll hands, tiny autumn-leaf girl-hands! . . . Gee, Pansetta! . . . The Doors of Life . . . the great big doors. . . . Sandy was asleep . . . of life.

Simple Discusses Colleges and Color

"Delbert is going to college," said Simple, "so if I live and nothing happens—and I get straight—I am going to send him the money for his first pair of football shoes."

"Who on earth is Delbert?" I asked. "I never heard of him before."

"He's my second cousin on my father's step-sister's side. He lives in Brooklyn," said Simple, "and seldom comes to Harlem, being a quiet young man."

"Oh," I said. "Well, if Delbert is going to college, what you should think about helping him buy is not football shoes, but books. Men go to college to study, not to play football."

"Footballing is all I ever read about them doing," said Simple. "Since I do not know any college boys, I thought they went there to play."

"They do not," I said. "Of course, the ones who play good football get their names in the papers. But there are thousands of others who graduate with honors and never even see a football game. What sort of college is Delbert going to, may I ask? A white college? Or a colored college?"

"I hope to a colored college," said Simple.

"Why?" I inquired.

"So he can get a rest from white folks."

"You have entirely the wrong idea about colleges," I said. "A man doesn't go to college to rest. He goes to get educated. Besides, why would a Northern boy want to go to a Negro school when he has been going to mixed schools all his life?"

"So he can dance with the girls," said Simple, "and not be no wall-flower, neither a floor walker."

"A man is hardly likely to be a wallflower," I said. "But I see what you mean—so he can be among his own and have a well-rounded social life. Still, I insist, you don't go to college to dance. You go to get educated."

"If I was going to college," said Simple, "I might not get educated, but I would come out with a educated wife."

"Hopeless!" I said. "Football, dancing, marriage are all side issues. A college is for the propagation of knowledge, my good man—not fun and sex."

"I don't see how you are going to keep sex out of a young boy's life," said Simple, "nor fun, neither. And if Delbert was a son of mine, not just a second step-cousin, I would say, 'Delbert, son, go have yourself a good time whilst you are also learning, because in due time you will be married and cannot have a good time, also you will have responsibilities and cannot enjoy yourself like you can in school. Since you have been going to school with white folks all your life, it is about time for you to go to school with colored folks now. Otherwise, how are you ever going to get to know your own folks? When you come out of college, if you don't work *with* colored folks, you are going to have to work *for* white folks. And the jobs white folks have for educated colored mens are few and far between. If you get to be a doctor, you are going to doctor *me*. I am black. Now, how can you doctor me good if you don't know me?' That is what I would say to Delbert."

"You have a point there," I said, "but I still insist the prime purpose of college is education."

"Do you mean book-learning?" asked Simple.

"Approximately that."

"Then you are approximately wrong," said Simple. "I do not care what you know out of a book, you also have got to know something out of life. And *life* is hard for a colored boy in the manhood stage to learn around white folks. If Delbert does learn it around white folks, he is going to learn it the hard way. That might make him mad, or else sad. If he gets mad, he is going to be bad. And if he's sad, he is going to just give up and maybe not get nowheres. No, I will tell Delbert not to go to no white school, and be snubbed when he asks a girl for a dance, and be barred out of the hotels, where his football team stays—no matter how smart he gets in his head. Facts is, I cares more about Delbert's heart, anyhow, than I do his head."

"I admit there has to be a balance," I said, "and certainly there are good Negro colleges where a boy can learn a great deal and have fun, too. But the way you talk, fun is first and foremost. And you imply that there is no fun to be had around white folks."

"I never had none," said Simple.

"You have a color complex," I said.

"A colored complexion," said Simple.

"I said, '*complex!*' not complexion."

"I added the 'shun' myself," said Simple. "I'm colored, and being around white folks makes me feel more colored—since most of them shuns me."

"Full proof of what I've just stated—a complex!"

"Call it what you want to," said Simple, "but my cousin is not white. Facts, he's not even light. Delbert would show up very dark in a white college."

"That might make him outstanding," I said.

"*Standing out*, you mean," said Simple, "standing out *all by himself*—and that is just where the '*shun*' comes in I was talking about."

"You are confusing the issue," I said.

"I had rather confuse the issue than confuse Delbert," said Simple.

Simple and the Rosenwald Fund

Walking down the street this evening I ran into my Simple Minded Friend who looked very gloomy indeed.

I said, "What're you doing around here?"

He said, "You're liable to see me *any* place, *any* time. Sometimes I just stomps the streets, to keep my problems from stomping me."

"What's the matter?" I said. "You do look rather down in the mouth."

Simple said, "Daddy-o, as bad as I'm feeling tonight, I could call Lena Horne an ugly woman."

"You've gone too far now," I said. "Why on earth are you feeling so badly?"

"Why?" yelled Simple. "You're asking me *why?* When the Rosenwald Fund's going out of existence and I have never had one of them Fellowships! I see in *The Defender* where they gave away twenty-two million dollars. Not nary one of them dollars did I see."

"No doubt that is true," I said, "but you have benefited indirectly—as has the Race—as has America."

"I would like to have benefited *directly*," said Simple. "A dollar in my pocket is worth two in somebody else's."

"Wrong," I said. "A dollar invested in educational, social, or cultural progress is worth many dollars to many more persons than merely the individual carrier of culture in whom it is invested."

"Says what?" asked Simple.

"For example, when you read Willard Motley's *Knock On Any Door* you are benefiting by the Rosenwald dollar. American culture is enriched. In that way you, me, everybody benefits by it. Indirectly maybe, yes. But then you've not been working in the cultural field yourself."

"I have just been *working*," said Simple.

"That's right, ordinary work," I said. "Well, the Fund has helped highly trained, talented people be of more service to ordinary folks. In other words, to benefit society as a whole, the Fund has taken care of extra-ordinary people."

"But we *ordinary* people have to take care of ourselves," said Simple.

"That's about right," I agreed. "There isn't enough money in the world to go *all* the way around."

"Which is why practically none of it ever comes around to me," said Simple. "I wonder will I ever hit that jackpot at the end of the rainbow. Don't no rainbows end on my street, so I guess I won't be that lucky."

"You don't get Fellowships through luck," I said. "You get them through qualifications."

"It would seem like luck to me," said Simple. "I have never seen a Fellowship in all my life, and I reckon I never will.

"Probably not," I said, "because not every fellow can have a Fellowship. Fellowships are granted to help enrich the world, I told you—that is how we benefit—through those capable people to whom the Fellowships are given. Don't you understand? Maybe I can make it clear to you in this way: Suppose a young doctor has a Rosenwald. He studies for a year and learns some very valuable things that enrich medical science as a whole. Then this knowledge is made available to other physicians. Well, those things benefit you. When you go to your doctor, perhaps something realized from that year of Rosenwald study will save *your life.*

"My doctor will charge *me* three dollars," said Simple.

"Of course, but you are getting knowledge worth many thousands of dollars—socially shared knowledge—which saves many lives."

"But if I don't have three dollars, it won't save mine," said Simple.

"Oh, you are just being difficult, as usual—making an argument. But even if you were to die for lack of funds—you never seem to have heard of a free clinic—wouldn't you still be proud to see somebody else of your race live and get ahead?"

"I damn sure would!" said Simple. "But don't kill me off, Buddy-o! I do not intend to die. I intend to make my own way in this world just like I been doing, Fund or no Fund."

"That's the spirit!" I said. "Certainly if it were not for millions of ordinary people like you, there wouldn't have been anybody anyhow for the Rosenwald Fund to help, either directly or indirectly—so that is your value."

"My value? You mean to tell me that I have been of some value to the Rosenwald Fund?" asked Simple.

"Of course you have," I said. "You *are!* You are the very problems the Fund has been trying to solve."

"Thank God for me then!" said Simple. "Even if they never gave me a Fellowship, at least I gave them a fellow!"

"Right! You did. You posed the problem."

"Then treat me to a beer," said Simple, "and I hope a dime poses no problems to you."

"It does not pose a problem," I said, "but it does pose a question."

"What question?"

"How come you're always broke, and never have a dime yourself?"

"*That* is a $64.00 question," said Simple. "To find the answer to that question requires a mighty lot of research—for which I don't just need a Fellowship, daddy-o, I needs a *whole* Fund! . . . Two beers, bartender—so I can drink to my needs!"

"Let's drink to your problems!" I said.

"O.K.," said Simple, "because I'm *still* one."

"Here's to you!" I said.

"Wait a minute before we drink," said Simple. "I want to say a toast. Listen fluently now and take note. This is it:

When you look at this life you'll find
That it ain't nothing but a race.
If you can't be the winning hoss, daddy-o,
At least—try to place!"

ARNA BONTEMPS
(1902-1973)

Arna Bontemps was born in Louisiana and reared in California. After college he spent several years in New York until the Depression forced him to leave in order to support his growing family. He eventually became librarian of Fisk University, a post which he held for many years.

The total range of Arna Bontemps' work is enormous. It includes fiction, poetry, history, and criticism. In his subdued manner, he has been consistently the most race-conscious of the black writers who began writing in the twenties. Without fanfare or histrionics he has held firm to the vision expressed in "Golgotha Is a Mountain":

> *Black men are bowing*
> *Naked in that grass.*
> *I am one of them:*
> *Those mountains should be ours.*

In fiction Bontemps has explored race-track life in God Sends Sunday *(1931),* Gabriel's *insurrection in* Black Thunder *(1936) and the Haitian revolution in* Drums at Dusk *(1939). His writing for children includes history as well as fiction. His earliest children's book was written in collaboration with Langston Hughes,* Popo and Fifina: Children of Haiti *(1932); others are* Sad-faced Boy *(1937) and* The Fast Sooner Hound *(1942), as well as* Story of the Negro *(1958).*

Bontemps again joined with Langston Hughes in editing Poetry of the Negro *and* The Book of American Negro Folklore *(1958).*

Bontemps' critical writings are scattered in articles, introductions, and occasional essays. A collection of them would illuminate the story of Afro-American letters in recent times.

Nocturne at Bethesda

I thought I saw an angel flying low.
I thought I saw the flicker of a wing
Above the mulberry trees—but not again.
Bethesda sleeps. This ancient pool that healed
A host of bearded Jews does not awake.
This pool that once the angels troubled does not move.
No angel stirs it now, no Saviour comes
with healing in His hands to raise the sick
and bid the lame man leap upon the ground.

The golden days are gone. Why do we wait
so long upon the marble steps, blood
falling from our open wounds? And why
do our black faces search the empty sky?
Is there something we have forgotten? some precious thing
we have lost, wandering in strange lands?

There was a day, I remember now,
I beat my breast and cried 'Wash me God,
wash me with a wave of wind upon
the barley; O quiet One, draw near, draw near!
walk upon the hills with lovely feet
and in the waterfall stand and speak.

Dip white hands in the lily pool and mourn
upon the harps still hanging in the trees
near Babylon along the river's edge,
but oh, remember me, I pray, before
the summer goes and rose leaves lose their red.'

The old terror takes my heart, the fear
of quiet waters and of faint twilights.
There will be better days when I am gone
and healing pools where I cannot be healed.
Fragrant stars will gleam forever and ever
above the place where I lie desolate.

Yet I hope, still I long to live.
And if there can be returning after death
I shall come back. But it will not be here:
if you want me you must search for me
beneath the palms of Africa. Or if
I am not there you may call to me
across the shining dunes, perhaps I shall
be following a desert caravan.

I may pass through centuries of death
with quiet eyes, but I'll remember still
a jungle tree with burning scarlet birds.
There is something I have forgotten, some precious thing
I shall be seeking ornaments of ivory,
I shall be dying for a jungle fruit.

You do not hear, Bethesda.
O still green water in a stagnant pool!
Love abandoned you and me alike.
There was a day you held a rich full moon
upon your heart and listened to the words
of men now dead and saw the angels fly.
There is a simple story on your face:
years have wrinkled you. I know, Bethesda!
You are sad. It is the same with me.

From *Black Thunder*

Juba moped. She stood outside the circle of savage gossiping hags and settled her weight on one leg. She had given them her left shoulder and an arm set akimbo on her hip, and now, running nervous fingers through her wild shock of hair, she cut her eyes at them spitefully.

At intervals the others leaned forward confidently, their heads coming together near the ground, their blunt posteriors rising and broadening simultaneously. At the center of the circle, beside the outdoor fire, squatted a woman with a baby. She was moistening a rag in a cup of gruel and offering it to the infant. Her teeth jutted between sagging lips; lean wrinkled breasts hung against her belly.

"The way that gal is putting on you'd think he's the last man in the state what's got a seed to give."

An older woman, wrinkled and witchlike, clasping a clay pipe in her mouth, picked at the toenails of a scaly foot.

"Gabriel's all right. He a mighty fine boy, even if he is got a face longer'n a mule's. But all this Jesus talk I hears ain't helping him none."

The sleeves were torn from Juba's garment, and the rag that remained of the upper half was drawn tight around her breasts. It had parted from the skirt, too, and there was a streak of nakedness at her waist. Now that she knew what they were getting at, she gave her hips a twitch and moved a few steps.

"You ain't never heard Gabriel moaning and praying. What you talking about?"

The others looked a little surprised, but they were far from displeased with their success in piquing her interest. She had ignored them so long they had begun to imagine that she failed to hear them, even when they talked in her presence. The woman with the baby leaned forward and spat into the fire.

"No sense of you trying to get yo'self hanged, though. You's a fool; that's what you is."

"Ne' mind about that. If I don't care do I get hanged, that's me. If I's a plum fool, that's me too. On'erstand?"

The shadows gathered quickly, almost hastily, and now, in no time at all, it was night at the cooking place. Juba walked completely around the circle of slave women. Somewhere among the folds of her butternut garment she found a pipe and a moment later she was kneeling at the fire. But she was not one of the crowd on the ground; even when she brushed against them while holding her pipe to the flame, she was as haughty and aloof as a harlot. The old woman scraping at her crusted toenails did not look up.

'A man, do he 'spect to win, is obliged to fight the way he know. That's what's ailing Gabriel and all them. He is obliged to go at it with something he can manage."

Juba looked perplexed, but she did not speak till she was on her feet again.

"What you mean, woman?"

"They talks about Toussaint over yonder in San Domingo. They done forget something."

Her face grew more hideous in the firelight. A frayed stick that she had been chewing hung on her lip.

"Go on. What Gabriel forget?"

"I don't know about all that reading in the Book. All that what say God is going to fight against them what oppresses the po'. That might be well and good—I don't know. Toussaint and them kilt a hog in the woods. Drank the blood."

"He did, hunh?"

"H'm. Gabriel done forget to take something to protect hisself. The stars wasn't right. See? All that rain. Too much listening to Mingo read a white man's book. They ain't paid attention to the signs."

"Gabriel don't know a heap of conjure and signs and charms. He ain't never had no head for nothing like that."

The old female drew up the other foot. Suddenly she seemed faraway and cruelly unconcerned.

"Nah, I reckon he ain't," she said.

"Well, he ain't done for yet. He going to be a peck of trouble to them yet, I bound you."

"Maybe. I tell you there's a heap of them what *is* done for, though. Criddle, Ditcher, Mingo and I don't know how many mo'. Then they's a lot mo' what nobody's seen hide or hair of and what's just as apt to be dead as they is apt to be live."

Juba shrugged.

"Plenty niggers died with Toussaint too, didn't they?"

"It didn't work out the same. You'll see. Toussaint kilt a hog. There's plenty things Gabriel could of done."

"Listen, woman. Maybe some time I might see Gabriel *now*— some night maybe. Has you got a good hand I can give him to put in his pocket?"

The infant, not satisfied with its rag, whimpered and presently set up a faint, croaking lamentation. The four or five women who were not smoking had snuff-smeared mouths; periodically they leaned forward and spat into the fire. Juba squatted down beside the old creature who was still preoccupied with her scaly black feet and waited for an answer.

"Maybe."

"Listen, woman," Juba said. "I don't know nothing about *maybe*. Is you going to make me a hand for Gabriel, one what'll keep him safe whilst he's running?"

"He ought to come hisself. That's the most surest way. I could make you one for him that might help some, though."

"Come on." Juba pulled at the other's rags. "Come on now. Some time I might can bring him to you, some night late, but that ain't now. Come on, woman."

"Take yo' hands off'n me, gal. See there, you done pulled it off. I can't be sitting out here buck naked, old as I'm getting."

Juba put the garment under her arm. The old female gave up her toes reluctantly, struggled to her feet.

"Come on now," Juba said. "Here's yo' rag."

"Gabriel should of come hisself. Matter of fact, he should of come long time ago, did he have any sense."

Night had come with emphasis, but bats were still leaving the peaked gable of the barn. They wavered upward, shadowy and fabulous, like legendary birds. When Juba and the old crone reached the door, a foul stench came out of the hut and assailed them like a plague. Juba halted and heard the women they had left cackling around the fire. Then, puffing fast to keep the smoke in her nostrils, she followed the older woman into the hovel.

(1936)

ZORA NEALE HURSTON
(1903-1960)

*Zora Neale Hurston, born in Eatonville, an all-black town in
Florida, achieved distinction as a writer of fiction and as a folklorist
and anthropologist. Miss Hurston's novels are* Jonah's Gourd Vine
(1934), Their Eyes Were Watching God *(1937),* Moses, Man of
the Mountain *(1939) and* Seraph on the Suwanee *(1948). She wrote
many short stories, beginning with* "Spunk," *published in* The New
Negro *in 1925.*

*Mules and Men (1935) is an account of folklore collecting in
her native Florida and in Louisiana, the land of "hoodoo." Miss Hurston went farther afield in* Tell My Horse, *which is a somewhat lurid
description of her search for folklore material in Haiti, an account
that should be contrasted with the sobriety of Katherine Dunham's
later* Journey to Accompong *(1945), reporting ethnographic research
in Jamaica.*

In her fascinating autobiography Dust Tracks on a Road *(1942)
Miss Hurston offers insights and judgments in her account of her
experiences in the black world, which included a friendship with
Ethel Waters. Her gift for infusing all that she considered with
vitality is especially evident in this work.*

*In recent years Hurston has excited great interest among literary critics, folk-
lorists, and militant feminists who see in the sadness of her later years, the toll taken
by a masculine world on an independent woman. Robert E. Hemenway's biography
of Hurston (1977) is both a product and a catalyst of the Hurston revival.*

Sweat

It was eleven o'clock of a Spring night in Florida. It was Sunday. Any other night, Delia Jones would have been in bed for two hours by this time. But she was a washwoman, and Monday morning meant a great deal to her. So she collected the soiled clothes on Saturday when she returned the clean things. Sunday night after church, she sorted them and put the white things to soak. It saved her almost a half day's start. A great hamper in the bedroom held the clothes that she brought home. It was so much neater than a number of bundles lying around.

She squatted in the kitchen floor beside the great pile of clothes, sorting them into small heaps according to color, and humming a song in a mournful key, but wondering through it all where Sykes, her husband, had gone with her horse and buckboard.

Just then something long, round, limp and black fell upon her shoulders and slithered to the floor beside her. A great terror took hold of her. It softened her knees and dried her mouth so that it was a full minute before she could cry out or move. Then she saw that it was the big bull whip her husband liked to carry when he drove.

She lifted her eyes to the door and saw him standing there bent over with laughter at her fright. She screamed at him.

"Sykes, what you throw dat whip on me like dat? You know it would skeer me—looks just like a snake, an' you knows how skeered Ah is of snakes."

"Course Ah knowed it! That's how come Ah done it." He slapped his leg with his hand and almost rolled on the ground in his mirth. "If you such a big fool dat you got to have a fit over a earth worm or a string, Ah don't keer how bad Ah skeer you."

"You aint got no business doing it. Gawd knows it's a sin. Some day Ah'm gointuh drop dead from some of yo' foolishness. 'Nother thing, where you been wid mah rig? Ah feeds dat pony. He aint fuh you to be drivin' wid no bull whip."

"Yo sho is one aggravatin' nigger woman!" he declared and stepped into the room. She resumed her work and did not answer him at once. "Ah done tole you time and again to keep them white folks' clothes outa dis house."

He picked up the whip and glared down at her. Delia went on with her work. She went out into the yard and returned with a galvanized tub and set it on the washbench. She saw that Sykes had kicked all of the clothes together again, and now stood in her way truculently, his whole manner hoping, *praying*, for an argument. But she walked calmly around him and commenced to re-sort the things.

"Next time, Ah'm gointer to kick 'em outdoors," he threatened as he struck a match along the leg of his corduroy breeches.

Delia never looked up from her work, and her thin, stooped shoulders sagged further.

"Ah aint for no fuss t'night Sykes. Ah just come from taking sacrament at the church house."

He snorted scornfully. "Yeah, you just come from de church house on a Sunday night, but heah you is gone to work on them clothes. You ain't nothing but a hypocrite. One of them amen-corner Christians—sing, whoop, shout, then come home and wash white folks clothes on the Sabbath."

He stepped roughly upon the whitest pile of things, kicking them helter-skelter as he crossed the room. His wife gave a little scream of dismay, and quickly gathered them together again.

"Sykes, you quit grindin' dirt into these clothes! How can Ah git through by Sat'day if Ah don't start on Sunday?"

"Ah don't keer if you never git through. Anyhow, Ah done promised Gawd and a couple of other men, Ah aint gointer have it in mah house. Don't gimme no lip neither, else Ah'll throw 'em out and put mah fist up side yo' head to boot."

Delia's habitual meekness seemed to slip from her shoulders like a blown scarf. She was on her feet; her poor little body, her bare knuckly hands bravely defying the strapping hulk before her.

"Looka heah, Sykes, you done gone too fur. Ah been married to you fur fifteen years, and Ah been takin' in washin' for fifteen years. Sweat, sweat, sweat! Work and sweat, cry and sweat, pray and sweat!

"What's that got to do with me?" he asked brutally.

"What's it got to do with you, Sykes? Mah tub of suds is filled yo' belly with vittles more times than yo' hands is filled it. Mah sweat is done paid for this house and Ah reckon Ah kin keep on sweatin' in it."

She seized the iron skillet from the stove and struck a defensive pose, which act surprised him greatly, coming from her. It cowed him and he did not strike her as he usually did.

"Naw you won't," she panted, "that ole snaggle-toothed black woman you runnin' with aint comin' heah to pile up on *mah* sweat and blood. You aint paid for nothin' on this place, and Ah'm gointer stay right heah till Ah'm toted out foot foremost."

"Well, you better quit gittin' me riled up, else they'll be totin' you out sooner than you expect. Ah'm so tired of you Ah don't know whut to do. Gawd! how Ah hates skinny wimmen!"

A little awed by this new Delia, he sidled out of the door and slammed the back gate after him. He did not say where he had gone, but she knew too well. She knew very well that he would not return until nearly daybreak also. Her work over, she went on to bed but not to sleep at once. Things had come to a pretty pass!

She lay awake, gazing upon the debris that cluttered their matrimonial trail. Not an image left standing along the way. Anything like flowers had long ago been drowned in the salty stream that had been pressed from her heart. Her tears, her sweat, her blood. She had brought love to the union and he had brought a longing for the flesh. Two months after the wedding, he had given her the first brutal beating. She had the memory of numerous trips to Orlando with all of his wages when he had returned to her penniless, even before the first year had passed. She was young and soft then, but now she thought of her knotty, muscled limbs, her harsh knuckly hands, and drew herself up into an unhappy little ball in the middle of the big feather bed. Too late now to hope for love, even if it were not Bertha it would be someone else. This case differed from the others only in that she was bolder than the others. Too late for everything except her little home. She had built it for her old days, and planted one by one the trees and flowers there. It was lovely to her, lovely.

Somehow before sleep came, she found herself saying aloud: "Oh well, whatever goes over the Devil's back, is got to come under his belly. Sometime or ruther, Sykes, like everybody else, is gointer reap his sowing." After that she was able to build a spiritual earthworks against her husband. His shells could no longer reach her. *Amen*. She went to sleep and slept until he announced his presence in bed by kicking her feet and rudely snatching the cover away.

"Gimme some kivah heah, an' git yo' damn foots over on yo' own side! Ah oughter mash you in yo' mouf fuh drawing dat skillet on me."

Delia went clear to the rail without answering him. A triumphant indifference to all that he was or did.

The week was as full of work for Delia as all other weeks, and Saturday found her behind her little pony, collecting and delivering clothes.

It was a hot, hot day near the end of July. The village men on Joe Clarke's porch even chewed cane listlessly. They did not hurl the caneknots as usual. They let them dribble over the edge of the porch. Even conversation had collapsed under the heat.

"Heah comes Delia Jones," Jim Merchant said, as the shaggy pony came 'round the bend of the road toward them. The rusty buckboard was heaped with baskets of crisp, clean laundry.

"Yep," Joe Lindsay agreed. "Hot or col', rain or shine, jes ez reg'lar ez de weeks roll roun' Delia carries 'em an' fetches 'em on Sat'day."

"She better if she wanter eat," said Moss. "Syke Jones aint wuth de shot an' powder hit would tek tuh kill 'em. Not to *huh* he aint."

"He sho' aint," Walter Thomas chimed in. "It's too bad, too, cause she wuz a right pritty lil trick when he got huh. Ah'd uh mah'ied huh mahseff if he hadnter beat me to it."

Delia nodded briefly at the men as she drove past.

"Too much knockin' will ruin *any* 'oman. He done beat huh 'nough tuh kill three women, let 'lone change they looks," said Elijah Mosely. "How Syke kin stommuck dat big black greasy Mogul he's layin' roun' wid, gits me. Ah swear dat eight-rock couldn't kiss a sardine can Ah done thowed out de back do' 'way las' yeah."

"Aw, she's fat, thass how come. He's allus been crazy 'bout fat women," put in Merchant. "He'd a' been tied up wid one long time ago if he could a' found one tuh have him. Did Ah tell yuh 'bout him come sidlin' roun *mah* wife—bringin' her a basket uh pee-cans outa his yard fuh a present? Yes-sir, mah wife! She tol' him tuh take 'em right straight back home, cause Delia works so hard ovah dat washtub she reckon everything on de place taste lak sweat an' soapsuds. Ah jus' wisht Ah'd a' caught 'im 'roun' dere! Ah'd a' made his hips ketch on fiah down dat shell road."

"Ah know he done it, too. Ah sees 'im grinnin' at every 'oman dat passes," Walter Thomas said. "But even so, he useter eat some mighty big hunks uh humble pie tuh git dat lil' 'oman he got. She wuz ez pritty ez a speckled pup! Dat wuz fifteen yeahs ago. He useter be so skeered uh losin' huh, she could make him do some parts of a husband's duty. Dey never wuz de same in de mind."

"There oughter be a law about him," said Lindsay. "He aint fit tuh carry guts tuh a bear."

Clarke spoke for the first time. "Taint no law on earth dat kin make a man be decent if it aint in 'im. There's plenty men dat takes a wife lak dey do a joint uh sugar-cane. It's round, juicy an' sweet when dey gits it. But dey squeeze an' grind, squeeze an' grind an' wring tell dey wring every drop uh pleasure dat's in 'em out. When dey's satisfied dat dey is wrung dry, dey treats 'em jes lak dey do a cane-chew. Dey thows 'em away. Dey knows whut dey is doin' while dey is at it, an' hates theirselves fuh it but they keeps on hangin' after huh tell she's empty. Den dey hates huh fuh bein' a cane-chew an' in de way."

"We oughter take Syke an' dat stray 'oman uh his'n down in Lake Howell swamp an' lay on de rawhide till they cain't say 'Lawd a' mussy.' He allus wuz uh ovahbearin' niggah, but since dat white 'oman from up north done teached 'im how to run a automobile, he done got too biggety to live—an' we oughter kill 'im," Old Man Anderson advised.

A grunt of approval went around the porch. But the heat was melting their civic virtue and Elijah Moseley began to bait Joe Clarke.

"Come on, Joe, git a melon outa dere an' slice it up for yo' customers. We'se all sufferin' wid de heat. De bear's done got *me!*"

"Thass right, Joe, a watermelon is jes' whut Ah needs tuh cure de eppizudicks," Walter Thomas joined forces with Moseley. "Come on dere, Joe. We all is steady customers an' you aint set us up in a long time. Ah chooses dat long, bowlegged Floridy favorite."

"A god, an' be dough. You all gimme twenty cents and slice away," Clarke retorted. "Ah needs a col' slice m'self. Heah, everybody chip in. Ah'll lend y'll mah meat knife."

The money was quickly subscribed and the huge melon brought forth. At that moment, Sykes and Bertha arrived. A determined silence fell on the porch and the melon was put away again.

Merchant snapped down the blade of his jackknife and moved toward the store door.

"Come on in, Joe, an' gimme a slab uh sow belly an' uh pound uh coffee—almost fuhgot 'twas Sat'day. Got to git on home." Most of the men left also.

Just then Delia drove past on her way home, as Sykes was ordering magnificently for Bertha. It pleased him for Delia to see.

"Git whutsoever yo' heart desires, Honey. Wait a minute, Joe. Give huh two botles uh strawberry soda-water, uh quart uh parched ground-peas, an' a block uh chewin' gum."

With all this they left the store, with Sykes reminding Bertha that this was his town and she could have it if she wanted it.

The men returned soon after they left, and held their watermelon feast. "Where did Syke Jones git dat 'oman from nohow?" Lindsay asked.

"Ovah Apopka. Guess dey musta been cleanin' out de town when she lef'. She don't look lak a thing but a hunk uh liver wid hair on it."

"Well, she sho' kin squall," Dave Carter contributed. "When she gits ready tuh laff, she jes' opens huh mouf an' latches it back tuh de las' notch. No ole grandpa alligator down in Lake Bell ain't got nothin' on huh."

Bertha had been in town three months now. Sykes was still paying her room rent at Della Lewis'—the only house in town that would have taken her in. Sykes took her frequently to Winter Park to "stomps." He still assured her that he was the swellest man in the state.

"Sho' you kin have dat lil' ole house soon's Ah kin git dat 'oman outa dere. Everything b'longs tuh me an' you sho' kin have it. Ah sho' 'bominates uh skinny 'oman. Lawdy, you sho' is got one portly shape on you! You kin git *anything* you wants. Dis is *mah* town an' you sho' kin have it."

Delia's work-worn knees crawled over the earth in Gethsemane and up the rocks of Calvary many, many times during these months. She avoided the villagers and meeting places in her efforts to be blind and deaf. But Bertha nullified this to a degree, by coming to Delia's house to call Sykes out to her at the gate.

Delia and Sykes fought all the time now with no peaceful interludes. They slept and ate in silence. Two or three times Delia had attempted a timid friendliness, but she was repulsed each time. It was plain that the breaches must remain agape.

The sun had burned July to August. The heat streamed down like a million hot arrows, smiting all things living upon the earth. Grass withered, leaves browned, snakes went blind in shedding and men and dogs went made. Dog days!

Delia came home one day and found Sykes there before her. She wondererd, but started to go on into the house without speaking, even though he was standing in the kitchen door and she must either stoop under his arm or ask him to move. He made no room for her. She noticed a soap box beside the steps, but paid no particular attention to it, knowing that he must have brought it there. As she was stooping to pass under his outstretched arm, he suddenly pushed her backward, laughingly.

"Look in de box dere Delia, Ah done brung yuh somethin'!"

She nearly fell upon the box in her stumbling, and when she saw what it held, she all but fainted outright.

"Syke! Syke, mah Gawd! You take dat rattlesnake 'way from heah! You *gottuh*. Oh, Jesus, have mussy!"

"Ah aint gut tuh do nuthin' uh de kin'—fact is Ah aint got tuh do nothin' but die. Taint no use uh you puttin' on airs makin' out lak you skeered uh dat snake—he's gointer stay right heah tell he die. He wouldn't bite me cause Ah knows how tuh handle 'im. Nohow he wouldn't risk breakin' out his fangs 'gin yo' skinny laigs."

"Naw, now Syke, don't keep dat thing 'roun' heah tuh skeer me tuh death. You knows Ah'm even feared uh earth worms. Thass de biggest snake Ah evah did see. Kill 'im Syke, please."

"Doan ast me tuh do nothin' fuh yuh. Goin' 'roun' tryin' to be so damn asterperious. Naw, Ah aint' gonna kill it. Ah think uh damn sight mo' uh him dan you! Dat's a nice snake an' anybody doan lak 'im kin jes' hit de grit."

The village soon heard that Sykes had the snake, and came to see and ask questions.

"How de hen-fire did you ketch dat six-foot rattler, Syke?" Thomas asked.

"He's full uh frogs so he caint hardly move, thass how Ah eased up on 'm. But Ah'm a snake charmer an' knows how tuh handle 'em. Shux, dat aint nothin'. Ah could ketch one eve'y day if Ah so wanted tuh."

"Whut he needs is a heavy hick'ry club leaned real heavy on his head. Dat's de bes 'way tuh charm a rattlesnake."

"Naw, Walt, y'll jes' don't understand dese diamon' backs lak Ah do," said Sykes in a superior tone of voice.

The village agreed with Walter, but the snake stayed on. His box remained by the kitchen door with its screen wire covering. Two or three days later it had digested its meal of frogs and literally came to life. It rattled at every movement in the kitchen or the yard. One day as Delia came down the kitchen steps she saw his chalky-white fangs curved like scimitars hung in the wire meshes. This time she did not run away with averted eyes as usual. She stood for a long time in the doorway in a red fury that grew bloodier for every second that she regarded the creature that was her torment.

That night she broached the subject as soon as Sykes sat down to the table.

"Syke, Ah wants you tuh take dat snake 'way fum heah. You done starved me an' Ah put up widcher, you done beat me an Ah took dat, but you done kilt all mah insides bringin' dat varmint heah."

Sykes poured out a saucer full of coffee and drank it deliberately before he answered her.

"A whole lot Ah keer 'bout how you feels inside uh out. Dat snake aint goin' no damn wheah till Ah gits ready fuh 'im tuh go. So fur as beatin' is concerned, yuh aint took near all dat you gointer take ef yuh stay 'roun' *me*."

Delia pushed back her plate and got up from the table. "Ah hates you, Sykes," she said calmly. "Ah hates you tuh de same degree dat Ah useter love yuh. Ah done took an' took till mah belly is full up tuh mah neck. Dat's de reason Ah got mah letter fum de church an' moved mah membership tuh Woodbridge—so Ah don't haftuh take no sacrament wid yuh. Ah don't wantuh see yuh 'round' me atall. Lay 'roun' wid dat 'oman all yuh wants tuh, but gwan 'way fum me an' mah house. Ah hates yuh lak uh suck-egg dog."

Sykes almost let the huge wad of corn bread and collard greens he was chewing fall out of his mouth in amazement. He had a hard time whipping himself to the proper fury to try to answer Delia.

"Well, Ah'm glad you does hate me. Ah'm sho' tiahed uh you hangin' ontuh me. Ah don't want yuh. Look at yuh stringey ole neck! Yo' raw-bony laigs an' arms is enough tuh cut uh man tuh death. You looks jes' lak de devvul's doll-baby tuh *me*. You cain't hate me no worse dan Ah hates you. Ah been hatin' *you* fuh years.

"Yo' ole black hide don't look lak nothin' tuh me, but uh passle uh wrinkled up rubber, wid yo' big ole yeahs flappin' on each side lak up paih uh buzzard wings. Don't think Ah'm gointuh be run 'way fum mah house neither. Ah'm goin' tuh de white folks about *you*, mah young man, de very nex' time you lay yo' han's on me. Mah cup is done run ovah." Delia said this with no signs of fear and Sykes departed from the house, threatening her, but made not the slighest move to carry out any of them.

That night he did not return at all, and the next day being Sunday, Delia was glad that she did not have to quarrel before she hitched up her pony and drove the four miles to Woodbridge.

She stayed to the night service—"love feast"—which was very warm and full of spirit. In the emotional winds her domestic trials were borne far and wide so that she sang as she drove homeward,

> *"Jurden water, black an' col'*
> *Chills de body, not de soul*
> *An' Ah wantah cross Jurden in uh calm time."*

She came from the barn to the kitchen door and stopped.

"Whut's de mattah, ol' satan, you aint kickin' up yo' racket?" She addressed the snake's box. Complete silence. She went on into the house with a new hope in its birth struggles. Perhaps her threat to go to the white folks had frightened Sykes! Perhaps he was sorry! Fifteen years of misery and suppression had brought Delia to the place where she would hope *anything* that looked towards a way over or through her wall of inhibitions.

She felt in the match safe behind the stove at once for a match. There was only one there.

"Dat niggah wouldn't fetch nothin' heah tuh save his rotten neck, but he kin run thew whut Ah brings quick enough. Now he done toted off nigh on tuh haff uh box uh matches. He done had dat 'oman heah in mah house, too."

Nobody but a woman could tell how she knew this even before she struck the match. But she did and it put her into a new fury.

Presently she brought in the tubs to put the white things to soak. This time she decided she need not bring the hamper out of the bedroom; she would go in there and do the sorting. She picked up the pot-bellied lamp and went in. The room was small and the hamper stood hard by the foot of the white iron bed. She could sit and reach through the bed-posts—resting as she worked.

"Ah wantah cross Jurden in uh calm time." She was singing again. The mood of the "love feast" had returned. She threw back the lid of the basket almost gaily. Then, moved by both horror and terror, she sprang back toward the door. *There lay the snake in the basket!* He moved sluggishly at first, but even as she turned round and round, jumped up and down in an insanity of fear, he began to stir vigorously. She saw him pouring his awful beauty from the basket upon the bed, then she seized the lamp and ran as fast as she could to the kitchen. The wind from the open door blew out the light and the darkness added to her terror. She sped to the darkness of the yard, slamming the door after her before she thought to set down the lamp. She did not feel safe even on the ground, so she climbed up in the hay barn.

There for an hour or more she lay sprawled upon the hay a gibbering wreck.

Finally she grew quiet, and after that, coherent thought. With this, stalked through her a cold, bloody rage. Hours of this. A period of intro-spection, a space of retrospection, then a mixture of both. Out of this an awful calm.

"Well, Ah done de bes' Ah could. If things aint right, Gawd knows taint mah fault."

She went to sleep—a twitchy sleep—and woke up to a faint gray sky. There was a loud hollow sound below. She peered out. Sykes was at the wood-pile, demolishing a wire-covered box.

He hurried to the kitchen door, but hung outside there some minutes before he entered, and stood some minutes more inside before he closed it after him.

The gray in the sky was spreading. Delia descended without fear now, and crouched beneath the low bedroom window. The drawn shade shut out the dawn, shut in the night. But the thin walls held back no sound.

"Dat ol' scratch is woke up now!" She mused at the tremendous whirr inside, which every woodsman knows, is one of the sound illusions. The rattler is a ventriloquist. His whirr sounds to the right, to the left, straight ahead, behind, close under foot—everywhere but where it is. Woe to him who guesses wrong unless he is prepared to hold up his end of the argument! Sometimes he strikes without rattling at all.

Inside, Sykes heard nothing until he knocked a pot lid off the stove while trying to reach the match safe in the dark. He had emptied his pockets at Bertha's.

The snake seemed to wake up under the stove and Sykes made a quick leap into the bedroom. In spite of the gin he had had, his head was clearing now.

"Mah Gawd!" he chattereed, "ef Ah could on'y strack uh light!"

The rattling ceased for a moment as he stood paralyzed. He waited. It seemed that the snake waited also.

"Oh, fuh de light! Ah thought he'd be too sick"—Sykes was muttering to himself when the whirr began again, closer, right underfoot this time. Long before this, Sykes' ability to think had been flattened down to primitive instinct and he leaped—onto the bed.

Outside Delia heard a cry that might have come from a maddened chimpanzee, a stricken gorilla. All the terror, all the horror, all the rage that man possibly could express, without a recognizable human sound.

A tremendous stir inside there, another series of animal screams, the intermittent whirr of the reptile. The shade torn violently down from the window, letting in the red dawn, a huge brown hand seizing the window stick, great dull blows upon the wooden floor punctuating the gibberish of sound long after the rattle of the snake had abruptly subsided. All this Delia could see and hear from her place beneath the window, and it made her ill. She crept over to the four-o'clocks and stretched herself on the cool earth to recover.

She lay there. "Delia, Delia!" She could hear Sykes calling in a most despairing tone as one who expected no answer. The sun crept on up, and he called. Delia could not move—her legs were gone flabby. She never moved, he called, and the sun kept rising.

"Mah Gawd!" She heard him moan, "Mah Gawd fum Heben!" She heard him stumbling about and got up from her flower-bed. The sun was

growing warm. As she approached the door she heard him call out hopefully, "Delia, is dat you Ah heah?"

She saw him on his hands and knees as soon as she reached the door.
He crept an inch or two toward her—all that he was able, and she saw his
horribly swollen neck and his one open eye shining with hope. A surge of
pity too strong to support bore her away from that eye that must, could
not, fail to see the tubs. He would see the lamp. Orlando with its doctors
was too far. She could scarcely reach the Chinaberry tree, where she
waited in the growing heat while inside she knew the cold river was creeping up and up to extinguish that eye which must know by now that she
knew.

STERLING BROWN
(b. 1901)

Although a contemporary of such Harlem Renaissance figures as Bontemps and Hughes, Sterling Brown has always maintained the fact of his distance from that movement, sometimes even denying the existence of the movement itself. Brown's career as poet, literary historian, critic, folklorist, and lecturer is one of the most impressive in the twentieth century.

Born in Washington, D.C., Brown spent the greater part of his life there as a professor at Howard University, where he inspired such writers as Amiri Baraka and Toni Morrison. Brown was a close student of the folk life of black people. Connoisseur of blues, he made a notable collection of blues recordings. A pioneer in the study of Afro-American literature, he collaborated with James Weldon Johnson in the 1931 revision of the Book of American Negro Poetry, *writing the appreciation of Johnson and preparing a study guide for use with the anthology. He was literary editor of* Opportunity, *and the author of two invaluable and pioneering studies,* Negro Poetry and Drama *and* The Negro in American Fiction *(1937). In 1941, in collaboration with Arthur P. Davis and Ulysses Lee, he produced* The Negro Caravan, *a landmark anthology, based on much firsthand research and publishing important material from manuscript.*

As a poet, Brown was eulogized by Alain Locke for his successful incorporation of the folk idiom in his work. It is in the authenticity of its folk voice that the poetry of Brown has achieved a pinnacle in Afro-American literature. An important adjunct of Brown's literary talent has been his dramatic gifts, which have made him a magnificent oral interpreter of his work and of that of others.

Brown's volume of poems Southern Road *(1932) was for years supplemented only by periodical publication.*

The Collected Poems of Sterling A. Brown, *selected by Michael S. Harper (1980), reprints* Southern Road, The Last Ride of Wild Bill *(1975), and the previously unpublished* No Hiding Place. *It also includes an essay by Sterling Stuckey and a bibliography by Robert C. O'Meally.*

Long Gone

I laks yo' kin' of lovin',
    Ain't never caught you wrong,
But it jes' ain' nachal
    Fo' to stay here long;

It jes' ain' nachal
    Fo' a railroad man,
With a itch fo' travelin'
    He caint understan'. . . .

I looks at de rails,
    An' I looks at de ties,
An' I hears an ole freight
    Puffin' up de rise,

An' at nights on my pallet,
    When all is still,
I listens fo' de empties
    Bumpin' up de hill;

When I oughta be quiet,
    I is got a itch
Fo' to hear de whistle blow
    Fo' de crossin' or de switch,

An' I knows de time's a-nearin'
    When I got to ride,
Though it's homelike and happy
    At yo' side.

You is done all you could do
      To make me stay;
'Taint no fault of yours I've leavin'—
      I'se jes dataway.

I is got to see some people
      I ain't never seen,
Gotta highball thu some country
      Whah I never been.

I don't know which way I'm travelin'—
      Far or near,
All I knows fo' certain is
      I cain't stay here.

Ain't no call at all, sweet woman,
      Fo' to carry on—
Jes' my name and jes' my habit
      To be Long Gone. . . .

Slim in Hell

I

Slim Greer went to heaven;
      St. Peter said, "Slim,
You been a right good boy."
      An' he winked at him.

"You been a travelin' rascal
        In yo day.
You kin roam once mo';
        Den you comes to stay.

"Put dese wings on yo' shoulders,
        An' save yo' feet."
Slim grin, and he speak up,
        "Thankye, Pete."

        Den Peter say, "Go
                To Hell an' see,
        All dat is doing, and
                Report to me.

"Be sure to remember
        How everything go."
Slim say, "I be seein' yuh
        On de late watch, bo."

        Slim got to cavortin'
                Swell as you choose,
        Like Lindy in de Spirit
                Of St. Louis Blues.

He flew an' he flew,
        Till at last he hit
A hangar wid de sign readin'
        DIS IS IT.

        Den he parked his wings,
                An' strolled aroun',
        Gittin' used to his feet
                On de solid ground.

II

Big bloodhound came aroarin'
    Like Niagry Falls,
Sicked on by white devils
    In overhalls.

Now Slim warn't scared,
    Cross my heart, it's a fac',
An de dog went on a bayin'
    Some po' devil's track.

        Den Slim saw a mansion
            An' walked right in;
        De Devil looked up
            Wid a sickly grin.

"Suttinly didn't look
    Fo' you, Mr. Greer,
How it happen you comes
    To visit here?"

        Slim say—"Oh, jes' thought
            I'd drop by a spell."
        "Feel at home, seh, an' here's
            De keys to hell."

Den he took Slim around
    An' showed him people
Raisin' hell as high as
    De First Church Steeple.

        Lots of folks fightin'
            At de roulette wheel,
        Like old Rampart Street,
            Or leastwise Beale.

Showed him bawdy houses
    An' cabarets,
Slim thought of New Orleans
    An' Memphis days.

Each devil was busy
    Wid a devilish broad,
An' Slim cried, "Lawdy,
    Lawd, Lawd, Lawd."

Took him in a room
    Where Slim see
De preacher wid a brownskin
    On each knee.

    Showed him giant stills,
        Going everywhere,
    Wid a passel of devils
        Stretched dead drunk there.

Den he took him to de furnace
    Dat some devils was firing,
Hot as hell, an' Slim start
    A mean presspirin'.

    White devils, wid pitchforks
        Threw black devils on,
    Slim thought he'd better
        Be gittin' along.

An' he says—"Dis makes
    Me think of home—
Vicksburg, Little Rock, Jackson,
    Waco and Rome."

    Den de devil gave Slim
        De big Ha Ha;
    An' turned into a cracker,
        Wid a sheriff's star.

Slim ran fo' his wings,
    Lit out from de groun'
Hauled it back to St. Peter,
    Safety boun'.

III

St. Peter said, "Well,
　　You got back quick.
How's de devil? An' what's
　　His latest trick?"

An' Slim say, "Peter,
　　I really cain't tell,
The place was Dixie
　　That I took for hell."

Then Peter say, "You must
　　Be crazy, I vow,
Where'n hell dja think Hell *was*,
　　Anyhow?

"Git on back to de yearth,
　　Cause I got de fear,
You'se a leetle too dumb,
　　Fo' to stay up here . . ."

Southern Road

Swing that hammer—hunh—
Steady, bo';
Swing that hammer—hunh—
Steady, bo';
Ain't no rush, bebby,
Long ways to go.

Burner tore his—hunh—
Black heart away;
Burner tore his—hunh—
Black heart away;
Got me life, bebby,
An' a day.

Gal's on Fifth Street—hunh—
Son done gone;
Gal's on Fifth Street—hunh—
Son done gone;
Wife's in de ward, bebby
Babe's not bo'n.

My ole man died—hunh—
Cussin' me;
My ole man died—hunh—
Cussin' me;
Ole lady rocks, bebby,
Huh misery.

Doubleshackled—hunh—
Guard behin';
Doubleshackled—hunh—
Guard behin';
Ball and chain, bebby,
On my min'.

White man tells me—hunh—
Dam yo' soul;
White man tells me—hunh—
Dam yo' soul;
Got no need, bebby,
To be tole.

Chain gang nevah—hunh—
Let me go;
Chain gang nevah—hunh—
Let me go;
Po' los' boy, bebby,
Evahmo' . . .

Strong Men

The strong men keep coming on.
—Sandburg.

They dragged you from homeland,
They chained you in coffles,
They huddled you spoon-fashion in filthy hatches.
They sold you to give a few gentlemen ease.

They broke you in like oxen,
They scourged you,
They branded you,
They made your women breeders,
They swelled your numbers with bastards. . . .
They taught you the religion they disgraced.

You sang:
  Keep a-inchin' along
  Lak a po' inch worm. . . .

You sang:
  Bye and bye
  I'm gonna lay down dis heavy load. . . .

You sang:
  Walk togedder, chillen,
  Dontcha git weary. . . .

     The strong men keep a-comin' on
     The strong men git stronger.

They point with pride to the roads you built for them,
They ride in comfort over the rails you laid for them.
They put hammers in your hands
And said—Drive so much before sundown.

You sang:
  Ain't no hammah
  In dis lan',
  Strikes lak mine, bebby,
  Strikes lak mine.

They cooped you in their kitchens,
They penned you in their factories,
They gave you the jobs that they were too good for,
They tried to guarantee happiness to themselves
By shunting dirt and misery to you.

You sang:
    Me an' muh baby gonna shine, shine
    me an' muh baby gonna shine.
        The strong men keep a-comin' on
        The strong men git stronger. . . .

They bought off some of your leaders
You stumbled, as blind men will . . .
They coaxed you, unwontedly soft-voiced. . . .
You followed a way,
Then laughed as usual.

They heard the laugh and wondered;
Uncomfortable;
Unadmitting a deeper terror. . . .
        The strong men keep a-comin' on
        Gittin' stronger. . . .

What, from the slums
Where they have hemmed you,
What, from the tiny huts
They could not keep from you—
What reaches them
Making them ill at ease, fearful?
Today they shout prohibition at you
"Thou shalt not this"
"Thou shalt not that"
"Reserved for whites only"
You laugh.

One thing they cannot prohibit—
        The strong men . . . coming on
        The strong men gittin' stronger.
        Strong men. . . .
        Stronger. . . .

414

Sister Lou

Honey
When de man
Calls out de las' train
You're gonna ride,
Tell him howdy.

Gather up yo' basket
An' yo' knittin' an' yo' things,
An' go on up an' visit
Wid frien' Jesus fo' a spell.

Show Marfa
How to make yo' greengrape jellies,
An' give po' Lazarus
A passel of them Golden Biscuits.

Scald some meal
Fo' some rightdown good spoonbread
Fo' li'l box-plunkin' David.

An' sit aroun'
An' tell them Hebrew Chillen
All yo' stories. . . .

Honey
Don't be feared of them pearly gates,
Don't go 'round to de back,
No mo' dataway
Not evah no mo'.

Let Michael tote yo' burden
An' yo pocketbook an' evah thing
'Cept yo' Bible,
While Gabriel blows somp'n
Solemn but loudsome
On dat horn of his'n.

Honey
Go Straight on to de Big House,
An' speak to yo' God
Widout no fear an' tremblin'.

Then sit down
An' pass de time of day awhile.

Give a good talkin' to
To yo' favorite 'postle Peter,
An' rub the po' head
Of mixed-up Judas,
An' joke awhile wid Jonah.

Then, when you gits de chance,
Always rememberin' yo' raisin',
Let 'em know youse tired
Jest a mite tired.

Jesus will find yo' bed fo' you
Won't no servant evah bother wid yo' room.
Jesus will lead you
To a room wid windows
Openin' on cherry trees an' plum trees
Bloomin' everlastin'.

An' dat will be yours
Fo' keeps.

Den take yo' time. . . .
Honey, take yo' bressed time.

Negro Folk Expression: Spirituals, Seculars, Ballads and Work Songs

The Spirituals

Thomas Wentworth Higginson, one of the very first to pay respectful attention to the Negro spiritual, called it a startling flower growing in dark soil. Using his figure, we might think of this flower as a hybrid, as the American Negro is a hybrid. And though flowers of its family grew in Africa, Europe, and other parts of America, this hybrid bloom is uniquely beautiful.

A large amount of recent scholarship has proved that the spirituals are not African, either in music or meaning (a claim made once with partisan zeal), that the American Negro was influenced by the religious music of rural America from the Great Awakening on, that at the frontier camp meetings he found to his liking many tunes both doleful and brisk, and that he took over both tunes and texts and refashioned them more to his taste. But careful musicologists, from studying phonograph records of folk singing rather than, as earlier, inadequate, conventional notations of "art" spirituals, are coming around to the verdict of Alan Lomax that "no amount of scholarly analysis and discussion can ever make a Negro spiritual sound like a white spiritual."

A new music, yes. But what of the poetry? Scholars have discovered that many phrases, lines, couplets, and even whole stanzas and songs, once thought to be Negro spirituals, were popular in white camp meetings. A full comparison of the words of white and Negro spirituals is out of the question here. It might be said that some of the parallels turn out to be tangents. Thus, "At his table we'll sit down, Christ will gird himself and serve us with sweet manna all around" is supposed to be the white source of "Gwine to sit down at the welcome table, gwine to feast off milk and honey," and "To hide yourself in the mountain top, to hide yourself from God" is supposed to have become "Went down to the rocks to hide my face, the rocks cried out no hiding place." Even when single lines were identical, the Negro made telling changes in the stanza. Briefly, the differences seem to result from a looser line, less tyrannized over by meter and rhyme, with the accent shifted unpredictably, from a more liberal use of refrains, and from imagery that is terser and starker. The improvising imagination seems freer. Some of the changes of words arose from confusion: "Paul and Silas bound in jail" has been sung: "bounded Cyrus born in jail"; and "I want to cross over into campground" has been sung as "I want to cross over in a calm time." Some of the changes, however, result from the truly poetic imagination at work on material deeply felt and pondered: "Tone de bell easy, Jesus gonna make up my dying bed." "I'll lie in de grave and stretch out my arms, when I lay dis body down." "Steal away, steal away, steal away to Jesus. Steal away, steal away home; I ain't got long to stay here."

Many spirituals tell of the joys of Christian fellowship. "Ain't you glad you got out de wilderness?" "I been bawn of God, no condemnation; no condemnation in my soul." "I been down in the valley; Never turn back no mo.'"

> I went down in the valley to pray
> My soul got happy and I stayed all day.

"Just like a tree, planted by the waters, I shall not be moved." Belonging to the glorious company, the slaves found comfort, protection. Sinners would find no hole in the ground, but those of the true faith had "a hiding place, around the throne of God." "I got a home in that rock, don't you see?" "In God's bosom gonna be my pillow." Their souls were witnesses for their Lord. "Done done my duty; Got on my travelin' shoes." "I done crossed the separatin' line; I done left the world behind."

The world could be left behind in visions.

> I've got two wings for to veil my face
> I've got two wings for to fly away. . . .

Gabriel and his trumpet caught the imagination. "Where will you be when the first trumpet sounds; sounds so loud its gonna wake up the dead?" "O My Lord, what a morning, when the stars begin to fall!" "When the sun refuse to shine, when the moon goes down in blood!" In that great getting up morning, "you see the stars a falling, the forked lightning, the coffins bursting, the righteous marching." "The blind will see, the dumb will talk; the deaf will hear; the lame will walk." This apocalyptic imagery, clear to the initiated, is a release, a flight, a message in code, frequently used by oppressed people.

> Then they'll cry out for cold water
> While the Christians shout in glory
> Saying Amen to their damnation
> Fare you well, fare you well.

It was not only to the far-off future of Revelations that the dreams turned. Heaven was a refuge too. In contrast to the shacks of slave row and the slums of the cities, to the work clothes and the unsavory victuals, would be the throne of God, the streets of gold, the harps, the robes, the milk and honey.

> A-settin' down with Jesus
> Eatin' honey and drinkin' wine
> Marchin' round de throne
> Wid Peter, James, and John. . . .

But the dream was not always so extravagant. Heaven promised simple satisfactions, but they were of great import to the slaves. Shoes for instance, as well as a harp. Heaven meant home: "I'm gonna feast at de welcome table." Heaven meant rest: just sitting down was one of the high privileges often mentioned. And acceptance as a person: "I'm going to walk and talk with Jesus." Moreover, the Heaven of escape is not a Heaven bringing forgetfulness of the past. The River Jordan is not Lethe.

> I'm gonna tell God all my troubles,
> When I get home . . .
> I'm gonna tell him the road was rocky
> When I get home.

The makers of the spirituals, looking toward heaven, found their triumphs there. But they did not blink their eyes to the troubles here. As the best expression of the slaves' deepest thoughts and yearnings, they speak with convincing finality against the legend of contented slavery. This world was not their home. "Swing low, sweet chariot, coming for to carry me home." They never tell of joy in the "good old days." The only joy in the spirituals is in dreams of escape.

That the spirituals were otherworldly, then, is less than half-truth. In more exact truth, they tell of this life, of "rollin' through an unfriendly world." "Oh, bye and bye, bye and bye, I'm going to lay down this heavy load." "My way is cloudy." "Oh, stand the storm, it won't be long, we'll anchor by and by." "Lord keep me from sinking down." And there is that couplet of tragic intensity:

> Don't know what my mother wants to stay here fuh,
> Dis ole world ain't been no friend to huh.

Out of the workaday life came figures of speech: "Keep a-inchin' along lak a po' inch-worm"; such a couplet as:

Better mind that sun and see how she run
And mind! Don't let her catch you wid yo' work undone.

And such an allegory: "You hear de lambs a-crying; oh, shepherd, feed-a my sheep." Out of folk wisdom came: "Oh de ole sheep, they know de road; young lambs gotta find de way," and "Ole Satan is like a snake in the grass."

Sister, you better watch how you walk on the cross
Yo' foot might slip, and' yo' soul git lost.

The spirituals make an anthology of Biblical heroes and tales, from Genesis where Adam and Eve are in the Garden, picking up leaves, to John's calling the roll in Revelations. There are numerous gaps, of course, and many repetitions. Certain figures are seen in an unusual light; Paul, for instance, is generally bound in jail with Silas, to the exclusion of the rest of his busy career. Favored heroes are Noah, chosen of God to ride down the flood; Samson, who tore those buildings down; Joshua, who caused the walls of Jericho to fall (when the rams' lambs' sheephorns began to blow); Jonah, symbol of hard luck changed at last; and Job, the man of tribulation who still would not curse his God. These are victors over odds. But losers, the wretched and despised, also serve as symbols. There is Lazarus, "poor as I, don't you see?" who went to heaven, in contrast to "Rich man Dives, who lived so well; when he died he found a home in hell." And finally there is Blind Barnabas, whose tormented cry found echoes in slave cabins down through the long, dark years:

Oh de blind man stood on de road an' cried
Cried, "Lord, oh, Lord, save-a po' me!"

In telling the story of Jesus, spirituals range from the tender "Mary had a little baby" and "Little Boy, how old are you" to the awe-inspiring "Were You There" and "He Never Said A Mumbalin' Word." Jesus is friend and brother, loving counselor, redeemer, Lord and King. The Negro slave's picturing of Calvary in such lines as

Dey whupped him up de hill . . .
Dey crowned his head with thorns . . .
Dey pierced him in de side,
An' de blood come a-twinklin' down;
But he never said a mumbalin' word;
Not a word; not a word.

belongs with the greatest Christian poetry. It fused belief and experience; it surged up from most passionate sympathy and understanding.

Some scholars who have found parallels between the words of Negro and white spirituals would have us believe that when the Negro sang of freedom, he meant only what the whites meant, namely freedom from sin. Free, individualistic whites on the make in a prospering civilization, nursing the American dream, could well have felt their only bondage to be that of sin, and freedom to be religious salvation. But with the drudgery, the hardships, the auction-block, the slave-mart, the shackles, and the lash so literally present in the Negro's experience, it is hard to imagine why for the Negro they would remain figurative. The scholars certainly do not make it clear, but rather take refuge in such dicta as: "The slave did not contemplate his low condition." Are we to believe that the slave singing "I been rebuked, I been scorned; done had a hard time sho's you bawn," referred to his being outside of the true religion? Ex-slaves, of course, inform us differently. The spirituals speak up strongly for freedom not only from sin (dear as that freedom was to the true believer) but from physical bondage. Those attacking slavery as such had to be as rare as anti-Hitler marching songs in occupied France. But there were oblique references. Frederick Douglass has told us of the double-talk of the spirituals: Canaan, for instance, stood for Canada; and over and beyond hidden satire the songs also were grapevines for communications. Harriet Tubman, herself called the Moses of her people, has told us that *Go Down, Moses* was tabu in the slave states, but the people sang it nonetheless.

Fairly easy allegories identified Egypt-land with the South, Pharaoh with the masters, the Israelites with themselves, and Moses with their leader. "So Moses smote de water and the children all passed over; Children, ain't you glad that they drowned that sinful army?"

> Oh, Mary don't you weep, don't you moan;
> Pharaoh's army got drownded,
> Oh, Mary, don't you weep.

Some of the references were more direct:

> Didn't my Lord deliver Daniel,
> And why not every man?

In the wake of the Union army and in the contraband camps spirituals of freedom sprang up suddenly. The dry grass was ready for the quickening flame. Some celebrated the days of Jubilo: "O Freedom; O Freedom!, And before I'll be a slave, I'll be buried in my grave! And go home to my Lord and be free." Some summed up slavery starkly: "No more driver's lash for me, no more, no more. . . . No more peck of corn for me; Many thousand go." "Slavery's chain done broke at last; gonna praise God till I die." And in all likelihood old spirituals got new meanings: "Ain't you glad you got out the wilderness?" "In That Great Gittin' Up Morning!" "And the moon went down in blood."

The best of the spirituals are, in W.E.B. Du Bois's phrase, "the sorrow-songs of slavery." In spite of indifference and resentment from many educated and middle class Negroes, the spirituals are still sung, circulated, altered and created by folk Negroes. Some of the new ones, started in the backwoods, have a crude charm; for instance Joseph and Mary in Jerusalem "to pay their poll-taxes," find the little boy Jesus in the temple confounding with his questions the county doctor, lawyer, and judge. Some of them mix in more recent imagery: "Death's little black train is coming!" "If I have my ticket, Lord, can I ride?" and a chant of death in which the refrain "Same train. Same train" is repeated with vivid effect:

> Same train took my mother.
> Same train. Same train.

Some use modern inventions with strained incongruity: "Jus' call up Central in Heaven, tell Jesus to come to the phone"; and "Jesus is my aeroplane, He holds the whole world in his hands"; and "Standing in the Safety Zone." But there is power in some of the new phrasing:

> God's got your number; He knows where you live;
> Death's got a warrant for you.

Instead of college choirs, as earlier, today it is groups closer to the folk like the Golden Gates, the Silver Echoes, the Mitchell Christian Singers, the Coleman Brothers, the Thrasher Wonders and the Original Harmony Kings, who carry the spirituals over the land. These groups and soloists like the Georgia Peach, Mahalia Jackson, Marie Knight and Sister Rosetta Tharpe, once churched for worldly ways but now redeemed, are extremely popular in churches, concert halls, and on records. They swing the spirituals, using a more pronounced rhythm and jazz voicing (some show-groups, alas, imitate even the Mills Brothers and the Ink Spots). Even the more sincere singers, however, fight the devil by using what have been considered the devil's weapons. Tambourines, cymbals, trumpets and even trombones and bass fiddles are now accepted in some churches. The devil has no right to all that fine rhythm, so a joyful noise is made unto the Lord with bounce and swing.

The Gospel Songs, sung "out of the book" as signs of "progress," are displacing the spirituals among the people. These are even more heavily influenced by jazz and the blues. One of the most popular composers of Gospel Songs is Thomas Dorsey, who once played barrelhouse piano under the alias of Georgia Tom. Many lovers of the older spirituals disdain the Gospel Songs as cheap and obvious. But this new urban religious folk music should not be dismissed too lightly. It is vigorously alive with its own musical values, and America turns no unwilling ear to it. And to hear some fervent congregations sing "Just a Closer Walk With Thee," "He Knows How Much You Can Bear," and "We Sure Do Need Him Now" can be unforgettable musical experiences. In sincerity, musical manner, and spirit, they are probably not so remote from the old prayer songs in the brush arbors.

Seculars and Ballads

The slaves had many other moods and concerns than the religious; indeed some of these ran counter to the spirituals. Irreverent parodies of religious songs, whether coming from the black-face minstrelsy or from tough-minded cynical slaves, passed current in the quarters. Other-worldliness was mocked: "I don't want to ride no golden chariot; I don't want no golden crown; I want to stay down here and be, Just as I am without one plea." "Live a humble to the Lord" was changed to "Live a humbug." Bible stories, especially the creation, the fall of Man, and the flood, were spoofed. "Reign, Master Jesus, reign" became "Rain, Mosser, rain hard! Rain flour and lard and a big hog head, Down in my back yard." After couplets of nonsense and ribaldry, slaves sang with their fingers crossed, or hopeless in defeat: "Po' mourner, you shall be free, when de good Lord set you free."

Even without the sacrilege, many secular songs were considered "devil-tunes." Especially so were the briskly syncopated lines which, with the clapping of hands and the patting of feet, set the beat for swift, gay dancing. "Juba dis, Juba dat; Juba skin a yeller cat; Juba, Juba!" Remnants of this syncopation are today in such children's play songs as

> "Did you feed my cow?" "Yes, Maam."
> "Will you tell-a me how?" "Yes, Maam."
> "Oh, what did you give her?" "Cawn and hay."
> "Oh, what did you give her?" "Cawn and hay."

Verses for reels made use of the favorite animals of the fables. "Brer Rabbit, Brer Rabbit, yo' eare mighty long; Yes, My Lord, they're put on wrong; Every little soul gonna shine; every little soul gonna shine!" Often power and pomp in the guise of the bullfrog and bulldog have the tables turned on them by the sassy blue-jay and crow:

> A bullfrog dressed in soldier's clothes
> Went in de field to shoot some crows,
> De crows smell powder and fly away,
> De bullfrog mighty mad dat day.

Even the easygoing ox or sheep or hog acquired characteristics:

> De ole sow say to de boar
> I'll tell you what let's do,
> Let's go and git dat broad-axe
> And die in de pig-pen too.
> Die in de pig-pen fighting,
> Die wid a bitin' jaw!

Unlike Stephen Foster's sweet and sad songs such as "Massa's in the Cold, Cold Ground," the folk seculars looked at slavery ironically. And where Foster saw comic nonsense, they added satiric point. Short comments flash us back to social reality: "Ole Master bought a yaller gal, He bought her from the South"; "My name's Ran, I wuks in de sand, I'd rather be a nigger dan a po' white man." Frederick Douglass remembers his fellow slaves singing "We raise de wheat, dey gib us de corn; We sift de meal, de gib us de huss; We peel de meat, dey gib us de skin; An dat's de way dey take us in." Grousing about food is common: "Milk in the dairy getting mighty old, Skippers and the mice working mighty bold. . . . A long-tailed rat an' a bowl of souse, Jes' come down from de white folk's house." With robust humor, they laughed even at the dread patrollers:

> Run, nigger, run, de patterollers will ketch you
> Run, nigger, run; its almost day.
> Dat nigger run, dat nigger flew;
> Dat nigger tore his shirt in two.

The bitterest secular begins:

> My ole Mistis promise me
> Fo' she died, she'd set me free;
> She lived so long dat her head got bald,
> And she give out de notion dyin' at all.

Ole marster also failed his promise. Then, with the sharp surprise of the best balladry: "A dose of poison helped him along, May de devil preach his funeral song!"

Under a certain kind of protection the new freedmen took to heart the songs of such an abolitionist as Henry C. Work, and sang exultantly of jubilo. They sang his lines lampooning ole master, and turned out their own:

> Missus and mosser a-walkin' de street,
> Deir hands in deir pockets and nothin' to eat.
> She'd better be home a-washin' up de dishes,
> An' a-cleanin' up de ole man's raggitty britches. . . .

But when the protection ran out, the freedmen found the following parody too true:

> Our father, who is in heaven,
> White man owe me eleven and pay me seven,
> Thy kingdom come, thy will be done,
> And if I hadn't took that, I wouldn't had none.

Toward the end of the century, there was interplay between the folk seculars and the vaudeville stage, and the accepted stereotypes appeared. "Ain't no use my working so hard, I got a gal in the white folks yard." From tent shows and roving guitar players, the folks accepted such hits as the "Bully Song" and the "coon-songs." "Bill Bailey, Won't You Please Come Home," and "Alabama Bound" shuttled back and forth between the folk and vaudeville. In the honky-tonks ribald songs grew up to become standbys of the early jazz: "Make Me a Pallet on The Floor," "Bucket Got A Hole In It," "Don't you leave me here; if you must go, baby, leave me a dime for beer." "Jelly Roll" Morton's autobiography, now released from the Library of Congress Archives, proves this close connection between the rising jazz and the old folk seculars. In the honky-tonks, songs handled sex freely, even licentiously; and obscenity and vituperation ran rampant in songs called the "dirty dozens."

One of the heroes of secular balladry is Uncle Bud, who was noted for his sexual prowess, a combination Don Juan and John Henry. His song is perhaps as uncollected as it is unprintable. Appreciative tales are told of railroading, of crack trains like The Cannon Ball and The Dixie Flyer, and The Rock Island Line, which is praised in rattling good verses. Such folk delights as hunting with the yipping and baying of the hounds and the yells and cheering of the hunters are vividly recreated. "Old Dog Blue" has been memorialized over all of his lop-eared kindred. The greatest trailer on earth, Old Blue keeps his unerring sense in heaven; there he treed a possum in Noah's ark. When Old Dog Blue died,

> I dug his grave wid a silver spade
> I let him down wid a golden chain

And every link I called his name;
Go on Blue, you good dog, you!

The above lines illustrate a feature of Negro folksong worth remarking. Coming from an old sea-chantey "Stormalong," their presence in a song about a hunting dog show the folk habit of lifting what they want and using it how they will. Like southern white groups, the Negro has retained many of the old Scotch-English ballads. Still to be found are Negroes singing "In London town where I was born" and going on to tell of hard-hearted Barbara Allen. John Lomax found a Negro mixing up "Bobby Allen" with the cowboy song "The Streets of Laredo," burying "Miss Allen in a desert of New Mexico with six pretty maidens all dressed in white for her pallbearers." But Negroes hand down fairly straight versions of "Lord Lovel," "Pretty Polly," and "The Hangman's Tree," which has special point for them with its repetend: "Hangman, hangman, slack on the line." The Elizabethan broadside "The Frog Went A-Courtin'" has long been a favorite Negro lullaby. From "The Lass of Roch Royal" two stanzas beginning "Who's gonna shoe yo' little feet" have found their way into the ballad of John Henry. The famous Irish racehorse Stewball reappears in Negro balladry as Skewball and Kimball. English nonsense refrains appear in songs like "Keemo-Kimo" and "Old Bangum." Even the Gaelic "Schule Aroon" has been found among Negroes, though the collector unwarily surmises it to be Guinea or Ebo. Similarly the Negro folk singer lends to and borrows from American balladry. "Casey Jones," though about an engineer, is part of the repertory; it has been established that a Negro engine-wiper was the first author of it. "Frankie and Johnnie," the most widely known tragedy in America, is attributed to both white and Negro authorship. It could come from either; it probably comes from both; the tenderloin cuts across both sections. Current singers continue the trading of songs: Leadbelly sings cowboy songs, yelling "Ki-yi-yippy-yippy-yay" with his own zest; and Josh White sings "Molly Malone" and "Randall, My Son" with telling power. But it is in narratives of their own heroes that Negro ballad makers have done best.

Prominent among such heroes are fugitives who outtrick and outspeed the law. "Travelin' Man" is more of a coon-song than authentically folk, but the hero whom the cops chased from six in the morning till seven the next afternoon has been warmly adopted by the people. Aboard the Titanic he spied the iceberg and dove off, and "When the old Titanic ship went down, he was shooting crap in Liverpool." More genuine is "Long Gone, Lost John" in which the hero outmatches the sheriff, the police, and the bloodhounds: "The hounds ain't caught me and they never will."

Fast enough to hop the Dixie Flyer—"he missed the cow catcher but he caught the blind"—Lost John can even dally briefly with a girl friend, like Brer Rabbit waiting for Brer Tortoise. But when he travels, he goes far: "the funniest thing I ever seen, was Lost John comin' through Bowlin' Green," but "the last time I seed him he was jumping into Mexico."

When Lost John "doubled up his fist and knocked the police down," his deed wins approval from the audience as much as his winged heels do. With bitter memories and suspicion of the law, many Negroes admire outlaws. Some are just tough killers; one is "a bad, bad man from bad, bad land"; another is going to start "a graveyard all of his own"; another, Roscoe Bill, who sleeps with one ear out because of the rounders about, reports to the judge blandly that

> I didn't quite kill him, but I fixed him so dis mornin'
> He won't bodder wid me no mo'
> Dis mornin', dis evenin', so soon.

But the favorites, like such western desperadoes as Jesse James, Billy the Kid, and Sam Bass, stand up against the law. Railroad Bill (an actual outlaw of southern Alabama) "shot all the buttons off the sheriff's coat." On the manhunt, "the policemen dressed in blue, come down the street two by two." It took a posse to bring him in dead. Po' Lazarus also told the deputy to his face that he had never been arrested "by no one man, Lawd, by no one man." Unlike his Biblical namesake in nature, Po' Lazarus broke into the commissary. The high sheriff sent the deputy to bring him back, dead or alive. They found him "way out between two mountains" and they "blowed him down."

> They shot Po' Lazarus, shot him with a great big number
> Number 45, Lawd, Lawd, number 45.

They laid Po' Lazarus on the commissary counter, and walked away. His mother, always worrying over the trouble she had with Lazarus, sees the body and cries.

> Dat's my only son, Lawd, Lawd, dat's my only son.

In contrast "Stackolee" ends on a hard note. At Stack's murder trial, his lawyer pleads for mercy because his aged mother is lying very low. The prosecutor states that

> Stackolee's aged mammy
> Has been dead these 'leven years.

Starting from a murder in Memphis in a dice game (some say over a Stetson Hat), Stackolee's saga has travelled from the Ohio River to the Brazos;

in a Texas version, Stack goes to hell, challenges the devil to a duel—pitchfork versus forty-one revolver—and then takes over the lower world.

One of America's greatest ballads tells of John Henry. Based on the strength and courage of an actual hammer-swinging giant, though in spite of what folk-singers say, his hammer cannot be seen decorating the Big Bend Tunnel on the C. & O. Road, John Henry reflects the struggle of manual labor against the displacing machine. The ballad starts with ill omens. Even as a boy John Henry prophesies his death at the Big Bend Tunnel. But he stays to face it out. Pitting his brawn and stamina against the new-fangled steam drill, John Henry says to his captain:

> A man ain't nothing but a man.
> But before I'll let that steam driver beat me down
> I'll die with my hammer in my hand.

The heat of the contest makes him call for water (in one variant for tom-cat gin). When John Henry is momentarily overcome, his woman, Polly Ann, spelled him, hammering "like a natural man." At one crucial point, John Henry gave "a loud and lonesome cry," saying, "A hammer'll be the death of me." But the general tone is self confidence. John Henry throws the hammer from his hips on down, "Great gawd amighty how she rings!" He warns his shaker (the holder of the drill) that if ever he misses that piece of steel, "tomorrow'll be yo' burial day." His captain, hearing the mighty rumbling, thinks the mountain must be caving in. John Henry says to the captain: "It's my hammer swinging in the wind." Finally he defeats the drill, but the strain kills him. The people gather round, but all he asks is "a cool drink of water 'fo I die." Polly Ann swears to be true to the memory (although in another version she turns out to be as fickle as Mrs. Casey Jones). John Henry was buried near the railroad where

> Every locomotive come a-roarin' by
> Says, "There lies a steel-drivin' man, Lawd, Lawd;
> There lies a steel-drivin' man."

The topical nature of American balladry is seen in "Boll Weevil," a ballad that grew up almost as soon as the swarm of pests descended. "Come up from Mexico, they say."

> The first time I seed the boll weevil
> He was sitting on the square—

(The folk poet puns on the "square" of the cotton boll, and the familiar southern town square.) A tough little rascal is celebrated who, when buried in the hot sand, says "I can stand it like a man"; when put into ice, he says: "This is mighty cool and nice," and thrives and breeds right on, until finally he can take over:

> You better leave me alone
> I done et up all your cotton,
> And now I'll start on your corn.

The ballad has grim side glances; the boll weevil didn't leave "the farmer's wife but one old cotton dress"; made his nest in the farmer's "best Sunday hat"; and closed the church doors since the farmer couldn't pay the preacher.

> Oh, de Farmer say to de Merchant
> I ain't made but only one bale
> An' befo' I bring you dat one
> I'll fight an' go to jail
> I'll have a home
> I'll have a home.

The stanzaic forms and general structure of "John Henry" and "The Boll Weevil" are fairly developed. One of the best folk ballads, however, is in the simpler, unrhymed African leader-chorus design. This is "The Grey Goose," a ballad about a seemingly ordinary fowl who becomes a symbol of ability to take it. It is a song done with the highest spirits; the "Lord, Lord, Lord" of the responding chorus expressing amazement, flattery, and good-humored respect for the tough bird:

> Well, last Monday mornin'
> Lord, Lord, Lord!
> Well, last Monday mornin'
> Lord, Lord, Lord!

They went hunting for the grey goose. When shot "Boo-loom!" the grey goose was six weeks a-falling. Then it was six weeks a-finding, and once in the white house, was six weeks a-picking. Even after the great feather-picking he was six months parboiling. And then on the table, the forks couldn't stick him; the knife couldn't cut him. So they threw him in the hog-pen where he broke the sow's jawbone. Even in the sawmill, he broke the saw's teeth out. He was indestructible. Last seen the grey goose was flying across the ocean, with a long string of goslings, all going "Quank-quink-quank." Yessir, it was one hell of a gray goose. Lord, Lord, Lord!

Work Songs and Social Protest

More work songs come from the Negro than from any other American folk group. Rowing the cypress dug-outs in Carolina low-country, slaves timed their singing to the long sweep of the oars. The leader, a sort of coxswain, chanted verse after verse; the rowers rumbled a refrain. On the docks Negroes sang sailors' chanteys as metronomes to their heaving and hauling. Some chanteys, like "Old Stormy," they took over from the white seamen; others they improvised. Along the Ohio and Mississippi waterfronts Negro roustabouts created "coonjine" songs, so-called after the shuffling dance over bucking gang-planks in and out of steamboat holds. Unless the rhythm was just right a roustabout and his bale or sack of cottonseed might be jolted into the brown waters. The singers cheered the speed of the highballing paddlewheelers: "left Baton Rouge at half pas' one, and got to Vicksburg at settin of de sun." But they griped over the tough captains "workin' hell out of me" and sang

> Ole Roustabout ain't got no home
> Makes his livin' on his shoulder bone.

For release from the timber and the heavy sacks there was always some city around the bend—Paducah, Cairo, Memphis, Natchez, and then

> Alberta let yo' hair hang low . . .
> I'll give you mo' gold
> Than yo' apron can hold . . .
> Alberta let yo' hair hang low.

These songs flourished in the hey-day of the packets; today they are nearly lost.

Another type of work song was chanted as a gang unloaded steel rails. Since these rails weighed over a ton apiece and were over ten yards long, any break in the rhythm of lifting them from the flat cars to the ground was a good way to get ruptured, maimed, or killed. So a chanter was employed to time the hoisting, lowering, and the getting away from it. He was a coach, directing the teamwork, and in self-protection the men had to learn his rhythmic tricks. In track-lining, a similar chanter functioned to keep the track straight in line. As he called, the men jammed their bars under the rails and braced in unison:

> Shove it over! Hey, hey, can't you line it!
> Ah shack-a-lack-a-lack-a-lack-a-lack-a-lack-alack (Grunt)
> Can't you move it? Hey, hey, can't you try.

As they caught their breath and got a new purchase, he turned off a couplet. Then came the shouted refrain as the men strained together.

More widely spread and known are the Negro work songs whose rhythm is timed with the swing back and down and the blow of broadaxe, pick, hammer, or tamper. The short lines are punctuated by a grunt as the axe bites into the wood, or the hammer finds the spike-head.

> Dis ole hammer—hunh
> Ring like silver—hunh (3)
> Shine like gold, baby—hunh
> Shine like gold—hunh.

The leader rings countless changes in his words and melody over the unchanging rhythm. When he grows dull or forgets, another singer takes over. The song is consecutive, fluid; it is doubtful if any one version is ever exactly repeated. Ballads, blues, even church-songs are levied on for lines, a simple matter since the stanzas are unrhymed. Some lines tell of the satisfaction of doing a man's work well:

> I got a rainbow—hunh
> Tied 'round my shoulder—hunh—(3)
> Tain't gonna rain, baby—hunh
> Tain't gonna rain.

(The rainbow is the arc of the hammer as the sunlight glints on the moving metal.) Sometimes a singer boasts of being a "sun-down man," who can work the sun down without breaking down himself. Lines quite as popular, however, oppose any speed-up stretch-out system:

> Dis ole hammer—hunh
> Killt John Henry—hunh—(3)
> Twon't kill me, baby—hunh
> Twon't kill me.

Some lines get close to the blues: "Every mail day / Gits a letter / Son, come home, baby / Son, come home." Sometimes they tell of a hard captain (boss)

> Told my captain—hunh
> Hands are cold—hunh—(3)
> Damn yo' hands—hunh
> Let de wheelin' roll.

The new-fangled machine killed John Henry; its numerous offspring have killed the work songs of his buddies. No hammer song could compete now with the staccato roaring drill even if the will to sing were there. The steamboat is coming back to the Mississippi but the winches and cranes do not call forth the old gang choruses. A few songs connected with work survive such as the hollers of the lonely worker in the fields and woods, or the call boy's chant to the glory-hole.

> Sleeping good, sleeping good,
> Give me them covers, I wish you would.

At ease from their work in their bunkhouses, the men may sing, but their fancies ramble from the job oftener than they stay with it. Song as a rhythmic accompaniment to work is declining. John and Alan Lomax, whose bag of Negro work songs is the fullest, had to go to the penitentiaries, where labor-saving devices were not yet numerous, in order to find the art thriving. They found lively cotton-picking songs:

> A-pick a bale, a-pick a bale
> Pick a bale of cotton
> A-pick a bale, a-pick a bale
> Pick a bale a day.

Slower songs came from gangs that were cutting cane or chopping weeds or hewing timber. Prison work is of course mean and tough: "You oughta come on de Brazo in nineteen-fo'; you could find a dead man on every turn-row." So the convicts cry out to the taskmaster sun:

> Go down, Ol' Hannah, doncha rise no mo'
> Ef you rise any mo' bring judgment day.

They grouse about the food: ever "the same damn thing," and at that the cook isn't clean. An old evangelical stand-by, "Let the Light of the Lighthouse Shine On Me," becomes a hymn of hope that the Midnight Special, a fast train, will some day bring a pardon from the governor. They sing of their long sentences:

> Ninety-nine years so jumpin' long
> To be here rollin' an' cain' go home.

If women aren't to be blamed for it all, they are still to be blamed for a great deal:

> Ain't but de one thing worries my min'
> My cheating woman and my great long time.

One song, like the best balladry, throws a searchlight into the darkness:

> "Little boy, what'd you do for to get so long?"
> Said, "I killed my rider in the high sheriff's arms."

From these men—long-termers, lifers, three-time losers—come songs brewed in bitterness. This is not the double-talk of the slave seculars, but the naked truth of desperate men telling what is on their brooding minds. Only to collectors who have won their trust—such as the Lomaxes, Lawrence Gellert, and Josh White—and only when the white captain is far enough away, do the prisoners confide these songs. Then they sing not loudly but deeply their hatred of the brutality of the chain-gang:

> If I'd a had my weight in lime
> I'd a whupped dat captain, till he went stone blind.
>
> If you don't believe my buddy's dead
> Just look at that hole in my buddy's head.

A prisoner is told: "Don't you go worryin' about forty [the years of your sentence], Cause in five years you'll be dead."

They glorify the man who makes a crazy dare for freedom; Jimbo, for instance, who escapes almost under the nose of his captain, is described as "a big Goliath," who walks like Samson and "totes his talker." They boast: "Ef ah git de drop / Ah'm goin' on / Dat same good way / Dat Jimbo's gone / Lawd, Lawd, Lawd." They reenact with graphic realism the lashing of a fellow-prisoner; the man-hunting of Ol' Rattler, "fastest and smellingest bloodhound in the South"; and the power of Black Betty, the ugly bull-whip. They make stark drama out of the pain, and hopelessness, and shame.

> All I wants is dese cold iron shackles off my leg.

It is not only in the prison songs that there is social protest. Where there is some protection or guaranteed secrecy other *verboten* songs come to light. Coal miners, fortified by a strong, truculent union, sing grimly of the exorbitant company stores:

> What's de use of me working any more, my baby? (2)
> What's de use of me working any more,
> When I have to take it up at de company store,
> My baby?

Or they use the blues idiom with a new twist:

> Operator will forsake you, he'll drive you from his do' . . .
> No matter what you do, dis union gwine to stand by you
> While de union growing strong in dis land.

And the sharecroppers sharply phrase their plight:

Go in the store and the merchant would say,
'Your mortgage is due and I'm looking for my pay.'
Down in his pocket with a tremblin' hand
'Can't pay you all but I'll pay what I can,'
Then to the telephone the merchant made a call,
They'll put you on the chain-gang, an' you don't pay at all.

Big Bill Broonzy is best known as a blues singer, but in the cotton belt of Arkansas he learned a great deal that sank deep. His sharp "Black, Brown, and White Blues" has the new militancy built up on the sills of the old folksong. In an employment office, Big Bill sings. "They called everybody's number / But they never did call mine." Then working side by side with a white man:

He was getting a dollar an hour
When I was making fifty cents.

Onto this new protest he ties an old vaudeville chorus, deepening the irony:

If you's black, ah brother.
Git back, git back, git back.

Such songs, together with the blues composed by Waring Cuney and Josh White on poverty, hardship, poor housing, and jim crow military service, come from conscious propagandists, not truly folk. They make use of the folk idiom in both text and music, however, and the folk listen and applaud. They know very well what Josh White is talking about in such lines as:

Great gawdamighty, folks feelin' bad
Lost everything they ever had.

Prospect

It is evident that Negro folk culture is breaking up. Where Negro met only with Negro in the black belt the old beliefs strengthened. But when mud traps give way to gravel roads, and black tops and even concrete highways with buses and jalopies and trucks lumbering over them, the world comes closer. The churches and schools, such as they are, struggle against some of the results of isolation, and the radio plays a part. Even in the backwoods, aerials are mounted on shanties that seem ready to collapse from the extra weight on the roof, or from a good burst of static against the walls. The phonograph is common, the television set is by no means unknown, and down at the four corners store, a jukebox gives out the latest jive. Rural folk closer to towns and cities may on Saturday jaunts even see an occasional movie, where a rootin'-tootin' Western gangster film introduces them to the advancements of civilization. Newspapers, especially the Negro press, give the people a sense of belonging to a larger world. Letters from their boys in the army, located in all corners of the world, and the tales of the returning veterans, true Marco Polos, also prod the inert into curiosity. Brer Rabbit and Old Jack no longer are enough. Increasingly in the churches the spirituals lose favor to singing out of the books or from broadsides, and city-born blues and jive take over the jook-joints.

The migration of the folk Negro to the cities, started by the hope for better living and schooling, and greater self-respect, quickened by the industrial demands of two world wars is sure to be increased by the new cotton picker and other man-displacing machines. In the city the folk become a submerged proletariat. Leisurely yarn-spinning, slow-paced aphoristic conversation become lost arts; jazzed-up gospel hymns provide a different sort of release from the old spirituals; the blues reflect the distortions of the new way of life. Folk arts are no longer by the folk for the folk; smart businessmen now put them up for sale. Gospel songs often become showpieces for radio slummers, and the blues become the double-talk of the dives. And yet, in spite of the commercializing, the folk roots often show a stubborn vitality. Just as the transplanted folk may show the old credulity, though the sophisticated impulse sends them to an American Indian for nostrums, or for fortune-telling to an East Indian "madame" with a turban around her head rather than to a mammy with a bandanna around her's; so the folk for all their disorganization may keep something of the fine quality of their old tales and songs. Assuredly even in the new gospel songs and blues much is retained of the phrasing and the distinctive musical manner. Finally, it should be pointed out that even in the transplanting, a certain kind of isolation—class and racial—remains. What may come of it, if anything, is unpredictable, but so far the vigor of the creative impulse has not been snapped, even in the slums.

Whatever may be the future of the folk Negro, American literature as well as American music is the richer because of his expression. Just as Huckleberry Finn and Tom Sawyer were fascinated by the immense lore of their friend Jim, American authors have been drawn to Negro folk life and character. With varying authenticity and understanding, Joel Chandler Harris, Du Bose Heyward, Julia Peterkin, Roark Bradford, Marc Connelly, E.C.L. Adams, Zora Neale Hurston, and Langston Hughes have all made rewarding use of this material. Folk Negroes have themselves bequeathed a wealth of moving song, both religious and secular, of pithy folk-say and entertaining and wise folk-tales. They have settled characters in the gallery of American heroes—resourceful Brer Rabbit and Old Jack, and indomitable John Henry. They have told their own story so well that all men should be able to hear it and understand.

MARGARET WALKER ALEXANDER
(b. 1915)

Winner of the Yale Younger Poets Award for 1942, Margaret Walker Alexander was the most distinctive Afro-American poet to appear in the thirties. She was born in Birmingham, Alabama, and educated at Northwestern and Iowa. She has been a teacher during most of her career, notably at Jackson State College where she has organized festivals and conferences devoted to black art and black studies.

Her verse celebrates the struggles, the lore, the hopes of Southern black people attempting to deal with the manifold problems of their existence. She has been quite consciously a people's poet. The title poem of her 1942 volume For My People *appeared in 1937 in the magazine* Poetry. *It was published in the* Negro Caravan *in 1941 and has become one of the emblem poems of black America. Its incantatory coda is gripping and assertive:*

Let a new earth rise. Let another world be born. Let a bloody peace be written in the sky. . . . Let the martial songs be written, let the dirges disappear. Let a race of men now rise and take control!

Alexander published in 1966 a novel on slavery, Jubilee, *which is set in Georgia. Many readers have found its story line too enmeshed in the details of slave life uncovered by Miss Alexander's research, but it has enjoyed a continuing and increasing reputation.*

Southern Song

I want my body bathed again by southern suns, my soul reclaimed
    again from southern land. I want to rest again in southern fields,
    in grass and hay and clover bloom; to lay my hand again upon
    the clay baked by a southern sun, to touch the rain-soaked earth
    and smell the smell of soil.

I want my rest unbroken in the fields of southern earth; freedom to
    watch the corn wave silver in the sun and mark the splashing
    of a brook, a pond with ducks and frogs and count the clouds.

I want no mobs to wrench me from my southern rest; no forms to
    take me in the night and burn my shack and make for me a
    nightmare full of oil and flame.
I want my careless song to strike no minor key; no fiend to stand
    between my body's southern song—the fusion of the South, my
    body's song and me.

Memory

I can remember wind-swept streets of cities
on cold and blustery nights, on rainy days;
heads under shabby felts and parasols
and shoulders hunched against a sharp concern;
seeing hurt bewilderment on poor faces,
smelling a deep and sinister unrest
these brooding people cautiously caress;
hearing ghostly marching on pavement stones
and closing fast around their squares of hate.
I can remember seeing them alone,
at work, and in their tenements at home.
I can remember hearing all they said:
their muttering protests, their whispered oaths,
and all that spells their living in distress.

438

Childhood

When I was a child I knew red miners
dressed raggedly and wearing carbide lamps.
I saw them come down red hills to their camps
dyed with red dust from old Ishkooda mines.
Night after night I met them on the roads,
or on the streets in town I caught their glance;
the swing of dinner buckets in their hands,
and grumbling undermining all their words.

I also lived in low cotton country
where moonlight hovered over ripe haystacks,
or stumps of trees, and croppers' rotting shacks
with famine, terror, flood, and plague near by;
where sentiment and hatred still held sway
and only bitter land was washed away.

We Have Been Believers

We have been believers believing in the black gods of an old land,
believing in the secrets of the seeress and the magic of the
charmers and the power of the devil's evil ones.

And in the white gods of a new land we have been believers believing
in the mercy of our masters and the beauty of our brothers,
believing in the conjure of the humble and the faithful and the
pure.

Neither the slavers' whip nor the lynchers' rope nor the bayonet
could kill our black belief. In our hunger we beheld the welcome
table and in our nakedness the glory of a long white robe. We
have been believers in the new Jerusalem.

We have been believers feeding greedy grinning gods, like a Moloch demanding our sons and our daughters, our strength and our wills and our spirits of pain. We have been believers, silent and stolid and stubborn and strong.

We have been believers yielding substance for the world. With our hands have we fed a people and out of our strength have they wrung the necessities of a nation. Our song has filled the twilight and our hope has heralded the dawn.

Now we stand ready for the touch of one fiery iron, for the cleansing breath of many molten truths, that the eyes of the blind may see and the ears of the deaf may hear and the tongues of the people be filled with living fire.

Where are our gods that they leave us asleep? Surely the priests and the preachers and the powers will hear. Surely now that our hands are empty and our hearts too full to pray they will understand. Surely the sires of the people will send us a sign.

We have been believers believing in our burdens and our demigods too long. Now the needy no longer weep and pray; the long-suffering arise, and our fists bleed against the bars with a strange insistency.

Part IV

The Forties to 1970

Instead of peace, the end of World War II brought a new era of struggle. For America the era was one of internal as well as international tensions, material progress and moral regression, wars and rumor of wars, apparently never to cease. Internationally America had become involved in numerous conflicts, the space race, and the cold war with Russia, which infused virtually all events of the period. Internally America was beset with troubles—the deterioration of the cities, inflation and recession, the revolt of youth, and most of all, the increasingly vociferous demands of black people for full citizenship. All conflicts, national and international, culminated in the savage and morally disastrous war in Vietnam, which caused many to doubt the basic American institutions and involved leaders and laymen alike in loud and endless harangue.

The result was a milieu of almost unbearable tension. Crime in the streets, corruption in high places, assassinations of charismatic leaders, murder of civil rights workers, government spying on dissenting groups and individuals, pollution of the environment—these and other influences generated an atmosphere of frustration, confusion, and violence. A spirit of rebellion was evident as white youth, black people of all ages, idealists of all kinds revolted against the System, rejecting its alleged values and fleeing, often to a dubious "freedom," to drug-induced tranquility, or to despair. For many contemporary Americans, alienated and afraid, life was disturbingly existential.

In this milieu the black American was in perpetual motion—

whether forward or backward depends upon what yardstick one uses. The years since World War II have found him unraveling his own personal truths about his dual heritage, his evaluation of his American experience, his role and his rights as a worthy human being. In the 1960s the black American was poised between rejection of his old "assumed" self and a positive assertion of his real identity.

One of the influences which brought us to this point was the emergence of independent nations in Africa, as European imperialism tumbled. The formation of the Organization of African States in 1962, conferences bringing together intellectuals and artists from among the African diaspora, and the development of Afro-centric culture in this country quickened the Afro-American's sense of pride in his ancestry and lessened his need to pursue the ever-receding horizon of whiteness as a psychological goal. The older concepts of Pan-Africanism and Negritude took on a wider meaning.

Various milestones in recent American history also contributed to black America's heightened self-awareness. In 1954 the Supreme Court outlawed racial discrimination in public schools, thus setting the stage for years of violent confrontation and legal debate. In 1956 the Montgomery bus boycott proved the effectiveness of concerted mass action and propelled Martin Luther King and nonviolence into eminence. King's philosophy of nonviolence, influenced in part by Henry David Thoreau and Gandhi, was based upon Christian brotherhood and redemptive suffering. It guided countless sit-ins, freedom rides, and marches in the fifties and reached a dramatic climax in 1963 when thousands of people, white and black, converged on the nation's capitol to demand jobs and civil liberties.

In spite of the various civil rights acts passed by Congress, the hopes raised in 1963 never came to fruition. In the wake of this failure, other philosophies and other leaders surfaced. The Student Nonviolent Coordination Committee (SNCC), led by Stokely Carmichael, enunciated the concept of Black Power—a concept vigorously aggressive rather than passive. Influenced by Frantz Fanon, a black psychiatrist and writer from Martinique, black leaders adopted the theory that black people must attain political and economic power before they can hope to be free. The recognition of power as a necessary ingredient in the struggle had a tremendous impact upon the black psyche and changed the tone of the struggle. Whites who had been "tolerant" and even "liberal" were now seen as a part of the backlash that threatened to call a halt to the Afro-American's gains.

One of the most significant leaders to emerge during this period was Malcolm X. His appeal to the grass roots, who had been untouched by any recent leader, his far-reaching vision, his plans to unite all black peoples, his magnetic personality and earthy eloquence gained him a large and dedicated following. It also made him dangerous enemies. But Malcolm's influence continued to grow, even after his assassination in 1965. For blacks from many socioeconomic strata, Malcolm provided an image of courageous manhood and a measure of insight into their situation.

In the years immediately following World War II, Richard Wright was the dominant figure in black letters. The bitter protest of *Native Son* (1940), which had been a best-selling novel as well as a critical success, keynoted the novels of the entire decade to follow. His autobiography, *Black Boy* (1945), reinforced the image of the black man as victim of his environment, degraded and all but dehumanized. The Wright hero became more sophisticated and more consciously existential in Wright's subsequent works, but he was always alienated, always the victimized native son of a hostile parent land.

Other novelists in the late forties used a tough, realistic style on the order of Wright's in works that effectively protested the ills which befall society's outcasts. The best of these were Chester Himes' *If He Hollers Let Him Go* (1945), and Ann Petry's *The Street* (1946). But nobody approached Wright's artistry in style and creation of characters, his skillful interweaving of naturalism and existentialism, his exposure of the ironies of black life in America.

An interesting feature of the late forties and early fifties was the fact that side by side with the literature of protest was the literature of integration. Often the same writers would use both modes. Some black writers of the period felt that one should write not as a "Negro" but as an "American"—should write, that is, "raceless" works centering on white characters (which is hardly being raceless). Thus Ann Petry's second novel, *Country Place* (1947), revolved around white characters in a small town. Willard Motley's *Knock on Any Door* (1947) involved an Italian-American ghetto family. His later novels, too, avoided blackness. Frank Yerby's lucrative historical novels, which appeared yearly (sometimes more often), concerned white characters. In poetry it was difficult to tell who was black, since many poems published did not deal with racial themes.

In reality, the paradox here is only apparent. Protest literature and "raceless" literature are both addressed primarily to the same audience—white America. One protests to the oppressor, not to one's oppressed fellows.

Perhaps encouraged by the success of Wright and Yerby, black novelists were more active than poets and playwrights during the first few years after the end of the war. Several older, established writers published novels during this period. Zora Neale Hurston rounded out a career begun in the years of the Harlem Renaissance of the twenties with her work *Seraph on the Suwanee*, which appeared in 1948. Several exciting new novelists began to publish in these years. William Gardner Smith's *Last of the Conquerors* was published in 1948, and was followed two years later by *Anger at Innocence*. Also in 1950, another new novelist, William Demby, brought out his first novel, *Beetle-Creek*, a semiautobiographical novel about troubled youth. Another semi-autobiographical novel was Owen Dodson's *Boy at the Window* (1951). Poet Gwendolyn Brooks issued her only novel to date, *Maud Martha* (1953).

In shorter fiction, several collections appeared. Langston Hughes' Simple sketches were gathered in *Simple Speaks His Mind* (1950)—the first of several Simple volumes. Two years later Hughes published a volume of short stories, *Laughing to Keep from Crying*. Shorter fiction of many authors was collected by Nick Aaron Ford and H. C. Faggett in *The Best Short Stories by Negro Authors* (1950).

Poetry during the early postwar years was high in merit. For the most part, poets used traditional forms and themes. Protest poems were still appearing, but nonracial themes were also being used, as many poets strove to shed what they regarded as the onus of race. In addition to the usual themes of love, death, and nature, poets were writing of the evil of war (Owen Dodson and Gwendolyn Brooks) and the variegated patterns in the life of a woman (Gwendolyn Brooks).

Several extremely competent poets produced volumes of high artistry. Owen Dodson's *Powerful Long Ladder* (1946) and Robert Hayden's and Myron O'Higgins' *The Lion and the Archer* (1948) showed virtuosity in traditional forms. Langston Hughes' *Fields of Wonder* (1947) and *One-Way Ticket* (1949) were more innovative, continuing Hughes' practice of using black folk patterns for theme and form. The most exciting new personality to emerge during these years was Gwendolyn Brooks. Her ability as a lyricist was immediately apparent in her first volume, *A Street in Bronzeville* (1945). Her second volume, *Annie Allen* (1949), won the Pulitzer Prize.

The publication of Ralph Ellison's novel *Invisible Man* in 1952 marked the beginning of a new emphasis in black writing. In a sense, the novel symbolized the thrust of the forties. Like the nameless hero of the novel, the black writer had tried on the many identities which the culture had assigned him, had played the various roles that America had demanded, had written raceless works, dialect works, and protest works. Like the hero, he discovered in time that each identity was false. But in a sense, too, the novel anticipated the passionate probing of blackness which the next two decades were to bring. For Ellison dipped deep into black folk experience: folk characters like Brer Rabbit and Jack the Bear, strains of jazz and children's chants, the warm rhythms and vivid idioms of black speech are the means of exploring the basic theme of the novel, the search for identity, a theme of crucial importance to black Americans of dual heritage.

Invisible Man was the first major novel since *Native Son* and probably the most acclaimed novel yet written by an Afro-American for its artistry. With consummate skill Ellison orchestrates complex symbols, multiple themes, and a style which moves easily from realism to fantasy and back.

One indication that the black man was beginning to search himself (rather than white America) for answers was the deepening interest in biography and autobiography. Since the days of the slave narratives, autobiography and biography had been an important genre in black writing—as if the voices from the dark land had to be heard, to tell what it was like. In the forties, only one important autobiography was published, Richard Wright's *Black Boy* (1945). In the fifties, however, autobiographies (sometimes "as told to") became abundant. Popular entertainers as well as writers and scholars told their stories. Autobiographies of Ethel Waters, Lena Horne, Louis Armstrong, Eartha Kitt, Marian Anderson, Billie Holiday, Sidney Bechet, and Katherine Dunham appeared in the fifties. Sports figures Willie Mays and Roy Campanella also were subjects of autobiographies. Ruby Berkley Goodwin's *It's Good to Be Black* (1953) anticipates the later emphasis on black beauty. Langston Hughes' second autobiography, *I Wonder As I Wander* (1956), gave insights into a man whose works constitute a vital part of black American literature. Important autobiographical essays appeared in James Baldwin's *Notes of a Native Son* (1955). Biographies included Helen Chesnutt's *Charles W. Chesnutt: Pioneer of the Color Line* (1952), and Lawrence D. Riddick's *Crusader without Violence: A Biography of Martin Luther King, Jr.* (1955).

The fiction of the fifties, then, bespoke the re-emergence of self-examination. There were, of course, still novels that were not on black themes. One was Ann Petry's *The Narrows* (1953), set in a small New England town and concerned with the town's reactions to an interracial romance. Another was James Baldwin's *Giovanni's Room* (1956), set in Europe and centering around a young white American's homosexual affair with an Italian. During the fifties the Wright tradition of protest flickered and dimmed. Wright himself, living in Paris, published *The Outsider* (1953), heavily existential, which explored the meaning of life in an absurd universe. Still bitterly ironic, still oriented to violence, the novel nevertheless has a limited view of blackness. The hero, Cross Damon, is a Negro, but his Negro-ness is merely a symbol for his alienation. The very title implied a viewpoint more white than black.

In the same year that *The Outsider* was published, another novel appeared which plunged deep into several aspects of blackness and held them up for critical examination. James Baldwin's first novel, regarded by some as his best, *Go Tell It on the Mountain* (1953) is an autobiographical story of painful growing up. The fourteen-year-old protagonist is buffeted by tensions arising from his ambivalent relationship to his harsh father, the demands of their restrictive religion, his own sensitivity and feeling of being "different," his growing sense of alienation. Baldwin captures family life in the black ghetto and creates an unforgettable young black at a crucial period of his life.

In the following years other novels looked closely into the life of black Americans. John O. Killens' first novel, *Youngblood* (1954), traced the fortunes of a black family in Georgia through two generations of struggle for human dignity in the face of racism. Julian Mayfield's *The Hit* (1957) and *The Long Night* (1958), and Paule Marshall's *Brown Girl, Brownstones* (1959) examined the various dilemmas and complex relationships of the urban Afro-American. W. E. B. Du Bois published *The Ordeal of Mansart* (1957), *Mansart Builds a School* (1959), and *Worlds of Color* (1961), his Black Flame trilogy.

Generally speaking, the novel was by far a more innovative genre during the fifties than was poetry. No major new poet arose; rather, poets of the preceding decade developed their techniques. Langston Hughes brought out *Montage of a Dream Deferred* (1951); Gwendolyn Brooks, *Bronzeville Boys and Girls* (1956); Melvin B.

Tolson, *Libretto for the Republic of Liberia* (1953); Naomi Long Madgett, *One of the Many* (1956).

With the dawn of the sixties, a number of varied forces converged to produce a new black literature. Student protest and a growing awareness on the part of the masses produced a climate conducive to an outpouring of literature.

One vital factor in the growth of black writing was the proliferation of publications edited by Afro-Americans. The older publications thickened with creative and critical works: *Phylon*, CLA *Journal*, and the *Negro History Bulletin* published scholarly works; *Freedomways*, *The Liberator*, and *Ebony* published essays and articles of popular appeal. A number of small magazines appeared and provided outlets for the rapidly increasing number of writers: *Journal of Black Poetry*, *Umbra*, *Black Dialogue*, and *Soulbook* were a few of the many new names.

Perhaps the most important single periodical was *Negro Digest*, which in 1970 changed its name to *Black World*. Its editor, Hoyt Fuller, was a vital force in the literary flowering. *Negro Digest/Black World* became one of the best sources of contemporary information about literary matters from the sixties on, with its articles of general interest to Afro-Americans. It reviewed new books at the time of their publication, and published articles, stories and poems by new as well as established writers, and special issues on subjects of particular interest. Also, through its pages older writers offered prizes to younger writers. With its change of name, the magazine announced its aim to encompass the entire black world.

In addition to magazines, publishing companies with a primary focus on blackness arose. Of these, Dudley Randall's Broadside Press has a central importance. White publishers began to hire black editors and to broaden their offerings in black literature. Several companies reprinted and promoted older works which had long since gone out of print but which were now demanded by the new Black Studies programs being organized in colleges across the nation.

The arts flourished in all directions. Art began to be seen as a major road to liberation. As the decade passed, Le Roi Jones' Black Arts Movement articulated the place of Black Arts: "The Black Artist must draw out of his soul the correct image of the world. He must use this image to band his brothers and sisters together in common understanding of the nature of the world (and the nature of America) and the nature of the human soul."

All genres experienced an upsurge of activity during this period. The essay took on new significance as black writers probed the perplexing questions of a new age. James Baldwin was one of the most talented. His mastery of this genre had been evident in his first volume, *Notes of a Native Son* (1955), in which he recalled poignantly his search for and discovery of his American identity. In the sixties he published two new collections, each a landmark in the American essay. *Nobody Knows My Name* (1961) contains autobiographical and critical essays that discuss frankly the state of black life and literature. *The Fire Next Time* (1963) contains two angry and masterfully written essays.

Other notable volumes of essays by other authors followed. Martin Luther King expounded his philosophy of nonviolence in *Strength to Love* (1963), *Why We Can't Wait* (1964), and *Where Do We Go from Here: Chaos or Community* (1967). The theories of black power were discussed in *Black Power* (1967) by Stokely Carmichael and Charles V. Hamilton. Malcolm X's speeches were published, edited usually from the many tapes of his public appearances. Meanwhile, serious creative writers expounded their views on the black situation in such volumes as *Home* (1966) by Le Roi Jones, *Black Man's Burden* (1965) by John O. Killens, and *Soul on Ice* (1968) by Eldridge Cleaver.

Biography and autobiography continued to flourish. The sixties brought life stories of both prominent and unknown people important because of their recording of black life. W. E. B. Du Bois' *Autobiography* (1968), published posthumously, and *The Autobiography of Malcolm X* (written with Alex Haley) were the most compelling. Claude Brown's *Manchild in the Promised Land* (1965) told the story of the author's childhood in ghetto Harlem.

Imaginative literature reached a high point in skill and quantity during the sixties. As the decade progressed and the tensions of the black revolt became more and more taut, fiction, poetry, and plays increased and grew angrier. At the same time, many writers turned to folk culture, as had their predecessors in the Harlem Renaissance of the twenties, for themes and language. The literature is characterized by great variety, a spirit of youth, freedom of expression, a growing sense of awareness of the black man's worth, and increasing rejection of standards that were regarded as white.

In fiction, several writers of the past decade remained. Wright's last books, *Eight Men* (1961) and *Lawd, Today* (1963) were published, but were actually much earlier works. Baldwin wrote, his rising anger observable in successive works, two novels, *Another Country* (1962) and *Tell Me How Long the Train's Been Gone* (1967), and a collection of stories, *Going to Meet the Man* (1965). John O. Killens followed his first novel in the fifties with *And Then We Heard the Thunder* (1963) and *'Sippi* (1967), angry and often violent works. Le Roi Jones published two impressionistic works: an autobiographical novel, *The System of Dante's Hell*, and a collection of stories, *Tales* (1967). Both probe into the unconscious. Langston Hughes published two Simple volumes, *The Best of Simple* (1961) and *Simple's Uncle Sam* (1965).

But there were also many perceptive new writers. John A. Williams wrote tough, tight novels about rugged black men—*Night Song* (1961), *Sissie* (1963), *The Man Who Cried I Am* (1967), and *Sons of Darkness, Sons of Light* (1970). Ernest J. Gaines wrote about personal relations in his novels *Catherine Carmier* (1964) and *Of Love and the Dust* (1967). His stories, collected in *Bloodline* (1968), show his adept handling of regional language and his skillful manipulation of point of view. William Melvin Kelley wrote allegorically in his novels, *A Drop of Patience* (1965), *A Different Drummer* (1962), and *Dem* (1967), and in his collected stories, *Dancers on the Shore* (1964). Charles Wright wrote with ferocious irony in his symbolic novels *The Wig* (1966) and *The Messenger* (1963), as did Ronald Fair in *Hog Butcher* (1966) and *Many Thousand Gone* (1965).

Poetry, which had been relatively sparse in the fifties, exploded during the sixties. The decade began fairly quietly with works by older established authors. Robert Hayden wrote with power and control in traditional lyric forms in *A Ballad of Remembrance* (1962) and later in his *Selected Poems* (1966). Melvin Tolson wrote in the ironic metaphysical tradition in *Harlem Gallery* (1965). Still, the anger and the search for new forms that characterized the new poetry were observable in some of the established poets. Two, in particular, grew with the times. Langston Hughes' *Ask Your Mama: Twelve Moods of Jazz* (1961) continued his use of musical forms and themes inspired by folk life. *The Panther and the Lash* (1967) collected his militant poems. Gwendolyn Brooks' *The Bean Eaters* (1960) used lyric forms and free verse in strong, feminine poems. Her mounting anger during the decade was apparent in *In the Mecca* (1968), a long symbolic poem about the murder of a ghetto child, and *Riot* (1969), a poem probing implications of the Chicago riots in 1968.

Le Roi Jones was undoubtedly the dominant poet of the period. His early poetry was characterized by avant garde conventions. His language was highly complex and heavy with symbolism, an existential poetry with a fairly logical unfolding of statement. By the end of the decade he had become immersed in blackness. He had changed his name to Amiri Baraka. His poetry sought direct communication with the inarticulate masses.

Other voices added to the crescendo in poetry. A group formed in Chicago under the aegis of Hoyt Fuller, called the Organization of Black American Culture, produced a number of poets—Don L. Lee, Carolyn Rodgers, Johari Amini, and others. Quincy Troupe came from the Watts Workshop, a group formed after the riots in the Watts area of Los Angeles.

Groups of young black poets sprang up all over the nation. Other poets of the decade were James A. Emanuel, Dudley Randall, Nikki Giovanni, Sonia Sanchez, Eugene Redmond, Mari Evans. Unhampered by the opinion of a white audience, they wrote for blacks; some attempted to abandon the conventions of standard English writing, which they felt were tools of the enemy. Poetry left the sanctuary of the study and took to the streets, where it found a warm welcome. A concomitant increase in public reading of poetry was the result.

In many ways the decade of the 1960s was the most crowded and exciting in the annals of Afro-American life and literature. However, its resonances in life as well as art can best be considered as an intensified reflection of the long, arduous road Black America has trod from its beginning.

MELVIN B. TOLSON
(1900-1966)

Though a member of an older generation, Melvin B. Tolson became an important poet of the forties and fifties. A native of Moberly, Missouri, Tolson attended Fisk and Lincoln Universities and received his Master of Arts degree from Columbia University. For many years he taught at Wiley College, Texas; Langston University, Oklahoma; and Tuskegee Institute. His charisma made him not only a popular teacher, debating coach, and drama director, but also mayor of Langston for four terms.

Tolson's first volume, Rendezvous with America *(1944), contained his prize-winning poem, "Dark Symphony," as well as a number of neo-metaphysical poems traditional in form. In 1947 he was commissioned Poet Laureate of Liberia and wrote* Libretto for the Republic of Liberia *(1953), a condensed verse epic. The high point of his career was* Harlem Gallery *(1965), an intricate, brilliant, highly allusive poem which has received both praise and disfavor from critics.*

An admirer of Pound and Eliot, Tolson artfully utilized the satiric possibilities of obscure allusions and complexity of form, and combined them with the milieu of black urban life. In the mid-sixties, when black poets were looking to their own literary forebears for models and were seeking simple and direct forms and themes to express the tragic overtones of black experience, Tolson's style was considered anachronistic. Nevertheless, the florid verbalism in his work is best understood as a product of black culture.

The posthumous publication of A Gallery of Harlem Portraits *(1979), completed in 1935, revealed Tolson as adept in the anecdotal style of Edgar Lee Masters'* Spoon River Anthology *and provided illumination of the sources of* Harlem Gallery. Cabbage and Caviar *(1981) collects some of Tolson's insightful newspaper columns.*

There are biographical studies of Tolson by Joy Flasch (1972) and Robert Farnsworth (1984), and a detailed study of Harlem Gallery *by Mariann Russell (1980).*

Dark Symphony

1
ALLEGRO MODERATO

Black Crispus Attucks taught
          Us how to die
Before white Patrick Henry's bugle breath
Uttered the vertical
          Transmitting cry:
"Yea, give me liberty or give me death."

Waifs of the auction block,
          Men black and strong
The juggernauts of despotism withstood,
Loin-girt with faith that worms
          Equate the wrong
And dust is purged to create brotherhood.

No Banquo's ghost can rise
          Against us now,
Aver we hobnailed Man beneath the brute,
Squeezed down the thorns of greed
          On Labor's brow,
Garroted lands and carted off the loot.

2
LENTO GRAVE

The centuries-old pathos in our voices
Saddens the great white world,
And the wizardry of our dusky rhythms
Conjures up shadow-shapes of ante-bellum years:

Black slaves singing *One More River to Cross*
In the torture tombs of slave-ships,
Black slaves singing *Steal Away to Jesus*
In jungle swamps,
Black slaves singing *The Crucifixion*
In slave-pens at midnight,
Black slaves singing *Swing Low, Sweet Chariot*
In cabins of death,
Black slaves singing *Go Down, Moses*
In the canebrakes of the Southern Pharaohs.

3
ANDANTE SOSTENUTO

They tell us to forget
The Golgotha we tread . . .
We who are scourged with hate,
A price upon our head.
They who have shackled us
Required of us a song,
They who have wasted us
Bid us condone the wrong.

They tell us to forget
Democracy is spurned.
They tell us to forget
The Bill of Rights is burned.
Three hundred years we slaved,
We slave and suffer yet:
Though flesh and bone rebel,
They tell us to forget!

Oh, how can we forget
Our human rights denied?
Oh, how can we forget
Our manhood crucified?
When Justice is profaned
And plea with curse is met,
When Freedom's gates are barred,
Oh, how can we forget?

4

TEMPO PRIMO

The New Negro strides upon the continent
In seven-league boots . . .
The New Negro
Who sprang from the vigor-stout loins
Of Nat Turner, gallows-martyr for Freedom,
Of Joseph Cinquez, Black Moses of the Amistad Mutiny
Of Frederick Douglass, oracle of the Catholic Man,
Of Sojourner Truth, eye and ear of Lincoln's legions,
Of Harriet Tubman, Saint Bernard of the Underground
    Railroad.

The New Negro
Breaks the icons of his detractors,
Wipes out the conspiracy of silence,
Speaks to *his* America:

"My history-moulding ancestors
Planted the first crops of wheat on these shores,
Built ships to conquer the seven seas,
Erected the Cotton Empire,
Flung railroads across a hemisphere,
Disemboweled the earth's iron and coal,
Tunneled the mountains and bridged rivers,
Harvested the grain and hewed forests,
Sentineled the Thirteen Colonies,
Unfurled Old Glory at the North Pole,
Fought a hundred battles for the Republic."

The New Negro:
His giant hands fling murals upon high chambers,
His drama teaches a world to laugh and weep,
His music leads continents captive,
His voice thunders the Brotherhood of Labor,
His science creates seven wonders,
His Republic of Letters challenges the Negro-baiters.

The New Negro,
Hard-muscled, Fascist-hating, Democracy-ensouled,
Strides in seven-league boots
Along the Highway of Today
Toward the Promised Land of Tomorrow!

5
LARGHETTO

None in the Land can say
To us black men Today:
You send the tractors on their bloody path,
And create Okies for *The Grapes of Wrath*.
You breed the slum that breeds a *Native Son*
To damn the good earth Pilgrim Fathers won.

None in the Land can say
To us black men Today:
You dupe the poor with rags-to-riches tales,
And leave the workers empty dinner pails.
You stuff the ballot box, and honest men
Are muzzled by your demagogic din.

None in the Land can say
To us black men Today:
You smash stock markets with your coined blitzkriegs,
And make a hundred million guinea pigs.
You counterfeit our Christianity,
And bring contempt upon Democracy.

None in the Land can say
To us black men Today:
You prowl when citizens are fast asleep,
And hatch Fifth Column plots to blast the deep
Foundations of the State and leave the Land
A vast Sahara with a Fascist brand.

6
TEMPO DI MARCIA

Out of abysses of Illiteracy,
Through labyrinths of Lies,
Across waste lands of Disease . . .
We advance!

Out of dead-ends of Poverty,
Through wilderness of Superstition,
Across barricades of Jim Crowism . . .
We advance!

With the Peoples of the World . . .
We advance!

Zeta
From *Harlem Gallery*

My thoughts tilted at the corners like long Nepalese eyes,
I entered, under the Bear, a catacomb Harlem flat
(grotesquely vivisected like microscoped maggots)
where the caricature of a rat
weathercocked in squeals
to be or not to be
and a snaggle-toothed toilet
grumbled its obscenity.
The half-blind painter,
spoon-shaped like an aged parrot-fish,
hauled up out of the ruin of his bed
and growled a proverb in Yiddish.

His smiting stare
was a Carib's forefinger prizing
Vuelta tobacco leaves in the butt of a pipe.
No half-man disguising,
he wore his odds and ends
like a mandarin's worked gold
and seated image nodding in silk,
as his bold
thumb motioned me to an expendable chair.
His sheaf of merino hair
an agitated ambush,
he bottomed upon the hazard of a bed—sighing:
"The eagle's wings,
as well as the wren's,
grow weary of flying."

His vanity was a fast-day soup—thin, cold.
Through a glass darkly I saw the face
of a fantast, heard the undated voice of a poet crying,
among scattered bones in a stony place,
"No man cares for my soul!"

Perhaps the isle of Patmos
was like this.
Here emerges the imago
from the impotence of the chrysalis
in the dusk of a people's dawn—
this, this,
thought I as I gazed at his *Black Bourgeoisie:*
colors detonating
fog signals on a railroad track,
lights and shadows rhythming
fog images in a negative pack:
this, somehow, a synthesis
(savage—sanative)
of Daumier and Gropper and Picasso.
As a Californian, I thought *Eureka;*
but as Ulfilas to the dusky Philistines I said,
"Oh!"

Although
the Regents of the Harlem Gallery are as eye-
less as knitting needles, *Black Bourgeoisie*
(retching foulness like Goya's etching,
She Says Yes to Anyone)
will wring from their babbitted souls a Jeremian cry!!

John Laugart,
alive beyond the bull of brass,
measured my interior—and said:
"A work of art
is an everlasting flower
in kind or unkind hands;
dried out,
it does not lose its form and color
in native or in alien lands."

Was he a radical leaf
created upon an under stem
at the behest
of the uncreated Diadem?
A fish of passage,
by hook unseen or crook unheard?
My curious art tried to gull his face,
the mug of a male umbrella bird,
haply black and mute.

This castaway talent
and I,
bent by paths coincident
on the lunar day
of Saint Crispin
(no matter how, by the heels, the land lay)
were fated to be
the Castor and Pollux of St. Elmo's fire,
on Harlem's Coalsack Way.

The Regents of the Harlem Gallery
suffer the carbon monoxide of ignorance
which—undetected in the
conference chamber—
leaves my budget as the
corpse of a chance.

John Laugart
—a Jacob that wrestles Tribus and sunders bonds—
discovers, in the art of the issues
of Art, our pros, as well as our cons,
fused like silver nitrate used
to destroy dead tissues.

Derisive ha-has of the half-alive
may gird the loins of the soul,
or rive
the ribs of the mind.
Yet, in the
grime and the sublime
of illusion and reality
(among olivets and pearls),
sometimes irony
bends back the cues,
like a reflective verb,
and gives the Gomorrhean blues
to the bulls of Bashan
that loose the full
butt of the bull
of blurb.

Again and again
huddled into a *cul-de-sac*
and skewed into sticks-in-the-mud
as to what shade of black
the villain Ultra should wear,
the dogs in the Harlem manger fret away their nails,
rake their hair,
initiate a game of pitch-and-toss;
then (wried by the seventh facial nerve) confuse
the T-shape of the gibbet with the T-shape of the cross.

Laugart's epitaphic words,
permanent as terre verte, are cooped
in my psyche.
A Bleak House grotesque,
his lower lip a drooped
whispering bell,
he wove—impressionistically,
like a Degas weaver,
and in a manner Gallic, *dégagé*—
coral stitches of the signature of an Apelles
in his *pièce d'identité:*

"Since dish on dish of tripe often put
our master Rodin under a spell,
perhaps this bootleg liquor eclipses my will
as dram steps on the heels of dram;
yet, I shall never sell
mohair for alpaca
to ring the bell!"

At once the ebony of his face
became moodless—bare
as the marked-off space
between the feathered areas of a cock;
then, his
spoon-shape straightened.
His glance
as sharp as a lance-
olate leaf, he said:
"It matters not a tinker's dam
on the hither or thither side of the Acheron
how many rivers you cross
if you fail to cross the Rubicon!"

Postscript:
He was robbed and murdered in his flat,
and the only witness was a Hamletian rat.
But out of *Black Bourgeoisie* came—
for John Laugart—
a bottle of Schiedam gin
and Charon's grin
and infamy,
the Siamese twin
of fame.

SAUNDERS REDDING
(b. 1906)

Saunders Redding has been a leading scholar, critic, and literary historian. A native of Wilmington, Delaware, Redding graduated from Brown University, where he was a member of Phi Beta Kappa. He has worked· with the National Endowment for the Humanities and has been a professor at Morehouse College, Hampton Institute, George Washington University and Cornell. He has lectured in numerous schools and colleges, as well as during a State Department tour of India. Among his honors have been the Guggenheim and Rockefeller fellowships and the Mayflower Award from the North Carolina Literary and Historical Society.

His works include To Make a Poet Black *(1939), a literary history;* No Day of Triumph *(1944), an autobiography;* Stranger and Alone *(1950), a novel;* On Being Black in America *(1951), a collection of essays;* The Lonesome Road *(1958), and* The Negro *(1967), histories. Redding has also published many articles in periodicals such as* The American Mercury, Antioch Review, *and* The American Scholar.

Redding has been a consistent defender of the position that the Afro-American in all essential ways should be viewed from the mainstream of American life, a position which created a degree of tension between his critical stance and that of the black aestheticians. However, his solid achievement, towering intelligence, and insistence upon excellence assure him a continuing role in black literature.

The Negro Writer and His Relationship to His Roots

I do not feel in the least controversial or argumentative about the announced subject. Indeed, I have touched upon it so often in one way or another that I long ago exhausted my store of arguments, and if I now revert to a kind of expressionistic way of talking, my excuse for it is patent. "The Negro Writer and his Relationship to his Roots" is the kind of subject which, if one talked directly on it for more than twenty minutes, he would have to talk at least a year. I shan't talk directly on it, and I shan't talk a year. An exhaustive treatment? Heaven forbid—or anything near it. Suggestive? Well, I can only hope.

And anyway, I realize now that my position here is that of the boy who, through native disability, cannot himself play but is perfectly willing to furnish the ball for others to play in exchange for the pleasure of watching the game.

Since my theme is that the American situation has complex and multifarious sources and that these sources sustain the emotional and intellectual life of American Negro writers, let me take as my starting point a classic oversimplification. This is that the meaning of American society and of the American situation to the Negro is summed up in such works as *Native Son*, *Invisible Man*, and the *Ordeal of Mansart*, and in two or three volumes of poetry, notably *Harlem Shadows*, *The Black Christ*, and *The Weary Blues*, and that the American Negro writer's entire spirit is represented by such writers as Richard Wright, Ralph Ellison and William Burghardt Du Bois—by realists, surrealists, and romantic idealists.

Please understand me. Wright, Ellison and Du Bois are not mendacious men, and they are doing what writers must always do. They are telling the truth as they see it, which happens to be largely what it is, and they are producing from the examined, or at least the observed causes, the predictable effects; and no one should blame them if the impression they give of the American situation is deplorable. They have been blamed, you know. But let those who blame these writers blame themselves for forgetting that fiction is fiction, and that no novel can pretend to be an exact photographic copy of a country or of the people in a country.

Moreover, dishonor, bigotry, hatred, degradation, injustice, arrogance and obscenity do flourish in American life, and especially in the prescribed and proscriptive American Negro life; and it is the right and the duty of the Negro writer to say so—to complain. He has cause. The temptation of the moral enthusiast is not only strong in him; it is inevitable. He never suspends social and moral judgment. Few actions and events that touch him as a man fail to set in motion his machinery as an artist. History is as personal to him as the woman he loves; and he is caught in the flux of its events, the currents of its opinion and the tides of its emotion; and he believes that the mood is weak which tolerates an impartial presentment of these, and that this weak mood cannot be indulged in a world where the consequences of the actions of a few men produce insupportable calamities for millions of humble folk. He is one of the humble folk. He forages in the cause of righteousness. He forgets that he is also one of Apollo's company.

On the one hand, the jungle; on the other, the resourceful hunter to clear it. The jungle, where lurk the beasts, nourishes the hunter. It is there that he has that sum of relationships that make him what he is. It is where he lives. It is precisely because the jungle is there and is terrible and dangerous that the Negro writer writes and lives at all.

But first, I suppose you must grant me, if only for the sake of this brief exposition, that the American Negro writer is not just an American with a dark skin. If he were, I take it, the theme of this conference would be mighty silly and the conference itself superfluous. This granted, you want to know what the frame of reference is, and about this I shall be dogmatic.

Neither the simplest nor the subtlest scrutiny reveals to an honest man that he has two utterly diverse kinds of experience, that of sense data and that of purpose. Psychology seems to have no difficulty establishing the natural gradation of impulse to purpose. In varying degrees, all our experiences are complications of physical processes.

Shifting from the dogmatic to the apologetic, I must eliminate from view a period of nearly three hundred years from 1619 to 1900. It was the period that saw the solid establishment here in America of a tradition of race relations and of the concepts that supported the tradition. It was a period that need not be rehearsed. Within the frame of reference thus established, let us look at a certain chain of events.

In 1902 came Thomas Dixon's *The Leopard's Spots*, and three years later *The Clansman*. Both were tremendously popular, and both were included in the repertoires of traveling theatrical companies; and I think it is significant—though we will only imply how—that even a colored company, The Lafayette Players, undertook an adaptation of *The Leopard's Spots*. In 1903 there was a race riot in New York. In 1906 race riots occurred in Georgia and Texas; in 1908 in Illinois. By this latter year, too, all the Southern states had disfranchised the Negro, and color caste was legalized or had legal status everywhere. The Negro's talent for monkeyshines had been exploited on the stage, and some of the music that accompanied the monkeyshines was created by James Weldon Johnson and his brother Rosamond. Meantime, in 1904, Thomas Nelson Page had written the one true canonical book of the law and the prophets, *The Negro, The Southerner's Problem*. And, most cogent fact of all, Booker Washington, having sworn on this bible of reactionism, had been made the undisputed leader of American Negroes because, as he had pledged to do, he advocated a race policy strictly in line with the tradition and the supporting concepts of race relations.

If there had been a time when this tradition seemed to promise the Negro a way out, that time was not now. He had been laughed at, tolerated, amusingly despaired of, but all his own efforts were vain. All the instruments of social progress—schools, churches, lodges —adopted by colored people were the subjects of ribald jokes and derisive laughter. "Mandy, has you studied you' Greek?" "I's sewing, Ma." "Go naked, Gal. Git Dat Greek!"

Any objective judgment of Booker Washington's basic notion must be that it was an extension of the old tradition framed in new terms. Under the impact of social change, the concept was modified to include the stereotype of the Negro as a happy peasant, a docile and satisfied laborer under the stern but kindly eye of the white boss, a creature who had a place and knew it and loved it and would keep it unless he got bad notions from somewhere. The once merely laughable coon had become now also the cheap farm grub or city laborer who could be righteously exploited for his own good and for the greater glory of America. By this addition to the concept, the Negro-white status quo, the condition of inferior-superior race and caste could be maintained in the face of profound changes in the general society.

What this meant to the Negro writer was that he must, if he wished an audience, adhere to the old forms and the acceptable patterns. It meant that he must create within the limitations of the concept, or that he must dissemble completely, or that he must ignore his racial kinship altogether and leave unsounded the profoundest depths of the peculiar experiences which were his by reason of that kinship. Some chose the first course; at least one—Dunbar—chose the second (as witness his sickly, sticky novels of white love life and his sad epithalamium to death); and a good many chose the third: Braithwaite's anthologies of magazine verse, James Weldon Johnson's contributions to the *Century Magazine*, and the writing of Alice Dunbar, Anne Spenser, and Angelina Grimke.

But given the whole web of circumstances—empirical, historic, psychological—these writers must have realized that they could not go on and that the damps and fevers, chills and blights, terrors and dangers of the jungle could not be ignored. They must have realized that with a full tide of race-consciousness bearing in upon them, they could not go on forever denying their racehood and that to try to do this at all was a symptom of psychotic strain. Rather perish now than escape only to die of slow starvation.

What had happened was that Booker Washington, with the help of the historic situation and the old concepts, had so thoroughly captured the minds of white people that his was the only Negro voice that could be heard in the jungle. Negro schools needing help could get it only through Booker Washington. Negro social thought wanting a sounding board could have it only on Washington's say-so. Negro political action was weak and ineffective without his strength. Many Negro writers fell silent, and for the writer, silence is death.

Many, not but all. There were stubborn souls and courageous, and the frankly mad among them. There was the Boston *Guardian*, and the Chicago *Defender*, and the Atlanta University Pamphlets, and *The Souls of Black Folk*, and finally the *Crisis;* and this latter quickly developed a voice of multi-range and many tones. It roared like a lion and cooed like a dove and screamed like a monkey and laughed like a hyena. And always it protested. Always the sounds it made were the sounds of revolt in the jungle, and protestation and revolt were becoming—forgive me for changing my figure—powerful reagents in the social chemistry that produced the "new" Negro.

Other factors contributed to this generation too. The breath of
academic scholarship was just beginning to blow hot and steadily
enough to wither some of the myths about the Negro. The changes
occurring with the onset of war in Europe sloughed off other emotional and intellectual accretions. The Negro might be a creature of
"moral debate," but he was also something more. "I ain't a problem,"
a Negro character was made to say, "I's a person." And that person
turned out to be a seeker after the realities in the American dream.
When he was called upon to protect that dream with his blood, he
asked questions and demanded answers. Whose dream was he protecting, he wanted to know, and why and wherefore? There followed such promises as only the less scrupulous politicians had made
to him before. Then came the fighting and the dying, and finally
came a thing called peace.

By this time, the Negro was already stirring massively along
many fronts. He cracked Broadway wide open. The Garvey movements swept the country like wildfire. *Harlem Shadows*, *The Gift of
Black Folk*, *Color*, *Fire in the Flint*, *The Autobiography of an Ex-
coloured Man*. The writers of these and other works were declared
to be irresponsible. A polemical offensive was launched against them,
and against such non-artist writers as Philip Randolph, Theophilus
Lewis, William Patterson, Angelo Herndon. They were accused of
negativism; they were called un-American. Cultural nationalism raised
its head and demanded that literature be patriotic, optimistic, positive,
uncritical, like *Americans All*, and *American Ideals*, and *America Is
Promises*, and *It Takes a Heap O'Living*, which were all written and
published in the period of which I speak. But democracy encourages
criticism, and it is true that even negative criticism implies certain
positive values like veracity, for instance, and these Negro writers had
positive allegiances. Their sensibilities were violently irritated, but
their faith and imaginations were wonderfully nourished by the very
environment which they saw to be and depicted as being bad.

Fortunately there was more than faith and fat imagination in
some of these works. There was also talent. Had this not been so,
Negro writing would have come to nothing for perhaps another
quarter century, for the ground would not have been plowed for the
seeds of later talents. But DuBois, Johnson, McKay, Fisher, Cullen,
Hughes knew what they were about. Their work considerably
furthered the interest of white writers and critics. Whatever else
O'Neill, Rosenfeld, Connelly, Calverton and Heyward did, they gave

validity to the notion that the Negro was material for serious literary treatment.

Beginning then and continuing into the forties, Negro writing had two distinct aspects. The first of these was arty, self-conscious, somewhat precious, experimental, and not truly concerned with the condition of man. Some of the "little reviews" printed a lot of non-sense by Negro writers, including the first chapter of a novel which was to be entirely constructed of elliptical sentences. Then there was *Cane:* sensibility, inwardness, but much of it for the purpose of being absorbed into the universal oneness. Nirvana. Oblivion. Transcend-ence over one's own personality through the practice of art for art's sake. The appropriate way of feeling and thinking growing out of a particular system of living. And so eventually Gurdjieff.

But the second aspect was more important. The pathos of man is that he hungers for personal fulfillment and for a sense of com-munity with others. And these writers hungered. There is no Ameri-can national character. There is only an American situation, and within this situation these writers sought to find themselves. They had always been alienated, not only because they were Negroes, but because democracy in America decisively separates the intel-lectual from everyone else. The intellectual in America is a radi-cally alienated personality, the Negro in common with the white, and both were hungry and seeking, and some of the best of both found food and an identity in communism. But the identity was only partial and, the way things turned out, further emphasized their alienation. So—at least for the Negro writers among them—back into the American situation, the jungle where they could find themselves. A reflex of the natural gradation of impulse to purpose.

Surely this is the meaning of *Native Son.* "Bigger Thomas was not black all the time," his creator says. "He was white too, and there were literally millions of him. . . . Modern experiences were creating types of personalities whose existence ignored racial . . . lines." Iden-tity. Community. Surely this is the meaning of *Invisible Man* and the poignant, pain-filled, pain-relieving humor of simple Jesse B. It is the meaning of *Go Tell It on the Mountain,* and it is explicitly the mean-ing of four brilliant essays in part three of a little book of essays called *Notes of a Native Son.* (How often that word "native" ap-pears, and how meaningful its implications!) Let me quote a short, concluding passage from one of these essays.

"Since I no longer felt that I could stay in this cell forever, I was

beginning to be able to make peace with it for a time. On the 27th
. . . I went again to trial . . . and the case . . . was dismissed. The story
of the *Drap De Lit*, . . . caused great merriment in the courtroom. . . .
I was chilled by their merriment, even though it was meant to warm
me. It could only remind me of the laughter of those who consider
themselves to be at a safe remove from all the wretched, for whom
the pain of living is not real. I had heard it so often in my native land
that I had resolved to find a place where I would never hear it anymore. In some deep, black, stony and liberating way, my life, in my
own eyes, began during that first year in Paris, when it was borne in
on me that this laughter is universal and never can be stilled." Explicit.

The human condition, the discovery of self. Community. Identity. Surely this must be achieved before it can be seen that a particular identity has a relation to a common identity, commonly described as human. This is the ultimate that the honest writer seeks. He
knows that the dilemmas, the perils, the likelihood of catastrophe in
the human situation are real and that they have to do not only with
whether men understand each other but with the quality of man
himself. The writer's ultimate purpose is to use his gifts to develop
man's awareness of himself so that he, man, can become a better instrument for living together with other men. This sense of identity is
the root by which all honest creative effort is fed, and the writer's
relation to it is the relation of the infant to the breast of the mother.

ROBERT HAYDEN
(1913-1980)

Robert Hayden is one of the most honored black poets of the forties, fifties, and sixties. He was born in Detroit and attended Wayne State University and the University of Michigan. He taught English first at the University of Michigan, then at Fisk University for twenty-two years; he then returned to the University of Michigan.

Hayden is a very deliberate craftsman, skilled in the traditional forms and uses of poetry. His poetry is often weighted with a burden of allusion and reference which many readers find excessive. His poetic gifts were recognized as early as 1938 and 1942, when he received the Avery Hopwood Award for poetry. He received fellowships from the Special Services Committee of Ann Arbor in 1946, the Julius Rosenwald Fund in 1947, and the Ford Foundation in 1954. He has published five volumes of poetry: Heart-Shape in the Dust *(1940),* The Lion and the Archer *(with Myron O'Higgins, 1949),* Figure of Time *(1955),* A Ballad of Remembrance *(1962), and* Selected Poems *(1966). Hayden has edited an anthology,* Kaleidoscope: Poems by American Negro Poets *(1967), and has written a play,* Go Down, Moses. *He has published poetry in* The Atlantic Monthly, Poetry, Cross Section, Phylon, Midwest Journal, *and other periodicals and collections. He supervised research in Negro history and folklore for the Federal Writers Project and has written criticism in music and drama.*

Hayden has objected to the fact that Afro-American poets are considered black poets rather than simply poets. *In* Kaleidoscope, *for example, he asserts that the effect of being labeled a spokesman for one's race places the author in "a kind of literary ghetto where the*

470

standards applied to other writers are not likely to be applied to him, since he . . . is not considered primarily a writer but a species of race-relations man, the leader of a cause, the voice of protest." However, he himself often uses racial themes; in some of his best poems he has woven black history, folklore, heroes, and experiences into beautiful, highly artistic creations.

Middle Passage

Jesús, Estrella, Esperanza, Mercy:

Sails flashing to the wind like weapons,
sharks following the moans the fever and the dying;
horror the corposant and compass rose.

Middle Passage:
      voyage through death
          to life upon these shores.

"10 April 1800—
Blacks rebellious. Crew uneasy. Our linguist says
their moaning is a prayer for death,
ours and their own. Some try to starve themselves.
Lost three this morning leaped with crazy laughter
to the waiting sharks, sang as they went under."

Desire, Adventure, Tartar, Ann:

Standing to America, bringing home
black gold, black ivory, black seed.

    Deep in the festering hold thy father lies,
    of his bones New England pews are made,
    those are altar lights that were his eyes.

Jesus Saviour Pilot Me
Over Life's Tempestuous Sea

We pray that Thou wilt grant, O Lord,
safe passage to our vessels bringing
heathen souls unto Thy chastening.

Jesus Saviour

"8 bells. I cannot sleep, for I am sick
with fear, but writing eases fear a little
since still my eyes can see these words take shape
upon the page & so I write, as one
would turn to exorcism. 4 days scudding,
but now the sea is calm again. Misfortune
follows in our wake like sharks (our grinning
tutelary gods). Which one of us
has killed an albatross? A plague among
our blacks—Ophthalmia: blindness—& we
have jettisoned the blind to no avail.
It spreads, the terrifying sickness spreads.
Its claws have scratched sight from the Capt.'s eyes
& there is blindness in the fo'c'sle
& we must sail 3 weeks before we come
to port."

What port awaits us, Davy Jones'
or home? I've heard of slavers drifting, drifting,
playthings of wind and storm and chance, their crews
gone blind, the jungle hatred
crawling up on deck.

Thou Who Walked On Galilee

"Deponent further sayeth The Bella J
left the Guinea Coast
with cargo of five hundred blacks and odd
for the barracoons of Florida:

"That there was hardly room 'tween-decks for half
the sweltering cattle stowed spoon-fashion there;
that some went mad of thirst and tore their flesh
and sucked the blood:

"That Crew and Captain lusted with the comeliest
of the savage girls kept naked in the cabins;
that there was one they called The Guinea Rose
and they cast lots and fought to lie with her:

"That when the Bo's'n piped all hands, the flames
spreading from starboard already were beyond
control, the negroes howling and their chains
entangled with the flames:

"That the burning blacks could not be reached,
that the Crew abandoned ship,
leaving their shrieking negresses behind,
that the Captain perished drunken with the wenches:

"Further Deponent sayeth not."

Pilot Oh Pilot Me

II.

Aye, lad, and I have seen those factories,
Gambia, Rio Pongo, Calabar;
have watched the artful mongos baiting traps
of war wherein the victor and the vanquished

Were caught as prizes for our barracoons.
Have seen the nigger kings whose vanity
and greed turned wild black hides of Fellatah,
Mandingo, Ibo, Kru to gold for us.

And there was one—King Anthracite we named him—
fetish face beneath French parasols
of brass and orange velvet, impudent mouth
whose cups were carven skulls of enemies:

He'd honor us with drum and feast and conjo
and palm-oil glistening wenches deft in love,
and for tin crowns that shone with paste,
red calico and German-silver trinkets

Would have the drums talk war and send
his warriors to burn the sleeping villages
and kill the sick and old and lead the young
in coffles to our factories.

Twenty years a trader, twenty years,
for there was wealth aplenty to be harvested
from those black fields, and I'd be trading still
but for the fevers melting down my bones.

III.

Shuttles in the rocking loom of history,
the dark ships move, the dark ships move,
their bright ironical names
like jests of kindness on a murderer's mouth;
plough through thrashing glister toward
fata morgana's lucent melting shore,
weave toward New World littorals that are
mirage and myth and actual shore.

Voyage through death,
        voyage whose chartings are unlove.

A charnel stench, effluvium of living death
spreads outward from the hold,
where the living and the dead, the horribly dying,
lie interlocked, lie foul with blood and excrement.

    Deep in the festering hold thy father lies,
    the corpse of mercy rots with him,
    rats eat love's rotten gelid eyes.

But, oh, the living look at you
with human eyes whose suffering accuses you,
whose hatred reaches through the swill of dark
to strike you like a leper's claw.

You cannot stare that hatred down
or chain the fear that stalks the watches
and breathes on you its fetid scorching breath;
cannot kill the deep immortal human wish,
the timeless will.

"But for the storm that flung up barriers
of wind and wave, *The Amistad*, señores,
would have reached the port of Principe in two,
three days at most; but for the storm we should
have been prepared for what befell.
Swift as the puma's leap it came. There was
that interval of moonless calm filled only
with the water's and the rigging's usual sounds,
then sudden movement, blows and snarling cries
and they had fallen on us with machete
and marlinspike. It was as though the very
air, the night itself were striking us.
Exhausted by the rigors of the storm,
we were no match for them. Our men went down
before the murderous Africans. Our loyal
Celestino ran from below with gun
and lantern and I saw, before the cane-
knife's wounding flash, Cinquez,
that surly brute who calls himself a prince,
directing, urging on the ghastly work.
He hacked the poor mulatto down, and then
he turned on me. The decks were slippery
when daylight finally came. It sickens me
to think of what I saw, of how these apes
threw overboard the butchered bodies of
our men, true Christians all, like so much jetsam.
Enough, enough. The rest is quickly told:
Cinquez was forced to spare the two of us
you see to steer the ship to Africa.
and we like phantoms doomed to rove the sea

voyaged east by day and west by night,
deceiving them, hoping for rescue,
prisoners on our own vessel, till
at length we drifted to the shores of this
your land, America, where we were freed
from our unspeakable misery. Now we
demand, good sirs, the extradition of
Cinquez and his accomplices to La
Havana. And it distresses us to know
there are so many here who seem inclined
to justify the mutiny of these blacks.
We find it paradoxical indeed
that you whose wealth, whose tree of liberty
are rooted in the labor of your slaves
should suffer the august John Quincy Adams
to speak with so much passion of the right
of chattel slaves to kill their lawful masters
and with his Roman rhetoric weave a hero's
garland for Cinquez. I tell you that
we are determined to return to Cuba
with our slaves and there see justice done. Cinquez—
or let us say 'the Prince'—Cinquez shall die."

The deep immortal human wish,
the timeless will:

    Cinquez its deathless primaveral image,
    life that transfigures many lives.

Voyage through death
        to life upon these shores.

Tour 5

The road winds down through autumn hills
in blazonry of farewell scarlet
and recessional gold,
past cedar groves, through static villages
whose names are all that's left
of Choctaw, Chickasaw.

We stop a moment in a town
watched over by Confederate sentinels,
buy gas and ask directions of a rawboned man
whose eyes revile us as the enemy.

Shrill gorgon silence breathes behind
his taut civility
and in the ever-tautening air,
dark for us despite its Indian summer glow.
We drive on, following the route
of highwaymen and phantoms,

Of slaves and armies.
Children, wordless and remote,
wave at us from kindling porches.
And now the land is flat for miles,
the landscape lush, metallic, flayed,
its brightness harsh as bloodstained swords.

478

Veracruz

I.

Sunday afternoon,
and couples walk the breakwater
heedless of the bickering spray.
Near the shoreward end,
Indian boys idle and fish.
A shawled brown woman
squinting against
the ricocheting brilliance
of sun and water
shades her eyes and gazes
toward the fort,
fossil of Spanish power,
looming in the harbor.

At the seaward end,
a pharos like a temple rises.
From here the shore
seen across marbling waves
is arabesque ornately green
that hides the inward-falling slum,
the stains and dirty tools of struggle;
appears a destination dreamed of,
never to be reached.

Here only the sea is real—
the barbarous multifoliate sea
with its rustling of leaves,
fire, garments, wind;
its clashing of phantasmal jewels,
its lunar thunder,
animal and human sighing.

Leap now
and cease from error.
Escape. Or shoreward turn,
accepting all—
the losses and farewells,
the long warfare with self,
with God.

The waves roar in and break
roar in and break
with granite spreeing hiss
on bronzegreen rocks below
and glistering upfling of spray.

II.
Thus reality
    bedizened in the warring colors
        of a dream
parades through these
    arcades ornate with music and
        the sea.

Thus reality
    become unbearably a dream
        beckons
out of reach in flyblown streets
    of lapsing rose and purple, dying
        blue.

Thus marimba'd night
    and multifoliate sea become
    phantasmal
space, and there,
    light-years away, one farewell image
        burns and fades and burns.

The Diver

Sank through easeful
azure. Flower
creatures flashed and
shimmered there—
lost images
fadingly remembered.
Swiftly descended
into canyon of cold
nightgreen emptiness.
Freefalling, weightless
as in dreams of
wingless flight,
plunged through infra-
space and came to
the dead ship,
carcass that swarmed with
voracious life.
Angelfish, their
lively blue and

yellow prised from
darkness by the
flashlight's beam,
thronged her portholes.
Moss of bryozoans
blurred, obscured her
metal. Snappers,
gold groupers explored her,
fearless of bubbling
manfish. I entered
the wreck, awed by her silence,
feeling more keenly
the iron cold.
With flashlight probing
fogs of water
saw the sad slow
dance of gilded
chairs, the ectoplasmic
swirl of garments,
drowned instruments
of buoyancy,
drunken shoes. Then
livid gesturings,
eldritch hide and
seek of laughing
faces. I yearned to
find those hidden
ones, to fling aside
the mask and call to them,
yield to rapturous
whisperings, have
down with self and
every dinning
vain complexity.
Yet in languid
frenzy strove, as
one freezing fights off
sleep desiring sleep;
strove against the
cancelling arms that
suddenly surrounded

me, fled the numbing
kisses that I craved.
Reflex of life-wish?
Respirator's brittle
belling? Swam from
the ship somehow;
somehow began the
measured rise.

GWENDOLYN BROOKS

(b. 1917)

For three decades Gwendolyn Brooks has captured the surges of her time in moving and excellent poetry. She has received many awards and is currently Poet Laureate of Illinois. Equally important, she has played a vital part in encouraging young black people to fine literary expressioin. In her own poetry she has revealed in the tempo of black urban life the quest for meaning and truth.

Gwendolyn Brooks was born in Topeka, Kansas, and reared in Chicago, where she still lives and works. She wrote her first poem at the age of seven and began publishing poetry at thirteen.

In 1945 she published her first volume, A Street in Bronzeville, *which views black American life (and all human life) through the sensibilities of a perceptive black woman. For this volume she received enthusiastic praise from critics, an award from the American Academy of Arts and Letters, and a two-year Guggenheim Fellowship. In 1949 she published her second volume of poetry,* Annie Allen, *the theme of which is the growth and development of a young black woman who searches out important truths through her feminine perceptions. This volume received the Pulitzer Prize for Poetry in 1950. Three years later she published her only novel,* Maud Martha, *a delicate and poetic work about a sensitive black girl's growing into maturity. Other volumes of poems followed:* Bronzeville Boys and Girls *(1956) for children,* The Bean Eaters *(1960), and* Selected Poems *(1963).*

In the Mecca (1968) is a long poem which uses the futile search for a murdered ghetto child as a vehicle for a compassionate portrayal of the people who live in a Chicago slum, and for a commentary on their lives. Riot (1969) is the poet's passionate response to the April 1968, riots following Martin Luther King's death.*

sponse to the April, 1968, riots following Martin Luther King's death.

With Riot *Brooks made in her poetry a conscious break with the earlier "conditioned" work in which she attempted to explain her selfhood to a hostile white world. The autobiographical* Report From Part I *(1972) gives us a portrait of the poet growing to maturity. Brooks has been extremely active in encouraging young writers, particularly poets.*

She is the subject of numerous critical essays and studies, including a major book-length one by critic George Kent.

Piano After War

On a snug evening I shall watch her fingers,
Cleverly ringed, declining to clever pink,
Beg glory from the willing keys. Old hungers
Will break their coffins, rise to eat and thank.
And music, warily, like the golden rose
That sometimes after sunset warms the west,
Will warm that room, persuasively suffuse
That room and me, rejuvenate a past.
But suddenly, across my climbing fever
Of proud delight—a multiplying cry.
A cry of bitter dead men who will never
Attend a gentle maker of musical joy.
Then my thawed eye will go again to ice.
And stone will shove the softness from my face.

Mentors

For I am rightful fellow of their band.
My best allegiances are to the dead.
I swear to keep the dead upon my mind,
Disdain for all time to be overglad.
Among spring flowers, under summer trees,
By chilling autumn waters, in the frosts
Of supercilious winter—all my days
I'll have as mentors those reproving ghosts.
And at that cry, at that remotest whisper,
I'll stop my casual business. Leave the banquet.
Or leave the ball—reluctant to unclasp her
Who may be fragrant as the flower she wears,
Make gallant bows and dim excuses, then quit
Light for the midnight that is mine and theirs.

The Mother

Abortions will not let you forget.
You remember the children you got that you did not get,
The damp small pulps with a little or with no hair,
The singers and workers that never handled the air.
You will never neglect or beat
Them, or silence or buy with a sweet.
You will never wind up the sucking-thumb
Or scuttle off ghosts that come.
You will never leave them, controlling your luscious sigh,
Return for a snack of them, with gobbling mother-eye.

I have heard in the voices of the wind the voices of my dim killed
    children.
I have contracted. I have eased
My dim dears at the breasts they could never suck.
I have said, Sweets, if I sinned, if I seized
Your luck
And your lives from your unfinished reach,
If I stole your births and your names,
Your straight baby tears and your games,
Your stilted or lovely loves, your tumults, your marriages, aches,
    and your deaths,
If I poisoned the beginnings of your breaths,
Believe that even in my deliberateness I was not deliberate.
Though why should I whine,
Whine that the crime was other than mine?—
Since anyhow you are dead.

Or rather, or instead,
You were never made.
But that too, I am afraid,
Is faulty: oh, what shall I say, how is the truth to be said?
You were born, you had body, you died.
It is just that you never giggled or planned or cried.

Believe me, I love you all.
Believe me, I knew you, though faintly, and I loved, I loved you
All.

We Real Cool

THE POOL PLAYERS
SEVEN AT THE GOLDEN SHOVEL.

We real cool. We
Left school. We

Lurk late. We
Strike straight. We

Sing sin. We
Thin gin. We

Jazz June. We
Die soon.

The Chicago Defender Sends a Man to Little Rock

FALL, 1957

In Little Rock the people bear
Babes, and comb and part their hair
And watch the want ads, put repair
To roof and latch. While wheat toast burns
A woman waters multiferns.

Time upholds or overturns
The many, tight, and small concerns.

In Little Rock the people sing
Sunday hymns like anything,
Through Sunday pomp and polishing.

And after testament and tunes,
Some soften Sunday afternoons
With lemon tea and Lorna Doones.

I forecast
And I believe

Come Christmas Little Rock will cleave
To Christmas tree and trifle, weave,
From laugh and tinsel, texture fast.

In Little Rock is baseball; Barcarolle.
That hotness in July . . . the uniformed figures raw and
    implacable
And not intellectual,
Batting the hotness or clawing the suffering dust.
The Open Air Concert, on the special twilight green. . . .
When Beethoven is brutal or whispers to lady-like air.
Blanket-sitters are solemn, as Johann troubles to lean
To tell them what to mean. . . .

There is love, too, in Little Rock. Soft women softly
Opening themselves in kindness,
Or, pitying one's blindness,
Awaiting one's pleasure
In azure
Glory with anguished rose at the root. . . .
To wash away old semi-discomfitures.
They re-teach purple and unsullen blue.
The wispy soils go. And uncertain
Half-havings have they clarified to sures.

In Little Rock they know
Not answering the telephone is a way of rejecting life,
That it is our business to be bothered, is our business
To cherish bores or boredom, be polite
To lies and love and many-faceted fuzziness.
I scratch my head, massage the hate-I-had.
I blink across my prim and pencilled pad.
The saga I was sent for is not down.
Because there is a puzzle in this town.
The biggest News I do not dare
Telegraph to the Editor's chair:
"They are like people everywhere."

The angry Editor would reply
In hundred harryings of Why.

And true, they are hurling spittle, rock,
Garbage and fruit in Little Rock.
And I saw coiling storm a-writhe
On bright madonnas. And a scythe
Of men harassing brownish girls.
(The bows and barrettes in the cirls
And braids declined away from joy.)

I saw a bleeding brownish boy. . . .

The lariat lynch-wish I deplored.

The loveliest lynchee was our Lord.

Life for My Child Is Simple

Life for my child is simple, and is good
He knows his wish. Yes, but that is not all.
Because I know mine too.
And we both want joy of undeep and unabiding things,
Like kicking over a chair or throwing blocks out of a window
Or tipping over an icebox pan
Or snatching down curtains or fingering an electric outlet
Or a journey or a friend or an illegal kiss.
No. There is more to it than that.
It is that he has never been afraid.
Rather, he reaches out and lo the chair falls with a beautiful crash,
And the blocks fall, down on the people's heads,
And the water comes slooshing sloppily out across the floor.
And so forth.

Not that success, for him, is sure, infallible.
But never has he been afraid to reach.
His lesions are legion.
But reaching is his rule.

Takes Time
From *In the Mecca*

"Takes time," grated the gradualist.
"Starting from when?" asked Amos.
Amos (not Alfred) says,
"Shall we sit on ourselves; shall we wait behind roses and veils
for monsters to maul us,
    for bulls to come butt us forever and ever,
shall we scratch in our blood,
    point air-powered hands at our wounds,
reflect on the aim of our bulls?" And Amos
(not Alfred) prays, for America prays:

"Bathe her in her beautiful blood.
A long blood bath will wash her pure.
Her skin needs special care.
Let this good rage continue out beyond
her power to believe or to surmise.
Slap the false sweetness from that face.
Great-nailed boots
must kick her prostrate, heel-grind that soft breast,
outrage her saucy pride,
remove her fair fine mask.

Let her lie there, panting and wild, her pain
red, running roughly through the illustrious ruin—
with nothing to do but think, think
of how she was so long grand,
flogging her dark one with her own hand,
watching in meek amusement while he bled.
Then shall she rise, recover.
Never to forget."

An Aspect of Love, Alive in the Ice and Fire
From *Riot*

LA BOHEM BROWN

It is the morning of our love.

In a package of minutes there is this We.
How beautiful.
Merry foreigners in our morning,
we laugh, we touch each other,
are responsible props and posts.

A physical light is in the room.

Because the world is at the window
we cannot wonder very long.

You rise. Although
genial, you are in yourself again.
I observe
your direct and respectable stride.
You are direct and self-accepting as a lion
in African velvet. You are level, lean,
remote.

There is a moment in Camaraderie
when interruption is not to be understood.
I cannot bear an interruption.
This is the shining joy;
the time of not-to-end.

On the street we smile.
We go
in different directions
down the imperturbable street.

RALPH ELLISON

(b. 1914)

American literature was considerably enriched in 1952 by the publication of Ellison's novel Invisible Man. *Many years in the making, the novel propelled its author into the first rank of American writers.*

Ralph Ellison was born in Oklahoma City. He entered Tuskegee Institute in 1933 to study music, expecting to become a composer. However, in the summer of his junior year he left school to go to New York to seek employment and to study sculpture. He never returned to Tuskegee.

In New York, Ellison met Richard Wright and witnessed the creation of Native Son. *Wright introduced him to the works of classic European novelists and encouraged him to learn the exacting craft of writing. Ellison began his writing career with a book review and several stories. In 1952 he published* Invisible Man *and immediately became a celebrity. The novel received the National Book Award in 1952, and in 1964 it was named by two hundred writers and critics as "the most distinguished single work in the last twenty years." Since the publication of* Invisible Man, *Ellison has written a number of stories and essays. Some of his essays were collected in* Shadow and Act *in 1964.*

Invisible Man *reveals Ellison's virtuosity as a literary artist. His style is rich in a symbolism the complexity of which permits various levels of interpretation. The novel uses black folk culture to develop the theme of the search for identity.*

Ellison's literary stature and career have been, to an extent, unparalleled in modern letters, based upon a single novel and the amplifications he and others have made of its meanings and resources. Certainly the initial impact of the work has been sustained and Ellison has, in consequence, been the subject of countless analyses and studies. His work has been included in every major survey of American fiction, and no listing of the major novelists of the twentieth century can omit his name.

From *Invisible Man*

CHAPTER 1

It goes a long way back, some twenty years. All my life I had been looking for something, and everywhere I turned someone tried to tell me what it was. I accepted their answers too, though they were often in contradiction and even self-contradictory. I was naïve. I was looking for myself and asking everyone except myself questions which I, and only I, could answer. It took me a long time and much painful boomeranging of my expectations to achieve a realization everyone else appears to have been born with: That I am nobody but myself. But first I had to discover that I am an invisible man!

And yet I am no freak of nature, nor of history. I was in the cards, other things having been equal (or unequal) eighty-five years ago. I am not ashamed of my grandparents for having been slaves. I am only ashamed of myself for having at one time been ashamed. About eighty-five years ago they were told that they were free, united with others of our country in everything pertaining to the common good, and, in everything social, separate like the fingers of the hand. And they believed it. They exulted in it. They stayed in their place, worked hard, and brought up my father to do the same. But my grandfather is the one. He was an odd old guy, my grand-father, and I am told I take after him. It was he who caused the trouble. On his deathbed he called my father to him and said, "Son, after I'm gone I want you to keep up the good fight. I never told you, but our life is a war and I have been a traitor all my born days, a spy in the enemy's country ever since I give up my gun back in the Reconstruction. Live with your head in the lion's mouth. I want you to overcome 'em with yeses, undermine 'em with grins, agree 'em to death and destruction, let 'em swoller you till they vomit or bust wide open." They thought the old man had gone out of his mind. He had been the meekest of men. The younger children were rushed from the room, the shades drawn and the flame of the lamp turned so low that it sputtered on the wick like the old man's breathing. "Learn it to the younguns," he whispered fiercely; then he died.

But my folks were more alarmed over his last words than over his dying. It was as though he had not died at all, his words caused so much anxiety. I was warned emphatically to forget what he had said and, indeed, this is the first time it has been mentioned outside the family circle. It had a tremendous effect upon me, however. I could never be sure of what he meant. Grandfather had been a quiet old man who never made any trouble, yet on his deathbed he had called himself a traitor and a spy, and he had spoken of his meekness as a dangerous activity. It became a constant puzzle which lay unanswered in the back of my mind. And whenever things went well for me I remembered my grandfather and felt guilty and uncomfortable. It was as though I was carrying out his advice in spite of myself. And to make it worse, everyone loved me for it. I was praised by the most lily-white men of the town. I was considered an example of desirable conduct—just as my grandfather had been. And what puzzled me was that the old man had defined it as *treachery*. When I was praised for my conduct I felt a guilt that in some ways I was doing something that was really against the wishes of the white folks, that if they had understood they would have desired me to act just the opposite, that I should have been sulky and mean, and that that really would have been what they wanted, even though they were fooled and thought they wanted me to act as I did. It made me afraid that some day they would look upon me as a traitor and I would be lost. Still I was more afraid to act any other way because they didn't like that at all. The old man's words were like a curse. On my graduation day I delivered an oration in which I showed that humility was the secret, indeed, the very essence of progress. (Not that I believed this—how could I, remembering my grandfather?—I only believed that it worked.) It was a great success. Everyone praised me and I was invited to give the speech at a gathering of the town's leading white citizens. It was a triumph for our whole community.

It was in the main ballroom of the leading hotel. When I got there I discovered that it was on the occasion of a smoker, and I was told that since I was to be there anyway I might as well take part in the battle royal to be fought by some of my schoolmates as part of the entertainment. The battle royal came first.

All of the town's big shots were there in their tuxedoes, wolfing down the buffet foods, drinking beer and whiskey and smoking black cigars. It was a large room with a high ceiling. Chairs were arranged in neat rows around three sides of a portable boxing ring. The fourth side was clear, revealing a gleaming space of polished floor. I had some misgivings over the battle royal, by the way. Not from a distaste for fighting, but because I didn't care too much for the other fellows who were to take part. They were tough guys who seemed to have no grandfather's curse worrying their minds. No one could mistake their toughness. And besides, I suspected that fighting a battle royal might detract from the dignity of my speech. In those pre-invisible days I visualized myself as a potential Booker T. Washington. But the other fellows didn't care too much for me either, and there were nine of them. I felt superior to them in my way, and I didn't like the manner in which we were all crowded together into the servants' elevator. Nor did they like my being there. In fact, as the warmly lighted floors flashed past the elevator we had words over the fact that I, by taking part in the fight, had knocked one of their friends out of a night's work.

We were led out of the elevator through a rococo hall into an anteroom and told to get into our fighting togs. Each of us was issued a pair of boxing gloves and ushered out into the big mirrored hall, which we entered looking cautiously about us and whispering, lest we might accidentally be heard above the noise of the room. It was foggy with cigar smoke. And already the whiskey was taking effect. I was shocked to see some of the most important men of the town quite tipsy. They were all there—bankers, lawyers, judges, doctors, fire chiefs, teachers, merchants. Even one of the more fashionable pastors. Something we could not see was going on up front. A clarinet was vibrating sensuously and the men were standing up and moving eagerly forward. We were a small tight group, clustered together, our bare upper bodies touching and shining with anticipatory sweat; while up front the big shots were becoming increasingly excited over something we still could not see. Suddenly I heard the school superintendent, who had told me to come, yell, "Bring up the shines, gentlemen! Bring up the little shines!"

We were rushed up to the front of the ballroom, where it smelled even more strongly of tobacco and whiskey. Then we were pushed into place. I almost wet my pants. A sea of faces, some hostile, some amused, ringed around us, and in the center, facing us, stood a magnificent blonde—stark naked. There was dead silence. I felt a blast of cold air chill me. I tried to back away, but they were behind me and around me. Some of the boys stood with lowered heads, trembling. I felt a wave of irrational guilt and fear. My teeth chattered, my skin turned to goose flesh, my knees knocked. Yet I was strongly attracted and looked in spite of myself. Had the price of looking been blindness, I would have looked. The hair was yellow like that of a circus kewpie doll, the face heavily powdered and rouged, as though to form an abstract mask, the eyes hollow and smeared a cool blue, the color of a baboon's butt. I felt a desire to spit upon her as my eyes brushed slowly over her body. Her breasts were firm and round as the domes of East Indian temples, and I stood so close as to see the fine skin texture and beads of pearly perspiration glistening like dew around the pink and erected buds of her nipples. I wanted at one and the same time to run from the room, to sink through the floor, or go to her and cover her from my eyes and the eyes of the others with my body; to feel the soft thighs, to caress her and destroy her, to love her and murder her, to hide from her, and yet to stroke where below the small American flag tattooed upon her belly her thighs formed a capital V. I had a notion that of all in the room she saw only me with her impersonal eyes.

And then she began to dance, a slow sensuous movement; the smoke of a hundred cigars clinging to her like the thinnest of veils. She seemed like a fair bird-girl girdled in veils calling to me from the angry surface of some gray and threatening sea. I was transported. Then I became aware of the clarinet playing and the big shots yelling at us. Some threatened us if we looked and others if we did not. On my right I saw one boy faint. And now a man grabbed a silver pitcher from a table and stepped close as he dashed ice water upon him and stood him up and forced two of us to support him as his head hung and moans issued from his thick bluish lips. Another boy began to plead to go home. He was the largest of the group, wearing dark red fighting trunks much too small to conceal the erection which projected from him as though in answer to the insinuating low-registered moaning of the clarinet. He tried to hide himself with his boxing gloves.

And all the while the blonde continued dancing, smiling faintly at the big shots who watched her with fascination, and faintly smiling at our fear. I noticed a certain merchant who followed her hungrily, his lips loose and drooling. He was a large man who wore diamond studs in a shirtfront which swelled with the ample paunch underneath, and each time the blonde swayed her undulating hips he ran his hand through the thin hair of his bald head and, with his arms upheld, his posture clumsy like that of an intoxicated panda, wound his belly in a slow and obscene grind. This creature was completely hypnotized. The music had quickened. As the dancer flung herself about with a detached expression on her face, the men began reaching out to touch her. I could see their beefy fingers sink into the soft flesh. Some of the others tried to stop them and she began to move around the floor in graceful circles, as they gave chase, slipping and sliding over the polished floor. It was mad. Chairs went crashing, drinks were spilt, as they ran laughing and howling after her. They caught her just as she reached a door, raised her from the floor, and tossed her as college boys are tossed at a hazing, and above her red, fixed-smiling lips I saw the terror and disgust in her eyes, almost like my own terror and that which I saw in some of the other boys. As I watched, they tossed her twice and her soft breasts seemed to flatten against the air and her legs flung wildly as she spun. Some of the more sober ones helped her to escape. And I started off the floor, heading for the anteroom with the rest of the boys.

Some were still crying and in hysteria. But as we tried to leave we were stopped and ordered to get into the ring. There was nothing to do but what we were told. All ten of us climbed under the ropes and allowed ourselves to be blindfolded with broad bands of white cloth. One of the men seemed to feel a bit sympathetic and tried to cheer us up as we stood with our backs against the ropes. Some of us tried to grin. "See that boy over there?" one of the men said. "I want you to run across at the bell and give it to him right in the belly. If you don't get him, I'm going to get you. I don't like his looks." Each of us was told the same. The blindfolds were put on. Yet even then I had been going over my speech. In my mind each word was as bright as flame. I felt the cloth pressed into place, and frowned so that it would be loosened when I relaxed.

But now I felt a sudden fit of blind terror. I was unused to darkness. It was as though I had suddenly found myself in a dark room filled with poisonous cottonmouths. I could hear the bleary voices yelling insistently for the battle royal to begin.

"Get going in there!"

"Let me at that big nigger!"

I strained to pick up the school superintendent's voice, as though to squeeze some security out of that slightly more familiar sound.

"Let me at those black sonsabitches!" someone yelled.

"No, Jackson, no!" another voice yelled. "Here, somebody help me hold Jack."

"I want to get at that ginger-colored nigger. Tear him limb from limb," the first voice yelled.

I stood against the ropes trembling. For in those days I was what they called ginger-colored, and he sounded as though he might crunch me between his teeth like a crisp ginger cookie.

Quite a struggle was going on. Chairs were being kicked about and I could hear voices grunting as with a terrific effort. I wanted to see, to see more desperately than ever before. But the blindfold was as tight as a thick skin-puckering scab and when I raised my gloved hands to push the layers of white aside a voice yelled, "Oh, no you don't, black bastard! Leave that alone!"

"Ring the bell before Jackson kills him a coon!" someone boomed in the sudden silence. And I heard the bell clang and the sound of the feet scuffling forward.

A glove smacked against my head. I pivoted, striking out stiffly as someone went past, and felt the jar ripple along the length of my arm to my shoulder. Then it seemed as though all nine of the boys had turned upon me at once. Blows pounded me from all sides while I struck out as best I could. So many blows landed upon me that I wondered if I were not the only blindfolded fighter in the ring, or if the man called Jackson hadn't succeeded in getting me after all.

Blindfolded, I could no longer control my motions. I had no dignity. I stumbled about like a baby or a drunken man. The smoke had become thicker and with each new blow it seemed to sear and further restrict my lungs. My saliva became like hot bitter glue. A glove connected with my head, filling my mouth with warm blood. It was everywhere. I could not tell if the moisture I felt upon my body was sweat or blood. A blow landed hard against the nape of my neck. I felt myself going over, my head hitting the floor. Streaks of blue light filled the black world behind the blindfold. I lay prone, pretending that I was knocked out, but felt myself seized by hands and yanked to my feet. "Get going, black boy! Mix it up!" My arms were like lead, my head smarting from blows. I managed to feel my way to the ropes and held on, trying to catch my breath. A glove landed in my mid-section and I went over again, feeling as though the smoke had become a knife jabbed into my guts. Pushed this way and that by the legs milling around me, I finally pulled erect and discovered that I could see the black, sweat-washed forms weaving in the smoky-blue atmosphere like drunken dancers weaving to the rapid drum-like thuds of blows.

Everyone fought hysterically. It was complete anarchy. Everybody fought everybody else. No group fought together for long. Two, three, four, fought one, then turned to fight each other, were themselves attacked. Blows landed below the belt and in the kidney, with the gloves open as well as closed, and with my eye partly opened now there was not so much terror. I moved carefully, avoiding blows, although not too many to attract attention, fighting from group to group. The boys groped about like blind, cautious crabs crouching to protect their mid-sections, their heads pulled in short against their shoulders, their arms stretched nervously before them, with their fists testing the smoke-filled air like the knobbed feelers of hypersensitive snails. In one corner I glimpsed a boy violently punching the air and heard him scream in pain as he smashed his hand against a ring post. For a second I saw him bent over holding his hand, then going down as a blow caught his unprotected head. I played one group against the other, slipping in and throwing a punch then stepping out of range while pushing the others into the melee to take the blows blindly aimed at me. The smoke was agonizing and there were no rounds, no bells at three minute intervals to relieve our exhaustion. The room spun round me, a swirl of lights, smoke, sweating bodies surrounded by tense white faces. I bled from both nose and mouth, the blood spattering upon my chest.

The men kept yelling, "Slug him, black boy! Knock his guts out!"

"Uppercut him! Kill him! Kill that big boy!"

Taking a fake fall, I saw a boy going down heavily beside me as though we were felled by a single blow, saw a sneaker-clad foot shoot into his groin as the two who had knocked him down stumbled upon him. I rolled out of range, feeling a tinge of nausea.

The harder we fought the more threatening the men became. And yet, I had begun to worry about my speech again. How would it go? Would they recognize my ability? What would they give me?

I was fighting automatically when suddenly I noticed that one after another of the boys was leaving the ring. I was surprised, filled with panic, as though I had been left alone with an unknown danger. Then I understood. The boys had arranged it among themselves. It was the custom for the two men left in the ring to slug it out for the winner's prize. I discovered this too late. When the bell sounded two men in tuxedoes leaped into the ring and removed the blindfold. I found myself facing Tatlock, the biggest of the gang. I felt sick at my stomach. Hardly had the bell stopped ringing in my ears than it clanged again and I saw him moving swiftly toward me. Thinking of nothing else to do I hit him smash on the nose. He kept coming, bringing the rank sharp violence of stale sweat. His face was a black blank of a face, only his eyes alive—with hate of me and aglow with a feverish terror from what had happened to us all. I became anxious. I wanted to deliver my speech and he came at me as though he meant to beat it out of me. I smashed him again and again, taking his blows as they came. Then on a sudden impulse I struck him lightly and as we clinched, I whispered, "Fake like I knocked you out, you can have the prize."

"I'll break your behind," he whispered hoarsely.

"For *them?*"

"For *me*, sonofabitch!"

They were yelling for us to break it up and Tatlock spun me half around with a blow, and as a joggled camera sweeps in a reeling scene, I saw the howling red faces crouching tense beneath the cloud of blue-gray smoke. For a moment the world wavered, unraveled, flowed, then my head cleared and Tatlock bounced before me. That fluttering shadow before my eyes was his jabbing left hand. Then falling forward, my head against his damp shoulder, I whispered,

"I'll make it five dollars more."

"Go to hell!"

But his muscles relaxed a trifle beneath my pressure and I breathed, "Seven?"

"Give it to your ma," he said, ripping me beneath the heart.

And while I still held him I butted him and moved away. I felt myself bombarded with punches. I fought back with hopeless desperation. I wanted to deliver my speech more than anything else in the world, because I felt that only these men could judge my ability, and now this stupid clown was ruining my chances. I began fighting carefully now, moving in to punch him and out again with my greater speed. A lucky blow to his chin and I had him going too— until I heard a loud voice yell, "I got my money on the big boy."

Hearing this, I almost dropped my guard. I was confused: Should I try to win against the voice out there? Would not this go against my speech, and was not this a moment for humility, for nonresistance? A blow to my head as I danced about sent my right eye popping like a jack-in-the-box and settled my dilemma. The room went red as I fell. It was a dream fall, my body languid and fastidious as to where to land, until the floor became impatient and smashed up to meet me.

A moment later I came to. An hypnotic voice said FIVE emphatically. And I lay there, hazily watching a dark red spot of my own blood shaping itself into a butterfly, glistening and soaking into the soiled gray world of the canvas.

When the voice drawled TEN I was lifted up and dragged to a chair. My eye pained and swelled with each throb of my pounding heart and I wondered if now I would be allowed to speak. I was wringing wet, my mouth still bleeding. We were grouped along the wall now. The other boys ignored me as they congratulated Tatlock and speculated as to how much they would be paid. One boy whimpered over his smashed hand. Looking up front, I saw attendants in white jackets rolling the portable ring away and placing a small square rug in the vacant space surrounded by chairs. Perhaps, I thought, I will stand on the rug to deliver my speech.

Then the M.C. called to us, "Come on up here boys and get your money."

We ran forward to where the men laughed and talked in their chairs, waiting. Everyone seemed friendly now.

"There it is on the rug," the man said. I saw the rug covered with coins of all dimensions and a few crumpled bills. But what excited me, scattered here and there, were the gold pieces.

"Boys, it's all yours," the man said. "You get all you grab."

"That's right, Sambo," a blond man said, winking at me confidentially.

I trembled with excitement, forgetting my pain. I would get the gold and the bills, I thought. I would use both hands. I would throw my body against the boys nearest me to block them from the gold.

"Get down around the rug now," the man commanded, "and don't anyone touch it until I give the signal."

"This ought to be good," I heard.

As told, we got around the square rug on our knees. Slowly the man raised his freckled hand as we followed it upward with our eyes.

I heard, "These niggers look like they're about to pray!"

Then, "Ready," the man said. "Go!"

I lunged for a yellow coin lying on the blue design of the carpet, touching it and sending a surprised shriek to join those rising around me. I tried frantically to remove my hand but could not let go. A hot, violent force tore through my body, shaking me like a wet rat. The rug was electrified. The hair bristled up on my head as I shook myself free. My muscles jumped, my nerves jangled, writhed. But I saw that this was not stopping the other boys. Laughing in fear and embarrassment, some were holding back and scooping up the coins knocked off by the contortions of the others. The men roared above us as we struggled.

"Pick it up, goddamnit, pick it up!" someone called like a bass-voiced parrot. "Go on, get it!"

I crawled rapidly around the floor, picking up the coins, trying to avoid the coppers and to get greenbacks and the gold. Ignoring the shock by laughing, as I brushed the coins off quickly, I discovered that I could contain the electricity—a contradiction, but it works. Then the men began to push us onto the rug. Laughing embarrassedly, we struggled out of their hands and kept after the coins. We were all wet and slippery and hard to hold. Suddenly I saw a boy lifted into the air, glistening with sweat like a circus seal, and dropped, his wet back landing flush upon the charged rug, heard him yell and saw him literally dance upon his back, his elbows beating a frenzied tattoo upon the floor, his muscles twitching like the flesh of a horse stung by many flies. When he finally rolled off, his face was gray and no one stopped him when he ran from the floor amid booming laughter.

"Get the money," the M.C. called. "That's good hard American cash!"

And we snatched and grabbed, snatched and grabbed. I was careful not to come too close to the rug now, and when I felt the hot whiskey breath descend upon me like a cloud of foul air I reached out and grabbed the leg of a chair. It was occupied and I held on desperately.

"Leggo, nigger! Leggo!"

The huge face wavered down to mine as he tried to push me free. But my body was slippery and he was too drunk. It was Mr. Colcord, who owned a chain of movie houses and "entertainment palaces." Each time he grabbed me I slipped out of his hands. It became a real struggle. I feared the rug more than I did the drunk, so I held on, surprising myself for a moment by trying to topple *him* upon the rug. It was such an enormous idea that I found myself actually carrying it out. I tried not to be obvious, yet when I grabbed his leg, trying to tumble him out of the chair, he raised up roaring with laughter, and, looking at me with soberness dead in the eye, kicked me viciously in the chest. The chair leg flew out of my hand and I felt myself going and rolled. It was as though I had rolled through a bed of hot coals. It seemed a whole century would pass before I would roll free, a century in which I was seared through the deepest levels of my body to the fearful breath within me and the breath seared and heated to the point of explosion. It'll all be over in a flash, I thought as I rolled clear. It'll all be over in a flash.

But not yet, the men on the other side were waiting, red faces swollen as though from apoplexy as they bent forward in their chairs. Seeing their fingers coming toward me I rolled away as a fumbled football rolls off the receiver's fingertips, back into the coals. That time I luckily sent the rug sliding out of place and heard the coins ringing against the floor and the boys scuffling to pick them up and the M.C. calling, "All right, boys, that's all. Go get dressed and get your money."

I was limp as a dish rag. My back felt as though it had been beaten with wires.

When we had dressed the M.C. came in and gave us each five dollars, except Tatlock. Tatlock, who got ten for being last in the ring. Then he told us to leave. I was not to get a chance to deliver my speech, I thought. I was going out into the dim alley in despair when I was stopped and told to go back. I returned to the ballroom, where the men were pushing back their chairs and gathering in groups to talk.

The M.C. knocked on a table for quiet. "Gentlemen," he said, "we almost forgot an important part of the program. A most serious part, gentlemen. This boy was brought here to deliver a speech which he made at his graduation yesterday . . ."

"Bravo!"

"I'm told that he is the smartest boy we've got out there in Greenwood. I'm told that he knows more big words than a pocket-sized dictionary."

Much applause and laughter.

"So now, gentlemen, I want you to give him your attention."

There was still laughter as I faced them, my mouth dry, my eye throbbing. I began slowly, but evidently my throat was tense, because they began shouting, "Louder! Louder!"

"We of the younger generation extol the wisdom of that great leader and educator," I shouted, "who first spoke these flaming words of wisdom: 'A ship lost at sea for many days suddenly sighted a friendly vessel. From the mast of the unfortunate vessel was seen a signal: "Water, water; we die of thirst!" The answer from the friendly vessel came back: "Cast down your bucket where you are." The captain of the distressed vessel, at last heeding the injunction, cast down his bucket, and it came up full of fresh sparkling water from the mouth of the Amazon River.' And like him I say, and in his words, 'To those of my race who depend upon bettering their condition in a foreign land, or who underestimate the importance of cultivating friendly relations with the Southern white man, who is his next-door neighbor, I would say: "Cast down your bucket where you are"—cast it down in making friends in every manly way of the people of all races by whom we are surrounded . . .' "

I spoke automatically and with such fervor that I did not realize that the men were still talking and laughing until my dry mouth, filling up with blood from the cut, almost strangled me. I coughed, wanting to stop and go to one of the tall brass, sand-filled spittoons to relieve myself, but a few of the men, especially the superintendent, were listening and I was afraid. So I gulped it down, blood, saliva and all, and continued. (What powers of endurance I had during those days! What enthusiasm! What a belief in the rightness of things!) I spoke even louder in spite of the pain. But still they talked and still they laughed, as though deaf with cotton in dirty ears. So I spoke with greater emotional emphasis. I closed my ears and swallowed blood until I was nauseated. The speech seemed a hundred times as long as before, but I could not leave out a single word. All had to be said, each memorized nuance considered, rendered. Nor was that all. Whenever I uttered a word of three or more syllables a group of voices would yell for me to repeat it. I used the phrase "social responsibility" and they yelled:

"What's that word you say, boy?"

"Social responsibility," I said.

"What?"

"Social . . ."

"Louder."

". . . responsibility."

"More!"

"Respon—"

"Repeat!"

"—sibility."

The room filled with the uproar of laughter until, no doubt, distracted by having to gulp down my blood, I made a mistake and yelled a phrase I had often seen denounced in newspaper editorials, heard debated in private.

"Social . . ."

"What?" they yelled.

". . . equality—"

The laughter hung smokelike in the sudden stillness. I opened my eyes, puzzled. Sounds of displeasure filled the room. The M.C. rushed forward. They shouted hostile phrases at me. But I did not understand.

A small dry mustached man in the front row blared out, "Say that slowly, son!"

"What sir?"

"What you just said!"

"Social responsibility, sir," I said.

"You weren't being smart, were you, boy?" he said, not unkindly.

"No, sir!"

"You sure that about 'equality' was a mistake?"

"Oh, yes, sir," I said. "I was swallowing blood."

"Well, you had better speak more slowly so we can understand. We mean to do right by you, but you've got to know your place at all times. All right, now, go on with your speech."

I was afraid. I wanted to leave but I wanted also to speak and I was afraid they'd snatch me down.

"Thank you, sir," I said, beginning where I had left off, and having them ignore me as before.

Yet when I finished there was a thunderous applause. I was surprised to see the superintendent come forth with a package wrapped in white tissue paper, and, gesturing for quiet, address the men.

"Gentlemen, you see that I did not overpraise this boy. He makes a good speech and some day he'll lead his people in the proper paths. And I don't have to tell you that that is important in these days and times. This is a good, smart boy, and so to encourage him in the right direction, in the name of the Board of Education I wish to present him a prize in the form of this . . ."

He paused, removing the tissue paper and revealing a gleaming calfskin brief case.

". . . in the form of this first-class article from Shad Whitmore's shop.

"Boy," he said, addressing me, "take this prize and keep it well. Consider it a badge of office. Prize it. Keep developing as you are and some day it will be filled with important papers that will help shape the destiny of your people."

I was so moved that I could hardly express my thanks. A rope of bloody saliva forming a shape like an undiscovered continent drooled upon the leather and I wiped it quickly away. I felt an importance that I had never dreamed.

"Open it and see what's inside," I was told.

My fingers a-tremble, I complied, smelling the fresh leather and finding an official-looking document inside. It was a scholarship to the state college for Negroes. My eyes filled with tears and I ran awkwardly off the floor.

I was overjoyed; I did not even mind when I discovered that the gold pieces I had scrambled for were brass pocket tokens advertising a certain make of automobile.

When I reached home everyone was excited. Next day the neighbors came to congratulate me. I even felt safe from grandfather, whose deathbed curse usually spoiled my triumphs. I stood beneath his photograph with my brief case in hand and smiled triumphantly into his stolid black peasant's face. It was a face that fascinated me. The eyes seemed to follow everywhere I went.

That night I dreamed I was at a circus with him and that he refused to laugh at the clowns no matter what they did. Then later he told me to open my brief case and read what was inside and I did, finding an official envelope stamped with the state seal; and inside the envelope I found another and another, endlessly, and I thought I would fall of weariness. "Them's years," he said. "Now open that one." And I did and in it I found an engraved document containing a short message in letters of gold. "Read it," my grandfather said. "Out loud."

"To Whom It May Concern," I intoned. "Keep This Nigger-Boy Running."

I awoke with the old man's laughter ringing in my ears.

(It was a dream I was to remember and dream again for many years after. But at that time I had no insight into its meaning. First I had to attend college.)

Brave Words for a Startling Occasion
Address For Presentation Ceremony
National Book Award, 1956

First, as I express my gratitude for this honor which you have bestowed on me, let me say that I take it that you are rewarding my efforts rather than my not quite fully achieved attempt at a major novel. Indeed, if I were asked in all seriousness just what I considered to be the chief significance of *Invisible Man* as a fiction, I would reply: Its experimental attitude, and its attempt to return to the mood of personal moral responsibility for democracy which typified the best of our nineteenth-century fiction. That my first novel should win this most coveted prize must certainly indicate that there is a crisis in the American novel. You as critics have told us so, and current fiction sales would indicate that the reading public agrees. Certainly the younger novelists concur. The explosive nature of events mocks our brightest efforts. And the very "facts" which the naturalists assumed would make us free have lost the power to protect us from despair. Controversy now rages over just what aspects of American experience are suitable for novelistic treatment. The prestige of the theorists of the so-called novel of manners has been challenged. Thus after a long period of stability we find our assumptions concerning the novel being called into question. And though I was only vaguely aware, it was this growing crisis which shaped the writing of *Invisible Man*.

After the usual apprenticeship of imitation and seeking with delight to examine my experience through the discipline of the novel, I became gradually aware that the forms of so many of the works which impressed me were too restricted to contain the experience which I knew. The diversity of American life with its extreme fluidity and openness seemed too vital and alive to be caught for more than the briefest instant in the tight well-made Jamesian novel, which was, for all its artistic perfection, too concerned with "good taste" and stable areas. Nor could I safely use the forms of the "hard-boiled" novel, with its dedication to physical violence, social cynicism and understatement. Understatement depends, after all, upon commonly held assumptions and my minority status rendered all such assumptions questionable. There was also a problem of language, and even dialogue, which, with its hard-boiled stance and its monosyllabic utterance, is one of the shining achievements of twentieth-century American writing. For despite the notion that its rhythms were those of everyday speech, I found that when compared with the rich babel of idiomatic expression around me, a language full of imagery and gesture and rhetorical canniness, it was embarrassingly austere. Our speech I found resounding with an alive language swirling with over three hundred years of American living, a mixture of the folk, the Biblical, the scientific and the political. Slangy in one instance, academic in another, loaded poetically with imagery at one moment, mathematically bare of imagery in the next. As for the rather rigid concepts of reality which informed a number of the works which impressed me and to which I owe a great deal, I was forced to conclude that reality was far more mysterious and uncertain, and more exciting, and still, despite its raw violence and capriciousness, more promising. To attempt to express that American experience which has carried one back and forth and up and down the land and across, and across again the great river, from freight train to Pullman car, from contact with slavery to contact with a world of advanced scholarship, art and science, is simply to burst such neatly understated forms of the novel asunder.

A novel whose range was both broader and deeper was needed. And in my search I found myself turning to our classical nineteenth-century novelists. I felt that except for the work of William Faulkner something vital had gone out of American prose after Mark Twain. I came to believe that the writers of that period took a much greater responsibility for the condition of democracy and, indeed, their works were imaginative projections of the conflicts within the human heart which arose when the sacred principles of the Constitution and the Bill of Rights clashed with the practical exigencies of human greed and fear, hate and love. Naturally I was attracted to these writers as a Negro. Whatever they thought of my people per se, in their imaginative economy the Negro symbolized both the man lowest down and the mysterious, underground aspect of human personality. In a sense the Negro was the gauge of the human condition as it waxed and waned in our democracy. These writers were willing to confront the broad complexities of American life and we are the richer for their having done so.

Thus to see America with an awareness of its rich diversity and its almost magical fluidity and freedom, I was forced to conceive of a novel unburdened by the narrow naturalism which has led, after so many triumphs, to the final and unrelieved despair which marks so much of our current fiction. I was to dream of a prose which was flexible, and swift as American change is swift, confronting the inequalities and brutalities of our society forthrightly, but yet thrusting forth its images of hope, human fraternity and individual self-realization. It would use the richness of our speech, the idiomatic expression and the rhetorical flourishes from past periods which are still alive among us. And despite my personal failures, there must be possible a fiction which, leaving sociology to the scientists, can arrive at the truth about the human condition, here and now, with all the bright magic of a fairy tale.

What has been missing from so much experimental writing has been the passionate will to dominate reality as well as the laws of art. This will is the true source of the experimental attitude. We who struggle with form and with America should remember Eidothea's advice to Menelaus when in the *Odyssey* he and his friends are seeking their way home. She tells him to seize her father, Proteus, and to hold him fast "however he may struggle and fight. He will turn into all sorts of shapes to try you," she says, "into all the creatures that live and move upon the earth, into water, into blazing fire; but you must hold him fast and press him all the harder. When he is himself, and questions you in the same shape that he was when you saw him in his bed, let the old man go; and then, sir, ask which god it is who is angry, and how you shall make your way homewards over the fish-giving sea."

For the novelist, Proteus stands for both America and the inheritance of illusion through which all men must fight to achieve reality; the offended god stands for our sins against those principles we all hold sacred. The way home we seek is that condition of man's being at home in the world, which is called love, and which we term democracy. Our task then is always to challenge the apparent forms of reality—that is, the fixed manners and values of the few, and to struggle with it until it reveals its mad, vari-implicated chaos, its false faces, and on until it surrenders its insight, its truth. We are fortunate as American writers in that with our variety of racial and national traditions, idioms and manners, we are yet one. On its profoundest level American experience is of a whole. Its truth lies in its diversity and swiftness of change. Through forging forms of the novel worthy of it we achieve not only the promise of our lives, but we anticipate the resolution of those world problems of humanity which for a moment seem to those who are in awe of statistics completely insoluble.

Whenever we as Americans have faced serious crises we have returned to fundamentals; this, in brief, is what I have tried to do.

JOHN O. KILLENS
(b. 1916)

John O. Killens was born in Macon, Georgia. He attended Edward Waters College and Howard University, and studied law at Columbia University. After nearly two years of service in the U.S. Amphibian Forces in the South Pacific, Killens worked with the National Labor Relations Board for six years. He was subsequently writer-in-residence at Fisk University, and later taught at Columbia University and Howard University. He has traveled extensively in West Africa and has used this experience in his positions as chairman of the Harlem Writers Guild Workshop and chairman of the Writers Committee of the American Society of African Culture.

Killens has continuously explored black culture as a source for theme, setting, and language in his writing. His first novel, Youngblood *(1954), utilizes his own Georgia background in relating the lives of two generations of a black family. His second novel,* And Then We Heard the Thunder *(1963), reflects Killens' observations in the military service—the racism which black servicemen endured and the psychological effects of racism upon men who must struggle with both the enemy and their own countrymen. A third novel,* 'Sippi *(1967), deals with the South since 1964 and the uphill struggle for civil rights there. It is a realistic, often brutal novel. A fourth* The Cotillion, *was published in 1971. In all of his novels, Killens uses effectively the colorful idiom of black language and the stark realities of black experience.*

In addition to novels, Killens has produced a volume of essays, Black Man's Burden *(1965), containing social commentary on American racism and critical commentary on the direction of black writing. He has written motion picture scripts, and a play with Lofton Mitchell,* Ballad of the Winter Soldiers, *about black people who have struggled for freedom.*

The Black Psyche

When I was a boy in Macon, Georgia, one of the greatest compliments a benevolent white man could give a Negro was usually found in the obituary column of the local newspaper: "He was a black man, but he had a white heart." And the burden of every black man was supposedly just a little easier to bear that day. It was a time when many of us black folk laughed at the antics of *Amos 'n' Andy* and wept copious tears at a ridiculous movie very aptly titled *Imitation of Life*. Most of us looked at life through the eyes of white America.

The great fictional (and film) masterpieces on the American racial theme usually fell into two categories. One theme dealt with the utter heartbreak of the mulatto, who rejected his black blood and was in turn rejected by his white blood. A variation of this theme was the shattering experience of "passing." The other theme was the "Uncle Tom," or what I prefer to call the "Gunga Din," theme. This one also had many variations, but over all there was the image created by that great apologist for colonialism, Rudyard Kipling, of a man who

> . . . *For all 'is dirty 'ide*
> *'E was white, clear white, inside*
> *When 'e went to tend the wounded*
> *under fire!*

With some "additional touches" by Hollywood, dear old "white inside" Gunga evolved as a marvelous figment of Western man's wistful imagination, the personification of his wish fulfillment. Remember Gunga? He was a water boy for the British regiment and in the movie version, finally blew the bugle against his own people. And how much "whiter" inside could a "noble savage" be?

I am waging a quiet little campaign at the moment to substitute the term "Gunga Din" for that much maligned character "Uncle Tom" in designating the contemporary water boys who still blow the bugles for old Massa. For although Mrs. Stowe's beloved "Uncle Tom" was indeed an Uncle Tom, as we understand the term today, he nevertheless, in the final confrontation, chose death rather than blow the whistle on his people.

Variations of the Gunga Din theme were seen in a rash of movie epics, like *Gone with the Wind* and *Virginia* and *Kentucky*, etc., *ad infinitum, ad nauseam,* always played magnificently with tongue in cheek by such stalwarts as Hattie McDaniel and Louise Beavers. In the great emotional scene the black "mammy" was usually in the big house, weeping and moaning over little pure-white-as-the-driven-snow Missy Anne, who had just sneezed, while Mammy's own young-un was dying of double pneumonia, unattended, down in the cabins. All in all, the slaves were presented as carefree and contented in their idyllic degradation. If the black man really believed in this romantic version of American slavery, he would have long since wasted away, pining for those good old happy-go-lucky days of bondage.

Last year I did considerable research on that bygone "utopian" era, and I got a very different picture, slightly less romantic. I found that the slaves were so happy that most of the plantation owners couldn't afford the astronomical rates of fire insurance. These rapturous slaves kept setting fire to the cotton patches, burning down the plantation, every day the good Lord sent them. They organized count-less insurrections, killed their masters, poisoned their mistresses, even put spiders in the Big House soup. They demonstrated their content-ment in most peculiar ways.

The point is, most white Americans cling desperately to these wish-fulfillment fantasies, but most of us Negroes have become un-believers. We don't break into cheers any more when the cowboys chase the Indians across the movie screen, or when the Army finally captures old John Brown, Indeed, our favorite epic of the west has become Custer's Last Stand. Sitting Bull is a colored hero. Many black folk wish that this mighty warrior had been an American Negro.

I shall never forget an evening I spent in a movie house in Holly-wood watching the closed-circuit television broadcast of the first

Patterson-Johannson fight, and the great shame I felt for my white countrymen that night as they began to sense a possible victory for the white foreigner over the black American. Forgotten entirely was the fact that softhearted Floyd Patterson was fellow countryman. Color superseded patriotism. As I sat there hearing shouted exhortations, like "Kill the nigger!", I felt that Patterson and I were aliens in a strange and hostile country, and that Ingemar was at home among his people. In fairness to my countrymen in the closed circuits of America that night, their reactions were not intellectual, not even willful. They were spontaneous, not unlike a conditioned reflex. This ecstasy at the sudden emergence of a new white hope came from their hearts, their souls, their bellies. It was their white insides reacting.

I have been told that this incident had no racial implications at all, that these rabid Johannson fans were merely upholding the old American tradition of rooting for the underdog. Well, I was also rooting for the underdog, and I knew that, win or lose, the underdog in America was Floyd Patterson, Harry Belafonte, Emmett Till, Rosa Parks, Meredith, Poitier, the black American, I, *me*. The words "Kill the nigger!" could not possibly have come screaming from my throat, subconsciously, or otherwise. Nor could they from any other black man's throat.

Just as surely as East is East and West is West, there is a "black" psyche in America and there is a "white" one, and the sooner we face up to this psychological, social, and cultural reality, the sooner the twain shall meet. Our emotional chemistry is different from white America's. Your joy is very often our anger, and your despair our hope. Most of us came here in chains, and many of you came here to escape your chains. Your freedom was our slavery, and therein lies the bitter difference in the way we look at life. You created the myth of the faithful slave, but we know that the "loyal slave" is a contradiction in terms. We understand, though, that the master must always make himself believe in the undying love of his slave.

Ironically enough, the fathers of our magnificent Revolution, Washington and Jefferson, themselves owned hundreds of human chattels, and even though the great Thomas Jefferson made many speeches against the peculiar institution, he was never able to convince himself to the extent of manumitting his own slaves during his lifetime. Surely the great irony of the situation did not escape my ancestors back in the days of the Revolution. And now, today, it does not escape their great-great-grandchildren. When we hear some white statesman use the phrase "the Free World," even though the same white statesman may very well be the Governor of the State of Mississippi or Alabama, or even President of these United States, for that matter, we—as the slaves of Washington and Jefferson must have done—stare at him incredulously and cannot believe our ears. And we wonder how this word "freedom" can have such vastly different meanings, such conflicting connotations.

But the time has come for you (white America) and me (black America) to work this thing out once and for all, to examine and evaluate the difference between us and the difference inside us. Time is swiftly running out, and a new dialogue is indispensable. It is so long overdue it is already half past midnight.

And let us be clear on one thing. My fight is not to be a white man in a black skin, but to inject some black blood, some black intelligence, some black humaneness, into the pallid mainstream of American life—culturally, socially, psychologically, philosophically. This is the truer, deeper meaning of the Negro revolt which is not yet a revolution—to get America ready for the middle of the twentieth century, which is already magnificently here.

This new epoch has caught our country (yours and mine) dozing in a sweet nostalgia of the good old days. Our country slumbers in a world of yesteryears, before Africa and Asia got up off their knees and threw off the black man's burden. The good old days when you threw pennies to the "natives." And there were gunboats in the China Sea and Big Stick policies and Monroe Doctrines and "Gold Coasters" from the U.K. sipped their gin-and-tonics in Accra and Lagos and talked about the "natives," as they basked in their roles of Great White Fathers in the best of all possible worlds.

That world is gone forever, and black and brown men everywhere are glad, deep in their hearts, though most Western men are chagrined, which may be the understatement of the century. The title of the great Duke Ellington's song has come true: "Things Ain't What They Used To Be." And the good news, or the bad news, depending on your point of view, is: Things ain't never going to be anything like they used to be. This is why the world is becoming too much for Western men, however liberal, even some radical Western men, whoever you are, and wherever. But the world is becoming more and more to my liking, to my taste and in my image. It gladdens my heart to see black and brown men and women walk with dignity in the United Nations, in affirmation of the manhood and the selfhood of the entire human race.

The American Negro, you see, is an Anglo-Saxon invention, a

role the Anglo-Saxon gentleman created for the black man in this drama known euphemistically as the American Way of Life. It began as an economic expedient, frankly, because you wanted somebody to work for nothing. It is still that, but now it is much more than that. It has become a way of life within a way of life, socially, economically, psychologically, philosophically. The Negro Invention, hatched in the brave New World, ultimately and rapidly became a rationalization for the colonializing of three-quarters of the earth's peoples. All non-whites throughout the world became "niggers" and therefore proper material for "civilizing" and "Christianizing" (cruel euphemisms for colonization, exploitation, genocide, and slavery).

And now, in the middle of the twentieth century, I, the Negro, like my counterparts in Asia and Africa and South America and on the islands of the many seas, am refusing to be your "nigger" any longer. Even some of us "favored," "talented," "unusual," ones are refusing to be your educated, sophisticated, split-leveled "niggers" any more. We refuse to look at ourselves through the eyes of white America.

We are not fighting for the right to be like you. We respect ourselves too much for that. When we advocate freedom, we mean freedom for us to be black, or brown, and you to be white and yet live together in a free and equal society. This is the only way that integration can bring dignity for both of us. I, for one, am growing weary of those well-meaning white liberals who are forever telling me they don't know what color I am. The very fact they always single me out at every cocktail party to gratuitously make me the beneficiary of their blessed assurances gives the lie to their pronouncements.

My fight is not for racial sameness but for racial equality and against racial prejudice and discrimination. I work for the day when black people will be free of the racist pressures to be white like you; a day when "good hair" and "high yaller" and bleaching cream and hair straighteners will be obsolete. What a tiresome place America would be if freedom meant we all had to think alike or be the same color or wear that same gray flannel suit! That road leads to the conformity of the graveyard.

If relationships are to improve between us Americans, black and white and otherwise, if the country is to be changed and saved, we will have to face up to the fact that differences do exist between us. All men react to life through man-made symbols. Even our symbolic reactions are different from yours. To give a few examples:

In the center of a little Southern town near the border of Mississippi there is a water tower atop which sits a large white cross, illumined at night with a lovely (awesome to Negroes) neon brightness, which can be seen for miles. To most white Americans, seeing it for the first time, it is a beacon that symbolizes the Cross upon which Jesus died, and it gives them a warm feeling. But it puts an angry knot in a black man's belly. To him it symbolizes the very "Christian" K.K.K. Just as to the average white man, a courthouse, even in Mississippi, is a place where justice is dispensed. Yet to me, the black man, it is a place where justice is dispensed with.

We even have a different historical perspective. Most white Americans, even today, look upon the Reconstruction period as a horrible time of "carpetbagging," and "black politicians," and "black corruption," the absolutely lowest ebb in the Great American Story. Oh, the oceans of bitter tears American writers have wept for that ill-begotten era. Oh, the shame of it all, the way those Southern patriots were treated after that unfortunate war, that horrendous misunderstanding.

We black folk, however, look upon Reconstruction as the most democratic period in the history of this nation; a time when the dream the founders dreamed was almost within reach and right there for the taking; a time of democratic fervor the like of which was never seen before and never since. For all we know, it was a time when America could have won the world but lost it, probably forever. We don't share your feeling that the Negro was not ready for the franchise. We think that the first slaves on that first slave ship were men and women and therefore capable of being citizens anywhere. This is our understanding of democracy. We are not impressed with the mess white Americans (educated and illiterate ones) have made of this Republic, and apparently, because of their whiteness, they were born ready. Apparently, they were endowed by "their creator."

For us, Reconstruction was the time when two black men were Senators in the Congress of the United States from the State of Mississippi; when black men served in the legislatures of all the states in Dixie; and when those "corrupt" legislatures gave to the South its first public-school education. And the lowest ebb for us black folk came on the heels of the Great Betrayal, when the government in Washington turned us over to the benevolent Ku Klux Klan and the Knights of the Camellias.

Nor do we share your romantic view of Rob Lee and Jeff Davis. Certainly, to most of us who have thought about the matter, they were traitors, pure and simple. We put them in the same inglorious category as the infamous Benedict Arnold.

I shall never forget the feeling I had one morning in the fall of 1957, in a Hollywood hotel, when I awoke and tuned into the outside world of television. There before my eyes were American soldiers, black and white, rolling into Little Rock, Arkansas, with their rifles at the ready. I cried that morning, I unashamedly wept. Wept for the moment that had been so long in the coming, the moment when for the first time in my life I felt that the nation gave a damn about *me*. One courageous black woman and eight innocent beautiful black children had laid down the gauntlet and brought the nation to the brink of human decency.

Whatever the political considerations that dictated the move, I felt that the nation had committed itself again, in a way it had not done since Reconstruction. When I saw the Star-Spangled Banners waving from those jeeps and tanks as they rolled endlessly into Little Rock that morning, Old Glory meant more to me, the black American, *me*, than ever before in my life's brief span, including the forty-one months I spent in the service of my country during World War II. Oh yes, we black folk find it difficult to understand the nation's hesitation about sending troops to Mississippi to guarantee free elections when we read of American boys dying thousands of miles from home to ensure freedom for the Vietnamese. The subtlety escapes us.

Even our white hero symbols are different from yours. You give us moody Abe Lincoln, but many of us prefer John Brown, whom most of you hold in contempt as a fanatic; meaning, of course, that the firm dedication of any white man to the freedom of the black man is *prima-facie* evidence of perversion or insanity.

You look upon these times as the Atomic Age, the Space Age, the Cold War Era. But I believe that when the history of our times is written, it will not be so important who reached the moon first or who made the largest bomb. I believe the great significance will be that this was the century when most of mankind achieved freedom and human dignity, the age when racial prejudices became obsolete. For me, this is the Freedom Century.

So now it is time for you to understand us, because it is becoming increasingly hazardous for you not to. Dangerous for both of us. As Richard Wright said in his *Twelve Million Black Voices*, voices you chose not to heed: "Each day when you see us black folk upon the dusty land of your farms or upon the hard pavement of your city streets, you usually take us for granted and think you know us, but our history is far stranger than you suspect, and we are not what we seem." The Rev. Ralph Abernathy of Montgomery put it more humorously when he said that the new Negro of Montgomery had stopped laughing when he wasn't tickled and scratching when he didn't itch.

At the turn of the century, Negro prophet William Edward Burghardt Du Bois warned the Western world: "The problem of the twentieth century is the problem of the color line." But who listens to a black prophet at such a time of endless frontiers for the white pioneers and missionaries? Now, in the middle of that same century, we are bringing down the curtain on this role you cast us in, and we will no longer be a party to our own degradation. We have become unbelievers, no longer believing in the absolute superiority of the white man's juju. You have never practiced what you preached. Why should we believe in you? Why should we want to be like you?

Yes, we are different from you and we are not invisible men, Ralph Ellison notwithstanding. We are the most visible Americans.

Last Spring, Charles Harris, Negro editor for Doubleday, and I had drinks at the Playboy Club in New York. We were so visible, everybody who came into the place stared at us more than they did the semi-naked bunnies. "Who're they? Ralph Bunche and Sonny Liston, or Joe Louis and Sammy Davis, Junior? Or maybe Willie Mays and Martin Luther King?" Oh yes, we have a very high degree of visibility.

But white Americans are great pretenders. Millions of you wish we were invisible, and so make you believe we are. You'd like to wish us out of existence so that the whole world would not see us, because our very life in this country, as black people, gives the lie before the world to your protestations of freedom and human brotherhood. The white man's juju is powerful stuff, but it cannot wish the Negro into invisibility. So you try the next best thing, pretending you can't tell one of us from the other.

The point is: Since we no longer look at ourselves through *your* eyes, our visibility, to *your* eyes, is a total irrelevance, to *us*. We no longer look to you for our identity. But this self-delusion on *your* part (that you don't see us and that you can't tell us one from the other) is dangerous for you and for *our* country. You always knew the difference between the "field" slave and the "house" one; between the "bad nigger" and the "good" one; between Gunga Din and old Nat Turner, between Du Bois and Booker Washington.

In the summer and fall of 1961 I traveled in a Land Rover 12,000 miles through Africa. I talked to people in the cities, on the farms, in the villages. I talked with workers, farmers, artists, market women, ministers of state, politicians, teachers, and the same question was asked me everywhere I went: "How can we believe your country's professions of good will to us, with whom they have not lived, when they deny human dignity to you who come from us and have lived with them for centuries and helped to build their great civilization?"

It is a question that America has to answer to the entire New World of Africa and Asia. The only way we Americans, black and white, can answer it affirmatively is to make freedom and democracy work at home, here and now. Most Negroes still believe that the ultimate solution for us is in America, and I am as firmly convinced that the ultimate salvation of America is in the Negro.

The Negro loves America enough to criticize her fundamentally. Most white Americans simply can't be bothered. Ironically enough, in the middle of the twentieth century, the Negro is the new white hope. To live castrated in a great white harem and yet somehow maintain our black manhood and humanity—this is the essence of the new man created out of the Negro Invention. History may render the verdict that this was the greatest legacy handed to the New World by the West.

There are glaring exceptions to every rule, but it is a truism that American Negroes are the only people in America who, as a people, are for change. This is true, again, not innately because of our color, but because of what America made of our color. The *status quo* has ever been the bane of black existence.

We black folk have learned many lessons during our sojourn in this place. One of them is the truth of the Ghana proverb, "Only a fool points to his origin with his left hand." We are becoming prouder and prouder of our origins. And we know the profound difference between pride and arrogance; the difference, if you will, between James Meredith and Ross Barnett, both of Mississippi. Our dialogue will not be protest but affirmation of the human dignity of all people everywhere. Yes, our aim is to create a dialogue in full vindication of every lonesome disinherited "nigger," every black and brown man born of woman who ever dwelt upon this alien earth, which means, of course, that all mankind would be vindicated regardless of race, color, or religion. Our dialogue is anti-racist.

Sure, I know that there are white folk who want America to be the land of the free and the home of the brave, but there are far too few of them, and many of them are rarely brave. I cherish old John Brown and Garrison and William Moore and Mike Schwerner and Andy Goodman and all the other winter soldiers. Let the winter patriots increase their ranks. Let those who truly love America join the valiant Negro Revolt and change and save our country.

JAMES BALDWIN

(b. 1924)

A brilliant essayist and inspired writer of fiction and drama, James Baldwin verbalized the experiences and attitudes of black America from the Wright-Ellison generation to the revolutionary 1960s.

Baldwin was born and reared in the slums of Harlem, the oldest child of a large family. His childhood was full of tensions arising not only from the family's economic struggles, but also from his ambivalent feelings toward his father. From age fourteen to seventeen Baldwin was a child-preacher. At eighteen he left home to earn a living and to begin his writing career. After a few years Baldwin went to Europe to wrestle with the problem of his black American identity and to complete his first novel, Go Tell It On the Mountain *(1953). This phase of his life is described in his early essays, collected in 1955 in the volume* Notes of a Native Son. *These two works established Baldwin as a major writer.*

Since these early works Baldwin has divided his time between Europe and America. During the fifties and early sixties he made many public appearances in which he shocked white audiences with his frank revelation of black truths as he saw them.

Baldwin's essays are an important part of American literature. He articulates the experiences and views of the urban black American in a style characterized by expert use of rhetorical devices, firm and decisive imagery, precision in wording, and effective use of irony. In the fifties, when many black writers were producing "nonracial" works, Baldwin's voice was raised in angry protest. A chronological study of Baldwin's works reveals deepening anger, increasing bitterness, and rising militancy. Undoubtedly Baldwin's anger and his art influenced the young writers who were to bloom in the sixties.

Baldwin's output as a writer is enormous. Among his collections of essays are Nobody Knows My Name *(1961),* The Fire Next Time *(1963),* No Name in the Street *(1972), and* The Devil Finds Work *(1976); the novels include* Giovanni's Room *(1956),* Another Country *(1962),* Tell Me How Long The Train's Been Gone *(1968),* If Beale Street Could Talk *(1974), and* Just Above My Head *(1978); two plays are* The Amen Corner *(1955; 1968), and* Blues For Mr. Charlie *(1964); and short stories are collected in* Going To Meet the Man *(1965). This abundant production has been the subject of numerous studies and commentary in many languages. An introduction to this vast domain is provided by Fred L. Standley and Nancy V. Standley in* James Baldwin: A Reference Guide *(1980).*

From *Nobody Knows My Name*

A LETTER FROM THE SOUTH

I walked down the street, didn't
have on no hat,
Asking everybody I meet,
Where's my man at?

—Ma Rainey

Negroes in the north are right when they refer to the South as the Old Country. A Negro born in the North who finds himself in the South is in a position similar to that of the son of the Italian emigrant who finds himself in Italy, near the village where his father first saw the light of day. Both are in countries they have never seen, but which they cannot fail to recognize. The landscape has always been familiar; the speech is archaic, but it rings a bell; and so do the ways of the people, though their ways are not his ways. Everywhere he turns, the revenant finds himself reflected. He sees himself as he was before he was born, perhaps; or as the man he would have become had he actually been born in this place. He sees the world, from an angle odd indeed, in which his fathers awaited his arrival, perhaps in the very house in which he narrowly avoided being born. He sees, in effect, his ancestors, who, in everything they do and are, proclaim his inescapable identity. And the Northern Negro in the South sees, whatever he or anyone else may wish to believe, that his ancestors are both white and black. The white men, flesh of his flesh, hate him for that very reason. On the other hand, there is scarcely any way for him to join the black community in the South: for both he and this community are in the grip of the immense illusion that their state is more miserable than his own.

This illusion owes everything to the great American illusion that our state is a state to be envied by other people: we are powerful, and we are rich. But our power makes us uncomfortable and we handle it very ineptly. The principal effect of our material well-being has been to set the children's teeth on edge. If we ourselves were not so fond of this illusion, we might understand ourselves and other peoples better than we do, and be enabled to help them understand us. I am very often tempted to believe that this illusion is all that is left of the great dream that was to have become America; whether this is so or not, this illusion certainly prevents us from making America what we say we want it to be.

But let us put aside, for the moment, these subversive speculations. In the fall of last year, my plane hovered over the rust-red earth of Georgia. I was past thirty, and I had never seen this land before. I pressed my face against the window, watching the earth come closer; soon we were just above the tops of trees. I could not suppress the thought that this earth had acquired its color from the blood that had dripped down from these trees. My mind was filled with the image of a black man, younger than I, perhaps, or my own age, hanging from a tree, while white men watched him and cut his sex from him with a knife.

My father must have seen such sights—he was very old when he died—or heard of them, or had this danger touch him. The Negro poet I talked to in Washington, much younger than my father, perhaps twenty years older than myself, remembered such things very vividly, had a long tale to tell, and counseled me to think back on those days as a means of steadying the soul. I was to remember that time, whatever else it had failed to do, nevertheless had passed, that the situation, whether or not it was better, was certainly no longer the same. I was to remember that Southern Negroes had endured things I could not imagine; but this did not really place me at such a great disadvantage, since they clearly had been unable to imagine what awaited them in Harlem. I remembered the Scottsboro case, which I had followed as a child. I remembered Angelo Herndon and wondered again, whatever had become of him. I remembered the soldier in uniform blinded by an enraged white man, just after the Second World War. There had been many such incidents after the First War, which was one of the reasons I had been born in Harlem. I remembered Willie McGhee, Emmett Till, and the others. My

younger brothers had visited Atlanta some years before. I remembered
what they had told me about it. One of my brothers, in uniform, had
had his front teeth kicked out by a white officer. I remembered my
mother telling us how she had wept and prayed and tried to kiss the
venom out of her suicidally embittered son. (She managed to do it,
too; heaven only knows what she herself was feeling, whose father
and brothers had lived and died down here.) I remembered myself as
a very small boy, already so bitter about the pledge of allegiance that
I could scarcely bring myself to say it, and never, never believed it.

I was, in short, but one generation removed from the South,
which was now undergoing a new convulsion over whether black
children had the same rights, or capacities, for education as did the
children of white people. This is a criminally frivolous dispute, absolutely unworthy of this nation; and it is being carried on, in complete
bad faith, by completely uneducated people. (We do not trust educated people and rarely, alas, produce them, for we do not trust the
independence of mind which alone makes a genuine education possible.) Educated people, of any color, are so extremely rare that it is
unquestionably one of the first tasks of a nation to open all of its
schools to all of its citizens. But the dispute has actually nothing to
do with education, as some among the eminently uneducated know.
It has to do with political power and it has to do with sex. And this
is a nation which, most unluckily, knows very little about either.

The city of Atlanta, according to my notes, is "big, wholly segregated, sprawling; population variously given as six hundred thousand
or one million, depending on whether one goes beyond or remains
within the city limits. Negroes 25 to 30 per cent of the population.
Racial relations, on the record, can be described as fair, considering
that this is the state of Georgia. Growing industrial town. Racial
relations manipulated by the mayor and a fairly strong Negro middle
class. This works mainly in the areas of compromise and concession
and has very little effect on the bulk of the Negro population and
none whatever on the rest of the state. No integration, pending or
actual." Also, it seemed to me that the Negroes in Atlanta were "very
vividly *city* Negroes"—they seemed less patient than their rural
brethren, more dangerous, or at least more unpredictable. And:
"Have seen one wealthy Negro section, very pretty, but with an un-
paved road. . . . The section in which I am living is composed of
frame houses in various stages of disrepair and neglect, in which two
and three families live, often sharing a single toilet. This is the other
side of the tracks; literally, I mean. It is located, as I am told in the

case in many Southern cities, just beyond the underpass." Atlanta contains a high proportion of Negroes who own their own homes and exist, visibly anyway, independently of the white world. Southern towns distrust this class and do everything in their power to prevent its appearance. But it is a class which has a certain usefulness in Southern cities. There is an incipient war, in fact, between Southern cities and Southern towns—between the city, that is, and the state— which we will discuss later. Little Rock is an ominous example of this and it is likely—indeed, it is certain—that we will see many more such examples before the present crisis is over.

Before arriving in Atlanta I had spent several days in Charlotte, North Carolina. This is a bourgeois town, Presbyterian, pretty—if you like towns—and socially so hermetic that it contains scarcely a single decent restaurant. I was told that Negroes there are not even licensed to become electricians or plumbers. I was also told, several times, by white people, that "race relations" there were excellent. I failed to find a single Negro who agreed with this, which is the usual story of "race relations" in this country. Charlotte, a town of 165,000, was in a ferment when I was there because, of its 50,000 Negroes, four had been assigned to previously all-white schools, one to each school. In fact, by the time I got there, there were only three. Dorothy Counts, the daughter of a Presbyterian minister, after several days of being stoned and spat on by the mob—"spit," a woman told me, "was hanging from the hem of Dorothy's dress"—had withdrawn from Harding High. Several white students, I was told, had called— not called *on*—Miss Counts to beg her to stick it out. Harry Golden, editor of *The Carolina Israelite*, suggested that the "hoodlum element" might not so have shamed the town and the nation if several of the town's leading businessmen had personally escorted Miss Counts to school.

I saw the Negro schools in Charlotte, saw, on street corners, several of their alumni, and read about others who had been sentenced to the chain gang. This solved the mystery of just what made Negro parents send their children out to face mobs. White people do not understand this because they do not know, and do not want to know, that the alternative to this ordeal is nothing less than a lifelong ordeal. Those Negro parents who spend their days trembling for their children and the rest of their time praying that their children have not been too badly damaged inside, are not doing this out of "ideals" or "convictions" or because they are in the grip of a perverse desire to send their children where "they are not wanted." They are doing it because they want the child to receive the education which will allow him to defeat, possibly escape, and not impossibly help one day abolish the stifling environment in which they see, daily, so many children perish.

This is certainly not the purpose, still less the effect, of most Negro schools. It is hard enough, God knows, under the best of circumstances, to get an education in this country. White children are graduated yearly who can neither read, write, nor think, and who are in a state of the most abysmal ignorance concerning the world around them. But at least they are white. They are under the illusion—which, since they are so badly educated, sometimes has a fatal tenacity—that they can do whatever they want to do. Perhaps that is exactly what they *are* doing, in which case we had best all go down in prayer.

The level of Negro education, obviously, is even lower than the general level. The general level is low because, as I have said, Americans have so little respect for genuine intellectual effort. The Negro level is low because the education of Negroes occurs in, and is designed to perpetuate, a segregated society. This, in the first place, and no matter how much money the South boasts of spending on Negro schools, is utterly demoralizing. It creates a situation in which the Negro teacher is soon as powerless as his students. (There are exceptions among the teachers as there are among the students, but, in this country surely, schools have not been built for the exceptional. And, though white people often seem to expect Negroes to produce nothing but exceptions, the fact is that Negroes are really just like everybody else. Some of them are exceptional and most of them are not.)

The teachers are answerable to the Negro principal, whose power over the teachers is absolute but whose power with the school board is slight. As for this principal, he has arrived at the summit of his career; rarely indeed can he go any higher. He has his pension to look forward to, and he consoles himself, meanwhile, with his status among the "better class of Negroes." This class includes few, if any, of his students and by no means all of his teachers. The teachers, as long as they remain in this school system, and they certainly do not have much choice, can only aspire to become the principal one day. Since not all of them will make it, a great deal of the energy which ought to go into their vocation goes into the usual bitter, purposeless rivalry. They are underpaid and ill treated by the white world and rubbed raw by it every day; and it is altogether understandable that they, very shortly, cannot bear the sight of their students. The children know this; it is hard to fool young people. They also know why they are going to an overcrowded, outmoded plant, in classes so large that even the most strictly attentive student, the most gifted teacher cannot but feel himself slowly drowning in the sea of general helplessness.

It is not to be wondered at, therefore, that the violent distractions of puberty, occurring in such a cage, annually take their toll, sending female children into the maternity wards and male children into the streets. It is not to be wondered at that a boy, one day, decides that if all this studying is going to prepare him only to be a porter or an elevator boy—or his teacher—well, then, the hell with it. And there they go, with an overwhelming bitterness which they will dissemble all their lives, an unceasing effort which completes their ruin. They become the menial or the criminal or the shiftless, the Negroes whom segregation has produced and whom the South uses to prove that segregation is right.

In Charlotte, too, I received some notion of what the South means by "time to adjust." The NAACP there had been trying for six years before Black Monday to make the city fathers honor the "separate but equal" statute and do something about the situation in Negro schools. Nothing whatever was done. After Black Monday, Charlotte begged for "time": and what she did with this time was work out legal stratagems designed to get the least possible integration over the longest possible period. In August of 1955, Governor Hodges, a moderate, went on the air with the suggestion that Negroes segregate themselves voluntarily—for the good, as he put it, of both races. Negroes seeming to be unmoved by this moderate proposal, the Klan reappeared in the counties and was still active there when I left. So, no doubt, are the boys on the chain gang.

But "Charlotte," I was told, "is not the South." I was told, "You haven't seen the South yet." Charlotte seemed quite Southern enough for me, but, in fact, the people in Charlotte were right. One of the reasons for this is that the South is not the monolithic structure which, from the North, it appears to be, but a most various and divided region. It clings to the myth of its past but it is being inexorably changed, meanwhile, by an entirely unmythical present: its habits and its self-interest are at war. Everyone in the South feels this and this is why there is such panic on the bottom and such impotence on the top.

It must also be said that the racial setup in the South is not, for a Negro, very different from the racial setup in the North. It is the etiquette which is baffling, not the spirit. Segregation is unofficial in the North and official in the South, a crucial difference that does nothing, nevertheless, to alleviate the lot of most Northern Negroes. But we will return to this question when we discuss the relationship between the Southern cities and states.

Atlanta, however, *is* the South. It is the South in this respect, that it has a very bitter interracial history. This is written in the faces of the people and one feels it in the air. It was on the outskirts of Atlanta that I first felt how the Southern landscape—the trees, the silence, the liquid heat, and the fact that one always seems to be traveling great distances—seems designed for violence, seems, almost, to demand it. What passions cannot be unleashed on a dark road in a Southern night! Everything seems so sensual, so languid, and so private. Desire can be acted out here; over this fence, behind that tree, in the darkness, there; and no one will see, no one will ever know. Only the night is watching and the night was made for desire. Protestantism is the wrong religion for people in such climates; America is perhaps the last nation in which such a climate belongs. In the Southern night everything seems possible, the most private, unspeakable longings; but then arrives the Southern day, as hard and brazen as the night was soft and dark. It brings what was done in the dark to light. It must have seemed something like this for those people who made the region what it is today. It must have caused them great pain. Perhaps the master who had coupled with his slave saw his guilt in his wife's pale eyes in the morning. And the wife saw his children in the slave quarters, saw the way his concubine, the sensual-looking black girl, looked at her—a woman, after all, and scarcely less sensual, but white. The youth, nursed and raised by the black Mammy whose arms had then held all that there was of warmth and love and desire, and still confounded by the dreadful taboos set up between himself and her progeny, must have wondered, after his first experiment with black flesh, where, under the blazing heavens, he could hide. And the white man must have seen his guilt written somewhere else, seen it all the time, even if his sin was merely lust, even if his sin lay in nothing but his power: in the eyes of the black man. He may not have stolen his woman, but he had certainly stolen his freedom—this black man, who had a body like his, and passions like his, and a ruder, more erotic beauty. How many times has the Southern day come up to find that black man, sexless, hanging from a tree!

It was an old black man in Atlanta who looked into my eyes and directed me into my first segregated bus. I have spent a long time thinking about that man. I never saw him again. I cannot describe the look which passed between us, as I asked him for directions, but it made me think, at once, of Shakespeare's "the oldest have borne most." It made me think of the blues: *Now, when a woman gets the blues, Lord, she hangs her head and cries. But when a man gets the blues, Lord, he grabs a train and rides.* It was borne in on me, suddenly, just why these men had so often been grabbing freight trains as the evening sun went down. And it was, perhaps, because I was getting on a segregated bus, and wondering how Negroes had borne this and other indignities for so long, that this man so struck me. He seemed to know what I was feeling. His eyes seemed to say that what I was feeling he had been feeling, at much higher pressure, all his life. But my eyes would never see the hell his eyes had seen. And this hell was, simply, that he had never in his life owned anything, not his wife, not his house, not his child, which could not, at any instant, be taken from him by the power of white people. This is what paternalism means. And for the rest of the time that I was in the South I watched the eyes of old black men.

Atlanta's well-to-do Negroes never takes buses, for they all have cars. The section in which they live is quite far away from the poor Negro section. They own, or at least are paying for, their own homes. They drive to work and back, and have cocktails and dinner with each other. They see very little of the white world; but they are cut off from the black world, too.

Now, of course, this last statement is not literally true. The teachers teach Negroes, the lawyers defend them. The ministers preach to them and bury them, and others insure their lives, pull their teeth, and cure their ailments. Some of the lawyers work with the NAACP and help push test cases through the courts. (If anything, by the way, disproves the charge of "extremism" which has so often been made against this organization, it is the fantastic care and patience such legal efforts demand.) Many of the teachers work very hard to bolster the morale of their students and prepare them for their new responsibilities; nor did those I met fool themselves about the hideous system under which they work. So when I say that they are cut off from the black world, I am not sneering, which, indeed, I scarcely have any right to do. I am talking about their position as a class—*if* they are a class—and their role in a very complex and shaky social structure.

The wealthier Negroes are, at the moment, very useful for the administration of the city of Atlanta, for they represent there the potential, at least, of interracial communication. That this phrase is a euphemism, in Atlanta as elsewhere, becomes clear when one considers how astonishingly little has been communicated in all these generations. What the phrase almost always has reference to is the fact that, in a given time and place, the Negro vote is of sufficient value to force politicians to bargain for it. What interracial communication also refers to is that Atlanta is really growing and thriving, and because it wants to make even more money, it would like to prevent incidents that disturb the peace, discourage investments, and permit test cases, which the city of Atlanta would certainly lose, to come to the courts. Once this happens, as it certainly will one day, the state of Georgia will be up in arms and the present administration of the city will be out of power. I did not meet a soul in Atlanta (I naturally did not meet any members of the White Citizen's Council, not, anyway, to talk to) who did not pray that the present mayor would be re-elected. Not that they loved him particularly, but it is his administration which holds off the holocaust.

Now this places Atlanta's wealthy Negroes in a really quite sinister position. Though both they and the mayor are devoted to keeping the peace, their aims and his are not, and cannot be, the same. Many of those lawyers are working day and night on test cases which the mayor is doing his best to keep out of court. The teachers spend their working day attempting to destroy in their students—and it is not too much to say, in themselves—those habits of inferiority which form one of the principal cornerstones of segregation as it is practiced in the South. Many of the parents listen to speeches by people like Senator Russell and find themselves unable to sleep at night. They are in the extraordinary position of being compelled to work for the destruction of all they have bought so dearly—their homes, their comfort, the safety of their children. But the safety of their children is merely comparative; it is all that their comparative strength as a class has bought them so far; and they are not safe, really, as long as the bulk of Atlanta's Negroes live in such darkness. On any night, in that other part of town, a policeman may beat up one Negro too many, or some Negro or some white man may simply go berserk. This is all it takes to drive so delicately balanced a city mad. And the island on which these Negroes have built their handsome houses will simply disappear.

This is not at all in the interests of Atlanta, and almost everyone there knows it. Left to itself, the city might grudgingly work out compromises designed to reduce the tension and raise the level of

Negro life. But it is not left to itself; it belongs to the state of Georgia. The Negro vote has no power in the state, and the governor of Georgia—that "third-rate man," Atlantans call him—makes great political capital out of keeping the Negroes in their place. When six Negro ministers attempted to create a test case by ignoring the segregation ordinance on the buses, the governor was ready to declare martial law and hold the ministers incommunicado. It was the mayor who prevented this, who somehow squashed all publicity, treated the ministers with every outward sign of respect, and it is his office which is preventing the case from coming into court. And remember that it was the governor of Arkansas, in an insane bid for political power, who created the present crisis in Little Rock—against the will of most of its citizens and against the will of the mayor.

This war between the Southern cities and states is of the utmost importance, not only for the South, but for the nation. The Southern states are still very largely governed by people whose political lives, insofar, at least, as they are able to conceive of life or politics, are dependent on the people in the rural regions. It might, indeed, be more honorable to try to guide these people out of their pain and ignorance instead of locking them within it, and battening on it; but it is, admittedly, a difficult task to try to tell people the truth and it is clear that most Southern politicians have no intention of attempting it. The attitude of these people can only have the effect of stiffening the already implacable Negro resistance, and this attitude is absolutely certain, sooner or later, to create great trouble in the cities. When a race riot occurs in Atlanta, it will not spread merely to Birmingham, for example. (Birmingham is a doomed city.) The trouble will spread to every metropolitan center in the nation which has a significant Negro population. And this is not only because the ties between Northern and Southern Negroes are still very close. It is because the nation, the entire nation, has spent a hundred years avoiding the question of the place of the black man in it.

That this has done terrible things to black men is not even a question. "Integration," said a very light Negro to me in Alabama, "has always worked very well in the South, after the sun goes down." "It's not miscegenation," said another Negro to me, "unless a black man's involved." Now, I talked to many Southern liberals who were doing their best to bring integration about in the South, but met scarcely a single Southerner who did not weep for the passing of the old order. They were perfectly sincere, too, and, within their limits, they were right. They pointed out how Negroes and whites in the

South had loved each other, they recounted to me tales of devotion and heroism which the old order had produced, and which, now, would never come again. But the old black men I looked at down there—those same black men that the Southern liberal had loved; for whom, until now, the Southern liberal—and not only the liberal—has been willing to undergo great inconvenience and danger—they were not weeping. Men do not like to be protected, it emasculates them. This is what black men know, it is the reality they have lived with; it is what white men do not want to know. It is not a pretty thing to be a father and be ultimately dependent on the power and kindness of some other man for the well-being of your house.

But what this evasion of the Negro's humanity has done to the nation is not so well known. The really striking thing, for me, in the South was this dreadful paradox, that the black men were stronger than the white. I do not know how they did it, but it certainly has something to do with that as yet unwritten history of the Negro woman. What it comes to, finally, is that the nation has spent a large part of its time and energy looking away from one of the principal facts of its life. This failure to look reality in the face diminishes a nation as it diminishes a person, and it can only be described as unmanly. And in exactly the same way that the South imagines that it "knows" the Negro, the North imagines that it has set him free. Both camps are deluded. Human freedom is a complex, difficult—and private—thing. If we can liken life, for a moment, to a furnace, then freedom is the fire which burns away illusion. Any honest examination of the national life proves how far we are from the standard of human freedom with which we began. The recovery of this standard demands of everyone who loves this country a hard look at himself, for the greatest achievements must begin somewhere, and they always begin with the person. If we are not capable of this examination, we may yet become one of the most distinguished and monumental failures in the history of nations.

Beauford Delaney

I learned about light from Beauford Delaney, the light contained in every thing, in every surface, in every face. Many years ago, in poverty and uncertainty, Beauford and I would walk together through the streets of New York City. He was then, and is now, working all the time, or perhaps it would be more accurate to say that he is *seeing* all the time; and the reality of his seeing caused me to begin to see. Now what I began to see was not, at that time, to tell the truth, his painting; that came later; what I saw, first of all, was a brown leaf on black asphalt, oil moving like mercury in the black water of the gutter, grass pushing itself up through a crevice in the sidewalk. And because I was seeing it with Beauford, because Beauford caused me to see it, the very colors underwent a most disturbing and salutary change. The brown leaf on the black asphalt, for example—what colors were these, really? To stare at the leaf long enough, to try to apprehend the leaf, was to discover many colors in it; and though black had been described to me as the absence of light, it became very clear to me that if this were true, we would never have been able to see the color, black: the light is trapped in it and struggles upward, rather like that grass pushing upward through the cement. It was humbling to be forced to realize that the light fell down from heaven, on everything, on everybody, and that the light was always changing. Paradoxically, this meant for me that memory is a traitor and that life does not contain the past tense: the sunset one saw yesterday, the leaf that burned, or the rain that fell, have not really been seen unless one is prepared to see them every day.

As Beauford is, to his eternal credit, and for our health and hope. Perhaps I am so struck by the light in Beauford's paintings because he comes from darkness—as I do, as, in fact, we all do. But the darkness of Beauford's beginnings, in Tennessee, many years ago, was a black-blue midnight indeed, opaque, and full of sorrow. And I do not know, nor will any of us ever really know, what kind of strength it was that enabled him to make so dogged and splendid a journey. —In any case, from Tennessee, he eventually came to Paris (I have the impression that he walked and swam) and for awhile lived in a suburb of Paris, Clamart. It was at this time that I began to see Beauford's painting in a new way, and it was also at this time that Beauford's paintings underwent a most striking metamorphosis into freedom. I know this sounds extremely subjective; but let it stand; it is not really as subjective as it sounds. There was a window in Beauford's house in Clamart before which we often sat—late at night, early in the morning, at noon. This window looked out on a garden; or, rather, it would have looked out on a garden if it had not been for the leaves and branches of a large tree which pressed directly against the window. Everything one saw from this window, then, was filtered through these leaves. And this window was a kind of universe, moaning and wailing when it rained, black and bitter when it thundered, hesitant and delicate with the first light of the morning, and as blue as the blues when the last light of the sun departed. Well, that life, that light, that miracle, are what I began to see in Beauford's paintings, and this light began to stretch back for me over all the time we had known each other, and over much more time than that, and this light held the power to illuminate, even to redeem and reconcile and heal. For Beauford's work leads the inner and the outer eye, directly and inexorably, to a new confrontation with reality. At this moment one begins to apprehend the nature of his triumph. And the beauty of his triumph, and the proof that it is a real one, is that he makes it ours. Perhaps I should not say, flatly, what I believe—that he is a great painter, among the very greatest; but I do know that great art can only be created out of love, and that no greater lover has ever held a brush.

The Rockpile

Across the street from their house, in an empty lot between two houses, stood the rockpile. It was a strange place to find a mass of natural rock jutting out of the ground; and someone, probably Aunt Florence, had once told them that the rock was there and could not be taken away because without it the subway cars underground would fly apart, killing all the people. This, touching on some natural mystery concerning the surface and the center of the earth, was far too intriguing an explanation to be challenged, and it invested the rockpile, moreover, with such mysterious importance that Roy felt it to be his right, not to say his duty, to play there.

Other boys were to be seen there each afternoon after school and all day Saturday and Sunday. They fought on the rockpile. Sure footed, dangerous, and reckless, they rushed each other and grappled on the heights, sometimes disappearing down the other side in a confusion of dust and screams and upended, flying feet. "It's a wonder they don't kill themselves," their mother said, watching sometimes from the fire escape. "You children stay away from there, you hear me?" Though she said "children" she was looking at Roy, where he sat beside John on the fire escape. "The good Lord knows," she continued, "I don't want you to come home bleeding like a hog every day the Lord sends." Roy shifted impatiently, and continued to stare at the street, as though in this gazing he might somehow acquire wings. John said nothing. He had not really been spoken to: he was afraid of the rockpile and of the boys who played there.

Each Saturday morning John and Roy sat on the fire escape and watched the forbidden street below. Sometimes their mother sat in the room behind them, sewing, or dressing their younger sister, or nursing the baby, Paul. The sun fell across them and across the fire escape with a high, benevolent indifference; below them, men and women, and boys and girls, sinners all, loitered; sometimes one of the church-members passed and saw them and waved. Then, for the moment that they waved decorously back, they were intimidated. They watched the saint, man or woman, until he or she had disappeared from sight. The passage of one of the redeemed made them consider, however vacantly, the wickedness of the street, their own latent wickedness in sitting where they sat; and made them think of their father, who came home early on Saturdays and who would soon be turning this corner and entering the dark hall below them.

But until he came to end their freedom, they sat, watching and longing above the street. At the end of the street nearest their house was the bridge which spanned the Harlem River and led to a city called the Bronx; which was where Aunt Florence lived. Nevertheless, when they saw her coming, she did not come from the bridge, but from the opposite end of the street. This, weakly, to their minds, she explained by saying that she had taken the subway, not wishing to walk, and that, besides, she did not live in *that* section of the Bronx. Knowing that the Bronx was across the river, they did not believe this story ever, but, adopting toward her their father's attitude, assumed that she had just left some sinful place which she dared not name, as, for example, a movie palace.

In the summertime boys swam in the river, diving off the wooden dock, or wading in from the garbage-heavy bank. Once a boy, whose name was Richard, drowned in the river. His mother had not known where he was; she had even come to their house, to ask if he was there. Then, in the evening, at six o'clock, they had heard from the street a woman screaming and wailing; and they ran to the windows and looked out. Down the street came the woman, Richard's mother, screaming, her face raised to the sky and tears running down her face. A woman walked beside her, trying to make her quiet and trying to hold her up. Behind them walked a man, Richard's father, with Richard's body in his arms. There were two white policemen walking in the gutter, who did not seem to know what should be done. Richard's father and Richard were wet, and Richard's body lay across his father's arms like a cotton baby. The woman's screaming filled all the street; cars slowed down and the people in the cars stared; people opened their windows and looked out and came rushing out of doors to stand in the gutter, watching. Then the small procession disappeared within the house which stood beside the rockpile. Then, "*Lord, Lord, Lord!*" cried Elizabeth, their mother, and slammed the window down.

One Saturday, an hour before his father would be coming home, Roy was wounded on the rockpile and brought screaming upstairs. He and John had been sitting on the fire escape and their mother had gone into the kitchen to sip tea with Sister McCandless. By and by Roy became bored and sat beside John in restless silence; and John began drawing into his school-book a newspaper advertisement which featured a new electric locomotive. Some friends of Roy passed beneath the fire escape and called him. Roy began to fidget, yelling down to them through the bars. Then a silence fell. John looked up. Roy stood looking at him.

"I'm going downstairs," he said.

"You better stay where you is, boy. You know Mama don't want you going downstairs."

"I be right *back*. She won't even know I'm gone, less you run and tell her."

"I ain't *got* to tell her. What's going to stop her from coming in here and looking out the window?"

"She's talking," Roy said. He started into the house.

"But Daddy's going to be home soon!"

"I be back before *that*. What you all the time got to be so *scared* for?" He was already in the house and he now turned, leaning on the window-sill, to swear impatiently, "I be back in *five* minutes."

John watched him sourly as he carefully unlocked the door and disappeared. In a moment he saw him on the sidewalk with his friends. He did not dare to go and tell his mother that Roy had left the fire escape because he had practically promised not to. He started to shout, *Remember, you said five minutes!* but one of Roy's friends was looking up at the fire escape. John looked down at his schoolbook: he became engrossed again in the problem of the locomotive.

When he looked up again he did not know how much time had passed, but now there was a gang fight on the rockpile. Dozens of boys fought each other in the harsh sun: clambering up the rocks and battling hand to hand, scuffed shoes sliding on the slippery rock; filling the bright air with curses and jubilant cries. They filled the air, too, with flying weapons: stones, sticks, tin cans, garbage, whatever could be picked up and thrown. John watched in a kind of absent amazement—until he remembered that Roy was still downstairs, and that he was one of the boys on the rockpile. Then he was afraid; he could not see his brother among the figures in the sun; and he stood up, leaning over the fire-escape railing. Then Roy appeared from the other side of the rocks; John saw that his shirt was torn; he was laughing. He moved until he stood at the very top of the rockpile. Then, something, an empty tin can, flew out of the air and hit him on the forehead, just above the eye. Immediately, one side of Roy's face ran with blood, he fell and rolled on his face down the rocks. Then for a moment there was no movement at all, no sound; the sun, arrested, lay on the street and the sidewalk and the arrested boys. Then someone screamed or shouted; boys began to run away, down the street, toward the bridge. The figure on the ground, having caught its breath and felt its own blood, began to shout. John cried, "Mama! Mama!" and ran inside.

"Don't fret, don't fret," panted Sister McCandless as they rushed down the dark, narrow, swaying stairs, "don't fret. Ain't a boy been born don't get his knocks every now and again. *Lord!*" they hurried into the sun. A man had picked Roy up and now walked slowly toward them. One or two boys sat silent on their stoops; at either end of the street there was a group of boys watching. "He ain't hurt bad," the man said, "wouldn't be making this kind of noise if he was hurt real bad."

Elizabeth, trembling, reached out to take Roy, but Sister McCandless, bigger, calmer, took him from the man and threw him over her shoulder as she once might have handled a sack of cotton. "God bless you," she said to the man, "God bless you, son." Roy was still screaming. Elizabeth stood behind Sister McCandless to stare at his bloody face.

"It's just a flesh wound," the man kept saying, "just broke the skin, that's all." They were moving across the sidewalk, toward the house. John, not now afraid of the staring boys, looked toward the corner to see if his father was yet in sight.

Upstairs, they hushed Roy's crying. They bathed the blood away, to find, just above the left eyebrow, the jagged, superficial scar. "Lord, have mercy," murmured Elizabeth, "another inch and it would've been his eye." And she looked with apprehension toward the clock. "Ain't it the truth," said Sister McCandless, busy with bandages and iodine.

"When did he go downstairs?" his mother asked at last.

Sister McCandless now sat fanning herself in the easy chair, at the head of the sofa where Roy lay, bound and silent. She paused for a moment to look sharply at John. John stood near the window, holding the newspaper advertisement and the drawing he had done.

"We was sitting on the fire escape," he said. "Some boys he knew called him."

"When?"

"He said he'd be back in five minutes."

"Why didn't you tell me he was downstairs?"

He looked at his hands, clasping his notebook, and did not answer.

"Boy," said Sister McCandless, "you hear your mother a-talking to you?"

He looked at his mother. He repeated:

"He said he'd be back in five minutes."

"He said he'd be back in five minutes," said Sister McCandless with scorn, "don't look to me like that's no right answer. You's the man of the house, you supposed to look after your baby brothers and sisters—you ain't supposed to let them run off and get half-killed. But I expect," she added, rising from the chair, dropping the cardboard fan, "your Daddy'll make you tell the truth. Your Ma's way too soft with you."

He did not look at her, but at the fan where it lay in the dark red, depressed seat where she had been. The fan advertised a pomade for the hair and showed a brown woman and her baby, both with glistening hair, smiling happily at each other.

"Honey," said Sister McCandless, "I got to be moving along. Maybe I drop in later tonight. I don't reckon you going to be at Tarry Service tonight?"

Tarry Service was the prayer meeting held every Saturday night at church to strengthen believers and prepare the church for the coming of the Holy Ghost on Sunday.

"I don't reckon," said Elizabeth. She stood up; she and Sister McCandless kissed each other on the cheek. "But you be sure to remember me in your prayers."

"I surely will do that." She paused, with her hand on the door knob, and looked down at Roy and laughed. "Poor little man," she said, "reckon he'll be content to sit on the fire escape *now*."

Elizabeth laughed with her. "It sure ought to be a lesson to him. You don't reckon," she asked nervously, still smiling, "he going to keep that scar, do you?"

"Lord, no," said Sister McCandless, "ain't nothing but a scratch. I declare, Sister Grimes, you worse than a child. Another couple of weeks and you won't be able to *see* no scar. No, you go on about your house-work, honey, and thank the Lord it weren't no worse." She opened the door; they heard the sound of feet on the stairs. "I expect that's the Rever-end," said Sister McCandless, placidly, "I *bet* he going to raise cain."

"Maybe it's Florence," Elizabeth said. "Sometimes she get here about this time." They stood in the doorway, staring, while the steps reached the landing below and began again climbing to their floor. "No," said Elizabeth then, "that ain't her walk. That's Gabriel."

"Well, I'll just go on," said Sister McCandless, "and kind of prepare his mind." She pressed Elizabeth's hand as she spoke and started into the hall, leaving the door behind her slightly ajar. Elizabeth turned slowly back into the room. Roy did not open his eyes, or move; but she knew that he was not sleeping; he wished to delay until the last possible moment any contact with his father. John put his newspaper and his notebook on the table and stood, leaning on the table, staring at her.

"It wasn't my fault," he said. "I couldn't stop him from going down-stairs."

"No," she said, "you ain't got nothing to worry about. You just tell your Daddy the truth."

He looked directly at her, and she turned to the window, staring into the street. What was Sister McCandless saying? Then from her bedroom she heard Delilah's thin wail and she turned, frowning, looking toward the bedroom and toward the still open door. She knew that John was watching her. Delilah continued to wail, she thought, angrily, *Now that girl's getting too big for that*, but she feared that Delilah would awaken Paul and she hurried into the bedroom. She tried to soothe Delilah back to sleep. Then she heard the front door open and close—too loud, Delilah raised her voice, with an exasperated sigh Elizabeth picked the child up. Her child and Gabriel's, her children and Gabriel's: Roy, Delilah, Paul. Only John was nameless and a stranger, living, unalterable testimony to his mother's days in sin.

"What happened?" Gabriel demanded. He stood, enormous, in the center of the room, his black lunchbox dangling from his hand, staring at the sofa where Roy lay. John stood just before him, it seemed to her aston-ished vision just below him, beneath his fist, his heavy shoe. The child stared at the man in fascination and terror—when a girl down home she had seen rabbits stand so paralyzed before the barking dog. She hurried past Gabriel to the sofa, feeling the weight of Delilah in her arms like the weight of a shield, and stood over Roy, saying:

"Now, ain't a thing to get upset about, Gabriel. This boy sneaked downstairs while I had my back turned and got hisself hurt a little. He's alright now."

Roy, as though in confirmation, now opened his eyes and looked gravely at his father. Gabriel dropped his lunchbox with a clatter and knelt by the sofa.

"How you feel, son? Tell your Daddy what happened?"

Roy opened his mouth to speak and then, relapsing into panic, began to cry. His father held him by the shoulder.

"You don't want to cry. You's Daddy's little man. Tell your Daddy what happened."

"He went downstairs," said Elizabeth, "where he didn't have no business to be, and got to fighting with them bad boys playing on that rockpile. That's what happened and it's a mercy it weren't nothing worse."

He looked up at her. "Can't you let this boy answer me for hisself?"

Ignoring this, she went on, more gently: "He got cut on the forehead, but it ain't nothing to worry about."

"You call a doctor? How you know it ain't nothing to worry about?"

"Is you got money to be throwing away on doctors? No, I ain't called no doctor. Ain't nothing wrong with my eyes that I can't tell whether he's hurt bad or not. He got a fright more'n anything else, and you ought to pray God it teaches him a lesson."

"You got a lot to say *now*," he said, "but I'll have *me* something to say in a minute. I'll be wanting to know when all this happened, what you was doing with your eyes *then*." He turned back to Roy, who had lain quietly sobbing eyes wide open and body held rigid: and who now, at his father's touch, remembered the height, the sharp, sliding rock beneath his feet, the sun, the explosion of the sun, his plunge into darkness and his salty blood; and recoiled, beginning to scream, as his father touched his forehead. "Hold still, hold still," crooned his father, shaking, "hold still. Don't cry. Daddy ain't going to hurt you, he just wants to see this bandage, see what they've done to his little man." But Roy continued to scream and would not be still and Gabriel dared not lift the bandage for fear of hurting him more. And he looked at Elizabeth in fury: "Can't you put that child down and help me with this boy? John, take your baby sister from your mother—don't look like neither of you got good sense."

John took Delilah and sat down with her in the easy chair. His mother bent over Roy, and held him still, while his father, carefully—but

still Roy screamed—lifted the bandage and stared at the wound. Roy's
sobs began to lessen. Gabriel readjusted the bandage. "You see," said
Elizabeth, finally, "he ain't nowhere near dead."

"It sure ain't your fault that he ain't dead." He and Elizabeth considered each other for a moment in silence. "He came mightly close to losing
an eye. Course, his eyes ain't as big as your'n, so I reckon you don't think
it matters so much." At this her face hardened; he smiled. "Lord, have
mercy," he said, "you think you ever going to learn to do right? Where
was you when all this happened? Who let him go downstairs?"

"Ain't nobody let him go downstairs, he just went. He got a head just
like his father, it got to be broken before it'll bow. I was in the kitchen."

"Where was Johnnie?"

"He was in here?"

"Where?"

"He was on the fire escape."

"Didn't he know Roy was downstairs?"

"I reckon."

"What you mean, you reckon? He ain't got your big eyes for nothing,
does he?" He looked over at John. "Boy, you see your brother go
downstairs?"

"Gabriel, ain't no sense in trying to blame Johnnie. You know right
well if you have trouble making Roy behave, he ain't going to listen to his
brother. He don't hardly listen to me."

"How come you didn't tell your mother Roy was downstairs?"

John said nothing, staring at the blanket which covered Delilah.

"Boy, you hear me? You want me to take a strap to you?"

"No, you ain't," she said. "You ain't going to take no strap to this
boy, not today you ain't. Ain't a soul to blame for Roy's lying up there
now but you—you because you done spoiled him so that he thinks he can
do just anything and get away with it. I'm here to tell you that ain't no
way to raise no child. You don't pray to the Lord to help you do better
than you been doing, you going to live to shed bitter tears that the Lord
didn't take his soul today." And she was trembling. She moved, unseeing,
toward John and took Delilah from his arms. She looked back at Gabriel,
who had risen, who stood near the sofa, staring at her. And she found in
his face not fury alone, which would not have surprised her; but hatred so
deep as to become insupportable in its lack of personality. His eyes were
struck alive, unmoving, blind with malevolence—she felt, like the pull of
the earth at her feet, his longing to witness her perdition. Again, as though
it might be propitiation, she moved the child in her arms. And at this his
eyes changed, he looked at Elizabeth, the mother of his children, the help-

meet given by the Lord. Then her eyes clouded; she moved to leave the room; her foot struck the lunchbox lying on the floor.

"John," she said, "pick up your father's lunchbox like a good boy."

She heard, behind her, his scrambling movement as he left the easy chair, the scrape and jangle of the lunchbox as he picked it up, bending his dark head near the toe of his father's heavy shoe.

MARGARET DANNER
(d. 1984)

Margaret Danner has lived and written poetry in two prolific urban centers of black culture. In Chicago she wrote poems and was an assistant editor of Poetry *magazine, and in Detroit she continues to produce many excellent poems. In 1962 a special issue of* Negro History Bulletin *featured her works and those of the Detroit poets with whom she was closely associated. She has received a John Hay Whitney Fellowship for poetry and has served as poet-in-residence at Wayne State University and at Virginia Union University. Among the magazines in which she has published poetry are* Accent, Poetry, Chicago Magazine, Chicago Review, Negro Digest, Negro History Bulletin, *and* Quicksilver; Broadside Press *has published a poster poem of hers,* "Not Light, Nor Bright, Nor Feathery." *Her volumes include* Impressions of African Art Forms, To Flower, *and* The Iron Lace. *She is co-author of* Poem: Counterpoem *with Dudley Randall. In 1966 she traveled to Dakar to participate in the First World Festival of Negro Arts.*

Margaret Danner's poems are delicately feminine but firm and clear in their conception and execution. Bold colors heighten their intense visual imagery. With restrained but evident passion she writes of the themes of contemporary black life. Perhaps her most impressive poems are those which combine her love of art with her love of Africa.

Dance of the Abakweta

Imagine what Mrs. Haessler would say
If she could see the Watusi youth dance
Their well-versed initiation. At first glance
As they bend to an invisible barre
You would know that she had designed their costumes.

For though they were made of pale beige bamboo straw
Their lines were the classic tutu. Nothing varied.
Each was cut short at the thigh and carried
High to a degree of right angles. Nor was there a flaw
In their leotards. Made of leopard skin or the hide

Of a goat, or the Gauguin-colored Okapi's striped coat
They were cut in her reverenced "tradition."
She would have approved their costumes and positions.
And since neither Iceland nor Africa is too remote
For her vision she would have wanted to form

A "traditional" ballet. Swan Lake, Scheherazade or
(After seeing their incredible leaps)
Les Orientales. Imagine the exotic sweep
Of such a ballet, and from the way the music pours

Over these dancers (this tinkling of bells, talking
Of drums, and twanging of tan, sandalwood harps)
From this incomparable music, Mrs. Haessler of Vassar can
Glimpse strains of Tchaikovsky, Chopin
To accompany her undeviatingly sharp
"Traditional" ballet. I am certain that if she could
Tutor these potential protégés, as
Quick as Aladdin rubbing his lamp, she would.

Visit of the Professor of Aesthetics

To see you standing in the sagging bookstore door
So filled me with chagrin that suddenly you seemed as
Pink and white to me as a newborn, hairless mouse. For

I had hoped to delight you at home. Be a furl
Of faint perfume and Vienna's cordlike lace.
To shine my piano till a shimmer of mother-of-pearl

Embraced it. To pleasantly surprise you with the grace
That transcends my imitation and much worn
"Louis XV" couch. To display my Cathedrals and ballets.

To plunge you into Africa through my nude
Zulu Prince, my carvings from Benin, forlorn
Treasures garnered by much sacrifice of food.

I had hoped to delight you, for more
Rare than the seven-year bloom of my
Chinese spiderweb fern is a mind like yours

That concedes my fetish for this substance
Of your trade. And I had planned to prove
Your views of me correct at even every chance

Encounter. But you surprised me. And the store which
Had shown promise until you came, arose
Like a child gone wild when company comes or a witch

At Hallowe'en. The floor, just swept and mopped,
Was persuaded by the northlight to deny it.
The muddy rag floor rugs hunched and flopped

Away from the tears in the linoleum that I wanted
Them to hide. The drapes that I had pleated
In clear orchid and peach feverishly flaunted

Their greasiest folds like a banner.
The books who had been my friends, retreated—
Became as shy as the proverbial poet in manner

And hid their better selves. All glow had been deleted
By the dirt. And I felt that you whose god is grace
Could find no semblance of it here. And unaware

That you were scrubbing, you scrubbed your hands.
Wrung and scrubbed your long white fingers. Scrubbed
Them as you smiled and I lowered my eyes from despair.

Gold Is the Shade Esperanto

Long green symbolized by
Gold is the shade Esperanto. Gold is the paragon.
The tint of the sun at noon or at setting
is gold; gold the first tinge of dawn.

for gold, gold, gold and the effort of getting
more gold is labored toward, focused on.
and tots are soon weaned of their baby girl pinks
denied their babyboy blues,

Early taught
gold the lion, the owl, the link
to this chain. Cold the juggernaut.

and gold is the color that all poets use;
golden lights, golden days are never cliche.
Gold is coined without tricks or excuse.

and few turn a hand toward a rainbow tint.
Few of ebony, flesh, or tan tone stray.
Few dare daub a sunset or hazard a hint

of the urge to sonnet to one. So the bold
indigo witchery and tangerine haze with
which our African ancestors colored their gaze
has nearly grown cold,
and the sunset today, like a beacon glaze
is a vision of glittering gold.

And Through the Caribbean Sea

We, like shades that were first conjured up
by an African witch-doctor's ire,
(indigo for the drum and the smoke of night,

tangerine for the dancing smudged fire)
have been forced to exist in a huge kaleidoscope world.
We've been shifting with time and sifting through space,

at each whimsical turn of the hands that have thrown
the kaleidoscope, until any pattern or place
or shade is our own.

The indigo sifted from its drum-like vein
toward the blue of the sky that the Goths attained.
The tangerine became the orange of the tango, again

the red of the Susy Q., and each time the turning invaded
one pattern, a new one was formed
and in forming each pattern, we traded.

Until, who questions whether we'd be prone to yearn
for a Louis Quinze frame, a voodoo fire,
Rococo, Baroque, an African mask or a Gothic spire
or any style of any age or any place or name.

MARTIN LUTHER KING, JR.

(1929-1968)

The forceful personality of Martin Luther King, Jr., his philosophy of nonviolence and his methods of passive resistance were vital influences in the development of the civil rights movement. For black art, Dr. King was, in a sense, the modern personification of the black folk preacher, who exhorted his congregation and spread his influence in many areas of secular life.

Born in Atlanta, King was educated at Morehouse College, Crozier Theological Seminary, and Boston University, where he earned a doctorate in theology. He became pastor of the Dexter Avenue Baptist Church in Montgomery, Alabama, and soon after found himself designated leader of a boycott undertaken to protest bus segregation. In 1957 King organized the Southern Christian Leadership Conference to extend the range of protest.

The story of this organization and of the many activities inspired by it is the story of the 1950s and early 1960s. Nineteen sixty-three was probably the year of peak power: The demonstrations in Birmingham, which Dr. King regarded as a focal point of racial segregation, and the "I Have a Dream" speech at the March on Washington were the highwater marks of the movement. In 1964 Dr. King was awarded the Nobel Peace Prize. In his last years he turned his attention to the war in Vietnam, which he regarded as immoral and as a drain upon resources which might be better used to build humanity rather than to destroy it. In 1968, while supporting a strike of garbagemen in Memphis, Tennessee, Dr. King was assassinated.

Dr. King's writing puts into literary form the rhetorical devices of the preacher—metaphor, parallelism, juxtaposition, contrast, repetition. His thoughts and the progress of his activities are recorded in his written works: Stride Toward Freedom: The Montgomery Story

(1958); Why We Can't Wait *(1963);* Where Do We Go from Here: Chaos or Community? *(1967). His essay, "Letter from a Birmingham Jail," and his speech, "I Have a Dream," are his best known works.*

There is a large and growing literature on all aspects of King's life and work. A book dealing with the basis of his meticulously developed philosophy is John J. Ansbro, Martin Luther King, Jr.: The Making of A Mind *(1982).*

Facing the Challenge of a New Age
Speech at Montgomery, Alabama, December 1956

Those of us who live in the Twentieth Century are privileged to live in one of the most momentous periods of human history. It is an exciting age filled with hope. It is an age in which a new social order is being born. We stand today between two worlds—the dying old and the emerging new.

Now I am aware of the fact that there are those who would contend that we live in the most ghastly period of human history. They would argue that the rhythmic beat of the deep rumblings of discontent from Asia, the uprisings in Africa, the nationalistic longings of Egypt, the roaring cannons from Hungary, and the racial tensions of America are all indicative of the deep and tragic midnight which encompasses our civilization. They would argue that we are retrogressing instead of progressing. But far from representing retrogression and tragic meaninglessness, the present tensions represent the necessary pains that accompany the birth of anything new. Long ago the Greek philosopher Heraclitus argued that justice emerges from the strife of opposites, and Hegel, in modern philosophy, preached a doctrine of growth through struggle. It is both historically and biologically true that there can be no birth and growth without birth and growing pains. Whenever there is the emergence of the new we confront the recalcitrance of the old. So the tensions which we witness in the world today are indicative of the fact that a new world order is being born and an old order is passing away.

We are all familiar with the old order that is passing away. We have lived with it for many years. We have seen it in its international aspect, in the form of colonialism and imperialism. There are approximately two billion four hundred million (2,400,000,000) people in this world, and the vast majority of these people are colored—about one billion six hundred million (1,600,000,000) of the people of the world are colored. Fifty years ago, or even twenty-five years ago, most of these one billion six hundred million people lived under the yoke of some foreign power. We could turn our eyes to China and see there six hundred million men and women under the pressing yoke of British, Dutch, and French rule. We could turn our eyes to Indonesia and see a hundred million men and women under the domination of the Dutch. We could turn to India and Pakistan and notice four hundred million brown men and women under the pressing yoke of the British. We could turn our eyes to Africa and notice there two hundred million black men and women under the pressing yoke of the British, the Dutch and the French. For years all of these people were dominated politically, exploited economically, segregated and humiliated.

But there comes a time when people get tired. There comes a time when people get tired of being trampled over by the iron feet of oppression. There comes a time when people get tired of being plunged across the abyss of exploitation where they experience the bleakness of nagging despair. There comes a time when people get tired of being pushed out of the glittering sunlight of life's July and left standing in the piercing chill of an Alpine November. So in the midst of their tiredness these people decided to rise up and protest against injustice. As a result of their protest more than one billion three hundred million (1,300,000,000) of the colored peoples of the world are free today. They have their own governments, their own economic systems, and their own educational systems. They have broken loose from the Egypt of colonialism and imperialism, and they are now moving through the wilderness of adjustment toward the promised land of cultural integration. As they look back they see the old order of colonialism and imperialism passing away and the new order of freedom and justice coming into being.

We have also seen the old order in our own nation, in the form of segregation and discrimination. We know something of the long history of this old order in America. It had its beginning in the year 1619 when the first Negro slaves landed on the shores of this nation. They were brought here from the soils of Africa. And unlike the Pilgrim Fathers who landed at Plymouth a year later, they were brought here against their wills. Throughout slavery the Negro was treated in a very inhuman fashion. He was a thing to be used, not a person to be respected. He was merely a depersonalized cog in a vast plantation machine. The famous Dred Scott Decision of 1857 well illustrates the status of the Negro during slavery. In this decision the Supreme Court of the United States said, in substance, that the Negro is not a citizen of the United States; he is merely property subject to the dictates of his owner. Then came 1896. It was in this year that the Supreme Court of this nation, through the *Plessy V. Ferguson* Decision, established the doctrine of separate-but-equal as the law of the land. Through this decision segregation gained legal and moral sanction. The end result of the Plessy Doctrine ended up making for tragic inequalities and ungodly exploitation.

Living under these conditions, many Negroes came to the point of losing faith in themselves. They came to feel that perhaps they were less than human. The great tragedy of physical slavery was that it led to mental slavery. So long as the Negro maintained this subservient attitude and accepted this "place" assigned to him, a sort of racial peace existed. But it was an uneasy peace in which the Negro was forced patiently to accept insult, injustice and exploitation. It was a negative peace. True peace is not merely the absence of some negative force—tension, confusion, or war; it is the presence of some positive force—justice, goodwill and brotherhood. And so the peace which existed between the races was a negative peace devoid of any positive and lasting quality.

Then something happened to the Negro. Circumstances made it necessary for him to travel more. His rural plantation background was gradually being supplanted by migration to urban and industrial communities. His economic life was gradually rising to decisive proportions. His cultural life was gradually rising through the steady decline of crippling illiteracy. All of these factors conjoined to cause the Negro to take a new look at himself. Negro masses began to re-evaluate themselves. The Negro came to feel that he was somebody. His religion revealed to him that God loves all of His children, and that every man, from a bass black to a treble white, is significant on God's keyboard. So he could now cry out with the eloquent poet:

Fleecy locks and black complexion
Cannot forfeit nature's claim.
Skin may differ, but affection
Dwells in black and white the same.
And were I so tall as to reach the pole
Or to grasp the ocean at a span,
I must be measured by my soul.
The mind is the standard of the man.

With this new self respect and new sense of dignity on the part of the Negro, the South's negative peace was rapidly undermined. And so the tension which we are witnessing in race relations today can be explained, in part, by the revolutionary change in the Negro's evaluation of himself, and his determination to struggle and sacrifice until the walls of segregation have finally been crushed by the battering rams of surging justice.

Along with the emergence of a "New Negro," with a new sense of dignity and destiny, came that memorable decision of May 17, 1954. In this decision the Supreme Court of this nation unanimously affirmed that the old Plessy Doctrine must go. This decision came as a legal and sociological death blow to an evil that had occupied the throne of American life for several decades. It affirmed in no uncertain terms that separate facilities are inherently unequal and that to segregate a child because of his race is to deny him equal protection of the law. With the coming of this great decision we could gradually see the old order of segregation and discrimination passing away, and the new order of freedom and justice coming into being. Let nobody fool you, all of the loud noises that you hear today from the legislative halls of the South in terms of "interposition" and "nullification," and of outlawing the NAACP are merely the death groans from a dying system. The old order is passing away, and the new order is coming into being. We are witnessing in our day the birth of a new age, with a new structure of freedom and justice.

Now as we face the fact of this new, emerging world, we must face the responsibilities that come along with it. A new age brings with it new challenges. Let us consider some of the challenges of this new age.

First, we are challenged to rise above the narrow confines of our individualistic concerns to the broader concerns of all humanity. The New World is a world of geographical togetherness. This means that no individual or nation can live alone. We must all learn to live together, or we will be forced to die together. This new world of geographical togetherness has been brought about, to a great extent, by man's scientific and technological genius. Man through his scientific genius has been able to dwarf distance and place time in chains; he has been able to carve highways through the stratosphere. And so it is possible today to eat breakfast in New York City and dinner in Paris, France. Bob Hope has described this new jet age in which we live. It is an age in which we will be able to get a non-stop flight from Los Angeles, California to New York City, and if by chance we develop hiccups on taking off, we will "hic" in Los Angeles and "cup" in New York City. It is an age in which one will be able to leave Tokyo on Sunday morning and, because of time difference, arrive in Seattle, Washington on the preceding Saturday night. When your friends meet you at the airport in Seattle inquiring when you left Tokyo, you will have to say, "I left tomorrow." This, in a very humorous sense, says to us that our world is geographically one. Now we are faced with the challenge of making it spiritually one. Through our scientific genius we have made of the world a neighborhood; now through our moral and spiritual genius we must make of it a brotherhood. We are all involved in the single process. Whatever affects one directly affects all indirectly. We are all links in the great chain of humanity. This is what John Donne meant when he said years ago:

> No man is an island, entire of it selfe; every man is a piece of the Continent, a part of the maine; if a clod bee washed away by the Sea, Europe is the lesse, as well as if a Promontorie were, as well as if a Mannor of thy friends or of thine owne were; any man's death diminishes me, because I am involved in Mankind; And therefore never send to know for whom the bell tolls; it tolls for thee.

A second challenge that the new age brings to each of us is that of achieving excellency in our various fields of endeavor. In the new age many doors will be opening to us that were not opened in the past, and the great challenge which we confront is to be prepared to enter these doors as they open. Ralph Waldo Emerson said in an essay back in 1871:

> If a man can write a better book, or preach a better sermon, or make a better mouse trap than his neighbor, even if he builds his house in the woods the world will make a beaten path to his door.

In the new age we will be forced to compete with people of all races and nationalities. Therefore, we cannot aim merely to be good Negro teachers, good Negro doctors, good Negro ministers, good

Negro skilled laborers. We must set out to do a good job, irrespective
of race, and do it so well that nobody could do it better.

Whatever your life's work is, do it well. Even if it does not fall
in the category of one of the so-called big professions, do it well. As
one college president said, "A man should do his job so well that the
living, the dead, and the unborn could do it no better." If it falls your
lot to be a street sweeper, sweep streets like Michelangelo painted
pictures, like Shakespeare wrote poetry, like Beethoven composed
music; sweep streets so well that all the host of Heaven and earth will
have to pause and say, "Here lived a great street sweeper, who swept
his job well." As Douglas Mallock says:

> If you can't be a pine on the top of the hill
> Be a scrub in the valley—but be
> The best little scrub by the side of the hill,
> Be a bush if you can't be a tree.
>
> If you can't be a highway just be a trail
> If you can't be the sun be a star;
> It isn't by size that you win or fail—
> Be the best of whatever you are.

A third challenge that stands before us is that of entering the new
age with understanding goodwill. This simply means that the Christian
virtues of love, mercy and forgiveness should stand at the center of
our lives. There is the danger that those of us who have lived so long
under the yoke of oppression, those of us who have been exploited
and trampled over, those of us who have had to stand amid the tragic
midnight of injustice and indignities will enter the new age with hate
and bitterness. But if we retaliate with hate and bitterness, the new age
will be nothing but a duplication of the old age. We must blot out
the hate and injustice of the old age with the love and justice of the
new. This is why I believe so firmly in non-violence. Violence never
solves problems. It only creates new and more complicated ones. If
we succumb to the temptation of using violence in our struggle for
justice, unborn generations will be the recipients of a long and desolate night of bitterness, and our chief legacy to the future will be an
endless reign of meaningless chaos.

We have before us the glorious opportunity to inject a new di-

mension of love into the veins of our civilization. There is still a voice
crying out in terms that echo across the generations, saying:

> Love your enemies, bless them that curse you, pray for them
> that despitefully use you, that you may be the children of your
> Father which is in Heaven.

This love might well be the salvation of our civilization. This is why
I am so impressed with our motto for the week, "Freedom and Justice through Love." Not through violence; not through hate; no, not
even through boycotts; but through love. It is true that as we struggle
for freedom in America we will have to boycott at times. But we
must remember as we boycott that a boycott is not an end within
itself; it is merely a means to awaken a sense of shame within the
oppressor and challenge his false sense of superiority. But the end is
reconciliation; the end is redemption; the end is the creation of the
beloved community. It is this type of spirit and this type of love that
can transform opposers into friends. It is this type of understanding
goodwill that will transform the deep gloom of the old age into the
exuberant gladness of the new age. It is this love which will bring
about miracles in the hearts of men.

Now I realize that in talking so much about love it is very easy
to become sentimental. There is the danger that our talk about love
will merely be empty words devoid of any practical and true meaning. But when I say love those who oppose you I am not speaking of
love in a sentimental or affectionate sense. It would be nonsense to
urge men to love their oppressors in an affectionate sense. When I
refer to love at this point I mean understanding goodwill. The Greek
language comes to our aid at this point. The Greek language has three
words for love. First it speaks of love in terms of *Eros*. Plato used this
word quite frequently in his dialogues. *Eros* is a type of esthetic love.
Now it has come to mean a sort of romantic love. I guess Shakespeare
was thinking in terms of *Eros* when he said:

> Love is not love which alters when it alteration finds, or bends
> with the remover to remove. It is an ever fixed mark that looks
> on tempest and is never shaken. It is a star to every wandering
> bark. . . .

This is *Eros*. And then the Greek talks about *philia*. *Philia* is a sort of intimate affectionateness between personal friends. It is a sort of reciprocal love. On this level a person loves because he is loved. Then the Greek language comes out with another word which is the highest level of love. It speaks of it in terms of *agape*. *Agape* means nothing sentimental or basically affectionate. It means understanding, redeeming goodwill for all men. It is an overflowing love which seeks nothing in return. It is the love of God working in the lives of men. When we rise to love on the *agape* level we love men not because we like them, not because their attitudes and ways appeal to us, but because God loves us. Here we rise to the position of loving the person who does the evil deed while hating the deed that the person does. With this type of love and understanding goodwill we will be able to stand amid the radiant glow of the new age with dignity and discipline. Yes, the new age is coming. It is coming mighty fast.

Now the fact that this new age is emerging reveals something basic about the universe. It tells us something about the core and heartbeat of the cosmos. It reminds us that the universe is on the side of justice. It says to those who struggle for justice, "You do not struggle alone, but God struggles with you." This belief that God is on the side of truth and justice comes down to us from the long tradition of our Christian faith. There is something at the very center of our faith which reminds us that Good Friday may occupy the throne for a day, but ultimately it must give way to the triumphant beat of the drums of Easter. Evil may so shape events that Caesar will occupy a palace and Christ a cross, but one day that same Christ will rise up and split history into AD and BC, so that even the life of Caesar must be dated by His name. There is something in this universe that justifies Carlyle in saying, "No lie can live forever." There is something in this universe which justifies William Cullen Bryant in saying, "Truth crushed to earth will rise again." There is something in this universe that justifies James Russell Lowell in saying:

Truth forever on the scaffold
Wrong forever on the throne
Yet that scaffold sways the future
And behind the dim unknown stands God
Within the shadows keeping watch above his own.

And so here in Montgomery, after more than eleven long months, we can walk and never get weary, because we know there is a great camp meeting in the promised land of freedom and justice.

Before closing I must correct what might be a false impression. I am afraid that if I close at this point many will go away misinterpreting my whole message. I have talked about the new age which is fastly coming into being. I have talked about the fact that God is working in history to bring about this new age. There is the danger, therefore, that after hearing all of this you will go away with the impression that we can go home, sit down, and do nothing, waiting for the coming of the inevitable. You will somehow feel that this new age will roll in on the wheels of inevitability, so there is nothing to do but wait on it. If you get that impression you are the victims of a dangerous optimism. If you go away with that interpretation you are the victims of an illusion wrapped in superficiality. We must speed up the coming of the inevitable.

Now it is true, if I may speak figuratively, that old man segregation is on his death-bed. But history has proven that social ssytems have a great last minute breathing power, and the guardians of a status quo are always on hand with their oxygen tents to keep the old order alive. Segregation is still a fact in America. We still confront it in the South in its glaring and conspicuous forms. We still confront it in the North in its hidden and subtle forms. But if Democracy is to live, segregation must die. Segregation is a glaring evil. It is utterly unchristian. It relegates the segregated to the status of a thing rather than elevate him to the status of a person. Segregation is nothing but slavery covered up with certain niceties of complexity. Segregation is a blatant denial of the unity which we all have in Christ Jesus.

So we must continue the struggle against segregation in order to speed up the coming of the inevitable. We must continue to gain the ballot. This is one of the basic keys to the solution of our problem. Until we gain political power through possession of the ballot we will be convenient tools of unscrupulous politicians. We must face the appalling fact that we have been betrayed by both the Democratic and Republican parties. The Democrats have betrayed us by capitulating to the whims and caprices of the southern Dixiecrats. The Republicans have betrayed us by capitulating to the blatant hypocrisy of right-wing reactionary Northerners. This coalition of Southern Democrats and Northern right-wing Republicans defeats every proposed bill on civil rights. Until we gain the ballot and place proper public officials in office this condition will continue to exist. In communities where we confront difficulties in gaining the ballot, we must use all legal and moral means to remove these difficulties.

We must continue to struggle through legalism and legislation. There are those who contend that integration can come only through education, for no other reason than that morals cannot be legislated. I choose, however, to be dialectical at this point. It is neither education nor legislation; it is both legislation and education. I quite agree that it is impossible to change a man's internal feelings merely through law. But this really is not the intention of the law. The law does not seek to change one's internal feelings; it seeks rather to control the external effects of those internal feelings. For instance, the law cannot make a man love—religion and education must do that—but it can control his efforts to lynch. So in order to control the external effects of prejudiced internal feelings, we must continue to struggle through legislation.

Another thing that we must do in pressing on for integration is to invest our finances in the cause of freedom. Freedom has always been an expensive thing. History is a fit testimony to the fact that freedom is rarely gained without sacrifice and self-denial. So we must donate large sums of money to the cause of freedom. We can no longer complain that we do not have the money. Statistics reveal that the economic life of the Negro is rising to decisive proportions. The annual income of the American Negro is now more than sixteen billion dollars, almost equal to the national income of Canada. So we are gradually becoming economically independent. It would be a tragic indictment on both the self respect and practical wisdom of the Negro if history reveals that at the height of the Twentieth Century the Negro spent more for frivolities than for the cause of freedom. We must never let it be said that we spend more for the evanescent and ephemeral than for the eternal values of freedom and justice.

Another thing that we must do in speeding up the coming of the new age is to develop intelligent, courageous and dedicated leadership. This is one of the pressing needs of the hour. In this period of transition and growing social change, there is a dire need for leaders who are calm and yet positive, leaders who avoid the extremes of "hot-headedness" and "Uncle Tomism." The urgency of the hour calls for leaders of wise judgment and sound integrity—leaders not in love with money, but in love with justice; leaders not in love with publicity, but in love with humanity; leaders who can subject their particular egos to the greatness of the cause. To paraphrase Holland's words:

> God give us leaders!
> A time like this demands strong minds, great hearts,
>   true faith and ready hands;
> Leaders whom the lust of office does not kill;
> Leaders whom the spoils of life cannot buy;
> Leaders who possess opinions and a will;
> Leaders who have honor; leaders who will not lie;
> Leaders who can stand before a demagogue
>   and damn his treacherous flatteries without winking!
> Tall leaders, sun crowned, who live above the fog
>   in public duty and private thinking.

Finally, if we are to speed up the coming of the new age we must have the moral courage to stand up and protest against injustice wherever we find it. Wherever we find segregation we must have the fortitude to passively resist it. I realize that this will mean suffering and sacrifice. It might even mean going to jail. If such is the case we must be willing to fill up the jail houses of the South. It might even mean physical death. But if physical death is the price that some must pay to free their children from a permanent life of psychological death, then nothing could be more honorable. Once more it might well turn out that the blood of the martyr will be the seed of the tabernacle of freedom.

Someone will ask, how will we face the acts of cruelty and violence that might come as results of our standing up for justice? What will be our defense? Certainly it must not be retaliatory violence. We must find our defense in the amazing power of unity and courage that we have demonstrated in Montgomery. Our defense is to meet every act of violence toward an individual Negro with the facts that there are thousands of others who will present themselves in his place at potential victims. Every time one school teacher is fired for standing up courageously for justice, it must be faced with the fact that there are four thousand more to be fired. If the oppressors bomb the home of one Negro for his courage, this must be met with the fact that they must be required to bomb the homes of fifty thousand more

Negroes. This dynamic unity, this amazing self respect, this willingness to suffer, and this refusal to hit back will soon cause the oppressor
to become ashamed of his own methods. He will be forced to stand
before the world and his God splattered with the blood and reeking
with the stench of his Negro brother.

There is nothing in all the world greater than freedom. It is
worth paying for; it is worth losing a job; it is worth going to jail for.
I would rather be a free pauper than a rich slave. I would rather die
in abject poverty with my convictions than live in inordinate riches
with the lack of self respect. Once more every Negro must be able
to cry out with his forefathers: "Before I'll be a slave, I'll be buried
in my grave and go home to my Father and be saved."

If we will join together in doing all of these things we will be
able to speed up the coming of the New World—a new world in
which men will live together as brothers; a world in which men will
beat their swords into ploughshares and their spears into pruning-
hooks; a world in which men will no longer take necessities from the
masses to give luxuries to the classes; a world in which all men will
respect the dignity and worth of all human personality. Then we will
be able to sing from the great tradition of our Nation:

> My Country 'tis of thee,
> Sweet land of liberty,
> Of thee I sing;
> Land where my fathers died;
> Land of the pilgrim's pride;
> From every mountain side
> Let Freedom ring!

This must become literally true. Freedom must ring from every
mountain side. Yes, let it ring from the snow-capped Rockies of
Colorado, from the prodigious hilltops of New Hampshire, from the
mighty Alleghenies of Pennsylvania, from the curvaceous slopes of
California. But not only that. Let Freedom ring from every mountain
side—from every mole hill in Mississippi, from Stone Mountain of
Georgia, from Lookout Mountain of Tennessee, yes, and from every
hill and mountain of Alabama. From every mountain side let freedom
ring. When this day finally comes "The morning stars will sing together and the sons of God will shout for joy."

HOYT W. FULLER
(1925-1981)

One of the most influential figures in Afro-American letters in the sixties and seventies was Hoyt Fuller. Born in Atlanta, Fuller was educated in Detroit. After a career in editing and as a free-lance writer residing abroad, he revived the Johnson Publishing Company's Negro Digest, *converting it to a major forum of black-world opinion, a fact duly commemorated by the change of the name of the magazine to* Black World *in 1970.*

During a decade and a half in Chicago, while editing Negro Digest/Black World, *Fuller also nurtured a group of young writers and other artists in the weekly OBAC workshop. After the cancellation of the monthly magazine in 1975, he moved to Atlanta to launch a magazine of literature and opinion called* First World.

His deep concern for Africa is reflected in the brief volume of selections, Journal to Africa *(1971), in which he sets forth his reactions to the postcolonial ethos of a continent still dominated in many respects by Europe.*

As editor and critic, Fuller was preeminent in the articulation of the black aesthetic, insisting that works emanating from the black experience be judged by persons saturated in that experience.

Dinner at Diop's

The restaurant Chez Diop was only a short walk from my hotel, La Savoie—a distance of four blocks, in fact—but I allowed myself a full fifteen minutes to negotiate it. It was 7:45 and the sun still hung high—if somewhat hazy—over the squat, tin-roofed, dust-daubed houses. If I walked leisurely, I had decided, I would not arrive for my dinner appointment dripping with perspiration, my cool shower nullified. M. Drin had been emphatic about the time, his crooked, red-lipped smile mischievous beneath the inch-thick black mustache. "At eight, M'sier, we will be waiting." The "we" was to include the "two charming young ladies" he had seemed so eager that I meet. "Conakry's most superb attractions will await you tomorrow evening," he had promised. "The cuisine of Diop and the company of my friends."

I was, frankly, both intrigued and apprehensive. I had first heard of the delights of Chez Diop from a proud Guinean student at a café on Boulevard St. Michel in Paris. "African food in the French manner," he had bragged, closing his eyes and shaking his head in pleasurable recall. "You are an American Negro and have never eaten African food, so you must go there." Later, aboard the liner *Foch*, sailing round the western bulge of Africa, a Dakar-bound French salesman who was familiar with all the French-speaking territories of the continent also had spoken enthusiastically of M. Diop's culinary artistry. In fact, the products of M. Diop's kitchen had been about all the Frenchman had spoken of favorably in Africa. The gentleman had not found it convenient to remain in Casablanca after the Moroccans assumed control of the country. And now, in January, 1959, with the dissolution of France's black African empire imminent, he was hard put to lavish any sentiment on the area. But Chez Diop was that extraordinary. "Ah, the food is excellent there," he affirmed.

"Diop was a chef in Paris, you know. Yes, yes, you must go there."
But on reflection, the Frenchman had offered a word of precaution.
"You should dine at Diop's for the experience, yes, but there is another restaurant just around the corner where the food is also excellent and much less dear. Le Paradis. Perhaps, if you do not have
unlimited funds, it would be wiser to dine regularly at Le Paradis.
But do not leave Conakry without dining at Chez Diop."

With such high recommendations, then, I looked forward to
dinner at Diop's with some anticipation. However, the prospect of
meeting M. Drin's "two charming young ladies" left me with feelings
considerably more ambiguous. I had only just met M. Drin the night
before, and the sketchy information he had volunteered about himself
gave me no clue as to what could be expected under the circumstances.
He had introduced himself in the bar in which I had sought refuge
from the wrenching heat. I was en route to my hotel after a rather
exhausting all-day visit to the extensive Fria aluminum mining works
in the interior, and I desperately needed refreshing. The bar was a
modern, cozy-looking little establishment which proved to be as cool
on the inside as it had seemed from the outside. When I entered, it
was empty except for three white men clustered on the customer
side of the counter, a strikingly handsome brown man behind the
counter talking with them, and an African bartender busy polishing
glasses at the far end of the bar. The African immediately put aside
his cloth and rushed to serve me, bubbling out an eager, "Bon soir,
M'sieur." It was when I asked, in French, if Dutch or German beer
was available that the four men down the counter abruptly ceased
conversing and focused attention on me. The bartender had hardly
produced the bottle of Dutch beer before the quartet sidled within
touching distance.

I suppose M. Drin was natural spokesman for the group, since
only he knew English. He was tall and solidly built, with thick black
hair and matching mustache over a thin, crooked mouth that seemed
perpetually on the verge of a sneer. He introduced himself in fluent
English. "I can tell you are an American," he said. "Your accent is
unmistakable."

I confessed that I was an American and braced myself for the
inevitable rush of questions. But M. Drin was tactful. Before asking
me who I was and why I was in Guinea, he proceeded to lay a
groundwork conducive to friendly exchange by volunteering information about himself. He was of Polish-French descent, he said, and had
lost his family during the war. He had spent several years with the

U.S. Army, part of the time in the United States. Now he was a salesman of books, school supplies, and office machinery. He did not say he was Jewish, which he was, and which fact helped to explain the others.

Having broken the ice, M. Drin introduced me to his friends. The short, pale gentleman was M. Berard, an official of a local trucking firm. The taller, thinner, and tanner man, hawkish and balding, was M. Foucher, manager of a variety store. M. Drin's smile grew plain wicked at the next introduction. This was M. Derval, the proprietor, the amber-colored man behind the counter. M. Derval shook hands warmly, studying my face through intense hazel eyes. "Welcome to Conakry," he said. I thanked him and sipped my beer.

Reverting to English, M. Drin now proceeded to ask the expected questions. In reply, I explained that I had come to Guinea to do a series of articles for the *Haagse Post*, a newspaper in Amsterdam. This was true, but only a part of the truth. I also had come out of curiosity and excitement, moved by the courage and drama of Sekou Touré who, a few weeks earlier, had severed the umbilical cord joining the territory with France. I also was doing a series of articles for the *Michigan Chronicle*, a weekly Detroit newspaper for which I formerly had worked as a feature editor. However, I saw no reason to divulge these further motives for making the journey to Guinea.

"You came all the way from America?" M. Drin asked, obviously impressed at the idea.

"No, I came to Africa from Spain."

"Ah, you live in Spain?"

"I have lived there for a year."

"And you like it?"

"I like it very much."

He considered a moment, scrutinizing my face with hard brown eyes—eyes which were, incidentally, much darker than M. Derval's. "Is this your first time in Africa?"

"Yes, in West Africa. I was in Algeria and Morocco."

"And what do you think of Guinea?"

I hesitated, partly out of caution. M. Drin's sly smile warned of a trap. "I find it most interesting," I said vaguely. "Of course, I have never before been in a country governed by Negroes. It is a new experience."

"They will fail."

The simple emphatic tone was surprising. "But how can you know?" I asked.

M. Drin gave the familiar Gallic shrug. "How can they run a country? They know nothing. Without Frenchmen, there would be no electricity, the water system would not operate, there would be no telephone or telegraph service . . ."

"The Africans will learn." My words sounded helplessly banal, even to me. "They must have time."

"Time!" he gave a derisive laugh.

"These things always take time," I found myself saying defensively.

"Then they should have waited," he said. "Why didn't they wait until they knew what is necessary to run a country?"

The other three men had been straining to understand the exchange between M. Drin and me, and now M. Berard, the short, pale Frenchman, impatiently tapped M. Drin on the shoulder. "What does he say?" he demanded. "Why don't you speak French?"

As M. Drin repeated our argument, it dawned on me that I had been drawn into a sort of running debate on the question of African independence. The four men conferred for a moment, and then M. Derval leaned toward me over the counter, his expression kindly, his tone rather patronizing. I had been told frequently by Frenchmen that the most elegant French was spoken by Africans and Antillians, and M. Derval's command of the language was a case in support of the claim. His French was lovely. "It is true, M'sieur," he said, as if his word on any subject sealed the matter forever. "I am African, my mother is Guinean, and so I speak without malice. It is true. The Africans do not have the experience in running a government. It would have been better to wait."

"Wait until when?" I asked him.

He shrugged, "Until they knew."

The answer to that seemed obvious, but it also seemed useless to try to point it out. After all, the Guineans *had* independence now, so it was pointless to debate whether they should have it. Nevertheless, I thought I should remind him of what he apparently had forgotten. "If the Africans do not know, it is because the French chose not to teach them," I said, silently wishing I could extricate myself from involvement in the quarrel. "You say the Africans should have waited, but you do not say how long they should have waited. The French have been here eighty years. They might have preferred staying another eighty. I suppose the Guineans thought they had to begin learning at some time. Why not now?"

M. Derval simply shrugged again, but M. Drin was more persistent. "They will fail," he repeated. "They have no doctors, no nurses, no teachers, no architects or builders, and they do not know the meaning of the word 'efficiency.' "

I smiled at that. Just that very afternoon I had felt like telling the postal clerks at the main post office those very words—that they did not understand the meaning of efficiency. I had stood in a long line that extended out of the building and onto the sidewalk, waiting to buy stamps, and I had watched the clerks engaging in gossip and tom-foolery behind the counters. They were not merely indifferent to the discomfort of the queuers; the clerks actually were enjoying their ability to make the people wait. But then, recognizing that power of any kind was new to them—and heady—it was easier for me to bear the inconvenience. Still, I understood M. Drin's exasperation, and even his malice.

However, I wondered why M. Drin remained in Guinea if he had so little faith in the ability of the Guineans. In the first weeks after Sekou Touré opted for independence, hundreds of Frenchmen packed up their belongings and took the first available boat or plane back to France. Others waited only until they could wind up their affairs and find passage on Europe-bound carriers. Why, then, I asked M. Drin, had he chosen to stay behind?

"I like it here," he replied. "It is something you could not understand. I love the smell of Africa, the people, the weather, and all the other things which Europeans are supposed to dislike about it. I am at home in Africa. Even if they drive me out of Guinea, I will go someplace else in Africa. It is in my blood. No other place in the world gives me the same satisfaction."

I laughed. "No, I don't understand that."

"But it is true, M'sieur. I am at home in Africa."

M. Drin then began to recount his voyages among his beloved Africans and I listened in silence but with growing weariness. There was an uncomfortable similarity between M. Drin's affection for the Africans and that celebrated "love" of the Negro so often avowed by white American southerners. When I had finished my beer, I paid for it and started to leave. But M. Drin mistook my fatigue for pique and begged that I have another beer at his expense. I assured him that I was not displeased, that I merely wanted to return to the hotel and have a shower and a rest before dinner.

"Well, then, promise that you will have dinner with me tomorrow," he said, thumping me on the shoulder. "That will prove that our little disagreement does not mean we cannot be friends. What do you say?"

"Very well," I agreed.

"Ah, good. We will dine at Chez Diop. Do you know the restaurant?"

"I have heard of it."

"It is just down the street. At eight o'clock."

"Very well."

M. Drin gave me another thump on the shoulder. "If you don't mind, I will bring along two charming young ladies to make the evening complete . . ."

I suppose I stared.

"Ah, you did not expect that," he said, his smile more crooked than ever. "I want you to meet these young ladies. Conakry's most superb attractions will await you tomorrow evening. The cuisine of Diop and the company of my friends. At eight, M'sieur, we will be waiting."

I thanked him, shook hands, and said good evening. I also nodded a farewell to the frustrated trio of listeners before walking out into the sweltering evening heat.

Several Citröens, a Dauphine or two, and those French motor roustabouts that resemble a cross between the American Jeep and the English Land Rover were parked on both sides of the dusty street in front of Chez Diop. The restaurant snuggled between two giant baobab trees. The sidewalk in front of the restaurant was washed and shaded by a blue-and-white striped canopy. Several French couples occupied the tables on the hedge-bordered terrace and, as I turned into the main dining room, I saw that most of the customers inside were also French. I did not see M. Drin at first but—hearing him call "hello" in English—I turned to find him standing at the end of the terrace waving to me. I started in his direction, but then I must have stopped dead in my tracks. What so startled me was the sight of M. Drin's companions. Having already labeled the man a full-blown racist, I had not considered that his "two charming young ladies" might be Africans.

By the time I reached M. Drin's table, I had regained composure. He greeted me with more effusiveness than I thought necessary, grasping my hand with extra vigor, and it might have been my imagination that painted his smile with adding cunning. He introduced the girls, pausing as he did to permit me a fleeting appraisal. A white-jacketed African waiter appeared to assist me into my chair and to take my order for an aperitive. The others were sipping Cinzano, so I asked for one. That done, I settled down to getting acquainted with the young ladies. The one seated opposite me, apparently my partner for the evening, was Therèse. She had a small head, bright-darting eyes, a tiny round nose, a permanently pursed mouth, and a long elegant throat. Her silk-smooth skin had the slightly blueish undertone of the Senegalese, and large pearl-white earrings framed her face. Therèse wore her short hair brushed straight back and held in place with white combs. The other young lady, Efua, was the more striking of the two. Her black eyes were slanted, doelike, her nose small and round like Therèse's, but her mouth wide and full. Her skin was the color of creamed cocoa and seemed to benefit from some inner radiance. She had captured her full crown of tangled black hair in a snood on her neck. Both girls were mannequin slender and Paris chic and, it developed, possessed airs as sophisticated as women bred in the cosmopolitan world of France although, in fact, neither had ever been out of Guinea. M. Drin had explained my purposes in the country and now, to make conversation, Therèse asked what places I had visited. I started to list the landmarks I had seen thus far, became suddenly conscious of the beauty of Therèse's French and the awkwardness of my own, and proceeded to apologize. Therèse mumbled something about my French being more than adequate, but Efua was not inclined toward indulgence. "Go right ahead and talk," she said coolly. "We will understand."

Stripped of all crutches, I recited the places I had visited—the presidential palace where I had interviewed Sekou Touré, the Department of the Interior where I had talked with Keita Fodeba, the drive to the Maison des Jeunes to see the director, the previous day's tour of the new city rising around the aluminum mines . . .

"You have been very busy," Therèse said. "You already have seen things I have not seen, and I have lived here all my life."

"That is often true of tourists," I small-talked. "They are always rushing off to see landmarks the local people take for granted."

"I suppose you have been taking photographs?"

"Yes," I admitted. "I am not a professional photographer, but I wish I were. I am especially intrigued by the different costumes the women wear in the various localities. I am learning to identify the tribes by the costumes . . . "

Efua broke into laughter, "Can you tell *our* tribes by our costumes?"

"Of course not," I said, flustered. "I had reference to the people in the villages . . ."

"Can you name our tribes then?"

I had guessed that Thérèse was Senegalese but decided it probably was more prudent not to hazard an opinion. I shook my head. "No."

"I am Senegalese," Thérèse said at once. "My parents came from St. Louis."

"And I am half-caste." Efua smiled.

"A half-caste?"

"Don't be astonished, M'sieur," she said. "It is not unusual."

"But you don't look like a mulatto at all . . ."

"Mulatto!" Efua joined Thérèse and M. Drin in uproarious laughter.

"But you said you were a half-caste," I said to Efua.

"Yes, but not a mulatto," M. Drin spoke up. "M. Derval, you will remember last night, is a mulatto. Not Efua."

"My father is Malinké, my mother is Soussou," Efua explained. "That makes me a half-caste."

"Oh, it is a new idea for me," I confessed.

Suddenly, pointing toward a tall blond Frenchman in khaki shorts who had just entered the restaurant, Efua cried: "Look, there is that stupid pig Vistel!"

"The ape!" Thérèse gasped, almost loud enough for the man to hear.

Noting my astonishment, M. Drin put a hand on my arm. "M. Vistel is a particular enemy of Thérèse," he explained.

"Oh, forgive me," Thérèse said, not smiling, her bright eyes burning in the direction of the blond man. "I am sorry, but he has his nerve coming here!"

"Why shouldn't he come here?" I ventured to ask.

The two girls glanced at me, then at each other, and then at M. Drin. M. Drin, expanding his off-balance smile, bent toward me. "He is head of the clinic where Thérèse's friend, Dr. Musard, is an associate. He has given Musard an ultimatum—either to stop seeing Thérèse or to leave the clinic."

"Dr. Musard is French?" I asked.

"Yes, of course."

"Oh."

"Vistel behaved in a beastly manner," Efua said, consolingly, to Thérèse. "He should be run out of the country."

"I would like to see him murdered," Thérèse said convincingly.

M. Drin again leaned forward to explain. "It was at the Hôtel de France. We had arrived for dinner, the four of us—Efua, Thérèse, Musad, and I. Vistel was there with a party. Immediately, they all got up and stalked out, leaving their dinner uneaten."

"You would have thought Thérèse was a common whore," Efua said. "It was so insulting."

I had not expected to find this kind of racism in an independent African country, particularly one steeped in French culture. I said this to M. Drin.

"Well, it is not racism, really," M. Drin said slyly. "Musard's wife is a very close friend of Madame Vistel . . ."

I dared not look at Thérèse.

"You are shocked, M'sieur?" she asked.

"No," I replied truthfully. I was not shocked, but I was embarrassed.

"I suppose it is natural if you are," she said generously. "Many people are. No one seems to approve, really. The neighbors have complained to my father."

"And what does your father say?"

She shrugged. "He is not concerned. He says it is my life to live as I choose."

"And are you in love with this Dr. Musard?"

Thérèse laughed. "I am very fond of him."

During the brief silence that followed, the glances of Thérèse and Efua wandered again to the blond man who had joined two other Frenchmen at a table. M. Drin brought their attention back to the table. "We have a guest, ladies," he said, "and I don't think he is interested in Vistel and his bad manners."

"Of course not," Efua said charmingly. "Tell us some of the things that interest you, M'sieur."

There was something vaguely hostile about the enchanting Efua. It intrigued me.

"I am secretary to the Minister of Transportation," Efua said.

"I am interested in your country, mademoiselle," I said, and added, including Thérèse in my smile, "and in what you do in it."

"Thérèse is assistant at the pharmacist's."

"And you are a journalist," Thérèse said, ambiguously.

"Well, yes . . . "

"What will you say about us—about our country?"

"Well, it is too early to know," I said. "After all, I have only been here a few days. There is still much to see."

"Do you like what you have seen?"

"Yes, I find your country very stimulating."

"It is so different from your United States," she said, again ambiguously.

"Yes . . ."

Efua leaned forward, smiling sweetly. "Here, you are free," she said.

I turned to look at her. Now it was quite clear that Efua had been taunting me. I was suddenly annoyed. But it was ridiculous! Being patronized by an African girl in a steamy, dusty, backward little acorn of a nation! The irony of the whole thing overwhelmed me, and I had to force control of my emotions. But then I realized that I had revealed to myself, sentiment aside, what I really felt about the girl and, indeed, the country. The realization was sobering. After all, the burden of communication was mine. I had come to Africa— Africa had not sent for me.

"What, exactly, do you mean?" I asked Efua, carefully modulating my voice.

She stared at me a moment, whether with pity or contempt I could not be certain. "We read the papers, M'sieur. We know of how you are treated in the United States of America."

"Perhaps you get a distorted view of conditions in my country," I said. At that moment, as at many other times before and afterward in Europe and Africa, I found myself making an effort to put into a pleasanter perspective the racial situation in America. Defending it was the last thing on earth I wanted to do, and yet all attempts at explanation automatically had the effect of defense. In frustration, I shifted to M. Drin. After all, he had lived in America. He knew what it was like. "Perhaps things are not quite the way they seem from stories in the papers," I said.

M. Drin's viscous smile was monumentally noncommittal.

"Perhaps," Efua said, with deliberate doubtfulness.

Thérèse extended cool fingers to touch my hand, a gesture of compassion. "Tell us how long you will stay in Conakry," she said.

I withdrew my hand. Mere annoyance threatened to become

violent anger. "No, I don't want you to change the subject," I told her. "I want to know what both of you think about America and American Negroes."

Efua gave a little laugh. "But, M'sieur, I never think of them at all. What has your country to do with us? And American Negroes? Obviously, they can do nothing at all."

I started to speak and, I suppose, I would have gone into a long and probably futile recitation of the achievements of American Negroes, but M. Diop, himself, arrived at the table at that moment. M. Diop was a tall, purplish-skinned Senegalese, round-faced and hard-eyed, with the universal girth of the chef and the imperious bearing of his race. He spoke familiarly to M. Drin and the two young women and, in acknowledgment of M. Drin's introduction of me, smiled graciously. Then, for several minutes, he and M. Drin discussed what would be served us for dinner. M. Drin explained that he wanted a very special African dinner for the occasion and M. Diop assured him everything would be perfect. M. Diop snapped his plump fingers and a waiter darted forward. The chef uttered some orders, apparently in Wolof and the waiter disappeared into the kitchen. M. Diop gave me a little bow, smiled at M. Drin and the women, and moved off across the dining room to another table.

"You are going to have a fabulous meal," M. Drin told me.

I nodded.

"M'sieur might not like African food," Therèse suggested.

"Oh, I probably will . . ."

"It is impossible not to like M. Diop's food," M. Drin insisted.

I nodded.

"M'sieur seems preoccupied," Efua mocked.

"I suppose I am," I said. "I would like you and Therèse to know more about my people and my country."

"But why?" Efua shrugged. "I have no interest."

"But you know nothing about America and yet you have made up your mind. Had you ever even met another American Negro before me?"

"No."

"And yet you were not even curious about them?"

"No."

I laughed in disbelief.

"It is not exactly as though we knew nothing at all," Therèse injected. "As Efua has said, we read the papers and magazines and books. And then, of course, there is the cinema . . ."

"The cinema?"

"Yes, of course." Thérèse was all sympathy. "We see American Negroes in the movies. They are always servants. Or else they are singers and dancers, entertainers for the white Americans. We are not very impressed by these occupations."

"But the cinema has very little to do with the facts of American life," I began. And then, finally, I recognized the futility of my argument, the ridiculousness of my position. There was nowhere to begin. Their image of America had been formed by reports of racial conflict and of the endless struggle over civil rights and the inanities of Hollywood. This was French-speaking Africa, where not even copies of *Ebony* magazine logically would have found their way, telling their glamorized story of the Negro in America. Depression settled over me like some smothering invisible cloak. I shook my head in defeat.

"Come now, you are here to enjoy yourself," M. Drin said gaily, leaning back so that the waiter could deposit a tray of steaming aromatic meats, garnished by dark herbs and held on skewers. "Let us forget serious matters for the rest of the evening."

"But you could have explained to them," I said to him in English. "You know what the situation is. You were in America."

"Oh, my friend," he said chidingly, and the twisted smile seemed revolting. "Forget it. Forget it. Here is food for a king. Let us eat and be happy."

The waiter gingerly slid the morsels of barbecue from the skewers onto the plates. M. Drin and the girls watched transfixed, their mouths almost visibly salivating in anticipation. I felt as removed from them as though they were figures in an exotic mural. And my appetite had fled. I was afraid that M. Diop's famous cuisine was going to be wasted on me.

Towards a Black Aesthetic

The black revolt is as palpable in letters as it is in the streets, and if it has not yet made its impact upon the Literary Establishment, then the nature of the revolt itself is the reason. For the break between the revolutionary black writers and the "literary mainstream" is, perhaps of necessity, cleaner and more decisive than the noisier and more dramatic break between the black militants and traditional political and institutional structures. Just as black intellectuals have rejected the NAACP, on the one hand, and the two major political parties, on the other, and gone off in search of new and more effective means and methods of seizing power, so revolutionary black writers have turned their backs on the old "certainties" and struck out in new, if uncharted, directions. They have begun the journey toward a black aesthetic.

The road to that place—if it exists at all—cannot, by definition, lead through the literary mainstreams. Which is to say that few critics will look upon the new movement with sympathy, even if a number of publishers might be daring enough to publish the works which its adherents produce. The movement will be reviled as "racism-in-reverse," and its writers labeled "racists," opprobrious terms which are flung lightly at black people now that the piper is being paid for all the long years of rejection and abuse which black people have experienced at the hands of white people—with few voices raised in objection.

Is this too harsh and sweeping a generalization? White people might think so; black people will not; which is a way of stating the problem and the prospect before us. Black people are being called "violent" these days, as if violence is a new invention out of the ghetto. But violence against the black minority is in-built in the established American society. There is no need for the white majority to take to the streets to clobber the blacks, although there certainly is *enough* of that; brutalization is inherent in all the customs and practices which bestow privileges on the whites and relegate the blacks to the status of pariahs.

These are old and well-worn truths which hardly need repeating. What is new is the reaction to them. Rapidly now, black people are turning onto that uncertain road, and they are doing so with the approval of all kinds of fellow-travellers who ordinarily are considered "safe" for the other side. In the fall 1967 issue of the *Journal of the National Medical Asso-*

ciation (all-black), for example, Dr. Charles A. De Leon of Cleveland, Ohio, explained why the new turn is necessary: "If young Negroes are to avoid the unnecessary burden of self-hatred (via identification with the aggressor) they will have to develop a keen faculty for identifying, fractionating out, and rejecting the absurdities of the conscious as well as the unconscious white racism in American society from what is worthwhile in it."

Conscious and unconscious white racism is everywhere, infecting all the vital areas of national life. But the revolutionary black writer, like the new breed of militant activist, has decided that white racism will no longer exercise its insidious control over his work. If the tag of "racist" is one the white critic will hang on him in dismissing him, then he is more than willing to bear that. He is not going to separate literature from life.

But just how widespread is white racism—conscious and unconscious—in the realm of letters? In a review of Gwendolyn Brook's *Selected Poems* in the old *New York Herald Tribune Book Week* back in October 1963, poet Louis Simpson began by writing that the Chicago poet's book of poems "contains some lively pictures of Negro life," an ambiguous enough opener which did not necessarily suggest a literary putdown. But Mr. Simpson's next sentence dispelled all ambiguity. "I am not sure it is possible for a Negro to write well without making us aware he is a Negro," he wrote. "On the other hand, if being a Negro is the only subject, the writing is not important."

All the history of American race relations is contained in that appraisal, despite its disingenuousness. It is civilized, urbane, gentle and elegant; and it is arrogant, condescending, presumptuous and racist. To most white readers, no doubt, Mr. Simpson's words, if not his assessment, seemed eminently sensible; but it is all but impossible to imagine a black reader not reacting to the words with unalloyed fury.

Both black and white readers are likely to go to the core of Mr. Simpson's statement, which is: "if being a Negro is the only subject, the writing is not important." The white reader will, in all probability, find that clear and acceptable enough; indeed, he is used to hearing it. "Certainly," the argument might proceed, "to be important, writing must have *universal values, universal implications*; it cannot deal exclusively with Negro problems." The plain but unstated assumption being, of course, that there are no "universal values" and no "universal implications" in Negro life.

Mr. Simpson is a greatly respected American poet, a winner of the Pulitzer Prize for poetry, as is Miss Brooks, and it will be considered the depth of irresponsibility to accuse him of the viciousness of racism. He is probably the gentlest and most compassionate of men. Miss Brooks, who met Mr. Simpson at the University of California not many months after the review was published, reported that the gentleman was most kind and courteous to her. There is no reason to doubt it. The essential point here is not the presence of overt hostility; it is the absence of clarity of vision. The glass through which black life is viewed by white Americans is, inescapably (it is a matter of extent), befogged by the hot breath of history. True "objectivity" where race is concerned is as rare as a necklace of Hope diamonds.

In October 1967, a young man named Jonathan Kozol published a book called *Death at an Early Age*, which is an account of his experiences as a teacher in a predominantly Negro elementary school in Boston. Mr. Kozol broke with convention in his approach to teaching and incurred the displeasure of a great many people, including the vigilant policeman father of one of his few white pupils. The issue around which the young teacher's opponents seemed to rally was his use of a Langston Hughes poem in his classroom. Now the late Langston Hughes was a favorite target of some of the more aggressive right-wing pressure groups during his lifetime, but it remained for an official of the Boston School Committee to come to the heart of the argument against the poet. Explaining the opposition to the poem used by Mr. Kozol, the school official said that "no poem by any Negro author can be considered permissible if it involves suffering."

There is a direct connecting line between the school official's rejection of Negro poetry which deals with suffering and Mr. Simpson's facile dismissal of writing about Negroes "only." Negro life, which is characterized by suffering imposed by the maintenance of white privilege in America, must be denied validity and banished beyond the pale. The facts of Negro life accuse white people. In order to look at Negro life unflinchingly, the white viewer either must relegate it to the realm of the subhuman, thereby justifying an attitude of indifference, or else the white viewer must confront the imputation of guilt against him. And no man who considers himself humane wishes to admit complicity in crimes against the human spirit.

There is a myth abroad in American literary criticism that Negro writing has been favored by a "double standard" which judges it less stringently. The opposite is true. No one will seriously dispute that, on occasions, critics have been generous to Negro writers, for a variety of reasons; but there is no evidence that generosity has been the rule. Indeed, why should it be assumed that literary critics are more sympathetic to blacks than are other white people? During any year, hundreds of mediocre volumes of prose and poetry by white writers are published, little noted, and forgotten. At the same time, the few creative works by black writers are seized and dissected and, if not deemed of the "highest" literary quality, condemned as still more examples of the failure of black writers to scale the rare heights of literature. And the condemnation is especially strong for those black works which have not screened their themes of suffering, redemption and triumph behind frail façades of obscurity and conscious "universality."

Central to the problem of the irreconcilable conflict between the black writer and the white critic is the failure of recognition of a fundamental and obvious truth of American life—that the two races are residents of two separate and naturally antagonistic worlds. No manner of well-meaning rhetoric about "one country" and "one people," and even about the two races' long joint-occupancy of this troubled land, can obliterate the high, thick dividing walls which hate and history have erected—and maintain—between them. The breaking down of those barriers might be a goal, worthy or unworthy (depending on viewpoint), but the reality remains. The world of the black outsider, however much it approximates and parallels and imitates the world of the white insider, by its very nature is inheritor and generator of values and viewpoints which threaten the insiders. The outsiders' world, feeding on its own sources, fecundates and vibrates, stamping its progeny with its very special ethos, its insuperably logical bias.

The black writer, like the black artist generally, has wasted much time and talent denying a propensity every rule of human dignity demands that he possess, seeking an identity that can only do violence to his sense of self. Black Americans are, for all practical purposes, colonized in their native land, and it can be argued that those who would submit to subjection without struggle deserve to be enslaved. It is one thing to accept the guiding principles on which American republic ostensibly was founded; it is quite another thing to accept the prevailing practices which violate those principles.

The rebellion in the streets is the black ghetto's response to the vast distance between the nation's principles and its practices. But that rebellion has roots which are deeper than most white people know; it is many-veined, and its blood has been sent pulsating to the very heart of black life. Across this country, young black men and women have been infected with a fever of affirmation. They are saying, "We are black and beautiful," and the ghetto is reacting with a liberating shock of realization which transcends mere chauvinism. They are rediscovering their heritage and their history, seeing it with newly focused eyes, struck with the wonder of that strength which has enabled them to endure and, in spirit, to defeat the power of prolonged and calculated oppression. After centuries of being told, in a million different ways, that they were not beautiful, and that whiteness of skin, straightness of hair, and aquilineness of features constituted the only measures of beauty, black people have revolted. The trend has not yet reached the point of avalanche, but the future can be clearly seen in the growing number of black people who are snapping off the shackles of imitation and are wearing their skin, their hair, and their features "natural" and with pride. In a poem called "Nittygritty," which is dedicated to poet LeRoi Jones, Joseph Bevans Bush put the new credo this way:

> . . . We all gonna come from behind
>   those
> Wigs and start to stop using those
> Standards of beauty which can never
> Be a frame for our reference; wash
> That excess grease out of our hair,
> Come out of that bleach bag and get
> Into something meaningful to us as
> Nonwhite people—Black people . . .

If the poem lacks the resonances of William Shakespeare, that is intentional. The "great bard of Avon" has only limited relevance to the revolutionary spirit raging in the ghetto. Which is not to say that the black revolutionaries reject the "universal" statements inherent in Shakespeare's works; what they do reject, however, is the literary assumption that the style and language and the concerns of Shakespeare establish the appropriate limits and "frame of reference" for black poetry and people. This is above and beyond the doctrine of revolution to which so many of the brighter black intellectuals are committed, that philosophy articulated by the late Frantz Fanon which holds that, in the time of revolutionary struggle, the traditional Western liberal ideals are not merely irrelevant but they must be assiduously opposed. The young writers of the black ghetto have set out in search of a black aesthetic, a system of isolating and evaluating the artistic works of black people which reflect the special character and imperatives of black experience.

That was the meaning and intent of poet-playwright LeRoi Jones' aborted Black Arts Theater in Harlem in 1965, and it is the generative idea behind such later groups and institutions as Spirit House in Newark, the Black House in San Francisco, the New School of Afro-American

Thought in Washington, D.C., the Institute for Black Studies in Los Angeles, Forum '66 in Detroit, and the Organization of Black American Culture in Chicago. It is a serious quest, and the black writers themselves are well aware of the possibility that what they seek is, after all, beyond codifying. They are fully aware of the dual nature of their heritage, and of the subtleties and complexities; but they are even more aware of the terrible reality of their outsideness, of their political and economic powerlessness, and of the desperate racial need for unity. And they have been convinced, over and over again, by the irrefutable facts of history and by the cold intransigence of the privileged white majority that the road to solidarity and strength leads inevitably through reclamation and indoctrination of black art and culture.

In Chicago, the Organization of Black American Culture has moved boldly toward a definition of a black aesthetic. In the writers' workshop sponsored by the group, the writers are deliberately striving to invest their work with the distinctive styles and rhythms and colors of the ghetto, with those peculiar qualities which, for example, characterize the music of a John Coltrane or a Charlie Parker or a Ray Charles. Aiming toward the publication of an anthology which will manifest this aesthetic, they have established criteria by which they measure their own work and eliminate from consideration those poems, short stories, plays, essays and sketches which do not adequately reflect the black experience. What the sponsors of the workshop most hope for in this delicate and dangerous experiment is the emergence of new black critics who will be able to articulate and expound the new aesthetic and eventually set in motion the long overdue assault against the restrictive assumption of the white critics.

It is not that the writers of OBAC have nothing to start with. That there exists already a mystique of blackness even some white critics will agree. In the November 1967 issue of *Esquire* magazine, for instance, George Frazier, a white writer who is not in the least sympathetic with the likes of LeRoi Jones, nevertheless did a commendable job of identifying elements of the black mystique. Discussing "the Negro's immense style, a style so seductive that it's little wonder that black men are, as Shakespeare put it in *The Two Gentlemen of Verona*, 'pearls in beauteous ladies' eyes,'" Mr. Frazier singled out the following examples:

"The formal daytime attire (black sack coats and striped trousers) the Modern Jazz Quartet wore when appearing in concert; the lazy amble with which Jimmy Brown used to return to the huddle; the delight the late 'Big Daddy' Lipscomb took in making sideline tackles in full view of the crowd and the way, after crushing a ball carrier to the ground, he would chivalrously assist him to his feet; the constant cool of 'Satchel' Paige; the

chic of Bobby Short; the incomparable grace of John Bubbles—things like
that are style and they have nothing whatsoever to do with ability (although the ability, God wot, is there, too). It is not that there are no white
men with style, for there is Fred Astaire, for one, and Cary Grant, for another, but that there are so very, very few of them. Even in the dock, the
black man has an air about him—Adam Clayton Powell, so blithe, so self-
possessed, so casual, as contrasted with Tom Dodd, sanctimonious, whining, an absolute disgrace. What it is that made Miles Davis and Cassius
Clay, Sugar Ray Robinson and Archie Moore and Ralph Ellison and
Sammy Davis, Jr. seem so special was their style. . . .

"And then, of course, there is our speech.

"For what nuances, what plays of light and shade, what little sharp-
nesses our speech has are almost all of them, out of the black world—the
talk of Negro musicians and whores and hoodlums and whatnot. 'Cool'
and all the other words in common currency came out of the mouths of
Negroes.

"'We love you madly,' said Duke Ellington, and now the phrase is almost a cliché. But it is a quality of the Negro's style—that he is forever
creative, forever more stylish. There was a night when, as I stood with
Duke Ellington outside the Hickory House, I looked up at the sky and
said, 'I hope it's a good day tomorrow. I want to wake up early.'

"'Any day I wake up,' said Ellington, 'is a good day.'

"And that was style."

Well, yes. . . .

Black critics have the responsibility of approaching the works of black
writers assuming these qualities to be present, and with the knowledge
that white readers—and white critics—cannot be expected to recognize
and to empathize with the subtleties and significance of black style and
technique. They have the responsibility of rebutting the white critics and
of putting things in the proper perspective. Within the past few years, for
example, Chicago's white critics have given the backs of their hands to
worthy works by black playwrights, part of their criticism directly attributable to their ignorance of the intricacies of black style and black
life. Oscar Brown, Jr.'s rockingly soulful *Kicks and Company* was panned for
many of the wrong reasons; and Douglas Turner Ward's two plays, *Day of
Absence* and *Happy Ending*, were tolerated as labored and a bit tasteless.
Both Brown and Ward had dealt satirically with race relations, and there
were not many black people in the audiences who found themselves in
agreement with the critics. It is the way things are—but not the way
things will continue to be if the OBAC writers and those similarly concerned elsewhere in America have anything to say about it.

MARI EVANS

Mari Evans is a poet whose commitment to her art and to the use of that art in the service of her social vision is total. This commitment is accompanied by a complete reticence in matters of biography. Unlike many, perhaps most, poets, Mari Evans speaks in her poems not so much directly from her person as from a persona whose structure can only be inferred.

Mari Evans' poems are usually brief and incisive, especially the early ones, achieving a startling effect through understatement and irony. She speaks in the tone and idiom of the urban black folk and with biting wit probes the paradoxes of black American life. Her themes are black realities—old women singing gospel songs, tired domestics, status-seeking bourgeois Negroes, strong and beautiful and loving black women. In her poetry she encompasses the tone of the sixties.

Her friend, the critic Hoyt Fuller, said of her work, "The poetry of Mari Evans is like fine architecture—solid at base, elegant of line, delightful to contemplate, and, most important of all, designed to fulfill a vital human need." Her art is encapsulated in the volumes Where Is All the Music? *(1968) and* I Am a Black Woman *(1970).*

Status Symbol

i
Have Arrived

i
am the
New Negro

i
am the result of
President Lincoln
World War I
and Paris
the
Red Ball Express
white drinking fountains
sitdowns and
sit-ins
Federal Troops
Marches on Washington
    and
prayer meetings . . .

today
They hired me
it
is a status
job . . .
along
with my papers

They
gave me my
Status Symbol
the
key
to the
White . . . Locked . . .
John

Black Jam for Dr. Negro

Pullin me in off the corner to wash my face an
cut my afro turn
my collar
down
when that aint my
thang I
walk heels first
nose round an tilted
up
my ancient
eyes
see your thang
baby
an it aint
shit
your thang
puts my eyes out baby
turns my seeking fingers
  into splintering fists

messes up my head
an I scream you out
your thang
is whats wrong
  an you keep
  pilin it on rubbin it
in
smoothly
  doin it
  to death

what you sweatin
baby
      your guts
puked an rotten
waitin
to be defended

Vive Noir!

i
am going to rise
en masse
from Inner City
        sick
          of newyork ghettos
        chicago tenements
      l a's slums

weary
      of exhausted lands
      sagging privies
      saying yessur yessah
      yesSIR
      in an assortment
      of geographical dialects i
have seen my last
broken down plantation
even from a
distance

        i
will load all my goods
in '50 Chevy pickups '53
Fords fly United and '66
caddys I
      have packed in
      the old man and the old lady and
      wiped the children's noses

        I'm tired
          of hand me downs
            shut me ups
              pin me ins
                keep me outs
                  messing me over have
              just had it
            baby
          from
        you . . .

i'm
gonna spread out
over America
        intrude
my proud blackness
all
      over the place
          i have wrested wheat fields
          from the forests

594

turned rivers
from their courses

leveled mountains
at a word
festooned the land with
bridges

    gemlike
  on filaments of steel
    moved
glistening towers of Babel in place

sweated a whole
civilization
    now

      i'm
gonna breathe fire
through flaming nostrils BURN
    a place for

     me
in the skyscrapers and the
schoolrooms on the green
lawns and the white
beaches

      i'm
gonna wear the robes and
sit on the benches
make the rules and make
the arrests say
who can and who
can't

      baby you don't stand
      a
      chance

i'm

gonna put black angels
in all the books and a black
Christchild in Mary's arms i'm
gonna make black bunnies black
fairies black santas black
nursery rhymes and

black

ice cream

i'm

gonna make it a
crime
to be anything BUT   black
pass the coppertone
gonna make white
a twentyfourhour
lifetime
J.O.B.
an' when all the coppertone's gone . . . ?

The Writers

Where did they go
the Writers?

    chests pulsing under kente cloth The
    Word clenched in sweaty fists
    Strength so awesome none approached
    without a questioning, a quickening
    "Am I incorrect?" "O tell me, brother!
    Am I incorrect?"

Where did they go
the Writers?

    With the wisdoms learned from bluesteel
    butts from cement crypts and
    With their ancient sealed potential

They have gone to whiteland, sister
              There they lie

healed by white lips
    soothed by white hands
        stoned in white beds
            bound again in silken chains
whispering in an alien tongue
                litanies
    None but me/ Miss Annie
    None but me/ pale comrade
            with the quick tongue
            with the rockblue eyes

Where did they go
the Writers?
        Beautiful
        Black
    chests pulsing under kente cloth The
    Word clenched in sweaty fists

They have gone to whiteland, sister

    Am I incorrect?
        O tell me, brother
        Am I incorrect?

conceptuality

        I am a wisp of energy
    flung from the core of the Universe
          housed
        in a temple
    of flesh and bones and blood

          in the temple
          because it is there
          that I make my home
          Free
    of the temple
    not bound
          by the temple
    but housed

    no distances
    I am everywhere
energy and will of the universe expressed
    realizing my oneness my
        indivisibility/ I

        I am
    the One Force

      I . . .

AMIRI BARAKA

(b. 1934)

Amiri Baraka easily dominates his generation of Afro-American poets and playwrights, and his writing extends to virtually every genre including fiction, social and political criticism, and music criticism. His public letters, occasioned by the need to protest and clarify, place him among the major practitioners of the epistolary genre.

Born as Le Roi Jones in Newark, New Jersey, he has established an identification with his natal city, which he re-christened New Ark, having returned there after attending Howard University, spending time in the United States Air Force, and enjoying a career in Greenwich Village as an avant-garde poet, editor, and publisher, followed by a period in Harlem as a theater director.

As much as any of the work of black poets who emerged in the sixties, the poetry of Baraka is best encompassed by the designation "manifesto-poetry," coined by critic Carolyn Fowler in an important Black World *essay. One could extend the designation to describe all of Baraka's work, characterized as it is by strong colloquial and polemical features.*

Central to Baraka's writings is the succession of literary and political orientations he has assumed in the course of his career. Before his return to Newark, his concerns had first been aesthetic and then were black protest. His return to Newark marked the beginning of a decade-long Black Nationalist commitment associated with Spirit House, the cultural center he founded. Subsequently he abandoned his "cultural" orientation for a politico-economic one and began to adopt a position based on Marxist insights. A part of this impassioned personal odyssey is disclosed in The Autobiography of Le Roi Jones *(1983).*

Baraka's prodigious output up to 1984 of nearly thirty volumes and hundreds of uncollected poems, dramas, fiction, and essays has invited a corresponding battery of explication and criticism. Among the most useful critical works, two deserving special note are Theodore Hudson's From Le Roi Jones to Amiri Baraka *(1973) and Werner Sollers'* Amiri Baraka/Le Roi Jones *(1978). A discussion of Baraka's militant theater appears in Genevieve Fabre's* Drumbeats, Masks and Metaphor, *translated by Melvin Dixon (1983).*

Preface to a Twenty Volume Suicide Note

Lately, I've become accustomed to the way
The ground opens up and envelops me
Each time I go out to walk the dog.
Or the broad edged silly music the wind
Makes when I run for a bus—

Things have come to that.

And now, each night I count the stars,
And each night I get the same number.
And when they will not come to be counted
I count the holes they leave.

Nobody sings anymore.

And then last night, I tiptoed up
To my daughter's room and heard her
Talking to someone, and when I opened
The door, there was no one there . . .
Only she on her knees,
Peeking into her own clasped hands.

A Poem for Black Hearts

For Malcolm's eyes, when they broke
the face of some dumb white man, For
Malcolm's hands raised to bless us
all black and strong in his image
of ourselves, For Malcolm's words
fire darts, the victor's tireless
thrusts, words hung above the world
change as it may, he said it, and
for this he was killed, for saying,
and feeling, and being/ change, all
collected hot in his heart, For Malcolm's
heart, raising us above our filthy cities,
for his stride, and his beat, and his address
to the grey monsters of the world, For Malcolm's
pleas for your dignity, black men, for your life,
black man, for the filling of your minds
with righteousness, For all of him dead and
gone and vanished from us, and all of him which
clings to our speech black god of our time.
For all of him, and all of yourself, look up,
black man, quit stuttering and shuffling, look up,
black man, quit whining and stooping, for all of him,
For Great Malcolm a prince of the earth, let nothing in us rest
until we avenge ourselves for his death, stupid animals
that killed him, let us never breathe a pure breath if
we fail, and white men call us faggots till the end of
the earth.

State/Ment

The Black Artist's role in America is to aid in the destruction of America as he knows it. His role is to report and reflect so precisely the nature of the society, and of himself in that society, that other men will be moved by the exactness of his rendering and, if they are black men, grow strong through this moving, having seen their own strength, and weakness; and if they are white men, tremble, curse, and go mad, because they will be drenched with the filth of their evil.

The Black Artist must draw out of his soul the correct image of the world. He must use this image to band his brothers and sisters together in common understanding of the nature of the world (and the nature of America) and the nature of the human soul.

The Black Artist must demonstrate sweet life, how it differs from the deathly grip of the White Eyes. The Black Artist must teach the White Eyes their deaths, and teach the black man how to bring these deaths about.

> We are unfair, and unfair.
> We are black magicians, black art
> s we make in black labs of the heart.
>
> The fair are
> fair, and death
> ly white.
>
> The day will not save them
> and we own
> the night.

PAULE MARSHALL
(b. 1929)

In Paule Marshall are combined two segments of the African heritage—West Indian and Afro-American. Following the First World War, her parents had migrated from their native Barbados to Brooklyn, New York, where Miss Marshall was born. Before her tenth birthday she had begun writing.

After graduating cum laude *from Brooklyn College in 1953, she became a librarian for the New York Public Libraries and a writer of feature stories for* Our World *magazine, for which her writing assignments took her to the West Indies and Brazil. In 1959 she published the novel* Brown Girl, Brownstones, *about a Barbadian girl growing up in Brooklyn. A year later she published* Soul Clap Hands and Sing, *a volume of four stories placed in four settings especially familiar and meaningful to her—Barbados, Brooklyn, British Guiana, and Brazil. Her second novel,* The Chosen Place, The Timeless People *(1969), is a story of Barbados. Miss Marshall's stories have appeared in periodicals and anthologies, and she has received a Guggenheim Fellowship (1961-2), the Rosenthal Award from the National Institute of Arts and Letters (1962), the Ford Foundation Theater Award (1964-5), and a grant from the National Endowment for the Arts (1967).*

In a style that is clear, economical, and rich in imagery, Paule Marshall describes the cane fields of Barbados as vividly as she does the row houses of Brooklyn. Her characters are three-dimensional people portrayed with compassion, and she captures in their easy, natural dialogue the intonations of both West Indian and urban Afro-American speech.

As an exacting writer, broodingly concerned with the crafting of fiction, Paule Marshall has taken increasingly long periods of time to produce new work. Praisesong for the Widow *(1983), the work of over a decade, was greeted by critics and readers with both exaltation and relief. The novel explores with lyricism and deep psychological penetration the search for affirmation and joy of Avey Johnson, a woman of sixty-two. In the process of this delineation, Paule Marshall plumbs the resonances of black culture in a powerful synthesis.*

To Da-duh, In Memoriam

". . . Oh Nana! all of you is not involved in this evil business Death,
Nor all of us in Life."
            —From "At My Grandmother's Grave," by Lebert Bethune

I did not see her at first I remember. For not only was it dark
inside the crowded disembarkation shed in spite of the daylight flooding in from outside, but standing there waiting for her with my
mother and sister I was still somewhat blinded from the sheen of
tropical sunlight on the water of the bay which we had just crossed in
the landing boat, leaving behind us the ship that had brought us
from New York lying in the offing. Besides, being only nine years
of age at the time and knowing nothing of islands I was busy attending to the alien sights and sounds of Barbados, the unfamiliar smells.

I did not see her, but I was alerted to her approach by my
mother's hand which suddenly tightened around mine, and looking
up I traced her gaze through the gloom in the shed until I finally
made out the small, purposeful, painfully erect figure of the old
woman headed our way.

Her face was drowned in the shadow of an ugly rolled-brim
brown felt hat, but the details of her slight body and of the struggle
taking place within it were clear enough—an intense, unrelenting
struggle between her back which was beginning to bend ever so
slightly under the weight of her eighty odd years and the rest of her
which sought to deny those years and hold that back straight, keep
it in line. Moving swiftly toward us (so swiftly it seemed she did not
intend stopping when she reached us but would sweep past us out
the doorway which opened onto the sea and like Christ walk upon

the water!), she was caught between the sunlight at her end of the building and the darkness inside—and for a moment she appeared to contain them both: the light in the long severe old-fashioned white dress she wore which brought the sense of a past that was still alive into our bustling present and in the snatch of white at her eye; the darkness in her black high-top shoes and in her face which was visible now that she was closer.

It was as stark and fleshless as a death mask, that face. The maggots might have already done their work, leaving only the framework of bone beneath the ruined skin and deep wells at the temple and jaw. But her eyes were alive, unnervingly so for one so old, with a sharp light that flicked out of the dim clouded depths like a lizard's tongue to snap up all in her view. Those eyes betrayed a child's curiosity about the world, and I wondered vaguely seeing them, and seeing the way the bodice of her ancient dress had collapsed in on her flat chest (what had happened to her breasts?), whether she might not be some kind of child at the same time that she was a woman, with fourteen children, my mother included, to prove it. Perhaps she was both, both child and woman, darkness and light, past and present, life and death—all the opposites contained and reconciled in her.

"My Da-duh," my mother said formally and stepped forward. The name sounded like thunder softly in the distance.

"Child," Da-duh said, and her tone, her quick scrutiny of my mother, the brief embrace in which they appeared to shy from each other rather than touch, wiped out the fifteen years my mother had been away and restored the old relationship. My mother, who was such a formidable figure in my eyes, had suddenly with a word been reduced to my status.

"Yes, God is good," Da-duh said with a nod that was like a tic. "He has spared me to see my child again."

We were led forward then, apologetically because not only did Da-duh prefer boys but she also liked her grandchildren to be "white," that is, fair-skinned; and we had, I was to discover, a number of cousins, the outside children of white estate managers and the like, who qualified. We, though, were as black as she.

My sister being the oldest was presented first. "This one takes after the father," my mother said and waited to be reproved.

Frowning, Da-duh tilted my sister's face toward the light. But her frown soon gave way to a grudging smile, for my sister with her large mild eyes and little broad winged nose, with our father's high-cheeked Barbadian cast to her face, was pretty.

"She's goin' be lucky," Da-duh said and patted her once on the cheek. "Any girl-child that takes after the father does be lucky."

She turned then to me. But oddly enough she did not touch me. Instead leaning close, she peered hard at me, and then quickly drew back. I thought I saw her hand start up as though to shield her eyes. It was almost as if she saw not only me, a thin truculent child who it was said took after no one but myself, but something in me which for some reason she found disturbing, even threatening. We looked silently at each other for a long time there in the noisy shed, our gaze locked. She was the first to look away.

"But Adry," she said to my mother and her laugh was cracked, thin, apprehensive. "Where did you get this one here with this fierce look?"

"We don't know where she came out of, my Da-duh," my mother said, laughing also. Even I smiled to myself. After all I had won the encounter. Da-duh had recognized my small strength—and this was all I ever asked of the adults in my life then.

"Come, soul," Da-duh said and took my hand. "You must be one of those New York terrors you hear so much about."

She led us, me at her side and my sister and mother behind, out of the shed into the sunlight that was like a bright driving summer rain and over to a group of people clustered beside a decrepit lorry. They were our relatives, most of them from St. Andrews although Da-duh herself lived in St. Thomas, the women wearing bright print dresses, the colors vivid against their darkness, the men rusty black suits that encased them like straitjackets. Da-duh, holding fast to my hand, became my anchor as they circled round us like a nervous sea, exclaiming, touching us with their calloused hands, embracing us shyly. They laughed in awed bursts: "But look Adry got big-big children!"/ "And see the nice things they wearing, wrist watch and all!/" "I tell you, Adry has done all right for sheself in New York . . ."

Da-duh, ashamed at their wonder, embarrassed for them, admonished them the while. "But oh Christ," she said, "why you all got to get on like you never saw people from 'Away' before? You would think New York is the only place in the world to hear wunna. That's why I don't like to go anyplace with you St. Andrews people, you know. You all ain't been colonized."

We were in the back of the lorry finally, packed in among the barrels of ham, flour, cornmeal and rice and the trunks of clothes that my mother had brought as gifts. We made our way slowly through Bridgetown's clogged streets, part of a funereal procession of cars and open-sided buses, bicycles and donkey carts. The dim little limestone shops and offices along the way marched with us, at the same mournful pace, toward the same grave ceremony—as did the people, the women balancing huge baskets on top their heads as if they were no more than hats they wore to shade them from the sun. Looking over the edge of the lorry I watched as their feet slurred the dust. I listened, and their voices, raw and loud and dissonant in the heat, seemed to be grappling with each other high overhead.

Da-duh sat on a trunk in our midst, a monarch amid her court. She still held my hand, but it was different now. I had suddenly become her anchor, for I felt her fear of the lorry with its asthmatic motor (a fear and distrust, I later learned, she held of all machines) beating like a pulse in her rough palm.

As soon as we left Bridgetown behind though, she relaxed, and while the others around us talked she gazed at the canes standing tall on either side of the winding marl road. "C'dear," she said softly to herself after a time. "The canes this side are pretty enough."

They were too much for me. I thought of them as giant weeds that had overrun the island, leaving scarcely any room for the small tottering houses of sunbleached pine we passed or the people, dark streaks as our lorry hurtled by. I suddenly feared that we were journeying, unaware that we were, toward some dangerous place where the canes, grown as high and thick as a forest, would close in on us and run us through with their stiletto blades. I longed then for the familiar: for the street in Brooklyn where I lived, for my father who had refused to accompany us ("Blowing out good money on foolishness," he had said of the trip), for a game of tag with my friends under the chestnut tree outside our aging brownstone house.

"Yes, but wait till you see St. Thomas canes," Da-duh was saying to me. "They's canes father, bo," she gave a proud arrogant nod. "Tomorrow, God willing, I goin' take you out in the ground and show them to you."

True to her word Da-duh took me with her the following day out into the ground. It was a fairly large plot adjoining her weathered board and shingle house and consisting of a small orchard, a good-sized canepiece and behind the canes, where the land sloped abruptly down, a gully. She had purchased it with Panama money sent her by her eldest son, my uncle Joseph, who had died working on the canal. We entered the ground along a trail no wider than her body and as devious and complex as her reasons for showing me her land. Da-duh strode briskly ahead, her slight form filled out this morning by the layers of sacking petticoats she wore under her working dress to protect her against the damp. A fresh white cloth, elaborately arranged around her head, added to her height, and lent her a vain, almost roguish air.

Her pace slowed once we reached the orchard, and glancing back at me occasionally over her shoulder, she pointed out the various trees.

"This here is a breadfruit," she said. "That one yonder is a papaw. Here's a guava. This is a mango. I know you don't have anything like these in New York. Here's a sugar apple [the fruit looked more like artichokes to me]. This one bears limes. . . ." She went on for some time, intoning the names of the trees as though they were those of her gods. Finally, turning to me, she said, "I know you don't have anything this nice where you come from." Then, as I hesitated: "I said I know you don't have anything this nice where you come from. . . ."

"No," I said and my world did seem suddenly lacking.

Da-duh nodded and passed on. The orchard ended and we were on the narrow cart road that led through the canepiece, the canes clashing like swords above my cowering head. Again she turned and her thin muscular arms spread wide, her dim gaze embracing the small fields of canes, she said—and her voice almost broke under the weight of her pride, "Tell me, have you got anything like these in that place where you were born?"

"No."

"I din' think so. I bet you don't even know that these canes here and the sugar you eat is one and the same thing. That they does throw the canes into some damn machine at the factory and squeeze out all the little life in them to make sugar for you all so in New York to eat. I bet you don't know that."

"I've got two cavities and I'm not allowed to eat a lot of sugar."

But Da-duh didn't hear me. She had turned with an inexplicably angry motion and was making her way rapidly out of the canes and down the slope at the edge of the field which led to the gully below. Following her apprehensively down the incline amid a stand of banana plants whose leaves flapped like elephants ears in the wind, I found myself in the middle of a small tropical wood—a place dense and damp and gloomy and tremulous with the fitful play of light and shadow as the leaves high above moved against the sun that was almost hidden from view. It was a violent place, the tangled foliage fighting each other for a chance at the sunlight, the branches of the trees locked in what seemed an immemorial struggle, one both necessary and inevitable. But despite the violence, it was pleasant, almost peaceful in the gully, and beneath the thick undergrowth the earth smelled like spring.

This time Da-duh didn't even bother to ask her usual question, but simply turned and waited for me to speak.

"No," I said, my head bowed. "We don't have anything like this in New York."

"Ah," she cried, her triumph complete. "I din' think so. Why, I've heard that's a place where you can walk till you near drop and never see a tree."

"We've got a chestnut tree in front of our house," I said.

"Does it bear?" She waited. "I ask you, does it bear?"

"Not anymore," I muttered. "It used to, but not anymore."

She gave the nod that was like a nervous twitch. "You see," she said. "Nothing can bear there." Then, secure behind her scorn, she added, "But tell me, what's this snow like that you hear so much about?"

Looking up, I studied her closely, sensing my chance, and then I told her, describing at length and with as much drama as I could summon not only what snow in the city was like, but what it would be like here, in her perennial summer kingdom.

". . . And you see all these trees you got here," I said. "Well, they'd be bare. No leaves, no fruit, nothing. They'd be covered in snow. You see your canes. They'd be buried under tons of snow. The snow would be higher than your head, higher than your house, and you wouldn't be able to come down into this here gully because it would be snowed under. . . ."

She searched my face for the lie, still scornful but intrigued. "What a thing, huh?" she said finally, whispering it softly to herself.

"And when it snows you couldn't dress like you are now," I said. "Oh no, you'd freeze to death. You'd have to wear a hat and gloves and galoshes and ear muffs so your ears wouldn't freeze and drop off, and a heavy coat. I've got a Shirley Temple coat with fur on the collar. I can dance. You wanna see?"

Before she could answer I began, with a dance called the Truck which was popular back then in the 1930's. My right forefinger waving, I trucked around the nearby trees and around Da-duh's awed and rigid form. After the Truck I did the Suzy-Q, my lean hips swishing, my sneakers sidling zigzag over the ground. "I can sing," I said and did so, starting with "I'm Gonna Sit Right Down and Write

Myself a Letter," then without pausing, "Tea for Two," and ending with "I Found a Million Dollar Baby in a Five and Ten Cent Store."

For long moments afterwards Da-duh stared at me as if I were a creature from Mars, an emissary from some world she did not know but which intrigued her and whose power she both felt and feared. Yet something about my performance must have pleased her, because bending down she slowly lifted her long skirt and then, one by one, the layers of petticoats until she came to a drawstring purse dangling at the end of a long strip of cloth tied round her waist. Opening the purse she handed me a penny. "Here," she said half-smiling against her will. "Take this to buy yourself a sweet at the shop up the road. There's nothing to be done with you, soul."

From then on, whenever I wasn't taken to visit relatives, I accompanied Da-duh out into the ground, and alone with her amid the canes or down in the gully I told her about New York. It always began with some slighting remark on her part: "I know they don't have anything this nice where you come from," or "Tell me, I hear those foolish people in New York does do such and such. . . ." But as I answered, recreating my towering world of steel and concrete and machines for her, building the city out of words, I would feel her give way. I came to know the signs of her surrender: the total stillness that would come over her little hard dry form, the probing gaze that like a surgeon's knife sought to cut through my skull to get at the images there, to see if I were lying; above all, her fear, a fear nameless and profound, the same one I had felt beating in the palm of her hand that day in the lorry.

Over the weeks I told her about refrigerators, radios, gas stoves, elevators, trolley cars, wringer washing machines, movies, airplanes, the cyclone at Coney Island, subways, toasters, electric lights: "At night, see, all you have to do is flip this little switch on the wall and all the lights in the house go on. Just like that. Like magic. It's like turning on the sun at night."

"But tell me," she said to me once with a faint mocking smile, "do the white people have all these things too or it's only the people looking like us?"

I laughed. "What d'ya mean," I said. "The white people have even better." Then: "I beat up a white girl in my class last term."

"Beating up white people!" Her tone was incredulous.

"How you mean!" I said, using an expression of hers. "She called me a name."

For some reason Da-duh could not quite get over this and repeated in the same hushed, shocked voice, "Beating up white people now! Oh, the lord, the world's changing up so I can scarce recognize it anymore."

One morning toward the end of our stay, Da-duh led me into a part of the gully that we had never visited before, an area darker and more thickly overgrown than the rest, almost impenetrable. There in a small clearing amid the dense bush, she stopped before an incredibly tall royal palm which rose cleanly out of the ground, and drawing the eye up with it, soared high above the trees around it into the sky. It appeared to be touching the blue dome of sky, to be flaunting its dark crown of fronds right in the blinding white face of the late moring sun.

Da-duh watched me a long time before she spoke, and then she said very quietly, "All right, now, tell me if you've got anything this tall in that place you're from."

I almost wished, seeing her face, that I could have said no. "Yes," I said. "We've got buildings hundreds of times this tall in New York. There's one called the Empire State building that's the tallest in the world. My class visited it last year and I went all the way to the top. It's got over a hundred floors. I can't describe how tall it is. Wait a minute. What's the name of that hill I went to visit the other day, where they have the police station?"

"You mean Bissex?"

"Yes, Bissex. Well, the Empire State Building is way taller than that."

"You're lying now!" she shouted, trembling with rage. Her hand lifted to strike me.

"No, I'm not," I said. "It really is, If you don't belive me I'll send you a picture postcard of it soon as I get back home so you can see for yourself. But it's way taller than Bissex."

All the fight went out of her at that. The hand poised to strike me fell limp to her side, and as she stared at me, seeing not me but the building that was taller than the highest hill she knew, the small stubborn light in her eyes (it was the same amber as the flame in the kerosene lamp she lit at dusk) began to fail. Finally, with a vague gesture that even in the midst of her defeat still tried to dismiss me and my world, she turned and started back through the gully, walking slowly, her steps groping and uncertain, as if she was suddenly no longer sure of the way, while I followed triumphant yet strangely saddened behind.

The next morning I found her dressed for our morning walk

but stretched out on the Berbice chair in the tiny drawing room where she sometimes napped during the afternoon heat, her face turned to the window beside her. She appeared thinner and suddenly indescribably old.

"My Da-duh," I said.

"Yes, nuh," she said. Her voice was listless and the face she slowly turned my way was, now that I think back on it, like a Benin mask, the features drawn and almost distorted by an ancient abstract sorrow.

"Don't you feel well?" I asked.

"Girl, I don't know."

"My Da-duh, I goin' boil you some bush tea," my aunt, Da-duh's youngest child, who lived with her, called from the shed roof kitchen.

"Who tell you I need bush tea?" she cried, her voice assuming for a moment its old authority. "You can't even rest nowadays without some malicious person looking for you to be dead. Come girl," she motioned me to a place beside her on the old-fashioned lounge chair, "give us a tune."

I sang for her until breakfast at eleven, all my brash irreverent Tin Pan Alley songs, and then just before noon we went out into the ground. But it was a short, dispirited walk. Da-duh didn't even notice that the mangoes were beginning to ripen and would have to be picked before the village boys got to them. And when she paused occasionally and looked out across the canes or up at her trees it wasn't as if she were seeing them but something else. Some huge, monolithic shape imposed itself, it seemed, between her and the land, obstructing her vision. Returning to the house she slept the entire afternoon on the Berbice chair.

She remained like this until we left, languishing away the mornings on the chair at the window gazing out at the land as if it were already doomed; then, at noon, taking the brief stroll with me through the ground during which she seldom spoke, and afterwards returning home to sleep till almost dusk sometimes.

On the day of our departure she put on the austere, ankle length white dress, the black shoes and brown felt hat (her town clothes she called them), but she did not go with us to town. She saw us off on the road outside her house and in the midst of my mother's tearful protracted farewell, she leaned down and whispered in my ear, "Girl, you're not to forget now to send me the picture of that building, you hear."

By the time I mailed her the large colored picture postcard of the

Empire State building she was dead. She died during the famous '37 strike which began shortly after we left. On the day of her death England sent planes flying low over the island in a show of force— so low, according to my aunt's letter, that the downdraft from them shook the ripened mangoes from the trees in Da-duh's orchard. Frightened, everyone in the village fled into the canes. Except Da-duh. She remained in the house at the window so my aunt said, watching as the planes came swooping and screaming like monstrous birds down over the village, over her house, rattling her trees and flattening the young canes in her field. It must have seemed to her lying there that they did not intend pulling out of their dive, but like the hard-back beetles which hurled themselves with suicidal force against the walls of the house at night, those menacing silver shapes would hurl themselves in an ecstasy of self-immolation onto the land, destroying it utterly.

When the planes finally left and the villagers returned they found her dead on the Berbice chair at the window.

She died and I lived, but always, to this day even, within the shadow of her death. For a brief period after I was grown I went to live alone, like one doing penance, in a loft above a noisy factory in downtown New York and there painted seas of sugarcane and huge swirling Van Gogh suns and palm trees striding like brightly-plumed Watusi across a tropical landscape, while the thunderous tread of the machines downstairs jarred the floor beneath my easel, mocking my efforts.

HAKI MADHUBUTI
(b. 1942)

Haki Madhubuti (originally known as Don L. Lee) is one of several poets who came out of the concentration of black cultural activity in Chicago in the mid-sixties and is one who remained to participate actively in the cultural and political life of that major black metropolis. He was a founding member of the Organization of Black American Culture (OBAC) and a participant in its writers' workshop directed by Hoyt Fuller. His dynamic stage presence made him one of the outstanding poet-readers and he became a favorite of college audiences, who probably responded more fully to his manner than his message.

Madhubuti's message, expressed in his poetry, in several books of essays, and in the Institute of Positive Culture which he founded, is one of black solidarity, communal living, and an absolute dedication to healing reform within the black community. In a brief poem he says

> *get fired up*
> *get excited about hue and dark colors*
> *ignite truth in the temple*
> *there will be many who will try to take you out*
> *watch the light shadows*
> *exemplify & scream cleanliness into the world*
> *leave yr mark*
> *the children must know that you*
> *& you   & you*
> *carried the message.*

In rapid fire fashion, Haki Madhubuti produced several volumes of poems: Think Black *(1968),* Black Pride *(1968),* Don't Cry, Scream *(1969), and* We Walk the Way of the New World *(1970). His concern with what other black writers were saying, and the absence of an adequate critical response to it, led him to the writing of* Dynamite Voices *(1970), intended to be the first of a series; however, this project was superseded by the political and social concerns of* From Plan to Planet *(1973) and* Enemies: The Clash of Races *(1978).*

Organizational concerns connected with the Institute of Positive Culture, the creation of Third World Press and Black Books Bulletin, *and a passionate commitment to cultural evangelism had seemed to still the poet in Haki Madhubuti, but this proved to not be the case with the publication of* Earthquakes and Survival Missions: Poetry and Essays of Black Renewal *(1984).*

Along the way, Haki Madhubuti has coedited both an anthology of black poetry, To Gwen With Love, *and* A Capsule Course in Black Poetry Writing. *His place in the circle of poets is secure.*

But He Was Cool
Or: He Even Stopped for Green Lights

super-cool
ultrablack
a tan/purple
had a beautiful shade.

he had a double-natural
that wd put the sisters to shame.
his dashikis were tailor made
& his beads were imported sea shells
    (from some blk/country i never heard of)
he was triple-hip.

his tikis were hand carved
out of ivory
& came express from the motherland.
he would greet u in swahili
& say good-by in yoruba.
wooooooooooooo-jim he bes so cool & ill tel li gent
        cool-cool is so cool he was un-cooled by other niggers' cool
        cool-cool ultracool was bop-cool/ice box cool so cool cold
            cool
        his wine didn't have to be cooled, him was air conditioned
            cool
        cool-cool/real cool made me cool—now ain't that cool
        cool-cool so cool him nick-named refrigerator.

cool-cool so cool
he didn't know,
after detroit, newark, chicago &c.,
we had to hip
        cool-cool/ super-cool/ real cool
   that
to be black
is
to be
very-hot.

Nigerian Unity
or little niggers killing little niggers

suppose those
who made
wars
had to fight them?

it's called blackgold.
& you.
my brothers/former warriors
who use to own the nights
that
knew no boarders
have acquired strings on yr/minds
& have knowingly sold yr/our/mothers.

there are no more tears.
tears will not stop bullets.
the dead don't cry,
the dead just grow; good crop this year,
wouldn't u say.

it's called blackgold
& u fight blindly,
swinging at yr/own mid-nights,
at yr/own children of tomorrow.

come one come two
against the middle is
a double feature starring the man from u.n.c.l.e.
with a nigger on his back
who played ping-pong with christ
and won.

little niggers
killing
little niggers: onetime/intime/outoftime
               theirtime/otherpeople'stime as
               niggers killed niggers everytime.

suppose those
who made
wars
had to fight them?

blackgold is not
the newnigger:
with a british accent
called me 'old chap' one day,
i rubbed his skin
it didn't come off. even him surprised.

him
another pipe-smoking faggot
who lost his balls in
a double-breasted suit
walking thru a nadinola commercial
with a degree in european history.
little nigger
choked himself with a hippies' tie
his momma didn't even know him/she thought he was a TWA
flashback or something out of a
polka-dot machine.

he
cursed at her in perfect english
called her:
Mother-Dear.

WANTED   WANTED:
black warriors to go south
to fight in Africa's mississippi.

go south young man.

everybody missed that train,
except one sister.
she wanted to fight the realenemy
but
she was "uneducated,"
wore the long-dress,
talked the native tongue
& had a monopoly on blackbeauty.
when we met—she smiled & said: "I'm the true-gold,
I'm the real-gold."

suppose those
who made
wars
had to fight them?

the real blackgold
was there before the drill,
before the dirty-eyed,
before the fence-builders,
before the wells,
before the british accent,
before christ,
before air condition,
before the cannon,
the real blackgold: was momma & sister; *is*, momma & sister.
was there before the "educated,"
before the pig-eaters,
before the cross-wearers,
before the pope,
before the nigger-warriors.
the real blackgold
was the first warrior.

go south young man.

little niggers
killing
little niggers.
the weak against the weak.
the ugly against the ugly.
the powerless against the powerless.
the realpeople becoming unpeople
& brothers we have more in common
than pigmentation & stupidity.
that same old two-for-one
was played on 47th & ellis—
invented on 125th & lenox
and now is double-dealing from
the mangrove swamps to the savannah grassland;
2 niggers for the price of nothing.

newnigger
lost his way
a whi-te girl gave him direction
him still lost
she sd. whi-te/he thought bite
been-eating everything in sight
including himself.

suppose those
who made
wars
had to fight them?

the lone ranger got a new tonto
he's 'brown' with a Ph.D. in
psy-chol-o-gy
& still walks around with
holes
in his brain.
losthismind.

saw him the other day
with his head across some railroad tracks—
tryen to get an untan.
will the real jesus christ
please stand up
and take a bow;
u got niggers tryen to be trains.

trained well.
european-african took a
double
at oxford.
wears ban-lon underwear & whi-te socks,
has finally got the killer's eye,
join the deathbringers club
& don't want more than two children.

622

the real blackgold
will be crippled,
raped,
and killed
in
that
order.

i will miss
the joy
of calling her
sister.

go south young man.

suppose those
who made
wars
had to fight *you*.

Bloodsmiles
(9/15/63 the day I left this society)

I remember the time
when I could
smile—
smiles of
ignorance.
This was about
? years ago,
now—smiles do not
come as easily
as they are
supposed
to.

My smiles are
now fixed
and
come slowly
like the gradual
movement of tomatoes—
in a near empty
ketchup bottle—
about to be
eaten.

Mixed Sketches

u feel that way sometimes
wondering:
as a nine year old sister
with burned out hair oddly
smiles at you and sweetly calls you
brother.

u feel that way sometimes
wondering:
as a blackwoman & her 6 children
are burned out of their apartment with no place
to go & a nappy-headed nigger comes running thru
our neighborhood with a match in his hand cryin
revolution.

u feel that way sometimes
wondering:
seeing sisters in two hundred dollar wigs & suits
fastmoving in black clubs in late surroundings   talking
about late thoughts in late language waiting for late men
that come in with, "i don't want to hear bout nothing black tonight."

u feel that way sometimes
wondering:
while eating on newspaper tablecloths
& sleeping on clean bed sheets that couldn't
stop bed bugs   as black children watch their
mothers leave the special buses returning from
special neighborhoods
to clean their "own" unspecial homes.
u feel that way sometimes
wondering:
wondering, how did we survive?

Part V

The Seventies and Beyond

As the seventies began, it seemed that the "New Black Renaissance," the literary movement begun in the sixties, would continue unabated. Books by and about black people poured from major publishing houses as well as from several shoestring enterprises. Small black presses tightened their hold on and continued their major role in the movement. Broadside Press published works such as Gwendolyn Brooks's autobiography, *Report From Part One* (1972), and began a series of volumes of literary criticism. Haki Madhubuti's Third World Press in Chicago published a number of significant books on various aspects of black culture, such as Chancellor Williams's historical analysis, *The Destruction of Black Civilization* (1974), and George E. Kent's *Blackness and the Adventure of Western Culture* (1972). A plethora of magazines, journals, and occasional publications came into being. In Chicago, Gwendolyn Brooks started a periodical, *The Black Position*, which carried essays by leading critics and commentators. Anthologies and collections continued to appear. Conferences and professional meetings provided opportunities for scholarly discourse on black culture. Still central to the movement was *Black World* magazine and its editor, Hoyt W. Fuller.

But change was in the wind. In the fall of 1971 a meeting of black writers was convened at the home of author John Henrik Clarke in Harlem. Some writers feared that the movement was even then disintegrating. A black editor at a major white publishing company asserted that the word had gone out to editors that black works were no longer money-makers and were not to be so readily accepted. In time publication of black-authored books did slow to a trickle, the new little magazines and presses died for lack of funds, the conferences tapered off, the black studies programs declined. As the decade ended, even Broadside Press virtually stopped publishing. In 1976 *Black World* had been terminated, reportedly to be replaced by a fashion magazine. The "black thing" seemed to be over.

In retrospect, 1968 probably marked the turning point in the black movement of which the literary burgeoning was a part. In April of 1968 Martin Luther King, the compelling spiritual leader of the nonviolent wing of the movement, was assassinated, and the cities were wracked with rioting and looting. That year Amiri Baraka and Larry Neal published their seminal anthology *Black Fire*, which defined and demonstrated the new black writing. In November, however, Richard Nixon was elected president, defeating his liberal opponent by a landslide, and America took a step back to conservatism. Under the subsequent administrations of Presidents Gerald Ford, Jimmy Carter, and Ronald Reagan, the conservatism deepened and racism in America thrived.

The continued health of racism was partly a result of the economic problems that gripped much of the world. In the United States, as prices skyrocketed and jobs became scarcer, white Americans increasingly protected their interests and vented their frustrations through reversion to old ways of race relations. By the early eighties virtually all of the economic gains seen in the sixties had vanished. The gap between white and black income had widened; a black college graduate was likely to earn about as much as a white high school graduate. Great numbers of black people, in fact, had no jobs at all. As the Reagan administration slowed inflation by inducing recession and cutting social programs, statistics revealed that a far greater proportion of the black community than of the white had been plunged into poverty and despair. Moreover, as technology progressed and educational opportunities for the poor and black decreased, it became apparent that many black people would remain indefinitely caught in a morass.

In "Division and Confusion: What Happened to the Black Movement?" (*Black World*, January 1976), psychologist Nathan Hare detailed a cycle through which he said black American thought constantly travels: integration to nationalism to Marxism, then back to integration. The cycle held true for the seventies and on into the eighties, as Amiri Baraka and other intellectuals turned from cultural nationalism to Marxism. The difference is profound. Marxism emphasizes economic oppression under a brutal class system as the source of misery for the downtrodden. The enemy is the affluent classes; the solution lies in unity of the poor, regardless of race or nationality. This emphasis is very different from that of the sixties, in which the enemy was seen as European predominance and the solution was thought to be found in unified action of black people worldwide. There was no mass exodus toward Marxism, but some of the intellectual vigor of the black movement was dispelled in that direction.

Another cause of the diffusion of the black movement was the women's movement. During the sixties numbers of white women joined the various black organizations in their push toward liberation. Others observed and were inspired and informed. By the early seventies the spotlight had shifted from the black movement to Women's Liberation, which became a powerful influence in American political and social institutions. Black women were a part of the surge toward women's rights. For this movement, however, the enemy was seen as men, and the solution was to be found in unified action by women. That the women's movement resulted in important gains in indisputable. Some young black women were seduced into a feminism which persuaded them that the black man was their enemy, the white woman their sister. While most were wary of alliance with white women, in their zeal against sexism they deemphasized racism, and differences between black men and black women were exacerbated.

There is no doubt that this has been the era of the black woman writer. In fiction, women have been in the vanguard of black writing. Their works have provided a dimension sorely needed—a more complete image of the black woman in literature and a view of the world through her perceptions. These perceptions, of course, varied widely. On the one hand, for example, there was Mari Evans's proud apostrophe to the black man in her poem "I Am a Black Woman":

I
am a black woman
tall as a cypress
strong
beyond all definition still
defying place
and time
and circumstance
assailed
impervious
indestructible
Look
on me and be
renewed

On the other hand, Ntozake Shange's popular "choreo-poems," *For Colored Girls Who Have Considered Suicide When the Rainbow Is Enuf*, portray black women as sexually and emotionally exploited by black men. Shange's drama ends with the women ritualistically healing themselves and each other, finding love and comfort in a god made in their own image—"I found God in myself and I loved her fiercely."

In theme, form, and world vision, the works of black women attained a wide range. For the first time, there were anthologies of works by and about black women. Prominent among these collections are *The Black Woman* (1970) by Toni Cade Bambara; *Sturdy Black Bridges* (1979) by Roseann P. Bell, Bettye J. Parker, and Beverly Guy-Sheftall; *Confirmation* (1983) by Amiri and Amina Baraka; and two collections of stories, *Black-Eyed Susans* (1975) and *Midnight Birds* (1980), edited by Mary Helen Washington. Another important collection, *Black Women Writers* (1984), edited by Mari Evans, contained the writers' own statements about their writing, and critical assessments of each author. Throughout the seventies and early eighties, women were at the forefront in virtually every genre.

Toni Morrison emerged as the most celebrated novelist of the period, winning acclaim for four popular novels. Alice Walker produced poetry and novels, and edited a collection of the works of Zora Neale Hurston. Walker's novel *The Color Purple* won the 1983 Pulitzer Prize. Toni Cade Bambara and Gayl Jones also made notable contributions to fiction. Important male fiction writers of this period were John Wideman, Leon Forrest, and David Bradley. Maya Angelou, Lucille Clifton, June Jordan, Eugene Redmond, and Michael Harper were among those publishing volumes of poetry. Maya Angelou's autobiographical *I Know Why the Caged Bird Sings* (1970) enjoyed a phenomenal and continuing success, being translated into many languages and adapted for a television film.

Established writers continued to produce. Paule Marshall, James Baldwin, Ishmael Reed, Chester Himes, John A. Williams, and Cyrus Colter brought forth new works of fiction. Larry Neal, Robert Hayden, Mari Evans, Sonia Sanchez, Dudley Randall, Lance Jeffers, Sarah Webster Fabio, Julia Fields, and Clarence Major were among those publishing volumes of poetry. Gwendolyn Brooks remained very active during the period, producing not only her autobiography but also several volumes of her own poetry and collections of the works of contemporary writers. Haki Madhubuti (formerly Don L. Lee) published not only poetry but also social commentary and *Dynamite Voices*, the first volume in the Broadside Press series of literary criticism. Television brought special prominence to Ernest J. Gaines's *The Autobiography of Miss Jane Pittman* (1971) and Alex Haley's *Roots* (1975). Both works were adapted to television by white writers and modified in the process, in essential ways, presumably for "television" purposes.

One of the most important consequences of the literary burgeoning of the sixties was the need for assessment by black critics. By the beginning of the seventies, a number of critics were elaborating a black aesthetic, maintaining that black art differed in important ways from the art of white people. Critics were making linkages with black art in Africa and throughout the diaspora and were searching the folk roots and the consequences of oppression to define and describe this aesthetic. Addison Gayle was, perhaps, the principal spokesman for this critical mode. In *The Black Aesthetic* (1971) he collected critical essays that contributed to the definition. Stephen Henderson's introduction to his anthology *Understanding the New Black Poetry* is perhaps the most complete statement of factors distinguishing black poetry from other poetry. Articles by Addison Gayle and Hoyt Fuller probed the subject of a black aesthetic. A fundamental element in the black aesthetic was the relationship of art to the community. Haki Madhubuti stated the case clearly in *From Plan to Planet* (1973):

> Black writers are first and foremost black men and black women functioning within the context of their respective communities as writers, which is to say that they are black men and women of their communities first and writers second. They are not writers who happen to be black, but are blacks who happen to write, thus understanding their fundamental relationship to their people.

Spurred by the interest in the black aesthetic, a number of critics looked deeply into black American culture as a basis for their analyses of individual authors and of literary trends. Books and articles of special significance were written by George E. Kent, Carolyn Fowler, Eleanor Traylor, Sherley Anne Williams, Bernard Bell, and Houston Baker.

As the decade progressed, the changes in the national situation were reflected in the assessments that the most vocal critics made of their literature. The concept of a black aesthetic came under fire as a new generation of critics arose, influenced by a return to the old dream of integration. Black American literature was placed squarely in the American tradition, with copious quotations from European and white American scholarship to support the process. On the other hand, a number of black women began to enunciate a feminist point of view. There had been astute women critics before, but now there were young women insisting that black men had received favored treatment while women writers had been largely ignored. Some pressed for a black lesbian criticism. The black aesthetic, for these critics, was totally irrelevant.

Both fiction and poetry have undergone changes since 1970. Both have responded to the retreat from militancy. There has been less concern with the sins of whites; there has been more turning inward to the black community itself for themes. Urban street life, so prevalent in the fiction poetry of the sixties, has dwindled in the works of the seventies and early eighties. The portrayal of the folk has, in fact, lost the aura of picaresque romanticism which imbued many of the works of the sixties. The folk are no longer heroic people struggling, and, in their way, prevailing through toughness of spirit. Rather, they are often aberrated or just plain mean. Language has been sanitized in both fiction and poetry. In poetry, innovative and experimental forms have given way to more conventional patterns.

The changes are due partly to the changing realities of the times. One no longer has to read about street people when one may walk through a city park in the morning to see homeless, destitute people sleeping on benches—and feel both guilty and menaced. The changes are due partly to the publication situation. Black presses, for the most part, have closed or curtailed activities for lack of funds. While white publishers have maintained lists of Black and African Studies, interest in and attention to black imaginative writing has either narrowed or declined, possibly in response to the increasingly conservative temper of the book-buying public.

In retrospect, however, from the vantage point of the mid-eighties, there has been an overall enrichment of the body of Afro-American writing, both by writers who were active in the period preceding 1970 and by a number of others who began to be heard from only after that date. And it is to this body of writing that we must turn both for insight and solace in the midst of social and political uncertainties.

ALBERT MURRAY

(b. 1916)

Born in Alabama, where he studied at and graduated from Tuskegee Institute, Albert Murray had from his earliest years a passionate attachment to literature and music. He taught at Tuskegee and then went to the U.S. Air Force, from which he retired as a major. Since 1970 he has frequently been writer in residence and special lecturer at schools, including the Columbia University School of Journalism and Emory University.

A collection of essays, The Omni-Americans *(1970), firmly established Murray as a major and distinctive voice in Afro-American letters. In it he took exception to white conservative and liberal attitudes toward blacks as well as to traditional and militant black views, demonstrating the fatuity of many of these. Murray notes: "The background experience of U.S. Negroes includes all of the negative things that go with racism and segregation; but it also includes all of the challenging things that make for ambition, integrity, and transcendent achievement."*

In 1972 Murray published South To A Very Old Place, *an account of a journey in space and time from Harlem, where he continues to live, to Alabama. En route he talks to distinguished Southerners, black and white, as well as to the humble, and once more he produced a Murray-esque counterportrait to the general picture painted both by partisans of the* status quo ante *and by proponents of change.* The Hero and the Blues *(1973), the Paul Anthony Brick lectures given at the University of Missouri, develops an insightful conception of contemporary literature in which attention is given to Joyce, Hemingway, Ellison, Mann, and Wright, as well as to urban folk music manifestations. In this work Murray ventures the dictum: "Such is the nature of art that the only thing the creative person is justified in straining for is his personal point of view, and paradoxically this probably has much to do not with straining but with learning to relax so as to discover how one actually feels about things."*

In Train Whistle Guitar *(1974), fiction about childhood and adolescence,*

Murray draws on his Alabama boyhood. In Stomping the Blues *(1976) Murray made a pivotal contribution to the history and interpretation of Afro-American music, demonstrating in the process both the shallowness and the factual weaknesses of much that had passed for jazz history.*

Murray continues to write literary and music criticism, as well as fiction. He contributed an important essay on Romare Bearden, "The Visual Equivalent of the Blues," to the retrospective catalogue Romare Bearden: 1970–1980.

A Clutch of Social Science
Fiction Fiction
From *The Omni-Americans*

Only a few American writers since the twenties have been able to create fiction with implications beyond the most obvious and tiresome of the clichés derived from social science. Even the most existentialistic and psychedelic avant-garde experimentalists seem as often as not to be circumscribed by assumptions that are essentially only Marxian or Freudian. Moreover, most book reviewers, no less than American readers in general, now seem to regard fiction as being little more than a very special extension of the social science case history.

Unlike the stories and novels of Hemingway, Fitzgerald, and Faulkner, which, like those of Melville, Mark Twain, and Henry James, embody the writer's insight into the poetic and dramatic dimensions of the human situation (man's aspirations and his possibilities), those of more recent American writers frequently read like interim research reports and position papers. Indeed, what most American fiction seems to represent these days is not so much the writer's actual sense of life as some theory of life to which he is giving functional allegiance, not so much his complex individual sensitivity to the actual texture of human experience as his intellectual reaction to ideas *about* experience.

Fiction about Negroes offers an obvious example. Instead of the imaginative writer's response to the infinitely fascinating mysteries, contradictions, and possibilities of human existence, what fiction about U.S. Negroes almost always expresses is some very highly specialized and extremely narrow psycho-political theory about American *Negro* existence. And what is even worse, these are the theories that, for the most part, only add up to the same old bigoted assumptions that underlie the doctrine of white supremacy.

Accordingly, although Negro life in the United States has always been the incarnation of the "very essence of adventure and romance" (Henrietta Buckmaster's phrase), most often fiction about it is specifically concocted as a documentation of U.S. Negro wretchedness. Seldom do American writers celebrate U.S. Negroes as heroes in fiction. There was William Faulkner, to be sure, who created Lucas Beauchamp, Dilsey, Sam Fathers, and Ned William McCaslin, but the best most other white American writers seem to be able to do by the Negro is show that he deserves economic and political assistance. Nor do many U.S. Negro writers do any better. (But that is another story—one about wailing-wall polemics.)

Here are three reviews of novels which deal with the subject of U.S. Negroes in various mixes of social science and fiction. The novels range from middle-brow ladies' entertainment to very serious efforts at fictional re-creation indeed.

Star-Crossed Melodrama

Perhaps the most significant thing about *Five Smooth Stones* (Crown, 1966), a first novel by Ann Fairbairn, is the fact that it represents a consistent and positive attitude toward the so-called U.S. Negro middle class. The author does not confuse middle income Negroes with white Americans who represent the middle class "norms" of the statistical surveys, and she avoids most of the other usual condescending clichés about educated middle and upper income Negroes. By and large she seems much more concerned with creating people who have human interest and historical resonance than with forcing some theory of class conflict into the interpretation of the behavior of people who make up what is perhaps the most open and intimately interrelated social class structure in the United States.

The career of her hero is nothing if not a testimony to the fluid nature of Negro life in America. David Champlin, who was born in poverty and segregation in New Orleans during the Depression, grows up with ever extending horizons of aspiration, graduates with honors from an integrated college in the Midwest, finishes Harvard Law School, becomes successful in his profession, and moves with assurance in the integrated social circles of Boston and London without ever losing contact with any area of Negro life he has ever known. Moreover, the higher he rises, the more his respect for the rich humanity of his "uneducated" grandfather increases. There are scientific studies and surveys, usually based on oversimplifications, that would have it otherwise, but in the case at least, it is the subjective observations of the fiction writer that come closest to the complexity of actuality.

Still, *Five Smooth Stones* has some curious inconsistencies in its treatment of Negro subject matter. In spite of the author's obvious personal and intellectual freedom from bigoted thinking, she is given to an exasperatingly sloppy overemphasis on race as a social category. Time and again as the omniscient narrator, she uses such expressions as "people of his own race," "one of his own race," "she was of his own race," when "Negroes," "Negro," and "she was a Negro" would be smoother as well as more accurate. And besides, her book demonstrates at every turn how Negroes are racially *interwoven* with other Americans. That U.S. Negroes make up a very distinct sociopolitical group with discernible cultural features peculiar to itself goes without saying, but by no ethnological definition or measurements are they a *race*.

Also Ann Fairbairn is all for intermarriage, as the saying goes, and illustrates her case in terms that are as human as you please. And her conception of the hero's grandfather reveals a rare understanding and magnificent feeling for the role of the older generation Negro as a source of "faith and courage." And yet the minute she has to consider Negroes in terms of "social problems," she becomes as cliché-ridden as a survey technician, and her writing degenerates to the level of the most irresponsible tabloid journalism. She obviously thinks she is making a big fat plea for social rehabilitation when she has one of her most dedicated do-gooders describe the Negroes of the Chicago South Side, East Philadelphia, Watts, and Harlem as being "gangsters at ten, addicts at fourteen, killers at seventeen and dead inside at twenty." But the best that can be said for such glib nonsense is that it reflects an incredibly stupid approach to polemics. It should take a certified imbecile less than fifteen seconds to realize that if the main problem of Negro children in Harlem and Watts is that they are gangsters, addicts, and killers, there would be no overcrowded classrooms and no serious agitation for school desegregation in these places. In fact, there would be no Northern civil rights movement at all! And besides, the Negro youths who are most troublesome to white people these days are not the hoodlums but the social reformers!

In many ways, then, *Five Smooth Stones* is another book of social science fiction despite its virtues. It has implications of an epic and overtones of tragedy, but it never gets beyond the platitudes of melodrama, which just might be the literary fate of such fiction at best. In any event, *Five Smooth Stones* is a melodrama with an unhappy ending. The good guy, in this instance, is David, who has the nicest and most humane white friends

and benefactors in the world. The bad guys are the ugly, snarling segrega-
tionists and the sneaky reactionaries. The great chase, of course, is the
civil rights movement. And the girl the good guy gets is Sara, an apple pie
of a white girl, who, as tiny as she is, just has too much of the pioneer
spirit of her ancestors in her to be restricted by the kind of people who
would not want their sisters and daughters "to marry one." The climax,
however, is only as American as a hysterical mob of white backlashers and
a Mississippi redneck with a sniper's rifle. But the momentum for constructive nonviolent social action is there, and Negroes are bound to show
up better on social science surveys hereafter.

Without denying any of David's obvious and often charming differences, the author of *Five Smooth Stones* can accept a Negro hero as being as
American as anyone else. The author of *Mojo Hand* (Simon & Schuster,
1966), Jane Phillips, cannot. Not only does she insist that middle income
Negroes are as dull and as square as she finds or imagines the white middle class to be, she even gives them pale faces and goes on to portray a mulatto girl as if she were really only a white girl who is fascinated by folk
Negroes, gin, awkward language in general, and foul-mouthed repeti-
tiousness in particular. Eunice, the unlikely heroine, has all the earmarks
of an overromantic unhip ofay beatnik who is hooked on folk music as a
form of "escape." Everything she does betrays her identity to the reader if
not to the other characters in the book, who after all are as unlikely as she
is. She says, does, and is interested in all the wrong things for the wrong
reasons.

The story line of *Mojo Hand*, although not easy to follow, is as simple
as it is unconvincing. Eunice hears a folk blues record by a guitar player
named Blacksnake, falls in love with him and Art and "real" life, leaves
her cotillion-oriented (wow!) middle class mulatto parents in California,
sets out for Louisiana with a guitar on her knee looking for Blacksnake.
She finds him and the blues, the blues as defined in ofay jazz mags—that
is, she talks nasty, does low down, gets pregnant, and so becomes a "real
person" among "real people" instead of being a paleface imitation of life.
Which gets pretty close to condemning Constance Baker Motley as a
phony because she finished law school instead of going on the road with,
say, T-Bone Walker. But then, look at all the confusion caused by white
people who mistake Congressman Adam Clayton Powell for good old Cab
Calloway of the Cotton Club days. One loud Hi-de Hi-de Hi-de-ho and
most of Powell's troubles with "the white world" would probably vanish
overnight.

Neither *Five Smooth Stones* nor *Mojo Hand* should be confused with literature. As for *Mojo Hand*, it is a fiasco from the very outset and can be

dismissed and forgotten as if it never happened. That its young author would rather be a novelist than a social science expert is somehow clear enough; but as yet her conception of the art of fiction is as aboriginal as that of certain widely patronized Negro literary figures who have yet to realize that banal sayings, slang anecdotes, dirty remarks, and bad song lyrics do not become literature simply because they are published in book form.

As for *Five Smooth Stones*, it seldom rises above the comfortable sentiments of the middle-brow ladies magazines and the TV serials. As fictional journalism, however, it is a fascinating and insightful behind-the-scenes account of some of the personal tribulations interwoven with the public political struggles of the civil rights movement. But even so, except where her key characters are involved, the author, like most other writers, shows little understanding and appreciation of what the Southern Negro's extremely complicated resistance to provocation really means. Thus, she not only oversimplifies and misrepresents it as fear, but also in the process she in effect de-emphasizes white insecurity-become-hysterical by treating it as if it were only high-handed callous brutality.

Whether or not *Five Smooth Stones* becomes the best-seller its publishers are hoping for, it seems definitely headed for most social science reading lists. And the author is not very likely to object in either case. It is obvious that she set out to write a popular star-crossed civil rights romance, a plea for good citizenship and a Black Primer for White Folks, all in one. What she seems to have forgotten, however, is the fact that, for those who do not already agree with you, fiction is most compelling as propaganda not when it is used primarily as an aspic for the ideas behind the writer's commitment to a cause but when the narration is compelling.

Warren Miller and His Black Face Vaudeville

Warren Miller is much too slick and much too superficial for his work to be mistaken as serious fiction. But you never know for sure. What with book promotion being what it is these days and what with his subject matter being life in Harlem, his very slapdash slickness may actually be the means by which he may yet slide into some highly important position as a very special expert on Negro Matters. All too often it happens.

One of his books, *The Cool World*, has already been made into a deadly serious avant-garde propaganda film, which has been generally dismissed as Art but praised as realistic documentation. It is no more realistic than the book itself, which was much more concerned about being cute about everything than about being accurate about anything. But so it goes, and it should surprise no one in Harlem if the mass media elect Warren Miller number one U.S. white Negro. So it went back in the days of the king of jazz and the king of swing and so it could go again. As a matter of fact, James Baldwin—who, by the way, knows much more about the goings on in Greenwich Village, Saint-Germain-des-Prés, and even Saint Tropez than he is ever likely to know about Harlem, who certainly knows infinitely more about the guerrilla warfare of New York intellectuals than he has ever actually known about uptown street gangs, and whose scintillating prose style is much closer to Oscar Wilde than to the vernacular of Harlem—has called *The Cool World*, "One of the finest novels about Harlem that has ever come my way." Stuff.

The Cool World is not only not fine, it is hardly a novel at all. Whatever his literary potential may be otherwise, when Warren Miller writes about Negroes and Harlem, he immediately becomes a second-rate blackface comedian, an opportunistic clown cutting topical capers for the entertainment of, as they say in Amagansett, the "white world" (*shitman get hot man stay cool man shitman soul man shitman*). Many white Americans have always gone for this kind of old razzmatazz, and they still pay well for it. And, of course, there are also those ever so smooth Negro con artists who operate in the sad, fuzzy world of the white U.S. liberal, and who will allow themselves to be sprayed with this kind of you-know-what just to prove how tolerant Negroes are, or how superior they are to it. One well-known NAACP bigwig, for instance, used to have one of those Aunt Jemima memo boards hanging in his kitchen during open house just to prove how sophisticated he was! He ain't. He something else. He white folks number one Negro mispronounced as Baldwin does it when referring to himself on TV.

Those who insist on working their way through the everlasting coyness of the language that screens *The Cool World* will not find themselves in a landscape created by an imaginative novelist. They will find a series of patently contrived situations hastily derived from the currently fashionable generalizations of the so-called social sciences. They will find themselves in the prefabricated world of the up to date social worker, a newspaper stage-set with crudely carved ebony and mahogany puppets moving their lips in a snazzy jazzy tempo while an inept ventriloquist mouths overworked Marxist and psychiatric clichés disguised as the untutored wisdom of the curbstones:

> Hurst live in a cellar an dont know whut the world all about. He dont know the world run by crooks pushers and hood from top to

bottom. In the white houses an in the vegetable stores on the corners all of them got big hands in the pie. Its no world to be nice in . . .

Harrison slam his book shut. It go Thuck. He stand up and go to the window an look out. He say to the window. "They make us live like animals. Is it any wonder then that some of us act like animals an some of us become animals. The fantastic thing is how few of us succum to their idea of us." An he went on like that standing there at the window not looking at us lookin out at Harlem.

And so on.

This kind of language is supposed to project the sensibility of four-teen-year-old Duke Custis, the first-person narrator protagonist, whose great ambition is to keep a pistol and become the absolute ruler of his gang. This boy's existence is represented as being so circumscribed that he has no significant awareness of the rich diversity of life about him in Har-lem, to say nothing of life in New York at large. Nor does his sensibility reflect any meaningful contact with the contents of radio programs, mov-ies, TV, magazines, or even comic books. His conception of space travel is that of an idiot. But Luann, the gang's teenage prostitute, takes the cake. She doesn't even know about the subway! What ever happened to the good old A train, so long familiar to every Negro cotton picker arriving from Alabama?

Now if a writer cannot, will not, or at any rate doesn't identify with his characters, he is not likely to write truly about life as he actually knows it. Certainly he cannot condescend to his characters and at the same time expect his readers to believe in them. The fact is, Warren Miller simply cannot imagine himself as Duke Custis. Much has been made of the fact that Miller is a white man who lived in Harlem for five years. This is all very well, but as a writer he seems unable to imagine himself living in Harlem as a Negro for five minutes.

The Harlem described by Warren Miller could never produce a James Baldwin. Thus Baldwin's endorsement of The Cool World would seem exaggerated to say the least. (But there is a curious consistency oper-ating here. For the Harlem described by James Baldwin himself could not possibly produce a James Baldwin either.)

II

The Cool World was a slapdash job. It was also slapstick, but one is not certain how much of the clowning was really intentional. The Seige of Har-lem (McGraw-Hill, 1964) is also slapdash, and here the slapstick is all too intentional. It is a minstrel show in which the writer comes pumping on stage doing a saggy bottomed, tangle footed buck and wing in the guise of Joel Chandler Harris, which he ain't; and he ain't no Octavus Roy Cohen either. Neither is he any Roark Bradford, however he may yearn for them good old green fried chicken pastures.

Here you find Uncle Remus uptown telling bedtime Amos and Andy war stories to a group of children who have such side splitting musical comedy names as M'bova, Jomo, N'Krumah, Ahmad, Shabad, and such like. Harlem has become a nation within New York City, has nationalized the numbers racket, and there are such hilarious vaudeville landmarks as Station WEB Du Bois, checkpoint Frederick Douglass, the Black House, and so on. No need to catalogue the cornballisms. Not even the best comedians at the Apollo theatre can bring stuff this thin to life. Not even the great Pigmeat Markham can make this stuff stack. (Not that you can't still make yourself a fortune by putting on a costume and conning the media into advertising you as a politicized Father Divine. After all, media people, who are nothing if not "committed" regard that as being far more "relevant" than such "razzmatazz" as "Stompin' at the Savoy.")

So much for *The Seige of Harlem*, unless somebody turns it into a TV spectacular. In color yet. But whenever you complain about how some white writer misrepresents Negro life, somebody always wants to know if you think it is possible for any white person to write accurately about any Negroes. The question almost always has racist implications, but the real issue is not racial but cultural. Of course it is possible. Why shouldn't it be possible? If Ernest Hemingway could write good stories about Italy, France, Spain, and Cuba, and if numerous other writers can produce outstanding books about people who lived not only in distant lands but in distant times, why the hell shouldn't a white writer be able to do an excellent book about contemporary Harlem?

The same question comes up when you complain about the inauthenticity of most white jazz musicians. Can a white man really play Negro music? Of course he can. If he is a good enough musician and respects the medium as he would any other art form. If he develops the same familiarity with its idiomatic nuances, the same love of it, and humility before it as the good Negro musician does. Why not? But certainly not if he is really ambivalent about it. Not if he hangs around with it for a while and then withdraws and allows himself to become a "white hope." Not if he allows his publicity to convince him that he is superior to the masters he knows damn well he is still plagiarizing.

Of course white writers can write well about Negroes. Some of William Faulkner's very finest characters are Negroes. And of course white writers are just as free to have as much fun with Negro characters as with any other. Most of Faulkner's Negroes in *The Reivers* are very funny indeed. But Warren Miller's feeble attempts at ridicule only expose his own provincialism, which he sadly mistakes for a superior sophistication. Routine Negro comics do a better job of spoofing the civil rights movement every night.

For one thing, Miller just doesn't seem to be able to resist the all-American temptation to put Negroes in their place by reducing them to stereotypes. Joel Chandler Harris was certainly no great shakes as a writer, but doggone my cats if his talking animals aren't infinitely more human than any character in either *The Cool World* or *The Seige of Harlem*.

Nevertheless Negroes would do well to keep an eye cocked on Warren Miller, slapdash, slapstick, and all. With your white Negro anything is possible. Say if the sequel to *The Seige of Harlem* is another mirthful matinee piece called *Porgy and Bess Stomping at the Savoy and the Walls Come Tumbling Down*, and then this very same Warren Miller grows a beard or something, goes serious and slaps together still another one about how once upon a time a boy in Boston heard a record nightmare by Artie Shaw and became an expert on jazz and the jazz life and had a cotton field romance with a Negro girl and became an expert on Negro sex life as it really is and then was befriended one night by a Negro hipster and became an expert on the narcotic life as it really is and went on to spout a steady stream of magazine articles explaining the civil rights movement as it really is, this very same Warren Miller could very easily be mistaken as a very genuine and understanding friend of Negroes. The trouble is that the Indians used to have friends like that. And look what happened to the Indians. They now live in ghettos. Or is it Casbahs? As Jelly Roll Morton or somebody said: *If you see dear Mrs. Equitone tell her I bring the horoscope myself: one must be so careful these days.*

William Styron and His Troublesome Property

The most fundamental shortcoming of almost all fiction written by white Americans about their black fellow countrymen is also almost always the most obvious. It is, given the deepseated racism of most Americans, also the most predictable. In almost every instance, the white American writer starts out either unable or unwilling to bring himself to make a truly intimate and profoundly personal identification with the black protagonist whose heroism he himself has chosen to delineate and whose sense of life he has elected to impersonate, if not emulate.

In fact, there are times when the emotional distance between the white writer and his black subject matter becomes so great that it seems like an act of deliberation or even calculation—as if what really matters most were not the fabulous self-extensions and enhancements inherent in the storyteller's magic of make believe but rather the writer's own petty provincialisms and preoccupations with social status. Such writers often behave as if the slightest notion of a black compatriot as a storybook hero compels them to equate the strongest Negroes with the most helpless. Or so it seems.

William Styron remarked several years ago that even so great a novelist as William Faulkner created Negro characters who, although marvelously drawn, were *observed* rather than *lived*. Even Faulkner, wrote Styron in "This Quiet Dust," an article for *Harper's* magazine (April, 1965), "hesitated to think Negro." Styron was also moved to point out that not even Dilsey, who, as he concedes, comes so richly alive in *The Sound and the Fury*, is created from what he calls a sense of withinness. At the last moment, he insists, "Faulkner draws back, and it is no mere happenstance that Dilsey alone among the four central figures from whose points of view the story is told is seen from the outside rather than from that intensely inner vantage point, the interior monologue."

It was also William Styron, the author of *Lie Down in Darkness*, *The Long March*, and *Set This House on Fire*, and hence a writer to be reckoned with, who contended, not without some deeply felt passion, that it had become the moral imperative of every white Southerner to break down the old law (which requires the denial of the most obvious of all Southern intanglements) and come to know Negroes. Nor was the fact that Styron himself comes from a lower middle class Tidewater Virginia background likely to strike most Negroes as being either surprising or even curious. On the contrary, many Negroes have long since come to feel that more forthright involvement can almost always be expected from reconstructed or even partially reconstructed Southerners than from any other white people in the United States.

Whatever degree of liberal fellowship the reconstructed Southerner has been able to attain—according to a number of Negroes who are anything but naive or sentimental about such matters—is thoroughgoing and dependable precisely because it is something achieved rather than recieved. The Northern liberal may or may not back up his protestations with action. But the Southerner's first liberal *remark* is likely to be a bridge burning action in itself. Thus, his statements are often a reliable index to the actual extent of his commitment. Or so many Negroes would have it, and there is the best of Robert Penn Warren, C. Vann Woodward, Ramsey Clark, and yes, Lyndon Johnson to bear them out.

In *The Confessions of Nat Turner* (Random House, 1966), however, Negroes will find very little evidence of the reconstruction many may have felt they had reason to anticipate. The very news that a writer of Styron's talent and determination had undertaken a novel about a Negro whose greatness is a matter of historical record (no matter how smudged) was itself cause enough for high hopes. But even better was the fact that a white Southerner had felt a moral imperative to go all the way and tell the story as his own. Those Negro intellectuals who keep check on such things were downright enthusiastic in their endorsement. Even the black nationalists who place race above literature were at least willing to wait and see. After all, Negritude, as the mulatto exponents of Afro-Americanisimus are wont to say, is only a state of mind, and of course there's that old saying about "room for many more." And besides, as black barber shop politicians were quick to acknowledge, it is infinitely more useful to The Cause for a William Styron to become Nat Turner than for Benny Goodman to become Jimmie Noone or for Stan Getz to become a paleface Lester Young, or numerous others to become Miles Davis and Charlie Parker.

But what Negroes will find in Styron's "confessions" is much the same old failure of sensibility that plagues most other fiction about black people. They will find a Nat Turner, that is to say, that many white people may accept at a safe distance but hardly one with whom Negroes will easily identify. The Nat Turner whom Southern Negro school children celebrate (or used to) in pageants during Negro History Week was a magnificent forefather enshrined in the national pantheon beside the greatest heroes of the Republic. There is an old song which goes:

> Well you can be milk-white and just as rich as cream
> And buy a solid gold carriage with a four-horse team
> But you caint keep the world from movering round
> Or stop old Nat Turner from gaining ground

These folk lyrics are about a dedicated man who did far more than declaim great phrases (later to become national clichés) about taxation without representation, liberty or death, and the times that try men's souls. He was, like all epic heroes, a special breed of man who had given his last full measure of devotion to liberation and dignity.

What Southern Negroes will find in Styron's version, alas, is not the black man's homeric Negro but a white man's Negro (specifically, Mister

Stanley M. Elkins') Sambo—a Nat Turner, that is to say, who has been emasculated and reduced to fit all too snugly into a personality structure based on highly questionable and essentially irrelevant conjectures about servility (to which Styron has added a neo-Reichean hypothesis about the correlation between sex repression and revolutionary leadership). Instead of the man of meditation who fasted and prayed to become the Moses of his people, the good shepherd who left a legacy of activism to American ministers which was never more operative than at present, both black and white men of the gospel will find here a black man who really wants to marry somebody's white sister—a man with a sex hangup who goes out into the wilderness to meditate only to get a simple thing like freedom all but hopelessly confused with masturbation while having fantasies about white women.

Ironically, in spite of Styron's expressed intention to get deeper inside his Negro hero than Faulkner did, he seems somehow to have begun by overlooking the fact that the *Negro* conception of Nat Turner was already geared to the dynamics of ritual and myth and hence to literature. In any event, his own seems to have been restricted to such assumptions as underlie sociopolitical science and hence the melodramatic success story. Thus, the Nat Turner who nourished the hopes of Negroes is a tragic hero who symbolizes the human spirit victorious in defeat. Whereas Styron has been able to concede him only "a kind of triumph"—a sort of social science B-plus for effort—for almost succeeding. As if the definition of success were suddenly limited to the consummation of a revolution (which would have annihilated all of Styron's great grandparents) and thus as if heroism were being measured only in terms of its concrete military contribution to the class struggle. (To concede a "kind of triumph" to Robert E. Lee is readily understandable and appropriate. Lee fought on the wrong side and became the biggest loser in the nation's history. But he also became one of the nation's greatest symbols of dignity in defeat.)

But then "This Quiet Dust" shows Styron, who ordinarily is anything but a dialectical materialist, falling into the trap of establishing a Marxist content at the very outset, misled perhaps by too many one-sided historians. Styron *disagrees* with Marxist historian Herbert Aptheker. But he does not reject Aptheker's frame of reference. Aptheker seems to be seeking revolutionary potential. Styron is talking about a failed potential of the same kind. Anyway, he seems to have begun by accepting the old pro-slavery image of white brutality and black docility recently resurrected by historian Elkins, the father of Samboism, in the interest of his own Marx-Freud or psychopolitical theory of black castration. Negro students are likely to find it absolutely incredible that a would-be soul brother could so fail to appreciate what "troublesome property" their ancestors were as to write, as Styron does, that for two hundred and fifty years slavery was "singularly free of organized uprisings, plots and rebellions." Compare this with the non-Marxist view of U.B. Phillips (in *Life and Labor in the Old South*): "The advertising columns of the newspapers bustled with notices of runaways; and no plantation record which has come to my hand is without mention of them."

Styron's failure of sensibility, because of which the best he has been able to do by his own choice of a darling protagonist is to make him a somewhat queer exception to black emasculation, is due at least in part to an overexposure to untenable historical information. After all, Elkins, perhaps too impressed by Nazi cold bloodedness, oversells the psychological damage of oppression on Negroes while making next to nothing of what the never relaxed preoccupation with black codes, fugitive slave laws, patrol systems, and disciplinary cruelty did to white people. The slave owners and drivers like many present-day police were not simply high-handed and callous, they were mostly always on the edge of hysteria from the fear of black uprisings.

Perhaps what on balance is almost certain to strike many Negroes as the pathetic rather than the heroic quality of the action in *The Confessions* also comes from not relying on Negro folk heritage. To Styron the story of Turner's insurrection is not an exemplary endeavor (ending with Nat in jail, echoing, say, Prometheus bound) but only a historical irony, "a decisive factor in the ultimate triumph of the pro-slavery forces."

It so happens, however, that the Nat Turner of Negro folklore is not only a figure ready-made for bards, gleemen, and dramatists but is also one that stands up well under careful documentation. He is, for example, also the Nat Turner of so scholarly a historian as Kenneth Stampp, for whom Turner's forty-eight-hour feat was "an event which produced in the South something resembling a mass trauma, from which the whites had not recovered three decades later. The danger that other Nat Turners might emerge, that even more serious insurrections might someday occur, became an enduring concern as long as the peculiar institution survived. Pro-slavery writers boldly asserted that Southerners did not fear their slaves—but fear of rebellion, sometimes vague, sometimes acute, was with them always."

Now, reviewers who have seized upon white postinsurrection atrocities as a precedent for an inevitable and overwhelming defeat of black militants by the white backlash have not only allowed their need for historical reassurance to becloud the actual historical significance of valid literary implications, but could only have done so by neglecting their homework in U.S. history in the process. "The shock of Nat Turner caused Southerners to take preventive measures," Stampp reports, "but these," he adds, "never eliminated their apprehension or the *actual danger*. [Italics added.] Hardly a year passed without some kind of alarming disturbance somewhere in the South. When no real conspiracy existed, wild rumors often agitated the whites and at times came close to creating an insurrection panic."

The fact is, slavery survived for only thirty-two years more. Emancipation was proclaimed in 1863. Moreover, almost every major figure of the Civil War was already alive at the time of Nat Turner's rebellion. Lincoln himself was twenty-two years old and a flatboatman about to enter politics. Grant was nine. Sherman was eleven. Jefferson Davis, twenty-three, and Robert E. Lee, twenty-four, were both officers already out of West Point. Frederick Douglass was fourteen. Harriet Tubman was eight. William Lloyd Garrison was twenty-six, and Harriet Beecher Stowe was twenty!

As for such a statement as, "Ask any Negro if he is prepared to kill a white man and if he says yes, you may be sure that he is indulging in the sheerest brag," which Styron puts into the mouth of Nat Turner, it would have been regarded as the sheerest nonsense by precisely those Confederate soldiers who defeated the Union's black regiment (the Massachusetts 54th), led by the splendid young white colonel, Robert Shaw, Harvard '60, in the Battle of Fort Wagner. But speaking of ironies, for a scene that at best has only a questionable basis in fact Styron has invented a white Major who, while counter-attacking Turner with integrated forces, says, "That's the spirit boys . . . fire away lads." Which should remind Negroes of nothing so much as Colonel Shaw's dying exhortation to his Negro troops, "Onward boys."

That William Styron is a novelist who is capable of extraordinary self-extension is obvious to anyone who is familiar with the effects he achieved with the interior monologue of Peyton, the central female character of *Lie Down in Darkness*. Nevertheless, he may have done better to use another or perhaps even several different points of view for *The Confessions of Nat Turner*. The withinness of the first-person narration, after all, is not necessarily the best way to tell a story. As the in-character speculations of white Southern types, some of Styron's misconceptions may have come off as brilliant, creative details. As the thoughts of Nat Turner they will probably strike most Negroes as ridiculous. It is hard to believe that either the author of Uncle Remus or William Faulkner could ever have written, "The life of a little nigger child is dull beyond recounting," to say nothing of presenting it as the conception of a Negro, certainly not one who has reached page 138 of a highly poetic 428-page confession.

The moral imperative to know Negroes does not necessarily require other people to "think Negro." But storytellers who would do so must in effect be able to sing the spirituals and/or swing the blues (as, for example, Stephen Vincent Benét did in his story "Freedom's a Hard Bought Thing"). A narrator who is properly tuned in on what underlies the spirituals would hardly allow the kind of vile language in the presence of a man of God like Nat Turner that a Harlem poolroom hoodlum would not tolerate in the presence of any known minister.

As for swinging the blues, the affirmative beat of which is always geared to the rugged facts of life, if you run Schillinger exercises instead of riffing down-home, you only *think* you're swinging. Which, of course, also applies to any Negro writer who assumes that "black consciousness" is only a matter of *saying* you're black while writing about black experience.

ADDISON GAYLE

(b. 1932)

Out of the ferment of civil rights and Black Power came pressing questions concerning the role of the black writer in the struggle. Addison Gayle was ready with a forceful reply. Gayle spent his formative years in tidewater Virginia at Newport News, where his interest in creative writing led him to write a novel before he left high school. His reputation was to be in the field of criticism, however, and notably as the major spokesman for the black aesthetic. In the "Introduction" to the volume he edited with the title, The Black Aesthetic *(1972), he states: "The question for the black critic today is not how beautiful is a melody, a poem, or a novel, but how much more beautiful has the poem, the melody, play, or novel made the life of a single black man. . . . The Black Aesthetic, then, as conceived by this writer, is a corrective—a means of helping black people out of the polluted mainstream of Americanism. . . ."*

The selections in The Black Aesthetic *range from essays from the twenties by Locke, Hughes, and J.A. Rogers, to a spate of contemporary essays by Hoyt Fuller, Dudley Randall, Carolyn Fowler (Gerald), and many others. The impact of the book was profound.*

In 1969 Gayle edited the anthology Black Expression. *He edited another anthology in 1971,* Bondage, Freedom and Beyond. *Gayle also showed himself to be a prolific literary biographer in volumes treating Dunbar (1971), McKay (1972), and Wright (1980). He also wrote* The Black Situation *(1972) and, perhaps precipitately, an autobiographical memoir,* Wayward Child *(1977).*

Gayle's major critical contribution, however, is The Way of the New World; The Black Novel in America *(1975), in which he passes in review, from his distinctive perspective, the fortunes of the black novel and novelist. The only comparable work approaching Gayle's study in discerning commitment is George Kent's* Blackness and the Adventure of Western Culture *(1972), the scope of which is not so broad.*

Introduction
From *The Way of the New World*

Questions concerning the function of literature and the role of the artist in society are as old as the dialogues of Plato. Yet such questions received little consideration from the African-American writer until the
twentieth century. Early black writers, forced into daily combat with an
almost completely closed society, believed that the function of literature
and the role of the artist were similar: Literature was an instrument to be
used in warfare against an oppressive society; it was, also, the medium
that allowed the black writer to serve as interpreter between the Black and
white society. The dual roles—that of the writer as combatant and that of
literature as a weapon in the struggle for human freedom—have received
condemnation over the years from critics, black and white, and led to accusations such as those forwarded by Allen Tate that the black writer has
been limited "to a provincial mediocrity in which feelings about one's difficulties become more important than [literature] itself."

Most African-American critics have been less dogmatic and more analytical than Tate. If the function of literature is to deal with the conditions under which men live—to analyze the effects of a hostile environment upon the human personality—then the proper label for such works,
according to some critics, is "sociology." This attempt to define literature
by pointing out what it is not has led Ralph Ellison to argue that "People
who want to write sociology should not write a novel." Literature, pure
artifact, is thus stripped of all save metaphors, myths, images, and symbols, and presented to us without substance or body, dazzling us not with
concreteness of message, but with the magic of words: ". . . If a moral or
perception is needed," writes Ellison, "let them [the readers] supply their
own. For me, of course, the narrative is the meaning."

Not surprisingly, the white critics have preferred Ellison's pronouncements to those of Tate, for black literature has presented obstacles difficult to overcome. If there is no such dichotomy as Ellison proposes—between sociology and literature—the white critic faces a serious dilemma. The literary artifact must be viewed as something more than form, something more than mechanical construct, which, concerned with the social, economic, and political ideas of the times, mandates the kind of exploration suggested by B. Traven. In a little recognized comment upon his own work, Traven admits that he cannot write about people, places, or things, of which he has little intimacy or direct knowledge: "I must have seen the things, landscapes, and persons, myself, before I can bring them to life in my works. . . . It is necessary for me to have been afraid almost to madness before I can describe terror; I must myself suffer all sadness and heartache before I can visit suffering on the figures which I have called into life."

Despite the differing functions between literature and criticism, Traven's remarks retain their import for both. The critic, the cultivator of the soil in which the best ideas might be nurtured, like the novelist, must possess a pervasive grasp of his subject, must know the landscape, the valleys, hedges, highways, and byways of the human soul. Only such knowledge enables him to evaluate the works of others. Unless one is to view literary criticism as an exact science, James Baldwin's comments in this respect have meaning for writer and critic alike, for one writes out of one thing only, his own experiences.

Ellison, on the other hand, argues that one writes out of other books—a view, which, if correct, defines literature as pure artifact and literary criticism as exact science. This definition gained modern import from the writings of the Agrarian critics of the nineteen twenties and thirties, who sought to establish rules for literary criticism which conformed to criteria established by an intellectual elite, designed to satisfy those for whom literature as history and sociology demanded too great a commitment to the world of practical experience. Those critics, whose chief nourishment has been "other books," turned from Baldwin to Ellison and received a much needed reprieve. For to evaluate the literary artifacts of black people from Phillis Wheatley to Don L. Lee entails little more than knowledge of the rudimentary aspects of literary criticism; to evaluate the black novel, for example, requires only such technical knowledge as that concerning plot, language, setting, and conflict.

These are the major elements in the new criticism forwarded by the Agrarian critics, and their modern-day followers have failed to recognize their limitations. The Agrarian critics did their best work in poetry, a genre which more readily lends itself to verbal gymnastics. In evaluating drama and the novel, the critics failed miserably, due to the complexity of the experiences which these two genres contained—experiences which supersede the form that contains them. Such genres are not autotelic, reach outside of themselves, feed upon the tensions in a universe alive with joy, despair, passivity, and rebellion; one where man, mammoth no longer, pits his feeble strength against the forces of his society, wanders from the planet Earth to the solar system in the never-ending quest to attain that which the followers of the Agrarians would deny him—the knowledge of human existence and purpose.

To define literature in terms of pure artifact, therefore, to evaluate it by methods applicable to science and technology, would make of every novel, poem, or play a hodgepodge of gibberish and would reduce each writer to the stature of a player in the witches' chorus in *Macbeth*, who, securely nestled upon his own tower of Babel, cackles ceaselessly, in tongues unintelligible to those who hold no magic key. Not autotelic, the novel, like its sister genres, depends upon the creative genius of the author, which, heightened by political, social, and historical factors, depicts the experiences of man and, reaching beyond form and structure, communicates with men everywhere. The novel is the one genre which attempts in dramatic and narrative form to answer the questions, What are we? and What is it all about?

These are social questions. They comprise such an essential part of the makeup of the novel that the evaluation of such novels requires an understanding of the social, political, and historical forces which produced them. What, asks Ellison, do we know of Sophocles' wounds? The answer is nothing. Yet to know of Sophocles' wounds might shed new light on *Oedipus Rex*. We know something of the wounds of Dostoevsky, Kafka, and Richard Wright, and as a result their works take on added significance.

Individual wounds are one thing. What does one make of racial wounds, those that make of one black man a black everyman, that hold meaning for each member of the race, that allow each black man, when confronted with injustice enacted against another, to avow that there, but for the grace of some God, go I. What does one make of such wounds buried, covertly or overtly, within the literary format? "I snuck the racial thing in," remarks Frank Yerby. What formula will enable the critic to evaluate literature replete with the effects of such wounds? One turns in answer to the real meaning of Traven's remarks, for to understand madness is to be a bit mad, to understand the Jewish experience, the Russian experience, the Chinese experience, is to be Jewish, Russian, and Chinese. No white man, argues Claude McKay, could have written my books. The message is clear: To evaluate the life and culture of black people, it is necessary that one live the black experience in a world where substance is more important than form, where the social takes precedence over the aesthetic, where each act, gesture, and movement is political, and where continual rebellion separates the insane from the sane, the robot from the revolutionary.

The history of Africans in America is one of rebellion and revolution, and the novelist who finds meaning in their survival upon this continent must be cognizant of the social, political, and historical milieu from which the necessity for rebellion springs. This is truer for the critic, who remains the final adjudicator. If he is to adequately separate truth from distortion, to pass judgment upon those who seek to create and recreate the artifacts of the racial past, he must be aware of those forces that have produced a distinctive history and a distinctive culture.

Ignoring their own history and culture, the early black writers attempted to create a literature patterned upon that of whites. With the possible exception of Martin Delany, the world of the early novelists—William Wells Brown, Frank Webb, and Francis Ellen Watkins—and that of the poets—Phillis Wheatley, Jupiter Hammon, and George Moses Horton—was modeled upon that of such Anglo-Saxons as Pope, Carlyle, Mills, and Byron. They were—Webb excepted—abolitionists, who, in fighting emancipation, adopted almost in total the mannerisms, language, and world view of their white allies. Influences from masters and abolitionist allies pushed the writers toward romanticism at a time when it was becoming the plaything of adolescents and led them to believe, that is, in the eventual assimilation of white and black cultures.

As a result they did not attempt to recreate legends of the past, create symbols, images, and metaphors anew, nor provide literary vehicles by which men, out of the marrow of suffering, might be redeemed in myth if not in actuality; instead, they either accepted the propaganda of their detractors or burned their talents into ashes in attempts to refuse them. They became the first proponents of the assimilation philosophy and helped to transform the Gabriel Prossers, Sojourner Truths, and Frederick Douglasses into Uncle Toms, Mingoes, and Aunt Sues. The courageous men and women who set examples for Blacks yet unborn, by stealing away from slavery, murdering masters and overseers, and committing untold acts of rebellion against the slave system, find little recognition in their poems and novels.

Yet, these writers were black men and women, and in their breasts, if sometimes only feebly, also dwelled the hell-fire of revolt. How then does one account for the failure of their works, for their commitment to the romantic dream, for their inability to come to grips with the fundamental realities of the society in which they lived? The answer is that they were firsts—those who came to maturity in the early decades of the republic. For them, the period between 1800 and 1865 was one in which slavery presented the major conundrum, a solution to which was viewed as a solution to the over-all problem between Blacks and whites. They knew no world other than that divided through sectional strife, centered around the conflict of slavery, and America, at that period of time, appeared as innocent to them, as it would later to such men as Henry James and Van Wyck Brooks.

America was a nation yet to be born and, despite slavery, the romantic belief was shared equally among the early writers that once slavery had ended, a better world would be erected upon the debris of the old. One finds this sense of innocence in the speeches of Douglass between 1863–65, in the poetry of Wheatley, the novels of Brown and Webb. For these writers, the new frontier lay beyond the boundaries erected by slavery; the new world was to be born on the seventh day of emancipation, the second coming ushered in by the last rifle shot fired in the "irrepressible conflict." Upon such a romantic foundation they constructed literature doomed to extinction in the years following Appomattox, and it is not surprising that during the fateful years of Reconstruction no major work is produced among them. Having failed to interpret American reality, they were jolted by the fact that the demise of slavery did not produce the new society, that the black man's condition was not appreciably altered. The America seen through the eyes of Thomas Jefferson, Henry David Thoreau, Ralph Waldo Emerson, and Walt Whitman was one which neither they nor their progeny were ever to know.

This failure to understand the country in which they lived produced an unfounded reservoir of hope and faith in America and its people that pervades the black novel from 1853 to 1962. The American dream, as set forth in legal documents, might become real if only certain blemishes upon the body politic were eradicated. Few questioned the thesis that the blemishes were part of the society's character and being, that the legal documents were the creations of men—Jefferson and Washington—for example, themselves corrupted by the issue of prejudice and racism. Failure to realize such facts led black people and black writers alike to visualize a world to be after the apocalypse—a theme which pervades African-American literature.

Each period—slavery, Reconstruction, early and late twentieth century—has its version of the apocalypse, each its Rubicon which must be forded, crossed, before the period of universal brotherhood, not to mention true creativity, is possible. One apocalypse gives way to another; one Rubicon is but a tributary stream, flowing, merging eventually with the other. The demise of slavery produced segregation and discrimination; the legal ending of segregation and discrimination produced economic and social problems of a magnitude as great as that of slavery and legal segregation. The first writers, therefore, were pioneers, foraging in the literary underbrush, believing always that reality was not what existed at the moment. They were literary visionaries: Brown, Delany, and Webb of one sort; Charles Chesnutt, Paul Laurence Dunbar, and Sutton Griggs of another. Each maintained a common belief and faith that America, after periods of overwhelming darkness, would lift the veil and eternal sunshine would prevail.

We do not know at what point this thesis first came under serious questioning. Martin Delany in *The Condition, Elevation, Emigration and Destiny of the Colored People of the United States* (1852) evidenced cynicism concerning American ideals and pretensions, some of which pervades his novel, *Blake; or the Huts of America* (1859). After two full-length novels designed to change the thinking of white men in regard to their treatment of Blacks, Charles Chesnutt evidences a sense of hopelessness in his final novel, *The Colonel's Dream* (1905). Paul Laurence Dunbar, more optimistic in fiction than in poetry, nevertheless, interjects a note of foreboding and despair in his final novel, *The Sport of the Gods* (1902). Serious, sustained questioning of American ideals by a sizable number of black writers does not occur until the late twentieth century, after the Supreme Court decision in Brown versus Board of Education, Topeka, Kansas (1954), the freedom riders, the crusades of Martin Luther King, Jr., and the rebellions in New York, California, Illinois, and Michigan. Re-examination, however, begins during the Harlem Renaissance, when black writers achieved success in the novel genre, both in terms of technical progress and readership acceptance.

This re-examination, never completed, was spurred in part by the Garvey movement, in part by the Pan-Africanism of W. E. B. Du Bois, and in part by a growing intellectual class, differing in educational attainments from their counterparts in the nineteenth century. William Wells Brown, Frederick Douglass, Jupiter Hammon, and Frank Webb were educated in the university of hard knocks; Alain Locke and W. E. B. Du Bois were educated at Harvard, Langston Hughes at Columbia, and James Weldon Johnson at Atlanta and Columbia. There was, in addition, the factor of time. The second coming was overdue by one hundred years—a long time had elapsed between the nineteen twenties, the beginning of the Renaissance years, and the day in 1865 when Douglass, with a group of

656

well-wishers, awaited news of the issuance of the Emancipation Proclamation. The dream, in short, had been too long deferred. The "Great Migration," which by 1920 resembled a small-scaled avalanche, was important in bringing about re-examination of the perceptions held by Blacks in regard to society, and the exodus of men, women, and children from the South had a profound effect upon black literature in general and the novel in particular. Unlike some of their more prosperous brothers, those who came north, following the great migration, were driven from their homes as a result of attacks by mobs, economic exploitation, and execution without benefit of trial by judge and jury. Langston Hughes sums up their hopes and disappointments in *The Dream Deferred:* "I've seen them come dark wondering/wide-eyed/dreaming out of Penn Station/. . . The gates open—but there are bars/at each gate."

The North failed to provide a locale and social climate much different from that of the region which they had fled. Many, as a result, soon came to surrender the American dream, to despair of ever witnessing a second coming upon these shores, and in protest and disillusionment, swelled the ranks of the new prophets—Marcus Garvey, Father Divine, and Bishop Grace. Their new-found disillusionment created new difficulties for the novelist. The yardstick of measurement by which change is recorded must, in the final analysis, be those for whom the system has not worked at all. Yet to accept these as the criterion of measurement is to suggest that the system cannot work, that the world envisioned by the earlier black writers and intellectuals was impossible of being brought into being.

The intellectuals of the Renaissance period attempted to deal with this difficulty by reverting to romanticism. They argued that the problem was not that American society could not work for Blacks, but only that it had not been sorely tested. Resentful of the dilemma proposed in the persons of the unlettered, primarily dark and poor migrants from the South, they sought to buttress their contention by postulating a questionable thesis structured upon the theory of the blessed and the dammed. Initiated early in the novel, *The Garies and Their Friends*, this thesis suggested that the denominator man was more important than the numerator Black, that the society envisioned in the Constitution was possible of attainment by those who equaled their white counterparts in terms of culture and material acquisition.

The theory divided black men along lines first devised by ingenious slaveholders, and the result of the schism accounts for much of the tension between black intellectuals and the black middle class in the nineteen seventies. Reacting, in part, against the division, Langston Hughes in "The Negro Artist and the Racial Mountain" struck a proletarian note in 1925:

"But then there are the low-down folks, the so-called common element, and they are the majority—may the Lord be praised." These common folk, distinguished by their unashamed adoration for such black artifacts as the spirituals and the blues, were those who had either survived the exodus themselves or children of those who had survived. In their refusal to follow the assimilationist route, they were, for the artist, those upon whom a viable literature might be founded, for they held "their own individuality in the face of American standardization."

"The Negro Artist and the Racial Mountain" is among the more significant critical documents written during the Renaissance years. Hughes suggested that the black writer confront the problem posed by a loss of faith in American society, not by creating divisions, but by rewriting the formula that defined the function and objectives of African-American literature. Return to William Wells Brown and Jupiter Hammon and the function of writer and work alike remain unchanged by most of their early twentieth-century counterparts: Literature is a weapon in the quest for black freedom, and the author is the interpreter of the ways of black folk to white folk. Hughes paid scant attention to the first supposition but sought to restructure the second. Empathizing with the new migrants to a degree impossible for most writers of the period, and knowing that their disillusionment had sunk deep indeed, he dreamed of a literature to describe accurately their hopes, fears, and anxieties, one to truthfully depict their experiences. He knew, contrary to Richard Wright's suppositions some forty years hence, that black people did not understand the meaning of their lives, were not cognizant of the rich cultural and historical milieu from whence they came, and that the black writer should waste little time and energy in directing his works to audiences composed of whites and the black middle class.

Thus, despite his difficulty in living up to his own prescriptions, Hughes demanded more important objectives from the black writer than had been demanded previously. The role of ambassador to the white world was to be exchanged by that of teacher to the black. The advocate for racial justice and democracy was to become the Lycurgus to the black masses; the entertainer to whites and the black middle class was to become the analyzer and explicator of African-American culture here and abroad. Not surprisingly, therefore, Jean Toomer, caroling softly, journeys back to the southland, the first home away from home, though despairingly, Countee Cullen broaches the question, "What is Africa to me?" Rudolph Fisher and Claude McKay look with critical eyes upon a Harlem struggling to be born; Arna Bontemps views the history of Haiti and America; Langston Hughes describes, in fiction, the ways of white folks.

Yet, literature directed toward explicating the lives of "the low-down folk" held dangers which the Renaissance men could not foresee. To deal truthfully with the history, culture, and sociology of the black masses is to deal openly with anger and resentment expressed in unabashed terms. To accurately analyze the life-style of the poor and embittered Blacks who followed Marcus Garvey and Sufi Abdul, the writer had to attack the false premise upon which the middle class and the romantics had structured their cosmology. From the vantage point of the migrants, America was desperately in need of revolution, and the writer who sought to function as their amanuensis would have to record this desire for violent change. That *Native Son* (1940) is the most celebrated novel of the post-Renaissance years evidences the black writer's disregard of the dangers inherent in accepting a new function for the black writer.

Native Son remains the most controversial book written by an African-American. Attacks upon the novel and its author have ranged from the hysterical utterances of Communists, to the bemused, bewildered comments of white liberal critics, and to the apologia of such black writers as James Baldwin and Ralph Ellison. The black and white critics—the Communists excluded—have this in common: an unbending faith in the American dream and an assumption that, despite the failure of Americans to live up to the ideals of justice and equality, hope should still spring eternally in the breast of the African-American. *Native Son* is not a novel for the hopeful or the faithful, but one which results from the inability of men to fulfill the tenets of their own tables of the law. It was written during a period of history wherein mass murder symbolized the moral depravity of Western man. It was written at a time when the incarceration of men of different skin color, ideas, and religion was the rule, in Europe and America as well. It is a novel which illuminates the reality of its time.

It succeeds, also, on a much more fundamental level, undoing the work of black novelists heretofore, pointing out the dangerous consequences of romanticism and unlimited faith in an America of the future, and calling for a total restructuring of the society along egalitarian lines. It mandates that black people forsake abstractionism and dedicate themselves to the possible. It avers that if Bigger Thomas, black everyman, is to be saved, he will not be saved in an integrated country in which each man walks the path of justice, equality, and brotherhood. Such postulates were difficult for the ideological descendants of Frederick Douglass to embrace. To accept Wright's thesis in total means to forego the attempt to achieve the integrated society. It means, moreover, that blacks who seek a sense of their own self-worth must dedicate themselves either to nihilism or revolution. For the most part, the black writer walked the ambivalent line between Wright's postulates and those adhered to by Douglass' ideological kinsmen, despite Wright's own insistence that if the African-American writer was to serve as a "purposeful agent" of his people, he would have to create those values by which they were "to live and die."

Yet, Wright and his followers, Chester Himes, William Gardner Smith, and Ann Petry, were the first black literary iconoclasts, modern-day Zarathustras, determined to bury the old dead god and his ideas. By nineteen-sixty they had succeeded in changing the course of the African-American novel, moving it in the direction that the younger writers of the Renaissance had wanted it to go. After Richard Wright, the novel of outright assimilationism and romanticism no longer appealed to a black reading audience. The novel that functioned as a vehicle for allaying the fears of whites and Blacks of some affluence was now the novel which depicted unadorned truth. When Chester Himes, writing of the hatred which each black man feels for his white countryman, assumed that much the same hatred forms part of the psychic makeup of the black writer as well and suggested that the real question for the writer was "How much does this hatred affect the Negro's personality?" he was signaling the end of the age of ambiguity and ushering in the age of truth—the age of the new black writer.

Before such a new writer could emerge, there were old plants to be plowed under; confrontations with old ideas and theories were necessary. Men who wage warfare with words must be conscious of the meaning of their existence. It is this that Richard Wright might have said to such detractors as James Baldwin, this that Langston Hughes might have said to the black bourgeois writers and their representatives who opposed him in the nineteen twenties—that to confront reality was to step outside of the realm of hate and fear, to posit a world far different from that vouchsafed by the Americans. The first step toward transforming reality is to admit the reality that exists at the moment. For only when black men have moved beyond romanticism and acknowledged the Bigger Thomas in their character, then and only then can the novelist truthfully explicate the world of black folks. It is this, in part, that the writers of the seventies have accomplished. They are indebted to Baldwin and Ellison in the same sense that the former are indebted to Attaway, Wright, and Himes, who in turn are indebted to the younger writers of the Renaissance. For the most part, each contributed to the steady eroding of the romanticism and futile faith which plagued their predecessors; each managed to purge himself of the hatred which consumed the works of many of the most talented of black writers. Acknowledging the existence of the Bigger Thomas living constantly in his skull, the black writer was capable of seeing newer visions, of moving back into the past, of coming to grips with the terrors and joys of those for whom visions of the river Jordan in days gone by were as bold, stark, and immediate as a newborn day.

In short, he embarked upon a new direction, and in so doing, repudiated the idea that the novel should be a vehicle for protest. He moved beyond the example of Richard Wright, seeing, more clearly than Du Bois, that the problem of the twentieth century centered upon power, not race. In the quest for power, the protest novel is a useless vehicle and the author who addresses himself to the power broker in obsequious, piteous pleadings and cajolings emphasizes his powerlessness. "I do not," wrote Richard Wright, "write for black people, but for whites," because whites know nothing of the problems confronting Blacks, whereas Blacks do. Read differently, the statement suggests that whites have the power to determine the destiny not only of the country, but of Blacks as well. The events of the nineteen sixties, however, evidence the fact that the white majority no longer has such frightening power.

On a hot summer night in 1965, the borough of Manhattan erupted in violence. Led by the young and the more defiant, men, women, and children took to the streets to articulate their grievances in terms almost too realistic for the printed page. Past and present merged as Molotov cocktails symbolized centuries of hostility transmitted from one generation to another. Before the decade of vengeance and redemption was over, Watts, Harlem, Detroit, and Chicago had added their names to a period of American history different from any that had preceded it. In the ashes and rubble of the major urban centers of America, the black power revolt had its genesis, and "the Black Aesthetic," its cultural and literary arm, was an outgrowth of the same historical events.

Had the rebellions of the sixties not taken place, black literature in general, and the African-American novel in particular, may not have continued along the road paved by the younger members of the Renaissance, might have veered sharply from the path prescribed by Wright and his followers into art for art's sake, abstractionism, or surrealism. The baptism by fire and blood produced the catharsis, violent in nature, that gave birth to a new literary Renaissance.

Traditional plots in the black novel, situations, and character became anachronistic. Form, as defined by the Europeans beginning with Cervantes, refined by Henry Fielding and Tobias Smollet, and brought forward as an accomplished instrument by Jane Austen, James Joyce, and Marcel Proust, was no longer the form which the serious black novelist deemed necessary of emulation. The Blacks who came north in the early part of the twentieth century had undergone almost complete alteration, recognized and transformed the Bigger Thomases in their skulls, and arrived at a sense of political and social awareness which mandated new literary forms. The novels of the early writers, based upon the Euro-American tradition in form and content, became obsolete; such novels as *Invisible Man* hailed for formalistic innovation were more important in terms of content and message. (For many of the younger writers, Ellison's novel, in terms of form, was a refinement of the genre handed to the Western world by Cervantes.)

These younger writers were now able to divine the real forces at work in the society, to understand the power that dominated the lives of black people in ways that Wright could hardly imagine. The symbol of the twentieth century, wrote Wright, is the man on the corner with a machine gun, and Imamu Baraka asks, "Will the machine gunner please step forward?" At long last, form and structure were recognized as little more than cousins to content, and the black novelist, machine gunner in the cause of mankind, prepared to move forward in the most monumental undertaking of the twentieth century—the task of redefining the definitions, creating new myths, symbols, and images, articulating new values, and recording the progression of a great people from social and political awareness to consciousness of their historical importance as a people and as a nation within a nation—a task which demanded, in the words of poet Don L. Lee, that black people walk the way of the New World.

MAYA ANGELOU

(b. 1928)

There are few writers better known to their readers than Maya Angelou since her poetic and analytical gifts have been consecrated to autobiography as a genre. The term multifaceted *can truly be applied to Angelou, whose career as actress, dancer, singer, and editor has unfolded in the United States, Egypt, Ghana, as well as in Europe. Although born in St. Louis, the chief segment of her life was spent in small town Arkansas, followed by a crowded and stressful period in California, and then an eventful career in a number of settings. The Arkansas years were distilled in* I Know Why The Caged Bird Sings *(1971), a work whose success was instantaneous and which has become virtually a classic, being translated into many languages and dramatized in a successful television film scripted by Angelou herself.*

As a poet Maya Angelou speaks in many voices—that of the sentient woman, that of the satirical observer, that of the folk consciousness.

> *You may write me down in history*
> *With your bitter, twisted lies,*
> *You may trod me in the very dirt*
> *But still, like dust, I'll rise.*

Her volumes of verse have been Just Give Me a Cool Drink of Water 'fore I Diiie *(1973),* Oh Pray My Wings Are Gonna Fit Me Well *(1975),* And Still I Rise *(1978), and* Shaker, Why don't You Sing *(1983).*

Following I Know Why the Caged Bird Sings, *she has continued the crafting of her autobiographical enterprise with* Gather Together in My Name *(1974),* Singin' and Swingin' and Gettin' Merry Like Christmas *(1976), and* The Heart of A Woman *(1981). The succeeding volumes of Angelou's recreation and reflection of her extraordinary life display an acute sensitivity to the human condition, going beyond feminism, racial protest, and anti-imperialism, causes which she understands and has aided, to a full concern for the integrity of the individual person.*

From *Gather Together in My Name*, chapter 16

There is a much-loved region in the American fantasy where pale white women float eternally under black magnolia trees, and white men with soft hands brush wisps of wisteria from the creamy shoulders of their lady loves. Harmonious black music drifts like perfume through this precious air, and nothing of a threatening nature intrudes.

The South I returned to, however, was flesh-real and swollen-belly poor. Stamps, Arkansas, a small hamlet, had subsisted for hundreds of years on the returns from cotton plantations, and until World War I, a creaking lumbermill. The town was halved by railroad tracks, the swift Red River and racial prejudice. Whites lived on the town's small rise (it couldn't be called a hill), while blacks lived in what had been known since slavery as "the Quarters."

After our parents' divorce in California, our father took us from Mother, put identification and destination tags on our wrists, and sent us alone, by train, to his mother in the South. I was three and my brother four when we first arrived in Stamps. Grandmother Henderson accepted us, asked God for help, then set about raising us in His way. She had established a country store around the turn of the century, and we spent the Depression years minding the store, learning Bible verses and church songs, and receiving her undemonstrative love.

We lived a good life. We had some food, some laughter and Momma's quiet strength to lean against. During World War II the armed services drew the town's youth, black and white, and Northern war plants lured the remaining hale and hearty. Few, if any, blacks or poor whites returned to claim their heritage of terror and poverty. Old men and women and young children stayed behind to tend the gardens, the one paved block of stores and the long-accepted way of life.

In my memory, Stamps is a place of light, shadow, sounds and entrancing odors. The earth smell was pungent, spiced with the odor of cattle manure, the yellowish acid of the ponds and rivers, the deep pots of greens and beans cooking for hours with smoked or cured pork. Flowers added their heavy aroma. And above all, the atmosphere was pressed down with the smell of old fears, and hates, and guilt.

On this hot and moist landscape, passions clanged with the ferocity of armored knights colliding. Until I moved to California at thirteen I had known the town, and there had been no need to examine it. I took its being for granted and now, five years later, I was returning, expecting to find the shield of anonymity I had known as a child.

Along with other black children in small Southern villages, I had accepted the total polarization of the races as a psychological comfort. Whites existed, as no one denied, but they were not present in my everyday life. In fact, months often passed in my childhood when I only caught sight of the thin hungry po' white trash (sharecroppers), who lived sadder and meaner lives than the blacks I knew. I had no idea that I had outgrown childhood's protection until I arrived back in Stamps.

Momma took my son in one arm and folded the other around me. She held us for one sweet crushing moment. "Praise God Almighty you're home safe."

She was already moving away to keep her crying private.

"Turned into a little lady. Sure did." My Uncle Willie examined me with his quiet eyes and reached for the baby. "Let's see what you've got there."

He had been crippled in early childhood, and his affliction was never mentioned. The right side of his body had undergone severe paralysis, but his left arm and hand were huge and powerful. I laid the baby in the bend of his good arm.

"Hello, baby. Hello. Ain't he sweet?" The words slurred over his tongue and out of the numb lips. "Here, take him." His healthy muscles were too strong for a year-old wriggler.

Momma called from the kitchen, "Sister, I made you a little something to eat."

We were in the Store; I had grown up in its stronghold. Just seeing the shelves loaded with weenie sausages and Brown Plug Chewing tobacco, salmon and mackerel and sardines all in their old places softened my heart and tears stood at the ready just behind my lids. But the kitchen, where Momma with her great height bent to pull cakes from the woodburning stove and arrange the familiar food on well-known plates, erased my control and the tears slipped out and down my face to plop onto the baby's blanket.

The hills of San Francisco, the palm trees of San Diego, prostitution and lesbians and the throat hurting of Curly's departure disappeared into a never-could-have-happened land. I was home.

"Now what you crying for?" Momma wouldn't look at me for fear my tears might occasion her own. "Give the baby to me, and you go wash your hands. I'm going to make him a sugar tit. You can set the table. Reckon you remember where everything is."

The baby went to her without a struggle and she talked to him without the cooing most people use with small children. "Man. Just a little man, ain't you? I'm going to call you Man and that's that."

Momma and Uncle Willie hadn't changed. She still spoke softly and her voice had a little song in it.

"Bless my soul, Sister, you come stepping up here looking like your daddy for the world."

Christ and Church were still the pillars of her life.

"The Lord my God is a rock in a weary land. He is a great God. Brought you home, all in one piece. Praise His name."

She was, as ever, the matriarch. "I never did want you children to go to California. Too fast that life up yonder. But then, you all's their children, and I didn't want nothing to happen to you, while you're in my care. Jew was getting a little too big for his britches."

Five years before, my brother had seen the body of a black man pulled from the river. The cause of death had not been broadcast, but Bailey (Jew was short for Junior) had seen that the man's genitals had been cut away. The shock caused him to ask questions that were dangerous for a black boy in 1940 Arkansas. Momma decided we'd both be better off in California where lynchings were unheard of and a bright young Negro boy could go places. And even his sister might find a niche for herself.

Despite the sarcastic remarks of Northerners, who don't know the region (read Easterners, Westerners, North Easterners, North Westerners, Midwesterners), the South of the United States can be so impellingly beautiful that sophisticated creature comforts diminish in importance.

For four days I waited on the curious in the Store, and let them look me over. I was that rarity, a Stamps girl who had gone to the fabled California and returned. I could be forgiven a few siditty airs. In fact, a pretesion to worldiness was expected of me, and I was too happy to disappoint.

When Momma wasn't around, I stood with one hand on my hip and my head cocked to one side and spoke of the wonders of the West and the joy of being free. Any listener could have asked me: if things were so grand in San Francisco, what had brought me back to a dusty mote of Arkansas? No one asked, because they all needed to believe that a land existed somewhere, even beyond the Northern Star, where Negroes were treated as people and whites were not the all-powerful ogres of their experience.

For the first time the farmers acknowledged my maturity. They didn't order me back and forth along the shelves but found subtler ways to make their wants known.

"You all have any long-grain rice, Sister?"

The hundred-pound sack of rice sat squidged down in full view.

"Yes, ma'am, I believe we do."

"Well then, I'll thank you for two pounds."

"Two pounds? Yes, ma'am."

I had seen the formality of black adult equals all my youth but had never considered that a time would come when I, too, could participate. The customs are as formalized as an eighteenth-century minuet, and a child at the race's knee learns the moves and twirls by osmosis and observation.

Values among Southern rural blacks are not quite the same as those existing elsewhere. Age has more worth than wealth, and religious piety more value than beauty.

There were no sly looks over my fatherless child. No cutting insinuations kept me shut away from the community. Knowing how closely my grandmother's friends hewed to the Bible, I was surprised not to be asked to confess my evil ways and repent. Instead, I was seen in the sad light which had been shared and was to be shared by black girls in every state in the country. I was young, yes, unmarried, yes—but I was a mother, and that placed me nearer to the people.

I was flattered to receive such acceptance from my betters (seniors) and strove mightily to show myself worthy.

Momma and Uncle Willie noted my inclusion into the adult stratum, and on my fourth day they put up no resistance when I said I was going for a night on the town. Since they knew Stamps, they knew that any carousing I chose to do would be severely limited. There was only one "joint" and the owner was a friend of theirs.

Age and travel had certainly broadened me and obviously made me more attractive. A few girls and boys with whom I'd had only generalities in common, all my life, asked me along for an evening at Willie Williams' café. The girls were going off soon to Arkansas Mechanical and Technical College to study Home Econmics and the boys would be leaving for Tuskegee Institute in Alabama to learn how to farm. Although I had no education, my California past and having a baby made me equal to an evening with them.

When my escorts walked into the darkened Store, Momma came from the kitchen, still wearing her apron, and joined Uncle Willie behind the counter.

"Evening, Mrs. Henderson. Evening, Mr. Willie."

"Good evening, children." Momma gathered herself into immobility.

Uncle Willie leaned against the wall. "Evening, Philomena, and Harriet and Johnny Boy and Louis. How you all this evening?"

Just by placing their big still bodies in the Store at that precise time, my grandmother and uncle were saying, "Be good. Be very very good. Somebody is watching you."

We squirmed and grinned and understood.

The music reached out for us when we approached the halfway point. A dark throbbing bass line whonked on the air lanes, and our bodies moved to tempo. The steel guitar urged the singer to complain

> "Well, I ain't go no
> special reason here.
> No, I ain't got no
> special reason here.
> I'm going leave
> 'cause I don't feel welcome here . . ."

The Dew Drop In café was a dark square outline, and on its wooden exterior, tin posters of grinning white women divinely suggested Coca-Cola, R.C. Cola and Dr Pepper for complete happiness. Inside the one-room building, blue bulbs hung down precariously close to dancing couples, and the air moved heavily like stagnant water.

Our entrance was noted but no one came rushing over to welcome me or ask questions. That would come, I knew, but certain formalities had first to be observed. We all ordered Coca-Cola, and a pint bottle of sloe gin appeared by magic. The music entered my body and raced along my veins with the third syrupy drink. Hurray, I was having a good time. I had never had the chance to learn the delicate art of flirtation, so now I mimicked the other girls at the table. Fluttering one hand over my mouth, while laughing as hard as I could. The other hand waved somewhere up and to my left as if I and it had nothing to do with each other.

"Marguerite?"

I looked around the table and was surprised that everyone was gone. I had no idea how long I had sat there laughing and smirking behind my hand. I decided they had joined the dancing throng and looked up to search for my, by now, close but missing friends.

"Marguerite." L.C. Smith's face hung above me like the head of a bodyless brown ghost.

"L.C., how are you?" I hadn't seen him since my return, and as I waited for his answer a wave of memory crashed in my brain. He was the boy who had lived on the hill behind the school who rode his own horse and at fifteen picked as much cotton as the grown men. Despite his good looks he was never popular. He didn't talk unless forced. His mother had died when he was a baby, and his father drank moonshine, even during the week. The girls said he was womanish, and the boys that he was funny that way.

I commenced to giggle and flutter and he took my hand.

"Come on. Let's dance."

I agreed and caught the edge of the table to stand. Half erect, I noticed that the building moved. It rippled and buckled as if a nest of snakes were mating beneath the floor. I was concerned, but the sloe gin had numbed my brain and I couldn't panic. I held on to the table and L.C.'s hand, and tried to straighten myself up.

"Sit down. I'll be right back." He took his hand away and I plopped back into the chair. Sometime later he was back with a glass of water.

"Come on. Get up." His voice was raspy like old corn shucks. I set my intention on getting up and pressed against the iron which had settled in my thighs.

"We're going to dance?" My words were thick and cumbersome and didn't want to leave my mouth.

"Come on." He gave me his hand and I stumbled up and against him and he guided me to the door.

Outside, the air was only a little darker and a little cooler, but it cleared one corner of my brain. We were walking in the moist dirt along the pond, and the café was again a distant outline. With soberness came a concern for my virtue. Maybe he wasn't what they said.

"What are you going to do?" I stopped and faced him, readying myself for his appeal.

"It's not me. It's you. You're going to throw up." He spoke slowly. "You're going to put your finger down your throat and tickle, then you can puke."

With his intentions clear, I regained my pose.

"But I don't want to throw up. I'm not in the least—"

He closed a hand on my shoulder and shook me a little. "I say, put your finger in your throat and get that mess out of your stomach."

I became indignant. How could he, a peasant, a nobody, presume to lecture me? I snatched my shoulder away.

"Really, I'm fine. I think I'll join my friends," I said and turned toward the café.

"Marguerite." It was no louder than his earlier tone but had more force than his hand.

"Yes?" I had been stopped.

"They're not your friends. They're laughing at you." He had misjudged. They couldn't be laughing at me. Not with my sophistication and city ways.

"Are you crazy?" I sounded like a San Francisco-born debutante.

"No. You're funny to them. You got away. And then you came back. What for? And with what to show for your travels?" His tone was as soft as the Southern night and the pond lapping. "You come back swaggering and bragging that you've just been to paradise and you're wearing the very clothes everybody here wants to get rid of."

I hadn't stopped to think that while loud-flowered skirts and embroidered white blouses caused a few eyebrows to be raised in San Diego, in Stamps they formed the bulk of most girl's wardrobes.

L.C. went on, "They're saying you must be crazy. Even people in Texarkana dress better than you do. And you've been all the way to California. They want to see you show your butt outright. So they gave you extra drinks of sloe gin."

He stopped for a second, then asked, "You don't drink, do you?"

"No." He had sobered me.

"Go on, throw up. I brought some water so you can rinse your mouth after."

He stepped away as I began to gag. The bitter strong fluid gurgled out of my throat, burning my tongue. And the thought of nausea brought on new and stronger contractions.

After the cool water we walked back past the joint, and the music, still heavy, throbbed like gongs in my head. He left the glass by the porch and steered me in the direction of the Store.

His analysis had confused me and I couldn't understand why I should be the scapegoat.

He said, "They want to be free, free from this town, and crackers, and farming, and yes-sirring and no-sirring. You never were very friendly, so if you hadn't gone anywhere, they wouldn't have liked you any more. I was born here, and will die here and they've never liked me." He was resigned and without obvious sorrow.

"But L.C., why don't you get away?"

"And what would my poppa do? I'm all he's got." He stopped me before I could answer, and went on, "Sometimes I bring home my salary and he drinks it up before I can buy food for the week. Your grandmother knows. She lets me have credit all the time."

We were nearing the Store and he kept talking as if I weren't there. I knew for sure that he was going to continue talking to himself after I was safely in my bed.

"I've thought about going to New Orleans or Dallas, but all I know is how to chop cotton, pick cotton and hoe potatoes. Even if I could save the money to take Poppa with me, where would I get work in the city? That's what happened to him, you know? After my mother died he wanted to leave the house, but where could he go? Sometimes when he's drunk two bottles of White Lightning, he talks to her. 'Reenie, I can see you standing there. How come you didn't take me with you, Reenie? I ain't got no place to go, Reenie, I want to be with you, Reenie.' And I act like I don't even hear him."

We had reached the back door of the Store. He held out his hand.

"Here, chew these Sen-sen. Sister Henderson ought not know you've been drinking. Good night, Marguerite. Take it easy."

And he melted into the darker darkness. The following year I heard that he had blown his brains out with a shotgun on the day of his father's funeral.

TONI MORRISON

(b. 1931)

Toni Morrison brings to her writing the background of a black community in a small town, Lorain, Ohio. This background is reflected in three novels, The Bluest Eye *(1970),* Sula *(1974), and* Song of Solomon *(1977); the angle of vision refracted in these novels brought a distinctive note into the American fiction of the seventies. After a brief career as a teacher at Howard University, Morrison became an editor in a major publishing house and conducted her own creative writing while working with other authors.*

Morrison's mastery of language and the startling personalities and traits, physical and psychological, of her characters give her fiction a cast which makes it truly unique in American fiction. Her work derives from a sense of folklore and myth which owes something to Latin American writers. Within the context of American fiction, Morrison's work may be considered to belong to the tradition of romance as defined by Nathaniel Hawthorne.

In Tar Baby *(1981) Morrison moved beyond the horizons essayed in her earlier fiction, thereby confusing and distressing some of her readers. The setting is an expatriate's villa on a Caribbean island; principal characters are white and black; there are flashbacks to plutocratic Philadelphia and jet-set Paris. In all, it seemed, a crowded canvas. In fact, Morrison's techniques and purposes had not changed. The heterogenous elements of* Tar Baby *are placed in the service of yet another Odyssey whose protagonist seeks individual fulfillment.*

From *The Bluest Eye*

Nuns go by as quiet as lust, and drunken men and sober eyes sing in the lobby of the Greek hotel. Rosemary Villanucci, our next-door friend who lives above her father's café, sits in a 1939 Buick eating bread and butter. She rolls down the window to tell my sister Frieda and me that we can't come in. We stare at her, wanting her bread, but more than that wanting to poke the arrogance out of her eyes and smash the pride of ownership that curls her chewing mouth. When she comes out of the car we will beat her up, make red marks on her white skin, and she will cry and ask us do we want her to pull her pants down. We will say no. We don't know what we should feel or do if she does, but whenever she asks us, we know she is offering us something precious and that our own pride must be asserted by refusing to accept.

School has started, and Frieda and I get new brown stockings and cod-liver oil. Grown-ups talk in tired, edgy voices about Zick's Coal Company and take us along in the evening to the railroad tracks where we fill burlap sacks with the tiny pieces of coal lying about. Later we walk home, glancing back to see the great carloads of slag being dumped, red hot and smoking, into the ravine that skirts the steel mill. The dying fire lights the sky with a dull orange glow. Frieda and I lag behind, staring at the patch of color surrounded by black. It is impossible not to feel a shiver when our feet leave the gravel path and sink into the dead grass in the field.

Our house is old, cold, and green. At night a kerosene lamp lights one large room. The others are braced in darkness, peopled by roaches and mice. Adults do not talk to us—they give us directions. They issue orders without providing information. When we trip and fall down they glance at us; if we cut or bruise ourselves, they ask us are we crazy. When we catch colds, they shake their heads in disgust at our lack of consideration. How, they ask us, do you expect anybody to get anything done if you all are sick? We cannot answer them. Our illness is treated with contempt, foul Black Draught, and castor oil that blunts our minds.

When, on a day after a trip to collect coal, I cough once, loudly, through bronchial tubes already packed tight with phlegm, my mother frowns. "Great Jesus. Get on in that bed. How many times do I have to tell you to wear something on your head? You must be the biggest fool in this town. Frieda? Get some rags and stuff that window."

Frieda restuffs the window. I trudge off to bed, full of guilt and self-pity. I lie down in my underwear, the metal in my black garters hurts my legs, but I do not take them off, for it is too cold to lie stockingless. It takes a long time for my body to heat its place in the bed. Once I have generated a silhouette of warmth, I dare not move, for there is a cold place one-half inch in any direction. No one speaks to me or asks how I feel. In an hour or two my mother comes. Her hands are large and rough, and when she rubs the Vicks salve on my chest, I am rigid with pain. She takes two fingers' full of it at a time, and massages my chest until I am faint. Just when I think I will tip over into a scream, she scoops out a little of the salve on her forefinger and puts it in my mouth, telling me to swallow. A hot flannel is wrapped about my neck and chest. I am covered up with heavy quilts and ordered to sweat, which I do—promptly.

Later I throw up, and my mother says, "What did you puke on the bed clothes for? Don't you have sense enough to hold your head out the bed? Now look what you did. You think I got time for nothing but washing up your puke?"

The puke swaddles down the pillow onto the sheet—green-gray, with flecks of orange. It moves like the insides of an uncooked egg. Stubbornly clinging to its own mass, refusing to break up and be removed. How, I wonder, can it be so neat and nasty at the same time?

My mother's voice drones on. She is not talking to me. She is talking to the puke, but she is calling it my name: Claudia. She wipes it up as best she can and puts a scratchy towel over the large wet place. I lie down again. The rags have fallen from the window crack, and the air is cold. I dare not call her back and am reluctant to leave my warmth. My mother's anger humiliates me; her words chafe my cheeks, and I am crying. I do not know that she is not angry at me, but at my sickness. I believe she despises my weakness for letting the sickness "take holt." By and by I will not get sick; I will refuse to. But for now I am crying. I know I am making more snot, but I can't stop.

My sister comes in. Her eyes are full of sorrow. She sings to me: "When the deep purple falls over sleepy garden walls, someone thinks of me. . . ." I doze, thinking of plums, walls, and "someone."

But was it really like that? As painful as I remember? Only mildly. Or rather, it was a productive and fructifying pain. Love, thick and dark as Alaga syrup, eased up into the cracked window. I could smell it—taste it—sweet, musty, with an edge of wintergreen in its base—everywhere in that house. It stuck, along with my tongue, to the frosted window-panes. It coated my chest, along with the salve, and when the flannel came undone in my sleep, the clear, sharp curves of air outlined its presence on my throat. And in the night, when my coughing was dry and tough, feet padded into the room, hands repinned the flannel, readjusted the quilt, and rested a moment on my forehead. So when I think of autumn, I think of somebody with hands who does not want me to die.

It was autumn too when Mr. Henry came. Our roomer. Our roomer. The words ballooned from the lips and hovered about our heads—silent, separate, and pleasantly mysterious. My mother was all ease and satisfaction in discussing his coming.

"You know him," she said to her friends. "Henry Washington. He's been living over there with Miss Della Jones on Thirteenth Street. But she's too addled now to keep up. So he's looking for another place."

"Oh, yes." Her friends do not hide their curiosity. "I been wondering how long he was going to stay up there with her. They say she's real bad off. Don't know who he is half the time, and nobody else."

"Well, that old crazy nigger she married up with didn't help her head none."

"Did you hear what he told folks when he left her?"

"Uh-uh. What?"

"Well, he run off with that trifling Peggy—from Elyria. You know."

"One of Old Slack Bessie's girls?"

"That's the one. Well, somebody asked him why he left a nice good church woman like Della for that heifer. You know Della always did keep a good house. And he said the honest-to-God real reason was he couldn't take no more of that violet water Della Jones used. Said he wanted a woman to smell like a woman. Said Della was just too clean for him."

"Old dog. Ain't that nasty!"

"You telling me. What kind of reasoning is that?"

"No kind. Some men just dogs."

"Is that what give her them strokes?"

"Must have helped. But you know, none of them girls wasn't too bright. Remember that grinning Hattie? She wasn't never right. and their Auntie Julia is still trotting up and down Sixteenth Street talking to her-self."

"Didn't she get put away?"

"Naw. County wouldn't take her. Said she wasn't harming anybody."

"Well, she's harming me. You want something to scare the living shit out of you, you get up at five-thirty in the morning like I do and see that old hag floating by in that bonnet. Have mercy!"

They laugh.

Frieda and I are washing Mason jars. We do not hear their words, but with grown-ups we listen to and watch out for their voices.

"Well, I hope don't nobody let me roam around like that when I get senile. It's a shame."

"What they going to do about Della? Don't she have no people?"

"A sister's coming up from North Carolina to look after her. I expect she wants to get aholt of Della's house."

"Oh, come on. That's a evil thought, if ever I heard one."

"What you want to bet? Henry Washington said that sister ain't seen Della in fifteen years."

"I kind of thought Henry would marry her one of these days."

"That old woman?"

"Well Henry ain't no chicken."

"No, but he ain't no buzzard, either."

"He ever been married to anybody?"

"No."

"How come? Somebody cut it off?"

"He's just picky."

"He ain't picky. You see anything around here you'd marry?"

"Well . . . no."

"He's just sensible. A steady worker with quiet ways. I hope it works out all right."

"It will. How much you charging?"

"Five dollars every two weeks."

"That'll be a big help to you."

"I'll say."

Their conversation is like a gently wicked dance: sound meets sound, curtsies, shimmies, and retires. Another sound enters but is upstaged by still another: the two circle each other and stop. Sometimes their words move in lofty spirals; other times they take strident leaps, and all of it is punctuated with warm-pulsed laughter—like the throb of a heart made of jelly. The edge, the curl, the thrust of their emotions is always clear to Frieda and me. We do not, cannot, know the meanings of all their words, for we are nine and ten years old. So we watch their faces, their hands, their feet, and listen for truth in timbre.

So when Mr. Henry arrived on a Saturday night, we smelled him. He smelled wonderful. Like trees and lemon vanishing cream, and Nu Nile Hair Oil and flecks of Sen-Sen.

He smilled a lot, showing small even teeth with a friendly gap in the middle. Frieda and I were not introduced to him—merely pointed out. Like, here is the bathroom; the clothes closet is here; and these are my kids, Frieda and Claudia; watch out for this window; it don't open all the way.

We looked sideways at him, saying nothing and expecting him to say nothing. Just to nod, as he had done at the clothes closet, acknowledging our existence. To our surprise, he spoke to us.

"Hello there. You must be Greta Garbo, and you must be Ginger Rogers."

We giggled. Even my father was startled into a smile.

"Want a penny?" He held out a shiny coin to us. Frieda lowered her head, too pleased to answer. I reached for it. He snapped his thumb and forefinger, and the penny disappeared. Our shock was laced with delight. We searched all over him, poking our fingers into his socks, looking up the inside back of his coat. If happiness is anticipation with certainty, we were happy. And while we waited for the coin to reappear, we knew we were amusing Mama and Daddy. Daddy was smiling, and Mama's eyes went soft as they followed our hands wandering over Mr. Henry's body.

We loved him. Even after what came later, there was no bitterness in our memory of him.

She slept in the bed with us. Frieda on the outside because she is brave—it never occurs to her that if in her sleep her hand hangs over the edge of the bed "something" will crawl out from under it and bite her fingers off. I sleep near the wall because that thought *has* occurred to me. Pecola, therefore, had to sleep in the middle.

Mama had told us two days earlier that a "case" was coming—a girl who had no place to go. The county had placed her in our house for a few days until they could decide what to do, or, more precisely, until the family was reunited. We were to be nice to her and not fight. Mama didn't know "what got into people," but that old Dog Breedlove had burned up his house, gone upside his wife's head, and everybody, as a result, was outdoors.

Outdoors, we knew, was the real terror of life. The threat of being outdoors surfaced frequently in those days. Every possibility of excess was curtailed with it. If somebody ate too much, he could end up outdoors. If somebody used too much coal, he could end up outdoors. People could gamble themselves outdoors, drink themselves outdoors. Sometimes mothers put their sons outdoors, and when that happened, regardless of what the son had done, all sympathy was with him. He was outdoors, and his own flesh had done it. To be put outdoors by a landlord was one thing—unfortunate, but an aspect of life over which you had no control, since you could not control your income. But to be slack enough to put oneself outdoors, or heartless enough to put one's own kin outdoors—that was criminal.

There is a difference between being put *out* and being put out*doors*. If you are put out, you go somewhere else; if you are outdoors, there is no place to go. The distinction was subtle but final. Outdoors was the end of something, an irrevocable, physical fact, defining and complementing our metaphysical condition. Being a minority in both caste and class, we moved about anyway on the hem of life, struggling to consolidate our weaknesses and hang on, or to creep singly up into the major folds of the garment. Our peripheral existence, however, was something we had learned to deal with—probably because it was abstract. But the concreteness of being outdoors was another matter—like the difference between the concept of death and being, in fact, dead. Dead doesn't change, and outdoors is here to stay.

Knowing that there was such a thing as outdoors bred in us a hunger for property, for ownership. The firm possession of a yard, a porch, a grape arbor. Propertied black people spent all their energies, all their love, on their nests. Like frenzied, desperate birds, they overdecorated everything; fussed and fidgeted over their hard-won homes; canned, jellied, and preserved all summer to fill the cupboards and shelves; they painted, picked, and poked at every corner of their houses. And these houses loomed like hothouse sunflowers among the rows of weeds that were the rented houses. Renting blacks cast furtive glances at these owned yards and porches, and made firmer commitments to buy themselves "some nice little old place." In the meantime, they saved, and scratched, and piled away what they could in the rented hovels, looking forward to the day of property.

Cholly Breedlove, then, a renting black, having put his family outdoors, had catapulted himself beyond the reaches of human consideration. He had joined the animals; was, indeed, an old dog, a snake, a ratty nigger. Mrs. Breedlove was staying with the woman she worked for; the boy, Sammy, was with some other family; and Pecola was to stay with us. Cholly was in jail.

She came with nothing. No little paper bag with the other dress, or a nightgown, or two pair of whitish cotton bloomers. She just appeared with a white woman and sat down.

We had fun in those few days Pecola was with us. Frieda and I stopped fighting each other and concentrated on our guest, trying to keep her from feeling outdoors.

When we discovered that she clearly did not want to dominate us, we liked her. She laughed when I clowned for her, and smiled and accepted gracefully the food gifts my sister gave her.

"Would you like some graham crackers?"

"I don't care."

Frieda brought her four graham crackers on a saucer and some milk in a blue-and-white Shirley Temple cup. She was a long time with the milk, and gazed fondly at the silhouette of Shirley Temple's dimpled face. Frieda and she had a loving conversation about how cu-ute Shirley Temple was. I couldn't join in their adoration because I hated Shirley. Not because she was cute, but because she danced with Bojangles, who was *my* friend, *my* uncle, *my* daddy, and who ought to have been soft-shoeing it and chuckling with me. Instead he was enjoying, sharing, giving a lovely dance thing with one of those little white girls whose socks never slid down under their heels. So I said, "I like Jane Withers."

They gave me a puzzled look, decided I was incomprehensible, and continued their reminiscing about old squint-eyed Shirley.

Younger than both Frieda and Pecola, I had not yet arrived at the turning point in the development of my psyche which would allow me to love her. What I felt at that time was unsullied hatred. But before that I had felt a stranger, more frightening thing than hatred for all the Shirley Temples of the world.

It had begun with Christmas and the gift of dolls. The big, the special, the loving gift was always a big, blue-eyed Baby Doll. From the clucking sounds of adults I knew that the doll represented what they thought was my fondest wish. I was bemused with the thing itself, and the way it looked. What was I supposed to do with it? Pretend I was its mother? I had no interest in babies or the concept of motherhood. I was interested only in humans my own age and size, and could not generate any enthusiasm at the prospect of being a mother. Motherhood was old age, and other remote possibilities. I learned quickly, however, what I was expected to do with the doll: rock it, fabricate storied situations around it, even sleep with it. Picture books were full of little girls sleeping with their dolls. Raggedy Ann dolls usually, but they were out of the question. I was physically revolted by and secretly frightened of those round moronic eyes, the pancake face, and orangeworms hair.

The other dolls, which were supposed to bring me great pleasure, succeeded in doing quite the opposite. When I took it to bed, its hard unyielding limbs resisted my flesh—the tapered fingertips on those dimpled hands scratched. If, in sleep, I turned, the bone-cold head collided with my own. It was a most uncomfortable, patently aggressive sleeping companion. To hold it was no more rewarding. The starched gauze or lace on the cotton dress irritated any embrace. I had only one desire: to dismember it. To see of what it was made, to discover the dearness, to find the beauty, the desirability that had escaped me, but apparently only me. Adults, older girls, shops, magazines, newspapers, window signs—all the world had agreed that a blue-eyed, yellow-haired, pink-skinned doll was what every girl child treasured. "Here," they said, "this is beautiful, and if you are on this day 'worthy' you may have it." I fingered the face, wondering at the single-stroke eyebrows; picked at the pearly teeth stuck like two piano keys between red bowline lips. Traced the turned-up nose, poked the glassy blue eyeballs, twisted the yellow hair. I could not love it. But I could examine it to see what it was that all the world said was lovable. Break off the tiny fingers, bend the flat feet, loosen the hair, twist the head around, and the thing made one sound—a sound they said was the sweet and plaintive cry "Mama," but which sounded to me like the bleat of a dying lamb, or, more precisely, our icebox door opening on rusty hinges in July. Remove the cold and stupid eyeball, it would bleat still, "Ahhhhhh," take off the head, shake out the sawdust, crack the back against the brass bed rail, it would bleat still. The gauze back would split, and I could see the disk with six holes, the secret of the sound. A mere metal roundness.

Grown people frowned and fussed: "You-don't-know-how-to-take-care-of-nothing. I-never-had-a-baby-doll-in-my-whole-life-and-used-to-cry-my-eyes-out-for-them. Now-you-got-one-a-beautiful-one-and-you-tear-it-up-what's-the-matter-with-you?"

How strong was their outrage. Tears threatened to erase the aloofness of their authority. The emotion of years of unfulfilled longing preened in their voices. I did not know why I destroyed those dolls. But I did know that nobody ever asked me what I wanted for Christmas. Had any adult with the power to fulfill my desires taken me seriously and asked me what I wanted, they would have known that I did not want to have anything to own, or to possess any object. I wanted rather to feel something on Christmas day. The real question would have been, "Dear Claudia, what experience would you like on Christmas?" I could have spoken up, "I want to sit on the low stool in Big Mama's kitchen with my lap full of lilacs and listen to Big Papa play his violin for me alone." The lowness of the stool made for my body, the security and warmth of Big Mama's kitchen, the smell of the lilacs, the sound of the music, and, since it would be good to have all my senses engaged, the taste of a peach, perhaps, afterward.

Instead I tasted and smelled the acridness of tin plates and cups designed for tea parties that bored me. Instead I looked with loathing on new dresses that required a hateful bath in a galvanized zinc tub before wearing. Slipping around on the zinc, no time to play or soak, for the water chilled too fast, no time to enjoy one's nakedness, only time to make curtains of soapy water careen down between the legs. Then the scratchy towels and the dreadful and humiliating absence of dirt. The irritable, unimaginative cleanliness. Gone the ink marks from legs and face, all my creations and accumulations of the day gone, and replaced by goose pimples.

I destroyed white baby dolls.

But the dismembering of dolls was not the true horror. The truly horrifying thing was the transference of the same impulses to little white girls. The indifference with which I could have axed them was shaken only by my desire to do so. To discover what eluded me: the secret of the magic they weaved on others. What made people look at them and say, "Awwwww," but not for me? The eye slide of black women as they approached them on the street, and the possessive gentleness of their touch as they handled them.

If I pinched them, their eyes—unlike the crazed glint of the baby doll's eyes—would fold in pain, and their cry would not be the sound of an icebox door, but a fascinating cry of pain. When I learned how repulsive this disinterested violence was, that it was repulsive because it was disinterested, my shame floundered about for refuge. The best hiding place was love. Thus the conversion from pristine sadism to fabricated hatred, to fraudulent love. It was a small step to Shirley Temple. I learned much later to worship her, just as I learned to delight in cleanliness, knowing, even as I learned, that the change was adjustment without improvement.

"Three quarts of milk. That's what was *in* that icebox yesterday. Three whole quarts. Now they ain't none. Not a drop. I don't mind folks coming in and getting what they want, but three quarts of milk! What the devil does *any*body need with *three* quarts of milk?"

The "folks" my mother was referring to was Pecola. The three of us, Pecola, Frieda, and I, listened to her downstairs in the kitchen fussing about the amount of milk Pecola had drunk. We knew she was fond of the Shirley Temple cup and took every opportunity to drink milk out of it just to handle and see sweet Shirley's face. My mother knew that Frieda and I hated milk and assumed Pecola drank it out of greediness. It was certainly not for us to "dispute" her. We didn't initiate talk with grown-ups; we answered their questions.

Ashamed of the insults that were being heaped on our friend, we just sat there: I picked toe jam, Frieda cleaned her fingernails with her teeth, and Pecola finger-traced some scars on her knee—her head cocked to one side. My mother's fussing soliloquies always irritated and depressed us. They were interminable, insulting, and although indirect (Mama never named anybody—just talked about folks and *some* people), extremely painful in their thrust. She would go on like that for hours connecting one offense to another until all of the things that chagrined her were spewed out. Then, having told everybody and everything off, she would burst into song and sing the rest of the day. But it was such a long time before the singing part came. In the meantime, our stomachs jellying and our necks burning, we listened, avoided each other's eyes, and picked toe jam or whatever.

". . . I don't know what I'm supposed to be running here, a charity ward, I guess. Time for me to get out of the *giving* line and get in the *getting* line. I guess I ain't sup*posed* to have nothing. I'm sup*posed* to end up in the poorhouse. Look like nothing I do is going to keep me out of there. Folks just spend all their time trying to figure out ways to send *me* to the poorhouse. I got about as much business with another mouth to feed as a cat has with side pockets. As if I don't have trouble enough trying to feed my own and keep out the poorhouse, now I got something else in here that's just going to *drink* me on in there. Well, naw, she ain't. Not long as I got strength in my body and a tongue in my head. There's a limit to everything. I ain't got nothing to just throw *away*. Don't *nobody* need *three* quarts of milk. Henry *Ford* don't need three quarts of milk. That's just downright *sin*ful. I'm willing to do what I can for folks. Can't nobody say I ain't. But this has got to stop, and I'm just the one to stop it. Bible say watch as *well* as pray. Folks just dump they children off on you and go on 'bout they business. Ain't nobody even *peeped* in here to see whether that child has a loaf of bread. Look like they would just *peep* in to see whether I had a loaf of bread to give her. But naw. That thought don't cross they mind. That old trifling Cholly been out of jail *two* whole days and ain't been here *yet* to see if his own child was 'live or dead. She could be *dead* for all he know. And that *mama* neither. What kind of something is that?"

When Mama got around to Henry Ford and all those people who didn't care whether she had a loaf of bread, it was time to go. We wanted to miss the part about Roosevelt and the CCC camps.

Frieda got up and started down the stairs. Pecola and I followed, making a wide arc to avoid the kitchen doorway. We sat on the steps of the porch, where my mother's words could reach us only in spurts.

It was a lonesome Saturday. The house smelled of Fels Naphtha and the sharp odor of mustard greens cooking. Saturdays were lonesome, fussy, soapy days. Second in misery only to those tight, starchy, cough-drop Sundays, so full of "don'ts" and "set'cha self downs."

If my mother was in a singing mood, it wasn't so bad. She would sing about hard times, bad times, and somebody-done-gone-and-left-me times. But her voice was so sweet and her singing-eyes so melty I found myself longing for those hard times, yearning to be grown without "a thin di-i-me to my name." I looked forward to the delicious time when "my man" would leave me, when I would "hate to see that evening sun go down . . ." 'cause then I would know "my man has left this town." Misery colored by the greens and blues in my mother's voice took all of the grief out of the words and left me with a conviction that pain was not only endurable, it was sweet.

But without song, those Saturdays sat on my head like a coal scuttle, and if Mama was fussing, as she was now, it was like somebody throwing stones at it.

". . . and here I am poor as a bowl of yak-me. What do they think I am? Some kind of Sandy Claus? Well, they can just take they stocking down 'cause it *ain't* Christmas. . . ."

We fidgeted.

"Let's do something," Frieda said.

"What do you want to do?" I asked.

"I don't know. Nothing." Frieda stared at the tops of the trees. Pecola looked at her feet.

"You want to go up to Mr. Henry's room and look at his girlie magazines?"

Frieda made an ugly face. She didn't like to look at dirty pictures. "Well," I continued, "we could look at his Bible. *That's* pretty." Frieda sucked her teeth and made a *phtt* sound with her lips. "O.K., then. We could go thread needles for the half-blind lady. She'll give us a penny."

Frieda snorted. "Her eyes look like snot. I don't feel like looking at them. What *you* want to do, Pecola?"

"I don't care," she said. "Anything you want."

I had another idea. "We could go up the alley and see what's in the trash cans."

"Too cold," said Frieda. She was bored and irritable.

"I know. We could make some fudge."

"You kidding? With Mama in there fussing? When she starts fussing at the walls, you know she's gonna be at it all day. She wouldn't even let us."

"Well, let's go over to the Greek hotel and listen to them cuss."

"Oh, who wants to do *that?* Besides, they say the same old words all the time."

My supply of ideas exhausted, I began to concentrate on the white spots on my fingernails. The total signified the number of boyfriends I would have. Seven.

Mama's soliloquy slid into the silence ". . . Bible say feed the hungry. That's fine. That's all right. But I ain't feeding no elephants. . . . Anybody need three quarts of milk to *live* need to get out of here. They in the wrong place. What is this? Some kind of *dairy* farm?"

Suddenly Pecola bolted straight up, her eyes wide with terror. A whinnying sound came from her mouth.

"What's the matter with *you?*" Frieda stood up too.

Then we both looked where Pecola was staring. Blood was running down her legs. Some drops were on the steps. I leaped up. "Hey. You cut yourself? Look. It's all over your dress."

A brownish-red stain discolored the back of her dress. She kept whinnying, standing with her legs far apart.

Frieda said, "Oh Lordy! I know. I know what that is!"

"What?" Pecola's fingers went to her mouth.

"That's ministratin'."

"What's that?"

"You know."

"Am I going to die?" she asked.

"Noooo. You won't die. It just means you can have a baby!"

"What?"

"How do *you* know?" I was sick and tired of Frieda knowing everything.

"Mildred told me, and Mama too."

"I don't believe it."

"You don't have to, dummy. Look. Wait here. Sit down, Pecola. Right here." Frieda was all authority and zest. "And you," she said to me, "you go get some water."

"Water?"

"Yes, stupid. Water. And be quiet, or Mama will hear you."

Pecola sat down again, a little less fear in her eyes. I went into the kitchen.

"What you want, girl?" Mama was rinsing curtains in the sink.

"Some water, ma'am."

"Right where I'm working, naturally. Well, get a glass. Not no clean one neither. Use that jar."

I got a Mason jar and filled it with water from the faucet. It seemed a long time filling.

"Don't nobody never want nothing till they see me at the sink. Then everybody got to drink water. . . ."

When the jar was full, I moved to leave the room.

"Where you going?"

"Outside."

"Drink that water right here!"

"I ain't gonna break nothing."

"You don't know what you gonna do."

"Yes, ma'am. I do. Lemme take it out. I won't spill none."

"You bed' not."

I got to the porch and stood there with the Mason jar of water. Pecola was crying.

"What you crying for? Does it hurt?"

She shook her head.

"Then stop slinging snot."

Frieda opened the back door. She had something tucked in her blouse. She looked at me in amazement and pointed to the jar. "What's that supposed to do?"

"You told me. You *said* get some water."

"Not a little old jar full. Lots of water. To scrub the steps with, dumbbell!"

"How was I supposed to know?"

"Yeah. How was you. Come on." She pulled Pecola up by the arm. "Let's go back here." They headed for the side of the house where the bushes were thick.

"Hey. What about me? I want to go."

"Shut uuuup," Frieda stage-whispered. "Mama will hear you. You wash the steps."

They disappeared around the corner of the house.

I was going to miss something. Again. Here was something important, and I had to stay behind and not see any of it. I poured the water on the steps, sloshed it with my shoe, and ran to join them.

Frieda was on her knees; a white rectangle of cotton was near her on the ground. She was pulling Pecola's pants off. "Come on. Step out of them." She managed to get the soiled pants down and flung them at me. "Here."

"What am I supposed to do with these?"

"Bury them, moron."

Frieda told Pecola to hold the cotton thing between her legs.

"How she gonna walk like that?" I asked.

Frieda didn't answer. Instead she took two safety pins from the hem of her skirt and began to pin the ends of the napkin to Pecola's dress.

I picked up the pants with two fingers and looked about for something to dig a hole with. A rustling noise in the bushes startled me, and turning toward it, I saw a pair of fascinated eyes in a dough-white face. Rosemary was watching us. I grabbed for her face and succeeded in scratching her nose. She screamed and jumped back.

"Mrs. MacTeer! Mrs. MacTeer!" Rosemary hollered. "Frieda and Claudia are out here playing nasty! Mrs. MacTeer!"

Mama opened the window and looked down at us.

"What?"

"They're playing nasty, Mrs. MacTeer. Look. And Claudia hit me 'cause I seen them!"

Mama slammed the window shut and came running out the back door.

"What you all doing? Oh. Uh-huh. Uh-huh. Playing nasty, huh?" She reached into the bushes and pulled off a switch. "I'd rather raise pigs than some nasty girls. Least I can slaughter *them!*"

We began to shriek. "No, Mama. No, ma'am. We wasn't! She's a liar! No, ma'am, Mama! No, ma'am, Mama!"

Mama grabbed Frieda by the shoulder, turned her around, and gave her three or four stinging cuts on her legs. "Gonna be nasty, huh? Naw you ain't!"

Frieda was destroyed. Whippings wounded and insulted her.

Mama looked at Pecola. "You too!" she said. "Child of mine or not!" She grabbed Pecola and spun her around. The safety pin snapped open on one end of the napkin, and Mama saw it fall from under her dress. The switch hovered in the air while Mama blinked. "What the devil is going on here?"

Frieda was sobbing. I, next in line, began to explain. "She was bleeding. We was just trying to stop the blood!"

Mama looked at Frieda for verification. Frieda nodded. "She's ministratin'. We was just helping."

Mama released Pecola and stood looking at her. Then she pulled both of them toward her, their heads against her stomach. Her eyes were sorry. "All right, all right. Now, stop crying. I didn't know. Come on, now. Get on in the house. Go on home, Rosemary. The show is over."

We trooped in, Frieda sobbing quietly, Pecola carrying a white tail, me carrying the little-girl-gone-to-woman pants.

Mama led us to the bathroom. She prodded Pecola inside, and taking the underwear from me, told us to stay out.

We could hear water running into the bathtub.

"You think she's going to drown her?"

"Oh, Claudia. You so dumb. She's just going to wash her clothes and all."

"Should we beat up Rosemary?"

"No. Leave her alone."

The water gushed, and over its gushing we could hear the music of my mother's laughter.

That night, in bed, the three of us lay still. We were full of awe and respect for Pecola. Lying next to a real person who was really ministratin' was somehow sacred. She was different from us now—grown-up-like. She, herself, felt the distance, but refused to lord it over us.

After a long while she spoke very softly. "Is it true that I can have a baby now?"

"Sure," said Frieda drowsily. "Sure you can."

"But . . . how?" Her voice was hollow with wonder.

"Oh," said Frieda, "somebody has to love you."

"Oh."

There was a long pause in which Pecola and I thought this over. It would involve, I supposed, "my man," who, before leaving me, would love me. But there weren't any babies in the songs my mother sang. Maybe that's why the women were sad: the men left before they could make a baby.

Then Pecola asked a question that had never entered my mind. "How do you do that? I mean, how do you get somebody to love you?" But Frieda was asleep. And I didn't know.

ISHMAEL REED

(b. 1938)

Ishmael Reed, mediating the intersection of social, aesthetic, and political tensions, has displayed in his fiction, poetry, and criticism a virtuosic zest which has both bedazzled and frustrated readers.

Born in Chattanooga, Tennessee, Reed educated himself in a number of places, East and West. He has created a mythos which embraces an occult world of values, vaguely African in inspiration, with Haiti and New Orleans as major reference points. His prose techniques—such as verbal accumulation, misquotation, and partial repetition—have suggested analogies with jazz composition, but one must reject the comparisons with Joyce and Stein offered by some critics. His chief mode is parody, both of form and content; he parodies the American western in Yellow Back Radio Broke-Down *(1969), the detective story in* The Last Days of Louisiana Red *(1974), and the slave narrative in* Flight to Canada *(1976). Reed's artistic motto may be that nothing is sacred because too much has been so.*

His first novel was The Free-Lance Pall-Bearers *(1969), a general critique of the American sociopolitical scene with not-so-veiled depictions of such figures as Lyndon Johnson and Cardinal Spellman. In his third novel,* Mumbo Jumbo *(1972), we reach the center of Reed's work, and it is this which the later fiction seems chiefly to amplify in diverse ways. In this novel, Reed looks for inspiration in sources ranging from the Harlem Renaissance to the Knights Templar. The text is followed by a "Partial Bibliography" of 104 items: New Orleans and Haiti are enshrined here as icons of the Reedian mythos. The novel* The Terrible Twos *(1982) continues Reed's destructive engagement with American culture.*

A collection of essays, Shrovetide in Old New Orleans *(1979), throws light on Reed's sources and critical concerns.* Conjure: Selected Poems *(1972) and* A Secretary to the Spirits *(1977) provide unexpected contrast for the reader,*

688

the poems being more readily accessible than the fiction. In "Sputin" from the latter volume, Reed tells us

Like Venus
My spin is retrograde
A rebel in more ways than one

From *Mumbo Jumbo*, chapters 25–27

It is 2:00 A.M. Rain has fallen and created many water puddles in the streets of Harlem. Moving on an invisible cord, H.V.V. climbs the steps, a spider swollen on snake venom, of the building where Abdul's office is located. All wormy and creepylike, H. "Safecracker" Gould follows behind. The strange pair reach the top of the landing and are confronted with the glass door of Abdul's office. It has the name of his magazine on it. They knock. Abdul comes to the door; he is putting his magazine together.

What do you want?

I would like to talk to you, Mr. Abdul. I am the publisher of the magazine the *Benign Monster*.

Hey man, what was the idea of you putting my picture there last week without my permission. Those weren't my views and you know it. And I didn't like the lewd photos that accompanied the article.

O we were merely trying to give you a friendly overture, perhaps boost the circulation of your magazine. According to our ratings we've climbed to 10,000 circulation. We plan to double that within a short time. We thought we could run some of the anthology you have . . .

What anthology are you referring to? Abdul says, eying the pair suspiciously.

Why the 1 you have. Woodrow Wilson Jefferson said so . . .

O him. Well I don't have it . . .

What do you mean, you don't have it?

I mean just that the words were unprintable.

But the tune was irresistible . . .

I don't think so. I don't like the lyricism. That kind at least. No, I don't have it.

"Safecracker" whispers to Hinckle Von Vampton. Let me talk to him, I know the jargon.

690

Look man, let's us cop the anthology; we may lay something on you.

Who is the corny guy you brought with you? Abdul asks, raising his head from the desk where he had been assembling the mag. Look, I don't have it.

We can have you arrested. The building code. I saw 14 violations downstairs myself. We can close down the magazine and your office. We have friends downtown.

"Safecracker" Gould reveals a pistol.

Move over, let's look into that safe. No use reasoning with this hot-head, H.

Gould points to a safe located behind Abdul.

Gould struggles with Abdul in an effort to reach the safe.

Hey man, what are you doing? Abdul swings Gould around but cries out in pain as the dagger pierces his back. After he falls to the floor mortally wounded, Hinckle Von Vampton removes the dagger from his back.

What's the procedure now, H.?

Open the safe.

"Safecracker" Gould puts his nimble fingers to work and soon the safe swings open.

Empty!!

Well it's not here.

Let's leave, Hubert S. Gould nervously remarks.

No wait, I have to cover my tracks. Take care of this, he says, pointing to Abdul's corpse.

The phone rings in Biff Musclewhite's office. Musclewhite talks after the person on the other end has identified himself and spoken.

O I thought you'd never call . . . I've been wanting to meet you but of course realizing you would be busy with phase 2 . . . A corpse you say to remove? Of course I will remove it at once, Grand Master. It will be done at once.

Tapping his obeah stick, PaPa LaBas climbs out of his Locomobile. He walks into Abdul Hamid's headquarters. His name appears on the glass door.

In the outer office is a desk, upon which lie magazines and newspapers including the newly published *Fire*. Its editor is Wallace Thurman; Langston Hughes and Zora Neale Hurston are associates. Countee Cullen, Langston Hughes and Gwendolyn Bennett have contributed poetry. Woodrow Wilson Jefferson has written a review in which he said that the magazine was pretty good but the contributors would have to go a long way to catch up because "their work didn't make you feel like you wanted to go out and pineapple a necktie store." The review has been clipped and filed.

Ornamenting the desk are amusing lampoons carved in wood, ivory, and cast in bronze by African sculptors. They depict Whites who went into Africa seeking skins, ivory, spices, feathers and furs. The subjects are represented giving bribes, drinking gin, leading manacled slaves, wearing curious, outlandish hats and holding umbrellas. Their chalk-faces appear silly, ridiculous. Outstanding in the collection is the figure of a monkey-like Portuguese explorer, carved by an Angolan. He is obviously juiced and is sitting on a barrel. What side-splitting, bellyaching, satirical ways these ancient craftsmen brought to their art! The African race had quite a sense of humor. In North America, under Christianity, many of them had been reduced to glumness, depression, surliness, cynicism, malice without artfulness, and their intellectuals, in America, only appreciated heavy, serious works. ('Tis the cause, Desdemona.) They'd really fallen in love with tragedy. Their plays were about bitter, raging members of the "nuclear family," and their counterpart in art was exemplified by the contorted, grimacing, painful social-realist face. Somebody, head in hands, sitting on a stoop. "Lawd, I'z so re-gusted." Bert Williams had captured the Afro-American mask with Northrop Frye's inverted U lips. But the figures on the desk, these grotesque, laughable wooden ivory and bronze cartoons represent the genius of Afro satire. They had been removed to Europe by the slavers, traders and sailors who had taken gunpowder and uniforms to Africa. They did not realize that the joke was on them. After all, how could "primitive" people possess wit. LaBas could understand the certain North American Indian tribe reputed to have punished a man for lacking a sense of humor. For LaBas, anyone who couldn't titter a bit was not Afro but most likely a Christian connoting blood, death, and impaled emaciated Jew in excruciation. Nowhere is there an account or portrait of Christ laughing. Like the Marxists who secularized his doctrine, he is always stern, serious and as gloomy as a prison guard. Never does I see him laughing until tears appear in his eyes like the roly-poly squint-eyed Buddha gaffawing with arms upraised, or certain African loas, Orishas.

LaBas believed that when this impostor, this burdensome archetype which afflicted the Afro-American soul, was lifted, a great sigh of relief would go up throughout the land as if the soul was like feet resting in mineral waters after miles of hiking through nails, pebbles, hot coals and prickly things. The young poet Nathan Brown, LaBas felt, was serious about his Black Christ, however absurd that may sound, for Christ is so unlike African loas and Orishas, in so many essential ways, that this alien becomes a dangerous intruder in the Afro-American mind, an unwelcome gatecrasher into Ifé, home of the spirits. Yes, Brown was serious, but the rest were hucksters who had invented this Black Christ, this fraud, simply in order to avoid an honest day's sweat.

PaPa LaBas looks over the figures again. He grins widely. Also on the table lies a book, *Bronze Casting in Benin*. Abdul had announced to the Race press his intention to teach a course on African sculpture to the neighborhood children. He was a hard worker. Some said he could learn a language in a week. In his own land, the land from which his ancestors had been captured during Africa's decline, Abdul would have been royalty. A prince. Here he was ridiculed and considered eccentric, even a dangerous character. No wonder he was so bitter. Who wouldn't be?

It was when PaPa LaBas walked into the room that he saw Abdul lying head down on his desk.

There is a letter on the desk. A pink rejection slip.

Dear Abdul:

We have read with interest the manuscript entitled "The Book of Tot," the sacred anthology. We have decided, however, things being what they are, that we cannot publish this book. It does have that certain panache, that picaresque characterization and zestful dialogue. I was also attracted to the strange almost mystical writing. But the market is overwrought with this kind of book. The "Negro Awakening" fad seems to have reached its peak and once more people are returning to serious writing, Mark Twain and Stephen Crane. A Negro editor here said it lacked "soul" and wasn't "Nation" enough. He suggested you read Claude Mckay's If We Must Die *and perhaps pick up some pointers. Whatever, thanks for permitting us to take a peek. Later Daddy*

S.S.

PaPa LaBas notices a piece of paper in Abdul's fist. He removes it. "Epigram on American-Egyptian Cotton"

> Stringy lumpy; Bales dancing
> Beneath this center
> Lies the Bird.

PaPa LaBas picks up the phone and calls the police. Just as he hears the 1st ring on the other end a man bopadoped into the room. It is one of the local fences. LaBas places the phone in its receiver. The man is stunned when he sees Abdul's corpse.

Hey what's wrong with Abdul?

He's been murdered.

The fence's eyes pop.

Murdered? I was just talking to him this morning and he said he had some boxes he wanted me to look at. Said the boxes were covered with jade, emeralds, jeweled bugs, birds and snakes. That Abdul . . . strange dude. Who do you think did it?

I don't know, PaPa LaBas says, dialing the phone once again.

Well I guess the bulls are going to be here. I'd better leave.

The man exits.

It must have been something to do with the anthology. Disgruntled contributor or something, LaBas thinks.

The authorities answer.

Would you please send an ambulance to Abdul Sufi Hamid's office on 125th St. and Lenox Ave.

We've already sent an ambulance to that place, buddy, answers the voice on the other end.

Strange, LaBas thinks, *perhaps someone has already discovered the corpse and phoned.* In fact he could hear the attendants carrying stretchers climbing the steps.

Monotonously, PaPa LaBas answers some routine questions. His mind is on other things.

Hinckle Von Vampton reads of PaPa LaBas' grim discovery on the front page of the New York *Sun*:

HATE MONGERER MEETS
WELL-DESERVED END
HINT WAR BETWEEN BLACK FACTIONS
NO SUSPECTS IN MURDER OF CULTIST
MU'TAFIKAH QUESTIONED

Later Hinckle Von Vampton's car pulls to the front of Buddy Jackson's cabaret. It is 1 of the more famous 1s in New York City along with Percy Brown's Gold Grabbers, Edmund's, Leroy's and Connie's. The basement is an Indonesian soul food restaurant featuring such exotic numbers as:

CHICKEN IN COCONUT MILK

BAR-BE-CUED FISH

BREGEDEL DJAGUNG

FRIED PINEAPPLE.

On the 2nd Floor is a theater where all the young Black actors come

694

to recite Shakespeare, dreaming of becoming a 2nd Ira Aldridge, the famed Negro thespian.

W.W., Hubert "Safecracker" Gould and Von Vampton alight from the car and head toward the entrance of the cabaret where the review is in progress. The mulatto doorman halts their progress.

What's wrong? queries Hinckle Von Vampton.

That man, sir, he's a mite too dark.

Too dark? an astonished Hinckle Von Vampton replies, but isn't this Harlem where the darkies cavort?

They cavorts, sir, but on stage; we cater to Brown Yellow and White.

That's ridiculous, Hubert "Safecracker" Gould remarks. I've seen Buddy Jackson in this place and he is as black as anthracite as black as ebony as black as the abyss, an Ethiopian if there ever was.

That's different, sir.

What do you mean different? Hinckle von Vampton asks.

He's the owner.

I see, Hinckle Von Vampton says, turning to W.W. You will have to wait outside in the car. Here is 3 cents, go and buy yourself an August Ham.

An August Ham, Hink? What's that?

Dammit, W.W.! An August Ham is watermelon. Don't you know your own people's argot? Get with it, Jackson, maybe it will enliven your articles a bit. You still haven't made a transition from that Marxist rhetoric to the Jazz prose we want.

Once inside Hinckle Von Vampton pornographic publisher begins to relax, drink champagne and savor the high-yellow chorus as they go through some dandy routines. They end their review with the internationally famous Cakewalk which already the French are calling "poetry-in-motion."

There is a hubbub at the door. A party of people, Brown, Yellow and White enter. They are directing their attention at a Brown man in the middle of all this. Vampton recognizes him as Major Young, a young man who is gaining a wide audience. The interracial revelers are having a good time. Langston Hughes, writing of this period, said: "We liked people of any race who smoked incessantly, drank liberally, wore complexion and morality with loose garments, made fun of those who didn't do likewise . . . After fish we went to two or three in the morning and drank until five." Abdul had accused them of "womanizing" and said they were merely trying to "show out" and should cultivate discipline by perhaps fasting sometimes: living off carrots and grasshoppers or even lying upon a bed of nails.

Hinckle Von Vampton, recognizing Major Young, ambles Hubert over to his table where Hubert places a note under his glass.

Major Young rises, excuses himself and walks over to Hinckle's table. He shakes hands with Hinckle, who rises slightly. "Safecracker" Gould "the only man of his generation who didn't go to jail" is too busy, writing down the "nigger mumbo jumbo words" he is hearing from the surrounding tables.

Safecracker! Hinckle says and the startled "Safecracker" turns to him.

We have a guest, say hello to Major Young.

They all sit down and Hinckle orders some more champagne and a Black, trucking waiter comes to his table.

I have read your poetry, my friend, and I must say that I am immensely impressed. Why it soars and it plumbs and it delights and saddens, it sounds like that great American poet Walt Whitman.

Major Young looks at him suspiciously. Walt Whitman never wrote about Harlem.

Well . . . let's just say it is polished as Whitman's attempts are.

Polished? I don't understand. Is writing glassware?

Insolent coon on my hands, Hinckle thinks. Well, let's just say that I enjoyed your work, my friend. The poems were quite raw and earthy; Harlem through and through.

Young smiles wryly.

I happen to run a little risqué sheet called the *Benign Monster*. It's to get White Americans a little loose. I've read Freud very much and my little sheet brings it all out into the open. Allows it to all hang out. We need a contribution from someone like yourself Mr . . . er . . . Mr . . . something in dialect with lots of razzledazzle in it.

Yes I've heard of your magazine, it employs that W. W. Jefferson, he's really dopey and glib. And why does he use that jargon so?

O don't worry about him. We just keep him around as a Go-Get.

As a Go-Get? I don't understand.

Well Go-Get cigarettes and coffee; if you wish we can easily dismiss him.

No, that won't be necessary because I haven't decided to submit anything. I didn't like those drawings you put on somebody's poems in the 1st issue. They were racist and insulting.

O you mean those. O they were just to perk up interest. Whatever you decide, we'll publish it. It will be an excellent welcome relief from that Nathan Brown. He's so arid and stuffy with his material that Phi Beta Kappa key must have gone to his head. Does he know what those references mean? Or is that just half-digested knowledge. He seems to pretend a good deal.

Nathan Brown happens to be a very accomplished poet and a friend of mine. Is it necessary for us to write the same way? I am not Wallace Thurman, Thurman is not Fauset and Fauset is not Claude McKay, McKay isn't Horne. We all have our unique styles; and if you'll excuse me I think I will join my friends.

Well here let me give you my card. Keep in touch.

If I was in my own territory Perry Street in Greenwich Village I'd give that nigger the caning he'd never forget. Who is he to tell me things like that? Hinckle thinks.

Gould lifts his head as Hinckle raises his voice.

Did you see that, "Safecracker"?

What do you expect from these New Negroes or whatever they call themselves. Uppity. Arrogant. If they were real Black men they would be out shooting officials or loitering on Lenox Ave. or panhandling tear-jerking pitiful autobiographies on the radio, wringing them for every cheap emotion they can solicit. They would be massacred in the street like heroes and then . . . why I could snap pictures of the corpses and make a pile of dough. That's why they should do this if they were real Black men.

Did you get what you wanted, "Safecracker"? The evening is not entirely lost?

Yes, the dances were difficult to write down though. Eccentric and individual. But soon I will have stolen enough to have my own Broadway musical. I think I'll call it *Harlem Tom-Toms*.

Hinckle laughs as he leaves the quarter. You know, "Safecracker," what we used to call you in the Templars. What . . . O yes . . . the "Caucasian blackamoor."

TONI CADE BAMBARA

(b. 1939)

With the publication of Gorilla, My Love *(1972), Toni Cade Bambara, a native of New York City, immediately established herself as a major short story writer, with a special gift for depicting the feelings and speech of young black urban folk. Her facility in the genre and the subject matter she presented so skillfully went hand-in-hand with a variety of interests and experiences. Bambara has studied mime in Paris, taught at Rutgers, and is an enthusiast for films. She edited two books:* The Black Woman *(1970) intended to respond to a white-based feminism that was insensitive to the black experience, and* Tales and Short Stories for Black Folks *(1971), a collection shaped to respond to black interests.*

With her second book of short stories The Sea Birds Are Still Alive *(1977), Bambara extended her range beyond the urban landscape, reflecting her Third World interests. Nevertheless, she reaffirmed her unusual control of the urban environment and urban speech. The use of a first-person female narrator in several of her stories provides a means of exploring the nuances, the surprises, the sheer creativity of urban folk discourse. Bambara's novel* The Salt Eaters *(1980) is dedicated to her mother, "who in 1948 having come upon me daydreaming in the middle of the kitchen floor, mopped around me." The dedication is especially appropriate for a novel concerned with hallucination and estrangement. The civil rights movement, treated in several of the short stories, here becomes the backdrop for a complex, musicalized narrative which partakes of allegory. The sharp features of urban life are intertwined with dreamlike visions in this book, in which Bambara attains a striking and complex vision.*

Christmas Eve at Johnson's Drugs N Goods
From *The Sea Birds Are Still Alive*

I was probably the first to spot them cause I'd been watching the entrance of the store on the lookout for my daddy, knowing that if he didn't show soon, he wouldn't be coming at all. His new family would be expecting him to spend the holidays with them. For the first half of my shift, I'd raced the cleaning cart down the aisles doing a slapdash job on the signs and glass cages, eager to stay in view of the doorway. And look like Johnson's kept getting bigger, swelling, sprawling itself all over the corner lot, just to keep me from the door, to wear me out in the marathon vigil.

In point of fact, Johnson's Drugs N Goods takes up less than one-third of the block. But it's laid out funny in crisscross aisles so you get to feeling like a rat in an endless maze. Plus the ceilings are high and the fluorescents a blazing white. And Mrs. Johnson's got these huge signs sectioning off the spaces—Tobacco Drugs Housewares, etc.—like it was some big-time department store. The thing is, till the two noisy women came in, it felt like a desert under a blazing sun. Piper in Tobacco even had on shades. The new dude in Drugs looked like he was at the end of a wrong-way telescope. I got to feeling like a nomad with the cleaning cart, trekking across the sands with no end in sight, wandering. The overhead lights creating mirages and racing up my heart till I'd realize that wasn't my daddy in the parking lot, just the poster-board Santa Claus. Or that wasn't my daddy in the entrance way, just the Burma Shave man in a frozen stance. Then I'd tried to make out pictures of Daddy getting off the bus at the terminal, or driving a rented car past the Chamber of Commerce building, or sitting jammed-leg in one of them DC point-o-nine brand X planes, coming to see me.

By the time the bus pulled into the lot and the two women in their big-city clothes hit the door, I'd decided Daddy was already at the house waiting for me, knowing that for a mirage too, since Johnson's is right across from the railroad and bus terminals and the house is a dollar-sixty cab away. And I know he wouldn't feature going to the house on the off chance of running into Mama. Or even if he escaped that fate, having to sit in the parlor with his hat in his lap while Aunt Harriet looks him up and down grunting, too busy with the latest crossword puzzle contest to offer the man some supper. And Uncle Henry talking a blue streak bout how he outfoxed the city council or somethin and nary a cold beer in sight for my daddy.

But then the two women came banging into the store and I felt better. Right away the store stopped sprawling, got fixed. And we all got pulled together from our various zones to one focal point—them. Changing up the whole atmosphere of the place fore they even got into the store proper. Before we knew it, we were all smiling, looking halfway like you supposed to on Christmas Eve, even if you do got to work for ole lady Johnson, who don't give you no slack whatever the holiday.

"What the hell does this mean, Ethel?" the one in the fur coat say, talking loud and fast, yanking on the rails that lead the way into the store. "What are we, cattle? Being herded into the blankety-blank store and in my fur coat," she grumbles, boosting herself up between the rails, swinging her body along like the kids do in the park.

Me and Piper look at each other and smile. Then Piper moves down to the edge of the counter right under the Tobacco sign so as not to miss nothing. Madeen over in Housewares waved to me to ask what's up and I just shrug. I'm fascinated by the women.

"Look here," the one called Ethel say, drawing the words out lazy slow. "Do you got a token for this sucker?" She's shoving hard against the turnstile folks supposed to exit through. Pushing past and grunting, the turnstile crank cranking like it gonna bust, her Christmas corsage of holly and bells and ajingling and hanging by a thread. Then she gets through and stumbles toward the cigar counter and leans back against it, studying the turnstile hard. It whips back around in place, making scrunching noises like it's been abused.

"You know one thing," she say, dropping her face onto her coat collar so Piper'd know he's being addressed.

"Ma'am?"

"That is one belligerent bad boy, that thing right there."

Piper laughs his prizewinning laugh and starts touching the stacks of gift-wrapped stuff, case the ladies in the market for pipe tobacco or something. Two or three of the customers who'd been falling asleep in the magazines coming to life now, inching forward. Phototropism, I'd call it, if somebody asked me for a word.

The one in the fur coat's coming around now the right way—if you don't count the stiff-elbow rail-walking she was doing—talking about "Oh, my God, I can walk, I can walk, Ethel, praise de lawd."

The two women watching Piper touch the cigars, the humidors, the gift-wrapped boxes. Mostly he's touching himself, cause George Lee Piper love him some George Lee Piper. Can't blame him. Piper be fine.

"You work on commissions, young man?" Fur Coat asking.

"No, ma'am."

The two women look at each other. They look over toward the folks inching forward. They look at me gliding by with the cleaning cart. They look back at each other and shrug.

"So what's his problem?" Ethel says in a stage whisper. "Why he so hot to sell us something?"

"Search me." Fur Coat starts flapping her coat and frisking herself. "You know?" she asking me.

"It's a mystery to me," I say, doing my best to run ole man Samson over. He sneaking around trying to jump Madeen in Housewares. And it is a mystery to me how come Piper always so eager to make a sale. You'd think he had half interest in the place. He says it's because it's his job, and after all, the Johnsons are Black folks. I guess so, I guess so. Me, I just clean the place and stay busy in case Mrs. J is in the prescription booth, peeking out over the top of the glass.

When I look around again, I see that the readers are suddenly very interested in cigars. They crowding around Ethel and Fur Coat. Piper kinda embarrassed by all the attention, though fine as he is, he oughta be used to it. His expression's cool but his hands give him away, sliding around the counter like he shuffling a deck of slippery cards. Fur Coat nudges Ethel and they bend over to watch the hands, doing these chicken-head jerkings. The readers take up positions just like a director was hollering "Places" at em. Piper, never one to disappoint an audience, starts zipping around these invisible walnut shells. Right away Fur Coat whips out a little red change purse and slaps a dollar bill on the counter. Ethel dips deep into her coat pocket, bending her knees and being real comic, then plunks down some change. Ole man Sampson tries to boost up on my cleaning cart to see the shells that ain't there.

"Scuse me, Mr. Sampson," I say, speeding the cart up sudden so that quite naturally he falls off, the dirty dog.

Piper is snapping them imaginary shells around like nobody's business, one of the readers leaning over another's shoulder, staring pop-eyed.

"All right now, everybody step back," Ethel announces. She weaves the crowd back and pushes up one coat sleeve, lifts her fist into the air and jerks out one stiff finger from the bunch, and damn if the readers don't lift their heads to behold in amazement this wondrous finger.

"That, folks," Fur Coat explains, "is what is known as the indicator finger. The indicator is about to indicate the indicatee."

"Say wha?" Dirty ole man Sampson decides he'd rather sneak up on Madeen than watch the show.

"What's going on over there?" Miz Della asks me. I spray the watch case and make a big thing of wiping it and ignoring her. But then the new dude in Drugs hollers over the same thing.

"Christmas cheer gone to the head. A coupla vaudevillians," I say. He smiles, and Miz Della says "Ohhh" like I was talking to her.

"This one," Ethel says, planting a finger exactly one-quarter of an inch from the countertop.

Piper dumb-shows a lift of the shell, turning his face away as though he can't bear to look and find the elusive pea ain't there and he's gonna have to take the ladies' money. Then his eyes swivel around and sneak a peek and widen, lighting up his whole face in a prizewinning grin.

"You got it," he shouts.

The women grab each other by the coat shoulders and jump each other up and down. And I look toward the back cause I know Mrs. J got to be hearing all this carrying-on, and on payday if Mr. J ain't handing out the checks, she's going to give us some long lecture about decorum and what it means to be on board at Johnson's Drugs N Goods. I wheel over to the glass jars and punch bowls, wanting alibi distance just in case. And also to warn Madeen about Sampson gaining on her. He's ducking down behind the coffeepots, walking squat and shameless.

"Pay us our money, young man," Fur Coat is demanding, rapping her knuckles on the counter.

"Yeah, what kind of crooked shell game is you running here in this joint?" say Ethel, finding a good foil character to play.

"We should hate to have to turn the place out, young man."

"It out," echoes Ethel.

The women nod to the crowd and a coupla folks giggle. And Piper tap-taps on the cash register like he shonuff gonna give em they money. I'd rather they turned the place out myself. I want to call my daddy. Only way any of us are going to get home in time to dress for the Christmas dance at the center is for the women to turn it out. Like I say, Piper ain't too clear about the worker's interest versus management's, as the dude in

Drugs would say it. So he's light-tapping and quite naturally the cash drawer does not come out. He's yanking some unseen dollar from the not-there drawer and handing it over. Damn if Fur Coat don't snatch it, deal out the bills to herself and her friend and then make a big production out of folding the money flat and jamming it in that little red change purse.

"I wanna thank you," Ethel says, strolling off, swinging her pocket-book so that the crowd got to back up and disperse. Fur Coat spreads her coat and curtsies.

"A pleasure to do business with you ladies," Piper says, tipping his hat, looking kinda disappointed that he didn't sell em something. Tipping his hat the way he tipped the shells, cause you know Mrs. J don't allow no hats indoors. I came to work in slacks one time and she sent me home to change and docked me too. I wear a gele some times just to mess her around, and you can tell she trying to figure out if she'll go for it or not. The woman is crazy. Not Uncle Henry type crazy, but Black property owner type crazy. She thinks this is a museum, which is why folks don't hardly come in here to shop. That's okay cause we all get to know each other well. It's not okay cause it's a drag to look busy. If you look like you ain't buckling under a weight of work, Mrs. J will have you count the Band-Aids in the boxes to make sure the company ain't pulling a fast one. The woman crazy.

Now Uncle Henry type crazy is my kind of crazy. The type crazy to get you a job. He march into the "saloon" as he calls it and tells Leon D that he is not an equal opportunity employer and that he, Alderman Henry Peoples, is going to put some fire to his ass. So soon's summer comes, me and Madeen got us a job at Leon D. Salon. One of them hushed, funeral type shops with skinny models parading around for customers corseted and strangling in their seats, huffin and puffin.

Madeen got fired right off on account of the pound of mascara she wears on each lash and them weird dresses she designs for herself (with less than a yard of cloth each if you ask me). I did my best to hang in there so's me and Madeen'd have hang-around money till Johnson started hiring again. But it was hard getting back and forth from the stockroom to this little kitchen to fix the espresso to the showroom. One minute up to your ass in carpet, the next skidding across white linoleum, the next making all this noise on ceramic tile and people looking around at you and all. Was there for two weeks and just about had it licked by stationing different kind of shoes at each place that I could slip into, but then Leon D stumbled over my bedroom slippers one afternoon.

But to hear Uncle Henry tell it, writing about it all to Daddy, I was working at a promising place making a name for myself. And Aunt Harriet listening to Uncle Henry read the letter, looking me up and down and grunting. She know what kind of name it must be, cause my name in the family is Miss Clumsy. Like if you got a glass-top coffee table with doo-dads on em, or a hurricane lamp sitting on a mantel anywhere near a door I got to come through, or an antique jar you brought all the way from Venice the time you won the crossword puzzle contest—you can rest assure I'll demolish them by and by. I ain't vicious, I'm just clumsy. It's my gawky stage, Mama says. Aunt Harriet cuts her eye at Mama and grunts.

My daddy advised me on the phone not to mention anything to the Johnsons about this gift of mine for disaster or the fact that I worked at Leon D. Salon. No sense the Johnson's calling up there to check on me and come to find I knocked over a perfume display two times in the same day. Like I say—it's a gift. So when I got to clean the glass jars and punch bowls at Johnson's, I take it slow and pay attention. Then I take up my station relaxed in Fabrics, where the worst that can happen is I upset a box of pins.

Mrs. J is in the prescription booth, and she clears her throat real loud. We all look to the back to read the smoke signals. She ain't paying Fur Coat and Ethel no attention. They over in Cosmetics messing with Miz Della's mind and her customers. Mrs. J got her eye on some young teen-agers browsing around Jewelry. The other eye on Piper. But this does not mean Piper is supposed to check the kids out. It means Madeen is. You got to know how to read Mrs. J to get along.

She always got one eye on Piper. Tries to make it seem like she don't trust him at the cash register. That may be part of the reason now, now that she's worked up this cover story so in her mind. But we all know why she watches Piper, same reason we all do. Cause Piper is so fine you just can't help yourself. Tall and built up, blue-black and smooth, got the nerve to have dimples, and wears this splayed-out push-broom mustache he's always raking in with three fingers. Got a big butt too that makes you wanna hug the customer that asks for the cartoons Piper keeps behind him, two shelfs down. Mercy. And when it's slow, or when Mrs. J comes bustling over for the count, Piper steps from behind the counter and shows his self. You get to see the whole Piper from the shiny boots to the glistening fro and every inch of him fine. Enough to make you holler.

Miz Della in Cosmetics, a sister who's been passing for years but fooling nobody but herself, she always lolligagging over to Tobacco talking bout are there any new samples of those silver-tipped cigars for women. Piper don't even squander energy to bump her off any more. She mostly just ain't even there. At first he would get mad when she used to act hinkty and had these white men picking her up at the store. Then he got sorrowful about it all, saying she was a pitiful person. Now that she's going out with the blond chemist back there, he just wiped her off the map. She tries to mess with him, but Piper ain't heard the news she's been born. Sometimes his act slips, though, cause he does take a lot of unnecessary energy to play up to Madeen whenever Miz Della's hanging around. He's not consistent in his attentions, and that spurs Madeen the dress designer to madness. And Piper really oughta put brakes on that, cause Madeen subject to walk in one day in a fishnet dress and no underwear and then what he goin do about that?

Last year on my birthday my daddy got on us about dressing like hussies to attract the boys. Madeen shrugged it off and went about her business. It hurt my feelings. The onliest reason I was wearing that tight sweater and that skimpy skirt was cause I'd been to the roller rink and that's how we dress. But my daddy didn't even listen and I was really hurt. But then later that night, I come through the living room to make some cocoa and he apologized. He lift up from the couch where he always sleeps when he comes to visit, lifted up and whispered it—"Sorry." I could just make him out by the light from the refrigerator.

"Candy," he calls to make sure I heard him. And I don't want to close the frig door cause I know I'll want to remember this scene, figuring it's going to be the last birthday visit cause he fixin to get married and move outta state.

"Sir?"

He pat the couch and I come on over and just leave the frig door open so we can see each other. I forgot to put the milk down, so I got this cold milk bottle in my lap, feeling stupid.

"I was a little rough on you earlier," he say, picking something I can't see from my bathrobe. "But you're getting to be a woman now and certain things have to be said. Certain things have to be understood so you can decide what kind of woman you're going to be, ya know?"

"Sir," I nod. I'm thinking Aunt Harriet ought to tell me, but then Aunt Harriet prefers to grunt at folks, reserving words for the damn crossword puzzles. And my mama stay on the road so much with the band, when she do come home for a hot minute all she has to tell me is "My slippers're in the back closet" or "Your poor tired Ma'd like some coffee."

He takes my hand and don't even kid me about the milk bottle, just holds my hand for a long time saying nothing, just squeezes it. And I know he feeling bad about moving away and all, but what can he do, he got a life to lead. Just like Mama got her life to lead. Just like I got my life to lead and'll probably leave here myself one day and become an actress or a director. And I know I should tell him it's all right. Sitting there with that milk bottle chilling me through my bathrobe, the light from the refrigerator throwing funny shadows on the wall, I know that years later when I'm in trouble or something, or hear that my daddy died or something like that, I'm going feel real bad that I didn't tell him—it's all right, Daddy, I understand. It ain't like he'd made any promises about making a home for me with him. So it ain't like he's gone back on his word. And if the new wife can't see taking in no half-grown new daughter, hell, I understand that. I can't get the words together, neither can he. So we just squeeze each other's hands. And that'll have to do.

"When I was a young man," he says after while, "there were girls who ran around all made up in sassy clothes. And they were okay to party with, but not the kind you cared for, ya know?" I nod and he pats my hand. But I'm thinking that ain't right, to party with a person you don't care for. How come you can't? I want to ask, but he's talking. And I was raised not to interrupt folk when they talking, especially my daddy. "You and Madeen cause quite a stir down at the barbershop." He tries to laugh it, but it comes out scary. "Got to make up your mind now what kind of woman you're going to be. You know what I'm saying?" I nod and he loosens his grip so I can go make my cocoa.

I'm messing around in the kitchenette feeling dishonest. Things I want to say, I haven't said. I look back over toward the couch and know this picture is going to haunt me later. Going to regret the things left unsaid. Like a coward, like a child maybe. I fix my cocoa and keep my silence, but I do remember to put the milk back and close the refrigerator door.

"Candy?"

"Sir?" I'm standing there in the dark, the frig door closed now and we can't even see each other.

"It's not about looks anyway," he says, and I hear him settling deep into the couch and pulling up the bedclothes. "And it ain't always about attracting some man either . . . not necessarily."

I'm waiting to hear what it is about, the cup shaking in the saucer and me wanting to ask him all over again how it was when he and Mama first met in Central Park, and how it used to be when they lived in Philly and had me and how it was when the two of them were no longer making any sense together but moved down here anyway and then split up. But I could hear that breathing he does just before the snoring starts. So I hustle on down the hall so I won't be listening for it and can't get to sleep.

All night I'm thinking about this woman I'm going to be. I'll look like Mama but don't wanna be no singer. Was named after Grandma Candestine but don't wanna be no fussy old woman with a bunch of kids. Can't see myself turning into Aunt Harriet either, doing crossword puzzles all day long. I look over at Madeen, all sprawled out in her bed, tangled up in the sheets looking like the alcoholic she trying to be these days, sneaking liquor from Uncle Henry's closet. And I know I don't wanna be stumbling down the street with my boobs out and my dress up and my heels cracking off and all. I write for a whole hour in my diary trying to connect with the future me and trying not to hear my daddy snoring.

Fur Coat and Ethel in Housewares talking with Madeen. I know they must be cracking on Miz Della, cause I hear Madeen saying something about equal opportunity. We used to say that Mrs. J was an equal opportunity employer for hiring Miz Della. But then she went and hired real white folks—a blond, crew-cut chemist and a pimply-face kid for the stockroom. If you ask me, that's running equal opportunity in the ground. And running the business underground cause don't nobody round here deal with no white chemist. They used to wrinkly old folks grinding up the herbs and bark and telling them very particular things to do and not to do working the roots. So they keep on going to Mama Drear down past the pond or Doc Jessup in back of the barbershop. Don't do a doctor one bit of good to write out a prescription talking about fill it at Johnson's, cause unless it's an emergency folk stay strictly away from a white root worker, especially if he don't tell you what he doing.

Aunt Harriet in here one day when Mama Drear was too sick to counsel and quite naturally she asks the chemist to explain what all he doing back there with the mortar and pestle and the scooper and the scales. And he say something about rules and regulations, the gist of which was mind your business, lady. Aunt Harriet dug down deep into her crossword-puzzle words and pitched a natural bitch. Called that man a bunch of choicest names. But the line that got me was—"Medication without explanation is obscene." And what she say that for, we ran that in the ground for days. Infatuation without fraternization is obscene. Insemination without obligation is tyranny. Fornication without contraception is obtuse, and so forth and so on. Madeen's best line came out the night we were watching a TV special about welfare. Sterilization without strangulation and hell's damnation is I-owe-you-one-crackers. Look like every situation called for a line like that, and even if it didn't, we made it fit.

Then one Saturday morning we were locked out and we standing around shivering in our sweaters and this old white dude jumps out a pickup truck hysterical, his truck still in gear and backing out the lot. His wife had given their child an overdose of medicine and the kid was out cold. Look like everything he said was grist for the mill.

"She just administered the medicine without even reading the label," he told the chemist, yanking on his jacket so the man couldn't even get out his keys. "She never even considered the fact it might be dangerous, the medicine so old and all." We follow the two down the aisle to the prescription booth, the old white dude talking a mile a minute, saying they tried to keep the kid awake, tried to walk him, but he wouldn't walk. Tried to give him an enema, but he wouldn't stay propped up. Could the chemist suggest something to empty his stomach out and sooth his inflamed ass and what all? And besides he was breathing funny and should be administer mouth-to-mouth resuscitation? The minute he tore out of there and ran down the street to catch up with his truck, we started in.

Administration without consideration is illiterate. Irrigation without resuscitation is evacuation without ambulation is inflammation without information is execution without restitution is. We got downright silly about the whole thing till Mrs. J threatened to fire us all. But we kept it up for a week.

Then the new dude in Drugs who don't never say much stopped the show one afternoon when we were trying to figure out what to call the street riots in the sixties and so forth. He say Revolution without Transformation is Half-assed. Took me a while to ponder that one, a whole day in fact just to work up to it. After while I would listen real hard whenever he opened his mouth, which wasn't often. And I jotted down the titles of the books I'd see him with. And soon's I finish up the stack that's by my bed, I'm hitting the library. He started giving me some of the newspapers he keeps stashed in that blue bag of his we all at first thought was full of funky jockstraps and sneakers. Come to find it's full of carrots and oranges and books and stuff. Madeen say he got a gun in there too. But then Madeen all the time saying something. Like she saying here lately that the chemist's jerking off there behind the poisons and the goopher dust.

The chemist's name is Hubert Tarrly. Madeen tagged him Herbert Tareyton. But the name that stuck was Nazi Youth. Every time I look at him I hear Hitler barking out over the loudspeaker urging the youth to measure up and take over the world. And I can see these stark-eyed gray kids in short pants and suspenders doing jump-ups and scissor kicks and turning they mamas in to the Gestapo for listening to the radio. Chemist looks like he grew up like that, eating knockwurst and beating on Jews, rounding up gypsies, saying *Sieg heil* and shit. Mrs. J said something to him one morning and damn if he didn't click his heels. I like to die. She blushing all over her simple self talking bout that's Southern cavalier style. I could smell the gas. I could see the flaming cross too. Nazi Youth and then some. The dude in Drugs started calling him that too, the dude whose name I can never remember. I always wanna say Ali Baba when I talk about him with my girl friends down at the skating rink or with the older sisters at the arts center. But that ain't right. Either you call a person a name that says what they about or you call em what they call themselves, one or the other.

Now take Fur Coat, for instance. She is clearly about the fur coat. She moving up and down the aisles talking while Ethel in the cloth coat is doing all the work, picking up teapots, checking the price on the dust mops, clicking a bracelet against the punch bowl to see if it ring crystal, hollering to somebody about whether the floor wax need buffing or not. And it's all on account of the fur coat. Her work is something other than that. Like when they were in Cosmetics messing with Miz Della, some white ladies come up talking about what's the latest in face masks. And every time Miz Della pull something out the box, Ethel shake her head and say that brand is crap. Then Fur Coat trots out the sure-fire recipe for the face mask. What she tells the old white ladies is to whip us some egg white to peaks, pour in some honey, some oil of wintergreen, some oil of eucalyptus, the juice of a lemon and a half a teaspoon of arsenic. Now any fool can figure out what lemon juice do to arsenic, or how honey going make the concoction stick, and what all else the oil of this and that'll do to your face. But Fur Coat in her fur coat make you stand still and listen to this madness. Fur Coat an authority in her fur coat. The fur coat is an act of alchemy in itself, as Aunt Harriet would put it.

Just like my mama in her fur coat, same kind too—Persian lamb, bought hot in some riot or other. Mama's coat was part of the Turn the School Out Outfit. Hardly ever came out of the quilted bag cept for that. Wasn't for window-shopping, wasn't for going to rehearsal, wasn't for church teas, was for working her show. She'd flip a flap of that coat back over her hip when she strolled into the classroom to get on the teacher's case bout saying something out of the way about Black folks. Then she'd pick out the exact plank, exact spot she'd take her stand on, then plant one of them black suede pumps from the I. Miller outlet she used to work at. Then she'd lift her chin arrogant proud to start the rap, and all us kids would lean forward and stare at the cameo brooch visible now on the wide-wale wine plush corduroy dress. Then she'd work her show in her outfit. Bam-bam that black suede pocketbook punctuating the points as Mama ticked off the teacher's offenses. And when she got to the good part, and all us kids would strain up off the benches to hear every word so we could play it out in the schoolyard, she'd take both fists and brush that fur coat way back past her hips and she'd challenge the teacher to either change up and apologize or meet her for a showdown at a school-board hearing. And of course ole teacher'd apologize to us all Black kids. Then Mama'd let the coat fall back into place and she'd whip around, the coat draping like queen robes, and march herself out. Mama was baad in her fur coat.

I don't know what-all Fur Coat do in her fur coat but I can tell it's hellafyin whatever it all is. They came into Fabrics and stood around a while trying to see what shit they could get into. All they had in their baskets was a teapot and some light bulbs and some doodads from the special gift department, perfume and whatnot. I waited on a few customers wanting braid and balls of macramé twine, nothing where I could show my stuff. Now if somebody wanted some of the silky, juicy cotton stuff I could get into something fancy, yanking off the yards, measuring it doing a shuffle-stick number, nicking it just so, then ripping the hell out the shit. But didn't nobody ask for that. Fur Coat and Ethel kinda finger some bolts and trade private jokes, then they moved onto Drugs.

"We'd like to see the latest in rubberized fashions for men, young man." Fur Coat is doing a super Lady Granville Whitmore the Third number. "If you would." She bows her head, fluttering her lashes.

Me and Madeen start messing around in the shoe-polish section so's not to miss nothing. I kind of favor Fur Coat, on account of she got my mama's coat on, I guess. On the other hand, I like the way Ethel drawl talk like she too tired and bored to go on. I guess I like em both cause they shopping the right way, having fun and all. And they got plenty of style. I wouldn't mind being like that when I am full-grown.

The dude in Drugs thinks on the request a while, sucking in his lips like he wanna talk to himself on the inside. He's looking up and down the counter, pauses at the plastic rain hats, rejects them, then squints hard at Ethel and Fur Coat. Fur Coat plants a well-heeled foot on the shelf with the tampons and pads and sighs. Something about that sigh I don't like. It's real rather than play snooty. The dude in Drugs always looks a little crumbled, a little rough dry, like he jumped straight out the hamper but not quite straight. But he got stuff to him if you listen rather than look. Seems to me ole Fur Coat is looking. She keeps looking while the dude moves down the aisle behind the counter, ducks down out of sight, reappears and comes back, dumping an armful of boxes on the counter.

"One box of Trojans and one box of Ramses," Ethel announces. "We want to do the comparison test."

"On the premises?" Lady G Fur says, planting a dignified hand on her collarbone.

"Egg-zack-lee."

"In your opinion, young man," Lady G Fur says, staying the arm of

710

the brand tester, "which of the two is the best? Uhmm—the better of the two, that is. In your vast experience as lady-killer and cock hound, which passes the X test?" It's said kinda snotty. Me and Madeen exchange a look and dust around the cans of shoe polish.

"Well," the dude says, picking up a box in each hand, "in my opinion, Trojans have a snappier ring to em." He rattles the box against his ear, then lets Ethel listen. She nods approval. Fur Coat will not be swayed. "On the other hand, Ramses is a smoother smoke. Cooler on the throat. What do you say in your vast experience as—er—"

Ethel is banging down boxes of Kotex cracking up, screaming, "He gotcha. He gotcha that time. Old laundry bag got over on you, Helen."

Mrs. J comes out of the prescription booth and hustles her bulk to the counter. Me and Madeen clamp down hard on giggles and I damn near got to climb in with the neutral shoe polish to escape attention. Ethel and Fur Coat don't give a shit, they paying customers, so they just roar. Cept Fur Coat's roar is phony, like she really mad and gonna get even with the dude for not turning out to be a chump. Meanwhile, the dude is standing like a robot, arms out at exactly the same height, elbows crooked just so, boxes displayed between thumb and next finger, the gears in the wrist click, clicking, turning. And not even cracking a smile.

"What's the problem here?" Mrs. J trying not to sound breathless or angry and ain't doing too good a job. She got to say it twice to be heard.

"No problem, Mrs. Johnson," the dude says straight-face. "The customers are buying condoms, I am selling condoms. A sale is being conducted, as is customary in a store."

Mrs. J looks down at the jumble of boxes and covers her mouth. She don't know what to do. I duck down, cause when folks in authority caught in a trick, the first they look for is a scapegoat.

"Well, honey," Ethel says, giving a chummy shove to Mrs. J's shoulder, "what do you think? I've heard that Trojans are ultrasensitive. They use a baby lamb brain, I understand."

"Membrane, dear, membrane," Fur Coat says down her nose. "They remove the intestines of a four-week-old lamb and use the membrane. Tough, resilient, sheer."

"Gotcha," says Ethel. "On the other hand, it is said by folks who should know that Ramses has a better box score."

"Box score," echoes Mrs. J in a daze.

"Box score. You know, honey—no splits, breaks, leaks, seeps."

"Seepage, dear, seepage," says Fur Coat, all nasal.

"Gotcha."

"The solution," says the dude in an almost robot voice, "is to take one small box of each and do the comparison test as you say. A survey. A random sampling of your friends." He says this to Fur Coat, who is not enjoying it all nearly so much as Ethel, who is whooping and hollering.

Mrs. J backs off and trots to the prescription booth. Nazi Youth peeks over the glass and mumbles something soothing to Mrs. J. He waves me and Madeen away like he somebody we got to pay some mind.

"We will take one super-duper, jumbo family size of each."

"Family size?" Fur Coat is appalled. "And one more thing, young man," she orders. "Wrap up a petite size for a small-size smart-ass acquaintance of mine. Gift-wrapped, ribbons and all."

It occurs to me that Fur Coat's going to present this to the dude. Right then and there I decide I don't like her. She's not discriminating with her stuff. Up till then I was thinking how much I'd like to trade Aunt Harriet in for either of these two, hang out with them, sit up all night while they drink highballs and talk about men they've known and towns they've been in. I always did want to hang out with women like this and listen to their stories. But they beginning to reveal themselves as not nice people, just cause the dude is rough dry on Christmas Eve. My Uncle Henry all the time telling me they different kinds of folks in the community, but when you boil it right down there's just nice and not nice. Uncle Henry say they folks who'll throw they mamas to the wolves if the fish sandwich big enough. They folks who won't whatever the hot sauce. They folks that're scared, folks that are dumb; folks that have heart and some with heart to spare. That all boils down to nice and not nice if you ask me. It occurs to me that Fur Coat is not nice. Fun, dazzling, witty, but not nice.

"Do you accept Christmas gifts, young man?" Fur Coat asking in icy tones she ain't masking too well.

"No. But I do accept Kwanza presents at the feast."

"Quan . . . hmm . . ."

Fur Coat and Ethel go into a huddle with the stage whispers. "I bet he thinks we don't know beans about Quantas . . . Don't he know we are The Ebony Jet Set . . . We never travel to kangaroo land except by . . ."

Fur Coat straightens up and stares at the dude. "Will you accept a watchamacallit gift from me even though we are not feasting, as it were?"

"If it is given with love and respect, my sister, of course." He was sounding so sincere, it kinda got to Fur Coat.

"In that case . . ." She scoops up her bundle and sweeps out the place. Ethel trotting behind hollering, "He gotcha, Helen. Give the boy credit. Maybe we should hire him and do a threesome act." She spun the turnstile round three times for she got into the spin and spun out the store.

"Characters," says Piper on tiptoe, so we all can hear him. He laughs and checks his watch. Madeen slinks over to Tobacco to be in asking distance in case he don't already have a date to the dance. Miz Della's patting some powder on. I'm staring at the door after Fur Coat and Ethel, coming to terms with the fact that my daddy ain't coming. It's gonna be just Uncle Henry and Aunt Harriet this year, with maybe Mama calling on the phone between sets to holler in my ear, asking have I been a good girl, it's been that long since she's taken a good look at me.

"You wanna go to the Kwanza celebrations with me sometime this week or next week, Candy?"

I turn and look at the dude. I can tell my face is falling and right now I don't feel up to doing anything about it. Holidays are depressing. Maybe there's something joyous about this celebration he's talking about. Cause Lord knows Christmas is a drag. The sister who taught me how to wrap a gele asked me was I coming to the celebration down at the Black Arts Center, but I didn't know nothing bout it.

"Look here," I finally say, "would you please get a pencil and paper and write your name down for me. And write that other word down too so I can look it up."

He writes his name down and spins the paper around for me to read.

"Obatale."

"Right," he says, spinning it back. "But you can call me Ali Baba if you want to." He was leaning over too far writing out Kwanza for me to see if that was a smile on his face or a smirk. I figure a smile, cause Obatale nice people.

ALICE WALKER

(b. 1944)

Alice Walker emerged from her college experience at Sarah Lawrence College as a promising writer of poetry, essay, and fiction, and she rapidly fulfilled that promise, becoming one of the most discussed American writers of the late seventies, winning in 1983 the Pulitzer Prize for The Color Purple. *She was born in Eatonton, a town of rural Georgia, and attended Spelman College in Atlanta in the midst of the Civil Rights Era.*

Her first novel, The Third Life of Grange Copeland *(1970) belongs to two Afro-American genres, the migration tale and the generational tale. In it she weaves together the dynamics of the move from the racism of the South to the racism of the North, and the impact that these have on three generations of the same family. Comparisons to themes of the fiction of Richard Wright could be made. With* Meridian *(1976) and* The Color Purple *(1982) Alice Walker moved, however, to a feminist assertion which affiliates her with currents prominent in the sixties and the seventies. She rejects the label feminist, though, preferring "womanist" to designate an aspect of female sensibility and experience pertinent, if not exclusive, to the black woman in America. Her short stories, while extending beyond the "womanist" limits, are a major vehicle of this fictional commitment. In* Love and Trouble: Stories of Black Women *(1974) and* You Can't Keep A Good Woman Down *(1981) are two important collections.*

Also a poet, Walker received applause for Revolutionary Petunias *(1973) and* Once *(1976), though it is quite clear that her fiction overshadows her poetry.*

As an essayist she has been a powerful and engaged observer and critic of the social scene, committed to understanding and redressing her perceived neglect of black women. Perhaps the major expression of this has been her personal crusade for the proper recognition of Zora Neale Hurston, a writer with whom she has closely identified. Her essay "In Search of Zora" (1975) has been reprinted several times and appears in the book In Search of Our Mothers' Gardens *(1983), a volume of womanist prose. Item 4 among the definitions of* womanist *which precede the collection reads: "Womanist is to feminist as purple to lavender."*

To Hell with Dying
From *In Love and Trouble*

"To hell with dying," my father would say. "These children want Mr. Sweet!"

Mr. Sweet was a diabetic and an alcoholic and a guitar player and lived down the road from us on a neglected cotton farm. My older brothers and sisters got the most benefit from Mr. Sweet, for when they were growing up he had quite a few years ahead of him and so was capable of being called back from the brink of death any number of times—whenever the voice of my father reached him as he lay expiring. "To hell with dying, man," my father would say, pushing the wife away from the bedside (in tears although she knew the death was not necessarily the last one unless Mr. Sweet really wanted it to be). "These children want Mr. Sweet!" And they did want him, for at a signal from Father they would come crowding around the bed and throw themselves on the covers, and whoever was the smallest at the time would kiss him all over his wrinkled brown face and begin to tickle him so that he would laugh all down in his stomach, and his moustache, which was long and sort of straggly, would shake like Spanish moss and was also that color.

Mr. Sweet had been ambitious as a boy, wanted to be a doctor or lawyer or sailor, only to find that black men fare better if they are not. Since he could become none of these things he turned to fishing as his only earnest career and playing the guitar as his only claim to doing anything extraordinarily well. His son, the only one that he and his wife, Miss Mary, had, was shiftless as the day is long and spent money as if he were trying to see the bottom of the mint, which Mr. Sweet would tell him was the clean brown palm of his hand. Miss Mary loved her "baby" however, and worked hard to get him the "li'l necessaries" of life, which turned out mostly to be women.

Mr. Sweet was a tall, thinnish man with thick kinky hair going dead white. He was dark brown, his eyes were very squinty and sort of bluish, and he chewed Brown Mule tobacco. He was constantly on the verge of being blind drunk, for he brewed his own liquor and was not in the least a stingy sort of man, and was always very melancholy and sad, though frequently when he was "feelin' good" he'd dance around the yard with us, usually keeling over just as my mother came to see what the commotion was.

Toward all of us children he was very kind, and had the grace to be shy with us, which is unusual in grownups. He had great respect for my mother for she never held his drunkenness against him and would let us play with him even when he was about to fall in the fireplace from drink. Although Mr. Sweet would sometimes lose complete or nearly complete control of his head and neck so that he would loll in his chair, his mind remained strangely acute and his speech not too affected. His ability to be drunk and sober at the same time made him an ideal playmate, for he was as weak as we were and we could usually best him in wrestling, all the while keeping a fairly coherent conversation going.

We never felt anything of Mr. Sweet's age when we played with him. We loved his wrinkles and would draw some on our brows to be like him, and his white hair was my special treasure and he knew it and would never come to visit us just after he had had his hair cut off at the barbershop. Once he came to our house for something, probably to see my father about fertilizer for his crops because, although he never paid the slightest attention to his crops, he liked to know what things would be best to use on them if he ever did. Anyhow, he had not come with his hair since he had just had it shaved off at the barbershop. He wore a huge straw hat to keep off the sun and also to keep his head away from me. But as soon as I saw him I ran up and demanded that he take me up and kiss me with his funny beard which smelled so strongly of tobacco. Looking forward to burying my small fingers into his woolly hair I threw away his hat only to find he had done something to his hair, that it was no longer there! I let out a squall which made my mother think that Mr. Sweet had finally dropped me in the well or something and from that day I've been wary of men in hats. However, not long after, Mr. Sweet showed up with his hair grown out and just as white and kinky and impenetrable as it ever was.

Mr. Sweet used to call me his princess, and I believed it. He made me feel pretty at five and six, and simply outrageously devastating at the blazing age of eight and a half. When he came to our house with his guitar the whole family would stop whatever they were doing to sit around him and listen to him play. He liked to play "Sweet Georgia Brown," that was what he called me sometimes, and also he liked to play "Caldonia" and all sorts of sweet, sad, wonderful songs which he sometimes made up. It was from one of these songs that I learned that he had had to marry Miss Mary when he had in fact loved somebody else (now living in Chi-ca-go, or De-stroy, Michigan). He was not sure that Joe Lee, her "baby," was also his baby. Sometimes he would cry and that was an indication that he was about to die again. And so we would all get prepared, for we were sure to be called upon.

I was seven the first time I remember actually participating in one of Mr. Sweet's "revivals"—my parents told me I had participated before, I had been the one chosen to kiss him and tickle him long before I knew the rite of Mr. Sweet's rehabilitation. He had come to our house, it was a few years after his wife's death, and was very sad, and also, typically, very drunk. He sat on the floor next to me and my older brother, the rest of the children were grown up and lived elsewhere, and began to play his guitar and cry. I held his woolly head in my arms and wished I could have been old enough to have been the woman he loved so much and that I had not been lost years and years ago.

When he was leaving, my mother said to us that we'd better sleep light that night for we'd probably have to go over to Mr. Sweet's before daylight. And we did. For soon after we had gone to bed one of the neighbors knocked on our door and called my father and said that Mr. Sweet was sinking fast and if he wanted to get in a word before the crossover he'd better shake a leg and get over to Mr. Sweet's house. All the neighbors knew to come to our house if something was wrong with Mr. Sweet, but they did not know how we always managed to make him well, or at least stop him from dying, when he was often so near death. As soon as we heard the cry we got up, my brother and I and my mother and father, and put on our clothes. We hurried out of the house and down the road for we were always afraid that we might someday be too late and Mr. Sweet would get tired of dallying.

When we got to the house, a very poor shack really, we found the front room full of neighbors and relatives and someone met us at the door and said that it was all very sad that old Mr. Sweet Little (for Little was his family name, although we mostly ignored it) was about to kick the bucket. My parents were advised not to take my brother and me into the "death room," seeing we were so young and all, but we were so much more accustomed to the death room than he that we ignored him and dashed in without giving his warning a second thought. I was almost in tears, for these deaths upset me fearfully, and the thought of how much depended on me and my brother (who was such a ham most of the time) made me very nervous.

The doctor was bending over the bed and turned back to tell us for at least the tenth time in the history of my family that, alas, old Mr. Sweet Little was dying and that the children had best not see the face of implacable death (I didn't know what "implacable" was, but whatever it was, Mr. Sweet was not!). My father pushed him rather abruptly out of the way saying, as he always did and very loudly for he was saying it to Mr. Sweet, "To hell with dying, man, these children want Mr. Sweet"— which was my cue to throw myself upon the bed and kiss Mr. Sweet all around the whiskers and under the eyes and around the collar of his nightshirt where he smelled so strongly of all sorts of things, mostly liniment.

I was very good at bringing him around, for as soon as I saw that he was struggling to open his eyes I knew he was going to be all right, and so could finish my revival sure of success. As soon as his eyes were open he would begin to smile and that way I knew that I had surely won. Once, though, I got a tremendous scare, for he could not open his eyes and later I learned that he had had a stroke and that one side of his face was stiff and hard to get into motion. When he began to smile I could tickle him in earnest because I was sure that nothing would get in the way of his laughter, although once he began to cough so hard that he almost threw me off his stomach, but that was when I was very small, little more than a baby, and my bushy hair had gotten in his nose.

When we were sure he would listen to us we would ask him why he was in bed and when he was coming to see us again and could we play with his guitar, which more than likely would be leaning against the bed. His eyes would get all misty and he would sometimes cry out loud, but we never let it embarrass us, for he knew that we loved him and that we sometimes cried too for no reason. My parents would leave the room to just the three of us; Mr. Sweet, by that time, would be propped up in bed with a number of pillows behind his head and with me sitting and lying on his shoulder and along his chest. Even when he had trouble breathing he would not ask me to get down. Looking into my eyes he would shake his white head and run a scratchy old finger all around my hairline, which was rather low down, nearly to my eyebrows, and made some people say I looked like a baby monkey.

My brother was very generous in all this, he let me do all the revivaling—he had done it for years before I was born and so was glad to be able to pass it on to someone new. What he would do while I talked to Mr. Sweet was pretend to play the guitar, in fact pretend that he was a young version of Mr. Sweet, and it always made Mr. Sweet glad to think that someone wanted to be like him—of course, we did not know this then, we

718

played the thing by ear, and whatever he seemed to like, we did. We were desperately afraid that he was just going to take off one day and leave us.

It did not occur to us that we were doing anything special; we had not learned that death was final when it did come. We thought nothing of triumphing over it so many times, and in fact became a trifle contemptuous of people who let themselves be carried away. It did not occur to us that if our own father had been dying we could not have stopped it, that Mr. Sweet was the only person over whom we had power.

When Mr. Sweet was in his eighties I was studying in the university many miles from home. I saw him whenever I went home, but he was never on the verge of dying that I could tell and I began to feel that my anxiety for his health and psychological well-being was unnecessary. By this time he not only had a moustache but a long flowing snow-white beard, which I loved and combed and braided for hours. He was very peaceful, fragile, gentle, and the only jarring note about him was his old steel guitar, which he still played in the old sad, sweet, down-home blues way.

On Mr. Sweet's ninetieth birthday I was finishing my doctorate in Massachusetts and had been making arrangements to go home for several weeks' rest. That morning I got a telegram telling me that Mr. Sweet was dying again and could I please drop everything and come home. Of course I could. My dissertation could wait and my teachers would understand when I explained to them when I got back. I ran to the phone, called the airport, and within four hours I was speeding along the dusty road to Mr. Sweet's.

The house was more dilapidated than when I was last there, barely a shack, but it was overgrown with yellow roses which my family had planted many years ago. The air was heavy and sweet and very peaceful. I felt strange walking through the gate and up the old rickety steps. But the strangeness left me as I caught sight of the long white beard I loved so well flowing down the thin body over the familiar quilt coverlet. Mr. Sweet!

His eyes were closed tight and his hands, crossed over his stomach, were thin and delicate, no longer scratchy. I remembered how always before I had run and jumped up on him just anywhere; now I knew he would not be able to support my weight. I looked around at my parents, and was surprised to see that my father and mother also looked old and frail. My father, his own hair very gray, leaned over the quietly sleeping old man, who, incidentally, smelled still of wine and tobacco, and said, as he'd done so many times, "To hell with dying, man! My daughter is home to see Mr. Sweet!" My brother had not been able to come as he was in the war in Asia. I bent down and gently stroked the closed eyes and gradually they began to open. The closed, wine-stained lips twitched a little, then parted in a warm, slightly embarrassed smile. Mr. Sweet could see me and he recognized me and his eyes looked very spry and twinkly for a moment. I put my head down on the pillow next to his and we just looked at each other for a long time. Then he began to trace my peculiar hairline with a thin, smooth finger. I closed my eyes when his finger halted above my ear (he used to rejoice at the dirt in my ears when I was little), his hand stayed cupped around my cheek. When I opened my eyes, sure that I had reached him in time, his were closed.

Even at twenty-four how could I believe that I had failed? that Mr. Sweet was really gone? He had never gone before. But when I looked up at my parents I saw that they were holding back tears. They had loved him dearly. He was like a piece of rare and delicate china which was always being saved from breaking and which finally fell. I looked long at the old face, the wrinkled forehead, the red lips, the hands that still reached out to me. Soon I felt my father pushing something cool into my hands. It was Mr. Sweet's guitar. He had asked them months before to give it to me; he had known that even if I came next time he would not be able to respond in the old way. He did not want me to feel that my trip had been for nothing.

The old guitar! I plucked the strings, hummed "Sweet Georgia Brown." The magic of Mr. Sweet lingered still in the cool steel box. Through the window I could catch the fragrant delicate scent of tender yellow roses. The man on the high old-fashioned bed with the quilt coverlet and the flowing white beard had been my first love.

A Gathering of Poets

The voices of the Afro-American poets of the seventies seemed to be different, on the whole, from those of the sixties. Whether one speaks of transposition or muting—in any case the analogy should be musical—a difference could surely be noted. Those public and manifesto poets who had characterized the sixties were still heard, but at lesser intervals, and more meditative, private themes began to emerge, even in the work of the sixties poets who remained active.

The concern with racism and injustice was still present, but other themes became clear and insistent, such as ancestral and kinship values, the joys and sorrows of womanhood, and the recurrence of death. Meditation on and experimentation in musical form continued and provides a sure bond with the prestigious jazz genre of the sixties. The elegiac poem commemorating both the famous and the humble became a distinctive genre in the seventies.

Overall, however, it is clear that poets and poetry in this period were and still are overshadowed by prose writers, many of whom have drawn upon their own achievements in the craft of poetry to create prose of great inventiveness and power. The poets gathered here are known primarily or exclusively as poets.

The group could have been enlarged. Jay Wright, the subject of a special issue of *Callaloo* (Fall, 1983), and Julia Fields, whose collection *Slow Coins* (1981) contains the incisive work of a decade, are but two among many poets whose work has enriched the poetic landscape of the seventies and eighties. Others who should be mentioned include Lance Jeffers, Everett Hoagland, and Sherley Anne Williams.

MICHAEL S. HARPER

(b. 1938)

Michael S. Harper has established a reputation as a major poet, teacher of writers, critic, and anthologist. For several years a teacher at Brown University, he collaborated with Sterling Brown to produce a much-needed volume of collected poems. With Robert B. Stepto, he edited a major anthology of Afro-American culture, Chant of Saints *(1979). His own output of verse, amounting to at least ten volumes, includes* Dear John, Dear Coltrane *(1970),* History is Your Own Heartbeat *(1973),* Images of Kin *(1977), and* Rhode Island *(1981).*

Dear John, Dear Coltrane

a love supreme, a love supreme
a love supreme, a love supreme

Sex fingers toes
in the marketplace
near your father's church
in Hamlet, North Carolina—
witness to this love
in this calm fallow
of these minds,
there is no substitute for pain:
genitals gone or going,
seed burned out,
you tuck the roots in the earth,
turn back, and move
by river through the swamps,
singing: *a love supreme, a love supreme;*
what does it all mean?

Loss, so great each black
woman expects your failure
in mute change, the seed gone.
You plod up into the electric city—
your song now crystal and
the blues. You pick up the horn
with some will and blow
into the freezing night:
a love supreme, a love supreme—

Dawn comes and you cook
up the thick sin 'tween
impotence and death, fuel
the tenor sax cannibal
heart, genitals and sweat
that makes you clean—
a love supreme, a love supreme—

Why you so black?
cause I am
why you so funky?
cause I am
why you so black?
cause I am
why you so sweet?
cause I am
why you so black?
cause I am
a love supreme, a love supreme:

So sick
you couldn't play *Naima*,
so flat we ached
for song you'd concealed
with your own blood,
your diseased liver gave
out its purity,
the inflated heart
pumps out, the tenor kiss,
tenor love:
a love supreme, a love supreme—
a love supreme, a love supreme—

We Assume: On the Death of Our Son, Reuben Masai Harper

We assume
that in 28 hours,
lived in a collapsible isolette,
you learned to accept pure oxygen
as the natural sky;
the scant shallow breaths
that filled those hours
cannot, did not make you fly —
but dreams were there
like crooked palmprints on
the twin-thick windows of the nursery —
in the glands of your mother.

We assume
the sterile hands
drank chemicals in and out
from lungs opaque with mucus,
pumped your stomach,
eeked the bicarbonate in
crooked, green-winged veins,
out in a plastic mask;

A woman who'd lost her first son
consoled us with an angel gone ahead
to pray for our family —
gone into that sky
seeking oxygen,
gone into autopsy,
a fine brown powdered sugar,
a disposable cremation:

We assume
you did not know we loved you.

Photographs: A Vision of Massacre

We thought the grass
would grow up quickly
to hide the bodies.
A brother sloped across
his brother, the patched
clay road slipping
into our rainy season
of red, our favorite color.

When the pictures came
we spoke of our love
for guns, oiled and glistening
in the rich blood of machines:
bodies, boys and girls, clutching
their private parts, oiled,
now slightly pink,
and never to be used.

Caves

Four M-48 tank platoons ambushed
near Dak To, two destroyed:
the Ho Chi Minh Trail boils,
half my platoon rockets
into stars near Cambodia,
foot soldiers dance from highland woods
taxing our burning half:

there were no caves for them to hide.

We saw no action,
eleven months twenty-two days
in our old tank
burning sixty feet away:
I watch them burn inside out:
hoisting through heavy crossfire,

hoisting over turret hatches,
hoisting my last burning man
alive to the ground,
our tank artillery shells explode
killing all inside:
hoisting blown burned squad
in tank's bladder,
plug leaks with cave blood:

there were no caves for them to hide—

LARRY NEAL

(1937–1981)

    Though born in Atlanta, Georgia, Larry Neal was reared in Philadelphia and attended both Lincoln University and the University of Pennsylvania. He collaborated with Amiri Baraka as co-editor of a pivotal anthology of literature of the Black Arts Movement, Black Fire *(1968). His collections of verse include* Black Boogaloo *(1969) and* Hoodoo Hollerin' Bebop Ghosts *(1975).*

Ghost Poem # 4

Dig night swinging there:
the cocaine sinners
as woven flesh; someone's sun melts, dark penis
explodes somewhere between the moist lips of the city.
and
the hully-gully victims of body
strip tease the moon
soon one of us will die, cheating the buried pimp
of his money and bitches.

If you could see me now, Momma
leaning like this against the shadows of Turk's Bar,
all did up like this, digging night swing in
with the coke and the moon-melting flesh;
somewhere you say
there is a way; that's cool for Bible readers.

But I know soon that either he or me will die
under these gaming stars.

The hitman's coming round the corner now
snorting blow for courage.
My problem is that I lingered too long;
and I was nervous on the trigger—some doom,
the after-hours spot, and the bitch, the heavy roll
in my pocket.
Yeah, if you could see now
Waycross Momma, the hitman coming
you would ask: "Is that my Junie Boy runnin
with that fast crowd?"

Rhythm Is a Groove # 2

Rhythm is a groove/packed against sweet flesh
an afternoon is Mt. Morris Park
Sun against black skin/hands moist/
/the beat/
/hands hot/the skins speak
Sun against beat
the beat against black motion
to flame and dance
while packed into the beat

ALL CLAP HANDS AND SING
do the foot shuffle/the colors/
shuffle the beat/and the skins speak

Sun come black, juju wonder song.
Sun come black, juju wonder song.
Drum sing/speak black/black skin skin

shuffle the beat/shuffle the color/the beat speaks
color the shuffle/black brotherbrother
brother/brother/hurl drum into sky
make Sun come, hot pulse flaming
YEAH! ! !

Shine's City

At the Heliopolis of Serapis
    we shoot crap
roll the world between our fingers
while we snap time
under neon light of Eighth Avenue summer.

I turn the corner, near the marketplace
    at Serapis
and dig the hiss of the blue serpent
his word whispers as light
a coil of red fire for his tongue.

So we tumble between worlds
we cling as word
to the sticky air.

Shine is the cosmic intruder
the pyramid tumbler
the hot sun's murmur
the summer singer.

AUDRE LORDE
(b. 1934)

Born in New York City, Audre Lorde has studied in Mexico, as well as at Hunter College and Columbia University. Her interests in feminism and in the African background are facets of her wide-flung commitment to transnational concerns. Her volumes include The First Cities *(1969),* Cables to Rage *(1970),* The Black Unicorn *(1978), and* Chosen Poems *(1982).*

Dahomey

"in spite of the fire's heat
the tongs can fetch it."

It was in Abomey that I felt
the full blood of my fathers' wars
and where I found my mother
Seboulisa
standing with outstretched palms hip high
one breast eaten away by worms of sorrow
magic stones resting upon her fingers
dry as a cough.

In the dooryard of the brass workers
four women joined together dying cloth
mock Eshu's iron quiver
standing erect and flamingly familiar
in their dooryard
mute as a porcupine in a forest of lead
In the courtyard of the cloth workers
other brothers and nephews
are stitching bright tapestries
into tales of blood.

   Thunder is a woman with braided hair
spelling the fas of Shango
asleep between sacred pythons
that cannot read
nor eat the ritual offerings
of the Asein.
My throat in the panther's lair
is unresisting.

Bearing two drums on my head I speak
whatever language is needed
to sharpen the knives of my tongue
the snake is aware although sleeping
under my blood
since I am a woman whether or not
you are against me
I will braid my hair
even
in the seasons of rain.

A Woman Speaks

Moon marked and touched by sun
thy magic is unwritten
but when the sea turns back
it will leave my shape behind.
I seek no favor
untouched by blood
unrelenting as the curse of love
permanent as my errors
or my pride
I do not mix
love with pity
nor hate with scorn
and if you would know me
look into the entrails of Uranus
where the restless oceans pound.

I do not dwell
within my birth nor my divinities
who am ageless and half-grown
and still seeking
my sisters
witches in Dahomey
wear me inside their coiled cloths
as our mother did
mourning.

I have been woman
for a long time
beware my smile
I am treacherous with old magic
and the noon's new fury
with all your wide futures
promised
I am
woman
and not white.

Rooming Houses Are Old Women

Rooming houses are old women
rocking dark windows into their whens
waiting incomplete circles
rocking
rent office to stoop to
community bathrooms to gas rings and
under-bed boxes of once useful garbage
city issued with a twice monthly check
and the young men next door
with their loud midnight parties
and fishy rings left in the bathtub
no longer arouse them
from midnight to mealtime no stops inbetween
light breaking to pass through jumbled up windows
and who was it who married the widow that Buzzie's son
    messed with?

To Welfare and insult from the slow shuffle
from dayswork to shopping bags
heavy with leftovers

Rooming houses
are old women waiting
searching
through darkening windows
the end or beginning of agony
old women seen through half-ajar doors
hoping
they are not waiting
but being
the entrance to somewhere
unknown and desired
but not new.

ETHERIDGE KNIGHT

(b. 1931)

Etheridge Knight was born in Corinth, Mississippi. Self-educated, he published his first book while he was a prison inmate and a second book shortly after being released from prison. Volumes by him include Poems From Prison *(1968),* Black Voices From Prison *(1970),* Belly Song & Other Poems *(1973), and* Born of A Woman *(1981). He has been poet-in-residence at several colleges, a Guggenheim Fellow, and a National Endowment For the Arts awardee.*

He Sees Through Stone

He sees through stone
he has the secret
eyes this old black one
who under prison skies
sits pressed by the sun
against the western wall
his pipe between purple gums

the years fall
like overripe plums
bursting red flesh
on the dark earth

his time is not my time
but I have known him
in a time gone

he led me trembling cold
into the dark forest
taught me the secret rites
to make it with a woman
to be true to my brothers
to make my spear drink
the blood of my enemies

now black cats circle him
flash white teeth

snarl at the air
mashing green grass beneath
shining muscles
ears peeling his words
he smiles
he knows
the hunt   the enemy
he has the secret eyes
he sees through stone

The Idea of Ancestry

1
Taped to the wall of my cell are 47 pictures: 47 black
faces: my father, mother, grandmothers (1 dead), grandfathers (both dead), brothers, sisters, uncles, aunts,
cousins (1st & 2nd), nieces, and nephews. They stare
across the space at me sprawling on my bunk. I know
their dark eyes, they know mine. I know their style,
they know mine. I am all of them, they are all of me;
they are farmers, I am a thief, I am me, they are thee.

I have at one time or another been in love with my mother,
1 grandmother, 2 sisters, 2 aunts (1 went to the asylum),
and 5 cousins. I am now in love with a 7 yr old niece
(she sends me letters written in large block print, and
her picture is the only one that smiles at me).

I have the same name as 1 grandfather, 3 cousins, 3 nephews,
and 1 uncle. The uncle disappeared when he was 15, just took
off and caught a freight (they say). He's discussed each year
when the family has a reunion, he causes uneasiness in
the clan, he is an empty space. My father's mother, who is 93
and who keeps the Family Bible with everybody's birth dates
(and death dates) in it, always mentions him. There is no
place in her Bible for "whereabouts unknown."

2
Each fall the graves of my grandfathers call me, the brown
hills and red gullies of mississippi send out their electric

messages, galvanizing my genes. Last yr / like a salmon quitting
the cold ocean-leaping and bucking up his birthstream / I
hitchhiked my way from L.A. with 16 caps in my pocket and a
monkey on my back. And I almost kicked it with the kinfolks.
I walked barefooted in my grandmother's backyard / I smelled the
    old
land and the woods / I sipped cornwhiskey from fruit jars with the
    men /
I flirted with the women / I had a ball till the caps ran out
and my habit came down. That night I looked at my grandmother
and split / my guts were screaming for junk / but I was almost
contented / I had almost caught up with me.
(The next day in Memphis I cracked a croaker's crib for a fix).

This yr there is a gray stone wall damming my stream, and when
the falling leaves stir my genes, I pace my cell or flop on my bunk
and stare at 47 black faces across the space. I am all of them,
they are all of me, I am me, they are thee, and I have no children
to float in the space between.

The Violent Space

(or when your sister sleeps around for money)

Exchange in greed the ungraceful signs. Thrust
The thick notes between green apple breasts.
Then the shadow of the devil descends,
The violent space cries and angel eyes,
Large and dark, retreat in innocence and in ice.
(Run sister run—the Bugga man comes!)

The violent space cries silently,
Like you cried wide years ago
In another space, speckled by the sun
And the leaves of a green plum tree,
And you were stung
By a red wasp and we flew home.
(Run sister run—the Bugga man comes!)

Well, hell, lil sis, wasps still sting.
You are all of seventeen and as alone now

In your pain as you were with the sting
On your brow.
Well, shit, lil sis, here we are:
You and I and this poem.
And what should I do? should I squat
In the dust and make strange markings on the ground?
Shall I chant a spell to drive the demon away?
(Run sister run—the Bugga man comes!)

In the beginning you were the Virgin Mary,
And you are the Virgin Mary now.
But somewhere between Nazareth and Bethlehem
You lost your name in the nameless void.
"O Mary don't you weep don't you moan"
O Mary shake your butt to the violent juke,
Absorb the demon puke and watch the white eyes pop,
(Run sister run—the Bugga man comes!)

And what do I do. I boil my tears in a twisted spoon
And dance like an angel on the point of a needle.
I sit counting syllables like Midas gold.
I am not bold. I cannot yet take hold of the demon
And lift his weight from you black belly,
So I grab the air and sing my song.
(But the air cannot stand my singing long.)

For Langston Hughes

Gone   Gone
  Another weaver of black dreams has gone
we sat in June Bug's pad with the shades drawn
and the air thick with holy smoke. and we heard
the Lady sing Langston before we knew his name.
and when Black Bodies stopped swinging June
But, TG and I went out and swung on some white cats.
now I don't think the Mythmaker meant for us to do *that*
but we didn't know what else to do.

Gone   Gone
  Another weaver of black dreams has gone

JUNE JORDAN

(b. 1936)

Born in New York, June Jordan studied at both Barnard College and the University of Chicago. She has worked on films and is the author of a number of books for young people, including a biography of Fannie Lou Hamer (1972). She edited the anthology Soulscript *(1976). Her volumes of poems include* Some Changes *(1971) and* Passion: New Poems, 1977–1980.

What Happens

What happens when the dog sits on a tiger
when the fat man sells a picture of himself
when a lady shoves a sword inside her
when an elephant takes tea cups from the shelf

or the giant starts to cry
and the grizzly loses his grip
or the acrobat begins to fly
and gorillas run away with the whip

What happens when a boy sits on a chair
and watches all the action on the ground and
in the air
or when the children leave the greatest
show on earth
and see the circus?

Poem from the Empire State

Three of us went to the top of the city
a friend, my son, and I
on that day when winter wrote like snow
across the moonlike sky

and stood there breathing a heavy height
as wide as the streets to see
so poor and frozen far below
that nothing would change for you and me
that swallowing death lay wallowing still
with the wind at the bloat of piled-up swill
And that was the day we conquered the air
with 100,000 tons of garbage.

No rhyme can be said
where reason has fled.

Index of Authors